September 1–4, 2014
Santiago, Chile

**Association for
Computing Machinery**

Advancing Computing as a Science & Profession

HT'14

Proceedings of the 25th ACM Conference on
Hypertext and Social Media

Sponsored by:
ACM SIGWEB

Supported by:
University of Concepción & Pontifical Catholic University of Chile

Association for Computing Machinery

Advancing Computing as a Science & Profession

The Association for Computing Machinery
2 Penn Plaza, Suite 701
New York, New York 10121-0701

Notice to Past Authors of ACM-Published Articles
ACM intends to create a complete electronic archive of all articles and/or other material previously published by ACM. If you have written a work that has been previously published by ACM in any journal or conference proceedings prior to 1978, or any SIG Newsletter at any time, and you do NOT want this work to appear in the ACM Digital Library, please inform permissions@acm.org, stating the title of the work, the author(s), and where and when published.

ISBN: 978-1-4503-3013-8 (Digital)

ISBN: 978-1-4503-3264-4 (Print)

Additional copies may be ordered prepaid from:

ACM Order Department
PO Box 30777
New York, NY 10087-0777, USA

Phone: 1-800-342-6626 (USA and Canada)
+1-212-626-0500 (Global)
Fax: +1-212-944-1318
E-mail: acmhelp@acm.org
Hours of Operation: 8:30 am – 4:30 pm ET

Printed in the USA

Preface

The 25th ACM Conference on Hypertext and Social Media - Hypertext 2014 - takes place in Santiago de Chile between September 1st and September 4th 2014. The Hypertext conference series is concerned with all aspects of modern hypertext research, including social media, the Semantic Web, dynamic and computed hypertext and hypermedia, as well as narrative systems and applications.

The ACM Hypertext 2014 conference focuses on the role of hypertext and hyperlink theory on the Web and beyond, as a foundation for approaches and practices in the wider community - ranging from the usage of social media to the semantics of the 'Internet of Things'. The conference also welcomes submissions that focus on the linguistic aspects of hypertext and user experience with linked entities, resources and events. Hypertext 2014 has the following tracks: Links and Connections between People, Open Data and the Semantics of Things, and User Experience and Adaptive Linking.

The focus of the track "Links and Connections between People" is on the analysis and exploitation of links between topics, people and events in social media and beyond. What structures can be found and exposed in conversations via Twitter or Facebook? What is the role of location in mobile communications? What characterizes people whom we talk with, meet, and listen to? And what are the topics that relate us with one another?

The track "Open Data and the Semantics of Things" focuses on the use of semantic web techniques and open data standards for the creation, aggregation, exploitation and analysis of data, information and knowledge in interlinked environments. Linked data formalisms constitute a solid basis for sharing, linking and integrating heterogeneous information, including descriptions and statistics of concrete events, buildings, persons and knowledge. Semantic technologies play an increasingly important role in analyzing and reasoning upon linked data and their connections to further hypertext structures.

The track "User Experience and Adaptive Learning" welcomes submissions related to user modeling, personalization, hypertext structuring mechanisms, user experience, and user studies. Adaptive hypermedia and contextual information access provide a means of suggesting user directions within the interwoven web, to achieve a particular goal or to acquire knowledge. Apart from semantic aspects, semiotics and linguistics play an important role in adaptive linking and enhanced user experience. Moreover, they inform how we can use and whether we should use particular links.

We received 86 submissions, of which 58 regular papers, 18 short papers and 10 posters and demos. Each submission was reviewed by at least three program committee members, followed by a metareview by the track chairs, who recommended acceptance or rejection of the papers. In several cases, full papers were accepted as short papers, and a number of interesting submissions that were not sufficiently mature yet have been accepted as posters. The final decisions were taken by the program chairs – with the exception of submissions with one of the organizing team's members involved, which have been handled separately by the general chairs. Finally, we have been able to accept 19 regular papers, 15 short papers and 15 posters and demos, which are included in these proceedings. Following tradition, Hypertext 2014 offers two awards: the Douglas Engelbart Best Paper Award and the Ted Nelson Newcomer Award. Three candidates for each award have been selected by the chairs. During the conference, an award committee will select the winners.

Hypertext 2014 features two invited talks with novel and stimulating ideas. César A. Hidalgo from MIT Media Lab discusses the visualization of the development of economics, cultural production and cities. The second talk is given by Ricardo Baeza-Yates from Yahoo! Research Labs and focuses on the wisdom of ad-hoc crowds.

We wish to thank the authors of all submitted papers, our fellow chairs for shaping this conference, the program committee and the subreviewers for their thoughtful and competent reviews, and to the ACM staff for its support of organizational issues. The Hypertext 2014 conference, and its workshops, tutorials, keynotes, social activities and student grants has been made possible through the sponsorship of ACM SIGWEB.

Leo Ferres
HT'14 General Chair
University of Concepción, Chile

Gustavo Rossi
HT'14 General Chair
University of La Plata, Argentina

Virgilio Almeida
HT'14 Program Chair
Federal University of Minas Gerais, Brazil

Eelco Herder
HT'14 Program Chair
L3S Research Center, Germany

Table of Contents

Posters and Demos

Author Index

Hypertext 2014 Conference Organization

General Chairs: Leo Ferres *(University of Concepción, Chile)*
Gustavo Rossi *(University of La Plata, Argentina)*

Program Chairs: Virgilio Almeida *(Federal University of Minas Gerais, Brazil)*
Eelco Herder *(L3S Research Center, Germany)*

Track Chairs: **Track 1: Links and Connections between People**
Daniele Quercia *(Yahoo! Labs, Spain)*
Johan Bollen *(Indiana University, USA)*

Track 2: Open Data and the Semantics of Things
Philippe Cudré-Mauroux *(University of Fribourg, Switzerland)*
Mathieu d'Aquin *(The Open University, UK)*

Track 3: User Experience and Adaptive Learning
Rosta Farzan *(University of Pittsburgh, USA)*
Vincent Wade *(Trinity College Dublin, Ireland)*

Workshop and Tutorial Chairs: Federica Cena *(University of Turin, Italy)*
Christoph Trattner *(Graz University of Technology, Austria)*

Demo and Poster Chairs: Carlos Castillo *(Qatar Computing Research Institute, Qatar)*
Jill Freyne *(CSIRO, Australia)*

Student Chairs: Julita Vassileva *(University of Saskatchewan, Canada)*
Martin Atzmüller *(University of Kassel, Germany)*

Local and Publicity Chair: Denis Parra *(Catholic University of Chile)*

Proceedings Chair: Altigran Soares da Silva *(Federal University of Amazonas, Brazil)*

Program Committee: Maristella Agosti *(University of Padua, Italy)*
Luca Aiello *(Yahoo! Research, Spain)*
Harith Alani *(KMI - The Open University, UK)*
Pramod Anantharam *(Kno.e.sis, Wright State University, USA)*
Sören Auer *(Leipzig University, Germany)*
Martin Atzmüller *(University of Kassel, Germany)*
Liliana Ardissono *(University of Turin, Italy)*
Amit Awekar *(Indian Institute of Technoloy, Guwahati, India)*
Alain Barrat *(CNRS, France)*
Shlomo Berkovsky *(NICTA, Australia)*
Maria Bielikova *(Slovak University of Technology, Slovakia)*
Eva Blomqvist *(Linköping University, Sweden)*
Paul De Bra *(Eindhoven University of Technology, the Netherlands)*
Peter Brusilovsky *(University of Pittsburgh, USA)*

Hypertext 2014 Sponsor & Supporters

Sponsor:  ACM SIGWEB

Supporters:  University of Concepción, Chile

 Pontifical Catholic University of Chile

The Wisdom of Ad-Hoc Crowds

Ricardo Baeza-Yates
Yahoo Labs
Barcelona, Spain & Santiago, Chile
rbaeza@acm.org

ABSTRACT

In this keynote we give an introduction to wisdom of crowds in the Web, the long tail of web content, and the bias involved in the generation of user generated content (UGC). This bias creates the wisdom of *ad hoc* crowds or the wisdom of a few. Although it is well known that user activity in most settings follows a power law, that is, few people do a lot, while most do nothing, there are few studies that characterize well this activity. In a recent analysis of social network data we corroborated that a small percentage of the active users (passive users are the majority) represent at least the 50% of the UGC. This implies that most of the wisdom comes from a few users, which is not that surprising, as the Web is a reflection of our own society, where economical or political power also is in the hands of minorities.

Categories and Subject Descriptors

H.2.8 [**Database Management**]: Database applications-Data mining;; J.4 [**Computer Applications**]: Social and Behavioral Sciences

General Terms

Human factors; Measurement.

Keywords

Social networks; user generated content; wisdom of crowds.

HT'14, September 1–4, 2014, Santiago, Chile.
ACM 978-1-4503-2954-5/14/09.
http://dx.doi.org/10.1145/2631775.2631813.

1. SUMMARY

The wisdom of crowds is a well known concept of how "large groups of people are smarter than an elite few, no matter how brilliant, they are better at solving problems, fostering innovation, coming to wise decisions, and even predicting the future" [3]. On the other hand, although all people that use Internet can contribute with content (or any type of activity), most people do not. In fact, in any social network, the set of people that just looks at the activity of others, *passive users*, is much larger than the people that is active. Similarly, among the active users most of them do little, while a few do a lot. We are interested in the interplay of these groups of people regarding the generation of content.

Let us take a specific case, say the world of blogs in the Web. Most people do not have a blog and few people have good blogs. Conversely, most blogs are not read and few blogs are well read. Indeed, people contribute with content in a social network or in the Web because they have the (probably wrong) perception that someone will look at and read their contribution. This perception that they are speaking to the whole world, when the truth is that most of the time they are speaking alone, creates a very long tail of content that nobody sees, a huge *digital desert* where people write to nobody, metaphorically speaking.

This bias in the generation of content was already pointed out in [4], and in in a recent study we analyzed further how people contributes to content and what is the impact of the content generation process in the so called wisdom of crowds [2]. This analysis was done on two social network samples, a small sample of New Orleans Facebook users and a large one coming from a micro-blogging platform, Twitter. We also compared our results to the creation of content in Wikipedia. The main results of this study are:

- The percentage of users that generate more than 50% of the content is small, less than 7% in the two cases mentioned;

- These top users are quite stable in time, more than 70% of the initial number stay for months (Twitter) or years (Facebook);

- The number of users that do not contribute to the generation of content is the majority of them;

- There is a non negligible volume of content that nobody sees; and

- This bias seems to be even worse in non social contexts such as content creation in Wikipedia.

We can represent all these results in a metaphorical map of the wisdom behind the crowd as shown in Figure 1, where the vertical axis represent all users in a logarithmic scale (highlighting the wisdom of a few) while the horizontal axis represent the generation of content for each user. Notice that the (sea of) potential content that can be generated by people is much larger than the actual content.

These results questions the independence principle that is needed to have a real wisdom of crowds [3] as the percentage of people that produces most of the content is really small (in addition to all social dependences). The diversity principle is also challenged, as many users do not contribute to the collective wisdom, either because they do not exercise this option or because their opinion is not taken in account (the digital desert).

Although we would like to believe that the Web is a more democratic environment as all the people has in principle the same opportunities (after taking in account educational, financial and digital gaps), at the end the Web mimics our society. Indeed, the economic or political power in most countries belongs to a minority of the people. Even when explicit decisions must be taken through elections or referendums, many people choose not to exercise their right to vote. On the other hand, at least the Web makes everything more measurable and hence, more transparent.

Finally, when doing web contextualization (that is, adapting the user experience to a given context, such as a task, a location, etc.), one good way to do it is to use the wisdom of all the people that has been in the same context in the past (see second challenge in [1]). For example, to recommend places to visit in Santiago de Chile we should use the people that has visited this city in the past. We call this the wisdom of *ad hoc* crowds which is another example of the wisdom of a few. This approach has several advantages. First, we do not need to know the user involved as we are not interested in the person but in the current context of such person. The main side effect is that there are no privacy issues as all users are hidden in this small crowd (natural k-anonymity). Second, in most cases we do not have enough data to personalize well, nor we are allowed to do it as the user may not be authenticated. However, in most contexts we have many people that will contribute more data as well as the right data because we are focusing on a given context. Therefore, to be successful in this approach we need to find the right context granularity such that the *ad-hoc* crowd is relevant and large enough to have enough data for the contextualization at hand.

2. REFERENCES

[1] R. Baeza-Yates, A. Broder and Y. Maarek. The new frontier of Web Search Technology: Seven challenges. In *Search Computing – Trends and Developments*, S. Ceri and M. Brambilla (eds). LNCS 6585, Springer, Berlin, 2011.

[2] R. Baeza-Yates and D. Saez-Trumper. Wisdom of the Crowd or Wisdom of a Few? An Analysis of Users' Content Generation. Submitted for publication, 2014.

[3] J. Surowiecki. *The Wisdom of Crowds: Why the Many Are Smarter Than the Few and How Collective Wisdom Shapes Business, Economies, Societies and Nations.* Random House, 2005.

[4] S. Wu, J. M. Hofman, W. A. Mason, and D. J. Watts. Who says what to whom on Twitter. In *WWW*, pages 705–714, 2011.

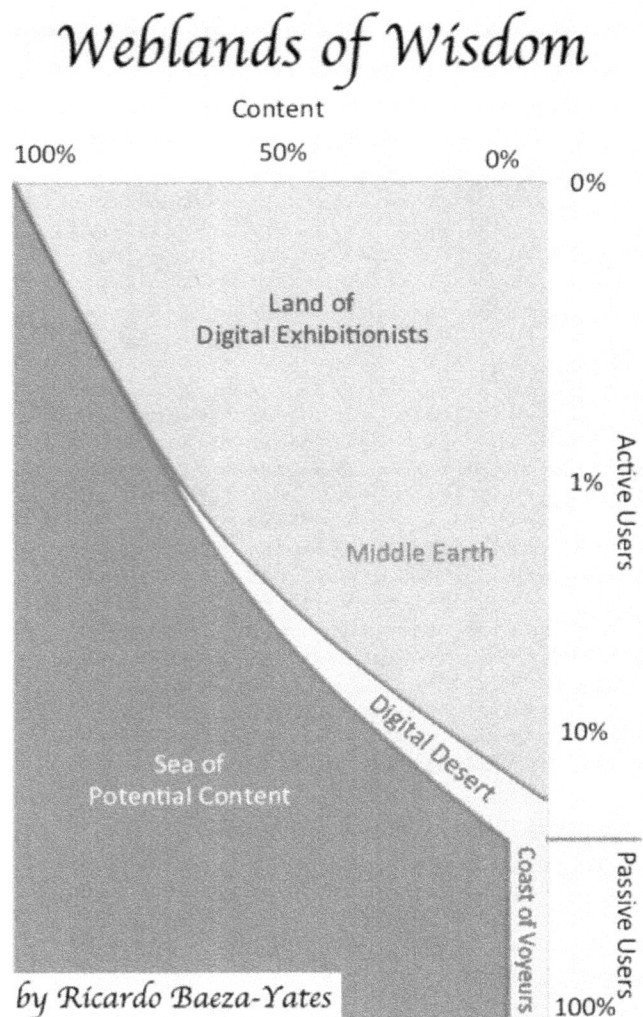

Figure 1: Metaphorical map of the wisdom of the Web. Notice that the users' axis is logarithmic while the content axis is linear.

Big Data Visualization Engines for Understanding the Development of Countries, Social Networks, Culture and Cities

Cesar A. Hidalgo
Macro Connections
The MIT Media Lab
75 Amherst St, Cambridge MA
hidalgo@mit.edu

ABSTRACT

Big data can be used for more than improving the targeting of marketing campaigns. In this talk I will present five big data visualization engines we have created at the MIT Media Lab's Macro Connections group and will show how we can use big data and visualizations to improve our understanding of the development of economies, cultures and cities. The data visualization engines I will demo include (i) the Observatory of Economic Complexity (atlas.media.mit.edu), which is the most comprehensive tool for exploring international trade data created to date; (ii) DataViva (dataviva.info), which is a tool we created to open up data for the entire formal sector economy of Brazil, including data on all of the working force, municipalities, industries, and occupations of Brazil; (iii) Pantheon (pantheon.media.mit.edu), a dataset and visualization engine we created to explore global patterns of cultural production; (iv) Immersion (immersion.media.mit.edu), which is a tool that inverts the email interface, by focusing it on people rather than messages; and (v) Place Pulse and StreetScore (pulse.media.mit.edu & streetscore.media.mit.edu), which are crowd-sourcing and machine learning tools we have developed to help understand the aesthetic aspects of cities and their evolution.

Categories and Subject Descriptors

H.5.4 Hypertext/Hypermedia: Architectures

Keywords

Data Visualization; Information Visualization; Big Data; Economic Complexity; Cultural Production; Urban Computing

HT'14, September 1–4, 2014, Santiago, Chile.
ACM 978-1-4503-2954-5/14/09.
http://dx.doi.org/10.1145/2631775.2631812

Scalable Learning of Users' Preferences Using Networked Data

Mohammad Ali Abbasi
Arizona State University
699 South Mill Ave
Tempe, AZ 85281
Ali.Abbasi@asu.edu

Jiliang Tang
Arizona State University
699 South Mill Ave
Tempe, AZ 85281
Jiliang.Tang@asu.edu

Huan Liu
Arizona State University
699 South Mill Ave
Tempe, AZ 85281
Huan.Liu@asu.edu

ABSTRACT

Users' personal information such as their political views is important for many applications such as targeted advertisements or real-time monitoring of political opinions. Huge amounts of data generated by social media users present opportunities and challenges to study these preferences in a large scale. In this paper, we aim to infer social media users' political views when only network information is available. In particular, given personal preferences about some of the social media users, how can we infer the preferences of unobserved individuals in the same network? There are many existing solutions that address the problem of classification with networked data problem. However, networks in social media normally involve millions and even hundreds of millions of nodes, which make the scalability an important problem in inferring personal preferences in social media. To address the scalability issue, we use social influence theory to construct new features based on a combination of local and global structures of the network. Then we use these features to train classifiers and predict users' preferences. Due to the size of real-world social networks, using the entire network information is inefficient and not practical in many cases. By extracting local social dimensions, we present an efficient and scalable solution. Further, by capturing the network's global pattern, the proposed solution, balances the performance requirement between accuracy and efficiency.

Categories and Subject Descriptors

H.2.8 [**Database Applications**]: Data Mining; G.2.2 [**Graph Theory**]: Network Problems

General Terms

Algorithms, Performance, Theory

Keywords

Social Media Mining; Preference Prediction; Relational Learning; Homophily

INTRODUCTION

Individuals extensively use online social networking sites to connect to each other, share content, express themselves, and benefit from the information provided by other users. Based on the degree of openness on their profiles, users publicly share some information and preferences such as geographic information, age, gender, political view, and interests. Many applications use this information to improve users' online experience or to monitor users' opinion and preferences. Online applications use these types of information to provide customized services to the users in many ways, such as recommending new products, friends, and content, or even providing better search results. Social media information also is used to monitor users' opinion on different topics. Political campaigns, for example, monitor the political views of social media users to predict the outcome of the general elections, and to evaluate the effectiveness of their political strategies. Gathering information of social media users is a key to success in both service and the product-oriented industries.

Despite the importance of social media information, many social media users do not reveal their personal information and preferences [37, 16]. These users usually are challenged to manage privacy concerns and balance trade-offs between disclosing and withholding their personal information. As a result, for some attributes such as political orientation, only a small fraction of the social media users, reveal their information. Two common solutions to this problem are: (i) explicitly asking users to provide the information, and (ii) inferring missing attributes and preferences by using other sources of information [14]. With the popularity of social media and huge amount of publicly available user-generated data, we are able to investigate users' preferences by studying their online activities in social media [27, 1]. There are considerable amount of work which show the possibility and effectiveness of using publicly available user-generated content in social networking sites to infer users' missing attributes and preferences [25, 17, 22]. Specifically, in a community of users involved in political discussions, and with sufficient user-generated content, researchers predict users' political alignment with more than 85% accuracy [5, 24].

However, the majority of regular social media users are reluctant to talk about controversial topics such as politics or share their political views publicly [4]. Consequently, their profiles and the content generated by them do not reveal sufficient clues about their political views [15]. Therefore, usually political views of only a small fraction of the social media users are given explicitly or can be inferred from their profiles and their user-generated content. For example, in a sample of more than 5.8 million fan pages we have collected from Facebook, only less than 1.0% of them revealed their political views. In this situation, the content generated by the social media users can be used to infer political views of only a small fraction of the users, and the majority of the users can not be covered. For many applications such as opinion mining it is important to infer more users' preferences or opinions. Therefore, we need to consider other sources of information to infer missing information of more users than, those with user-generated content. In response, the related work propose to utilize network information to predict more users' missing attributes and preferences [21]. *Network-based* approaches, leverage users' friendship or interaction information to predict their preferences.

In the presence of content information, classical classification algorithms such as support vector machines (SVMs) and logistic regression are commonly used to find patterns in a data set characterized by a collection of independent instances of a single relation. These patterns, are used to predict preferences for unlabeled users. However, when we use network information, we have to deal with new challenges. In network-based approaches, the predictor uses one's connections in the network to infer her preferences. Based on the homophily hypothesis, users are more likely connected to those who share common interests or preferences than to the random users [23]. Consequently, the data points in social networks are not independent and identically distributed. Naively applying classical statistical inferences algorithms such as SVM, which assume that instances are independent, can lead to inappropriate results [19, 10]. Dealing with this problem is one of the major challenges of predicting from linked data. Collective inference and relational learning are two common approaches to address the network-based inference problem. However, scalability of the algorithms to deal with millions of data points is the common challenge of the proposed algorithms in this area.

In this work, we address the scalability problems on predicting social media users' preferences, using a relational learning approach. We develop a network-based scheme to predict social media users' preferences taking into consideration the nature of network information (i.e., non-i.i.d. characteristics of network information). To this end, we design our solution based on the social influence theory, which indicates that a user's preferences are influenced by the influential users in her social circle [36]. This local pattern suggests that an influential user and those influenced by her, should share similar preferences. With this intuition, we use the influential users and their immediate neighbors or neighbors a few hops away, to construct local social dimensions. Users in the same local social dimensions are likely to share similar preferences. Then we use these local social dimensions as features to train classifiers and predict users' preferences. Instead of using the entire network information, which is inefficient for real-world social networks, our approach extracting local social dimensions, leads to an efficient and a scalable solution. Further, the proposed solution, capturing the network's global pattern, balances the trade-off between accuracy and efficiency while is highly scalable.

The remainder of this paper is organized as follows. We first introduce two representative network-based approaches of predicting users' preferences and use them as the baseline solutions. Next, In section 3, we propose our approach, local social dimensions method, to develop network-based prediction consistent with the nature of network information. Then, in Section 4, we describe the experiments and the results of the proposed algorithm and compare it against the baseline solutions. We give a brief literature review on preference prediction in Section 5. Finally, in Section 6, we discuss the results in details.

PREDICTION USING NETWORKED DATA

Network data is commonly used to model the relations between the entities of a system, such as relationship between social entities and paths between geographical locations. In such models, entities are represented by nodes whose labels give their types, and edges are relations between these entities. The task of inferring users' preferences is recovering the missing types of nodes based on the available information. In network-based approaches of predicting users' preferences, the predictor uses one's connections in the network to infer her preferences. The underlying reason for these algorithms to work is the homophily property, which is observed in many social networks, including directed social networks [2].

Based on the homophily effect, users are more likely connected to those with common interests or preferences than to the random users [23]. As a result, structural information of the network can be leveraged to infer properties about users that tend to associate with one another. Due to the homophily and the influence effects, the data points in social networks are not independent and identically distributed. Therefore, traditional classification algorithms such as SVM may not be directly applied in predicting users' labels or preferences. This is because those algorithms work based on i.i.d. assumptions of the input data. In this situation, the classification of a node may have an influence on the class membership of related nodes, and vice-versa [30]. To overcome this problem, different techniques are proposed. Among them, *collective classification* is a techniques that is widely used. The idea of the collective classification is to simultaneously infer the class membership of the nodes in the network [19, 31, 7]. In addition to the collective classification, researchers propose other classification methods built upon the ideas of social sciences such as homophily and influence.

Based on the homophily, similar nodes connect to each other, and based on the influence, connected nodes become similar to their neighbors. Based on perspectives to exploit the social network, the vast majority of existing algorithms can be roughly divided into two groups - *local algorithms* and *global algorithms*. Local algorithms only use the ego-centric networks of users, i.e., users' immediate neighbors or a local view of the social network. The basic assumption behind these methods is that *nearby nodes are likely to have the same label or preference*. Global algorithms, however, utilize the entire network (or a global view of the social network). The assumption behind global algorithms is that *users in the same structure (such as a cluster) are likely to have the same label or preference*. Both of local and global algorithms are based on the same assumption that connected users in social networks are likely to share similar characteristics or similar interests, hence, social networks are homogeneous with regard to many personal or behavioral characteristics [23, 35].

Local algorithms are easy to implement, are fast, and even in some cases produce accurate predictions [20]. As a results, in many studies, they are used as baseline solutions [21]. We describe and use weighted-vote relational neighbor (wvRN) algorithm [20] as a representative of the local algorithms and use it as a baseline solution. Global algorithms, split the network into clusters of users. Then by using the information from user's association to the clusters, the solutions infer user's preferences. The clustering assumption is similar to the idea of using dimensionality reduction algorithms such as singular value decomposition (SVD) or matrix factorization, since the central idea of these algorithms is to construct low-dimensional feature set preserving both local and global structure of the network [33]. In the class of global algorithms, we choose a framework based on *social dimensions* [31] for which its superiority over representative relational learning solutions is empirically verified.

Let $\mathcal{U} = \{u_1, u_2, \ldots, u_n\}$ be the set of users where n is the number of users. We use $\mathbf{X} \in \mathbb{R}^{n \times n}$ to denote the social network among these n users where $\mathbf{X}_{ij} = 1$ if u_i has a direct link to u_j, and zero otherwise. Let $\mathcal{C} = \{c_1, c_2, \ldots, c_m\}$ be the set of class labels where m is the number of labels. $\mathbf{Y} \in \mathbb{R}^{n \times m}$ is the label indicator matrix where $\mathbf{Y}_{ij} = 1$ if u_i is in the j-th class c_j, and zero otherwise. Assume that there are $N \leq n$ labeled users in the network, which indicates that there are only N non-zero entities in $\mathbf{Y}$ and the remaining $n - N$ rows of $\mathbf{Y}$ are zero.

Weighted-vote relational neighbor (wvRN)

Local prediction algorithms, infer user u_i's attributes via using attribute values observed from her "local" edges directly. A user's local edges are the edges which directly connect to her. However, in some cases we also might consider neighbors of up to 2 hops away from, as local connections. In this section, we use weighted-vote relational neighbor (wvRN) algorithm [21] to predict users' preferences. This algorithm performs relational classification via a weighted average of the class membership scores of the node's neighbors. The classifier works by making two strong, yet reasonable, assumptions: a) in the given network, some nodes' class labels are known, b) the network exhibits homophily effect. Both of these assumptions hold for the problem we try to solve. The algorithm estimates the class membership probability of a node u_i belonging to class $c_j \in \mathcal{C}$.

$$P(c_j|u_i) = \frac{1}{|\mathcal{N}(u_i)|} \sum_{u_k \in \mathcal{N}(u_i)} w_{ik} \mathbf{Y}_{kj}, \qquad (1)$$

where w_{ik} is the weight of the link between nodes u_i and u_j, and $\mathcal{N}(u_i)$ is the immediate neighbors of u_i, which is formally defined as

$$\mathcal{N}(u_i) = \{u_k | u_k \in \mathcal{U} \wedge \mathbf{X}_{ik} = 1\} \qquad (2)$$

The label of the user u_i is predicted as

$$c_j = \arg\max_{c_j \in \mathcal{C}} P(c_j|u_i) \qquad (3)$$

Local prediction algorithms, are easy to implement. However, as they only use local information to predict users' preference, they are expected to achieve lower accuracy than the global algorithms.

Social Dimensions

Global prediction algorithms, infer a user's attributes via using all the edges in the graph. Therefore, it is expected that these algorithms infer user's attributes more accurately than the local ones. Algorithms based on social dimensions are reported as the state-of-the-art global-based approaches to infer users' preferences by utilizing the network information [31]. Social dimension based techniques are usually composed of two steps - (1) extracting social dimensions and representing nodes with social dimensions, and (2) training a classifier on the user presentation by social dimensions. Social dimensions are extracted based on global network information to capture the potential affiliations of users. Then these social dimensions can be treated as features of users for the subsequent classifier learning process. Users in the same social dimension are likely to interact with each other more frequently. Hence to infer social dimensions, we need to find out a group of people who interact with each other more frequently than random, which boils down to a classical community detection problem. A typical example of a social dimension based technique is illustrated in Figure 1. A community detection algorithm is employed to extract social dimensions such as $\{S_1, S_2, S_3\}$ in Figure 1(a), and then users will

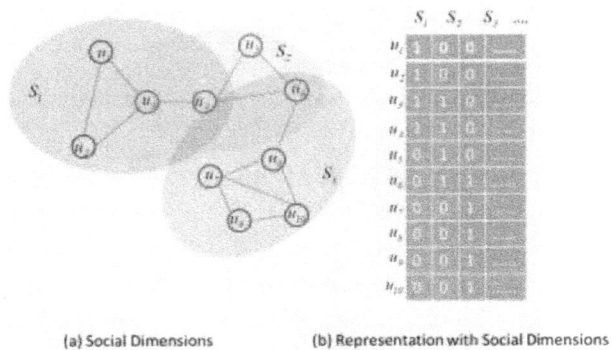

(a) Social Dimensions   (b) Representation with Social Dimensions

Figure 1: Social Dimension based Methods.

be presented by social dimensions as shown in Figure 1(b). Finally a classifier will be trained based on the new representation.

A typical implementation of these algorithms is formulated as follows,

$$\min_{\mathbf{U},\mathbf{V},\mathbf{W}} \|\mathbf{X} - \mathbf{U}\mathbf{V}\mathbf{U}^\top\|_F^2 + \lambda\|\mathbf{H}(\mathbf{U}\mathbf{W}^\top - \mathbf{Y})\|_F^2$$
$$+ \alpha(\|\mathbf{U}\|_F^2 + \|\mathbf{V}\|_F^2) + \beta\|\mathbf{W}\|_F^2 \qquad (4)$$

where $\mathbf{U} \in \mathcal{R}^{n \times d}$ captures the latent social dimension structure and d is the number of social dimensions. $\mathbf{W} \in \mathbb{R}^{m \times d}$ is a linear classifier, which is trained on the new representation of users $\mathbf{U}$ based on social dimensions. $\mathbf{H}$ is a diagonal matrix where $\mathbf{H}_{ii} = 1$ if u_i is labeled, and zero otherwise. The terms of $\alpha(\|\mathbf{U}\|_F^2 + \|\mathbf{V}\|_F^2) + \beta\|\mathbf{W}\|_F^2$ are added to avoid overfitting.

After learning the classifier $\mathbf{W}$ and the new representation $\mathbf{U}$ of users based on social dimensions, the label $\mathbf{y}_i$ of an unlabeled user u_i is predicted as

$$\mathbf{y}_i = \mathbf{u}_i \mathbf{W}^\top \qquad (5)$$

where $\mathbf{u}_i$ is the i-th row of $\mathbf{U}$ and is the new representation of u_i based on social dimensions.

THE PROPOSED SCALABLE ALGORITHM - LSOCDIM

Social influence theory suggests that a user's preference is likely to be influenced by influential users in her/his social networks. Therefore, wvRN directly uses the preferences of a user's neighbors to infer her preference and avoid to access the global network information in social dimension methods. Therefore, they are computationally efficient. However, they do not take into account the global structure patterns of network information, and need huge amount of labeled data to generate comparable results with social dimension methods. Social dimension based methods can access the whole network and extract global pattern (i.e, social dimensions) to represent users. Social dimensions can capture user preference dependence in the social network. Therefore with the social dimension representation, traditional powerful classifiers such as SVM can be trained. They can achieve high accuracy with a small fraction of labeled data. However, finding global structure patterns is very computationally expensive. Due to these shortcomings in each method, in this section we study a scalable algorithm which not only incorporates social influence theory as wvRN but also takes advantage of the power of traditional classifiers by finding a representation as social dimensions to capture user preference dependence.

Local Social Dimensions

Social influence theory indicates that a user's preference is influenced by influential users in her social networks [32] and this local pattern suggests that an influential user and users influenced by this user should share similar preferences. With this intuition, we define an influential user and her immediate neighbor or neighbors a few hops away as a local social dimension. Similar to global social dimensions, users in the same local social dimensions are likely to share similar preferences and local social dimensions also capture user preference dependency in the social network.

To extract K local social dimensions, we first find K influential users such that the number of users influenced by these K influential users is maximum, and then form a local social dimension with each influential user and users in her her immediate or a few hop neighbors. Therefore extracting local social dimensions boils down to find K influential users. We now formally define the problem of identifying K influential users as follow: *given a social network $G = (U, E)$ and a positive integer $K \leq |\mathbf{U}|$, identify a set of users $\mathbf{U}'$ such that a subset $\mathbf{U}' \subseteq \mathbf{U}$, $|\mathbf{U}'| \leq K$, and the number of users influenced by $\mathbf{U}'$ is maximum.*

The problem of finding K-influential users is tantamount to the maximization of a non-negative, non-decreasing, sub-modular function with a cardinality constraint. A greedy method gives a $(1 - 1/e)$−approximation for the maximization problem [12, 26]. The proposed algorithm to extract K local social dimensions is shown in Algorithm 1. It First starts with an empty output set $\mathbf{U}'$, and add one element from users set $\mathbf{U}$ to the output set that provides the largest marginal increase in the coverage; repeat the previous step until all the users are processed or the maximum cardinality bound K is reached. Then K local social dimensions are formed based on K influential users and their neighbors.

Algorithm 1 Local Social Dimension Extraction.

Input: The network information $\mathbf{X}$, K
Output: K Local Social Dimensions

1: Initialize $\mathbf{U}' \leftarrow \phi$
2: **while** $(|\mathbf{U}'| \leq K)$ and $(|\mathbf{U}'| \neq n)$ **do**
3:     Find $u_i \in \mathbf{U}$ such that difference between the amount of influenced users from $\mathbf{U}$ and $\mathbf{U}'$ is maximum.
4:     Update $\mathbf{U}' \leftarrow \mathbf{U}' \cup u_i$
5:     Update $\mathbf{U} \leftarrow \mathbf{U} - u_i$
6: **end while**
7: **for** Each Influential Users u_i in $\mathbf{U}'$ **do**
8:     Form a local social dimensions with u_i and immediate or a few hop neighbors
9: **end for**

An example of extracting local social dimensions from the network in Figure 1 is shown in Figure 2 where $\{u_3, u_6, u_7\}$ are three influential users and $\{LS_1, LS_2, LS_3\}$ are three local social dimensions formed by $\{u_3, u_6, u_7\}$.

User Preference Prediction with Local Social Dimensions

Local social dimensions can capture user preference dependency as social dimensions. Then users can be represented by local social dimensions and traditional powerful classifiers can be trained based on the new representation to facilitate the user preference prediction problem, which leads to a novel framework LSocDim as shown in Algorithm 2. Next, we briefly review the algorithm. In line 1, we use Algorithm 1 to extract K local social dimensions.

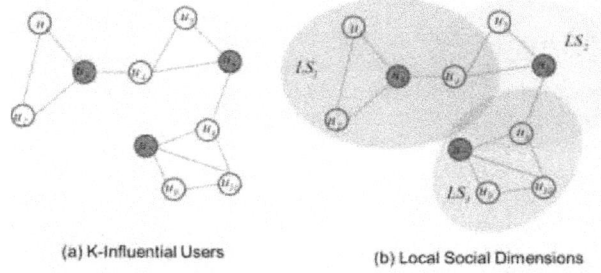

(a) K-Influential Users   (b) Local Social Dimensions

Figure 2: Local Social Dimension Extractions.

In line 2, similar to processes in [31], we treat local social dimensions as new features for users and represent users by local social dimensions. In line 3, we train a classifier based on the new representation.

Algorithm 2 The Proposed Local Social Dimension based Method.

Input: The network information $\mathbf{X}$, K
Output: A Classifier

1: Extract K local social dimensions by Algorithm 1
2: Represent users by local social dimensions
3: Train a classifier based on the new representation of users based on local social dimensions

---

Complexity Analysis

Due to the size of social networks, time complexity of the algorithm is an important parameter. In this section we analyze the time complexity of the proposed LSocDim algorithm and compare it against our two baseline algorithms, wvRN and SocDim. In the next section, we present the running time of the three algorithms. *Weighted Vote Relational Neighbors (wvRN) algorithm* Local predictions need only to look at the nodes' neighbors, therefore their execution time only depends on the size of nodes' neighborhood and is not a factor of size of the network. A theoretical analysis of time complexity shows that complexity of the local algorithm is $O(n)$, which n is the number of users in the network. *Social Dimensions algorithm* The original social dimension algorithm [31], uses an SVD approach to extract social dimensions from the network. The best algorithms for SVD computation of an $n \times n$ matrix take time that is proportional to $O(n^3)$ [1]. Then, the algorithm utilizes the social dimensions as features to train the classifier and predicts the missing labels. In this algorithm, extracting the social dimensions is the bottleneck which is the most contributor to the complexity of the algorithm. Overall, the algorithm has the time complexity proportional to $O(Kn^3)$, where K is number of social dimensions. *Local social dimensions algorithm* According to [12, 26], extracting K local social dimensions needs $O(Kn)$ operations. We treat local social dimensions as features. Since, the number of social dimensions is much smaller than the number of users $K \ll n$, the new representation is very low and sparse. Also the size of labeled data N should be much smaller than n. Most of popular classifiers can be trained with less than $O(Kn)$ operations. Hence, the overall time complexity of Algorithm 2 is $O(Kn)$

---

[1]http://rakaposhi.eas.asu.edu/s01-cse494-mailarchive/msg00028.html

EXPERIMENTS

In this section, we give a set of experiments where we use LSocDim for semisupervised classification. First we evaluate the efficiency of the proposed algorithm against the two representative algorithms: 1) weighted vote relational neighbor (wvRN) [20] and 2) social dimension (SocDim) [31]. We also study how the performance varies with the size of the labeled data. To evaluate the scalability of the algorithm, we use datasets with different sizes and run the experiments. For every experiment, we randomly sample a portion of nodes as labeled and report the average performance of 10 runs. The section starts with a quick introduction about the baseline algorithms. Then the dataset is described, and finally the results are presented.

Dataset

We use a directed dataset from Facebook. The nodes are Facebook fan pages and the links are formed by *like* relation between the pages. Each page can *like* or *be liked* by other pages. In our settings, if page u_i *like* page u_j, we consider u_j as u_i's *followee* and u_i as u_j's *follower*. In the network structure, each page is a node and liking another page creates a link from the follower to the followee. There is no limitation on the number of users that can like a Facebook page. The number of likes is a public property of the page., and is further considered as a measure of popularity in our experiments. Table 1 shows the statistics about the dataset.

Table 1: Our Facebook fan pages dataset

Number of nodes	5,856,000
Number of links	19,646,000
Size of labeled data	25,129 (0.43%)

Data collection process.

The dataset is collected by crawling Facebook pages through the site's public web interface. We start with a small set of seeds from the United States politicians, whose pages are publicly available on Facebook. We follow a *breadth first search (BFS)* algorithm to expand the nodes to the pages that are liked by the current page. Thus, after we crawl all of the seed pages, we continue with the pages liked by the seeds, and this process continued until all of the pages are collected. For every page, we collect the following publicly available attributes: *title*, *number of likes*, *political view*, *political party*, *category*, *gender*, and *list of liked pages*.

Table 2: Political views of self-reported Facebook fan-pages in our dataset

Political view	Distribution
Conservative	23%
Moderate	19%
Liberal	18%
Very Liberal	7%
Libertarian	7%
Very Conservative	4%
Apathetic	2%
Other	21%

In our experiments, labels are page's political view. Table 2 shows political views and their distribution in the dataset. Among more than 5.8 million Facebook pages in our dataset, only 25, 129 of them revealed their political views or parties which is about 0.43% of all pages. We use *page category* information to filter users affiliated with political issues. *Page category* is a public attribute of

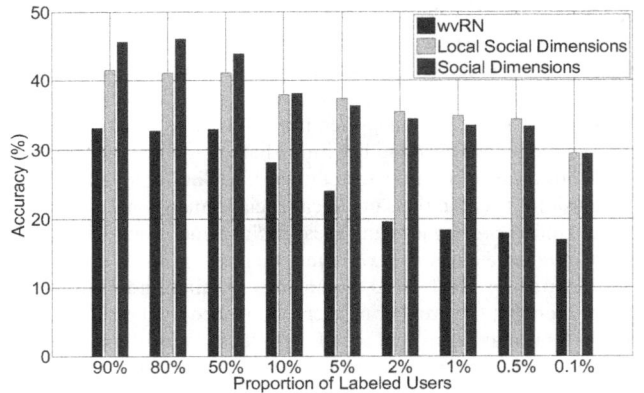

Figure 3: Accuracy of Local Social Dimensions comparing with wvRN [20] and Social Dimensions. The x-axis shows the fraction of the nodes that are labeled.

Facebook fan pages, which is usually chosen from a dropdown list of predefined values. In our dataset, *Community* with 16.8%, *Musician/Band* with 7.4%, *Non-Profit Organizations* with 4.1%, and *Public figure* with 3.8% popularity are the most popular categories. We choose *Public Figures*, *Politicians*, *Political Organizations*, and *Political Parties* categories in our experiments.

Performance Analysis

Accuracy of the prediction or precision is the most important factor in evaluating the performance of prediction algorithms. We define the accuracy as the fraction of the preferences correctly predicted as follows,

$$\frac{\sum_{c_i \in C} tp_{c_i}}{\sum_{c_i \in C} (tp_{c_i} + fn_{c_i})} \tag{6}$$

where C is the set of all class labels, tp_{c_i} is *true positive*, number of accurately classified nodes, and fn_{c_i} is *false negative*, number of misclassified nodes.

Figure 3 shows the accuracy of all three algorithms (wvRN, SocDim, and LSocDim). The second bar in the graph represents our proposed algorithm, Local Social Dimensions (LSocDim). It can be seen from the figure that the results of LSocDim algorithm are promising and are comparable with SocDim (the state-of-the-art prediction algorithm for networked data). Among the three algorithms, wvRN uses the minimum network information, and SocDim uses the maximum network information. LSocDim, however, uses local information but also considers the global patterns of the network. The local algorithm, wvRN, in all of the experiments take the third place in prediction accuracy among the three algorithms. Though the highest prediction accuracy of 45.6% belongs to SocDim method, according to Table 3 LSocDim outperforms SocDim for all of the experiments with less than 10% labeled data. These results confirm the effectiveness of LSocDim when only a small fraction of the data is labeled. When a small fraction of the data is labeled, nodes tend to associate with other like-minded nodes in local communities. In this situation, techniques that use the entire network information to extract the clusters, are not as effective as those focus more on local information but consider the global signals as well. LSocDim is an example of a local approach with global patterns. Recall our goal is to design a scalable algorithm where its accuracy is comparable with other state-of-the-art algorithms.

Table 3: Accuracy of the three algorithms, with respect to the size of labeled data.

Labels	90%	80%	50%	10%	5%	2%	1%	0.5%	0.1%	RND
LSocDim	41.5	41.1	41.1	37.9	**37.4**	**35.5**	**34.9**	**34.4**	**29.5**	18.6%
wvRN	33.1	31.8	35.0	28.1	23.9	19.6	18.4	17.9	17.0	18.6%
SocDim	**45.6**	**46.1**	**43.9**	**38.1**	36.4	34.5	33.6	33.4	29.4	18.6%

Table 4: Running time of the three algorithms, *wvRN*, *LSocDim*, and *SocDim* (all numbers are in Seconds). The first row shows the fraction of the labeled data. In *SocDim* and *LSocDim*, running time has a direct correlation with the fraction of revealed labels. In wvRN algorithm, running time is a constant value.

Labels	90%	80%	50%	10%	5%	2%	1%	0.5%	0.1%
Local	0.9	0.9	0.9	0.9	0.9	0.9	0.9	0.9	0.9
LSocDim	47.2	46.2	42.2	38	38	38	37.8	38	37.6
Global	1237	1255	1260	1308	1209	1278	878	888	876

Efficiency Analysis

It is always desired to design algorithms to be both efficient and accurate. However, usually there is a trade-off between performance and efficiency of prediction algorithms.

In this experiment we use the running time of each algorithm to measure the efficiency. Table 4 shows the running time of the three algorithms. Among the three methods, wvRN is the fastest with only 0.9 second for every experiment. On average, LSocDim algorithm needs 39.9 seconds to predict labels in a network with 26,240 nodes and 457,597 edges. SocDim algorithm however, needs much longer time to predict the labels with an average of 1107 seconds for each iteration. In both SocDim and LSocDim algorithms, running time positively correlates with the size of labeled data. The reason is that when size of the labeled data decreases, the training set size decreases. Therefore, the algorithms converges faster compared to the case where we use larger training set.

Figure 4 provides a comprehensive comparison between *LSocDim* and *SocDim* (global) algorithms. The experiments show that LSocDim is 23 to 34 times faster than SocDim, which is a huge improvement on the efficiency of the algorithm. However, there is a huge gap between LSocDim and wvRN algorithm. From efficiency point of view, LSocDim can be considered as a bridge between wvRN and SocDim algorithms.

Scalability Analysis

In this section, we study the scalability of the proposed algorithm, i.e., how the computational time of the algorithm (when running on a Core i7-4770 CPU and 16GB memory desktop) varies with the number of nodes in the network. To evaluate the scalability of the algorithm, we construct four smaller samples of the original network. Table 5 shows statistics about the networks.

Table 5: Smaller networks to test the scalability of the algorithms

	N_1	N_2	N_3	N_4
Nodes	529	900	1715	2498
Edges	2879	7507	10939	24201
Number of Clusters	137	313	492	1301

We run the experiments and measure the running time of each algorithm for all four networks. Table 6 shows the running time for the three algorithms with respect to different network sizes.

Table 6: Scalability analysis. The table shows the number of seconds each algorithm needs to predict labels for the given network.

	N_1	N_2	N_3	N_4
wvRN	0.011	0.025	0.042	0.079
SocDim	0.960	2.140	7.291	13.861
LSocDim	0.026	0.037	0.056	0.121

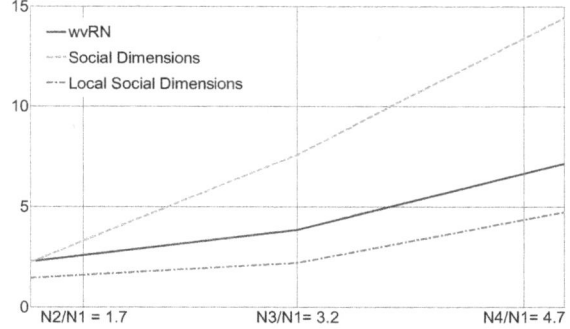

Figure 5: Scalability of the algorithms; x-axis shows the growth of the network size, and y-axis shows the running time increase.

Figure 5 shows how the running time increases when we use networks with larger sizes. In the figure, x-axis shows the growth of the network size, and y-axis shows the running time increase. Among the three algorithm, LSocDim has the minimum slope of increasing the running time, and SocDim has the maximum slope.

Sensitivity Analysis

In both supervised and semi-supervised learning algorithms, size of the labeled data is an important parameter that affects the prediction accuracy [34], which is also observed in the experiments of the previous sections. Table 3 shows the accuracy of the prediction algorithms with respect to the size of labeled data. The first column on the left hand side of the figure is the accuracy, when 90% of the users are labeled, and the algorithm needs to predict the remaining 10% non-labeled users. As the table suggests, for all of the three algorithms, there is a direct correlation between the size of labeled data and the accuracy of prediction. Further, the table and Figure 3 shows two trends. First, the prediction accuracy of both SocDim and LSocDim smoothly decreases when the labeled data decrease from 90% down to only 0.1%. It shows that these methods are more prone to the changes of the size of the labeled data. Even with only 1% of labeled data, the prediction accuracy of these algorithms are relatively high. Second, the results show that wvRN is highly sensitive to the size of the labeled data. In particular, when the fraction of the labeled data goes under 10%, the accuracy of wvRN decreases sharply, and the results become similar to the random prediction. In local approaches, algorithms usually use the nodes' immediate neighbors to make prediction. However, due to the size of nodesŠ neighbors and small fraction of the labeled nodes, most likely the algorithms are not able to find a labeled node. In addition, even small chance of existing noise in the data, leads to a huge prediction error. The need for a huge amount of labeled data can be considered as the main drawbacks of local algorithms, as the labeled data is not alway available.

Labeled Users	Accuracy (%)			Running time (Seconds)		
	SocDim	LSocDim	LSocDim vs SocDim	SocDim	LSocDim	LSocDim vs SocDim
90.0%	45.6%	41.5%	-9.1%	1237	47.2	3.8%
80.0%	46.1%	41.1%	-10.8%	1255	46.2	3.7%
50.0%	43.9%	41.1%	-6.4%	1260	42.2	3.3%
10.0%	38.1%	37.9%	-0.5%	1308	38.0	2.9%
5.0%	36.4%	37.4%	2.8%	1209	38.0	3.1%
2.0%	34.5%	35.5%	3.0%	1278	38.0	3.0%
1.0%	33.6%	34.9%	4.1%	878	37.8	4.3%
0.5%	33.4%	34.4%	2.9%	888	38.0	4.3%
0.1%	29.5%	29.5%	0.1%	876	37.6	4.3%

Figure 4: From performance point of view, LSocDim is comparable with SocDim, and from efficiency point of view LSocDim is comparable with wvRN. Therefore, LSocDim can be considered as a bridge between wvRN and SocDim algorithms.

Despite the local algorithms, SocDim and LSocDim use global patterns. This means that they use the entire network structure to extract the clusters, train a model, and then make prediction. Consequently, even small fraction of labeled nodes can be effectively used to achieve high prediction accuracy.

Table 3 shows that even when only 1% of the data points are labeled, the prediction accuracy of the global approaches are higher than the accuracy of local algorithm with 90% labeled data. Surprisingly, when the size of labeled data decreases from 90% down to only 0.1%, the accuracy of SocDim and LSocDim drops by only 30%. These results show the stability of the global approaches against the size of the labeled data.

Among the three algorithms, LSocDim is more efficient and reliable when smaller sizes of labeled data is available. The experiments show that when less than 10% of the users are labeled, LSocDim always outperform SocDim in prediction accuracy. Labeling the data point are an expensive and time consuming process, and in many cases it may be impossible to label enough data points. Therefore, it is important that the algorithm has the capability of prediction with reasonable accuracy even if a small set of labeled data is available. In this regard, LSocDim is preferred over the other two algorithms from our results.

In the literature, many of the proposed algorithms are evaluated with more than 10% up to 90% available labeled data points. This is far from many real world cases where the available labeled data can be as low as (or less than) 1%. One line of our future work is to evaluate the performance of the existing algorithms with respect to the size of labeled data.

LITERATURE REVIEW

Predicting an individual's interests and preferences based various cues from the individual and her environment has a long history in social science [8]. The advent of participatory web has enabled information consumers to become information producers via social media. This phenomenon has attracted researchers of different disciplines including social scientists, political parties, and market researchers to study social media as a source of data to explain human behavior in the physical world [1, 18]. With the availability of social media data and huge amount of user-generated data, it is shown that we are able to investigate users' preferences by studying their online activities, postings, and behavior in social media [27]. There are plenty of studies showing that it is possible to use information available in social networking sites to infer missing attributes such as age, gender, education, political orientation and users' interests and preferences [24, 25, 17, 22, 3].

According to the type of information the prediction algorithms use, we can categorize them into *Content-based*, *log-based*, and *network-based* approaches. *Content-based* approaches use user generated content, such as user profile, weblogs, product reviews, and status update, to predict user preferences. They usually use classification algorithms to predict the users' preferences. Support vector machines (SVMs) [28], latent dirichlet allocation (LDA) [5], and boosted decision trees are the most prominent algorithms used in this category. Content-based approaches also can use users' historical information, such as credit card purchases, rating history, buying history, or browsing information, to predict user preferences [6]. Preferences also could be directly inferred from analyzing the log information. [9], [25], and [22] investigate the use of website browsing logs and the content of personal websites to predict personal attributes. Mislove et al. [24] show that the attributes of users, in combination with the social network graph, can be used to predict the attributes of other users in the same network. They user Facebook data and show that when only 20% of the nodes in the network reveal their personal attribute (major, department, year), it is possible to predict other users' attributes with an accuracy of over 80%. Tan et al. [29] use Twitter mention (@) data to construct a network and show that users who mention each other in their tweets are more likely to hold similar opinions. Similar results also reported by [9] Conover et al. [5] report an accuracy of up to 95% when predicting users' political orientation by employing users' content in combination with network information on Twitter. Carter et al. in [11] use the network structure and users' positions within a friendship network on Facebook to accurately predict users' sexual orientation. Kosinski et al. [13] use users' Facebook records to show the degree to which relatively basic digital records of social media users' behavior can be used to accurately predict a wide range of personal attributes. They use Facebook *likes* to extract users' positive association with online content, such as photos, videos, Facebook pages of products, businesses, people, books, places, and websites.

Network-based approaches use users' friendship or interaction information to predict their preferences. Most of the algorithms in this category use the simple but effective social theory of *homophily*, which indicates the similarity of connected users [36].

Relational learning or within-network classification [21] refers to the classification when data instances are presented in a network format. The data instances in the network are not independently identically distributed (i.i.d.) as in conventional data mining. To capture the correlation between labels of neighboring data objects, typically a Markov dependency assumption is assumed. That is, the labels of one node depend on the labels (or attributes) of its neighbors. Normally, a relational classifier is constructed based on the relational features of labeled data, and then an iterative process is required to determine the class labels for the unlabeled data. The class label or the class membership is updated for each node while the labels of its neighbors are fixed [32]. This process is repeated until the label inconsistency between neighboring nodes is minimized. It is shown that [21] a simple weighted vote relational neighborhood classifier [20] works reasonably well on some benchmark relational data and is recommended as a baseline for comparison.

CONCLUSIONS AND FUTURE WORK

In this paper we studied the network-based approach of inferring users' personal preferences. We categorized the network-based algorithms into *local* and *global* algorithms. Local algorithms use usersŠ neighbors to predict their preferences, while the global approaches use the entire network information to predict user's preferences. Our experimental results show that local algorithms are fast and scalable, however they need large amount of labeled data to achieve reasonable prediction accuracy. Further their prediction accuracy is always less than the accuracy of global algorithms. *Global* algorithms, in contrast, are computationally expensive, but perform well even in cases where only a very small fraction of the data is labeled. We proposed a new algorithm called *LSocDim* based on social influence theory to bridge the efficiency of local algorithms and the accuracy of global algorithms. The experiments show the efficiency and the effectiveness of the proposed algorithm. In particular, we show that LSocDim achieves a prediction accuracy near to that of the state-of-the-art global algorithm, SoCDim, while decreasing the running time by upto 40 times.

By performing a sensitivity analysis with respect to the size of labeled data, we show that SocDim, performs better than the baseline local algorithm, wvRN, when the available labeled data is small. We also show that the proposed algorithm, LSocDim, performs better than SocDim, when less than 10% of the data is labeled. This is an important result, considering that labeling the data points is expensive and time consuming process, and in many cases it is even impossible to label enough data points. We also evaluate the scalability of the algorithms. The theoretical and experimental results show that the proposed algorithm is computationally less expensive that the SocDim algorithm, the baseline global algorithm. The scalability analysis also shows a promising result. As the networks in social media are normally involving millions and even hundreds of millions of nodes, it is important for inferring algorithms to be scalable.

According to our experiments, the size of the labeled data is an important parameter that affects the performance of the prediction algorithms. Therefore, as our future work, we plan to evaluate different prediction algorithms with respect to the size of the labeled data points. In addition, we are interested in evaluating the impact of data characteristics on the performance of the prediction algorithms.

ACKNOWLEDGMENT

We thank the anonymous reviewers for their useful comments. This research is, in part, sponsored by the Office of Naval Research grants (N000141110527 and N000141410095) and Army Research Office (025071).

REFERENCES

[1] M. A. Abbasi, S.-K. Chai, H. Liu, and K. Sagoo. Real-world behavior analysis through a social media lens. In *Social Computing, Behavioral-Cultural Modeling and Prediction*, pages 18–26. Springer, 2012.

[2] M. A. Abbasi, R. Zafarani, J. Tang, and H. Liu. Am i more similar to my followers or followees? homophily effect in directed online social networks. In *25th ACM Conference on Hypertext and Social Media*, 2014.

[3] A. Chaabane, G. Acs, M. A. Kaafar, et al. You are what you like! information leakage through users' interests. In *Proceedings of the 19th Annual Network & Distributed System Security Symposium (NDSS)*, 2012.

[4] R. Cohen and D. Ruths. Classifying political orientation on twitter: It's not easy! In *Seventh International AAAI Conference on Weblogs and Social Media*, 2013.

[5] M. D. Conover, B. Gonçalves, J. Ratkiewicz, A. Flammini, and F. Menczer. Predicting the political alignment of twitter users. In *Privacy, security, risk and trust (passat), 2011 ieee third international conference on and 2011 ieee third international conference on social computing (socialcom)*, pages 192–199. IEEE, 2011.

[6] K. De Bock and D. Van den Poel. Predicting website audience demographics forweb advertising targeting using multi-website clickstream data. *Fundamenta Informaticae*, 98(1):49–70, 2010.

[7] C. Desrosiers and G. Karypis. Within-network classification using local structure similarity. In *Machine Learning and Knowledge Discovery in Databases*, pages 260–275. Springer, 2009.

[8] S. D. Gosling, S. J. Ko, T. Mannarelli, and M. E. Morris. A room with a cue: personality judgments based on offices and bedrooms. *Journal of personality and social psychology*, 82(3):379, 2002.

[9] J. Hu, H.-J. Zeng, H. Li, C. Niu, and Z. Chen. Demographic prediction based on user's browsing behavior. In *Proceedings of the 16th international conference on World Wide Web*, pages 151–160. ACM, 2007.

[10] D. Jensen. Statistical challenges to inductive inference in linked data. In *Seventh International Workshop on Artificial Intelligence and Statistics*, pages 569–571, 1999.

[11] C. Jernigan and B. F. Mistree. Gaydar: Facebook friendships expose sexual orientation. *First Monday*, 14(10), 2009.

[12] D. Kempe, J. Kleinberg, and É. Tardos. Maximizing the spread of influence through a social network. In *Proceedings of the ninth ACM SIGKDD international conference on Knowledge discovery and data mining*, pages 137–146. ACM, 2003.

[13] M. Kosinski, D. Stillwell, and T. Graepel. Private traits and attributes are predictable from digital records of human behavior. *Proceedings of the National Academy of Sciences*, 110(15):5802–5805, 2013.

[14] J. A. Krosnick, C. M. Judd, and B. Wittenbrink. The measurement of attitudes. *The handbook of attitudes*, pages 21–76, 2005.

[15] S. Kumar, G. Barbier, M. Abbasi, and H. Liu. Tweettracker: An analysis tool for humanitarian and disaster relief. In *Fifth International AAAI Conference on Weblogs and Social Media, ICWSM*, 2011.

[16] S. Kumar, F. Morstatter, and H. Liu. Twitter data analytics, 2013.

[17] R. Li, S. Wang, H. Deng, R. Wang, and K. C.-C. Chang. Towards social user profiling: unified and discriminative influence model for inferring home locations. In *Proceedings of the 18th ACM SIGKDD international conference on Knowledge discovery and data mining*, pages 1023–1031. ACM, 2012.

[18] H. Liu and M. A. Abbasi. Measuring user credibility in social media. In *Social Computing, Behavioral-Cultural Modeling and Prediction*, pages 441–448. Springer, 2013.

[19] Q. Lu and L. Getoor. Link-based classification. In *ICML*, volume 3, pages 496–503, 2003.

[20] S. A. Macskassy and F. Provost. A simple relational classifier. Technical report, DTIC Document, 2003.

[21] S. A. Macskassy and F. Provost. Classification in networked data: A toolkit and a univariate case study. *The Journal of Machine Learning Research*, 8:935–983, 2007.

[22] B. Marcus, F. Machilek, and A. Schütz. Personality in cyberspace: personal web sites as media for personality expressions and impressions. *Journal of Personality and Social Psychology*, 90(6):1014, 2006.

[23] M. McPherson, L. Smith-Lovin, and J. M. Cook. Birds of a feather: Homophily in social networks. *Annual review of sociology*, pages 415–444, 2001.

[24] A. Mislove, B. Viswanath, K. P. Gummadi, and P. Druschel. You are who you know: inferring user profiles in online social networks. In *Proceedings of the third ACM international conference on Web search and data mining*, pages 251–260. ACM, 2010.

[25] D. Murray and K. Durrell. Inferring demographic attributes of anonymous internet users. In *Web Usage Analysis and User Profiling*, pages 7–20. Springer, 2000.

[26] G. L. Nemhauser, L. A. Wolsey, and M. L. Fisher. An analysis of approximations for maximizing submodular set functionsÛi. *Mathematical Programming*, 14(1):265–294, 1978.

[27] B. O'Connor, R. Balasubramanyan, B. R. Routledge, and N. A. Smith. From tweets to polls: Linking text sentiment to public opinion time series. *ICWSM*, 11:122–129, 2010.

[28] D. Rao and D. Yarowsky. Detecting latent user properties in social media. In *Proc. of the NIPS MLSN Workshop*, 2010.

[29] C. Tan, L. Lee, J. Tang, L. Jiang, M. Zhou, and P. Li. User-level sentiment analysis incorporating social networks. In *Proceedings of the 17th ACM SIGKDD international conference on Knowledge discovery and data mining*, pages 1397–1405. ACM, 2011.

[30] J. Tang, Y. Chang, and H. Liu. Mining social media with social theories: A survey. *SIGKDD Explorations*, 2014.

[31] L. Tang and H. Liu. Relational learning via latent social dimensions. In *Proceedings of the 15th ACM SIGKDD international conference on Knowledge discovery and data mining*, pages 817–826. ACM, 2009.

[32] L. Tang and H. Liu. Scalable learning of collective behavior based on sparse social dimensions. In *Proceedings of the 18th ACM conference on Information and knowledge management*, pages 1107–1116. ACM, 2009.

[33] F. Wang and C. Zhang. Label propagation through linear neighborhoods. *Knowledge and Data Engineering, IEEE Transactions on*, 20(1):55–67, 2008.

[34] F. Wang, C. Zhang, H. C. Shen, and J. Wang. Semi-supervised classification using linear neighborhood propagation. In *Computer Vision and Pattern Recognition, 2006 IEEE Computer Society Conference on*, volume 1, pages 160–167. IEEE, 2006.

[35] Y. Yang, P. Cui, W. Zhu, and S. Yang. User interest and social influence based emotion prediction for individuals. In *Proceedings of the 21st ACM international conference on Multimedia*, pages 785–788. ACM, 2013.

[36] R. Zafarani, M. A. Abbasi, and H. Liu. *Social Media Mining: An Introduction*. Cambridge University Press, 2014.

[37] E. Zheleva and L. Getoor. To join or not to join: the illusion of privacy in social networks with mixed public and private user profiles. In *Proceedings of the 18th international conference on World wide web*, pages 531–540. ACM, 2009.

Recognizing Skill Networks and Their Specific Communication and Connection Practices

Sergiu Chelaru, Eelco Herder, Kaweh Djafari Naini, Patrick Siehndel
L3S Research Center
Leibniz University Hannover, Germany
{chelaru, herder, naini, siehndel}@L3S.de

ABSTRACT

Social networks are a popular medium for building and maintaining a professional network. Many studies exist on general communication and connection practices within these networks. However, studies on expertise search suggest the existence of subgroups centered around a particular profession. In this paper, we analyze commonalities and differences between these groups, based on a set of 94,155 public user profiles. The results confirm that such subgroups can be recognized. Further, the average number of connections differs between groups, as a result of differences in intention for using social media. Similarly, within the groups, specific topics and resources are discussed and shared, and there are interesting differences in the tone and wording the group members use. These insights are relevant for interpreting results from social media analyses and can be used for identifying group-specific resources and communication practices that new members may want to know about.

Categories and Subject Descriptors

H.5.4 [**Hypertext/Hypermedia**]: Navigation; H.3.5 [**Online Information Services**]: Web-based services

Keywords

skills, expertise, social networks, connections, topics, sentiment, content

1. INTRODUCTION

People who work in similar professions typically share particular skills. Further, if people are asked to indicate their skills, it is expected that the skills they mention vary in granularity. For example, someone working in public relations may indicate skills in social networking and marketing, but also specific skills such as DTP software, writing press releases and time management.

It is also known that people from different professions or cultural backgrounds have different practices in how they

communicate with one another, the communication mechanisms that they choose and the topics that they discuss [12]. These differences can also be observed on a more private, personal level: programmers are usually more informal than bankers, people working in public relations are typically more active in social media than investors, and pastors will most likely talk about different topics than real-estate agents.

In this paper, we investigate differences in communities within self-reported skill networks. We are particularly interested in discovering differences in their communication practices: how well is a professional community connected, how often do people post updates via Twitter or Facebook, what are the topics that they talk about, and what is the overall tone or sentiment of these communications? Particularly for people who aim to identify and approach experts from a different profession, who wish to promote their services in other communities, or who consider a career switch, it is important to know the unwritten rules in a network. For example, what would programmers think of overly positive marketing language? How often can one repeat an announcement? Would it be a good idea to add a personal touch or will that be considered 'unprofessional'?

Being aware of differences between professional communities is also important for interpreting statistical data from social network analysis. For instance, in some communities the average number of followers is considerably higher than in other communities. As a consequence, a person from a well-connected community like online marketing with, say, 300 followers, may be considered isolated; for a programmer, this is actually a very good number. The same differences apply for interpreting centrality and other in- and out-degree measures.

The main contributions of our paper are: we provide an overview on how skills in professional networks are related and categorize these skills into professions. Further, we show to what extent different professions differ from one another in terms of connections, topics, sentiment and shared content. Finally, we discuss implications for social network analysis and the design of professional networking sites.

The remainder of this paper is structured as follows. In the next section we discuss related work, followed by a description of the dataset we used. In Section 4 we discuss the structure of the skill network derived from LinkedIn profiles and how this structure is reflected in the professions that we extracted using LDA. The results are presented in four subsections, covering: connections between people, topics that people discuss about, subjectivity and polarity of the wording, and the resources that they share. We end the paper with a discussion and concluding remarks.

2. RELATED WORK

Our work draws upon two related strands of research. First, our focus on skill and expertise networks fits in the research area of automated expert finding, in which both explicit and implicit information is used for identifying experts in a particular area. Our interest in differences between expertise domains in how people connect and communicate online follows the tradition of social media analysis.

Yimam-Seid and Kobsa [20] argue that for the effective use of knowledge in organizations, it is essential to exploit tacit knowledge that is hidden in various forms, including in the people's heads. The authors also separate the need for 'information' from the need for 'expertise': the need for people who can provide advise, help or feedback - or who can perform a social or organizational role. Their expertise recommender made use of a hand-tailored expertise model.

MacDonald et al [15] indicate that, in order to identify experts, documentary evidence is needed. This evidence may be based on documents, emails, web pages visited, or explicitly created profiles with an abstract or a list of their skills. This evidence will than be ranked with respect to a given query or goal skill profile. Based on the TREC W3C and CERC test collections, they evaluated to what extent additional evidence could improve expert retrieval. They found out that the proximity of a candidate name to query terms and clustering of main expertise areas are the best indicators. Extracted text from homepages and the number of inlinks did not have much influence.

Balog and De Rijke's experiments [3] with data from the 2005 TREC Enterprise track show that user expertise can effectively be derived from email content; the persons being cc'd in an email were often authorities on the content of the message. Ghosh et al [10] leveraged social media (Twitter) content for seeking experts on a topic. Their results indicate that *endorsement* in other users' Twitter Lists (of which the topics need to be extracted) infers a user's expertise more accurately than systems that rely on someone's biography or tweet content.

Guy et al [11] examined indicators for expertise and interest as expressed by users of enterprise social media. The results are based on a large-scale user survey. They separate 'expertise' (being knowledgeable or skilled) from 'interest' (curiosity, basic knowledge, desire to learn more). As expected, interest and expertise ratings are correlated, with values for interest higher than for expertise. Results indicate that blogs and microblog provide different, more useful, information than communities and forums.

The above-mentioned studies suggest that people's skills and expertise can be derived from both explicitly provided lists and from their connections and communication patterns. This is consistent with Cingano et al's [8] observation that better-connected unemployed individuals, particularly those whose contacts were employed, are more easily reemployed. However, all of these studies were conducted in a single professional area or they generalized results between different areas. It is likely that considerable differences can be found between communities. For example, Hong et al [12] found that Twitter users of different languages adopted different conventions with respect to the inclusion of URLs, hashtags and mentions, as well as on replying and retweet-ing behavior. The main conclusion they drew is that the 'average' behavior of the English-speaking community does not necessarily translate to other communities.

In our study, we will look at differences in how people from different professions are connected, the topics that they discuss, the subjectivity and polarity in their wording, and the type of resources or websites that they share. These topics have been subject of research in various studies, a small selection of them is discussed in the remainder of this section.

Kumar et al [13] analyzed the structure and evolution of online social networks. They showed that networks typically have one well-connected core region, but most users are located in one of several more or less isolated communities around it. These communities are typically centered around one central person, and it is unlikely that two isolated communities will merge at some point. In the next section, we will see that the structure of our skill-based network matches these observations.

Abel et al [2] compared different approaches for extracting professional interests from social media profiles. Results indicate that dedicated tag-based profiles and self-created user profiles are most suitable for this task. Twitter profiles are more diverse but also more noisy; this effect can be reduced by extracting entities from running text. In a follow-up study, Abel et al [1] analyzed the completeness of user profiles in different social media. The outcomes suggest that user profiles in networking services, such as LinkedIn, are more complete than those in services like Twitter. Further, the topics that users talk about differs between channels, but the overlap in topics is higher between services that are used for similar purposes. It was also shown that combining information from different services was beneficial for tag and resource recommendations.

Siersdorfer et al [17] investigated the usefulness of comments, as perceived by YouTube users. They found out that positive comments were considered more useful than negative comments. Differences between categories were also found: for example, science videos receive predominantly objective comments, politics relatively many negatively rated comments, and music videos mainly attract positively rated comments. These findings suggest that different communities have different norms with respect to commenting - we expect that the same effect can be observed if one compares different professions.

3. DATASET

In order to create our dataset, we first collected a set of 94,115 public user profiles from About.me, using the crawling strategy employed by Liu et al. in [14]. About.me is a personal profile site where users can include all their social-web accounts. From each profile, we collected the users' LinkedIn, Twitter and Facebook accounts.

For LinkedIn, our crawler gathered the public profile data, including skills and expertise tags, industry, job and number of connections.

For each account from Twitter, we gathered the complete user profile with information like number of followers and friends or number of lists the user is in. Beside that, we crawled the latest 200 Tweets using the Twitter Rest API [1]. The average number of Tweets posted by the users is 5,833,

---
[1] https://dev.twitter.com/docs/api

with a median of 1812. This indicates that most of our users are quite active in Twitter. We also had 33 users with more than 100.000 followers, which is already pretty influential.

The Facebook subset was collected using the Facebook API [2], which provides access to the public profile information of the users. Here, our crawl was focused on the Facebook timeline of the user, which mainly contains the shared posts. On average, the number of posts per user is 210 (median 23), with 34 users having more than 5,000 posts. Further, we collected data on the most popular features in Facebook, including the number of likes, number of comments, and number of shares on the users' posts.

In total, we have 33,516 users with a LinkedIn profile, 46,799 users with a Twitter profile and 34,523 users with a Facebook profile. Since the LinkedIn account serves as a source for our topics describing the users, we use for our analysis only Twitter and Facebook profiles that have a corresponding LinkedIn profile, resulting in a final set of 7,740 users. Our datasets are inherently noisy, as they represent human behavior. For example, the skills from LinkedIn are self-reported. Similarly, tweet content and Facebook posts are a mix of - among others - work-related announcements, private updates, and responses to others. However, this noise is reduced by the fact that our analysis is based on a fairly large collection of users.

4. SKILL NETWORKS

LinkedIn users can list their skills in their profiles. It is a reasonable assumption that basic, more generic skills - such as 'management' - are more often mentioned than more specific skills - such as 'competitive analysis'. Further, one would expect that related skills - such as 'search engine optimization' and 'Web analytics' are often mentioned together, and that subskills are connected to one or two more generic skills - for example, 'Microsoft Word' would be often mentioned together with 'Microsoft Office' and 'Creative Writing'.

To verify whether these assumptions hold in LinkedIn, we visualized the network of skills using the graph visualization software Gephi [4] - see Figure 1, using a force-based layout, with the edge weights determined by how often skills are mentioned together. The four inlays that show parts of the network confirm the above-mentioned assumptions.

The largest node in the network is 'Social Media', which suggests that our sample is dominated by people who are professionally active in social media. Further, the areas surrounding the 'social media hub' have clearly defined sub topics. Top-right from social media are skills that are related to blogging and writing - with a subgroup of graphic design skills. The more technical professions, such as web design and programming are located bottom-right. 'Search engine optimization' forms the bridge to the more marketing-related skills in the left part of the visualization. Top-left is dominated by more traditional management skills, including team building and planning.

4.1 Subgroups in skill networks

The skill network, as displayed in Figure 1, suggests that the LinkedIn network can be divided into skill-based groups, or 'professions'. As explained in the introduction, different professions are expected to have differences in terms of

communication behavior, the way people are connected, the topics they talk about, the resources they use, and the way they express themselves.

In order to study topics beyond individual tags and to obtain more context-related information, we additionally employed Latent Dirichlet Allocation (LDA) [5] and modeled each LinkedIn Skills and Expertise tag-based representation of a user as a mixture of latent topics. For this, we used the LDA implementation in the Mallet library[3]. Given a set of term sets (users u_i represented by their Skills and Expertise tags in our case) and the desired number of latent topics, k, LDA outputs the probabilities $P(z_j|u_i)$ that the Skills and Expertise topic z_j is contained (related) in the user profile u_i. In addition, LDA computes term probabilities $P(t_j|z_i)$ for tags t_j; the terms with the highest probabilities for a latent topic z_i can be used to represent that topic. We empirically chose the number of latent topics as 50 for our LinkedIn dataset.

Table 1 shows the top-10 most probable terms for the 50 latent topics (called *professions* in the next sections), as assigned by the LDA method. In addition, the table contains short topic labels which were manually assigned and will be used throughout the rest of this paper.

5. CONNECTIONS AND ACTIVITIES

In this section, we discuss the results obtained from our analysis of differences in connections and activities between professions. We start with an overview of the differences in connections: which professions are better connected and more active. We continue with an analysis of the differences in topics that users post and tweet about: how generic or specific are these topics? Then we show that the differences in reasons why professions engage in social media have an impact on the sentiment and objectivity of the wording. Finally, we investigate which types of links and resources are shared in different professions.

5.1 Differences in connections

In this section, we look which professions are most and least connected with one another. Based on the insights obtained from the related work, we expect that professions that are in the core of the network are most connected and most active. In order to identify these differences, we took the following features into account:

- **LinkedIn:** We used the number of contacts as an indicator for the connections, no activity information was available.

- **Twitter:** Here, the user connections are based on the followers (incoming links), friends (outgoing links) and presence in lists (curated group of Twitter users). Activity is measured by the number of tweets.

- **Facebook:** As measure for connectivity, we used the number of likes, comments and shares (from friends) on the user's 'wall'. The number of posts of the users himself is an indicator of their activity.

For each of the social networks we created two lists of the top-5 highest and the top-5 lowest values on connections, presented in Figure 2. All professions displayed in this picture appear at least in one of these lists - all others are omitted.

[2]https://developers.facebook.com/docs/graph-api/

[3]http://mallet.cs.umass.edu/

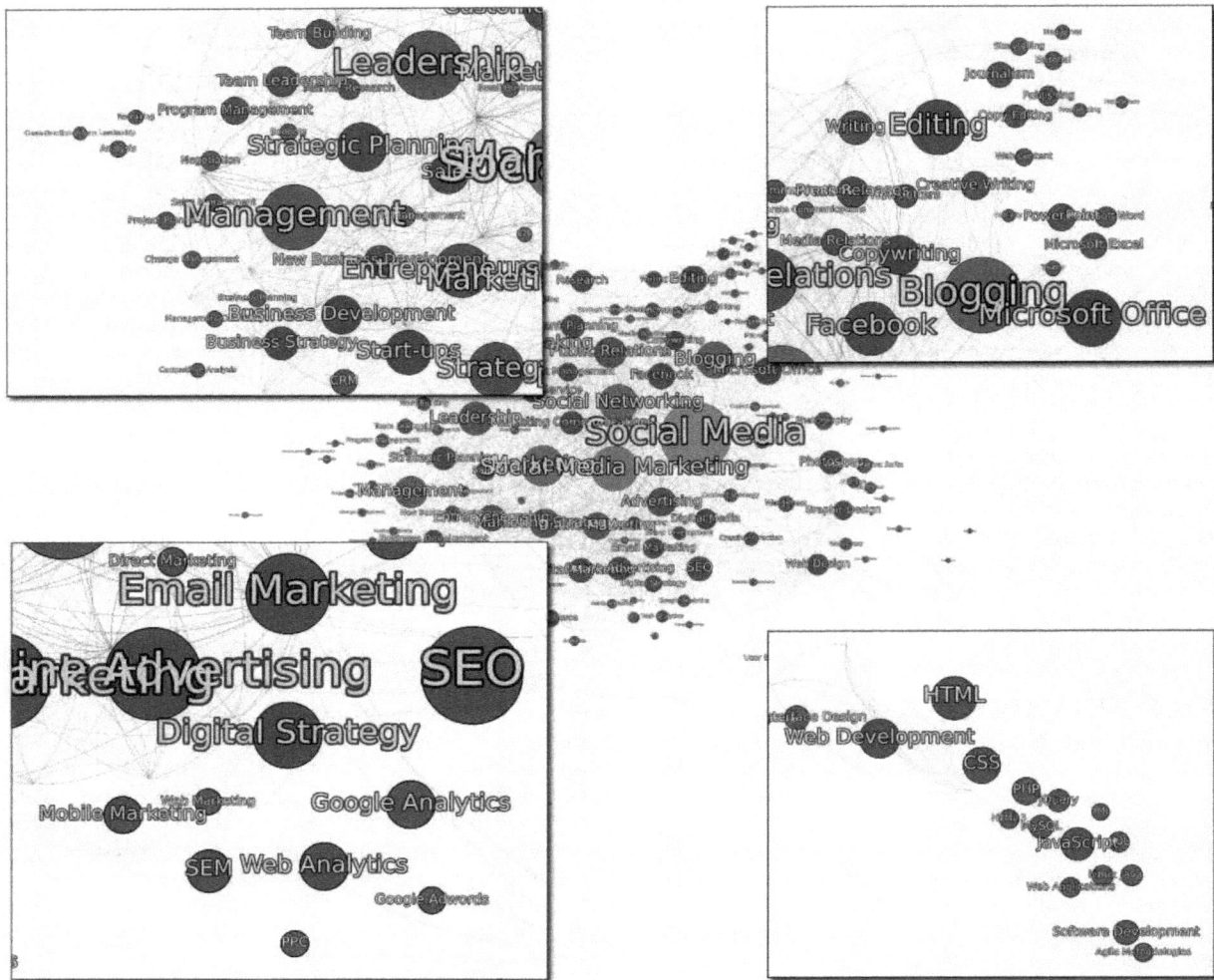

Figure 1: Skill network in LinkedIn. Larger nodes are more often mentioned. Skills that are often mentioned together are closer to one another. The four inlays are close-ups of parts of the network.

As can be seen, several professions have high connectivity scores in more than one network. These include Mobile Devices (actually startups in this field), Entrepreneurs, Marketing and Search Engine Optimization. Low connectivity scores in more than one network are found among Web Programmers, Software Engineers, Pastors, Team Managers and Health and Lifestyle Advisors. In general, the left side mainly contains marketing-oriented professions, the right side IT-oriented professions and 'offline' professions.

In Twitter, the number of followers is highly correlated with the number of friends ($r = .79$) and presence in lists ($r = .87$). The number of followers depends less ($r = .59$) on the number of status updates. Within Facebook, no significant correlations between the number of (public) posts and likes or comments can be found - apparently, Facebook is less 'quantity-driven'.

Interestingly, apart from the marketing-oriented professions, the top-5 professions in terms of status updates (tweets) also includes Content Creators, Journalists and Pastors. These people probably use Twitter for announcements and 'spread-

ing the word', even though - on average - they do not score very high in terms of followers.

5.2 Differences in topics

In order to compare what users of different areas talk about in different networks, we indexed the tweets and Facebook posts of the users into a Solr[4] Index. All the messages were processed trough a standard text processing pipeline, in which we removed stop words and used a stemming algorithm. Beside this, we also removed links from the text as we are only interested in the 'real words' used by a user. For tweets, we also removed the mentions of other users as well as the hash-symbol from hash tags.

This indexing allows us to compute the cosine similarity between different users and different professions. The similarity is calculated using the Solr 'more like this' functionality, which finds documents similar to a given document or a set of documents, based on the terms within the given document. These terms are selected based on their TF/IDF

---

[4]https://lucene.apache.org/solr/

16

Table 1: The manually assigned topic labels and the most probable top-10 terms (assigned by the LDA method) for the 50 "Skills and Expertise" (SE) topics.

Topic Label	Top-10 Topic Terms
E-commerce-Strategy	marketing media social digital online strategy advertising analytics web management
Marketing-Strategy	research analysis strategy market product business development strategic competitive innovation
Social Media-Public Relations	media social creative public relations writing editing blogging press releases
Graphic Designer-Hands-On	design creative graphic direction art adobe suite illustration graphics identity
System/Network Administrator	windows server security network administration microsoft system vmware linux networking
Entrepreneur-Startup	business development strategy management start up strategic entrepreneurship marketing planning
Search Engine Optimization-Tech.	marketing google web analytics online seo search advertising optimization sem
Web Designer-Graphical	web html design css wordpress photoshop adobe development graphic suite
Technical Support-Helpdesk	os mac office microsoft windows computer support technical hardware networking
Game Designer	design game games animation interior architecture video computer development planning
Social Media-'Spammer'/Analyst	social google media facebook twitter wordpress marketing analytics microsoft blogging
Manager or consultant	development community management program writing public leadership outreach planning education
Data Analysis-Programmer	data analysis science engineering research statistics computer design modeling matlab
Customer Management-People	customer management service sales retail team training satisfaction problem solving
Public Relations-International	policy public international research political relations english analysis writing government
Marketing-Events,Press	communications media marketing relations social management public strategic corporate event
Sustainability-Focused,Green	environmental energy management sustainability engineering sustainable construction project awareness water
Software Engineer-Commercial	software management cloud computing enterprise architecture data business integration saas
Financial Analyst	financial management analysis insurance finance planning business banking accounting risk
Marketing-Branding	marketing strategy media digital creative advertising brand social development online
Team Manager,Management	management team planning business project leadership development negotiation analysis strategy
Pastor-Church	pastoral church ministry youth leadership theology preaching studies development teaching
Professional Microsoft Product	microsoft office excel word powerpoint customer research service photoshop management
Marketing-Generic	marketing management media strategy social development advertising online brand business
Medical (Psychiatrists and co)	health healthcare medical clinical research psychology medicine counseling management mental
Beauty Industry	de fashion en styling trend beauty dise merchandising care comunicaci
Marketing-Networking	social marketing media public management event planning relations speaking networking
Marketing-Creator/Blogger	content media social marketing management web digital strategy online development
Web Programmer (#1)	sql net server asp development web microsoft software visual javascript
Manager-Project Planner	management business project process analysis improvement strategy leadership team planning
Real Estate	real estate homes home buyers sales property residential properties investment
Education-Teaching	learning education teaching technology development design curriculum educational training instructional
Creative Writer-Self-Employed	writing editing creative content publishing fiction copy blogging books articles
Web Programmer (#2)	development web html javascript css ruby java mysql php software
Journalist	journalism editing media writing news radio social style broadcast ap
Mobile Devices/Smart Phone	mobile product development devices applications strategy start web ups user
Film and Video Production	video production final pro cut media television producing
Marketing-Generic Online	social media marketing networking online blogging digital web facebook design
IPR Person,Legal Analyst	law legal litigation property writing corporate intellectual research contract civil
Sales Manager	sales management business marketing development strategy selling product strategic account
Health and Lifestyle Advisor	coaching training sports wellness fitness nutrition health lifestyle weight personal
Music and Entertainment	music production audio sound theatre recording entertainment industry acting film
Photo Journalism-Art	photography art digital fine image painting portrait editing portraits photoshop
Hospitality and Tourism	food management hospitality event events travel wine tourism industry beverage
Software Engineer-Management	management software project testing agile analysis requirements quality assurance development
Training and Coaching	development management coaching leadership training business team organizational speaking change
Supply Chain Manager	security management military manufacturing supply chain operations engineering process improvement
Human Resources,Team Manager	skills problem solving communication team leadership thinking creative people building
Recruiter	recruiting management talent recruitment employee human search career resources sourcing
Usability Engineer	design user experience interface web information interaction usability mobile architecture

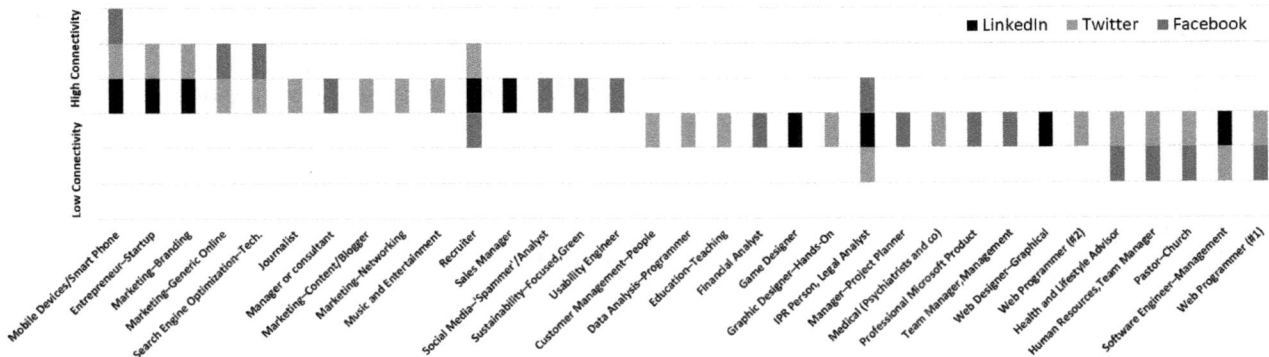

Figure 2: The professions with the highest and lowest connectivity for LinkedIn, Twitter, and Facebook.

17

values for the given document, which allows us to obtain a representative set of query terms for each user or profession. For all experiments, we selected the 500 most representative terms that occurred within at least five documents.

The different research questions we aim to answer with the experiments described in this section are the following:

- **Mentioning of skills.** Do people use Facebook and Twitter to talk about their professional skills as described in LinkedIn?

- **Similarity between networks.** How similar are users from the profession clusters in Twitter and in Facebook?

- **Specific & general topics.** Which profession clusters are very specific and which are very generic, based on the Facebook posts or Tweets?

To answer these questions, we built queries based on the terms used for the different skill and expertise groups (professions) from LinkedIn. Using these queries, we computed the score for the tweets or posts of every user. For each profession, we calculated the average score. The result of this computation is a matrix that shows how similar the users from the different professions are to the keywords of these professions. These matrices are shown in Figure 3. In order to make the differences better visible, we normalized the results for every query by dividing it by the maximum score. This ensures that the results are within a $[0, 1]$ interval and are comparable for every LinkedIn profession.

The diagonal lines in both diagrams show that most users use Facebook and Twitter to talk about their professional skills. In Twitter the diagonal is stronger than in Facebook, which indicates that Twitter is used for 'professional' communication to a larger extent than Facebook. Inside Twitter, we got an average self similarity (between the same profession cluster in LinkedIn and Twitter) of 0.884, while inside Facebook this values decreases to 0.741.

For answering the second question, how similar users behavior is in Facebook and Twitter, we indexed 50 users from each profession. We chose to use a similar amount of users per profession to remove the influence of the differences in cluster sizes. For each of the selected 2500 users, we computed the similarity to all other users based on the most representative terms used by the user in Facebook and in Twitter. The results are again two matrices, as shown in Figure 4. The matrix on the left uses the most common words in Twitter, the matrix on the right uses the most common words in Facebook. All values are normalized between 0 and 1.

Compared with the first two matrices, the first observation is that the diagonal is missing. This lack of within-cluster overlap indicates that users use Facebook and Twitter for different purposes. A remarkable difference between the two networks is the average similarity between random users: in Twitter, the average similarity is just 0.365 (the predominant green color in the left matrix); in Facebook, the average similarity is 0.818 (the predominant red color in the right matrix). The vertical lines in the left diagram indicate that some groups - particularly Creative Writing, Marketing and Social Media - write about very generic content within Twitter, while other groups use Twitter for more specific (professional) purposes. In summary, this indicates that Facebook is more general-purpose than Twitter, and that most profession clusters use Twitter for profession-specific purposes.

For analyzing the third question - which profession clusters discuss about more specific topics and which about more general topics - some first insights are already given by Figure 3, in which we ordered the LinkedIn profession clusters based on their average similarity to the users inside Twitter and Facebook. We see that professions related to Marketing and Social Media are listed on top in both diagrams, which indicates that the keywords used by these users are more generic and can be found in all professions. The bottom of both diagrams is dominated by technology-related professions as well as pastors, real estate and recruiters. Within these groups, the self-similarity is quite strong, which indicates that users within these professions exchange content-specific information.

We also indexed all messages from all networks and calculated the average similarity of one profession to all other professions, as shown in Figure 5. The blue bars show the similarity based on Facebook query terms and the red bars based on Twitter query terms. For some professions, like *E-commerce-Strategy* or *Usability Engineer*, we see large differences between the two networks. Other professions, like *Marketing*, *Journalist* or *Social Media*, are very general in both networks. The very general professions on the left seem all to be related to areas related to communication and marketing, the more specific professions on the right do not follow a clear scheme. Interesting to see is that many software-related topics are in the average area.

5.3 Differences in sentiment

In this section, we use the SentiWordNet [9] lexicon to study the connection between the users' professions and the sentiment features of tweets and Facebook posts written by these users. SentiWordNet is a lexical resource built on top of WordNet. It contains triples of sentivalues (pos, neg, obj) corresponding to positive, negative or objective sentiment of a word. The sentivalues are in the range of $[0, 1]$ and sum up to 1. For instance (pos, neg, obj) = (0.875, 0.0, 0.125) for the word 'good' and (0.25, 0.375, 0.375) for the word 'ill'.

We assigned a sentivalue to each tweet and Facebook post, in a similar manner as [17, 7], where the authors analyse sentiment in short texts (YouTube comments and Web queries). Similar to the method used in these works, we restrict our analysis to adjectives, as we observed the highest accuracy in SentiWordNet. Finally, we computed the average positivity, negativity and objectivity over all tweets and Facebook posts that belong to a profession.

Table 2 shows the top-5 most positive, negative and objective professions with respect to user-expressed sentiments in Facebook posts and tweets. The users with skills in computer technical support and data analysis programmers tend to post the most negative messages in both Facebook and Twitter. Their posts or tweets often offer or request help for problems, i.e., *'@user Sounds like a hard drive issue. Either it's hitting bad sectors or the drive has literally slowed down and is having read/write issues'*. On the other side, users related to human resources, logistics and health, as well as lifestyle advisors post the most positive content in our collection. Some hand-picked examples from Twitter include *'Best food moments of 2013 #food http://t.co/JdYO36wVAY'*, *'Kids Eat and Stay Free at the Holiday Inn Washington DC. Bring the entire family for a holiday trip http://t.co/RhYa3zuHgu'*.

Twitter Topics per Profession

Facebook Topics per Profession

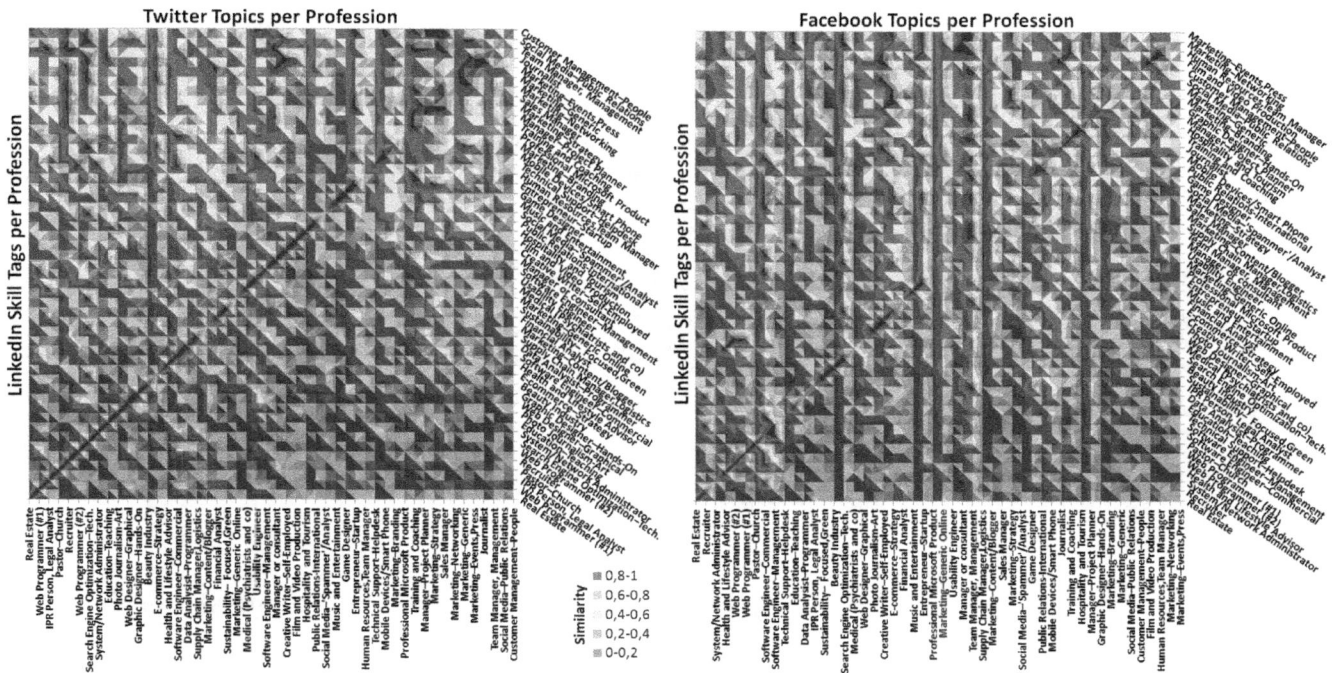

Figure 3: Similarity of skill tags from LinkedIn and terms used in Twitter (left) and Facebook (right). Similarities are summarized per profession.

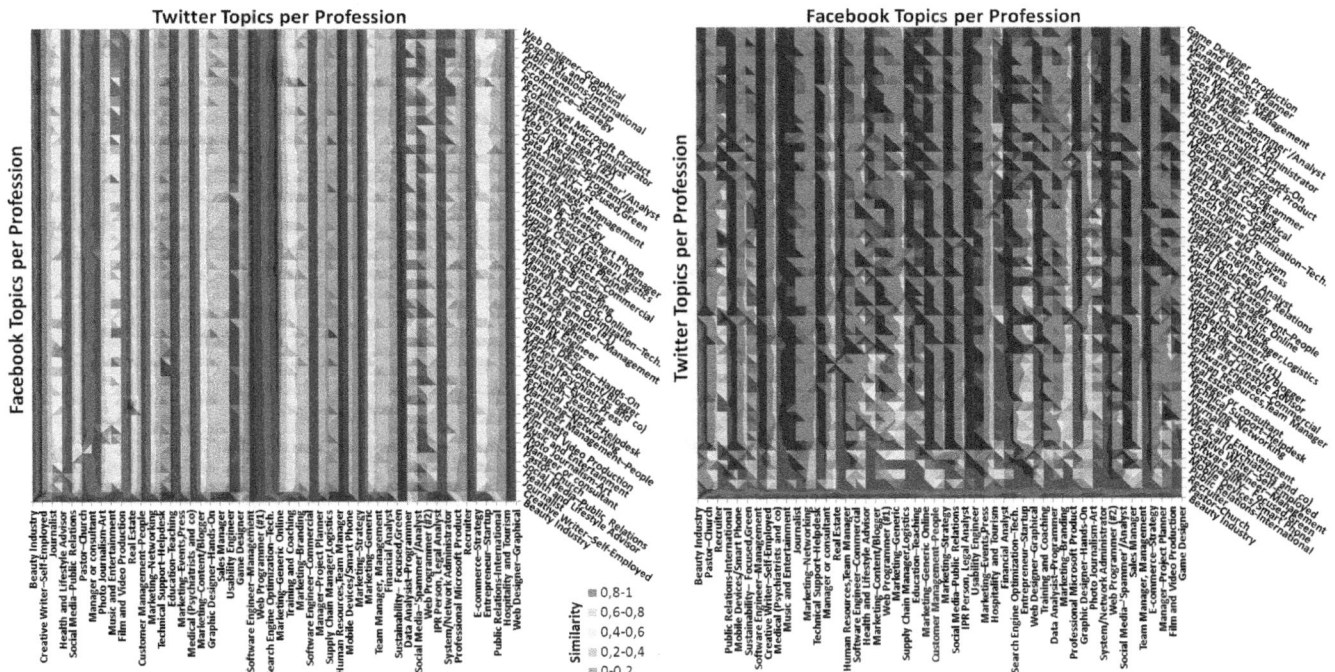

Twitter Topics per Profession

Facebook Topics per Profession

Figure 4: Similarity between topics that users talk about in Twitter (left) and Facebook (right), grouped by professions.

We also observed that users tend to be more objective in Twitter than Facebook, particularly for some of the professions. For instance, the average objectivity for *Pastors-Church* is up to 14% higher in Twitter than in Facebook. Many of the Facebook messages posted by users belonging to this profession express sympathy or commendation

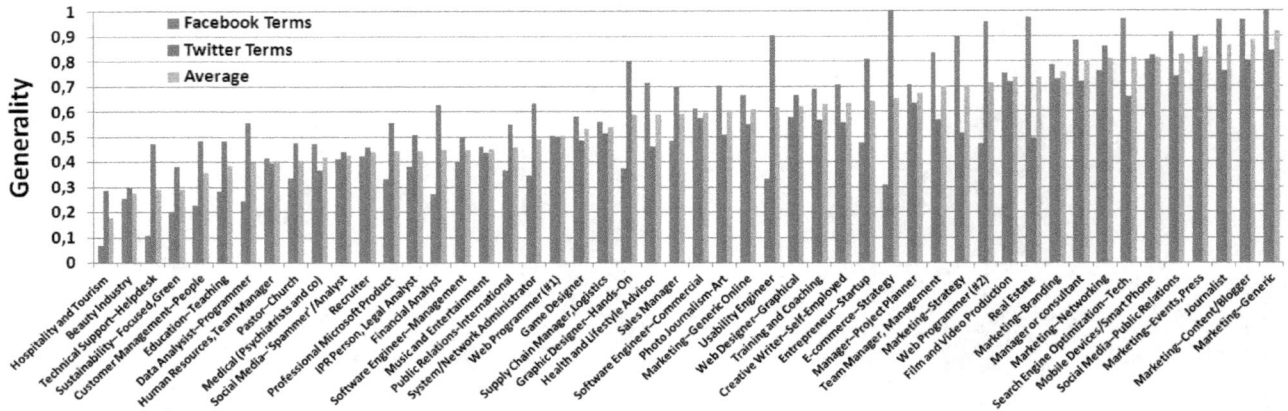

Figure 5: Comparison of generality of communication in different professions, based on terms from both Facebook and Twitter. Generality is the average similarity to all other professions.

Table 2: Top-5 most positive/negative/objective professions w.r.t. user-expressed sentiments in Facebook and Twitter.

Facebook	Twitter
Positive	
Supply Chain Manager,Logistics	Human Resources,Team Manager
Technical Support-Helpdesk	Hospitality and Tourism
Medical (Psychiatrists and co)	Health and Lifestyle Advisor
IPR Person,Legal Analyst	Customer Management
Pastor-Church	Marketing-Branding
Negative	
Pastor-Church	Technical Support-Helpdesk
Technical Support-Helpdesk	System/Network Administrator
Training and Coaching	Social Media-'Spammer'/Analyst
Film and Video Production	Human Resources,Team Manager
Data Analysis-Programmer	Journalist
Objective	
Manager-Project Planner	Recruiter
Recruiter	Public Relations-International
Team Manager,Management	Team Manager,Management
Beauty Industry	IPR Person,Legal Analyst
Professional Microsoft Product	Education-Teaching

towards a religious topic or event, such as: *'2013 EVAN-GELICAL HEALING CONVENTION "Arise, Go, Preach" (Jonah 3:2)'* or a religious greeting *'May God bless your day as you display responsible actions and superior performance'*.

The differences in sentiment between the different skills and expertise groups may reflect that people in some professions are more positive or negative in general, or that they tend to formulate their messages more positively or negatively. Our interpretation, however, is that the differences in sentiment are largely caused by differences in intentions of tweeting.

The most positive groups are professions that use social media for selling and promoting items and events; it seems natural that these promotional messages are positive and motivating. On the other hand, the most negative group consists of people who work individually on programming or writing tasks. We expect that these people mainly use social media for asking and providing help for problems and issues that they encounter. The least objective - or most subjective - topic groups mainly consist of people who provide advice and coaching in areas such as religion, health and lifestyle and entertainment. Most likely, these are people who aim to spread a particular message or opinion.

5.4 Differences in linked and shared content

Nowadays, a vast amount of content is shared by users through various social platforms. A recent study [18] shows that 71% of online users have shared some type of content on social media sites. The most popular shared items usually refer to a picture, an opinion/status update or a link to an article. Another user study [6] looks into the main motivation for sharing items, showing that most of the users (94%) carefully consider the usefulness of their shared content for the readers. While all of these recent studies imply the importance of users' shared content, there is no work that systematically investigates the link sharing patterns based on the users different expertise skills. We believe that our findings unleash the potential of analyzing users' shared links, which is a rather overlooked source of information up to now.

In this section, we first provide an overview on the amount of link-based content shared by different experts in their tweets and posts. Next, we investigate the type of content shared by different experts, by looking into the main web-domains extracted from the shared links.

Figure 6 shows the percentage of Facebook posts and tweets that contain links for each profession group. In Facebook, 60.97% of the posts share a link. Users belonging to the *Sustainability-Focused, Green*, *IPR Person, Legal Analyst* and *Public Relations-International* professions are most likely to post links. In contrast, software engineers, pastors or market strategists are less likely to include URLs in their posts. In Twitter, Web programmers and software professionals attach links less frequently. On the other side, real estate experts, photo-journalists and health care advisors contribute with a considerably higher amount of links across their tweets. This is in line with our observation in Section 5.1 that these professions make use of social media for posting announcements. Overall, 54.76% from the tweets in our collection contain a link.

As an illustrative example, we computed ranked lists of web-domains from a set of tweets and posts belonging to the top-3 and bottom-3 most active web-domain sharers in our dataset. For ranking the resulting web-domain terms, we used the Mutual Information measure [16, 19] from information theory, which can be interpreted as a measure of

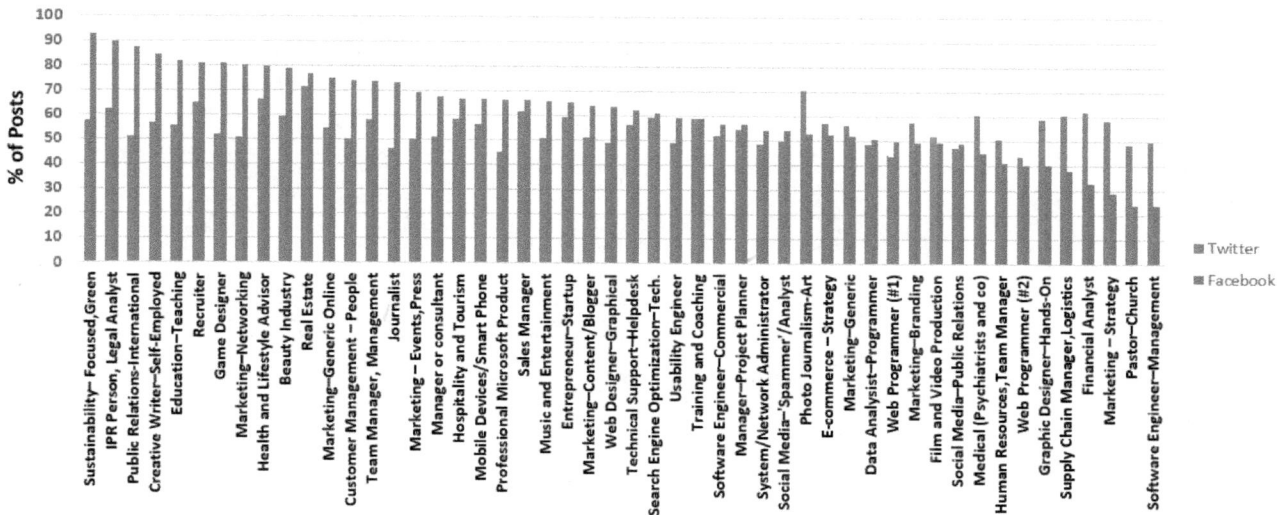

Figure 6: Percentage of Facebook posts and tweets sharing links, for each profession.

how much the joint distribution of features X_i (web-domain terms in our case) deviate from a hypothetical distribution in which features and categories (a specific profession versus all 'other' professions, in our case) are independent from each other. Table 3 shows the top-10 web-domains extracted from the links shared within: 1) the posts written by users belonging to top-3 and bottom-3 Facebook profession groups, based on the link-sharing frequency and 2) the tweets written by users belonging to top-3 and bottom-3 Twitter profession groups, based on the link-sharing frequency.

Different profession groups tend to prefer linking different type of content across their messages. In our collection, the most shared links refer to a Social Network. For instance, in Twitter, Web programmers show a preference for *foursquare.com* (a platform for discovering friends' best locations), while real estate users link a vast amount of Facebook content. Note that, while Table 3 indicates noticeable differences in the preference towards different Social Networks, analyzing the underlying reasons for such differences is beyond the scope of this study.

At the same time, people tend to include links related to their expertise domains, i.e., *activerain.com*, *houselogic.com* for Real-Estate users and *arstechnica.com*, techcrunch.com for Web Programmers. For Facebook, we noticed that most of the shared web-domains seem to be less connected to the user's profession.

6. DISCUSSION

In this paper, we investigated differences in communication and connection practices between professions, as represented by the skill and expertise groups that we extracted from a representative dataset.

In our analysis, we used a combination of exploratory analysis, visualization and interpretation. These methods are not suitable for drawing strong conclusions on the exact structure and growth of communities and the interactions between the members. Among others, Kumar et al [13] investigated these aspects as well. Our aim was to provide a complementary view on these structures and to give some insight in the people, professions and conversation topics that

constitute these structures. Necessarily, these insights are partially given by means of representative examples. Keeping this limitation in mind, there are several key insights that can be drawn from the results.

In professional networks, connections between people based on shared skills follow the same structure as explicit connections, such as following, endorsing or befriending in social networks. The majority of mentioned skills are quite detailed and closely connected to a frequently mentioned more generic skill. By separating the skill network into clusters, skill and expertise groups - or professions - can be recognized.

The core of the skill network mainly consists of people who professionally use social media for specific purposes, such as marketing, promoting, branding and recruiting. These persons are typically well-connected, talk about common topics, share links from common resources and usually have a positive tone.

By contrast, several niche groups that are further away from the core are typically less connected and centered around a particular representative skill. Professions in which (individual) productivity is more important than communication - such as programming and writing - seem to use social networks predominantly for specific purposes, such as providing or asking for help or feedback. Due to this different intention of use, the activity level, the topics discussed and the resources shared differ highly from what happens in 'the core'.

These observations have clear implications for social network analysis, particularly for professional networks. Firstly, it is clear that averages for the whole population - and interpretation of these averages - are often only meaningful for the central core. The dynamics in subgroups are in many cases quite different - based on our qualitative evidence mainly caused due to differences in intention of use.

Zooming into the topics and links that are specific for a subgroup, and providing these to users who are new to the community or who aim to connect to it, seems to be a promising approach to get these users acquainted with the community and to get a feeling on the unwritten conventions

Table 3: Top-10 web-domains according to their Mutual Information values for tweets/posts written by users belonging to "One" profession vs. "Other" professions.

Top-10 distinctive web-domains for top-three professions, according to their % of links.					
Twitter			Facebook		
Real Estate	Photo Journalism	Health and Lifestyle Advisor	Sustainability Focused, Green	IPR Person, Legal Analyst	Public Relations âĂ§ International
facebook.com	facebook.com	facebook.com	facebook.com	facebook.com	apps.facebook.com
foursquare.com	instagram.com	networkedblogs.com	change.org	dangerousminds.net	nytimes.com
youtube.com	etsy.com	youtube.com	ulink.tv	politicususa.com	npr.org
paper.li	zazzle.com	graph.facebook.com	elpais.com	addictinginfo.org	nyti.ms
activerain.com	plus.google.com	articles.mercola.com	youtube.com	huffingtonpost.com	youtube.com
yelp.com	about.me	paper.li	avaaz.org	alternet.org	washingtonpost.com
trulia.com	vimeo.com	ebay.com	librarything.com	thinkprogress.org	salon.com
inman.com	blipfoto.com	amazon.com	europapress.es	forwardprogressives.com	behance.net
houselogic.com	post.ly	about.me	actuable.es	dailykos.com	change.org
scoop.it	fineartamerica.com	fitbit.com	zimbio.com	fab.com	i.imgur.com

Top-10 distinctive web-domains for bottom-three professions, according to their % of links.					
Twitter			Facebook		
Web Programmer #1	Web Programmer #2	Profesional Microsoft Product	Software Engineer Management	Pastor-Church	Marketing Strategy
foursquare.com	foursquare.com	instagram.com	youtube.com	apps.facebook.com	nike.com
youtube.com	twitter.com	foursquare.com	apps.facebook.com	ludia.com	buff.ly
fancy.com	youtube.com	twitter.com	facebook.com	barackobama.com	youtube.com
getglue.com	i.imgur.com	twittascope.com	nblo.gs	instagr.am	tripit.com
blogs.msdn.com	techcrunch.com	youtube.com	bbc.co.uk	gofundme.com	groupon.com
arstechnica.com	theverge.com	plurk.com	livingsocial.com	facebook.com	act.credoaction.com
engadget.com	twitpic.com	justunfollow.com	ludia.com	eventbrite.ca	secure.sierraclub.org
path.com	twitter.yfrog.com	gofundme.com	meetup.com	amzn.com	generalassemb.ly
fplus.me	plurk.com	runkeeper.com	mashable.com	amzn.com	gr.pn
techcrunch.com	meetup.com	infojobs.net	amazon.co.uk	itunes.apple.com	animoto.com

and rules within these communities. In addition, the group-specific resources - such as technology-oriented websites - often serve as a useful starting point for exploring a new expertise area. These insights can be used as starting points for new browsing and search functionality in professional networking sites.

7. CONCLUSION

Within a skill network, several subgroups - or professions - centered around a particular skill can be recognized. Our analysis shows that these subgroups have specific unwritten conventions and rules, mainly caused by differences in intention for using social media. These insights call for separate analysis or treatment of activities within these subgroups, and provide several starting points for new functionality in professional networking sites.

8. ACKNOWLEDGMENTS

This work was partially supported by EU FP7 projects ForgetIT (Contract No. 600826) and QualiMaster (Contract No. 619525).

9. REFERENCES

[1] F. Abel, E. Herder, G.-J. Houben, N. Henze, and D. Krause. Cross-system user modeling and personalization on the social web. *User Modeling and User-Adapted Interaction*, 23(2-3):169–209, 2013.

[2] F. Abel, E. Herder, and D. Krause. Extraction of professional interests from social web profiles. *Proc. Augmented User Modeling at UMAP*, 34, 2011.

[3] K. Balog and M. de Rijke. Finding experts and their details in e-mail corpora. In *Proceedings of the 15th international conference on World Wide Web*, pages 1035–1036. ACM, 2006.

[4] M. Bastian, S. Heymann, and M. Jacomy. Gephi: an open source software for exploring and manipulating networks. In *ICWSM*, pages 361–362, 2009.

[5] D. M. Blei, A. Y. Ng, and M. I. Jordan. Latent dirichlet allocation. *J. Mach. Learn. Res.*, 3:993–1022, Mar. 2003.

[6] B. Brett. The psychology of sharing, 2012. Available at http://nytmarketing.whsites.net/mediakit/pos/.

[7] S. Chelaru, I. S. Altingovde, S. Siersdorfer, and W. Nejdl. Analyzing, detecting, and exploiting sentiment in web queries. *ACM Trans. Web*, 8(1):6:1–6:28, Dec. 2013.

[8] F. Cingano and A. Rosolia. People i know: job search and social networks. *Journal of Labor Economics*, 30(2):291–332, 2012.

[9] A. Esuli and F. Sebastiani. Sentiwordnet: A publicly available lexical resource for opinion mining. In *In Proceedings of the 5th Conference on Language Resources and Evaluation (LREC '06)*, pages 417–422, 2006.

[10] S. Ghosh, N. Sharma, F. Benevenuto, N. Ganguly, and K. Gummadi. Cognos: Crowdsourcing search for topic experts in microblogs. In *Proceedings of the 35th International ACM SIGIR Conference on Research and Development in Information Retrieval*, SIGIR '12, pages 575–590, New York, NY, USA, 2012. ACM.

[11] I. Guy, U. Avraham, D. Carmel, S. Ur, M. Jacovi, and I. Ronen. Mining expertise and interests from social media. In *Proceedings of the 22nd International Conference on World Wide Web*, WWW '13, pages 515–526, Republic and Canton of Geneva, Switzerland, 2013. International World Wide Web Conferences Steering Committee.

[12] L. Hong, G. Convertino, and E. H. Chi. Language matters in twitter: A large scale study. In *ICWSM*, 2011.

[13] R. Kumar, J. Novak, and A. Tomkins. Structure and evolution of online social networks. In P. S. Yu, J. Han, and C. Faloutsos, editors, *Link Mining: Models, Algorithms, and Applications*, pages 337–357. Springer New York, 2010.

[14] J. Liu, F. Zhang, X. Song, Y.-I. Song, C.-Y. Lin, and H.-W. Hon. What's in a name?: An unsupervised approach to link users across communities. In

Proceedings of the Sixth ACM International Conference on Web Search and Data Mining, WSDM '13, pages 495–504, New York, NY, USA, 2013. ACM.

[15] C. Macdonald, D. Hannah, and I. Ounis. High quality expertise evidence for expert search. In *Proceedings of the IR Research, 30th European Conference on Advances in Information Retrieval*, ECIR'08, pages 283–295, Berlin, Heidelberg, 2008. Springer-Verlag.

[16] C. Manning and H. Schuetze. *Foundations of Statistical Natural Language Processing*. MIT Press, 1999.

[17] S. Siersdorfer, S. Chelaru, W. Nejdl, and J. San Pedro. How useful are your comments?: Analyzing and predicting youtube comments and comment ratings. In *Proceedings of the 19th International Conference on World Wide Web*, WWW '10, pages 891–900, New York, NY, USA, 2010. ACM.

[18] J. Wiltfong. Majority (71%) of global internet users "share" on social media sites, 2013. Available at http://ipsos-na.com/news-polls/pressrelease.aspx?id=6254.

[19] Y. Yang and J. O. Pedersen. A comparative study on feature selection in text categorization. pages 412–420. Morgan Kaufmann Publishers, 1997.

[20] D. Yimam-Seid and A. Kobsa. Expert-finding systems for organizations: Problem and domain analysis and the demoir approach. *Journal of Organizational Computing and Electronic Commerce*, 13(1):1–24, 2003.

Online Popularity and Topical Interests through the Lens of Instagram

Emilio Ferrara
School of Informatics and Computing
Indiana University Bloomington, USA
ferrarae@indiana.edu

Roberto Interdonato, Andrea Tagarelli
DIMES
University of Calabria, Italy
{rinterdonato,tagarelli}@dimes.unical.it

ABSTRACT

Online socio-technical systems can be studied as proxy of the real world to investigate human behavior and social interactions at scale. Here we focus on Instagram, a media-sharing online platform whose popularity has been rising up to gathering hundred millions users. Instagram exhibits a mixture of features including social structure, social tagging and media sharing. The network of social interactions among users models various dynamics including follower/followee relations and users' communication by means of posts/comments. Users can upload and tag media such as photos and pictures, and they can "like" and comment each piece of information on the platform. In this work we investigate three major aspects on our Instagram dataset: *(i)* the structural characteristics of its network of heterogeneous interactions, to unveil the emergence of self organization and topically-induced community structure; *(ii)* the dynamics of content production and consumption, to understand how global trends and popular users emerge; *(iii)* the behavior of users labeling media with tags, to determine how they devote their attention and to explore the variety of their topical interests. Our analysis provides clues to understand human behavior dynamics on socio-technical systems, specifically users and content popularity, the mechanisms of users' interactions in online environments and how collective trends emerge from individuals' topical interests.

1. INTRODUCTION

The study of society through the lens of social media allows us to uncover questions about human behavior at scale [27]. Recent results unveiled complex dynamics in human behavior [44, 11], interactions [2, 15] and influence [3, 9]. Still, many open questions remain: for example, how do social interactions affect individual and collective behavior? Or, how does connectivity affect individual and collective topical interests? Yet, how do trends and popular content emerge from individuals' interactions?

In this paper we address these questions by studying an emerging socio-technical system, namely Instagram. The popularity of this platform has been growing during recent years: as of the beginning of 2014 Instagram gathers over one hundred million users. Instagram users generate an unparalleled amount of media content. Hence, it should not be surprising that Instagram has recently attracted the attention of the research community, fostering results in different areas including cultural analytics [23, 22] and urban social behavior [41]. Instagram represents an unprecedented environment of study, in that it mixes features of various social media and online social networks (including the ability of creating user-generated content in the form of visual media), the option of social tagging, and the possibility of establishing social relations (*e.g.*, followee/follower relationships), and social interactions (*e.g.*, commenting or liking media of other users.)

A natural comparison arises between Instagram and other photo sharing systems, particularly Flickr. The two systems appear rather different in terms of features and target of users. Flickr offers more professional-oriented features (*e.g.*, high-quality photos, thematic groups and communities, advanced media organization features.) Instagram, being designed for mobile users, resembles an amateur photo-blog, as it incorporates features to quickly take photos and apply visual effects, and it offers a minimal interface. In other words, Flickr can be seen as a more complete photo sharing platform with social network features, while Instagram resembles a Twitter-like online social network based on photo sharing.

Following the lead of studies based on similar platforms such as Flickr [37, 16, 33, 12], in this paper we address five different research questions, discussed in the following, spanning different areas of network-, semantic- and topical-based data analysis using signals from user activities and interactions.

1.1 Contribution and outline

We provide a framework to analyze the Instagram ecosystem, incorporating in our model the unique mixture of social interactions, social tagging and media sharing features provided by the platform. By using this framework, we conduct a rigorous analysis focusing on the following main aspects: *(i)* the structural characteristics of the Instagram network, *(ii)* the dynamics of content production and consumption, and *(iii)* the users' interests modeled via the social tagging mechanisms available to label media with topical tags. We elaborate on each and all these aspects to answer the following research questions:

Q1 *Network and community structure*: What are the salient structural features in the network built on the users' interactions?

Q2 *Content production and consumption*: How do users produce and consume content? That is, how do users get engaged on the platform and how do they interact with content produced by others?

Q3 *Social tagging*: How diverse is the set of tags exploited by each user? In other words, what is the user tagging behavior?

Q4 *Topical clusters of interest*: How can users be grouped based on the tags they use to annotate media?

Q5 *Popularity and topicality*: How does the topical interests of users affect their popularity? And, how large is the variety of topics covered by each user or by each media?

1.2 Scope of this work

To the best of our knowledge, this work is the first to study the Instagram network of users' interactions, social tagging activities, and topical interests. Therefore, our major goal is to fill a lack of knowledge concerning a number of research issues in Instagram. Within this view, we aimed at providing a first understanding of the above listed aspects of the Instagram network, being aware that all such aspects are interrelated and hence they should be preferably addressed together. It should also be noted that our experimental findings depend on the particular sampling mechanism used to build our dataset; as we shall discuss in the next section, this introduces a bias that does not allow us to provide an analysis of the full Instagram ecosystem, but only of users (and associated media) that are engaged in a public Instagram initiative.

2. METHODOLOGY

In this section we describe the challenges that we faced in gathering data from the Instagram network, and the technical choices that we adopted to build our dataset. Analogously to other studies, we had to cope with the impossibility of obtaining data directly from the network administrators; therefore, we collected an Instagram sample by querying the Instagram API.[1] Various features are made publicly available, including: *(i)* the *users API*, which allows sampling from the Instagram user space by querying for specific user account details; *(ii)* the *relationships API*, which retrieves information about specific users, their followers and followees; *(iii)* the *media API*, which queries for specific or popular media; *(iv,v)* the *comments* and the *likes* APIs, respectively, to extract comments and likes from specific media; and *(vi)* the *tags API*, which extracts the keywords associated with specific media, as attributed by the social tagging process of Instagram users.

2.1 Crawling strategy

Our primary objective in crawling the Instagram network was to ensure adequate levels of consistency in user relationships as well as topical variety in media properties, over a timespan possibly larger than the actual crawling period.

---

[1]See http://instagram.com/developer/

Table 1: Statistics on the Instagram media dataset.

No. Media	1,686,349
No. Distinct users	2,081
No. Tags	8,919,630
No. Distinct tags	269,359
No. Likes	1,242,923,022
No. Comments	41,341,783

We expected to detect a user interaction graph having topological properties (*e.g.*, clustering coefficient, average path length) as close as possible to those typically exhibited by other (directed) social media networks [49, 35]; at the same time, we aimed at collecting media whose thematic subjects could span over a predetermined, relatively large classification, while capturing time information about media and user relationships that would allow for trend evolution analysis.

Our initial crawling attempt consisted in retrieving media geolocalized w.r.t. a list of touristic/popular locations, which were selected based on their presumed potential to attract users with very different (photographic) tastes, concerning, *e.g.*, art and culture, entertainment and night life, wild life (sea/mountain), etc. Then, the user relations underlying the authors of the retrieved media were taken into account to build a user network. Our hypothesis here was that two users who take pictures within a limited area are more likely to be connected via a follower/followee relation (they may know each other in real life.) Unfortunately, despite the spatial proximity between the authors of the collected media, a poor number of followships were identified, resulting in a network overly disconnected (*e.g.*, clustering coefficient of 2.0E-6). Note that, by trying different sets of touristic locations, we obtained similar results in terms of connectivity.

We changed our crawling strategy based on retrieving users that belong to a relatively large "community" in Instagram. Here, our usage of term community corresponds to that of thematic channel, which is typical in many other social media networks (*e.g.*, YouTube); Instagram does not offer an explicit group/community feature, therefore we exploited the existence of public initiatives officially organized by Instagram. We focused our crawling on the Instagram *weekend hashtag project* (WHP) promoted by the Instagram's official blog.[2] The characteristics of the WHP initiative and their implications on our data crawling are described next.

2.2 Dataset construction

Every Friday, the Instagram team runs a photographic contest, through the Instagram's official blog. Each contest is assigned a specific topic, which is expressed by a unique (hash)tag prefixed with *#whp*. According to the project rules, submitted photos need to be marked with no more than one contest-specific tag.

We selected 72 popular contests and randomly picked up about 2,100 users that participated in at least one of those contests. All media uploaded by these users (including media that were not tagged with *#whp*-hashtags) were gathered and their information retrieved and stored into the *media dataset*. For each media, we retrieved its unique ID, the ID of the user who posted it, the timestamp of media cre-

---

[2]http://blog.instagram.com/tagged/
weekend-hashtag-project

Table 2: Relational Instagram network statistics.

No. Nodes	44,766
No. Links	677,686
Avg. In-degree	15.14
Avg. Path length	3.16
Clustering coefficient	4.1E-2
Diameter	11
Assortativity index	-0.097
No. Communities	151
Network modularity	0.578

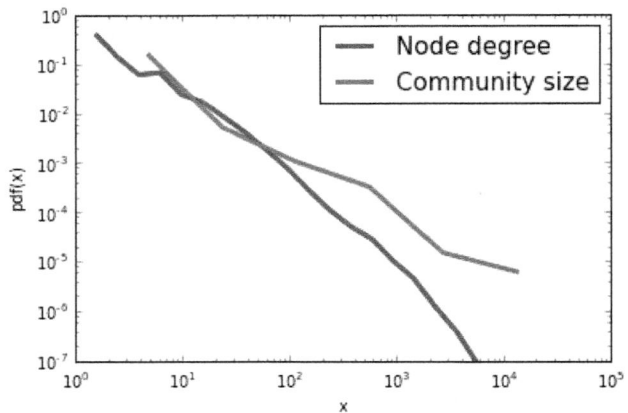

Figure 1: Distribution of node degree and community size of the Relational Instagram Network.

ation, the set of tags assigned to the media, the number of likes and comments it received.

We constructed the *Relational Instagram Network* (RIN) as a directed weighted graph. Edges were drawn to model asymmetric relationships of the form follower-followee, and edge weights were calculated proportionally to the number of likes and comments generated by a user (follower) towards media created by her/his followee. The users selected to build the media dataset were used as seed nodes for the construction of the RIN. Note that we conceived the RIN so to model (asymmetric) relationships that hold strictly among the participants in the contests. The reason for this choice is that including the whole topological neighborhood of the candidate nodes (*e.g.*, the individual egonets also including non-participants) would have resulted again in highly disconnected networks (with clustering coefficient of the order of 1.0E-6). Therefore, we started a breadth-first search process from the set of seed nodes, filtering out any user who did not participate in at least a *#whp* contest.

Our data were crawled over about one-month period (from Jan 20 to Feb 17, 2014). The obtained media dataset contains full information about over 2 thousand users and almost 1.7 million media, with about 9 million tags, 1.2 billion likes, and 41 million comments (see Table 1.) Details on our RIN are reported in Table 2. Here it can be noted that the network of user relations shows a negative, close-to-zero assortativity, which would indicate no tendency of users with similar degree to connect each other. Moreover, the characteristic path length and clustering coefficient are both low, while the modularity is rather high, which would indicate that the RIN has small modules, with moderately dense connections between the nodes within modules and sparse connections between nodes in different modules.[3]

Limitations.

As previously discussed, our dataset is intentionally built around the set of users and media that belong to a competition-driven, large, community in Instagram. Unlike previous work on the Flickr network (a major competitor of Instagram) [33], we were not able to perform a number of analyses such as, *e.g.*, preferential creation/reception and proximity bias in link creation, which rely on fellowship creation timestamps. This information is missing in our dataset, as the Instagram APIs do not make it available. Flickr APIs do not make it available either, but those authors inferred such temporal information by crawling the Flickr network daily, and monitoring the creation of new links [33]. Another

[3] Our data are available at http://uweb.dimes.unical.it/tagarelli/data/.

limitation concerns the analysis of latent interactions (*e.g.*, profile browsing), which has been shown to be a prominent activity in OSNs [7, 40, 25]: unfortunately, this information is not publicly available for Instagram, while obtaining significant clickstream data (like that used other studies [7, 40]) is challenging.

3. ANALYSIS AND RESULTS

We begin with explaining the five research questions that we will address to unveil the characteristics of Instagram.

Q1: Network and community structure.

Our first question aims at understanding what are the structural features of the Relational Instagram Network and the characteristic of its community structure. We want to determine the dynamics of social relations and interactions on the system and how they shape (if they do) the structure of the network. In addition, we want to determine whether or not the community structure reflects the self-organization principle [31] by which individuals in social networks tend to aggregate in communities oriented to topical discussions, and if this, in turn, yields the emergence of a *topically-induced community structure*.

Q2: Content production and consumption.

We want also to understand how the cycle of production and consumption of information (*e.g.*, media) is characterized on Instagram. We first aim at understanding what is the driving mechanism of content production; then, we aim to unveil whether content consumption, measured in some way (*e.g.*, via social interactions), follows similar patterns or if any striking difference emerges.

Q3: Social tagging dynamics.

In the third research question our goal is to study the dynamics of social tagging on Instagram. We want to study both the patterns of tag adoption at the user level, and at the global level, to characterize how popular tags emerge from the adoption of independent users. We also want to describe the variety of tagging usage by the users, to deter-

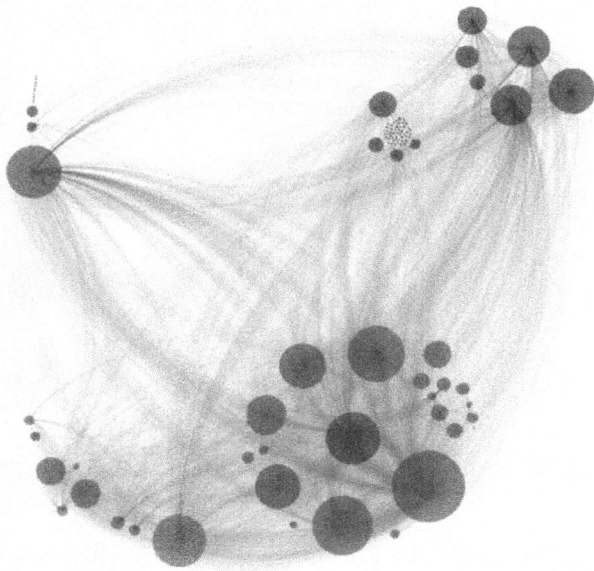

Figure 2: Visualization of the community structure of the Relational Instagram Network.

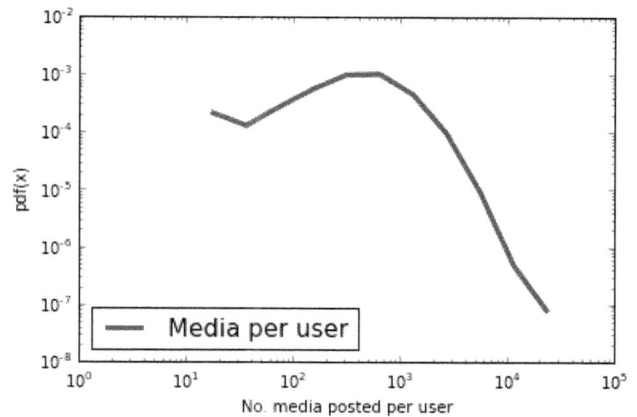

Figure 3: Distribution of user content production.

mine whether users focus their attention on few rather than many contexts.

Q4: Topical clusters of interests.

A fourth research questions aims at determining whether it is possible to cluster users exploiting their tagging behavior, and, in turn, if topical clusters emerge by means of such procedure.

Q5: Popularity and topicality.

Our final research questions aims at unveiling the dynamics of user popularity and how this relates to topical interests. We hypothesize that popular users might exhibit different patterns of attention and therefore different topical interests. We want to determine whether we can characterize user popularity as function of the variety of their interests, and, in turn, learn how topicality relates to social interactions.

3.1 Structural features of the Instagram Network

We discuss the analysis of the Relational Instagram Network (RIN) we carried out to answer our first research question (**Q1**). Our goal here is to study its topological features and determine whether they reflect any particular social process. In particular, we aim at unveiling whether this particular environment, at the boundary between a social network and a sharing media platform, exhibits any characteristic feature: for example, we will drive our attention on the effect of topical interests of users and how these reflect on the network structure. Figure 1 shows the distribution of node degree (in blue) and community size (in green) for the RIN. The community detection task has been carried out using two algorithms: the *Louvain method* [8], and OSLOM [26]. Results obtained with both methods are consistent (the

plot shows the results from the former algorithm.) Both the node degree and the community size distributions are broad and exhibit a fat-tail. A broad degree distribution suggests that the Relational Instagram Network growth may follow a preferential-attachment mechanism [5]: new social relations and social interactions are disproportionately more likely to occur between individuals who previously grew their social network and invested in interacting with others, rather than between users less prone to connect [42]. The formation of communities of heterogeneous size suggests the emergence of self organization [31], a principle explaining that individuals tend to aggregate in units (the communities) optimized for efficiency of communication (*e.g.*, around specific topics of conversation.) A self-organized network structure enjoys crucial properties, including that of enhancing the topicality of interests, or their scope, to smaller sets of individuals rather than to the entire system. By addressing research questions **Q2** and **Q3** in the following sections, we will determine whether these communities emerge from user relations and interactions around certain topics of interest; in other words, we will investigate whether the network exhibits a *topically-induced community structure*.

To visualize the community structure of the RIN we produced a graphical representation in Figure 2, by means of a circular hierarchical algorithm.[4] Here nodes (*i.e.*, users) belonging to the same community have the same colors, and the hue of the edges transitions from the color of the community of the source node to that of the target one. The RIN community structure clearly separates close clusters of individuals (*e.g.*, bottom-right ones) from clusters of isolated individuals (*e.g.*, top-right ones.) Note that the RIN has (multi)edges weighted by means of social relations and interactions (*i.e.*, follower/followee, likes and comments), being these weights accounted in the community detection and visualization tasks. Differently from other social networks [19, 21], Instagram does not exhibit a tight core-periphery structure, whereas communities of large size exist in peripheral areas of the network and they are interconnected with other communities of comparable size. Other basic statistics of the Relational Instagram Network are reported in Table 2.

---

[4]Cvis by Andrea Lancichinetti: `https://sites.google.com/site/andrealancichinetti/cvis`.

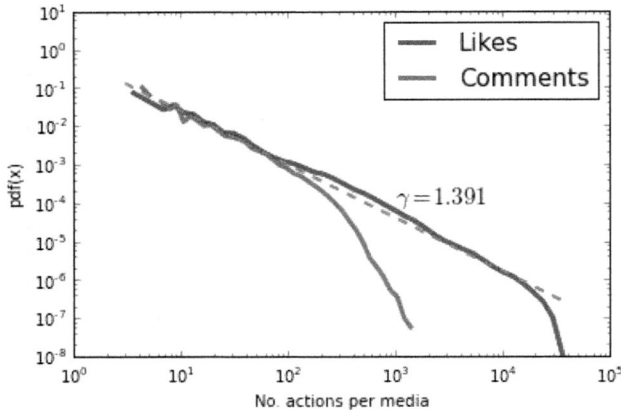

Figure 4: Distribution of social interactions.

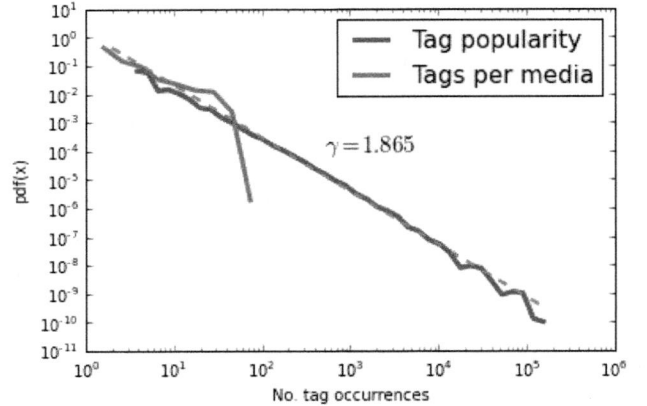

Figure 5: Tag adoption and global popularity.

3.2 Content production and consumption

We continue our analysis of the Instagram ecosystem by investigating how users produce and consume content (**Q2**.) Our goal is to determine whether any particular pattern emerges to describe how individuals' get engaged on the platform and how they interact with content produced by others. To this aim, we study *content production* from the user perspective. Figure 3 shows the probability density function (pdf(x)) of the amount x of media posted by each Instagram user in our dataset. This plot suggests peculiar content production dynamics on Instagram: users who already uploaded a large number of media are more likely to do so, causing the presence of a fat tail showing users with a disproportionate amount of media posted on the platform. Individuals exhibit higher tendency to posting new content if they already did that in the past. The lack of a scale-invariant content production dynamics differentiates Instagram from other platforms [33] (even if some caution is required given how the sample was constructed.) If our observation holds in general, this has an interesting impact from the perspective of system design, in that it suggests a neat separation between active and inactive users: those who are already engaged in using the platform are more likely to keep staying active users. Strategies to engage inactive users could be designed and implemented based on these findings to lower the heterogeneity (*i.e.*, the imbalance) in users involved in content production on the platform.

We now investigate *content consumption* on Instagram. Here with content consumption we intend that a given user on the platform has performed some specific action toward a media produced by another user (*e.g.*, liking or commenting it.) This draws an interesting parallel between content production and social interactions, and provides a slightly different perspective from usual studies on platform like social media such as Twitter, where content consumption is intended as users rebroadcast others' content (*e.g.*, via retweets) aiming at information diffusion rather than interactions. Figure 4 shows the distribution of two consumption dynamics, namely "like" and comment, of Instagram users. The plot includes the best fit of a power law to the likes distribution,[5] with an exponent $\gamma = 1.391$ ($x_{min} = 3$, $\sigma = 0.001$), whereas

no significant power law fit has been found for the comment distribution that clearly shows two different regimes, $x \lesssim 250$ and $x \gtrsim 250$. The "likes" distribution shows a cutoff in the tail due to the finite system size, and suggests that the behavior of likes and comments on Instagram might follow two different dynamics. Popularity of media measured by the number of likes grows by preferential attachment similarly to how, for example, scientific papers acquire citations [24]: resources with large number of likes (resp., citations) are more likely to acquire even more. Differently, the ecosystem is less prone to trigger large conversations (based on comments); this is consistent with the theory of user communication efficiency: the different costs (*e.g.*, in terms of time required to perform the action) between "liking" some content and writing a comment affect the nature of interactions among individuals on the platform.

3.3 Social tagging dynamics

To answer our question about the dynamics of social tagging on Instagram (**Q3**) we investigated three aspects: *(i)* the tag popularity at the global level and the distribution of tags per media; *(ii)* the distribution of total tags used by the users and their vocabulary size; and, *(iii)* the diversity in tag usage by each individual.

Our first goal is to understand how tags emerge in the system at the global level from the tagging patterns of individual media. To this end, we derived the distribution of tag popularity, as represented by the probability density function of observing a given total number of tag occurrences across all media. Then, we obtained the distribution of the number of tags assigned to each media. The results are shown in Figure 5. The plot reports the best fitting of a power law to the distribution of tag popularity with an exponent equal to $\gamma = 1.865$ ($x_{min} = 2$, $\sigma = 0.002$), whereas the tags-per-media distribution best fits an exponential-decay function. Two main observations stand out. First, the tag usage mechanism seems to follow an information economy principle of least effort, that is that the majority of media are labeled with just a few tags, and larger sets of tags assigned to the same media are increasingly more unlikely to be observed. Second, although the mechanism describing the as-

---

[5]The statistical significance of this fitting (and all the others in the paper) has been assessed by means of *powerlaw*, a

library by Alstott *et al.* [1], and it's based on a Kolmogorov-Smirnov test.

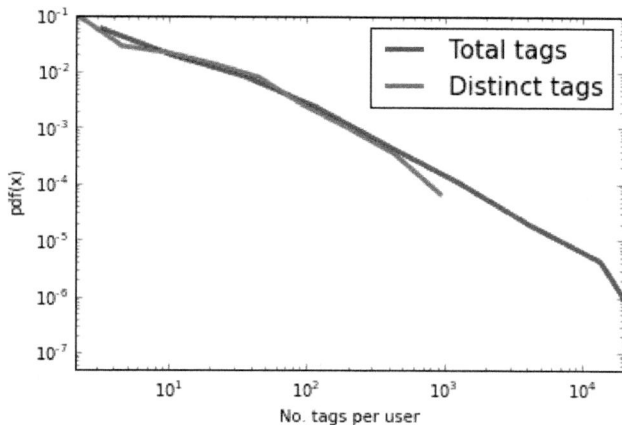

Figure 6: Tag usage and tagset size distributions.

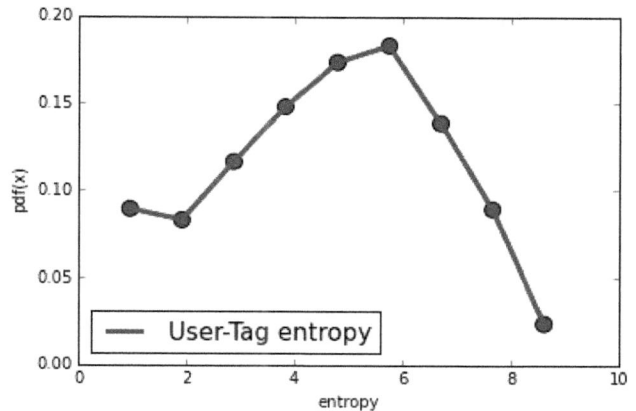

Figure 7: User-Tag entropy distribution.

signment of tags is not quite by preferential attachment, the outcome of the process, that is the overall tag popularity, follows a power law behavior. Similar findings have been observed in other popular systems, like Twitter, where popular (hash)tags emerge from individuals' adoption [45]. Limited attention of users and competition among (hash)tags have been hypothesized as explanation of the emergence of such broad distributions.

Moreover, we seek to understand what is the emerging behavior at the user level. We want to determine what patterns of tag adoption users follow, in terms of how many total tags they use, and how many of these tags are distinct. In other words, we establish their vocabulary size (*i.e.*, the number of "words" they are aware of) and we compare it against the total number of tags they produce. Figure 6 shows the distribution of, respectively, total and distinct tags used by each user. Both distributions are fat-tailed and show similar slopes. Vocabulary size reflects the information economy principle: the distribution of distinct tags per user spans above one order of magnitude less if compared with that of the total tags usage. This suggests that the actual user vocabulary size is limited, with a large majority of users adopting only few tags. This can be explained by considering that users cannot keep track of all tags emerging on the platform.

Finally, to the aim of studying how diverse is the set of tags used by each individual we proceeded as follows. First, we described each given user u in our dataset by means of a vector T_u where each entry represents the frequency $f(t)$ of adoption of tag t (*i.e.*, the total number of times user u adopted tag t to label one of the media she/he uploaded to Instagram), for all tags used by u. We define the entropy value $H(\cdot)$, to describe each user's entropy in the adoption of tags, in the classic Shannon way

$$H(u) = -\sum_{t \in T_u} p(t) \cdot \log p(t), \quad \text{with } p(t) = \frac{f(t)}{\sum_{t \in T_u} f(t)}.$$

Afterwards, we determined the probability density function of the distribution of users' tag adoption entropy, as shown in Figure 7. Note that the entropy ranges between 0 and the logarithm of the total number of tags of each user. The lower the entropy, the more focused a user's tagging

pattern is (that is, she/he tends to adopt less tags in a more concentrated ways), the more diverse is her/his tagging behavior. Figure 7 shows that the entropy is roughly normally distributed with a peak between 5 and 6, and a skewness towards lower values of entropy. This suggests that, while a fraction of about 50% of the users tend to exhibit an average tagging variety (corresponding to entropy values $4 \lesssim x \lesssim 7$), the remainder are either focused ($x \lesssim 4$) or extremely heterogeneous ($x \gtrsim 7$) in their tagging adoption. The analysis of tag adoption entropy reveals crucial features from the perspective of modeling user attention: tagging entropy is a proxy to measure how spread or focused users' attention is towards few or several contexts. A more refined analysis, that will take into account not only tags but the topics that emerge from their co-occurrences is presented later to address **Q5**.

3.4 Topical clusters of interest

To answer **Q4**, we conducted a number of experiments aimed at evaluating how users in the media dataset can be grouped together. Users were represented as term-frequency vectors in the space of media tags. We performed the clustering of these users based on Bisecting k-Means [43], which is well-suited to produce high-quality (hard) clustering solutions in high-dimensional, large datasets [50]. We used the CLUTO clustering toolkit[6] which provides a globally-optimized version of Bisecting k-Means. Feature selection was carried out to retain only the features (*i.e.*, tags) that accounted for 80% of the overall similarity of clusters. We experimented by varying the number k of clusters from 2 to 50, with unitary increment of k at each run. Our evaluation was both quantitative, based on standard within-cluster and across-cluster similarity criteria, and qualitative, based on the cluster characterization in terms of descriptive and discriminating features. The best-quality clustering solution corresponded to $k = 5$.

Figure 8 shows a color-intensity plot of the relations between the different clusters of users and features (*i.e.*, tags), corresponding to a 5-way clustering solution. Only a subset of the features is displayed, which corresponds to the union of the most descriptive and discriminating features of each cluster. Moreover, features are re-ordered according to a

---

[6]CLUTO: `www.cs.umn.edu/~karypis/cluto`

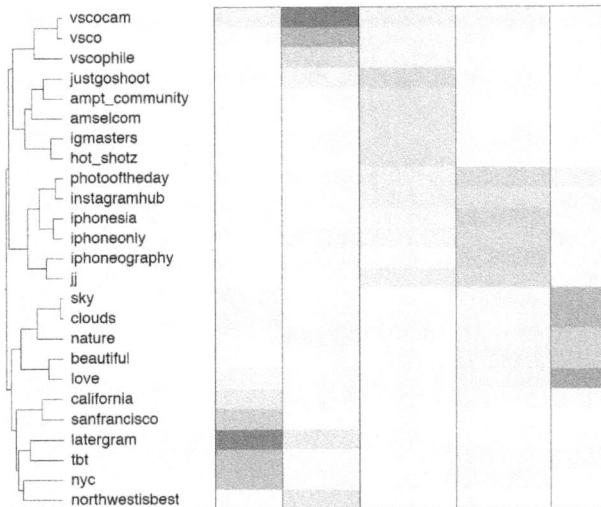

Figure 8: 5-way clustering of the users in the media dataset.

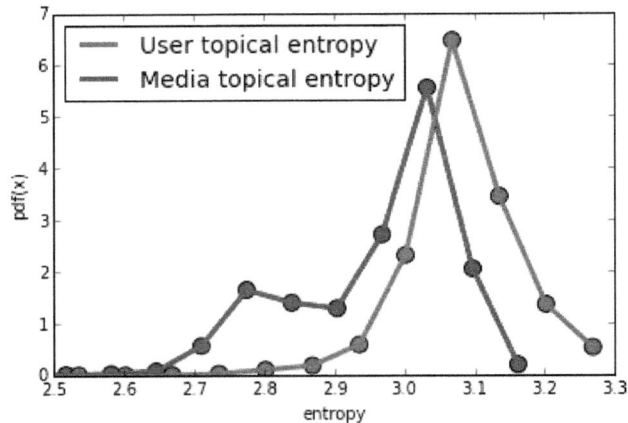

Figure 9: User and media topical entropy.

hierarchical clustering solution, which is visualized on the left-hand side of the figure. A brighter red cell corresponding to a pair feature-cluster indicates higher power of that feature to be, for that cluster, descriptive (*i.e.*, the fraction of within-cluster similarity that this feature can explain) and discriminating (*i.e.*, the fraction of dissimilarity between the cluster and the rest of the objects this feature can explain.) The width of each cluster-column is proportional to the logarithm of the corresponding cluster's size.

It can be noted that the five clusters are quite well-balanced. The first two clusters (*i.e.*, the two left-most columns) are strongly characterized by hashtags denoting the use of popular *applications*, namely VSCO Cam and Latergram. The former is commonly used to modify pictures by adding filters, while the latter is used to schedule the upload of a picture at different (later) time than that of its shot. The #latergram cluster is also characterized by another popular hashtag, #tbt, which is an acronym of Throwback Thursday (a "throwback" theme can pertain to some event that happened in the past), and at higher levels in the induced feature-cluster hierarchy, by geographical hashtags (*e.g.*, #nyc, #california.) While the fifth cluster is labeled by *subject-based* tags that are evocative of feelings (#love) or nature (#sky, #nature), the third and fourth clusters are instead characterized by either *attention-seeking* tags or *microcommunity-focused* tags: #photooftheday, #igmaster are representative of the former category, as users are seeking approval from their peers, whereas #amselcom, and #justgoshoot fall into the latter category along with #iphonesia (originally used by East-Asia users who share photos taken with their iPhones) and #instagramhub (which aims at helping users understand best practices and sharing tips.) Yet, #jj, which is run by prominent Instagram user Josh Johnson, denotes a community which asks their users to abide by the rule "for every one photo posted, comment on two others and like three more". Note that, in general, members of such microcommunities are often asked to share photos on a specific theme, and motivated to create more effective images. These challenges posed by the community continuously prompt their members to play active roles in Instagram.

3.5 User popularity and topicality

Our final research question (**Q5**) aims at exploring the topical interests space of users and how this affects their popularity. To learn the topics of interest exhibited by the users we employed a topic model which adopts the tags assigned by users to their media as the topical characterization feature. We filtered out tags occurring only once in our corpus, that account for roughly 20% of the total.

After experimenting with various topic models available in the *gensim python* library,[7] (including LDA and HDP), we adopted Latent Semantic Indexing (LSI) that provided the most interpretable model for a suitable number of topics set to 10. Note that, differently from topic modeling applications where the impact of the choice of the number of topics might affect the results, in our case we obtained consistent results by using larger number of topics as well (we tested with 5, 10, 20 and 30 topics obtaining consistent results.) We set up our topic model inferring the posterior probability distribution over the topics for each media in our dataset. To determine the topical interests of each user u, we simply averaged the probabilities of each topic being exhibited by the media produced by u. As concerns the variety of topics covered by each user (as well as that exhibited by a given media), we adopted the Shannon entropy. Similarly to the formula used in Section 3.3 for users and tags, we calculated the probability of observing the topics (rather than the tags.) Afterwards, we estimated the probability distribution of user (respectively, media) topical entropy, as illustrated in Figure 9. Here we observe that the topical entropy (both for users and media) is very concentrated and spans values between 2.5 and 3.5 as opposed to the broader entropy interval of user tags, which ranges between 0 and 9 (see Figure 7.) This suggests that, although users are equally likely to adopt either a narrow or broad vocabulary of tags, their topical interests tend to be in general more concentrated. At the end of this section we will discuss if there are deviations from this pattern, and how they relate to users' popularity. In other words, we will seek to understand whether popu-

---

[7]Gensim: `http://radimrehurek.com/gensim/`

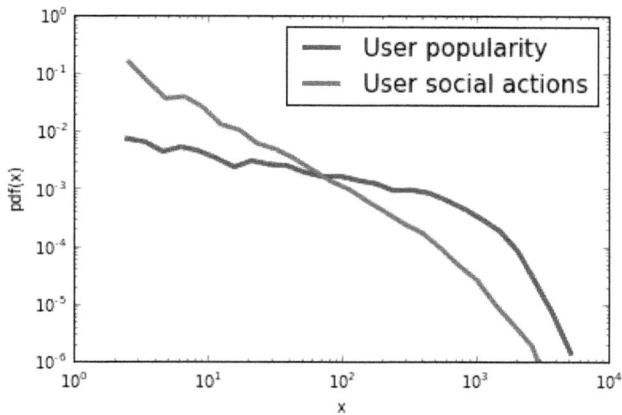

Figure 10: User popularity and social actions.

larity can be described by variety of topical interests. Note that user topical entropy and media topical entropy are similarly distributed, as it should be, suggesting the goodness of our approach to build users topical interest profiles.

In order to investigate the popularity of users, we measured the total number of likes and comments received by a user's media. We also account for the total number of times a user likes or comments someone else media, namely the number of *social actions* that this user performs. Such measures are clearly correlated since one is complementary to the other. In Figure 10 we show the distribution of user popularity and user social actions. From the two distributions some interesting facts emerge. First, they are both broadly distributed. The slope of the user popularity distribution is small. This implies the presence of many users with approximately the same (small) popularity. Around $x \gtrsim 1000$, the slope of the user popularity distribution drastically changes, becoming steeper as of identifying a cut-off due to the finite size of the sample. Values larger than this point coincide with the few extremely popular users who receive a lot many likes and comments to their media. The social actions distribution is still broad but with a steeper slope. This implies that there exist relatively less users (with respect to the popularity distribution) who produce many likes or comments to others' media.

Our final experiment aims to understand whether user popularity can be explained by means of variety of users' topical interests. Our goal is to determine whether different classes of popular users emerge, according to their topical interests. To this aim, we correlate user popularity with their topical entropy values discussed above. Figure 11 shows a boxplot that separates users in five logarithmic bins. For each bin, the corresponding box extends from the lower to upper quartile values of the data, whereas the whiskers extend from the box to show the range of the popularity values for that bin. A red line corresponds to the median value for each bin. Popularity once again is measured as the sum of likes and comments received from the media produced by each user. Results do not vary when considering the count instead of the sum of social actions, or when varying the number of topics in the topic model. The values of topical entropy span between 2.7 and 3.3 bits, in a spectrum of 0.6 bit overall.

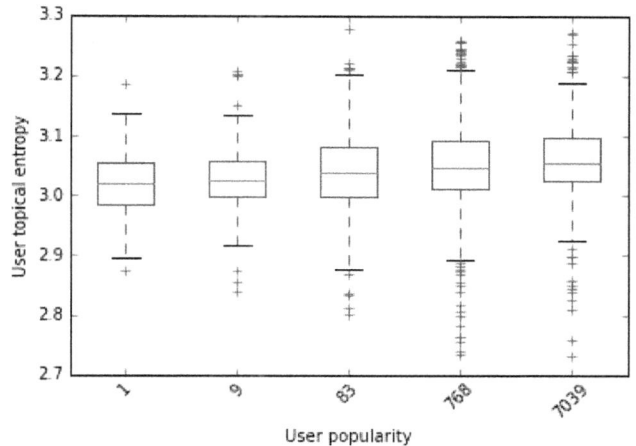

Figure 11: Boxplot on popularity and topical entropy.

From Figure 11 two interesting findings emerge. First, user popularity is somewhat affected by topical entropy. As popularity grows, the topical entropy increases accordingly. For example, the median topical entropy for very popular users ($768 < x \leq 7039$) is around 0.1 bits larger than that of unpopular users ($x \leq 9$). By comparing these two distributions we observe a statistically very significant difference: a two-sided t-test of the two independent samples yields a t-statistic of 3.674 corresponding to a p-value of 0.0005. The second observation is that various outliers are present among the popular users; this causes the presence of popular users with topical entropy much lower or much higher than average.

Our findings suggest that unpopular users tend to be more focused in their interests with respect to more popular users. However, there exist popular users who are either extremely specialized (very low values of topical entropy) or have extremely broad topical interests. These results complement the intriguing hypothesis, recently advanced by other studies [46, 47], that popularity might be affected by structural features and information diffusion patterns in addition to content production and topical interests.

4. DISCUSSION

In this section we summarize the results obtained addressing the five research questions we posed at the beginning of the paper, providing a final memorandum to the reader with the main findings of this work.

A1 *Network and community structure*: The network structure of the Relational Instagram Network exhibits two relevant characteristics: a scale-free distribution of node degree and a broad distribution of community size. This suggests that the network growth might happen by preferential attachment, whereas the emergence of the community structure might be driven by self organization of users around topics of interest.

A2 *Content production and consumption*: Regarding content production, the life-cycle of information generation on the platform might be explained in Simon's terms with a heightened likelihood that already engaged users produce more content. Content consumption, on the other hand, might be driven by the information economy principle of least effort: users tend to adopt the "like" behavior strikingly more than producing comments, in line with the intuition that a greater effort (in terms of time and communication economy) must be done to drive the social interaction towards conversation.

A3 *Social tagging*: Tag usage too is in line with the principle of least effort: the majority of media are labeled with just a few tags, yielding a power law distribution of tagging activity. A similar effect was recently observed in other platforms, like Twitter [45] due to limited attention in combination with competition among tags.

A4 *Topical clusters of interest*: Clusters of Instagram users can be detected by means of the tags they adopt to label the contents they produce (and how contents are produced), to indicate their intention to seek approval from other users, or to denote the microcommunity the users belong to.

A5 *Popularity and topicality*: User popularity is mildly affected by the breath of topical interests. Increasing values of topical entropy are positively correlated to higher user popularity; however, popular users exhibit more extreme topical entropy values, which means that some popular users are highly specialized, whereas other have very broad interests. This translates in the principle that users with general interests have the same chance to become popular than the specialized ones.

5. RELATED WORK

In recent literature, social media and online communities have been used as proxy to study human communication and behavior at scale in different scenarios, including social protests or mobilizations, social influence and political interests and much more [9, 13, 14]. Other research highlighted how trends emerge and diffuse in socio-technical systems, and how individuals' interacting in such environments devote their attention [30, 10].

In this work, we addressed popularity and trends emerging in Instagram. Trends are used to represent popular topics of interest as they are considered indicators of collective attention [28], and have been studied to detect exogenous real-world events [39, 6, 20]. Our work explores network features and diffusion patterns of social media content. Information diffusion and the network structure in social media have been extensively studied [29, 21, 48, 18]. A lot of attention has been devoted to explore the community structure of such socio-technical systems [19] and to study the formation and evolution of social groups therein [4]. The interplay between the dimensions of social interactions and those of topical interests of users have been also investigated showing a mutual reshaping based on mutual feedback mechanisms [38]. Moreover, our study touches on a mixture of ingredients commonly exhibited by socio-technical systems that digitally mediate communications among individuals: content, topics of discussion, language and tags. Content in social media well reflects socio-economic indicators of users,

in that languages highlight patterns of linguistic homogeneity [36], individual and collective satisfaction, demographic characteristics [34]. Social network data also exhibit cues of users' evolution, as discussed in this work. Existing literature witnesses that online content reflects the intuition that users are susceptible to changing their behavior along with experience, and common patterns of evolution emerge over time [17, 32].

Narrowing our focus on research investigating social media features similar to those of Instagram, an extensive analysis of the Flickr social network is reported in [33, 12]. Particular attention here is devoted to the understanding of the temporal evolution of network topology, picture popularity, and relating processes of information propagation. However, unlike in our work, no content information (*e.g.*, tags, comments) is taken into account. A study concerning user interactions in the 22 largest regional networks on Facebook is conducted in [49]. Results show that interaction activity on Facebook is significantly skewed towards a small portion of each user's social links, and consequently the interaction graph reveals different characteristics than the corresponding social graph. Note that we also leverage the importance of user interactions, as our RIN takes into account like and comment actions. In [7], clickstream data obtained by an aggregator of social networks (Orkut, Myspace, Hi5 and LinkedIn) are exploited to analyze various aspects of online lifetime of users, such as frequency and length of online sessions, activity sequences and types, dynamics of social interactions. The analysis of workloads has showed that the user browsing is the dominant behavior (accounting for 92% of all requests.) A similar study is performed in [40], where clickstream data from Facebook, LinkedIn, Hi5, and StudiVZ are used to characterize actual user interactions within the sites, in terms of session length, feature popularity and active/inactive time. In our work, we do not consider clickstream data as such information is not made available through the Instagram APIs. User latent interactions in Renren are investigated in [25]. Results show that latent interactions (*e.g.*, browsing of users profiles) are more numerous, non-reciprocal and they often connect non-friend strangers if compared to visible ones. In contrast to previously discussed works, the authors in [25] did not use clickstream data, but they exploited public data about visits to the crawled user profiles.

6. CONCLUSIONS

In this paper we presented a broad analysis of the Instagram ecosystem, exploiting its heterogeneous structure, part social network, part tagging environment, and part media sharing platform. We exploited users signals in the form of relationships and interactions to investigate a number of research questions spanning network-, semantic- and topical-based analysis on users, media and how these two dimensions are interrelated.

We first focused on the network and community structure, observing that the topical interests exhibited by the users might affect their inter-connectivity and interactions, shaping the network structure around topical communities that can possibly be explained by users' self organization. We then studied the patterns of content production and consumption on the platform, putting into evidence a strong heterogeneity in the mechanism of production of new information, and the emergence of an information economy principle in the case of content consumption. Our analysis shifted toward the study of social tagging behavior, and we highlighted that users exhibit vocabularies of limited size reflecting their limited attention capabilities, but, nonetheless, popular trends emerge. This can be explained by limited attention of individuals and competition among "memes" (*i.e.*, popular tags.) The study concludes by investigating topics and topicality in the network, and relating it to user popularity. We showed that clusters of users can be found around the tags. Furthering this analysis by learning a topic model on such tags, we showed that the variety of topical interests mildly affects user popularity: users with narrow interests tend to be less popular, whereas broader interests tend to yield higher popularity. However, popular users are special in a way because they exhibit more extreme behavior: they can produce either very topically specific content, or media of very broad interest.

Further work is needed to assess what role the structure of the network has in the determination of the popularity of content and users in online ecosystems based on social connectivity and content sharing, in the direction of recent work on Twitter [46, 47].

7. REFERENCES

[1] J. Alstott, E. Bullmore, and D. Plenz. powerlaw: a python package for analysis of heavy-tailed distributions. *PloS one*, 9(1):e85777, 2014.

[2] S. Aral, L. Muchnik, and A. Sundararajan. Distinguishing influence-based contagion from homophily-driven diffusion in dynamic networks. In *Proceedings of the National Academy of Sciences*, 106(51):21544–21549, 2009.

[3] S. Aral and D. Walker. Identifying influential and susceptible members of social networks. *Science*, 337(6092):337–341, 2012.

[4] L. Backstrom, D. Huttenlocher, J. Kleinberg, and X. Lan. Group formation in large social networks: membership, growth, and evolution. In *Proceedings of the 12th ACM SIGKDD international conference on Knowledge discovery and data mining*, pages 44–54, 2006.

[5] A.-L. Barabási and R. Albert. Emergence of scaling in random networks. *Science*, 286(5439):509–512, 1999.

[6] H. Becker, M. Naaman, and L. Gravano. Beyond trending topics: Real-world event identification on Twitter. In *Proceedings of the 5th International AAAI Conference on Weblogs and Social Media*, 2011.

[7] F. Benevenuto, T. Rodrigues, M. Cha, and V. A. F. Almeida. Characterizing user behavior in online social networks. In *Proceedings of the ACM SIGCOMM Conference on Internet Measurement*, pages 49–62, 2009.

[8] V. D. Blondel, J.-L. Guillaume, R. Lambiotte, and E. Lefebvre. Fast unfolding of communities in large networks. *Journal of Statistical Mechanics: Theory and Experiment*, 2008(10):P10008, 2008.

[9] R. M. Bond, C. J. Fariss, J. J. Jones, A. D. Kramer, C. Marlow, J. E. Settle, and J. H. Fowler. A 61-million-person experiment in social influence and political mobilization. *Nature*, 489(7415):295–298, 2012.

[10] C. Budak, D. Agrawal, and A. El Abbadi. Structural trend analysis for online social networks. In *Proceedings of the VLDB Endowment*, 4(10):646–656, 2011.

[11] D. Centola. The spread of behavior in an online social network experiment. *Science*, 329:1194–1197, 2010.

[12] M. Cha, A. Mislove, and K. P. Gummadi. A Measurement-driven Analysis of Information Propagation in the Flickr Social Network. In *Proceedings of the 18th International Conference on World Wide Web*, WWW '09, pages 721–730, 2009.

[13] M. D. Conover, C. Davis, E. Ferrara, K. McKelvey, F. Menczer, and A. Flammini. The geospatial characteristics of a social movement communication network. *PloS one*, 8:e55957, 2013.

[14] M. D. Conover, E. Ferrara, F. Menczer, and A. Flammini. The digital evolution of occupy wall street. *PloS one*, 8(5):e64679, 2013.

[15] D. J. Crandall, L. Backstrom, D. Cosley, S. Suri, D. Huttenlocher, and J. Kleinberg. Inferring social ties from geographic coincidences. In *Proceedings of the National Academy of Sciences*, 107(52):22436–22441, 2010.

[16] D. J. Crandall, L. Backstrom, D. Huttenlocher, and J. Kleinberg. Mapping the world's photos. In *Proceedings of the 18th international conference on World wide web*, pages 761–770. ACM, 2009.

[17] C. Danescu-Niculescu-Mizil, R. West, D. Jurafsky, J. Leskovec, and C. Potts. No country for old members: user lifecycle and linguistic change in online communities. In *Proceedings of the 22nd international conference on World Wide Web*, pages 307–318, 2013.

[18] P. De Meo, E. Ferrara, F. Abel, L. Aroyo, and G.-J. Houben. Analyzing user behavior across social sharing environments. *ACM Transactions on Intelligent Systems and Technology*, 5(1), 2013.

[19] E. Ferrara. A large-scale community structure analysis in Facebook. *EPJ Data Science*, 1:1–30, 2012.

[20] E. Ferrara, O. Varol, F. Menczer, and A. Flammini. Traveling trends: social butterflies or frequent fliers? In *Proceedings of the first ACM conference on Online social networks*, pages 213–222, 2013.

[21] P. A. Grabowicz, J. J. Ramasco, E. Moro, J. M. Pujol, and V. M. Eguiluz. Social features of online networks: The strength of intermediary ties in online social media. *PloS one*, 7(1):e29358, 2012.

[22] N. Hochman and L. Manovich. Zooming into an instagram city: Reading the local through social media. *First Monday*, 18(7), 2013.

[23] N. Hochman and R. Schwartz. Visualizing instagram: Tracing cultural visual rhythms. In *Proceedings of the Workshop on Social Media Visualization (SocMedVis) in conjunction with The Sixth International AAAI Conference on Weblogs and Social Media*, 2012.

[24] H. Jeong, Z. Néda, and A.-L. Barabási. Measuring preferential attachment in evolving networks. *EPL (Europhysics Letters)*, 61(4):567, 2003.

[25] J. Jiang, C. Wilson, X. Wang, P. Huang, W. Sha, Y. Dai, and B. Y. Zhao. Understanding latent interactions in online social networks. In *Proceedings of the ACM SIGCOMM Conference on Internet Measurement*, pages 369–382, 2010.

[26] A. Lancichinetti, F. Radicchi, J. J. Ramasco, and S. Fortunato. Finding statistically significant communities in networks. *PloS one*, 6(4):e18961, 2011.

[27] D. Lazer, A. S. Pentland, L. Adamic, S. Aral, A. L. Barabasi, D. Brewer, N. Christakis, N. Contractor, J. Fowler, M. Gutmann, et al. Life in the network: the coming age of computational social science. *Science*, 323(5915):721, 2009.

[28] J. Lehmann, B. Gonçalves, J. J. Ramasco, and C. Cattuto. Dynamical classes of collective attention in Twitter. In *Proceedings of the 21th International Conference on World Wide Web*, pages 251–260, 2012.

[29] K. Lerman and R. Ghosh. Information contagion: An empirical study of the spread of news on Digg and Twitter social networks. In *Proceedings of the 4th International AAAI Conference on Weblogs and Social Media*, pages 90–97, 2010.

[30] J. Leskovec, L. Backstrom, and J. Kleinberg. Meme-tracking and the dynamics of the news cycle. In *Proceedings of the 15th ACM SIGKDD International Conference on Knowledge Discovery and Data Mining*, pages 497–506. ACM, 2009.

[31] N. Luhmann, J. Bednarz, D. Baecker, and E. M. Knodt. *Social systems*, volume 1. Stanford University Press Stanford, 1995.

[32] J. J. McAuley and J. Leskovec. From amateurs to connoisseurs: modeling the evolution of user expertise through online reviews. In *Proceedings of the 22nd international conference on World Wide Web*, pages 897–908. ACM, 2013.

[33] A. Mislove, H. S. Koppula, K. P. Gummadi, P. Druschel, and B. Bhattacharjee. Growth of the Flickr Social Network. In *Proceedings of the First Workshop on Online Social Networks*, WOSN '08, pages 25–30, 2008.

[34] A. Mislove, S. Lehmann, Y.-Y. Ahn, J.-P. Onnela, and J. N. Rosenquist. Understanding the demographics of Twitter users. In *Proceedings of the 5th International AAAI Conference on Weblogs and Social Media*, 2011.

[35] A. Mislove, M. Marcon, P. K. Gummadi, P. Druschel, and B. Bhattacharjee. Measurement and analysis of online social networks. In *Proceedings of the ACM SIGCOMM Conference on Internet Measurement*, pages 29–42, 2007.

[36] D. Quercia, L. Capra, and J. Crowcroft. The social world of Twitter: Topics, geography, and emotions. In *Proceedings of the 6th International AAAI Conference on Weblogs and Social Media*, pages 298–305, 2012.

[37] T. Rattenbury, N. Good, and M. Naaman. Towards automatic extraction of event and place semantics from flickr tags. In *Proceedings of the 30th annual international ACM SIGIR conference on Research and development in information retrieval*, pages 103–110. ACM, 2007.

[38] D. M. Romero, C. Tan, and J. Kleinberg. On the interplay between social and topical structure. In *Proceedings of the 7th International AAAI Conference on Weblogs and Social Media*, 2013.

[39] H. Sayyadi, M. Hurst, and A. Maykov. Event detection and tracking in social streams. In *Proceedings of the 3rd International AAAI Conference on Weblogs and Social Media*, 2009.

[40] F. Schneider, A. Feldmann, B. Krishnamurthy, and W. Willinger. Understanding online social network usage from a network perspective. In *Proceedings of the ACM SIGCOMM Conference on Internet Measurement*, pages 35–48, 2009.

[41] T. H. Silva, P. O. Vaz de Melo, J. M. Almeida, J. Salles, and A. A. Loureiro. A comparison of foursquare and instagram to the study of city dynamics and urban social behavior. In *Proceedings of the 2nd SIGKDD International Workshop on Urban Computing*, page 4, 2013.

[42] H. A. Simon. On a class of skew distribution functions. *Biometrika*, 42(3/4):425–440, 1955.

[43] M. Steinbach, G. Karypis, and V. Kumar. A comparison of document clustering techniques. In *Proceedings of the KDD workshop on text mining*, pages 525–526. Boston, 2000.

[44] A. Vespignani. Predicting the behavior of techno-social systems. *Science*, 325(5939):425, 2009.

[45] L. Weng, A. Flammini, A. Vespignani, and F. Menczer. Competition among memes in a world with limited attention. *Scientific Reports*, 2, 2012.

[46] L. Weng, F. Menczer, and Y.-Y. Ahn. Virality prediction and community structure in social networks. *Scientific Reports*, 3:2522, 2013.

[47] L. Weng, F. Menczer, and Y.-Y. Ahn. Predicting successful memes using network and community structure. In *Proceedings of the 8th International Conference on Weblogs and Social Media (ICWSM 2014)*, 2014.

[48] L. Weng, J. Ratkiewicz, N. Perra, B. Gonçalves, C. Castillo, F. Bonchi, R. Schifanella, F. Menczer, and A. Flammini. The role of information diffusion in the evolution of social networks. In *Proceedings of the 19th ACM SIGKDD Conference on Knowledge Discovery and Data Mining (KDD 2013)*, pages 356–364, 2013.

[49] C. Wilson, B. Boe, A. Sala, K. P. N. Puttaswamy, and B. Y. Zhao. User interactions in social networks and their implications. In *EuroSys*, pages 205–218, 2009.

[50] Y. Zhao and G. Karypis. Empirical and theoretical comparisons of selected criterion functions for document clustering. *Machine Learning*, 55(3):311–331, 2004.

Scalable, Generic, and Adaptive Systems for Focused Crawling

Georges Gouriten
Institut Mines-Télécom
Télécom ParisTech; CNRS LTCI
75634 Parix Cedex 13, France
gouriten@telecom-paristech.fr

Silviu Maniu
Department of Computer Science
University of Hong Kong
Pokfulam Road, Hong Kong
smaniu@cs.hku.hk

Pierre Senellart
Institut Mines-Télécom
Télécom ParisTech; CNRS LTCI
75634 Parix Cedex 13, France
senellart@telecom-paristech.fr

ABSTRACT

Focused crawling is the process of exploring a graph iteratively, focusing on parts of the graph relevant to a given topic. It occurs in many situations such as a company collecting data on competition, a journalist surfing the Web to investigate a political scandal, or an archivist recording the activity of influential Twitter users during a presidential election. In all these applications, users explore a graph (e.g., the Web or a social network), nodes are discovered one by one, the total number of exploration steps is constrained, some nodes are more valuable than others, and the objective is to maximize the total value of the crawled subgraph.

In this article, we introduce scalable, generic, and adaptive systems for focused crawling. Our first effort is to define an abstraction of focused crawling applicable to a large domain of real-world scenarios. We then propose a generic algorithm, which allows us to identify and optimize the relevant subsystems. We prove the intractability of finding an optimal exploration, even when all the information is available.

Taking this intractability into account, we investigate how the crawler can be steered in several experimental graphs. We show the good performance of a greedy strategy and the importance of being able to run at each step a new estimation of the crawling frontier. We then discuss this estimation through heuristics, self-trained regression, and multi-armed bandits. Finally, we investigate their scalability and efficiency in different real-world scenarios and by comparing with state-of-the-art systems.

Categories and Subject Descriptors

H.3.7 [**Digital Libraries**]: Collection

Keywords

focused crawling, graph exploration, multi-armed bandits

1. INTRODUCTION

Thanks to better interfaces, better hardware, and the Internet, digital resources are omnipresent. People and institutions produce and consume more and more of them. Being able to efficiently collect

data thus becomes increasingly important. However, the challenge is not to simply collect any data but only relevant data. An electronic music publishing company, for instance, will be particularly interested in blog posts about electronic music and probably less in those about classic painting.

Many focused data collection operations can be formalized as a topic-driven exploration of a graph. Searching for Web content is performed by following hyperlinks in the Web graph. Looking for a file in a decentralized file sharing peer-to-peer network is done by exploring the graph of the connected peers. Influential users in an online social network are found by exploring its graph. Even some social tasks such as looking for job opportunities may amount to an iterative and recursive exploration of one's connections. In addition, in all these cases, those explorations are guided by a specific need: they are topic-driven.

Accessing data in these scenarios is not free. The cost of access can be in terms of bandwidth, processing power, available time, server policies, etc. One particularly relevant example is crawling Twitter. Twitter stores vast amounts of data but only allows a comparatively tiny number of requests in a 15-minute period on its API [24]. Furthermore, not only big companies with vast IT resources need to collect data, but also individuals or small companies with more modest means.

For all those reasons, being able to build better systems for focused crawling is crucial. This is the essence of the work presented in this article. In this direction, we propose a simple and widely applicable abstraction for focused crawling, practical considerations, various new systems adaptable to different use cases, and experiments on real-world datasets.

More specifically, we offer the following contributions:

- A generic model for focused crawling, as an optimization problem on a graph, with various examples of its application; [Section 2];

- A proof that it is intractable to compute optimal crawl sequences [Section 3];

- A flexible high-level algorithm to perform focused crawling [Section 4];

- A consistent experimental framework, based on real and large datasets[1] [Sections 2 and 5];

- Pragmatic considerations on how to drive the crawl [Section 6];

---

[1] All datasets and source code used in the experiments are available online at http://netiru.fr/research/14fc/index.

- A variety of techniques to estimate the value of unknown nodes, some inspired by the literature, some conceptually novel [Section 7];

- A detailed study of the behavior of these estimators in a variety of situations [Section 8].

We summarize the related work in Section 9, just before concluding. A preliminary version of this work was presented in a national conference without formal proceedings [14]; additions with respect to that version include estimators based on the second-level neighborhood, multi-armed bandit approaches, and final experiments.

2. MODEL AND USE CASES

In this section, we define focused crawling with a generic model, explain how it applies to real-world scenarios, then introduce our experimental datasets.

2.1 Generic Model for Focused Crawling

We fix a crawling space G to be a directed graph, $G = (V, E)$. The nodes, V, are the resources that we want to crawl (e.g., Web pages). The edges, E, are the links between those resources (e.g., hyperlinks).

We assume there are non-negative *weights* (or *scores*) on both edges and nodes. The weight of a node is its relevance to the topic (e.g., how much the Web page is related to the topic of the crawl). The weight of an edge is an *a priori* indication of the relevance of the node it links to (e.g., how much the hyperlink occurs in a context that is related to the topic of the crawl). In actual crawling scenarios, the weight of a node will only be known once this node has been crawled, while the weight of an edge will be known once its source has been crawled.

These weights are computed by functions. They can be any scoring technique. For instance, in the case of the Web, we may define the score of a node, given a term, to be the tf–idf of the Web page for this term. However, we stress the generality of our approach to any *edge scoring function*, noted $\alpha : E \to \mathbb{Q}^+$, and *node scoring function* $\beta : V \to \mathbb{Q}^+$. Weights are assumed to be rationals to be representable in machine format. For the crawling space, we assume α and β to be fixed.

From the score of an individual node, we define the score of a set of nodes. Let X be a subset of V, then by definition $\beta(X) := \sum_{v \in X} \beta(v)$. Other ways of aggregating node scores could be used, we chose the sum as it is intuitive, simple, and enough for most use cases. Any other monotonically increasing scoring function could be used; the sum has the advantage of simplicity.

We now introduce some concepts specific to the setting of graph crawling. For a subset V' of V, the *frontier* of V' is the set of nodes not in V' it directly connects to. Formally:

DEFINITION 1. *We define the* frontier *of any $V' \subseteq V$ as:*

$$\text{Frontier}(V') := \{ v \in V \setminus V' \mid \exists v' \in V', (v', v) \in E \}.$$

A crawl has a starting point, a set of nodes (e.g., some handpicked Web pages) the *seed set* which is a subset of V.

The *crawled set* is originally V_0. A *step* of the crawl consists in downloading a resource from the frontier of the crawled set, and adding it to the latter. A crawl has a limited number of steps, depending on the request rate, the bandwidth, or the hardware. We detail some typical use cases in the next part. This limit is the *crawl budget*, that we simply define to be a fixed non-negative integer n.

A *crawl sequence* is a sequence of n nodes, where each node is at the frontier of the crawled set:

DEFINITION 2. *A crawl sequence $(v_1 \dots v_n) \in V^n$ is any sequence of n nodes such that*

$$\forall 1 \leqslant i \leqslant n, \quad v_i \in \text{Frontier}(V_0 \cup \{v_1 \dots v_{i-1}\}).$$

The graph, the scoring functions, the seed set, and the budget define a *crawl configuration*. A *crawling system* or *crawler* returns a crawl sequence given a crawl configuration.

A crawl happens *online*, the crawler only has access to the information of the nodes of the current crawled set; their score, their outgoing edges, and their edges' scores. The scores of the nodes at the frontier are not known. We define the *performance* of a crawler as the aggregated score of the crawl sequence it returns.

For each crawl configuration, there is a fixed number of possible crawl sequences. The *optimal crawl sequences* are the crawl sequences with the highest score:

DEFINITION 3. *The set of* optimal crawl sequences *is defined as:*

$$\underset{(v_1 \dots v_n) \text{ crawl sequence}}{\arg \max} \beta(\{v_1, \dots, v_n\})$$

(arg max *returns a set as there may be different crawl sequences with the same score.*)

An *optimal crawler* is one that always returns an optimal crawl sequence. The unique β value of all the optimal crawl sequences is the *optimal score*. Edge weights are not part of the definition of optimality but, as we will see later, can be used to estimate the weights of the nodes at the frontier.

2.2 Example Use Cases

Our model covers different use cases, beyond classical focused Web crawling. The main ingredients V, E, α, β, V_0, and n can be instantiated for a variety of problems. We propose here examples of α and β, but other scoring techniques could be used in the same settings. To calculate n in the following use cases, we consider a crawl that lasts one week. For instance, in a Web crawling scenario, with one request per domain per second, it is possible to perform a total of $60 \times 60 \times 24 \times 7 \approx 6 \times 10^5$ crawling steps per domain.

Focused Web crawling [6]. This is the classical focused crawling scenario where the objective is to crawl the Web. We assume given a keyword query, used to focus the crawl.
V: Web pages;
E: hyperlinks;
α: tf–idf of the anchor text, w.r.t. the query;
β: tf–idf of the page, w.r.t. the query;
V_0: manually selected Web pages;
n: 6×10^5 requests for a unique domain, 6×10^8 for a thousand domains crawled in parallel.

In more elaborate settings [20], α and β are computed by automatically trained classifiers – this still fits within our model, with slight modification to the definition of these two functions.

Topic-centered Twitter user crawl [15]. The aim is to crawl Twitter users, retrieving their tweets from the API, and adding to the frontier the Twitter users they mention in them. We also assume a keyword query is given.
V: Twitter users;
E: mentioning relations, $(u, v) \in E$ if at least one tweet of user u mentions v;
α: tf–idf of all the tweets of u mentioning v w.r.t. the query;
β: tf–idf of all the tweets of u w.r.t. the query;
V_0: users obtained using the Twitter Search API;
n: 2×10^5 `statuses/user_timeline` requests [24].

Deep Web siphoning through a keyword search interface [3]. The goal is to siphon an entire database which is only accessible beyond an HTML form. Keyword queries are used through the form and new keywords are discovered from the pages given in response to the query.

V: keywords;

E: keyword relations, $(u,v) \in E$ if the keyword v appears in the response page obtained by submitting the form with the keyword u;

α: number of occurrences of the keyword v in the result pages for the keyword u;

β: number of records returned for a keyword;

V_0: initial small dictionary of keywords;

n: 6×10^5 requests for one domain.

In the examples so far, the crawling entity is centralized, but we can also consider cases where multiple entities perform a distributed crawl.

Gossiping peer-to-peer search [2]. One peer (e.g., in a file sharing network) issues a query and this query is propagated through gossiping to the neighboring peers.

V: peers;

E: peer-to-peer overlay network;

α: relevance, to the query, of the cached information about a remote peer;

β: relevance of a peer's data to the query;

V_0: peer issuing the query;

n: 10^4 propagation steps, limited to prevent flooding, e.g., one tenth of the total number of nodes in the network.

Using a real-world social network to answer a query [23, 11]. This example is a well-known sociological experiment where individuals are asked to use their direct social network to, e.g., forward a message to another person of the network that they are not directly connected to.

V: individuals;

E: acquaintance network;

α: assessment of an individual of her acquaintance's ability to forward the message to the right person;

β: 1 if the individual is the receiver, 0 otherwise;

V_0: user the query starts from;

n: 10^3 requests made from an individual to another, the collective effort allowed (how many people contribute).

These examples are from very different settings: the resources can be Web pages, users, machines; in some cases, a centralized entity governs the crawl, in others the process is distributed; the budget can be set to prevent flooding, or as a consequence of a time limit; etc. Yet, they all can be seen as instances of our general problem of finding the best crawl sequences starting from a given set of nodes.

We advocate that our general framework, and the algorithms we present hereafter, can be used in a wide range of scenarios, listed previously and beyond, as a basis to build efficient adaptive systems. Obviously, specific settings may also require specific adjustments. In particular, we chose to study centralized crawls. The question of managing distributed focused crawls is left for future work.

2.3 Experimental Use Cases

We chose five large and diverse datasets[2] from scenarios that correspond to actual needs.

---

[2]Available at http://netiru.fr/research/14fc/index.

Wikipedia datasets: bretagne and france. Wikipedia has a density of links and a diversity of content that makes it a good candidate to simulate a focused crawl on the Web, a very common use case.

We used scoring functions based on one keyword, *bretagne* in one dataset, and *france* in the other. The two keywords we sufficient in obtaining datasets that have realistic score distributions, and different crawling challenges, on one hand a very specialized topic, on the other a more generic one. We used the content of the French Wikipedia[3].

Let first f be a logarithm smoothening function $f : x \mapsto \log(1 + x)$ that maps non-negative numbers to non-negative numbers. If x is the number of occurrences of the keyword in a Wikipedia article u, we set $\beta(u) := f(x)$. Similarly, if y is the number of occurrences of the keyword in a 100-character window around a hyperlink from u to v, we set $\alpha(u,v) := f(y)$.

Twitter datasets: happy, jazz, and weird. Crawling social networks is of particular interest given the popularity of those platforms, and their graphs are structurally different from the graph of the Web.

We built three datasets simulating a user crawl on Twitter, one of the most popular social network. Here also, we used scoring functions based on one keyword to obtain realistic score distributions with three different degrees of specialization. The three keywords are *happy*, *jazz*, and *weird*. We used the SNAP Twitter dataset [25][4].

For x the number of occurrences of the keyword in the tweets of a user u, we define $\beta(u) := f(x)$. For y the number of occurrences of the keyword in the tweets of user u mentioning user v, we let $\alpha(u,v) := f(y)$.

Dataset	Nodes (million)	Non-zero nodes (%)	Edges (million)	Non-zero edges (%)
BRETAGNE	2.2	2.0	35.6	0.5
FRANCE	"	19.2	"	6.8
HAPPY	16.9	11.0	78.0	2.4
JAZZ	"	0.6	"	0.1
WEIRD	"	3.2	"	0.4

Table 1: Size of the experimental datasets

Experimental diversity. Our datasets correspond to popular use cases, and as shown in Table 1, they cover different graph settings, in terms of size and score distribution.

3. INTRACTABLE OPTIMAL CRAWLS

In Section 2, we defined the notion of optimality for a crawling system, which depends on optimal crawl sequences. In our effort to build efficient crawling systems, it is important to investigate these optimal crawl sequences. Unfortunately, even in an *offline setting*, a setting where it is possible to access the whole graph, to determine the optimal sequence is NP-hard.

---

[3]February 2013 dump downloaded from http://dumps.wikimedia.org/backup-index.html.

[4]Formerly available at http://snap.stanford.edu/data/twitter7.html, it contains an estimated 30 % of all the tweets published between June and December 2009, 476 million tweets. The dataset unfortunately had to be pulled out from this Web site by request of Twitter.

PROPOSITION 1. *Let G be a graph, β a PTIME-computable node scoring function, V_0 a subset of nodes of G, and n a budget. To determine if there is a crawl sequence of score greater than or equal to a given rational r for G, β, V_0, and n is an NP-complete problem. NP-hardness holds even if V_0 is a singleton and r is an integer.*

PROOF. Membership in NP is straightforward. We guess a node sequence of size n, check that it is a valid crawl sequence (easily done in PTIME), compute its score (feasible in PTIME by hypothesis), and compare it to r.

For NP-hardness, we exhibit a PTIME many-one reduction from the LST-Graph problem described in [17]. The edge-uniform LST-Graph problem is defined as follows: given two positive integers L and W, and a directed graph $G = (V, E)$ where each edge (u, v) is annotated with a nonnegative integer *weight* $w(u, v)$, does there exist a subtree T of G such that the number of edges in T is less than or equal to L and that the sum of edge weights is greater than or equal to W? Theorem 5 of [17] shows this problem is NP-hard, by reduction from Set-Cover.

First, observe that instead of weights w on edges and budgets L and W on total edge counts and total edge weights, we can as well have weights w on nodes and budgets L' on node counts and W on the sum of node weights. To reduce the former problem to the latter, just add nodes in the middle of each edge, with weight being the weight of the edge, set weight 0 to all nodes originally in the graph, and set budget on node count L' to $2L + 1$ (in a tree, there is one more node than the number of edges, and there are twice more edges now). It is straightforward to show the reduction from the original edge-uniform LST-Graph problem to this modified LST-Graph* problem, with weights on nodes and budgets on node counts and sum of node weights.

Let (L, W, G, w) be an instance of LST-Graph*. Without loss of generality, we can assume L to be at most $|V|$ (otherwise, just set L to $|V|$, the problem will have the same answer) and the graph to have at least 2 nodes (otherwise, just add one more node with no edges). Let G' be the graph obtained from $G = (V, E)$ by adding:

- an additional node r;
- for each node u of G, $L + 1$ new nodes $u_1, \ldots, u_{L+1}$;
- for each node u of G, a chain of $L + 2$ edges $(r, u_1), (u_1, u_2), \ldots, (u_L, u_{L+1}), (u_{L+1}, u)$.

Since L is at most $|V|$, this construction is in $O(|V|^2)$. The score of a node is their weight in the old graph, new nodes having score 0.

We claim that LST-Graph*(L, W, G, w) has a solution if and only if $(G', w, \{r\}, 2L + 1)$ admits a crawling sequence of score greater than or equal to W. This reduction is obviously polynomial-time. We shall prove both directions of the equivalence.

First, assume (L, W, G, w) is a "yes" instance of LST-Graph*. Let T be a subtree of G of total weight at least W and of size l at most L. Let $(v^1 \ldots v^l)$ be a topological sort of tree T (i.e., an ordering such that v^j descendant of v^i implies $i \leqslant j$). We consider the sequence $(v_1^1, \ldots, v_{L+1}^1, v^1, \ldots, v^l)$ of length $L + 1 + l \leqslant 2L + 1$; this is a valid crawl sequence starting from $\{r\}$. We complete this crawl sequence into a crawl sequence S of length exactly $2L + 1$ by adding $L - l$ additional nodes $u_1, u_2, \ldots, u_{L-l}$ for an arbitrary node $u \in V$ distinct of v^1. The score of S is the summed weight of T, and is thus $\geqslant W$.

Conversely, assume $(G', w, \{r\}, 2L + 1)$ admits a crawling sequence S of score greater than or equal to W. This crawling sequence S, together with r, naturally defines a tree T' in G': the root of this tree is r; for every node v in S there is an edge from u to v where u is first node u in the sequence (r, S) such that $(u, v) \in G'$. Consider the forest $F = T' \cap V$, the restriction of T' to the nodes of G. F is not empty since S has non-zero score. F is a forest of G of length at most L (because since F is not empty, T must include at least one chain $v_1, \ldots, v_{L+1}, v$) and of summed weight greater

than or equal to W (because new nodes do not contribute to weight). We just have to show that F is connected. Since T is connected, F is disconnected only if there are two chains $u_1, \ldots, u_{L+1}, u$ and $v_1, \ldots, v_{L+1}, v$ in T with $u \neq v$. But the length of these two chains combined is $2L + 2 > 2L + 1$, which is impossible to fit inside T. $\qquad\square$

An immediate corollary of Proposition 1 is that it is unfeasible for practical purposes to determine whether a specific crawl sequence is close enough in score to the optimal. Consequently, it is also intractable to find an optimal crawl sequence. As in [17], we leave as an open problem the possibility of approximating the optimal score or finding a crawling sequence with a score being a factor of the optimal one.

In order to be optimal, a crawler would have to produce an optimal crawling sequence – the result above shows that this is NP-hard. This implies that even a crawler using a greedy strategy with an oracle estimator (concepts that we introduce later) cannot be optimal in the general case.

On a side note, if we do not use the sum of individual node weights but the *count* of nodes having non-zero weight as subset scoring, a greedy solution *does* work as long as there are some non-zero nodes in the frontier. The proof is straightforward, as adding one non-zero node always adds one to the total score, which is the best that can be done at any given point.

4. HIGH-LEVEL ALGORITHM

We gave in Section 2 the intuition behind a crawling process. In this part, we clarify this introducing a generic algorithm and the subsystems that we will investigate later: `scoreFrontier`, `getBatchSize`, and `getNextNodes`.

Algorithm 1: High-level algorithm

input : seed subgraph G_0, budget n
output: crawl sequence V, with a score as high as possible

1   $V \leftarrow ()$;
2   $G' \leftarrow G_0$;
3   budgetLeft $\leftarrow n$;
4   **while** budgetLeft > 0 **do**
5   frontier $\leftarrow$ extractFrontier(G');
6   scoredFrontier $\leftarrow$ scoreFrontier$(G', \text{frontier})$;
7     $b \leftarrow$ getBatchSize$()$;
8   NodeSequence $\leftarrow$ getNextNodes$(\text{scoredFrontier}, b)$;
9     $V \leftarrow (V, \text{NodeSequence})$;
10   **for** u **in** NodeSequence **do**
11       $G' \leftarrow G' \cup$ crawlNode(u);
12   budgetLeft $=$ budgetLeft $- b$
13 **return** V

Algorithm 1 maintains a crawled graph G'. This is the union of the subgraph induced by the crawled set, and the set of its outgoing edges, pointing to the frontier. G' is initialized to G_0, the subgraph of G induced by V_0 (line 2), it is then updated as more nodes are crawled (lines 10–11). The main loop of the crawl (lines 4–12) iterates as long as there is some budget left. The method `getBatchSize` allows to create a *batch* of crawling steps of size b, which avoids estimating the frontier between each crawled node – instead, a batch of b nodes are crawled using the current estimation of the scored frontier.

The method `extractFrontier` extracts the frontier from the crawled graph (line 5). As we explained in Section 2, the crawler does not have access to the scores of the nodes at the frontier, so `scoreFrontier` assigns a score *estimation* to these nodes. For that purpose, it has access to the crawled graph, which can serve as a training set. `getNextNodes` decides which should be the b nodes to crawl, depending on the scored frontier. The crawl sequence V, the crawled graph, and the budget are then updated accordingly (line 9–12), `crawlNode` consisting in retrieving a node, its actual score, and its outgoing edges, which are added to G'.

The above pseudocode gives a high-level overview of a generic focused crawler, but the details might change slightly in practical implementations, for instance to implement incremental statistical learning models.

5. EXPERIMENTAL FRAMEWORK

Now that we have a good understanding of the general context, we will study different systems in detail and present several empirical findings. It is therefore important to understand the experimental framework we used in order to ensure the consistent quality of these findings.

Baseline. For any crawl configuration with a meaningful budget, it is not possible to find the optimal crawl sequence. We thus could not compare our crawlers to an absolute optimal baseline. However, we specified in each experiment a baseline crawler, and compared the different crawlers, including those from the literature, relatively.

Testing configuration. We also tested our crawlers with enough configurations to ensure statistical significance. We tested fifty different configurations. For each experimental dataset (introduced in Section 2.3), we built ten seed sets, made of fifty different nodes chosen uniformly at random among those having non-zero weights. We ran the crawler for each seed set to obtain a seed score. We then computed their arithmetic mean to obtain a *dataset score*. This score was divided by the dataset score of a baseline, specified in each experiment, to obtain a normalized score. We eventually computed the geometric mean of the normalized score among the different datasets to obtain a *global score*.

Crawl budget. The maximum crawl budget we used is 10^5. As explained in Section 2.2, this would be a crawl campaign of three days and a half on Twitter [24], and a bit more than one day on Wikipedia. It is reasonable both in terms of time and freshness of the crawled data.

Implementation. The running time and memory consumption of a crawler is critical. For the largest experiments, we used the C++ programming language and stored the graph and the crawler metadata in the RAM. The RAM memory cost of our datasets was important – especially for the Twitter graph. Thus, all experiments were run on a Linux PC with 48 GB RAM. The CPU model was an Intel(R) Core(TM) i7-3820 CPU @ 3.60GHz.

Each subsystem of the crawler was an abstract C++ class, with derived classes for different possible implementations (greedy vs altered greedy, different estimators), that provide a number of virtual methods, especially `scoreFrontier` and `getNextNodes`. The source code, the datasets, and instructions to run the experiments are available online.[5]

We used the *Boost* graph library[6]. For the linear regression, we used the *dlib* C++ library[7] that implements an *incremental* version of the recursive least squares algorithm.

---

[5] http://netiru.fr/research/14fc/index
[6] http://www.boost.org/libs/graph
[7] http://dlib.net/

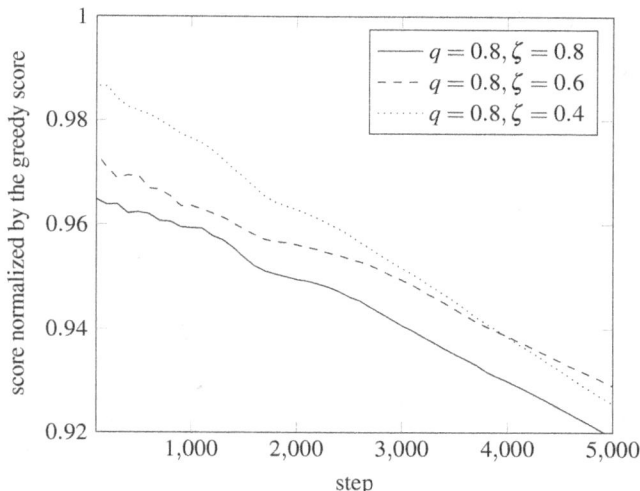

Figure 1: Best altered greedy parameters for JAZZ at step 5,000

6. STEERING THE CRAWLER

Before looking at how to build a good estimation of the frontier (`scoreFrontier`), we think here about which nodes to pick once the frontier has been estimated (`getNextNodes`), and what the impact of using batch processing is (`getBatchSize`).

To study those questions, in this section, we allow the crawlers not to worry about the estimation. They have access to the perfect estimator, the *oracle*, meaning that `scoreFrontier` returns the exact scores of the nodes at the frontier. The estimators that we use in practice are quite far from the oracle, as we will see in Section 8.1, so we consider only properties that look reasonable as invariants.

6.1 Rich People have Rich Friends

`getNextNodes` looks at the *estimated* frontier and returns the next nodes to crawl. We investigate here what this function should do, limiting ourselves to a batch size of 1, thus `getNextNodes` returns only one node. The estimated score of a node is noted $\tilde{\beta}(v)$. We also refer to `getNextNodes` as the *strategy* of the crawler.

In our online and incremental situation, a *greedy strategy* is a reasonable option:

STRATEGY 1. greedy strategy $= \underset{v \in \text{Frontier}(V')}{\arg\max} \tilde{\beta}(v)$

Yet, a pure greedy strategy could miss interesting parts of the graph. A node bridging to a rich subgraph with a low score would never be selected. This is the usual trade-off between exploitation and exploration. To test this risk, we consider *altered greedy* strategies, defined by a *probability* $q \in [0,1]$ and a *ratio* $\zeta \in [0,1]$.

STRATEGY 2. altered greedy $=$
with probability q, $\underset{v \in \text{Frontier}(V')}{\arg\max} \tilde{\beta}(v),$
with probability $1 - q$,
$\text{random}(\{ v \in \text{Frontier}(V') \mid \tilde{\beta}(v) \geqslant \tilde{\zeta} \times \max_u(\beta(u)) \})$

We tested the altered greedy strategies for $q = 0.2, 0.4, \ldots, 1.0$ and $\zeta = 0.0, 0.2, \ldots, 0.8$.

Figure 1 illustrates well what we found with all the datasets. For any number of steps greater or equal to a few thousands, the best altered greedy strategies are the one with the highest probability and ratio, and all the randomized strategies fall behind greedy.

39

We explain this with the "rich people have rich friends" property. The rich nodes (with a high score) cannot, statistically, have as friends (connected nodes) only poor nodes, they also have some rich nodes. When the frontier has a significant size, crawling the rich nodes is generally enough to get to the other rich nodes.

However, for experiments below a thousand steps, we sometimes saw altered greedy beat greedy, even with risky probability and ratio. With a small frontier, some rich parts can "hide" behind poor nodes, which then become more interesting. It is a phenomenon worth mentioning, but the gain was not very important and our work is mostly on large crawls so we did not investigate further on.

Greedy being a clear winner for any crawl of significant size, we use the greedy strategy for the rest of the study, `getNextNodes` returns the nodes with the top estimated scores.

6.2 The Batch Disadvantage

As introduced in Section 4, `getBatchSize` can be used to reduce the computation time. It does so by returning an integer, b, the *batch* size, greater than 1. It is then used to crawl a set of nodes of that size, instead of a unique node, before calling `scoreFrontier`, which is a relatively costly operation.

However, increasing the batch has a performance cost. We tested crawlers differing only by their batch sizes. The estimator was the *oracle*. For each crawler, we computed a global score according to the experimental framework defined in Section 5. The baseline for the score degradation was the score of the crawler with $b = 1$. If the crawler had no estimated node in the frontier, it picked the next node randomly.

	Step			
Batch size	100	1,000	10,000	100,000
2	0.4	2.2	3.9	6.4
8	1.3	6.5	12.8	18.3
32	6.6	6.5	17.5	24.3
128	38.8	10.7	19.9	29.5
1024	38.8	74.3	25.8	35.9

Table 2: Score degradation (%) for different batch sizes

In Table 2, we see the importance of the performance degradation, even for a batch size of 2. We explain it with two main arguments. First of all, the crawler is sometimes forced to pick nodes randomly, which, on average, degrades the performances (see Section 6.1). Secondly, the sooner a rich node is crawled, the sooner its connections are added to the frontier. Adding a rich node later creates a *score delay*, that will remain during the crawl, and increase if this delay is repeated.

Even for a batch size of 2, the performance degradation is notable. For this reason, we will, for the rest of the study, look for scalable estimation techniques, allowing to refresh of the estimation at each step.

7. FRONTIER ESTIMATORS

`scoreFrontier` is our last system to study, and the most difficult. It takes as an input the crawled graph and the frontier, and returns a `scoredFrontier`, an estimation of the β value of each node of the frontier, $\widetilde{\beta}$.

Thanks to the previous parts, we now have some precise ideas on what we would like for `scoreFrontier`. We look for a scalable system able to identify the top nodes of the frontier. We also call such a system an *estimator*.

In this part, we formalize frontier estimators, some adapted from the literature, some new. We are in the context of a specific crawl, V' is the set of crawled nodes, E' the set of known edges – including edges from V' to Frontier(V'), and $d_o : V \rightarrow \mathbb{N}$ (resp., d_i) the number of known outgoing (resp., incoming) edges of a node. The estimators are defined by their node weight estimation function $\widetilde{\beta} :$ Frontier$(V') \rightarrow \mathbb{Q}^+$. We defined a `short_name` for each estimator.

7.1 State-of-the-Art

We start our list looking at estimators from the literature that we adapted and translated using our model.

BFS. `bfs` is the *breadth-first search* estimator, a simple estimator based on a common crawling technique.

ESTIMATOR 1 (`bfs`). $\widetilde{\beta}(v) = \frac{1}{l(v)+1}$, *where* $l(v)$ *is the distance of* v *to* V_0.

This estimator is naive and we can expect poor results. We used it as a bottom line.

As we discuss in Section 9, most focused crawling systems from the literature mostly deal with how to compute the score of a node or an edge (i.e., how to define α and β), once they have been crawled [20]. Not many are about how to estimate those values *before* they are crawled (i.e., how to define $\widetilde{\beta}$). The exceptions are the following two approaches. They are inspired by PageRank and perform iterative computations on the crawled graph.

Navigational Rank. Navigational Rank [12] is a two-step node importance computation specifically designed for focused crawling. The first step is an iterative propagation from offsprings to ancestors, combined with the actual node score:

$$NR_1(v)^{t+1} = \eta \times \beta(v) + (1-\eta) \times avg_{(v,u)\in E'} \frac{NR_1(u)^t}{d_i(u)}$$

where $NR_1(u)^t$ is the node score at the iteration step t, and η is a parameter affecting convergence speed.

The second propagation step is performed only on the frontier nodes, and is from ancestors to offspring, as follows:

$$NR_2(v)^{t+1} \eta \times NR_1(v) + (1-\eta) \times avg_{(u,v)\in E'} \frac{NR_2(u)^t}{d_o(u)}.$$

We must make it clear that [12] contained an error in both equations (1) and (2). The senses of the propagations were reversed. It is fixed in the equations we just presented and has been confirmed with the authors of [12].

We define `nr`, the *Navigational Rank* estimator, as the NR_2 score.

ESTIMATOR 2 (`nr`). $\widetilde{\beta}(v) = NR_2(v)$.

One step of `nr` estimation requires two successive iterative computations (with perhaps a few dozens steps) on the whole crawled graph. This results in an overall quadratic complexity, with important multipliers, for each frontier estimation. As we will see in Section 8.1, this will have major consequences on the running time.

OPIC. OPIC [1] is an algorithm designed to estimate the PageRank of a node in a crawling situation.

OPIC maintains two per-node counters during the crawl: $C(v)$ – the *cash* value of of a node, initially set to 1, and $H(v)$, its cash history, starting at 0. It also keeps a global counter G, the entire cash accumulated in the system.

The estimation takes three steps:

1. the node v with the highest cash among all encountered nodes is selected (ties resolved arbitrarily), and its history is updated with the current cash value $H(v) = H(v) + C(v)$,
2. for each outgoing node u of v, the cash value is updated $C(u) = C(u) + \frac{C(v)}{d_{o(v)}}$,
3. the global counter is incremented and the cash value of v is reset, $G = G + C(v)$ and $C(v) = 0$.

Since OPIC does not take into account edge scores, we changed the second step with the following formula:

$$C(u) = C(u) + \frac{C(v)}{\sum_{(v,w) \in E'} \alpha(v,w) \times C(w)} \times \alpha(v,u) \times C(u)$$

`opic` is based on the three counters defined above.

ESTIMATOR 3 (`opic`). $\widetilde{\beta}(v) = \frac{H(v) + C(v)}{G+1}$.

7.2 Looking at the Neighborhood of a Node

The estimators from the research literature are not entirely satisfying for focused crawling. `nr` is computationally costly. `opic` is PageRank specific and initially does not take into account node and edge weights. We thus defined new estimators, starting here with intuitive heuristics.

For those heuristics, we combine in simple ways the scores of the nodes already crawled and of their outgoing edges. For a node of the frontier v, $P(v)$ is the *set of parent nodes*, or the *first-level neighborhood* of the node v. $P(v) = \{u \in V' \mid (u,v) \in E'\}$. The nodes of V' pointed to by the nodes of the first-level neighborhood constitute the *second-level neighborhood*.

The `fl_` estimators are based on the first-level neighborhood, and the `sl_` estimators on the second-level.

ESTIMATOR 4 (`fl_n fl_e fl_ne sl_n sl_e sl_ne`).
`fl_deg`: $\widetilde{\beta}(v) = d_i(v) = |P(v)|$
`fl_n`: $\widetilde{\beta}(v) = \sum_{u \in P(v)} \beta(u)$
`fl_e`: $\widetilde{\beta}(v) = \sum_{u \in P(v)} \alpha(u,v)$
`fl_ne`: $\widetilde{\beta}(v) = \sum_{u \in P(v)} \beta(u)\alpha(u,v)$
`sl_n`: $\widetilde{\beta}(v) = \sum_{u \in P(v)} \sum_{\substack{w \in V' \\ u \in P(w)}} \beta(w)$
`sl_e`: $\widetilde{\beta}(v) = \sum_{u \in P(v)} \sum_{\substack{w \in V' \\ u \in P(w)}} \alpha(u,w)$
`sl_ne`: $\widetilde{\beta}(v) = \sum_{u \in P(v)} \sum_{\substack{w \in V' \\ u \in P(w)}} \beta(w)\alpha(u,w)$

We will see how those heuristics perform later in the article. Before that, we looked at statistical correlations between the heuristics and the node scores. We used the Pearson correlation coefficients for this purpose. We obtained the results in a setting where the full graph is known so we have to look at those measures cautiously. However the intuitions we gain from this analysis proved, as we will see, robust enough for the online setting. We averaged the coefficients geometrically over the five graphs. Lastly, we looked also tried to smooth the values with the function $f : x \mapsto \log(1+x)$ (*log* row in the following table).

Type	fl_deg	fl_n	fl_e	fl_ne	sl_n	sl_e	sl_ne
orig.	0.063	0.127	0.073	0.090	0.170	0.199	0.203
log	0.269	0.373	0.402	0.412	0.273	0.360	0.356

Table 3: Pearson correlation coefficients

From Table 3, we learn several things. First of all, the correlation between any of the features and the actual node score is

positive. Secondly, logarithmic smoothening reinforces significantly the correlations (on a relative scale). We thus decided to use the smoothened version of those estimators in the rest of the study ($\widetilde{\beta}(v) = f(\widetilde{\beta}(v))$). Lastly, we observe some differences between the heuristics, but there is no clear winner as the coefficient remains small.

7.3 Linear Regression

These positive correlations gave us the intuition to use these estimators as features for a linear regression. We define `lr_fl` and `lr_sl`, respectively the *first-level* and *second-level linear regression* estimators.

These estimators are linear combinations for which the coefficients are trained. The crawled graph is used as the training data and the coefficients are updated before each frontier estimation. We used the *least-squares linear regression* with incremental solvers. This allowed us to not fully retrain the models for each estimation.

ESTIMATOR 5 (`lr_fl lr_sl`).
`lr_fl`: $\widetilde{\beta}(v) =$ *trained linear combination of the* `fl_` *estimators.*
`lr_sl`: $\widetilde{\beta}(v) =$ *trained linear combination of the* `fl_` *and* `sl_` *estimators.*

To have a first intuition on those estimators, we performed a R^2 analysis. It is a measure of the precision we can expect from the linear models, but shown here with full graph knowledge.

Type	lr_fl	lr_sl
orig.	0.030	0.075
log	0.221	0.230

Table 4: Linear regression fit (R^2), geometrically averaged over the five graphs

From Table 4, we confirm the logarithmic smoothening is beneficial, as well as the addition of the second level features to the training, which means we do not have an overfitting problem. However, we also see that, even if the R^2 fit is better for `lr_sl`, its value remains low in the absolute.

7.4 Reinforcement Learning

As we saw in the previous statistical analysis and as we will see more in details in Section 8.1, the intuition gained from the observation of the different estimators is that they perform differently at different stages. For instance, in some graphs, `fl_e` performs on average very well at the beginning of a crawl but poorly later. In this situation, reinforcement learning allows us to pick the right model at the right time.

Initial multi-armed bandit strategy. We chose to model our situation as a multi-armed bandit problem [22]. There is a room full of casino machines (the bandits) with different reward distributions. A player enters the room with a budget of n lever pulls and looks for a strategy to maximize its total reward. In our case, a slot machine is an estimator, and a reward is the weight of the top node returned. Playing a lever is the action of crawling the top node of an estimation model.

In this situation, the challenge is to balance properly the exploration (the player wants to test as many slot machines as possible) and the exploitation (if the player has found the best machine, he should focus on this one). A first usual way is to use an *epsilon-greedy* bandit strategy. Let $\varepsilon \in [0,1]$ be the *epsilon-greedy parameter*. With a probability ε the slot machine with the highest average reward is used. With a probability $1 - \varepsilon$, the slot machine used is chosen uniformly randomly.

ESTIMATOR 6 (mab_ε). $\widetilde{\beta}(v) =$ *output of an epsilon-greedy strategy*

With $\varepsilon = 0.1$, this estimator already gives interesting results. However, it has two major potential shortcomings. It gives the same importance to old and to new rewards, when we might want to favor new information. It also does not adapt well to variations of pace in the average reward changes. We want the exploitation–exploration ratio to vary with how dynamic the context is. We propose a new simple and robust solution to solve those two issues.

ε-first with variable reset strategy. Let $r \in \mathbb{N}$ be the *reset parameter*, a *bandit strategy with reset* is so that, every r steps, all the slot machines average rewards are set to 0. From a different perspective, let n be the number of lever pulls so far, the average reward is calculated with a weight of 1 for the rewards at the steps from $max(0, n-r)$ to n, and 0 for the more ancient ones.

This notion of reset is particularly intuitive in the context of an *epsilon-first bandit strategy*. Let $\varepsilon \in [0, 1]$ be the *epsilon-first parameter* and N the total amount of lever pulls. For the steps between 0 and $\lfloor \varepsilon \times N \rfloor$, the slot machine used is chosen uniformly randomly. For the rest of the steps, the slot machine with the highest average reward is used.

ESTIMATOR 7 (mab_ε-first). $\widetilde{\beta}(v) =$ *output of an epsilon-first strategy*

The *epsilon-first with reset bandit strategy* is a succession of $\lfloor \frac{N_{total}}{r} \rfloor + 1$ epsilon-first bandit strategies, all of them except the last one with $N = r$. The last one is so that $N = N_{total} - r \times \lfloor \frac{N_{total}}{r} \rfloor$.

Let $f : \mathbb{N}^2 \to \mathbb{N}$ be the *reset variation function*, p the number of times the best estimator at the end of the exploration phase has been the same, an *epsilon-first bandit strategy with variable reset* is an epsilon-first bandit strategy with reset where $r = h(p)$. Obviously, we will pick h increasing with respect to p.

ESTIMATOR 8 (mab_var). $\widetilde{\beta}(v) =$ *output of an epsilon-first with variable reset strategy*

8. COMPARING THE ESTIMATORS

We tested the quality of the different estimators in terms of precision, running times, and ability to lead a crawl. We chose to use a batch size of 1 and getNextNodes returning the top nodes (the greedy strategy from Section 6.1), due to the reasons explained in Section 6. The crawl is thus driven by the estimated top node.

8.1 With the Same Crawl Sequence

In this section, we force the crawlers to have the same crawl sequence, the crawl sequence returned by the crawler with the oracle as its estimator.

Running times. We look here at how long an estimator takes to compute its estimation. This running-time depends on the size of the estimated frontier and the scores of the crawled graph. Crawl sequences thus determine running times. That is why we chose to compare the crawlers with the same crawl sequence.

As explained in Section 2.2, the different use cases require different running-times. However, for the less demanding use cases, there is 1 second between two requests for a unique Web domain, and 3

seconds for the Twitter API. The estimators must at least scale to those examples.

We measured how long the frontier estimation took at different steps on a Wikipedia (FRANCE) and a Twitter (HAPPY) graph. We chose only one graph from Wikipedia and one from Twitter as the main variable affecting the running time is the topology of the graph, rather than the scores themselves.

Dataset	Evaluator	100	1,000	10,000	100,000
FRANCE	nr	2,832.1	19,720.5	N/A	N/A
	opic	1.9	2.5	4.6	4.7
	ne_fl	0.2	0.1	0.1	0.1
	lr_fl	0.2	0.2	0.1	0.1
	mab_var_fl	0.6	0.3	0.2	0.2
	ne_sl	8.5	27.1	2.0	6.1
	lr_sl	8.5	27.2	2.0	6.1
HAPPY	nr	45,965.7	105,209.3	N/A	N/A
	opic	1.8	1.6	1.9	2.5
	ne_fl	0.3	0.1	0.2	2.1
	lr_fl	0.5	0.1	0.2	2.1
	mab_var_fl	1.1	0.3	0.5	3.9
	ne_sl	111.1	24.5	63.3	240.5
	lr_sl	111.4	24.5	63.3	241.0

Table 5: Running-times (in ms) of the evaluators at various steps

From Table 5, we see that the nr running time is several orders of magnitude above what we require. Simulating a few thousand steps of crawl took hours, compared with seconds for the others estimators. The second-level neighborhood estimators can scale, but have a non negligible cost, and might not be usable for restricted running time budgets. The other estimators have sub-millisecond running-times on both graphs, and are thus able to fit for most crawling restrictions.

Regarding nr, we remarked that the analysis performed in [12] is based on graphs that are much smaller than those we use here, typically graphs of small individual websites.

Precision. A precise estimation will return, as a top node, a node that is not too far in score from the oracle top node. To quantify the precision of an estimator, we measured the distance between the score of the top node it returns to the score of the oracle node. The distance being the score difference.

Following the same crawl sequence allows us to see the variations in performance at the different stages. The results were noisy so we smoothed them, arithmetically averaging the distance in a window of 1,000 steps.

We computed the precision for the estimators based on the first-level neighborhood only. The intuitions we gained from them are similar for the second-level neighborhood. We also did not look at multi-armed bandit strategies at that time since those experiments led us to them.

Figure 2 illustrates well the general properties we observed. First of all, the average distance decreases in the long run. At the beginning, there are a lot of rich nodes that can easily be missed. In the long run, the richest nodes will have been consumed. The average distance logically tends to be lower. Secondly, making abstraction of this tendency, the estimators perform differently at different steps. Here, we can see that ne does very well at first, but then loses ground to n. Lastly, on average, we observed the common trend that the simple neighborhood-based estimators seem to perform best at the start, while the linear regression estimator catches up in the later stages of the crawl. However, we could not find a global winner

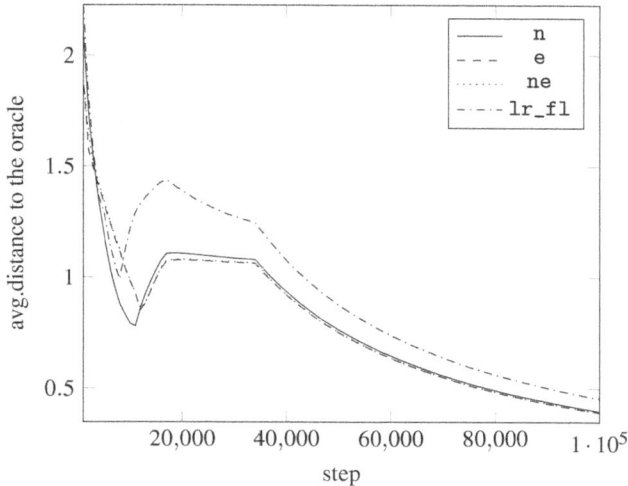

Figure 2: Estimators precision for BRETAGNE

among the different heuristics or regressions, which gave us the intuition of the multi-armed bandit strategies.

8.2 Driving the Crawl

In the previous part, we looked at situations where the crawl sequence was decided by the oracle. We investigate here what happens when the estimators are themselves leading the crawl.

Multi-armed bandit estimators. It is convenient to first study the estimators based on multi-armed bandit strategies. We experimented several of them with different parameters. For all these estimators, the slot machines are the estimators based on the first-level neighborhood, including the linear regression. The reason why we did not look at estimators based on the second-level neighborhood is explained in the next paragraph.

We used the generic experimental framework introduced in Section 5 to obtain global scores, using the oracle greedy as a baseline. Those global scores allow to gauge the overall potential of each estimator, disregarding as much as possible the particular cases.

`mab_ε` and `mab_ε-first` have been parametrized with $\varepsilon = 0.1$. `mab_var-0.1-1000` and `mab_var-0.2-200` have respectively for parameters $\varepsilon = 0.1, r = h(p) = 1000 \times (p + 1)$ and $\varepsilon = 0.2, h(p) = 200 \times (p + 1)$.

Type	100	1,000	10,000	100,000
ε	0.450	0.481	0.477	0.495
ε-first	0.409	0.501	0.484	0.490
var-0.1-1000	0.383	0.439	0.420	0.494
var-0.2-200	0.427	0.413	0.461	0.458

Table 6: Global performance of the multi-armed bandit estimators

Looking at Table 6, our first observation is that the multi-armed bandits are very comparable in terms of performances. We can also already notice that their global score is stable at different steps. As we will see below, this stability is a major difference with the other estimators. For the other experiments, in order not to overcrowd our figures, we chose to only consider `mab_var-0.2-200`.

Overall comparison. We ran crawls on the five datasets for the estimators introduced in Section 7, with a few exceptions. As explained in the previous paragraph, we only show one estimator based on multi-armed bandit, `mab_var-0.2-200`. We also excluded `nr` as its running-time was too long. Lastly, we studied the estimators based on the second-level neighborhood on a few examples, and found out that their crawl performances are not better than those of the first-level. Since their running times are too large, we decided not to compute the full results for those estimators.

Figure 3 shows the crawl performance for the different estimators in two scenarios. It illustrates interesting properties of the estimators. First of all, the breadth-first estimator, `bfs`, and the PageRank-based estimator, `opic`, are clearly worse than the other estimators. However, they remain interesting baselines. Note that we also tried the original OPIC, that does not use edge or node scores, without any improvement. The first-level neighborhood estimators, on the other hand, usually perform quite well, but with different quality in different situations. This confirms the results found in Section 8.1. Regarding the linear regression, it seems to do better at the end than at the beginning, and achieves good results at the end of the crawl. At last, the multi-armed bandit strategy seems to perform well all along the crawl, staying on the highest part.

Estimator	100	1,000	10,000	100,000
bfs	0.147	0.132	0.130	0.207
opic	0.283	0.184	0.205	0.287
n	0.358	0.280	0.362	0.467
e	0.594	0.560	0.457	0.377
ne	0.583	0.570	0.466	0.378
lr_fl	0.325	0.382	0.466	0.504
mab_var-0.2-200	0.427	0.413	0.461	0.458

Table 7: Global score of the estimators

Those results are confirmed by Table 7. It shows the global score (averaged over the five graphs), normalized with the oracle greedy. This score gives a general idea of the ability of an estimator to lead a crawl. `bfs` and `opic` are significantly worse than the rest. `n` behaves worse than the other heuristics at first, except in later stages of the crawl. `e` and `ne` are almost equivalent, leading a good crawl at the beginning but not towards the end. `lr_fl` is not great at the beginning but performs well in the long run. `mab_var` does stably well all along the crawl.

8.3 Building the Right Crawling System

We can now come up with reasonable recommendations in order to build a crawler that will perform generally well. This crawler will implement the high-level algorithm with `getNextNodes` as greedy, and `getBatchSize` as the constant 1.

To build `scoreFrontier` it is more complicated. First, we suggest to compute the estimators based on the first-level neighborhood. They are not very costly and usually helpful. From there, it is interesting to perform an incremental linear regression using those estimators as features. Eventually, combining those different estimators with a multi-armed bandit strategy should allow to pick the best estimator at different steps of the crawl.

9. RELATED WORK

General works. Most works on focused crawling addressed web page and hyperlink scoring or classification. Those works are com-

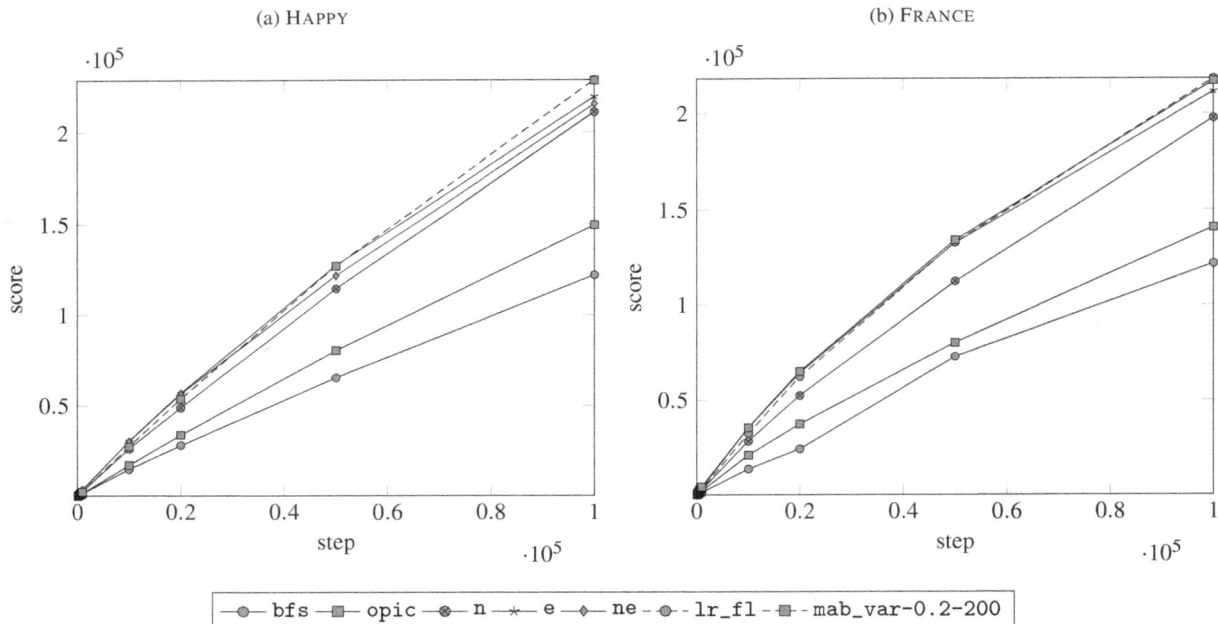

(a) HAPPY (b) FRANCE

Figure 3: Average graph scores for various estimators leading the crawl of two graphs

plementary with ours, and serve as inspiration for the scoring functions α and β. A 2005 survey [20] studied the different options available at that time for focused crawling classifiers and scorers. The Fish-search [9] and Shark-search [16] algorithms score pages and links with tf-idf measures. [7, 5] put forward a crawler made of a classifier, to distinguish relevant pages, and a distiller, to identify pages more likely to point to other relevant pages. Classifiers used range from SVMs [19], HMMs [18, 4], to reinforcement learning [21]. An experimental study [19] proved that a crawler using both link and page scores outperforms single-score techniques.

Steering the crawler. The complexity result regarding finding the optimal crawl score was proved by reduction to the length-constrained maximum-sum subtree problem [17]. The altered greedy strategy was inspired by greedy randomized adaptive search procedures [13]. To the best of our knowledge, the impact of using batch processing for the frontier estimation has not been studied before.

Frontier estimation. A first idea to use some graph properties to estimate a frontier node score is formulated in [10] but only applies to Web pages, requires that the crawler is aware of backlinks to pages, and is only compared to one other system.

We compared our crawler with two main state-of-the-art systems: OPIC [1], which aims at estimating a PageRank score (on a similar idea, the RankMass crawler [8] intends to maximize coverage of high Personalized PageRank nodes); and the Navigational Rank [12], that uses a two-way propagation to estimate frontier scores and found to perform better than previous approaches.

The multi-armed bandits with variable reset was inspired by the adaptive ε-greedy exploration for reinforcement learning [22].

10. CONCLUSIONS

In this paper, we formulated the focused crawling problem as a graph exploration problem, the graph having weighted nodes and weighted edges. We then illustrated how this model can be applied to different use cases. This formalization allowed us to

introduce a generic algorithm to perform focused crawling and to identify several important subproblems. From there, we studied those subproblems one by one. We demonstrated the NP-hardness of the offline optimal crawl problem, the "rich people have rich friends" property, and the batch disadvantage. Then, we looked at different techniques to estimate the frontier. We adapted state-of-the-art estimators to our formalization and proposed various new estimators. Finally, we dissected them and evaluated their running-times, their precision in identifying the best nodes, and their performance when leading a crawl.

Our formalization of focused crawling is novel and high-level. The results we present can be applied in many cases. The systems we propose have very good performance. We believe this is a significant contribution towards scalable, generic, and adaptive systems for focused crawling.

This work also allowed us to identify promising opportunities. As we proved the NP-hardness of the offline optimal crawl problem, finding an approximation technique is an interesting new challenge. The question of a distributed focused crawling systems is open and exciting. We also did not address the issue of refreshing a node already crawled, it should be possible to reuse our model to integrate it. Finally, a more thorough study on the multi-armed bandits techniques is worthy of investigation.

Acknowledgments

We are grateful to Bogdan Cautis for his valuable inputs. We also thank the Futur et Ruptures program of Institut Mines–Télécom, the France – Hong Kong PHC Procore 2012 grant 26893QA, as well as the French government under the X-Data project, for their financial support.

11. REFERENCES

[1] Serge Abiteboul, Mihai Preda, and Gregory Cobena. Adaptive on-line page importance computation. In *WWW*, 2003.

[2] André Allavena, Alan J. Demers, and John E. Hopcroft. Correctness of a gossip based membership protocol. In *PODC*, pages 292–301, 2005.

[3] Luciano Barbosa and Juliana Freire. Siphoning hidden-web data through keyword-based interfaces. *JIDM*, 1(1):133–144, 2010.

[4] Sotiris Batsakis, Euripides G M Petrakis, and Evangelos Milios. Improving the performance of focused web crawlers. *Data & Knowledge Engineering*, 68(10):1001–1013, 2009.

[5] Soumen Chakrabarti, Kunal Punera, and Mallela Subramanyam. Accelerated focused crawling through online relevance feedback. In *WWW*, pages 148–159, 2002.

[6] Soumen Chakrabarti, Martin van den Berg, and Byron Dom. Focused crawling: a new approach to topic-specific web resource discovery. *Computer Networks*, 1999.

[7] Soumen Chakrabarti, Martin van den Berg, and Byron Dom. Focused crawling: a new approach to topic-specific Web resource discovery. *Computer Networks*, 31(11-16):1623–1640, 1999.

[8] Junghoo Cho and Uri Schonfeld. RankMass Crawler: a Crawler with High Personalized PageRank Coverage Guarantee. In *VLDB*, pages 375–386, may 2007.

[9] Paul de Bra, Geert-Jan Houben, Yoram Kornatzky, and Reinier Post. Information Retrieval in Distributed Hypertexts. In *RIAO*, 1994.

[10] Michelangelo Diligenti, Frans Coetzee, Steve Lawrence, C. Lee Giles, and Marco Gori. Focused Crawling Using Context Graphs. In *VLDB*, pages 527–534, 2000.

[11] Peter Sheridan Dodds, Roby Muhamad, and Duncan J. Watts. An experimental study of search in global social networks. *Science*, 301(5634):827–829, August 2003.

[12] Shicong Feng, Li Zhang, Yuhong Xiong, and Conglei Yao. Focused crawling using navigational rank. In *CIKM*, pages 1513–1516, 2010.

[13] Thomas A. Feo and Mauricio G.C. Resende. Greedy randomized adaptive search procedures. *Journal of Global Optimization*, 6:109–133, 1995.

[14] Georges Gouriten, Silviu Maniu, and Pierre Senellart. Exploration adaptative de graphes sous contrainte de budget. In *BDA*, 2013.

[15] Georges Gouriten and Pierre Senellart. API Blender: A uniform interface to social platform APIs. In *WWW*, April 2012. Developer track.

[16] Michael Hersovici, Michal Jacovi, Yoelle S. Maarek, Dan Pelleg, Menanchem Shtalhaim, and Sigalit Ur. The Shark-Search algorithm. An application: tailored Web site mapping. In *WWW*, pages 317–326, 1998.

[17] Hoong Chuin Lau, Trung Hieu Ngo, and Bao Nguyen Nguyen. Finding a length-constrained maximum-sum or maximum-density subtree and its application to logistics. *Discrete Optimization*, 2006.

[18] Hongyu Liu, Jeannette Janssen, and Evangelos Milios. Using HMM to learn user browsing patterns for focused web crawling. *Data & Knowledge Engineering*, 59(2):270–291, 2006.

[19] Gautam Pant and P. Srinivasan. Link contexts in classifier-guided topical crawlers. *IEEE TKDE*, 18(1):107–122, 2006.

[20] Gautam Pant and Padmini Srinivasan. Learning to crawl: Comparing classification schemes. *ACM TOIS*, 23(4):430–462, 2005.

[21] Jason Rennie and Andrew Kachites McCallum. Using Reinforcement Learning to Spider the Web Efficiently. In *ICML*, 1999.

[22] Michel Tokic. Adaptive ε-greedy exploration in reinforcement learning based on value differences. In *KI*, 2010.

[23] Jeffrey Travers and Stanley Milgram. An experimental study of the small world problem. *Sociometry*, 34(4), December 1969.

[24] Twitter. GET statuses/user_timeline. `https://dev.twitter.com/docs/api/1.1/get/statuses/user_timeline`, 2013.

[25] Jaewon Yang and Jure Leskovec. Patterns of temporal variation in online media. In *WSDM*, pages 177–186, 2011.

An Author-Reader Influence Model for Detecting Topic-based Influencers in Social Media

Jonathan Herzig
IBM Haifa Research Lab
Haifa 31905, Israel
hjon@il.ibm.com

Yosi Mass
IBM Haifa Research Lab
Haifa 31905, Israel
yosimass@il.ibm.com

Haggai Roitman
IBM Haifa Research Lab
Haifa 31905, Israel
haggai@il.ibm.com

ABSTRACT

This work addresses the problem of detecting topic-based influencers in social media. For that end, we devise a novel behavioral model of authors and readers, where authors try to influence readers by generating *"attractive"* content, which is both *relevant* and *unique*, and readers can become authors themselves by further citing or referencing content made by other authors. The model is realized by means of a content-based citation graph, where nodes represent authors with their generated content and edges represent reader-to-author citations. To find the top influencers for a given topic, we first profile the content of authors (nodes) and citations (edges) and derive topic-based similarity scores to the topic, which further model the unique and relevant topic interests of users. We then present three different extensions of the Topic-Sensitive PageRank algorithm that exploit the similarity scores to find topic-based influencers. We evaluate our solution on a large real-world dataset that was gathered from Twitter by measuring information diffusion in social networks. We show that, overall, our methods outperform several state-of-the-art methods. This work further serves as an evidence that the topic uniqueness aspect in user interests within social media should be considered for the influencers detection task; this is in comparison to previous works that have solely focused on detecting topic-based influencers using the combination of link structure and topic-relevance.

Categories and Subject Descriptors

H.3.3 [**Information Storage and Retrieval**]: Information Search and Retrieval—*Information filtering*

Keywords

Social Media, Influencers Detection

1. INTRODUCTION

Nowadays, the detection of influential users (influencers) has become one of the most essential tasks in social media analysis. The influence of a user can be generally defined as the user's ability to disseminate interesting content, ideas or opinions to others, hoping to "stimulate" some "intended" reactions by potential "readers", e.g., be endorsed, followed, cited, or even trigger an active discussion [11, 9, 20, 2]. While some users may hold significant influence over a variety of topics, some may only gain influence by strictly focusing on a single topic which may *attract* the attention of others [8].

Influencers are recognized for playing an important role in many domains. As an example, in the marketing domain, the detection of influencers can be used to harness their viral power for spreading campaign relevant messages, maximizing the campaign's overall reach [13]. As another example, social-networking services, such as the popular professional networking service LinkedIn[1], utilize influencers for attracting the attention of "regular" users to promoted contents and services.

In many cases, a topic "oblivious" detection of influencers is insufficient, and sometimes, may even lead to erroneous decisions. Considering again the marketing scenario, a marketer may wish to discover only those influencers that are focused on her brand's related topics (e.g., products or offers) so to correctly allocate the budget for viral marketing purposes. Hence, the ability of users to influence others on specific topics should be further estimated.

The problem of influencers detection in social media has been long studied. Earlier works have commonly been topic-oblivious [11, 9, 14, 1, 2, 19]. Some works have proposed various influence measures based on the analysis of the link-structure of social-networks. Social-networks were usually derived from either explicit (e.g., followship, comments, etc) or implicit (e.g., retweets, mentions, etc) relationships among users. Influence was then measured relatively to the authority of users [1, 14]. Others tried to formally capture the *"information diffusion"* among users in social-networks, measuring influence in terms of information "cascades" or "propogation" within the network [11, 9, 2, 19].

Realizing that the influence of users may vary among topics, more recent works have further focused on the detection of topic-based influencers [24, 7, 3]. The common approach taken by such works is to consider the topic in mind as a facet of the problem. Similarly to topic-oblivious works, topic-based influencers are derived by such works either by using social-network analysis or information diffusion methods, considering the users' topic-relevance. Hence, the user's topic-relevance is used to determine which nodes and edges

[1]https://www.linkedin.com/today/influencers

in the social network should be considered (and how much) for authority analysis [24, 7] or how much information related to the topic may be prorogated [3].

1.1 Our Approach

In this work, we take a different point of view on the topic-based influencers detection problem. Through a *dual* representation of users as both content authors and readers, we provide a new interpretation to the notion of topic-based influence, where the influence of a given user is determined by her ability to author content that constantly satisfies the *unique* information needs of readers.

We propose a novel *behavioral model*, termed the *Author-Reader Influence* (ARI) model, which captures the various "behavioral" states of readers, whose main goal is to read *relevant* and *unique* content produced by authors. We therefore argue that, the ability of authors to influence their readers closely depends on their ability to generate *attractive* content. To estimate this ability, we propose a novel content-based citation graph representation, derived from content that is both generated by authors and contributed by readers via means of content references (i.e., either explicit or implicit "citations"). We then try to estimate the influence of various users on others by applying a *retrospective* analysis from an ordinary reader's point of view, in order to *simulate* the reader's behavioral model. We further show how the relevant and unique aspects of content generated by authors in general (i.e., independently of specific readers) and in the specific context of readers' citations, which represent an evidence of author influence, can be estimated.

Next, we introduce the main ideas behind our approach.

1.2 Main Ideas

Within the social-media, every user may "play" a *dual* role of an *author* (i.e., content producer) and a *reader* (i.e., content consumer). Therefore, a user may author some content, read the content of other authors, and possibly even contribute more content again as an author in response to "interesting" read content.

Each role is further driven by some goal that the user tries to satisfy. As an author, the user's main goal is to maximize its "social fingerprint" by generating content that may *attract* the attention of others and hence influence them. The author's main problem is, therefore, to determine which *relevant* and *unique* topics to discuss about, in order to attract the attention of as many readers as possible. As a reader, the user's main goal is to *discover* authors that generate *relevant* (interesting) content that satisfy some of her *unique* information needs, possibly not satisfied by existing authors that the reader already discovered and read their content.

It is important to note at this point that, a *unique* content does not immediately implies a "novel" content. It might be that some author generates content relevant to topics that are not novel to readers, yet may provide some *unique* point of view on those topics that some readers do find it to be interesting enough.

A reader may further wish to acknowledge that a certain author's content was relevant to her by referencing (citing) the original content generated by that author. The reader may even start a (relevant) "discussion", and in turn, may further assist the original content's author to influence more readers. The "reader-to-author" influence process can keep on as long as there will be some reader who will be willing to switch her role and become an author that continues to "discuss" about topics related to the original author's generated content (discussion). The more readers that cite the original author, the more *influence* this author has on others.

As an example, let us focus on Twitter. An author on Twitter generates content on various topics in the form of tweets. Whenever a reader user (being a direct follower of that author or having just discovered that author's tweet through another author) wishes to express her satisfaction from that author's tweet, she may either retweet (RT) that tweet, mention the author (@username) or even actively reply to that author's tweet and start an "active" discussion. In turn, other readers of that responding author (reader) now get exposed to the original tweet's author, who they may find also to be relevant to their information needs.

Without loss of generality, we now consider the influencers detection problem from a behavioral point of view of reader users. We identify two main reader behavioral patterns, which motivate our work, and can be summarized as follows:

- *Readers **follow** authors that they already know and **read** their content. If they are not satisfied by existing authors' content, they try to **discover** new authors who generate content that may be both **relevant** and **unique** to their information needs.*

- *Readers who are **satisfied** by the content of other authors may further **express** their satisfaction by actively referencing (or discussing) the authors' content which they find to be both **relevant** and **unique** to their information needs.*

Trying to "project" back the above two reader behavioral patterns on potential influencers, an influencer is such that constantly manages to attract the attention of other readers. For that, the influencer is expected to produce attractive (i.e., both relevant and unique) content that satisfies as much information needs of her readers as possible. In turn, those readers may become authors on their own and continue to "publish" the influencer's generated content to other potential readers.

1.3 Outline

The rest of this paper is organized as follows. We start by reviewing related works in Section 2. We then formally define the Author-Reader Influence (ARI) model and derive several algorithms for topic-based influencers detection in Section 3. Finally, we evaluate the various algorithms in Section 4 and conclude in Section 5.

2. RELATED WORK

Related works can be classified into two main types, namely: *topic-oblivious* and *topic-based*. Topic-oblivious works aim at identifying influencers independently of a specific topic. On the other hand, topic-based works detect influencers per topic or topics of interest.

2.1 Topic-oblivious

Early works on influencers detection in social media have commonly been topic-oblivious [11, 9, 14, 1, 20, 2, 23]. In these works, influence was measured either by the relative authority of individuals within their social-network or by measuring the information flow (also termed "information diffusion") within the network.

In this line of works, Kempe et al. [11] have proposed a formal graph theoretic model for information diffusion. For a given probabilistic influence (linear threshold or cascade) model, modeling the odds of influence among individuals, the spread of influence was maximized [11]. Gruhl et al. [9] borrowed ideas from epidemiology and modeled information diffusion through the blogsphere as an infectious process among users. According to [9], some users get "infected" by ideas and opinions of others, which in turn, continue to infect others and so forth.

Other works have tried to explain information diffusion by quantifying the influence of different individuals on others [14, 1, 20, 23]. Mathloudakis et al. [14] has quantified influence as the difference between the inlinks and outlinks of each individual. Therefore, according to [14], a better influencer (or discussion starter) has more inlinks to her content and less outlinks to others. Agarwal et at. [1] further extended this measure and considered also the number of comments each individual got from the community. Song et al. [20] modeled influence using *InfluenceRank*, a measure that captured novel information diffusion among individuals. According to this measure, an influencer produces novel content that diffuses to others who reuse it. Bakshy et al. [2] measured influence on Twitter according to the average size of all cascades originated from each user. Ver Steeg et al. [23] have modeled influence among users using an information theoretic approach. In their model, the causality among user actions was captured using the transfer entropy measure. Therefore, an influence between two users was attributed to the reduction in the uncertainty of one user's actions given the previous actions of the other [23].

Finally, Kwak et al. [12] has further studied the difference between influence and popularity on Twitter. They have found that influence inferred from the number of followers of a given user differs from that inferred from the user's popularity based on her retweeted content. Therefore, a user's popularity by its own cannot solely explain the user's influence on others [12].

2.2 Topic-based

Realizing that the influence of individuals may vary among topics, recent works have further focused on the detection of topic-based influencers [21, 8, 24, 7, 3, 19, 4]. Built on top of the basic ideas originated by topic-oblivious works, the primary extension behind these works is the consideration of the topic in mind as a facet of the problem. Therefore, a common approach taken by such works is to first estimate the topic relevance of individuals [8, 19, 4] or their relationships [21, 24, 7, 3, 4] and then incorporating such estimates within "similar" (topic-oblivious) influence models.

Tang et al. [21] proposed a two-step solution for topic-based social influence analysis. As a preliminary requirement in their solution, an input of *explicit* social network together with a *predefined* topic-model for user nodes, capturing topic interests of users, was assumed. At the first step, a Topical Factor Graph (TFG) model was employed to incorporate all the inputs into a unified probabilistic model. At the second step, a Topical Affinity Propagation (TAP) model was proposed for influence model learning. The detection of topic-based influencers was then casted in [21] into an *expert identification* problem. Therefore, topic based experts were detected using an extension to the Topic-Sensitive PageRank (TSPR) algorithm [10], where random graph transitions were derived from the TAP model's learned influence parameters [21].

Cha et al. [8] have studied topic-based influence on Twitter. Influence was measured using three measures, namely, indegree, number of retweets, and number of user mentions (i.e., @username). They have shown that an influence of a given user may differ per topic, where some influential users may hold significant influence over a variety of topics. Furthermore, they discovered that ordinary users usually gain influence by focusing on a single topic which they can contribute interesting tweets [8].

Weng et al. [24] have proposed *TwitterRank* - an extension to the PageRank algorithm which measures influence using the topic-similarity between users and the structure of the social-network induced from *explicit* user followship relationships. According to this measure, for each topic, a random-walk transition probability between a follower user u and user v being followed is given by the relative number of tweets published by user v to all the tweets published by all the other users followed by user u, further multiplied by the relative topic-similarity between user u and user v. Therefore, according to TwitterRank, the more two users are topic-similar and the more tweets generated by the followed user are consumed by the follower, the more influence is attributed. TwitterRank was shown to perform relatively well compared to traditional measures such as in-degree and TSPR.

Cano et al. [7] ranked topic-influencers on Twitter according to their topic-authority as derived from their retweets graph. For that, the damping vector of the Topic-Sensitive PageRank algorithm was modified to consider the relative number of retweets to each individual that were further relevant to the topic, hence implying on the topic relevance of the retweeted author [7].

Barbieri et al. [3] proposed an extension to Kempe et al.'s [11] influence maximization problem, by further incorporating topics within a generalized expectation maximization (GEM) method. Overall, a significant improvement in influence maximization compared to the topic-oblivious solution of Kempe et al. [3] was demonstrated.

Silva et al. [19] proposed *ProfileRank*, an influence measure that considered the relevance of content generated by individuals and consumed by others. The mutual relationship among users and contents was captured by a bipartite graph with user nodes on the one side and content nodes on the other and edges further represented the contents' generation and consumption by users. The ProfileRank of individuals was then derived by a random walk on the bipartite graph. Therefore, according to [19], a content is relevant to a given user if it was generated by another user that is influential to that user, and a given user has influence on another user if she generates content that is relevant to that user.

Finally, very recently, Bi et al. [4] proposed Followship-LDA (FLDA) - a mixed generative model that extends the LDA model [6] and considers both followship links and content on Twitter for detecting topic-based influencers. FLDA was demonstrated to provide superior performance to that of TwitterRank and other LDA variations (e.g., Link-LDA).

2.3 Main differences

Similarly to [21, 7], in this work, we also detect topic-based influencers based on an extension to the TSPR algorithm.

Yet, our solution differs from previous works in several aspects. Compared to [21, 24, 3, 4], we do not assume the input of an explicit social network graph or user topic models. Instead, similarly to [8, 7], we utilize explicit "feedback" of readers (e.g., retweets). In this work, such reader feedback is further used for inferring an *implicit* content-based citation graph from which topic-based influencers are detected. Furthermore, we propose a novel behavioral model that captures a new angle of topic-based influence based on the estimation of the *"attractiveness"* (a combination of topic uniqueness and relevance) of content generated by authors and consumed by their readers. Therefore, the random transition probabilities within the TSPR algorithm are differently derived and have a different semantic interpretation in our work. Finally, similarly to Silva et al. [19] we utilize profiles for learning the relevant topic interests of various authors and readers. Though, compared to [19], our profiles further capture the *uniqueness* aspect of topic interest of readers.

Unique user topic interests are learned in this work by adopting the user profiling method of Shmueli-Scheuer et. al [18] for deriving profiles of nodes (authors) and edges (reader-to-author citations) in a content-based citation graph. Few other works have also utilized Shmueli-Scheuer et. al's basic model for studying unique user interests, among others works on social network evolution [22], ad serving [17] and recommender systems [16]. To the best of our knowledge, this work is the first to consider the role of user uniqueness in the context of the influencers detection task.

3. FRAMEWORK

We now formalize the topic-based influencers detection problem. We begin with some preliminary notations that will be used throughout the rest of this paper and define the problem. We then present a formal model for topic-based influencers detection, and based on that model, we suggest several algorithms.

3.1 Preliminaries

Let $G(V, E)$ denote a citation graph, inferred from the content generated by different users. Therefore, each node $v \in V$ in the graph represents a single user. Recall that, every user can play the *dual* role of an author, a reader or both. Assuming the author's role, for a given author user u, let c_u denote a single piece of content generated by this author. For example, on Twitter, a single piece of content is a tweet, while on the Blogosphere, it is a single blog post. To ease the terminology, we use the term *post* to represent any single piece of a user generated content. We further denote by C_u the *overall* content generated by author u, given by the "concatenation" of all her posts c_u. Similarly, we denote by C the content generated by *all* the authors in V, further termed the graph's *corpus*.

Assuming the reader's role, an edge $e_{vu} \in E$ from reader user v to author user u exists in the graph, if reader v generated some post c_v that references some other post c_u previously generated by author u. For example, on Twitter, such references may include all the retweets, mentions and replies made by some users in response to the tweets of others. On the Blogosphere, content references represent citations among different user posts. Intuitively, an edge e_{vu} in the citation graph implies that author u has some sort of influence on reader v, evidenced by the fact that some

post generated by u has attracted the attention of v. Again, to ease the terminology, we use the term *citation* to represent all types of user content references. For a given edge $e = e_{vu}$ we also denote C_e the edge *overall* content, given by the concatenation of all posts c_v generated by reader v that cited some post c_u previously generated by author u.

It is important to note, that, while an analysis of an author's overall content C_u may indicate the author's overall interests, a similar analysis on an edge e_{vu} content (i.e., C_e) may indicate the interests of reader v in the content of author u.

Since the content C in the citation graph can be quite diversified and usually spans many topics, we would like to find topic-based influencers. We model a topic T as a set of terms (topic aspects) with a weight associated with each term denoting its importance to the topic. Therefore, let t now denote a single term in C's vocabulary $\mathcal{V}_C$. For a given topic T, let $\vec{w}_T$ represent the topic's "profile", which associates a weight $\vec{w}_T(t)$ with each term $t \in \mathcal{V}_C$ that captures t's importance in topic T.

Having set the definition of the citation graph, the topic-based influencers detection problem can be shortly defined as follows:

PROBLEM DEFINITION 1. *Given a citation graph $G(V, E)$ and a topic T, find the top-k most influential users for that topic among the users in V. The "influence" of an author $u \in V$ is measured by her ability to generate relevant and unique content that will be exposed to as many as possible readers (both directly and indirectly through other authors), which is evident by her reader's content citations*[2].

3.2 The Author-Reader Influence Model

We now propose a novel model for topic-based influencers detection, termed hereinafter the *"Author-Reader Influence Model"* (ARI for short). The ARI model closely tries to capture the two reader behavioral patterns that were described in Section 1.2.

Again, without loss of generality, we now consider the point of view of an "ordinary" reader who wishes to select authors that produce content that is both *relevant* and *unique* to her information needs. Being satisfied by the content of some author, the reader may further express her satisfaction by citing that author's content, with the goal of "encouraging" the author to continue generating attractive content.

We now assume a model of a "random reader" who represents an ordinary reader. On every point of time, the reader may choose (at random) to perform one of the following two actions:

1. *Author selection*: select an author and read her content. The author can be either one that the reader already knows or the reader may choose to read some new author's content.

2. *Author citation*: being satisfied by existing read content of some author, the reader may decide to further express her satisfaction by citing that author's content.

Note that new authors can be discovered either by their reference (such as mentions, replies or retweets) in a previously read content, or by querying the underline system (e.g., Twitter).

---

[2]A more formal definition will follow in the evaluation in Section 4.2.

Next, we propose a novel algorithm for the influencers detection problem, which closely captures the random reader's behavior defined by the ARI model.

3.3 ARI Algorithm

Given content generated by various authors, we first infer the citation graph $G(V, E)$. Our next step is, therefore, to detect influencer users based on the citation graph and content associated with its author nodes C_u and (reader-author) citation edges C_e, given its corpus C as a background.

Built on top of the Topic-Sensitive PageRank (TSPR) algorithm [10], our influencers detection solution further extends the basic TSPR algorithm to closely capture the behavior of the random reader defined in the ARI model.

Let T now denote a single topic discussed within the corpus C. For a given topic T and some user $u \in V$, let $R_T(u)$ now encode the relative influence that u has on other users in the graph.

Recall that, according to the ARI model, the random reader may choose at any step either to select an author and read her content or cite an author in order to "gratitude" that the author's generated content satisfied some of the reader's information needs.

We now capture the random reader's decision through three probability functions. The first function represents the probability that the random reader will decide to take the "author selection" action. This function is based on a *fixed* parameter d, also termed a "dumping factor" in PageRank [15]. So with probability d the random reader will select an author to read her content and with probability $1 - d$ she will cite an existing author.

The other two probability functions are used to estimate which author to select or to cite. The "author selection" probability function, denoted by $\alpha_T(u)$ measures the probability of the random reader to select user u, given that the "author selection" action was selected. The "author citation" probability function denoted $\beta_T(e_{vu})$ measures the probability that the random reader v will cite user u (out of all other already discovered authors by v), given that the "author citation" option was selected.

Having defined the two possible actions of the random reader and the probabilities for each action, we are now ready to formally derive the (recursive) influencer score of each user $u \in V$. The score is based on the basic TSPR model [10] score and is generally defined as follows:

$$R'_T(u) = d \cdot \alpha_T(u) + (1 - d) \cdot \sum_{v \in In(u)} R_T(v)\beta_T(e_{vu}) \quad (1)$$

where $R_T(u)$ and $R'_T(u)$ denote the influencer scores of user $u \in V$ before and after each iteration of the TSPR algorithm, respectively. $In(u)$ represents the set of readers that cited author u in the citation graph $G(V, E)$.

We assume that $\sum_{u \in V} \alpha_T(u) = 1$ and for a given reader v, $\sum_{u \in Out(v)} \beta_T(e_{vu}) = 1$, where $Out(v)$ is the set of authors already discovered by v. To acknowledge the amount of satisfaction the random reader has from the author u's content, the random reader v "rates" u's content as follows $R_T(v)\beta_T(e_{vu})$, hence letting the author u get more exposure to other potential readers.

It should be noted that the random reader v may just choose herself as an author and never cite other authors. This represents the self-beliefs the author has on her own

(unique) information interests. Such self-interest of authors exists in the citation graph $G(V, E)$ in the form of *dangling nodes* [5], i.e., nodes without out-going edges (citations). Such nodes require a special treatment in the algorithm for correctness [5], as we shall explained shortly.

For a given topic T, the higher $R_T(u)$ is, the more influence we attribute to user u as an author on that topic.

Finally, it is worth noting that, at the beginning of the algorithm, for each topic T, all $R_T(u)$ are initialized to $1/|V|$ such that $\sum_u R_T(u) = 1$. To keep this sum further equal to 1 after each iteration we need to deal with possible dangling nodes (i.e., those users in V that never provide feedback via citation to other users). The influence "mass" of dangling nodes is "lost" after each iteration; thus, similar to [5], we equally divide their total "mass" between all the graph nodes. Let RD_T be the sum of influence scores $R_T(u)$ of all the dangling nodes at the end of the previous iteration. The modified $R'_T(u)$ value is given by:

$$R'_T(u) = d \cdot \alpha_T(u) +$$
$$(1 - d) \cdot \left(RD_T(u)\alpha_T(u) + \sum_{v \in In(u)} R_T(v)\beta_T(e_{vu}) \right) \quad (2)$$

Next, we show how the random reader's author probabilities (i.e., $\alpha_T(u)$ and $\beta_T(e_{vu})$) can be estimated.

3.3.1 Estimating the ARI Probabilities

Recall that, a random reader's goal is to maximize the satisfaction of her information needs defined by one or more topics. Hence, the random reader may choose authors (at random) according to the combination of the *relevance* and *uniqueness* of each author's generated content.

Further recall that, for each random reader v, the topic-based probabilities of each author are captured in our model by the pair of probability functions $\langle \alpha_T(u), \beta_T(e_{vu}) \rangle$. Therefore, we now explain how the types of topic-based probabilities of each author $u \in V$ for any topic T can be estimated.

Each probability function should be built such that it considers both the relevant and unique topic-aspects of the random reader's information needs and that of the content generated by authors, who wish to satisfy the reader's needs and attract their attention.

We now take the "profile approach", and use profiles to *uniformly* model user information interests in some topic. A profile shall capture the "*unique*" topic-aspects embedded in content generated by authors and consumed by readers. We consider three profile types, one for the random reader, one for each author and one for each citation edge. The random reader's profile defines the various topic-aspects of her needs. Since we are modeling an *arbitrary* random reader information needs in some topic T, her profile is assumed to be similar to a *predefined* topic T whose influencers we try to detect.

We further maintain two other types of profiles, namely: "*selection profile*" and "*citation profile*". The selection profile (denoted $\vec{w}_u$) of a given author $u \in V$ is based on the analysis of the overall content that author u has generated and captures u's unique interests in general. A citation profile is further derived for each citation edge $e = e_{vu}$ in the citation graph, representing the *common* and *unique* interests of author u and her reader v in general (i.e., in the context of v's citations).

Given a topic-profile $\vec{w}_T$, representing the random reader v's information needs in topic T, the "author selection" ($\alpha_T(u)$) and the "author citation" ($\beta_{e_{vu}}$) probabilities of the random reader v are now estimated by the *relative similarity* between the relevant and unique topic aspects (terms) encoded within topic T's profile and those of the selection and citation profiles.

First, the unique topic aspects "hidden" within the content generated by authors (and may be "needed" by readers) should be derived. For this purpose, we adopt the user profiling method of Shmueli-Scheuer et. al [18] which weighs topic-aspects (terms) according to their uniqueness to the user needs. The main motivation behind Shmueli-Scheuer et. al's user profiling method is that, a given user's unique interests may be found by discovering those topic-aspects in her profile that cannot be covered by the profile of an average user [18]. For that, we cast the author profiling task into a feature selection task, where terms (features) are weighed according to their marginal contribution to the KL-divergence between the language model [25] induced from the author's content and the language model induced from the "background" corpus C [18], i.e.:

$$D_{KL}(P(C_x)\|P(C)) = \sum_{t \in \mathcal{V}_C} P(t|C_x) \log \frac{P(t|C_x)}{P(t|C)}. \quad (3)$$

where x represents either an author u or an author's citation e, denoting that we either weigh terms in author's u selection-profile (based on C_u) or those of some author's citation-e profile (based on C_e).

Therefore, the more a given term $t \in \mathcal{V}_C$ contributes to the KL-divergence between the two language models, the more this term captures unique and important aspects of the user interests [18]. Note that, each term may be a unigram or an n-gram.

Let $P(t|C_x)$ and $P(t|C)$ now denote the occurrence probabilities of a given term $t \in \mathcal{V}_C$ based on content C_x's language model and that of the corpus C, respectively. The two probabilities can be estimated using maximum likelihood estimation [25] as follows:

$$P_{MLE}(t|C') = \frac{tf(t,C')}{\sum_{t' \in \mathcal{V}} tf(t',C')} \quad (4)$$

where C' represents either C_u, C_e or C.

We further smooth the probabilities with the background language model as follows:

$$P(t|C_x) = (1-\lambda)P_{MLE}(t|C_x) + \lambda P_{MLE}(t|C) \quad (5)$$

where, λ is a smoothing parameter [25].

The importance (uniqueness) of each term with respect to the author u' selection-profile ($x = u$) or citation profile ($x = e$) is then derived by:

$$w_x(t) = \begin{cases} P(t|C_x) \log \frac{P(t|C_x)}{P(t|C)}, & P(t|C_x) > P(t|C) \\ 0, & otherwise \end{cases} \quad (6)$$

Having defined the term weights in every author u's profiles $\vec{w}_u$ and $\vec{w}_e$, we next show how the random reader's

Algorithm	$\alpha_T(u)$	$\beta_T(e)$
ARI_S	$rsim(u,T;V)$	$1/|Out(v)|$
ARI_C	$\begin{cases} 1/|V_T|, & T \in C_u \\ 0, & otherwise \end{cases}$	$rsim(e,T;E)$
ARA_{SC}	$rsim(u,T;V)$	$rsim(e,T;E)$

Table 1: Three algorithm instantiations

probabilities to select or cite a specific author u are estimated.

Let $sim(x,T)$ now denote the similarity between the profile $\vec{w}_x$ (either selection or citation profile) and the topic's T profile $\vec{w}_T$ which encodes the random reader's information needs in topic T. The similarity is then given by the cosine of the two weight vectors, as follows:

$$sim(x,T) = \frac{\vec{w}_x \cdot \vec{w}_T}{\|\vec{w}_x\|\|\vec{w}_T\|} \quad (7)$$

Finally, to make the similarity into a probability we define the normalized value of $sim(x,T)$, which is further denoted $rsim(x,T;X)$, where X represents the set of entities of x's type. Formally:

$$rsim(x,T;X) = \frac{sim(x,T)}{\sum_{x \in X} sim(x,T)} \quad (8)$$

For example, for a given author $u \in V$, $rsim(u,T;V)$ estimates the probability that the random reader (whose interests are represented by the topic T's profile) will select user u according to u's selection profile. Similarly, $rsim(e_{vu},T;E)$ estimates the probability that the random reader v will cite author u according to the author u's citation-e profile. In both cases, the normalization guarantees that that $rsim(x,T;X)$ will produce a correct probability space.

3.4 ARI Algorithm Instantiations

While the ARI algorithm *generically* captures the random reader's behavior, we wish to derive actual algorithms that check the various aspects of the model. Therefore, we now propose three instantiations based on the specific selection of various instances for the random reader's probability functions $\langle \alpha_T(u), \beta_T(e_{vu}) \rangle$. The first two algorithm instances capture a single aspect of the random reader's behavior (according to the behavioral patterns described in Section 1.2), while the third instance further combines the two.

The various random reader's probability function instances used to instantiate the three algorithms are summarized in Table 1, and we now shortly discuss their details. The first algorithm instance, denoted ARI_S (S stands for selection profile), assumes that the random reader's sole goal is to select relevant authors. Hence, for authors that the random reader already read their content, the chance of citation in case of content satisfaction is equal. Note that, the "author selection" probability $\alpha_T(u)$ depends only on the topic T and on the similarity of authors to the topic, given by $rsim(u,T;V)$ of Eq. 8. Thus, the probability does not distinguish between users that are already known to the reader, and between newly discovered authors. We leave it for future work to add such a distinction to the model.

The second algorithm instance, denoted ARI_C (C stands for citations profile), assumes that the random reader's sole goal is to "improve" the exposure of content consumed from existing authors by providing authors "feedback" on their content via citation, where an author that produces a more relevant content has a more chance for feedback. Hence,

similarly to the basic TSPR model, the random reader selects authors by chance, meaning that the random reader has no prior preference over authors' selection, except for the fact that the content they generate is (somehow) relevant to the topic.

Finally, the third algorithm, denoted ARI_{SC}, combines the two basic algorithms, and therefore, captures the two reader behavioral patterns.

4. EXPERIMENTS

We now describe the details of our evaluation of the ARI model and the three proposed topic-based influencers detection algorithms based on it. We start by describing the dataset used for the evaluation. We then describe the evaluation framework and the experimental setup. Finally, we report on the main results of the evaluation, comparing the proposed algorithms to several other state-of-the-art algorithms.

4.1 Dataset

Our evaluation is based on a large real-world Twitter dataset that was collected during the 2012 US Presidential Elections. The dataset was collected from Twitter's public stream using the twitter4j open source Twitter API library[3]. To focus the collection of tweets on related topics as much as possible, several seed keywords were further used to filter out the stream. Example seed keywords include both hashtags such as #Election2012, #Obama2012, #Mitt2012, #obama, #romney and mentions to related Twitter accounts such as @BarackObama, @TheDemocrats, @MittRomney, @JoeBiden, etc. Overall, 3,490,369 tweets were obtained, collected during the two days of the actual elections (i.e., November 6th-7th, 2012).

4.2 Evaluation Framework

As a first step, we "reconstructed" the citation graph based on the collected data as was described in Section 3.1, considering only tweets of users who cited (i.e., retweeted, mentioned, replied to) other's tweets or were cited by others.

Note that, the result of the influencer detection algorithms using our data collection is a list of top-k users presumed to be able to influence other users on US Elections related topics. Therefore, the "quality of influence" of these users should be *quantitatively* evaluated. In this work, we choose to evaluate the quality of suggested users by their ability to *spread information* to others. Such evaluation may simulate, for example, an application of word-of-mouth marketing, where a small set of influential users should be detected in order to assist in promoting a new product or service to targeted audience [13]. To accomplish that, we now borrow the information diffusion model of Kempe et al. [11] which allows to quantify the amount of information spread within networks.

The basic idea in Kempe et al.'s model is that information may propagate in the network between neighboring nodes (users). Initially, the information exists in some set of "seed" nodes, who can then propagate the information to their neighbors which, in turn, can then propagate the information to their neighbors and so on [11]. The influencers detection task is, therefore, to find the set of k seed nodes

[3]http://twitter4j.org

from which the largest set of nodes may be "reached" or the largest "amount" of information may be prorogated in the network [11].

We further use the linear threshold (LT) model suggested by [11] to model the information propagation in social networks. In this model, for a given citation graph $G = (V, E)$, its induced *influence graph* is defined as a directed graph $G' = (V, E, \delta_E, \theta_V)$. Note that, an edge e_{vu} in the citation graph G (and in G' as a consequence) means that v cited u; thus, the direction of actual information flow is in the opposite direction from u to v. In other words, u has generated some content which was then cited by v, and therefore, some information prorogated from u to v.

δ_E and θ_V are two functions used to control the information propagation in the graph, as follows. $\delta_E : E \to [0, 1]$ is a weight function defined on edges, such that for each node $v \in V$, the sum of weights of its outgoing edges is ≤ 1; formally:

$$\sum_{u \in Out(v)} \delta_E(e_{vu}) \leq 1. \qquad (9)$$

$\theta_V : V \to [0, 1]$ is a threshold function defined on nodes, used to determine whether an information will propagate to node v, and its usage will be shortly explained.

Following [11], the information diffusion process starts by choosing a seed of k nodes $S_0 \subseteq V$ that have some piece of information to prorogate. We now say that, a node $v \in V$ is *activated* in G' if it also includes that piece of information. Therefore, by definition, all members of the set S_0 are active.

Information propagates in rounds, where in round i all nodes that were activated up to round $i - 1$ (denoted S_{i-1}) remain active, and a node $v \in V \setminus S_{i-1}$ is activated if the total weight of the outgoing edges from v to its active neighbors is at least $\theta_V(v)$; formally:

$$\sum_{u \in S_{i-1} \cap Out(v)} \delta_E(e_{vu}) \geq \theta_V(v). \qquad (10)$$

Newly activated nodes are added to S_{i-1} to form S_i. This process stops when there is a round where no new nodes are activated (i.e., $|S_i| = |S_{i-1}|$).

There are several ways to measure the "quality" of the information diffusion process. In a simple model, we can just count the number of active nodes at the end of the process (i.e., $|S_i|$). Another way is to assign weights to nodes of the graph G' and then use the aggregated weight of the active nodes in S_i as the diffusion value. Thus, we further extend the influence graph to be $G' = (V, E, \delta_E, \theta_V, \psi_V)$, where $\psi_V : V \to [0, 1]$ is a weight function defined on nodes, such that $\sum_{v \in V} \psi_V(v) = 1$. ψ_V shall capture the marginal value of every node $v \in S_i$ given that it is active at the end of the diffusion process (in the simple model, for every node $v \in V$, we just have: $\psi_V(v) = 1/|V|$).

Having defined the information diffusion setting, the goal of an influencers detection algorithm is, therefore, to find a set of top-k (influencer) seed nodes $S_0 \subseteq V$ that *maximizes* the information diffusion in the network G'. Hence, the quality of top-k influencers selection S_0 of a given algorithm is measured as follows:

$$score(S_0) = \sum_{v \in S_i} \psi_V(v) \qquad (11)$$

Recall that, θ_V is used to determine the threshold of node activation during the information diffusion process. In this

#Tweets	#Nodes	#Edges
2,644,564	1,202,516	1,485,857

Table 2: Details of the citation graph reconstructed from the 2012 US Precedential Elections Twitter data collection, considering only retweet citations.

work, each node $v \in V$ activation threshold $\theta_V(v)$ is randomly determined (i.e., by tossing a fair coin). Therefore, during our experiments, we run the information diffusion process multiple times, using the same seed node S_0, and we report on the average $score(S_0)$ over all runs.

4.3 Experimental Setup

Recall that, we wish to detect influencers in specific topics, which in our case, are topics related to the 2012 US Presidential Elections. We therefore, define the influence graph G'_T per topic T as follows. First, according to G' construction, its nodes and edges are based on the citation graph G. We take the edge weights function δ_E to be the similarity between an edge content and the topic, i.e.: $rsim(e, T; E)$. Similarly, we take the nodes weight (value) function ψ_V to be the similarity between a node and the topic, i.e.: $rsim(u, T; V)$. Again, θ_V is randomly drawn by tossing a fair coin. Thus, the goal of a topic-based influencers detection algorithm in this topic-based setting is to find a set $S_0 \subseteq V_T$ that maximizes the value of information diffusion $score(S_0)$, based on the nodes' topic T relevance (which is determined by ψ_V).

4.3.1 Topics extraction

Given the citation graph corpus C, we extracted 30 different topics using `hadoop-lda`[4] - an open source implementation of the Latent Dirichlet Allocation (LDA) topic model [6]. As an example, the following are sample keywords from topic #27 (related to Obama's reelection and discussed during November 7th 2012) : "romnei", "obama2012", "down stop", "gop elect", "won reelect", "up christian", "dalai lama".

4.3.2 Parameter settings

In all our runs, unless otherwise specified, we used the following parameters. The citation graph was generated by considering only (implicit) retweet citations. The details of this graph are described in Table 2. The ARI probabilities were estimated according to Section 3.3.1. In order to generate the nodes and edges profiles, we considered both unigrams and bigrams in $\mathcal{V}_C$, where the top-100 features (terms) were chosen according to their contribution to the KL-divergence of the profile (using Eq. 6). Similarly to the edges and nodes profiles, a topic is described also by a set of unigrams and bigrams in $\mathcal{V}_C$. For the smoothing parameter of Eq. 5, we have used the Jelnik-Mercer smoothing [25], setting $\lambda = 0.1$. For the damping factor d of Eq. 2, we have followed the standard setting of TSPR and fixed it to $d = 0.15$ [10].

4.3.3 Baseline methods

We have compared the performance of our three algorithms with the following three different baselines.

1. *TwitterRank* [24] is used as a state-of-the-art baseline. We have implemented this algorithm with the following

ing modifications to fit the setup of our work. For the similarity of a user $u \in V$ to a topic T (see Eq. 4 in [24]), we used $rsim(u, T; V)$. This way, the performance of all algorithms is comparable on the topic level. We also used the citation graph instead of the followers graph when running TwitterRank, so all algorithms get the citation graph as an input. The last modification was made after observing that there could be a possible case where a tweet in the dataset contains a citation to some user, while no tweets authored by the cited user were actually collected. In this case, TwitterRank assigns no rank to the cited user. To avoid this behavior, we added one empty (dummy) tweet to each user who was cited, but had no tweets associated with her in the dataset.

2. *PageRank* [15] was implemented as an example of a topic-oblivious influencer detection algorithm over the citation graph. Dangling nodes were treated similarly to Eq. 2.

3. *Indegree centrality* of a node v is defined as the number of its incoming edges to v, i.e.: $|In(v)|$. In the citation graph this translates into the set of users in V that cited user v. We calculate this measure for each node in the citation graph, and output the top-k nodes with the largest indegree values.

The quality of each algorithm (ours and the three baselines) was measured by the average score (using Eq. 11) of the set of top-k suggested (influencers) seed nodes S_0. For each topic, we first built the graph $G' = (V, E, \delta_E, \theta_V, \psi_V)$ as described in Section 4.2 above, and then ran Kempe et al.'s [11] information diffusion model 100 times. Finally, the average score over the 30 topics (and runs) was measured for each algorithm.

The various algorithms (ours and the baselines) were implemented using the Apache's Hadoop Map/Reduce framework[5]. Further details are omitted due to space considerations.

4.4 Algorithms Comparison

Figure 1 shows the relative performance of the various algorithms in terms of the information spread (diffusion) scores obtained for varying number of top-k selected influencers.

First, we can observe that, an increase in the number of top-k selected influencers also results in a consistent increase in performance. This is attributed to the fact that, with a larger user seed set S_0, the better is the potential for reaching more users within the network using information diffusion that is originated from those seed users.

We can further observe that, overall, for all values of k, the combined algorithm ARI_{SC} provided the best performance. Moreover, both AR_{SC} and ARI_S (using the author selection profiles only) performed better than all other algorithms including the state-of-the-art TwitterRank algorithm which is also topic-based. For example, for $k = 100$, the combined algorithm ARI_{SC} achieved information diffusion score of 0.406, compared to 0.359 for TwitterRank (with a statistical significant improvement of 14%, paired two-tailed t-test with p-value $< 10^{-21}$). In addition, as we

---

[4]https://code.google.com/p/hadoop-lda/

[5]http://hadoop.apache.org/

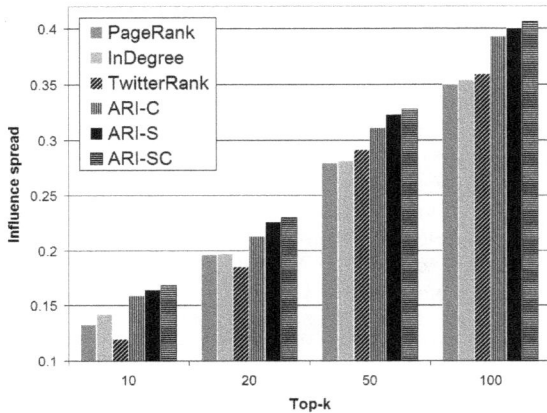

Figure 1: Average influence spread score over all 30 topics and 100 runs of the different algorithms for various number (

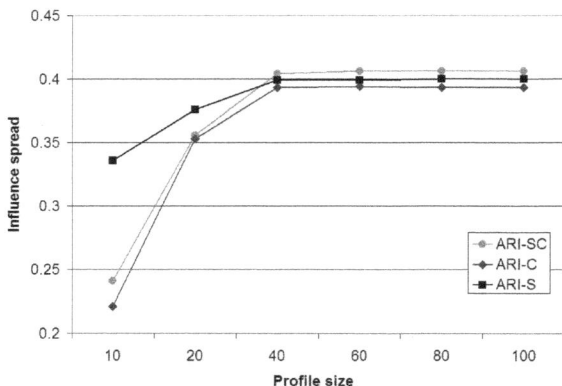

Figure 2: Average influence spread score of the three ARI-based algorithms for different profile sizes (using **retweet-only** citations)

might have expected, the topic-based algorithms were significantly better than the topic-oblivious algorithms (e.g., ARI_{SC} improved on PageRank by 19%, on average).

4.5 Effect of profile size

We next tested the effect of the profile size parameter on our ARI-based algorithms. Figure 2 shows the performance of the three algorithms using the top-100 suggested influencers with varying profile sizes. We can observe that, the influence spread improves with the increase in profile size. This improvement reaches its peak when the profile size is at least 40. For profile sizes 40-100 the influence spread remains constant. This in turn demonstrates that, the KL-divergence method used for building the various author profiles (Eq. 3) is quite effective even for a small number of selected topic features. In addition, we observe that, for small profile sizes (i.e., < 40), the ARI_S algorithm, which utilizes the author selection profiles, has a better performance than that of the two other ARI-based algorithms that utilize the author citation profiles. This may be explained by the fact that the author selection profiles are based on all the tweets authored by users, while the citation profiles are only based on (tweet) citations which are less common.

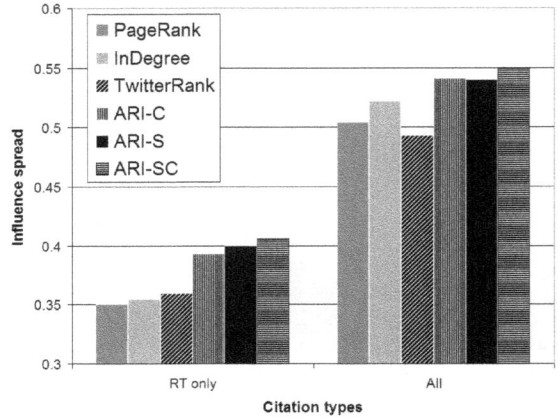

Figure 3: Comparison of the average influence spread score of the different algorithms using retweet-only (RT) citations and all types of citations (k=100)

Hence, author selection profiles are much more informative, and therefore, provide relatively good performance, even for very small sized profiles.

4.6 Effect of citation type

We next explored the difference between using only "passive" content citations (i.e., retweets only) and using all types of content citations (i.e., including "active" user mentions and replies). The results of this comparison are further depicted in Figure 3, where the top-100 suggested influencers were used for the information diffusion evaluation. First, we observe that, the consideration of the "active" content citations (i.e., mentions and replies) in addition to the "passive" citations (i.e., retweets) significantly boosts the overall performance, with up to 35% improvement for the best performing algorithm ARI_{SC}. This comes as no surprise, while a retweet only duplicates the original message of the retweeted user, a mention or a reply may further contribute more relevant and unique content to that of the original cited tweet, denoting a much stronger signal of influence [7]. Finally, comparing the ARI_S and ARI_C algorithms relative performance in the two citation type settings, we can observe that, ARI_C performance got (slightly) better than that of ARI_S. This may be attributed to the fact that the author citation profiles generated in the full citations setting allow better capture of influence indicators through user feedback.

5. CONCLUSIONS

In this work we suggested a novel solution for detecting topic-based influencers in social media. A main advantage of this solution is that it is solely based on analyzing the user generated content. To realize the interactions of users, we described the Author-Reader Influence (ARI) model, where authors generate attractive content and readers may either cite this content (and thus further diffuse it to other readers) or read new content from other relevant authors. To estimate the model, we built a content-based citation graph, where nodes dually represented authors and readers, and edges represented reader-to-author citations.

We then described three algorithms that are based on profiling the content of nodes and edges in the citation graph and on an extension of the Topic-Sensitive PageRank algorithm. We have evaluated the proposed algorithms on a large real-world dataset collected from Twitter. We demonstrated that our best method outperformed state-of-the-art methods. We further showed that we can achieve good results even with small sized profiles.

This work serves as an evidence that the topic uniqueness aspect in user interests within social media should be further considered for the influencers detection task; this is in comparison to previous works that have solely focused on detecting topic-based influencers using the combination of link structure and topic-relevance.

6. ACKNOWLEDGMENTS

This work was partially funded by the EU FP7 SocialSensor project, contract number 287975.

7. REFERENCES

[1] N. Agarwal, H. Liu, L. Tang, and P. S. Yu. Identifying the influential bloggers in a community. In *WSDM '08: Proceedings of the international conference on Web search and web data mining*, pages 207–218, New York, NY, USA, 2008. ACM.

[2] E. Bakshy, J. M. Hofman, W. A. Mason, and D. J. Watts. Everyone's an influencer: quantifying influence on twitter. In *Proceedings of WSDM*, WSDM '11, pages 65–74, New York, NY, USA, 2011. ACM.

[3] N. Barbieri, F. Bonchi, and G. Manco. Topic-aware social influence propagation models. In *Proceedings of the 2012 IEEE 12th International Conference on Data Mining*, ICDM '12, pages 81–90, Washington, DC, USA, 2012. IEEE Computer Society.

[4] B. Bi, Y. Tian, Y. Sismanis, A. Balmin, and J. Cho. Scalable topic-specific influence analysis on microblogs. In *Proceedings of the 7th ACM International Conference on Web Search and Data Mining*, WSDM '14, pages 513–522, New York, NY, USA, 2014. ACM.

[5] M. Bianchini, M. Gori, and F. Scarselli. Inside pagerank. *ACM Transactions on Internet Technology (TOIT)*, 5(1):92–128, 2005.

[6] D. M. Blei, A. Y. Ng, and M. I. Jordan. Latent dirichlet allocation. *the Journal of machine Learning research*, 3:993–1022, 2003.

[7] A. E. Cano, S. Mazumdar, and F. Ciravegna. Social influence analysis in microblogging platforms–a topic-sensitive based approach. *Semantic Web*, 2011.

[8] M. Cha, H. Haddadi, F. Benevenuto, and K. P. Gummadi. Measuring User Influence in Twitter: The Million Follower Fallacy. In *Proceedings of ICWSM*.

[9] D. Gruhl, R. Guha, D. Liben-Nowell, and A. Tomkins. Information diffusion through blogspace. In *WWW '04: Proceedings of the 13th international conference on World Wide Web*, pages 491–501, New York, NY, USA, 2004. ACM.

[10] T. H. Haveliwala. Topic-sensitive pagerank: A context-sensitive ranking algorithm for web search. *IEEE Transactions on Knowledge and Data Engineering*, 15:784–796, 2003.

[11] D. Kempe, J. Kleinberg, and E. Tardos. Maximizing the spread of influence through a social network. In *KDD '03: Proceedings of the ninth ACM SIGKDD*

[12] H. Kwak, C. Lee, H. Park, and S. Moon. What is twitter, a social network or a news media? In *Proceedings of WWW*, WWW '10, pages 591–600, New York, NY, USA, 2010. ACM.

[13] J. Leskovec, L. A. Adamic, and B. A. Huberman. The dynamics of viral marketing. *ACM Trans. Web*, 1(1), May 2007.

[14] M. Mathioudakis and N. Koudas. Efficient identification of starters and followers in social media. In *EDBT '09: Proceedings of the 12th International Conference on Extending Database Technology*, pages 708–719, New York, NY, USA, 2009. ACM.

[15] L. Page, S. Brin, R. Motwani, and T. Winograd. The pagerank citation ranking: Bringing order to the web. In *Stanford Digital Libraries Working Paper*, 1998.

[16] H. Roitman, D. Carmel, Y. Mass, and I. Eiron. Modeling the uniqueness of the user preferences for recommendation systems. In *Proceedings of SIGIR*, SIGIR '13, pages 777–780, New York, NY, USA, 2013. ACM.

[17] X. Shi, K. Chang, V. K. Narayanan, V. Josifovski, and A. J. Smola. A compression framework for generating user profiles. In *SIGIR Workshops*, 2010.

[18] M. Shmueli-Scheuer, H. Roitman, D. Carmel, Y. Mass, and D. Konopnicki. Extracting user profiles from large scale data. In *Proceedings of the 2010 Workshop on Massive Data Analytics on the Cloud*, MDAC '10, pages 4:1–4:6, New York, NY, USA, 2010. ACM.

[19] A. Silva, S. Guimarães, W. Meira, Jr., and M. Zaki. Profilerank: Finding relevant content and influential users based on information diffusion. In *Proceedings of the 7th Workshop on Social Network Mining and Analysis*, SNAKDD '13, pages 2:1–2:9, New York, NY, USA, 2013. ACM.

[20] X. Song, Y. Chi, K. Hino, and B. Tseng. Identifying opinion leaders in the blogosphere. In *CIKM '07: Proceedings of the sixteenth ACM conference on Conference on information and knowledge management*, pages 971–974, New York, NY, USA, 2007. ACM.

[21] J. Tang, J. Sun, C. Wang, and Z. Yang. Social influence analysis in large-scale networks. In *Proceedings of SIGKDD*, KDD '09, pages 807–816, New York, NY, USA, 2009. ACM.

[22] C. Teng, L. Gong, A. Livne, C. Brunetti, and L. A. Adamic. Coevolution of network structure and content. In *WebSci*, pages 288–297, 2012.

[23] G. Ver Steeg and A. Galstyan. Information transfer in social media. In *Proceedings of WWW*, WWW '12, pages 509–518, New York, NY, USA, 2012. ACM.

[24] J. Weng, E.-P. Lim, J. Jiang, and Q. He. Twitterrank: finding topic-sensitive influential twitterers. In *Proceedings of the third ACM international conference on Web search and data mining*, WSDM '10, pages 261–270, New York, NY, USA, 2010. ACM.

[25] C. Zhai and J. Lafferty. A study of smoothing methods for language models applied to information retrieval. *ACM Trans. Inf. Syst.*, 22(2):179–214, 2004.

Exploiting the Wisdom of the Crowds for Characterizing and Connecting Heterogeneous Resources

Ricardo Kawase, Patrick Siehndel, Bernardo Pereira Nunes,
Eelco Herder and Wolfgang Nejdl
Leibniz University of Hannover & L3S Research Center
Appelstrasse 9, 30167 Hannover, Germany
{kawase, siehndel, nunes, herder, nejdl}@L3S.de

ABSTRACT

Heterogeneous content is an inherent problem for cross-system search, recommendation and personalization. In this paper we investigate differences in topic coverage and the impact of topicstopics in different kinds of Web services. We use entity extraction and categorization to create 'fingerprints' that allow for meaningful comparison. As a basis taxonomy, we use the 23 main categories of Wikipedia Category Graph, which has been assembled over the years by the wisdom of the crowds. Following a proof of concept of our approach, we analyze differences in topic coverage and topic impact. The results show many differences between Web services like Twitter, Flickr and Delicious, which reflect users' behavior and the usage of each system. The paper concludes with a user study that demonstrates the benefits of fingerprints over traditional textual methods for recommendations of heterogeneous resources.

Categories and Subject Descriptors

H.5.m [**Information Interfaces and Presentation**]: Miscellaneous—*Classification, Navigation*

Keywords

Fingerprints; Classification; Comparison; Domain independent; Wikipedia

1. INTRODUCTION

When searching on the Web for a particular topic, many different kinds of resources can be found, varying from tweets or news items on this topic to movies that have this topic as a keyword. Which resources are found, depends on whether one uses a general-purpose search engine or a specific site such as Twitter[1] or IMDb[2]. As an example, a query on 'Farming' at Twitter may lead to tweets as 'Five reasons

_____

[1] http://twitter.com/

[2] http://www.imdb.com/

why urban farming is the most important movement of our time', while IMDb suggests the 1957 BBC series 'Farming' and even the movie 'There Will Be Blood'.

User interests are as diverse as the topics covered in Web content. However, it is unlikely that a user who is interested in concrete topics such as sustainable farming methods also likes to watch fictional movies that happen to be situated in the countryside. This raises several issues for cross-system search, recommendation and personalization. For instance, besides regular Web content, Google[3] usually includes images and videos in the search results, which in many cases seems to be a shot in the dark. Still, it is likely that more general user interests, for example in sports or in culture, will be reflected in preferences for news items as well as books or movies. Conversely, some topics may be more represented in one ecosystem than in the other. For example, one would expect that 'Politics' is less prominent in Flickr[4] pictures than in Twitter messages.

In this paper, we investigate the differences in *topic coverage* in different kinds of Web sites. Furthermore, we investigate the *impact* of a topic on user appreciation: are movies on agriculture more or less popular than people who tweet on this topic? Our approach relies on the assumption that heterogeneous resources will have similar scores on the coverage of more general categories, such as agriculture, health and politics. Thus, we propose a method to generate *fingerprints* for objects that allow for meaningful comparisons between heterogeneous domains.

The most important characteristic of our fingerprint approach is that it has a limited, yet broad coverage of topics, based on Wikipedia[5] top categories that are maintained by the overall agreement of millions of contributors. Fingerprints provide users a sense making categorization that is digestible and manageable. While other approaches like clustering and LDA provide means for categorization and recommendation of items, they do not support the end user in understanding or configuring parameters.

Our proposed fingerprint is composed of a 23-sized vector that corresponds to the 23 main top categories of Wikipedia. Thus, for each category we assign a weight that represents its relevance for the given object. After all categories have been weighted, the fingerprint is created as a histogram, which characterizes a given object. Due to the collaborative nature of Wikipedia and the large use as a source of knowledge by the Web users, we have adopted its categories as our

_____

[3] http://www.google.com/

[4] http://www.flickr.com/

[5] http://www.wikipedia.org/

knowledge base. Wikipedia currently contains over 4 million articles that have manually been categorized: one article may belong to one or more categories, and categories to one or more parent categories. However, although we use Wikipedia, any other classification scheme could be used along with our method, for instance, ODP[6], OpenCyc[7] or YAGO [19].

The process for creating the fingerprints is divided into 3-step process chain: (a) entity extraction; (b) categorization and (c) profile aggregation. Briefly, for any given object, our technique first recognizes its entities. After that, the entity categories are extracted and finally aggregated (following a weighting rule), creating the objects' fingerprint.

We validate and demonstrate our proposed approach with a set of experiments and analyses: (i) We validate our fingerprinting approach by comparing it with manual categorization (Section 4), (ii) we expose differences in topic coverage between several online systems (Section 5), (iii) we show the influence of topics on resources' *impact* (Section 6), and finally, (iv) we perform a user study that shows how fingerprints improve recommendations for heterogeneous resources (Section 7).

The results show that the 23 main categories of Wikipedia provide a solid base for reasoning about differences in topic coverage between, for example, Twitter and IMDb. Furthermore, the analysis of topic impact shows interesting differences in user appreciation of resources related to topics such as politics, nature and law, as expressed by the number of followers in Twitter and movie ratings in IMDb. As shown by the results of the user study, this opens the way for automatically identifying the most promising sites for finding resources that are relevant, but not necessarily directly related, to a topic and to incorporate this in the search results.

2. RELATED WORK

Ontologies and categories are commonly used as domain models in the field of user modeling and recommender systems [4]. Corresponding user models are represented as overlays of the domain model, in which the values represent the user's knowledge of or interest in a concept. Knowledge or interest levels are usually estimated based on user actions, such as the content of visited pages or the keywords of user queries. Propagation techniques, such as spreading activation [18], are used to ensure that evidence of interest in a particular concept also affects related concepts, such as its parents or children.

Wikipedia is a popular knowledge base for classification, categorization and even recommendations. Wikipedia is constantly refined by contributors and each article is assigned to a number of categories which are hierarchically organized, creating an implicit ontology [21]. In fact, numerous previous works leverage the use of Wikipedia categories. For example, Köhncke and Balke [11] exploit Wikipedia categories in order to generate useful descriptions for chemical documents. In their work, they identify chemical entities in documents and extract the categories of these entities. The resulting categories, combined with a tailored ontology, provided chemical documents with a better description (tagclouds) than terms from a domain-specific ontology. The main difference from our work is that they deal with a very

specific domain, and, they are not interested in co-relating objects with other fields. Thus, they only use the direct categories assigned to the entities, not exploring the category graph.

Chen et al. [5] exploit Wikipedia categories to improve Web video categorization. Their approach relies on identifying Wikipedia concepts in videos and exploiting the associated concepts' categories. Their outcomes describe a small improvement in the categorization task, however, in their work, Wikipedia concepts are manually identified from titles and tags of videos, and they manually performed a syntactical analysis to discriminate classes of concepts.

Blognoon [7] is a semantic blog search engine that leverages topic exploration and navigation. Blognoon provides faceted navigation for blog posts based on Wikipedia concepts. The main idea of the authors is to relate blog posts by the means of common concepts and, to some extent improve the exploration and serendipity in the blogosphere. Their work aligns with our goals of generating implicit relation between objects (in their case blog posts) by exploiting Wikipedia concepts. Unfortunately, the authors do not expose any evaluation. They claim that their query suggestion method, which is based on Wikipedia popularity, is more effective than alphabetical order. However, Wikipedia popularity of articles has been proven to be an ineffective foundation for recommendation [9]. Moreover, we believe that usability could be improved if categories were used instead of plain concepts.

Our approach of reducing the user profile to 23 topics differs significantly from the work of Michelson and Macskassy [14]. In their work, they propose a similar approach to annotate tweets with Wikipedia articles; but instead of considering all parent categories, they traverse the category graph only '5 levels deep'; they assume that a five stage traversal is sufficient to reach categories that are general enough for a user's profile. The limitation of their assumption is that a user's classification may have an unlimited number of categories, thereby preventing profiles from having a normalized length and comparison among all items.

Abel et al. [1] presented similar strategies to enhance Twitter user profiles, however their topic-based profile is built upon topics related to different types of news events. In our work, we consider the topics (categories) of each detected Wikipedia entity, thus the categories describe a wider area of fields. Moreover, they use as knowledge base the OpenCalais[8] ontology, which is a document categorization system that mainly focuses on news events.

Finally, regarding topic graph walk strategies (see Section 3), the method proposed by Kittur and Chi [10] to relate articles to categories is very similar to our approach. The main difference is that our approach is more focused on applications and not limited to articles inside Wikis. While the authors relate one article to the top-level category with the shortest path (or more if there is more than one shortest path) to see which content is inside Wikipedia, our approach relates articles to several top-level categories. This allows us a better comparison of profiles, due to the increased number of weights for each top-level category - in our case, no topic information is discarded.

---

[6] Open Directory Project - http://www.dmoz.org/
[7] http://www.opencyc.org/

[8] http://www.opencalais.com

3. FINGERPRINTS

As explained in the introduction, we aim to compare heterogeneous objects, based on fingerprint profiles of these objects. A common approach is to create a vector space model in which each field contains a score on a particular term or category.

There are several ways for selecting the terms or categories to be used for the vector. An IR approach would be to select the most frequent terms, excluding stop words. However, as our aim is to compare heterogeneous objects, it makes more sense to use an existing and well-accepted ontology or categorization.

There are many good candidate ontologies or knowledge bases, including YAGO, WordNet[9], and SUMO[10]. We decided to use the well established Wikipedia corpus as a semantic knowledge base. Wikipedia is arguably the most accessed reference Web site and each of the more than 4 million existing articles are manually classified by human curators to one or more categories. Additionally, categories are organized in a graph in which sub-categories reference to top-level categories. The English Wikipedia has a total of 23 top-level categories (*Main topic classifications*), which we use to represent a profile[11].

The creation of semantically enhanced profiles consists of three stages. During the first stage, *extraction*, entities are extracted from a given textual object. We first annotate the object to detect any mention of entities that can be linked to Wikipedia articles. For this purpose, we use the WikipediaMiner[15] service as an annotation tool. First, detected words are disambiguated using machine learning algorithms that take the context of the word into account. This step is followed by the detection of links to Wikipedia articles. Only those words that are relevant for the whole document are linked to articles. The goal of the whole process is to annotate a given document in the same way as a human would link a Wikipedia article.

In the second stage, *categorization*, we extract the categories of each entity that has been identified in the previous step. For each category, we follow the path of all parent categories, up to the root category. In some cases, this procedure results in the assignment of several top-level categories to a single entity. Following the parent categories (which are closer the root category), we compute values of distance and siblings categories, resulting in each entity receiving 23 categories' scores. In fact, there are different approaches that can be applied to walk Wikipedia's category graph. To achieve best results and accurately assign weights to each of the 23 categories, we experimented different graph walk and weighting strategies. A detailed evaluation is provided in Section 3.1.

Finally, in the *aggregation* stage, we perform a linear aggregation over all of the scores for a given object in order to generate the final profile.

3.1 Category Computation

We used the Wikipedia category graph for relating one article to the 23 main Wikipedia categories. The dataset we used contains 593,125 different categories. Each of these

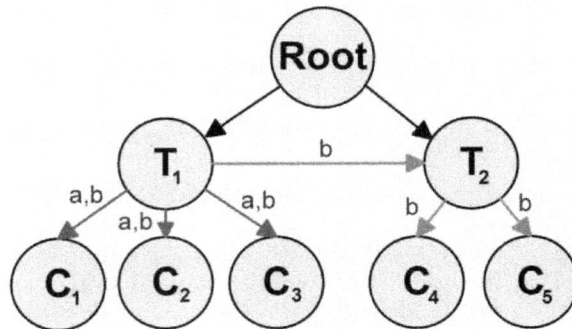

Figure 1: Subcategories of TC_1 for strategies 'A' and 'B'.

categories is linked to one or more of the main categories. Table 1 shows some statistics of the used graph.

We used two different graph walking algorithms for computing the relation of a category to the main categories. Both strategies follow a top-down approach that pre-computes main category weights for each article. The main difference between the two approaches is the size of the generated tree for each main category. The relation of an article to the main categories is based on a depth-first walk through the Wikipedia category graph: the algorithm remembers the distance from the root node, and follows only sub-category links of which the distance is larger (*strategy A*) or equal (*strategy B*) to the current distance to the root node.

Figure 1 shows a small graph that consists of a root, two top-level categories (T_i) and 5 normal categories (C_i). When strategy 'A' is applied on this graph, category T_1 will contain all articles that are related to the categories C_1, C_2, C_3 and T_1. The category T_2 will not be part of C_1 because there exists another way with equal length from the root to T_2. When strategy 'B' is used on this graph, all categories will be seen as part of T_1.

By following only links that match this pattern, we make sure not to include the entire category graph (and all articles) for each main category. Additionally, we avoid loops by storing visited nodes and not visiting these nodes again. For the subcategories that are reachable through the category graph, we get the corresponding articles that belong to the categories. With this approach, we get a relation map in which every category is related to many articles and, in which most articles are related to many categories.

A basic profile (fingerprint) for an object consists of weights for all of the main categories. The final weight θ of a topic $t \in T$ (top 23 Wikipedia categories) for an object $o \in O$ is given by Equation 1:

Table 1: Statistics on the Wikipedia Category Graph.

# of Categories	593,125
# of Category-Subcategory links	1,306,838
avg. # of Subcategories	2.2
# of Page-Category Links	11,220,967
avg. # of Pages per Category	18.9

---

[9] http://wordnet.princeton.edu/

[10] http://www.ontologyportal.org/

[11] http://en.wikipedia.org/wiki/Category:Main_topic_classifications

$$\theta(o_i, t_k) = \sum_{e \in c_i}^{l=|e|} \left(\sum_{c_j(e_l)}^{j=|c_j(e_l)|} w(c_j, t_k) \right), \qquad (1)$$

where e are the entities annotated in a given object o, $c(e)$ are the Wikipedia categories for $e \in o_i$ and w is a weight given to the link between a category c_j and a top-category t_k. In Section 4, we define the weight used in our experiments (see Equation 2).

3.2 Resource Fingerprints

With the proposed approach, we are able to generate fingerprints for different sources of information and in different domains. This subsection explains how our approach can be applied to generate fingerprints for user-generated content, and for tags that are associated with a particular resource or user. In addition, we explore the benefits of generating fingerprints for movies (Subsection 3.2.3).

3.2.1 User-content Fingerprint

In the last years, social networking has become the most prominent online activity: the most popular social networks, including Facebook[12], Twitter, Myspace[13], aggregate over a billion users. As a result, research interest in the area of social networks has grown considerably. User modeling, link prediction, sentiment analysis, community analysis, sociology and many other areas of Web Science are examples of research fields that exploit the public (and private) data available from such networks.

User-content fingerprints are based on the contents produced by a user (in our experiments, all tweets posted by a user). In order to generate a user fingerprint we utilize the content posted by the user as the input corpus for the *Extraction*, *Categorization* and *Aggregation* steps. The resulting fingerprint represents the users main interests in terms of the 23 Wikipedia top categories. As a downside, the fingerprints are not detailed enough to be useful for generating recommendations or other kinds of personalization. However, this 23-size vector has the advantage that the profile is human understandable and allows for easy comparison between users.

3.2.2 Tag-Based Fingerprints

Another application area is the generation of fingerprints for tagged resources. Considering the associated tags of a given resource or user, we use them as input for the profiling process. In this case, instead of exploiting the whole text of a resource that inevitably introduces noise, the resulting fingerprint is based solely on entities identified by the tags.

Tags are mainly applied for describing the content of an item in order to facilitate the organization and management of the resources, and for making search and retrieval more effective [8, 20]. Additionally, tags enhance the visibility of community content by associating related items with the same annotation(s) [3]. Thus, fingerprinting items based on tags allows our approach to be applied to any folksonomy, even on those where resources do not have a textual representation (e.g. images and videos), which results in profiles that are more concise and less noisy.

---
[12] http://www.facebook.com/
[13] http://www.myspace.com/

3.2.3 Text-Based Fingerprints

To exemplify text-based fingerprints, let us consider movie descriptions. Although a movie is often classified by its genre, rarely there is a content-based classification of it. In the field of movie recommendation, most approaches make use of features that are based on co-occurrence of movies with actors and genres, user ratings, contextual and temporal information, together with collaborative filtering [12]. Recommenders that exploit the actor-movie-genre network are able to provide movie recommendations that hold similar characteristics. Collaborative filtering - based on user data and ratings - is able to provide very good recommendations, but in many cases for dissimilar movies (e.g. people who liked "The Manchurian Candidate", a political thriller, may also like "A Beautiful Mind", the dramatization of a mathematician biography, even though the movies have nothing in common).

By creating fingerprints of movies, we generate sense making profiles that are solely based on the content, i.e. the movie description. Our example movie "The Manchurian Candidate" would, based on its description, have 'Politics' as its main category. The benefits of such profiles are twofold. First, the reduced representation of topics of interest is based on a well-established knowledge base that effectively aggregates the wisdom of the crowds. In this way, fingerprints are comparable among any different entity type. Second, the profiles are human comprehensible, thus, any person is able interpret a fingerprint and understand the rationale behind it.

4. PROOF OF CONCEPT

In this section, we describe a experiment to evaluate the quality of the profiling methods through the recognition of entities in a text.

4.1 Experimental setup

In order to validate the applicability of the profiling method, we use articles from the Wikipedia corpus itself. In Wikipedia, articles are manually annotated with categories. The idea is to utilize these categories as the input for our method (in this case, starting from stage two, *Categorization*) and use the output as ground truth. As a result of this profiling method, we have a 23-sized vector, representing the fingerprint of a given article, which are solely based on the article's own categories.

The validation comes with a comparison of these profiles against the ones generated by applying the whole method. Therefore, the evaluation will measure the similarity of profiles generated by the existing categories of an article against the profiles generated by the categories of articles mentioned in an article.

Given the fact that manually assigned categories are descriptive, we aim to demonstrate that it is possible to categorize textual objects through the extraction of mentioned entities. This experiment is divided in two different stages. In the first stage, we aim to show that our approach leads to a good description of the main category of an article. Therefore, we selected articles that have already been annotated with one of the main categories. This set of 1444 different Wikipedia articles is then processed based on their categories, to relate it automatically to the top categories. This experiment will show that the categories of articles men-

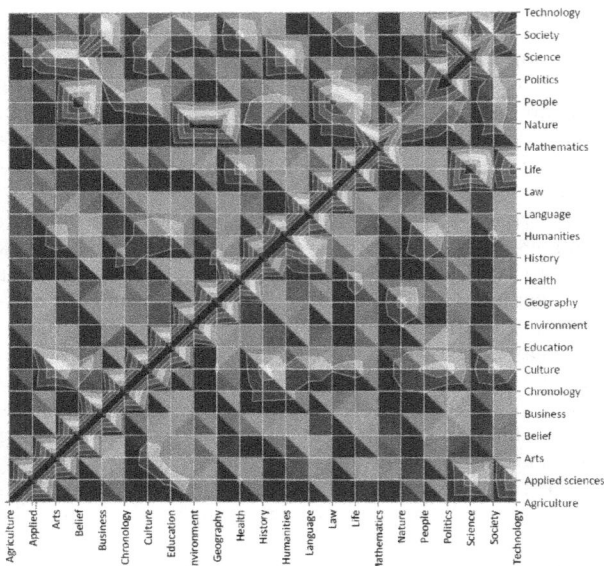

Figure 2: Relation between automatically assigned top category and ground truth.

tioned inside *containing articles* can be used to define the categories of the *containing article*.

In the second stage, we select a set of random articles from Wikipedia. With the second experiment we aim to evaluate if the categorization process leads to similar results when used with just the text of an article, or the categories directly related to an article. The set of articles contained in the set of the first article is very high in the category graph. Therefore, most of the articles in this set have very strong relations to just one of the main categories. The second set is randomly chosen and contains also articles which have strong relations to more than one of main categories. Additionally, we run the experiments using both graph walking strategies described in Section 3.1, in order to select the best performing one.

4.2 Experimental Results

The diagram in Figure 2 shows to which category articles from the different top categories are related. The diagonal line indicates that most articles from a certain top category are also classified as part of this category. Additionally, we see that there are strong relations between some of the categories. For instance, articles of the category 'Nature' are often classified with a high value in the categories 'Environment' and 'Geography'. The map was generated by using strategy 'B' together with a weighting scheme. The weighting is based on the distance of the article's categories to the root category and the probability of an article belonging to a certain top category.

There are big variances between the different categories. Categories like 'Mathematics', 'Agriculture' or 'Chronology' are relatively weakly represented. This leads to a classification in which these categories are underrepresented as well.

To achieve a more precise classification, we calculate the weight of the top categories taking into account the relative probability of an article belonging to one of the main categories. Additionally, we assume that a longer distance to

Table 2: Results of generated article category relations for articles of main categories

	Strategy A	Strategy B
Avg. Ranking	2.9863	3.5024
Success @ 1	0.5044	0.5073
Success @ 2	0.6568	0.6456
Success @ 5	0.8367	0.815
Success @ 10	0.9531	0.9085

Table 3: Results of generated article category relations for articles of subcategories of main categories

	Strategy A	Strategy B
Avg. Ranking	3.5198	4.0619
Success @ 1	0.4458	0.4102
Success @ 2	0.586	0.5585
Success @ 5	0.791	0.7627
Success @ 10	0.9314	0.8955

one of the main categories can be interpreted as a weaker relation to that category. The calculation is shown as Equation 2,

$$w(t_k, c_j) = \frac{1}{P(t_k)} * \frac{1}{\delta(t_k, c_j)} \qquad (2)$$

where $P(t_k)$ indicates the popularity of a given top-category and δ is the distance of a category c_j to the top-category t_k. To measure the performance in this experiment, we calculate the average rank of the correct main category inside the profile vector. For strategy 'A' we achieve an average rank of 2.9863 and for strategy 'B' we achieve 3.502. For the success@k we got very similar values for both strategies as shown in Table 2. To analyze how the performance changes when taking articles which are not so high in the Wikipedia category, we performed the same experiment with articles that belong to categories one level below the top categories. Overall, this dataset contained 33,262 different articles. The results are shown in Table 3 and as we can see, the overall performances of both algorithms are still good.

Beside the analysis of articles which are close to main categories, we performed an experiment to measure how the approach works for random articles. In order to select articles that contain enough content, we only selected articles with at least 20 inlinks, 30 outlinks and a minimum text length of 1000 characters. Overall we selected 10,000 different articles and applied our categorization method once on the content of the article, and once on the categories directly related to article. Since there are not necessarily any main categories directly related to the article, we measured the performance by means of cosine similarity between the generated profile based on the content and the profile based on the categories. The results of this experiment are shown in Table 4. As strategy 'B' performed better for random articles, we used this strategy for the remaining experiments in this paper.

5. TOPIC COVERAGE

As explained in the introduction, it is likely that there are differences in topic focus between Web services. In this section we use the fingerprint approach for identifying such differences in four distinct services: Flickr, Delicious[14], Twitter and IMDb, making use of an extensive dataset. As will

---

[14] http://delicious.com/

Table 4: Similarity results between the generated categories and the ground truth for 10000 random articles.

Depth of which Article	Strategy A cos-sim	Strategy B cos-sim	Number of Articles
ALL	0.8603	0.9275	10000
0-3	0.7314	0.8641	91
4	0.84	0.8897	536
5	0.8744	0.9214	2962
6	0.867	0.9320	2885
7	0.8631	0.9346	1904
8	0.8444	0.9390	1015
9	0.8208	0.9418	485
10	0.8081	0.9397	92
>10	0.7246	0.8689	30

Table 5: Datasets Statistics

	Data	Users	Identified Articles
Twitter	86,244 tags	1,574	32,569
Flickr	12,271,742 tags	14,450	5,341,331
Delicious	890,062 tags	2,005	558,409
IMDb	275,784 descriptions	-	1,351,433

be discussed in more detail in the remainder of this section, overall coverage per topic is quite consistent between all systems. However, when looking at the relative coverage of each topic, it becomes clear that, for instance, 'Mathematics' has a relatively high coverage in Delicious and Twitter, but - as one would expect - is less well represented in Flickr and IMDb.

5.1 Datasets

The tag-based datasets that are used in our evaluation were collected by Abel et al.[2] for the Mypes user profiling service. Flickr and Delicious data consist of tags that were assigned to resources, respectively pictures and bookmarks. In Twitter, the data consists of hashtags used in Tweets. As explained in subsection 3.2.2, these tags are the input to identify Wikipedia articles about the entities related to the resources, which on their turn were used for generating the fingerprints. For IMDb the input for generating the fingerprints was the descriptions of movies. Table 5 shows some statistics about the used datasets.

5.2 Fingerprints in different domains

We applied our profiling method to all users in the datasets described in the previous subsection. The collection of all users discriminated by each of the systems gives us an overall fingerprint for each domain (movies in the case of IMDb). All four systems receive a relative similar fingerprint profile. All have a very broad coverage in the categories 'Society' , 'Life' and 'Culture'. To make the results of the different systems easier to compare, we normalized the values based on the category with the highest coverage (in all cases 'Society').

For a better understanding of the coverage difference in each domain, we calculated the variation of topic coverage of all systems per category. Figure 3 quantifies the difference between each topic in each system and the global mean. The results show interesting aspects that uncover users' behavior

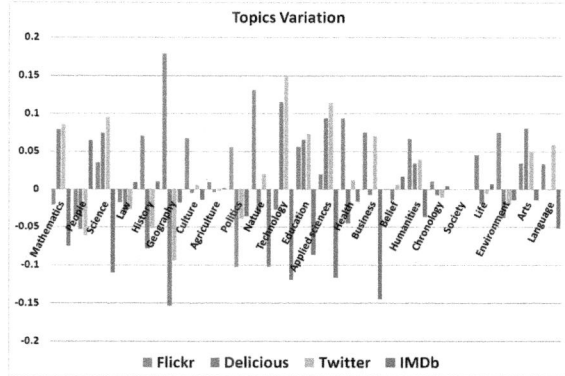

Figure 3: Variations in topic coverage in different systems.

and the usage of each system. For instance, Flickr is used to publish and tag pictures, many of these are tagged with locations, leading to a peak at the 'Geography' category. Other topics like 'Technology' are less covered in Flickr, but show a higher coverage for Twitter and Delicious. We also see that the graphs for Delicious and Twitter are very similar for most of the categories while the graphs for IMDb and Flickr show higher differences.

Many more differences can be observed in Figure 3, but a detailed analysis is beyond the scope of this paper. In general, the tendencies reflect expected differences between the different services.

5.2.1 Topic Breakdown

The fingerprinting approach is not limited to the generic top-level categories, but can also be used for breaking down a topic. To illustrate this, we also analyzed what the coverage of deeper categories looks like. Figure 4 shows how the different systems cover the subcategories of the 'Culture' (the plots do not include all subcategories of 'Culture', only those with significant coverage or variation). A closer look at the variations of each system against the global average shows that, for instance, Twitter and IMDb have strong relations to 'Entertainment' while Flickr shows peaks at 'Cultural spheres of influence', 'Cultural history' and 'Political culture'. The highest peak in 'Cultural spheres of influence' can be explained by the fact that this category has many subcategories which are related to geography. The peak in 'Cultural history' can be explained with tags on pictures of landmarks, a very representative set in Flickr [6].

6. TOPICS IMPACT

Given the differences in focus between domains and systems, it is likely that user appreciation of a tweet or a movie on a topic will be different. In other words, movies on certain topics may have a significantly lower or higher average rating in IMDb. Similarly, users who tweet on certain topics may have more or less followers than others.

6.1 Datasets

We applied our profiling method to the IMDb dataset from October 2012, consisting of over 2.3 million items (movies, tv series, etc). In total, we generated fingerprint profiles for

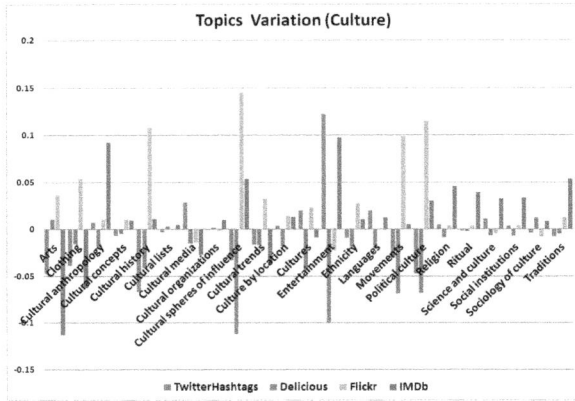

Figure 4: Variations in topic coverage of 'Culture' subcategories in different systems.

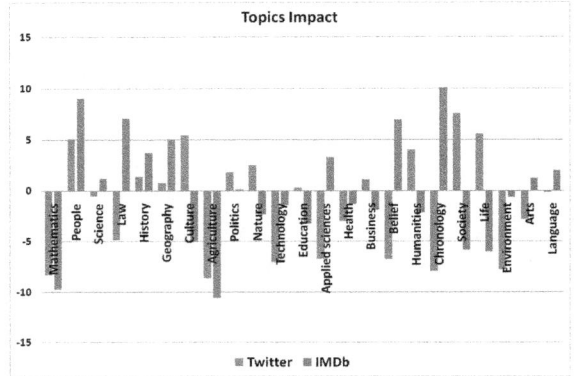

Figure 5: Percentual impact factors of topics on number of followers on Twitter and movies' ratings on IMDb.

275,784 movies - we ignored all identified episodes descriptions of series and other items apart from movies. With the movie fingerprints, we are now able to suggest movies that deal the same topics, without the compulsory attachment of genre, actors or ratings, and that are still interesting for the user. In the movies scenario, we use ratings as a success indicator.

While for movies higher ratings arguably indicate *better* movies, in the Twitter-user scenario, we used the number of followers as a parameter of *success* (the higher the number of followers the 'bette r' the user). Obviously, there are exceptions: celebrities on Twitter get millions of followers without posting anything interesting. Lim and Datta [13] propose an approach that involves identifying celebrities that are representative for a given topic of interest. In their work, they define a celebrity as a user that has more than 10,000 followers. Given this premise, we computed the impact factor of Wikipedia topics in Twitter based on the profiles of 1776 users - from these users we had information on the number of followers (average 74.7) and there were no celebrities. The resulting impact factors for Twitter users are depicted together with IMDb impact factors in Figure 5.

6.1.1 Topic-Based Movie Ratings

Arguably, ratings are the most prominent feature for recommending movies. As we have both ratings and topic weights for every movie, we can analyze the influence of topics in movies ratings.

To check the topic influence on ratings, we compute the difference between, on the one hand, the average percentages of topic distribution multiplied by movies' ratings, and, on the other hand, the average percentages of topic distribution multiplied by 6.54 (the global average of all ratings in IMDb).

To illustrate the analysis, imagine that there are 100 *Technology* movies and 100 *Politics* movies. The average distribution considering only these two categories is 50% for each. Now, let us assume that all *Technology* movies have ratings of 7.5 stars while *Politics* have ratings with 4.5 stars. By multiplying the distributions by the ratings, ($100 \times 7.5 = 750$ and $100 \times 4.5 = 450$), and the average rating ($100 \times 6.54 \cong 650$), and calculating the differences ($750 - 650 = 100$ and $450 - 650 = -200$), the absolute

variation of 300 indicates a 33.3% positive impact factor of *Technology* and a 66.6% negative impact factor of *Politics*. We calculated the topic impact factor based on the ratings of all movies that had at least 1000 votes - in total 16,374 movies.

The topic impact factor ω is then given by Equation 3:

$$
\omega(t_k) = \sum_{i=0}^{|m|} (\theta(m_i, t_k) \cdot \gamma(m_i)) \\
- \sum_{i=0}^{|m|} (\theta(m_i, t_k) \cdot \frac{\sum_{i=0}^{|m|} \cdot \gamma(m_i)}{|m|}),
$$

(3)

where the function θ gives the weight of topic for a movie m (see Section 3) and γ is the IMDb rating of a movie m.

As depicted in Figure 5, the topics 'Mathematics', 'Agriculture', 'Culture', 'Society' and 'Life' have a stronger negative impact on the movies ratings - or, in other perspective, movies that deal with those subjects are usually rated lower than others. These differences in topic impact largely match the variations in topic coverage, as discussed in the previous section. It should be noted that the differences in average movie rating may not be directly related to the topic per se: it may well be the case that the average movie on, for instance, 'Agriculture' is produced with a smaller budget and targets a particular audience - this in contrast to popular movie topics such as 'Law' or 'History'.

6.2 Topic Impact in Different Domains

To draw a comparison between people's interests and movie topics, we calculate the same *topic impact factors* for Twitter users. Not surprisingly, Twitter users tend to follow people who talk about popular topics as 'People', 'Society', 'Life' and 'Culture'.

Figure 5 also shows some interesting contrasts between both domains. People like movies about 'Law', but usually do not follow people who tweet about this topic - people tend not to be fond of lawyers. Additionally, 'Chronology', 'Applied Sciences' and 'Belief' seem to be topics that produce enjoyable movies, but are great turn-offs in Twitter.

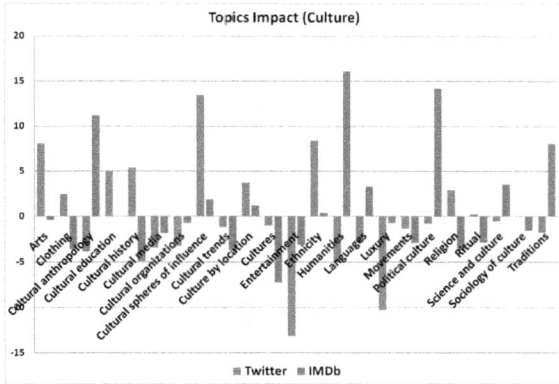

Figure 6: Impact factors (in percentage) of *'Culture'* subcategories on number of followers on Twitter and movies' ratings on IMDb.

6.2.1 Topic breakdown

Similar to the topic breakdown in Section 5, we apply impact analysis on subcategories of the main category 'Culture'. Figure 6 shows the impact factors for these subcategories - we only display those that have an influence higher than 1%. The chart shows interesting differences between both domains, where 'Cultural Anthropology', 'Humanities', 'Political Culture' and 'Tradition' have a positive impact for movies while in Twitter 'Arts', 'Cultural Spheres of Influence' and 'Ethnicity' provides the most positive impacts. Without going into further detail, the differences clearly show that users tend to rate movies on certain topics differently than tweets on the corresponding topics.

7. USER STUDY

This section presents the evaluation process used to validate our approach in terms of cross-domain recommendations. For this, we perform a user evaluation using a crowdsourcing platform to collect feedback. The goal is to compare recommendations given by the fingerprint approach against a text-based approach. The idea behind this study is to validate the usefulness of the fingerprint profiles to recommend heterogeneous resources in comparison to traditional text-based approaches. Specifically, the setup of our user study is to recommend movies that are relevant, but not necessarily directly related, to a given textual resource.

7.1 Datasets

In order to collect a useful dataset, we used the OAI-PMH protocol[15] to harvest resources that contain informative or educational content. We focus on repositories that provided an OAI-PMH target, among others *12Manage*[16], *INSEAD*[17], *LSE Research Online*[18].

After harvesting these different open repositories, we selected a random set of documents that were written in English and that contained at least 500 characters in its description. In total, we collected 1,416 resources to undergo our fingerprint method. For the movies dataset, we used

the same as described in Section 6.1, however we selected only movies that are annotated with the genre 'documentary' (31,991 in total), which are assumed to provide interesting facts on a given topic, to be rather informative and in many cases entertaining.

7.2 Approach and Baseline

In order to generate recommendations, we used cosine similarity between the fingerprints. Thus, given a learning object and its fingerprint, we rank the movies according to their fingerprint' cosine similarity. As a result, for each resource, a ranked list of 'contextualized' movies is produced. With the purpose of comparison, we also generated rankings based solely on textual similarities.

To measure the textual similarity among the resources and movies, in our study, we used *MoreLikeThis*, a standard function provided by the Lucene search engine library[19]. *MoreLikeThis* calculates similarity of two documents by computing the number of overlapping words and giving them different weights based on TF-IDF [16]. *MoreLikeThis* runs over the fields we specified as relevant for the comparison - in our case the description of the resource and the movies' plots - and generates a term vector for each analyzed item (excluding stop-words).

To measure the similarity between items, the method only considered words that are longer than 2 characters and that appear at least 2 times in the source document. Furthermore, words that occur in less than 2 different documents are not taken into account for the calculation. For calculating relevant items, the method used the 15 most representative words, based on their TD-IDF values, and generated a query with these words. The ranking of the resulting items is based on Lucene's scoring function which is based on the Boolean model of Information Retrieval and the Vector Space Model of Information Retrieval [17].

7.3 User Task

We set up our evaluation on CrowdFlower[20], a crowdsourcing platform. With CrowdFlower, we are able to reach a broad and unbiased audience to judge our outcomes. The task posted for the participants consisted of evaluating the relevance and relatedness between a resource and a movie. Each participant was presented with the description of the resource and the description of the top-ranked recommended movies (with the same descriptions as used for the fingerprinting process). After reading the descriptions, participants were asked the following two questions:

- *Q1: Do you think that the suggested movie is relevant for the given document?*

- *Q2: In which degree the movie is related to the main topic of the document?*

The responses were registered using a 5-point Likert scale model. The first question aims at measuring the quality of the movie recommendations in terms of informational value. The second one aims at uncovering the actual topic-based relatedness of a movie and a resource. These answers are

---

[15]http://www.openarchives.org/pmh

[16]http://12manage.com/

[17]http://knowledge.insead.edu/

[18]http://eprints.lse.ac.uk/

[19]http://lucene.apache.org/core/old_versioned_docs/versions/3_4_0/api/all/org/apache/lucene/search/similar/MoreLikeThis.html

[20]https://www.crowdflower.com/

not necessarily dependent: a movie may not be relevant, but still topic-wise related. For example, a document on the economical crisis in Greece is topically related to the movie 'My Big Fat Greek Wedding', but they are arguably hardly relevant for each other.

7.4 Results

In total, we had 60 participants in our evaluation. These participants evaluated 606 pairs of movie recommendations. The responses were evenly distributed between fingerprints and the text-based approach (303 judgments for each). In general, for the fingerprint-based strategy, 74% of the participants *agreed* or *strongly agreed* on the *relevance* of the recommendations. In contrast, the positive agreement results for the relevance of the text-based strategy sums up to only 55% (see Table 6). Regarding relatedness, the results turned out to be quite similar. Both strategies produced around 44% related (>3) recommendations.

To extend our analysis, we calculated the Pearson's coefficient of correlation between the first and the second question, resulting in 0.52 for the fingerprints strategy and 0.80 for the text-based. In both cases, we see a high correlation, specially for the text-based approach. The main reason is that the text-based approach is unable to capture different aspects other than explicit terms in the description. Thus, if it produces a relevant result, most probably it will also be related. On the other hand, fingerprints identify relevance without relatedness. In fact, results show that for the fingerprint approach, in 13.9% of the judged pairs, the participants stated that the movies were relevant (*agree* or *strong agree*) but not related (relatedness 1 or 2). For the opposite case, where movies were related (relatedness 4 or 5) but not relevant (*disagree* or *strong disagree*), it only happened in 1.3% of the judgments. Respectively, the numbers for the text-based approach are 7.2% and 1.3%. These numbers suggest that even though a movie is unrelated to the main topic of a document, it might still be relevant.

To summarize, the results show that the fingerprint approach produces significant (p<0.05) better recommendations in terms of relevance. Our *fingerprinting* approach is able to identify the context of a document (using the 23 main topic categories of Wikipedia) on a higher level of abstraction. In contrast, a text-based approach is not able to identify these general topics and relies solely on term-to-term identification. In general, text-based approaches fail to identify latent topics in rather short descriptions. Fingerprints overcome this problem by efficiently recognizing relevant and contextualized entities in the objects' descriptions.

8. CONCLUSION

In this paper, we presented a fingerprint-based approach for comparing different kinds of resources in different domains. Fingerprint-based profiles are created by extracting entities from free text, categorizing them into one of Wikipedia main categories and aggregating the results into one profile. We validated this approach by comparing manually assigned main categories of Wikipedia articles with automatically found categories. Fingerprint-based profiles of user content, textual descriptions and tags were used for identifying differences in topic coverage and topic impact in different domains and systems, among which Twitter, Flickr, IMDb and Delicious.

Experimental results show that the Fingerprint-based approach is able to quantify and visualize differences in focus of these systems, such as the focus of Twitter messages on recent events, with entertainment as a main interest. We also showed that certain topics receive significantly higher or lower ratings in a system. As an example, movies about agriculture usually receive lower ratings in IMDb and people who tweet about agriculture have a less-than-average number of followers. As we discussed, these tendencies need not to be caused by the topic per se.

There are numerous applications where fingerprints can be applied: assisting systems and users to disambiguate queries, to control diversity in results and to overcome language differences. Fingerprint-based profiles are especially useful in situations when apples need to be compared to oranges, a situation that is not uncommon. As an example, user profiles, which are used for recommendation and personalization, are usually specific to the domain and the system, and therefore cannot easily be applied elsewhere. Fingerprint-based profiles are less precise than regular user profiles, but provide a good basis for creating an initial interest profile in cold-start situations.

Fingerprints also provide users insight in differences in focus for different systems. For systems such as IMDb, knowledge on significant differences in user ratings per topic can be used for compensating for these differences, in order to better cater queries for specific (niche) topics or for users with a high interest in these specific topics.

To illustrate our approach, we deployed an online system[21] that allow users to generate fingerprints for Twitter users, Web resources and to browse IMDb movies fingerprints.

9. REFERENCES

[1] F. Abel, Q. Gao, G.-J. Houben, and K. Tao. Analyzing user modeling on twitter for personalized news recommendations. In *International Conference on User Modeling, Adaptation and Personalization (UMAP), Girona, Spain*. Springer, July 2011.

[2] F. Abel, N. Henze, E. Herder, and D. Krause. Linkage, aggregation, alignment and enrichment of public user profiles with mypes. In A. Paschke, N. Henze, and T. Pellegrini, editors, *Proceedings the 6the International Conference on Semantic Systems, I-SEMANTICS 2010, Graz, Austria, September 1-3, 2010*, ACM International Conference Proceeding Series. ACM, September 2010.

[3] M. Ames and M. Naaman. Why we tag: motivations for annotation in mobile and online media. In *Proceedings of the SIGCHI Conference on Human Factors in Computing Systems*, CHI '07, pages 971–980, New York, NY, USA, 2007. ACM.

[4] P. Brusilovsky, A. Kobsa, and W. Nejdl, editors. *The Adaptive Web, Methods and Strategies of Web Personalization*, volume 4321 of *Lecture Notes in Computer Science*. Springer, 2007.

[5] Z. Chen, J. Cao, Y. Song, Y. Zhang, and J. Li. Web video categorization based on wikipedia categories and content-duplicated open resources. In *Proceedings of the international conference on Multimedia*, MM '10, pages 1107–1110, New York, NY, USA, 2010. ACM.

---

[21] http://twikime.l3s.uni-hannover.de

Table 6: User study results.

(1st question) - Relevance			(2nd question) - Relatedness			
Agreement	Fingerprint-based(%)	Text-based(%)	Relatedness		Fingerprint-based(%)	Text-based(%)
Strongly Agree	25.74	22.55	Related	5	14.85	15.69
Agree	48.51	32.35		4	29.7	28.43
Undecided	3.96	13.73		3	19.8	17.65
Disagree	12.87	17.65		2	15.84	16.67
Strongly Disagree	8.91	13.73	Unrelated	1	19.8	21.57

[6] D. J. Crandall, L. Backstrom, D. Huttenlocher, and J. Kleinberg. Mapping the world's photos. In *Proceedings of the 18th international conference on World wide web*, WWW '09, pages 761–770, New York, NY, USA, 2009. ACM.

[7] M. Grineva, M. Grinev, D. Lizorkin, A. Boldakov, D. Turdakov, A. Sysoev, and A. Kiyko. Blognoon: exploring a topic in the blogosphere. In *Proceedings of the 20th international conference companion on World wide web*, WWW '11, pages 213–216, New York, NY, USA, 2011. ACM.

[8] A. Hotho, R. Jaschke, C. Schmitz, and G. Stumme. Information retrieval in folksonomies: search and ranking. In *Proceedings of the 3rd European conference on The Semantic Web: research and applications*, ESWC'06, pages 411–426, Berlin, Heidelberg, 2006. Springer-Verlag.

[9] R. Kawase, P. Siehndel, E. Herder, and W. Nejdl. Hyperlink of men. In *Proceedings of the 2012 Latin American Web Congress (la-web 2012)*, LA-WEB '12, Washington, DC, USA, 2012. IEEE Computer Society.

[10] A. Kittur, E. H. Chi, and B. Suh. What's in wikipedia?: mapping topics and conflict using socially annotated category structure. In *Proceedings of the SIGCHI Conference on Human Factors in Computing Systems*, CHI '09, pages 1509–1512, New York, NY, USA, 2009. ACM.

[11] B. Köhncke and W.-T. Balke. Using wikipedia categories for compact representations of chemical documents. In *Proceedings of the 19th ACM international conference on Information and knowledge management*, CIKM '10, pages 1809–1812, New York, NY, USA, 2010. ACM.

[12] Y. Koren. Collaborative filtering with temporal dynamics. In *Proceedings of the 15th ACM SIGKDD international conference on Knowledge discovery and data mining*, KDD '09, pages 447–456, New York, NY, USA, 2009. ACM.

[13] K. H. Lim and A. Datta. Finding twitter communities with common interests using following links of celebrities. In *Proceedings of the 3rd international workshop on Modeling social media*, MSM '12, pages 25–32, New York, NY, USA, 2012. ACM.

[14] M. Michelson and S. A. Macskassy. Discovering users' topics of interest on twitter: a first look. In *Proceedings of the fourth workshop on Analytics for noisy unstructured text data*, AND '10, pages 73–80, New York, NY, USA, 2010. ACM.

[15] D. Milne and I. H. Witten. Learning to link with wikipedia. In *CIKM '08: Proceeding of the 17th ACM conference on Information and knowledge management*, pages 509–518, New York, NY, USA, 2008. ACM.

[16] G. Salton and M. J. McGill. *Introduction to Modern Information Retrieval*. McGraw-Hill, New York, 1983.

[17] G. Salton, A. Wong, and C. S. Yang. A vector space model for automatic indexing. *Commun. ACM*, 18(11):613–620, Nov. 1975.

[18] A. Sieg, B. Mobasher, and R. Burke. Web search personalization with ontological user profiles. In *Proceedings of the sixteenth ACM Conference on information and knowledge management*, CIKM '07, pages 525–534, New York, NY, USA, 2007. ACM.

[19] F. M. Suchanek, G. Kasneci, and G. Weikum. Yago: A core of semantic knowledge. In *16th international World Wide Web conference*, New York, NY, USA, 2007. ACM Press.

[20] S. Xu, S. Bao, B. Fei, Z. Su, and Y. Yu. Exploring folksonomy for personalized search. In *Proceedings of the 31st annual international ACM SIGIR conference on Research and development in information retrieval*, SIGIR '08, pages 155–162, New York, NY, USA, 2008. ACM.

[21] J. Yu, J. A. Thom, and A. Tam. Ontology evaluation using wikipedia categories for browsing. In *Proceedings of the sixteenth ACM Conference on information and knowledge management*, CIKM '07, pages 223–232, New York, NY, USA, 2007. ACM.

Cross-Site Personalization: Assisting Users In Addressing Information Needs That Span Independently Hosted Websites

Kevin Koidl
Trinity College Dublin, Ireland
College Green, Dublin
Kevin.Koidl@scss.tcd.ie

Owen Conlan
Trinity College Dublin, Ireland
College Green, Dublin
Owen.Conlan@scss.tcd.ie

Vincent Wade
Trinity College Dublin, Ireland
College Green, Dublin
Vincent.Wade@scss.tcd.ie

ABSTRACT

This paper discusses Cross-Site Personalization (CSP) an approach to provide personalized assistance for the user in addressing information needs that span independently hosted websites. This is done by seamlessly personalizing the support offered to each individual user, as they browse across multiple websites, by modeling the user's interactions and then augmenting information access points, such as links, on each independent website. Cross-Site Personalization is realized as a third-party API offering Personalisation As a Service to ensure cross-site and cross-device usage. The personalized augmentations are provided through module extensions for the Web-based Content Management Systems (WCMS) Drupal. The approach is non-intrusive and does not limit or alter the user's information access paradigm. This is done by visually augmenting the existing hyperlinks on webpages. The design of the API ensures user's privacy by not disclosing personal browsing information to the websites. Rather, this approach recommends how each website may adapt their information and navigation structures to meet user's information needs. Finally, the approach ensures user control and scrutiny. The user can enable/disable CSP at any time and view any information collected. The evaluation of the approach was conducted with a real-world use case. This paper introduces the architecture, a prototype implementation and encouraging evaluation results.

Keywords

Web Personalization, Information Access, Hyperlink Augmentation, Adaptive Hypermedia, User Privacy, User Model Scrutiny and Control, User Experience, Adaptive Linking, Networked User Engagement.

HT'14, September 1–4, 2014, Santiago, Chile.
Copyright © 2014 ACM 978-1-4503-2954-5/14/09...$15.00.
http://dx.doi.org/10.1145/2631775.2631798

1. INTRODUCTION

The Web has become an essential commodity within modern societies allowing the access, creation, management and distribution of vast amounts of information. This has lead to an information explosion and has resulted in an increased difficulty to organize digital information based on the user's current and constantly changing information needs. To allow users to find and use information most effectively, it is essential to develop novel and innovative personalised assistance approaches helping the user find and explore relevant information. Several publications across different research areas, such as library and information science [1][2], cognitive science [3], social science [4] and medical science [5] have voiced this need, and the failure to address it properly can result in increased costs to the economy and the wider society [6].

In recent years, computer science has addressed this challenge by introducing systems that assist the user's information needs by applying a user model reflecting the users interests. Examples of systems using an interest focused user model are keyword-based search engines [7][8][14], browser based support mechanisms, such as bookmarking and browsing history tools [9][10], recommender systems to identify and recommend content related to the user's current interest [11] and Web personalization techniques that adapt different aspects of the web experience to the needs and preferences of the individual user and based on a individual user model [12][13]. In addition collaborative approaches were introduced. The main difference is that collaborative approaches implement a *'People that like x also liked y'* approach. One example is Amazon's product recommendations service [25][50]. A second example is Facebook's *'socially connect'* to recommend content that friends and peers 'like' [15].

Even though current approaches are successful in providing fast and accurate results for simple information needs, such as finding information related to a product via personalised search or collaborative recommendation system, most approaches cannot assist the user in more complex needs. For example, if a user's information needs span different subject domains, the user may need to gather information from several independently hosted websites. This cross-site browsing process can introduce friction based on different website layouts the user has to adapt to in order to identify the relevancy of the navigation choices presented [29][42]. To reduce this friction a browsing support approach is required that can unify the mostly fractured browsing experience across independent and unrelated websites [39]. Moreover users may choose to use multiple browsers and devices to address more complex information needs. Therefore, any supporting approach has to ensure that the user remains free in her choice of information access (not limiting the browsing space) and her choice in browser/device; thus not limiting the browsing process to a specific browser based plugin and/or device.

This paper introduces an overarching, service-based approach towards assisting the user in information needs that span independently hosted websites.

This paper is organized as follows. This introduction is followed by a discussion related to background and related work. After this design considerations are introduced that allow the addressing of the discussed challenges. This is followed by a brief discussion of the implementation. Finally, evaluation results are discussed.

2. BACKGROUND AND RELATED WORK

Providing personalized browsing support across independent websites is difficult due to the lack of communication between the websites. This can lead to a browsing experience that is mostly confined within a website; thus if a user is gathering information about a specific topic on one website and then decides to browse to a different website, the latter will not be informed about the user's previous information needs [16][17]. Furthermore any personalization techniques used by one websites will not be able to assist the user in relation a wider information needs across a second (independent) website. The effect of this siloing of information and personalization techniques can lead to the repetition of user actions, such as keyword based search queries, and navigational patterns throughout the different websites, such repetitive interaction is both frustrating and time consuming for the user [18].

A key challenge therefore remains in providing Web personalization techniques that assist users across the web and not only on isolated Websites. To address this problem Web personalization techniques have to balance both the needs of the website user and website publishers. For website users the introduced Web personalization technique should provide assistance across different websites, but in doing so honor the user's privacy needs and browsing freedom. For the website publisher the introduced Web personalization techniques should include simple and cost effective integration of Web personalization to existing websites and honor the website owner's control over the website. For example a publisher might want to ensure specific content is promoted based on commercial goals even if it the content does not reflect the current interest of the website user. Motivated by the discussion above following Figure 1 illustrates a high-level abstraction of the problem space a Cross-Site Personalisation (CSP) approach needs to addresses.

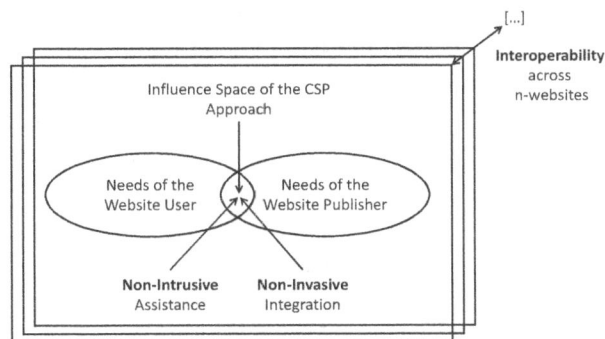

Figure 1 Cross-Site Personalisation Abstraction

Based on this illustration (Figure 1) it can be argued that a CSP approach requires influencing both areas (needs of the website user and website publishers) simultaneous and in real-time by creating a *state of equilibrium* in which the needs of the user and the website publisher are balanced. This state is introduced as *Equilibrium of Web Personalisation*. To ensure the needs of both sides are addressed adequately this paper argues that the resulting CSP assistance should be non-intrusive [37][38][40] for the user (not limiting the users free browsing paradigm) and non-invasive on the website (ensuring simple, light weight integration).

Within non-intrusive personalisation approaches three techniques stand out: Information Retrieval [51][22], Recommender Systems [50] and Rule Engine based techniques [52]. All three techniques have proven successful in personalization use cases, with limited impact on the users free browsing paradigm.

However, these techniques are not distinct, for example Content-based Recommender Systems are often based on Information Retrieval techniques [26][53]. Furthermore, many non-intrusive approaches have been extended towards personalisation since they have been introduced [54]. However, the main shortcoming of non-intrusive approaches still is the lacking focus on specific user needs and preferences. Most approaches apply a more generalized data driven approach resulting a 'User that viewed this page also viewed following pages' personalization scenario.

In relation to introducing CSP to websites in a non-invasive manner, two approaches can be discussed: (1) Non-Invasive integration of web personalisation techniques at design-time and (2) non-invasive integration of web personalisation at run-time.

Non-invasive integration at design-time refers the research and application field of Web Engineering, which addresses the shortcoming of integrating techniques and methods to existing websites. Here, a structured modularization of the website development process is introduced [55]. This process relies on modeling the overall website based on software engineering principals. Several web engineering design methods were introduced. The main design methods introduced are OOHDM [56], UWE [57] and OOWS [58]. In addition data modeling approaches, such as WebML [59] and WebRatio [60] were introduced as model-driven engineering environments.

The advantage of Web Engineering is in relying on strict design methodologies. For example OOHDM (Object Oriented Hypermedia Design Method) has following phases: requirements gathering, conceptual design, navigational design, abstract interface design and implementation. The result is UML like diagrams and re-usable design pattern. Most Web Engineering approaches include functionalities that assist the user in finding and exploring information. This includes techniques discussed above, such as Information Retrieval and Recommendation Systems [54].

The main shortcoming of Web Engineering is lack in flexibility in extending the websites functionality beyond what has been stated in the websites setup design. Furthermore any extension towards CSP would have to be considered in the early conceptual phase with limited flexibility during run-time.

In contrast the integration of personalisation methods and techniques at run-time is even more challenging. The main reason is the missing understanding of the interdependencies within a website. A promising approach is the use of website frameworks. Such frameworks are often referred to as Web Information Systems (WIS) and allow the implementation of an entire website as out-of-the-box deployment [61][62]. In certain environments this approach enables non-invasive extensibility during run-time.

However, WIS are traditionally proprietary software products limiting the extensibility without the vendors help and/or approval. A promising solution to this limitation are Web-based Content Management Systems (WCMS). They allow a simple and more flexible implementation, based on their Open-Source nature. The most important feature of WCMS is the extendable framework, which allows external modules to influence different level of the functional layer of the website without the need of re-design or re-deployment. The main shortcomings of WCMS are a lack of strict and coherent coding guidelines and documentations.

Applying CSP to WCMS provides the added benefit of giving the website owner control in deciding what area of the website should be affected by the link guidance provided by the CSP service.

A further related research area is known as Adaptive Hypermedia (AH). AH traditionally focuses on problems known as *information explosion* [27][28] and its resulting phenomena known as *information overload* [30][31] and *lost in hyperspace* [32]. The former refers to the user being overwhelmed by the amount of information choices. The latter refers to orientation difficulties of the user within and across different websites.

AH approaches seek to assist the user in addressing such phenomena by tailoring the web experience to the specific needs and preferences of the user (or a set of users) and at the same time avoid that the user is limited in its information freedom [19][20]. This is done by providing the information users want or need without expecting them to ask for it explicitly [21][23]. Methods and techniques enabling Web personalization have become important for both research and commercial applications [21][24]. Especially in domain specific application, such as e-Learning, the use of AH techniques and methods have been proven to be successful by increasing the learning performance of the student [33][35].

This domain focus however has also lead to a shortcoming known as the open-corpus problem described as: '*The problem to provide adaptation within a set of documents that is not known at design time and, moreover, can constantly change and expand*' [34][36].

This paper argues that the open-corpus problem of AH needs to be extended towards the *open-web problem* of AH for it to reflect personalization on the open web by adding '[…] *and which may reside in individually hosted websites on the open web.*'

To address the open-web problem of personalization this paper discusses the concept of Cross-Site Personalization (CSP) as a process in which a web user is individually assisted in addressing information needs that span independently hosted websites.

Finally, in relation to web personalization privacy and trust related issues have been discussed extensively [41][63]. A major shortcoming of AH and web personalization in general is the danger of filtering the information in a way that is not in the interest of the user; thus limiting the users information space. A typical solution is to provide transparency. This has been introduced by [40] as user model scrutiny. Here, the main limitation is related to the visualization of the model. The discussion of information visualisation however is out of scope for this paper. For an in-depth discussion about model visualization strategies see [40] and [64].

The following section introduces the architecture of the proposed CSP approach.

3. CSP ARCHITECTURE OVERVIEW

This architecture provides the conceptual basis for an introduced prototype implementation. The goal of the introduced architectural overview is to illustrate the responsibilities and capabilities of the different architectural components. In the following high-level architecture (Figure 2) is proposed and subsequently discussed.

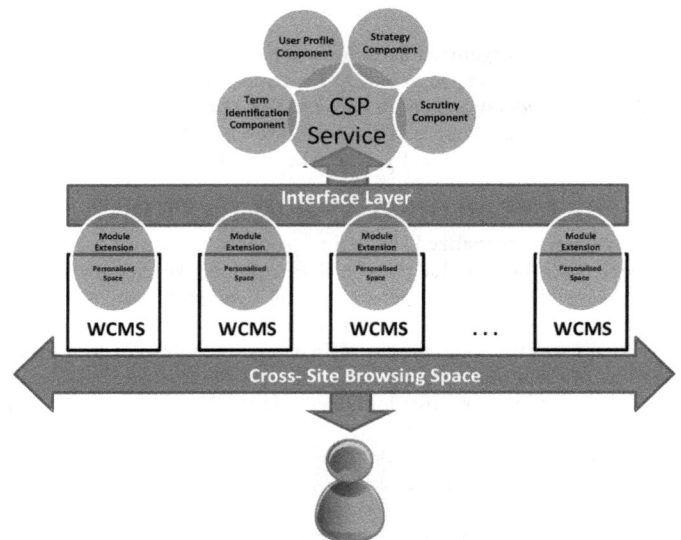

Figure 2 High-Level CSP architecture

3.1 Term Identification Component

The term identification component of the CSP architecture has the responsibility to facilitate the identification of terms. The terms indicate the meaning of the underlying content from the websites within the cross-site browsing space. This identification can be a result of using already existing (editorial) terms provided by the website or by using additional Natural Language Processing services/tools to identify terms (e.g. OpenCalais[1]). The main responsibility of this component is to ensure the creation of a *shared conceptualization* of the user's CSP enabled browsing space. This shared conceptualization is represented as term space and is based on the terms extracted from the content of the websites the user is browsing across. Once the terms are identified they can be used by the user profile component to represent the user's information needs. Furthermore, the term identification component requires means to facilitate continuous content updates to ensure the shared conceptualization of the user's cross-site browsing space is up-to-date. For this the term identification component needs access to the content on the different websites. Within the interface layer of this architecture it is proposed that the website sends the content to the website that is to be used for CSP. This ensures the independence of the approach from the websites.

3.2 User Profile Component

The user profile component is responsible for the correct storage and aggregation of terms related to the content the user is browsing. These terms are provided by the term identification component and are stored together with the engagement activity the user is conducting on the content. This activity can include

---

[1] http://www.opencalais.com/

mouse clicks, scrolls and keyboard presses. Together the terms and the activity form the base to create an informed decision by the strategy component. Furthermore, the terms are used within the Scrutiny Component to enable the representation of the user's profile. The User Profile Component requires the identification of the user. This identification can either be provided directly by the website or by a sign-on mechanism, such as OAuth.

3.3 Strategy Component

The strategy component is responsible to provide an *informed decision* to the website the user is currently browsing. An informed decision assists a website to identify relevant links based on the users overall cross-site browsing. It implements a decision process that facilitates elements of the user's current user profile and relates this with the current website the user is browsing. The resulting *informed decision* allows a website to receive relevant information to provide adaptive guidance based on the user's overall information needs. The component implements techniques that ensure fast and flexible calculation of an informed decision. The calculation has to take the users recent and long-term user engagement into account and also takes a depreciation factor is taken into account. This allows long terms interests to be reflected but not as strong as recent interests. Finally, the strategy component has to ensure that the user's privacy is honored. This is achieved by not passing any information related to the users cross-site needs to individual website. The design approach followed here is to allow the service to provide information on the relevancy of links, but to not provide information on why the links are relevant. The informed decision is closely linked with website extension. These extensions allow the simple application of CSP based on the informed decision.

3.4 Scrutiny Component

The scrutiny component addresses requirements related to privacy, trust and control needs of the user. It allows users to access their user profile and to influence the profile. Furthermore the user can receive information on where and how the user related data was collected and used. In its basic implementation the scrutiny component allows the visualisation of the terms that correspond to the webpage the user has accessed. Furthermore size of the terms can indicate the relevancy of the terms based on the users engagement with the different websites. This is visualized as term cloud that can be only accessed by the user.

3.5 Interface Layer

The interface layer provides an abstraction from the specific implementation of the different websites within the user's cross-site browsing space. For this it implements a RESTful API (Advanced Programming Interface) to facilitate the communication between the CSP Service and the websites the user is browsing. A key responsibility of the API is to ensure that the interface with the CSP approach is device independent and does not depend on a specific technology stack. Furthermore, it ensures fast and accurate interconnectivity between the interfacing websites and the CSP Service. The API can either interface with a website through bespoke integration or through provided website extensions.

3.6 Web-based Content Management System Module Extensions

Web-based Content Management Systems (WCMS) module[2] extensions allow a simple and non-invasive integration of CSP to existing website implementations. The responsibility of the WCMS module extensions is twofold: (1) To facilitate the communication between the website and the API of the CSP Service and (2) to provide non-intrusive personalization's to the user, within the website the user is currently browsing, based on an informed decision from the CSP Service. By using WCMS extensions it can be assured that CSP provides non-intrusive assistance for the user and non-invasive integration in existing websites (during run-time).

3.7 Cross-Site Browsing Space

The application of CSP to independently hosted websites introduces a Cross-Site Personalization Browsing Space. Within the browsing space the user receives CSP through navigational assistance. The navigational assistance is enabled either through direct integration with the API of the CSP service or by using the above introduces website extensions. Based on the back-end integration of the CSP service with the website it is possible that the user decides when the CSP is enabled and when disabled. This allows the user to control the mechanism and ensures the user's privacy is honored. The enabling/disabling of the service can either be facilitated though the user signing into the website or by directly signing into the service.

The following section discusses implementation considerations of the above-introduced CSP architecture.

4. IMPLEMENTATION

This section describes the technological architecture required for CSP based on the architectural overview discussed in the previous section. Figure 2 has been extended with implementation details (see Figure 3). In the following the implementation decisions of the different components are discussed.

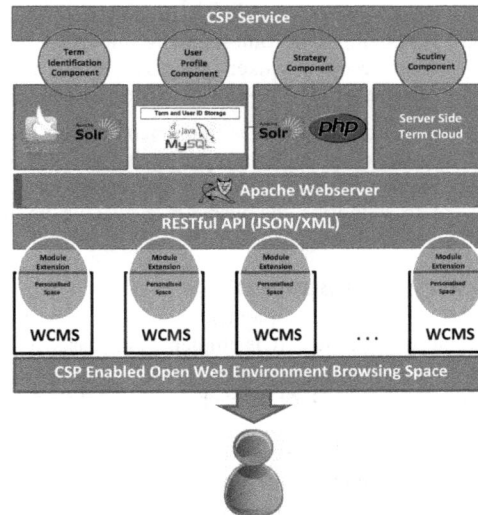

Figure 3 Implementation Overview of CSP

---

[2] For this research the WCMS Drupal (https://drupal.org/) was used.

4.1 Term Identification Component

The term identification component enables term identification as a constant and fast process. Furthermore it allows the identification of terms across several different subject domains, possibly including different languages. Based on this an extendible architecture was implemented. This allows the adding of additional external term identification services. Due to its reliability the current iteration of the CSP approach interfaces with OpenCalais[3]. An addition investigation was conducted in implementing a solution that provides the same flexibility and maturity as an external term identification service, but is deployable within the CSP Service. OpenNLP[4] was identified as one possible solution. However, it requires an extensive training phase and relies on pre-set (domain specific) content to train the service. Based on this shortcoming the Apache Stanbol Project[5] was investigated. It implements a pre-trained OpenNLP instance. However, at the time this research was conducted the project was still in incubation phase.

The process of term identification is initialized as soon as a website enables CSP (based on this topic by deploying an enabling the CSP extension module). After the website publisher enables the CSP module the module sends the content body, title, path id and any associated terms of the openly accessible content to the API of the CSP Service. The service then requests the term identification from OpenCalais for the content body sent, which returns social tags associated with a relevancy of either 0.5 or 1. The CSP Service stores the identified terms and the identified relevancy together with the path and website id. The CSP Service therefore implements a table representing all terms identified from the content of the CSP enabled website.

4.2 User Profile Component

The user profile is stored in MySQL and stores the terms related to the user's page views and related browsing activities on the page. A user activity is represented by a unique user id, a unique website id, the content path within the website, a list of the inferred terms related to the content path, scroll counter, click counter, touches counter, cut-and-paste counter, key pressed counter and timestamp. The timestamp is important to indicate when the last page access has taken place. This allows the strategy component to ensure more up-to-date activities are prioritized.

For user identification OAuth[6] was implemented. This mechanism allows the website to remain open by allowing the user to sign-in to the CSP Service via the website. Furthermore the approach enables users to authorize the website to receive an informed decision to assist the user.

4.3 Strategy Component

The strategy component implements an information retrieval query generation approach. It is implemented based on Apache Solr[7] and uses the existing content index built by the Term Identification Service. Once a website requests an informed decision the strategy component requests the user's current profile terms and the calculated relevancy of the terms. The terms and the related weight are used to create a query on the stored index of the

website that requested the informed decision. The result list is filtered based on the links the website has requested an informed decision for. The result of the filtering is a list containing links and the calculated relevancy (based on the relative position within the result list). The usage of IR was chosen due to its flexibility in relation to term usage and its performance.

Finally, in relation to data privacy requirements it is important to note that no terms are sent to the different websites. The website only receives a list of links with related relevancy indications.

4.4 Scrutiny Component

The scrutiny component allows the user to see the terms in the user profile together with the indicated relevancy as size. For this a word cloud can be used.

4.5 WCMS Client Integration

To enable a website to offer CSP to their users, a custom build Drupal 7 module extension was deployed.[8] The role of the module is:

1. To enable initial term identification within the CSP Service by sending content to the CSP Service.

2. To provide a sign-in mechanism for users to enable CSP. This sign-in is provided on the website the user wants to enable CSP on and is implemented via the CMS plugin. An additional sign-in is provided on the service website where the user can see and manage their user profile.

3. To enable user behavior tracking once the user has signed in.

4. To provide non-invasive visual assistance once the user is signed in and has authorized the website to receive an informed decision for CSP.

5. To send content updates to the CSP Service on a regular base independent from user being signed in or not.

6. Request an informed decision from the CSP Service.

Based on the API approach taken by the CSP Service the deployment of extensible modules is not necessary i.e. the website publisher and or the wider open-source community can chose to write addition website extensions/plug-ins. However, using the provided extension significantly decreases integration time and based on the extensive research in relation to non-intrusive visual assistance ensures that the user need in not being aversively guided or controlled is addressed.

The WCMS module extension is focused on a menu structure that is introduced as separate element or replacing element on a Drupal powered website. The website publisher therefore can replace the standard menu element with the CSP enabled menu element. The menu area looks identical and only is affected if the user enables CSP. The menu structure is tied in with the request of an informed decision. In this use case implementation the influence of the CSP Service is confined to the CSP enabled menu. Therefore the informed decision influences only links within the CSP enabled menu. Prior to rendering the webpage after the user has clicked the CSP module sends the links that the user will see on the resulting webpage to the CSP Service. The CSP Service generates an informed decision that is rendered within the CSP enabled menu.

---

[3] http://www.opencalais.com/

[4] http://opennlp.apache.org/

[5] http://stanbol.apache.org/

[6] http://oauth.net/

[7] http://lucene.apache.org/solr/

---

[8] Drupal was used in this use case implementation based on its wide adoption.

5. EVALUATION

This evaluation section introduces the result of a use case based user study in the tourism sector.

5.1 Experimental Setup

This experiment focused on a use case in the tourism space. The content was provided by Failte Ireland and is used live[9]. The experiment consisted of three websites. The first website acted as entry website and was based on health and fitness related content in the four activities Golfing, Hiking, Walking and Cycling. The purpose of the entry website was to train the users profile to enable CSP across the remaining two websites. The two additional websites were related to tourism and were deployed each relating to different locations (Killarney and Dingle). Each website was hosted as a separate WCMS implementation with different templates to ensure a different look and feel on each website. To evaluate the effect of CSP on the user's performance and to assess the self-reported feedback it was conducted as a between-subject experiment, with each cohort consisting of equal numbers. Each participant was randomly assigned to the CSP enabled or CSP disabled group. Two different system settings were used. The first system setting consisted of all four websites with CSP enabled the second with all four websites CSP disabled. The underlying websites including the layout and content were equal in both system settings.

Overall 60 participants took part in the user-focused study. The participants were sourced through school mailing lists and black board notices throughout Trinity College Dublin. The experiment was conducted in a closed lab environment to reduce distraction, and allowing further feedback through an unstructured interview. The evaluation data was collected through questionnaires, system logging and unstructured interviews.

The duration of each evaluation was approximately one hour and the overall evaluation including the two-phased design study was conducted over a timeframe of six months. One of the goals of the evaluation was to ensure the experiment setup was as natural as possible. To ensure a realistic browsing environment the tasks were based on real-world fact gathering tasks and the experiment environment was set up without any intrusive recording devices.

Each participant was asked to conduct one browsing tasks related to planning a holiday around the activity of Golf. The goal of the experiment was to explore and collect information that would allow the participant to convince friends that a holiday around the activity Golf is worth pursuing. After filling out the ethics form and informing the participant what information will be recorded, a short description of the task was presented. The participant was asked to provide all answers in handwritten form to ensure the participants were able to answer the task questions without interrupting the browsing setup (which would have been necessary in an online form). Finally, the participant was given a chance to ask questions. Once the participant was ready to start, task time was recorded and the examiner left the room. The participant was asked to stop the clock once the task was completed and then call the examiner back into the room.

After the task the participants were asked to complete an online survey with 22 questions. The cohort with the personalised setting was asked to fill out a second short paper questionnaire with the examiner in the room in order to trigger open questions and responses in relation to the introduced CSP approach. For this the participant was made aware of the introduced approach.

5.1.1 Baseline Comparison

The experiment was conducted comparatively as a between-subject design. Each cohort was presented with a total of three independently hosted websites. The first website was used to train the participant's profile. The latter two evaluated the appropriateness of the CSP approach. All three websites were hosting real world content in the area of recreation and tourism. The baseline system was deployed without any personalization features enabled. From the participants perspective there was a difference how the side menu presented links. The CSP enabled websites implemented a green link annotation icon beside every link in the menu. Each annotation icon was filled depending on the level of relevance the link had (based on a relevancy scale from 1-10). All other website features were identical. The following discussion of the findings is split into user performance and self-reported feedback. Note following image (Figure 4) for an overview of the annotations used.

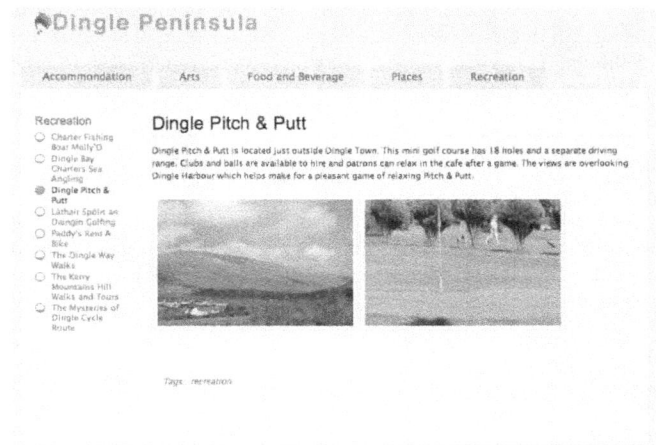

Figure 4 Open domain use case example

The annotations were implemented as green icons in the menu structure on the left hand side. This annotation was consistent across all websites ensuring the user was able to become familiar with the approach. It also has to be noted that only annotations were used. This forms an overlay on the existing visualisation of the page without applying content filtering or sorting. The icon was chosen based on user trials with different shapes and relevancy indications.

5.1.2 Results User Performance

The findings related to the user's performance is divided into click-related and time-related findings.

Click-related Findings

To discuss the influence of the CSP approach on the click behavior of the user, the overall clicks were analyzed.

The comparison of the total clicks (without outliers and including repeated page views) within the cohort assessing the CSP enabled websites was 173 vs. 268 in the CSP disabled websites. The individual results were 83 (enabled) vs. 111 (disabled) clicks in the first 'Health and Fitness' website, 52 (enabled) vs. 99 (disabled) in the Killarney website and 38 (enabled) vs. 58 clicks (disabled) in the final website 'Dingle'.

---

[9] http://www.discoverireland.ie

To further investigate this encouraging result the average clicks of each individual website were compared.

The highest difference in the mean value was in the 'Killarney' website. To identify if the difference in the mean values are statistically significant a t-test assuming equal variances with a hypothesized mean difference of 0 was conducted. The corresponding p-value resulted in 0.169 for 'Health and Fitness', 0.003 for 'Killarney' and 0.448 for Dingle concluding that there is a significant difference between the mean click values of 'Killarney' in both cohorts. A reason for this difference may lie in the fact that each website presented a different amount of links the participant could choose. On the 'Health and Fitness' website all five links were relevant. The Killarney website participants were presented with 14 links of which 4 were relevant. In the Dingle website 8 links were displayed of which 2 were relevant. The significant difference in the decrease of clicks in the crossover from the first to the second website can be judged as evidence as a positive impact of CSP on the users performance.

Finally, cumulative data was analyzed. Cumulative observations were not directly comparable with the observations above due to using all three website datasets as one dataset. Therefore the following comparison only serves investigative purposes. Overall the average values resulted in 10.42 clicks (median 9) for the CSP enabled websites and 14.3 clicks (median 12) in the CSP disabled websites.

Task Completion Time

The overall task completion time (in seconds) within the CSP enabled cohort was 23100 and within the CSP disabled cohort 21960. The overall mean times resulted in 1073.8 seconds vs. 933.6 seconds.

Following image (Figure 5) illustrates the overall mean time across the different website.

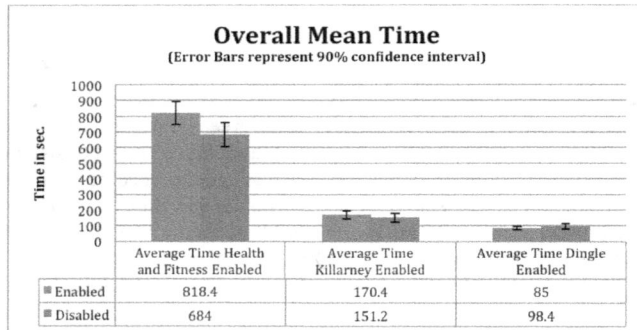

Overall Mean Time
(Error Bars represent 90% confidence interval)

	Average Time Health and Fitness Enabled	Average Time Killarney Enabled	Average Time Dingle Enabled
Enabled	818.4	170.4	85
Disabled	684	151.2	98.4

Figure 5 Overall Mean Times CSP in Open Domains

Interestingly, the gap between the means decreases. This trend is important and possibly indicates a performance increase of the introduced CSP approach as the users continue browsing across separate websites. Most encouraging is the decrease within the last website.

5.1.3 Results Self-Reported Feedback

To gather the self-reported feedback, the participants were asked to provide answers to 26 questions. The questionnaire had the objective of assessing the perceived appropriateness of the CSP approach, and whether it assisted users in addressing information needs in open domains. For this the participants were asked direct and indirect questions. Direct questions addressed key aspects of the CSP approach (e.g. perceived difficulty in browsing) and indirect questions assessed cognitive indicators, such as the perceived motivation and frustration.

The questionnaire was presented on a custom made online interface. The participants were presented with a slider to provide the answer on a scale from 0-100. Each participant was presented with visual markers at 0 for strongly disagree, 25 for disagree, 50 for neutral, 75 for agree and 100 for strongly agree. Yes and no questions were binary (0 for yes and 100 for no).

To assess the overall perceived mood of the participants both the perceived effect of the CSP approach on frustration and motivation was queried. The result indicated no statistically significant difference between both cohorts although with the average being slightly higher for the participants assessing the CSP enabled websites (averages 15.28 vs. 19.46 and median 15 vs. 11). The low level of frustration coincided with a high-level of motivation with the average of the CSP enabled websites feedback slightly higher (averages 80.29 vs. 74.93 and median 85 vs. 76).

To assess if the task was appropriate the participants were asked if the task reflected a real-world cross-site browsing task. Most users agreed with similar means in both cohorts (averages 75.52 vs. 76.65 and median 76 vs. 77). This result is encouraging and indicates that the participants were not negatively biased due to the pre-set nature of the task and the unnatural browsing setting with a lab.

To assess the appropriateness of the CSP approach participants were asked to rate the perceived influence of system guidance. As mentioned in the experiment setup, no participant was informed about the CSP approach prior to the experiment. The result is therefore encouraging (average 79.55 vs. 59.41 and median 78 vs. 58) with the mean being significantly higher than the CSP disabled (p-value of 0.0006). This result can be interpreted, as a key finding in relation to the participant's perceived appropriateness of the approach to assist in cross-site information needs.

A further encouraging result was found in the question related to the difficulty in browsing. The answers result in a significant difference towards the CSP enabled system setting (p-value 0.0216) with an average of 24.07 (media 25) in the CSP enabled based feedback and 36.52 in the CSP disabled 36.52 (median 38).

Finally, an interesting result was provided by the participants in the question related to privacy concerns. Here, the cohort assessing the CSP enabled websites indicated a higher average concern than the cohort assessing the CSP disabled websites (59 vs. 55.79 and mean 46 vs. 48). This is surprising given the fact that this question does not directly relate to CSP or the usage of personalization in general. In relation to this research the result can be interpreted as a higher awareness for the CSP approach within the cohort assessing the CSP enabled websites. Furthermore some participants indicated in the open interview at the end of the experiment that they felt watched and/or guided – a perception that might make users more curious about the source or motivation of the approach. Some participants stated they started to trust the guidance after a while and that they look for the visual indication first when accessing a website.

6. CONCLUSION AND FUTURE WORK

This paper discussed Cross-Site Personalization novel approach to assist users in addressing information needs that span independently hosted websites.

The Cross-Site Personalization approach was introduced as third-party API offering Personalisation As a Service. The personalized link augmentations were realized through module extensions for the Web-based Content Management Systems (WCMS) Drupal. The introduced architecture ensures not limiting or altering the users free browsing paradigm. Moreover, the design of the API ensures user's privacy by not disclosing personal browsing information to the websites. Finally, the approach introduced ensures user control and scrutiny by allowing the user to enable/disable the CSP assistance at any time and view any information collected by the service.

A prototype implementation was presented and subsequently evaluated. The evaluation indicated the usefulness and appropriateness of CSP a real-world use case. The results were encouraging motivating following future work.

Additional Use Case Evaluations

To ensure the above-introduced CSP approach can be applied widely on the open web further real-world CSP use cases need to be investigated. The main challenge in identifying such use cases is to ensure that they are motivate by complex information needs that require the user to browse independently hosted websites. These use-cases are among others retail (gathering reviews and feedback related to purchasing a products), e-Learning (gathering information to gain knowledge e.g. informal learning or conducting research projects) and Online Customer Care (gathering information related to solving a problem).

In addition the evaluation of CSP use cases needs further investigation. The above-introduced evaluation was conducted in a controlled lab setting. The main motivation for this was to allow unstructured interviewing and strict measurement of metrics without any distracting or disturbing factors. However, it can be argued that this artificial environment may limit the results. A more natural and familiar environment however would require a much large user group and sufficient A/B testing, which can be both time and resource intense. Moreover due to the different interests and interests of users (which would be uncontrolled in an open scenario) it would be unclear if the user clicked on a link due to a general interest (i.e. would have clicked in any case) or due to the personalized augmentation (i.e. is only clicking because of the augmentation).

On the contrary ensuring full insight the experiment would require the usage of more intrusive observation methods, such as eye tracking and/or video surveillance [44]. However, intrusive observations interfere with the natural open-web browsing behavior of the user. Therefore a balance between more intrusive observation and the participants' natural browsing environment should be found and aligned with additional use cases (possibly using browser plugins tracking users over a prolonged period). These evaluation challenges are not new to the research field of web personalization and have been highlighted throughout different publications [45][47].

Networked User Engagement

Networked user engagement is becoming increasingly popular with lager corporations owning multiple web properties. The most prominent examples are yahoo and AOL [48]. For owners of larger website federations it is becoming increasingly important to both understand and assist the user across the commonly owned web space. Based on the cross-site notion discussed and applied in this paper, future work can be conducted by using large datasets from a larger interconnected set of websites.

User Profile Management and Social Media

The CSP approach presented in this paper allows the user to view their interest model (model scrutiny) that relates to their overall cross-site information needs [49]. Through comments, several participants expressed their interest in actively engaging with their user profile and sharing it with peers and friends.

Flexible Intrusiveness

A core element of this research is to ensure that the introduced approach ensures non-intrusive assistance for the user and non-invasive integration to the website to address website publisher needs. The commonality of both aspects (non-intrusive assistance and non-invasive integration) is to balance the needs and requirement of the user and the website publisher (state of equilibrium). This paper argues that the means to establish this balance has been introduced by CSP. Extensions to the CSP approach could allow this balance to be adjusted to either side. For example the user may opt into more intrusive guidance that in the most extreme could result in a fully personalised website. This is possible due to the approach integrating directly with the website and therefore enabling deeper personalization scenarios. The main challenge related to increased intrusiveness is control. This paper argues that the control of intrusiveness should be based on the user's information needs. This however may conflict with the website publisher's economic need. An example of this conflict could be a user seeking full intrusiveness i.e. a fully guided and personal website, but not seeking any links that are of commercial benefit to the website publisher (such as promoted links, advertisement etc.). To overcome this shortcoming an adjustable or negotiable element could be introduced to the service that indicates the level of intrusiveness a user seeks and the level of invasiveness a website publisher allows.

Mobile and localization

The service-based approach ensures that CSP can be applied on websites rendered on a mobile device. This assists mobile use cases in which a user browses CSP enabled websites on a stationary desktop and then continues to browse the CSP enabled websites on a mobile device. This seamless Cross-Device Personalization can be extended by integrating CSP deeper into the mobile device. This would allow the CSP service to receive information about the user's location, and potentially allow the integration with other app information to enrich the user's cross-site profile and cross-site personalization. This extension might also include using the user's cross-site profile to provide location aware recommendations or by providing different apps with an informed decision.

A further, potentially mobile related, future work is in the context of localization. Specifically the application of CSP across different language sets. This would allow users to avail of CSP assistance on websites hosting content in different languages. An example of this would be in the tourism domain. Here a Non-English speaking user may seek to browse websites hosting in a local language and related to a specific hobby. The user could use CSP to seek visual assistance on English content-based websites, e.g. a tourist location, that match the user's hobby. To enable Cross-Lingual CSP two approaches could be studied. The first would translate all source (e.g. French) language based websites into one target language (e.g. English) and extract terms only from the target language corpus. The other, opposite approach, would be to extract terms in the source languages (e.g. French) and then translate the terms into one target language (e.g. English). Obviously the target language in both cases would relate to the user's mother tongue and/or language preference. Future work in this space relies strongly on the investigation of semi-automated machine translation and multi-language term identification.

Web Narratives

One of the main concepts introduced by CSP is the notion of an *informed decision* that allows websites to provide navigational assistance without compromising the user's privacy.

The main focus of the approach introduced in this paper is focused on assisting the user in exploration and fact gathering based browsing across independently hosted websites. However, in tasks that require a more structured guidance and which may underlie a specific goal or objective, such as informal learning, the approach can be extended towards a more narrative driven decision process. The notion of introducing a narrative has been successfully applied in Adaptive Hypermedia Systems (AHS) traditionally focused on the area of e-Learning [52]. Within AHS the usage of a narrative allows the sequencing of course material based on the course description of a pedagogical expert. This narrative can then be used to populate a course with content based on pre-defined concepts. By overlaying the content concepts with user model concepts a balance between user preferences (e.g. learning goals, current knowledge etc.) and narrative preferences (a defined sequence of the course) [65].

7. ACKNOWLEDGMENTS

This research is supported by the Science Foundation Ireland (Grant 07/CE/I1142) as part of the Centre for Next Generation Localization (www.cngl.ie) at Trinity College Dublin. We would like to acknowledge the contributions made by Symantec and Failte Ireland in relation to providing content.

8. REFERENCES

[1] D. O. Case, Looking for Information: A Survey of Research on Information Seeking, Needs, and Behavior. Emerald Group Publishing, 2012.

[2] H. F. Korth and A. Silberschatz, "Database research faces the information explosion," Commun ACM, vol. 40, no. 2, pp. 139–142, Feb. 1997.

[3] M. D. Kirchhoff, "Enaction: Toward a New Paradigm for Cognitive Science," Philos. Psychol., vol. 26, no. 1, pp. 163–167, 2013.

[4] Y.-C. Chen, R. A. Shang, and C. Y. Kao, "The effects of information overload on consumers' subjective state towards buying decision in the internet shopping environment," Electron. Commer. Res. Appl., vol. 8, no. 1, pp. 48–58, Jan. 2009.

[5] P. Epstein, "Beyond information: Exploring patients' preferences," JAMA J. Am. Med. Assoc., vol. 302, no. 2, pp. 195–197, Jul. 2009.

[6] A. Edmunds and A. Morris, "The problem of information overload in business organisations: a review of the literature," Int. J. Inf. Manag., vol. 20, no. 1, pp. 17–28, Feb. 2000.

[7] S. Brin and L. Page, "The anatomy of a large-scale hypertextual Web search engine," Comput. Networks ISDN Syst., vol. 30, no. 1–7, pp. 107–117, Apr. 1998.

[8] A. Broder, "A taxonomy of web search," SIGIR Forum, vol. 36, no. 2, pp. 3–10, Sep. 2002.

[9] M. G. Noll and C. Meinel, "Web Search Personalization Via Social Bookmarking and Tagging," in The Semantic Web, vol. 4825, K. Aberer, K.-S. Choi, N. Noy, D. Allemang, K.-I. Lee, L. Nixon, J. Golbeck, P. Mika, D. Maynard, R. Mizoguchi, G. Schreiber, and P. Cudré-Mauroux, Eds. Berlin, Heidelberg: Springer Berlin Heidelberg, 2007, pp. 367–380.

[10] P. Heymann, G. Koutrika, and H. Garcia-Molina, "Can social bookmarking improve web search?," in Proceedings of the international conference on Web search and web data mining, New York, NY, USA, 2008, pp. 195–206.

[11] G. Adomavicius and A. Tuzhilin, "Toward the next generation of recommender systems: a survey of the state-of-the-art and possible extensions," IEEE Trans. Knowl. Data Eng., vol. 17, no. 6, pp. 734– 749, Jun. 2005.

[12] S. S. Anand and B. Mobasher, "Intelligent Techniques for Web Personalization," in Intelligent Techniques for Web Personalization, vol. 3169, B. Mobasher and S. S. Anand, Eds. Berlin, Heidelberg: Springer Berlin Heidelberg, 2005, pp. 1–36.

[13] M. Gao, K. Liu, and Z. Wu, "Personalisation in web computing and informatics: Theories, techniques, applications, and future research," Inf. Syst. Front., vol. 12, no. 5, pp. 607–629, Jul. 2009.

[14] M. Speretta and S. Gauch, "Personalized search based on user search histories," in The 2005 IEEE/WIC/ACM International Conference on Web Intelligence, 2005. Proceedings, 2005, pp. 622 – 628.

[15] A. Dieberger, P. Dourish, K. Höök, P. Resnick, and A. Wexelblat, "Social navigation: techniques for building more usable systems," interactions, vol. 7, no. 6, pp. 36–45, Nov. 2000.

[16] P. Brusilovsky and M. T. Maybury, "From adaptive hypermedia to the adaptive web," Commun ACM, vol. 45, no. 5, pp. 30–33, 2002.

[17] F. Abel, E. Herder, G.-J. Houben, N. Henze, and D. Krause, "Cross-system user modeling and personalization on the social web," User Model. User-Adapt. Interact., vol. 23, no. 2–3, pp. 169–209, 2013.

[18] H. A. Feild, J. Allan, and R. Jones, "Predicting searcher frustration," in Proceeding of the 33rd international ACM SIGIR conference on Research and development in information retrieval, Geneva, Switzerland, 2010, pp. 34–41.

[19] E. Pariser, The filter bubble: What the Internet is hiding from you. Penguin Press HC, 2011.

[20] T. O'Callaghan, "Eli Pariser: The dark side of web personalisation," New Sci., vol. 211, no. 2822, p. 23, Jul. 2011.

[21] B. Mobasher, R. Cooley, and J. Srivastava, "Automatic personalization based on Web usage mining," Commun ACM, vol. 43, no. 8, pp. 142–151, Aug. 2000.

[22] K. Keenoy and M. Levene, "Personalisation of Web Search," in Intelligent Techniques for Web Personalization, vol. 3169, B. Mobasher and S. Anand, Eds. Springer Berlin / Heidelberg, 2005, pp. 201–228.

[23] M. D. Mulvenna, S. S. Anand, and A. G. Büchner, "Personalization on the Net using Web mining: introduction," Commun ACM, vol. 43, no. 8, pp. 122–125, Aug. 2000.

[24] S. Liewehr and M. Laplante, "Understanding Best Practices for Profiling, Personalizing, and Targeting Next Generation Engagement." Gilbane, Aug-2011.

[25] N. Nanas, A. Roeck, and M. Vavalis, "What Happened to Content-Based Information Filtering?," in Advances in Information Retrieval Theory, vol. 5766, L. Azzopardi, G. Kazai, S. Robertson, S. Rüger, M. Shokouhi, D. Song, and

E. Yilmaz, Eds. Berlin, Heidelberg: Springer Berlin Heidelberg, 2009, pp. 249–256.

[26] N. J. Belkin and W. B. Croft, "Information filtering and information retrieval: two sides of the same coin?," Commun ACM, vol. 35, no. 12, pp. 29–38, Dec. 1992.

[27] M. J. Rudd and J. Rudd, "The Impact of the Information Explosion on Library Users: Overload or Opportunity?," J. Acad. Librariansh., vol. 12, no. 5, pp. 304–06, 1986.

[28] L. Sweeney, Zayatz, P., and Doyle, J., Information Explosion. Confidentiality, Disclosure, and Data Access: Theory and Practical Applications for Statistical Agencies. Urban Institute, 2001.

[29] J. Sweller, "Cognitive load during problem solving: Effects on learning," Cogn. Sci., vol. 12, no. 2, pp. 257–285, 1988.

[30] A. Edmunds and A. Morris, "The problem of information overload in business organisations: a review of the literature," Int. J. Inf. Manag., vol. 20, no. 1, pp. 17–28, Feb. 2000.

[31] H. Berghel, "Cyberspace 2000: dealing with information overload," Commun ACM, vol. 40, no. 2, pp. 19–24, Feb. 1997.

[32] D. M. Edwards and L. Hardman, "Lost in hyperspace: cognitive mapping and navigation in a hypertext environment," pp. 90–105, 1999.

[33] P. Brusilovsky, "Adaptive Hypermedia," User Model. User-Adapt. Interact., vol. 11, no. 1–2, pp. 87–110, 2001.

[34] C. Bailey, W. Hall, D. E. Millard, and M. J. Weal, "Towards Open Adaptive Hypermedia," in AH, 2002, pp. 36–46.

[35] Conlan and Wade, "Evaluation of APeLS–an adaptive eLearning service based on the multi-model, metadata-driven approach," in Adaptive Hypermedia and Adaptive Web-Based Systems, 2004, pp. 291–295.

[36] P. Brusilovsky and N. Henze, "Open Corpus Adaptive Educational Hypermedia," Adapt. Web, vol. 4321/2007, pp. 671–696, 2007.

[37] F. Bohnert and I. Zukerman, "Non-intrusive personalisation of the museum experience," User Model. Adapt. Pers., pp. 197–209, 2009.

[38] K. Koidl, O. Conlan, and V. Wade, "Non-Invasive Adaptation Service for Web-based Content Management Systems," in International Workshop on Dynamic and Adaptive Hypertext: Generic Frameworks, Approaches and Techniques, Torino, Italy, 2009.

[39] B. Berendt and M. Spiliopoulou, "Analysis of navigation behaviour in web sites integrating multiple information systems," VLDB J., vol. 9, no. 1, p. 56, 2000.

[40] J. Kay, Scrutable Adaptation: Because We Can and Must. 2006.

[41] S. Y. X. Komiak and I. Benbasat, "The effects of personalization and familiarity on trust and adoption of recommendation agents," Mis Q., pp. 941–960, 2006.

[42] J. Park and J. Kim, "Effects of contextual navigation aids on browsing diverse Web systems," in Proceedings of the SIGCHI conference on Human Factors in Computing Systems, The Hague, The Netherlands, 2000, pp. 257–264.

[43] J. Brooke, "SUS-A quick and dirty usability scale," Usability Eval. Ind., vol. 189, p. 194, 1996.

[44] D. Hauger, A. Paramythis, and S. Weibelzahl, "Using browser interaction data to determine page reading behavior," User Model. Adapt. Pers., pp. 147–158, 2011.

[45] A. Paramythis, S. Weibelzahl, and J. Masthoff, "Layered evaluation of interactive adaptive systems: framework and formative methods," User Model. User-Adapt. Interact., vol. 20, no. 5, pp. 383–453, Dec. 2010.

[46] M. S. Bernstein, M. S. Ackerman, E. H. Chi, and R. C. Miller, "The trouble with social computing systems research," in Proceedings of the 2011 annual conference extended abstracts on Human factors in computing systems, 2011, pp. 389–398.

[47] R. Kohavi, A. Deng, B. Frasca, R. Longbotham, T. Walker, and Y. Xu, "Trustworthy online controlled experiments: five puzzling outcomes explained," in Proceedings of the 18th ACM SIGKDD international conference on Knowledge discovery and data mining, 2012, pp. 786–794.

[48] J. Lehmann, M. Lalmas, R. Baeza-Yates, and E. Yom-Tov, "Networked User Engagement."

[49] F. Abel, N. Henze, E. Herder, and D. Krause, "Interweaving Public User Profiles on the Web," in UMAP, 2010, pp. 16–27.

[50] Linden, Greg, Brent Smith, and Jeremy York. "Amazon. com recommendations: Item-to-item collaborative filtering." Internet Computing, IEEE 7.1 (2003): 76-80.

[51] M. Feuz, M. Fuller, and F. Stalder. Personal Web Searching in the Age of Semantic Capitalism: Diagnosing the Mechanisms of Personalisation. First Monday, 16(2), 2011.

[52] Conlan, Owen, and Vincent P. Wade. "Evaluation of APeLS–an adaptive eLearning service based on the multi-model, metadata-driven approach." Adaptive Hypermedia and Adaptive Web-Based Systems. Springer Berlin Heidelberg, 2004.

[53] Michael J. Pazzani and Daniel Billsus. 2007. Content-based recommendation systems. In The adaptive web, Peter Brusilovsky, Alfred Kobsa, and Wolfgang Nejdl (Eds.). Lecture Notes In Computer Science, Vol. 4321. Springer-Verlag, Berlin, Heidelberg 325-341.

[54] Sieg, Ahu, Bamshad Mobasher, and Robin Burke. "Web search personalization with ontological user profiles." Proceedings of the sixteenth ACM conference on Conference on information and knowledge management. ACM, 2007.

[55] Ginige, Athula, and San Murugesan. "Web engineering: An introduction." MultiMedia, IEEE 8.1 (2001): 14-18.

[56] Rossi, Gustavo, and Daniel Schwabe. "Modeling and implementing web applications with OOHDM." Web engineering: Modelling and implementing Web applications. Springer London, 2008. 109-155.

[57] Koch, Nora, et al. "UML-based web engineering." Web Engineering: Modelling and Implementing Web Applications. Springer London, 2008. 157-191.

[58] Pastor, Oscar, et al. "Conceptual modelling of web applications: the OOWS approach." Web Engineering. Springer Berlin Heidelberg, 2006. 277-302.

[59] Ceri, Stefano, Piero Fraternali, and Aldo Bongio. "Web Modeling Language (WebML): a modeling language for designing Web sites." Computer Networks 33.1 (2000): 137-157.

[60] Acerbis, Roberto, et al. "Webratio 5: An eclipse-based case tool for engineering web applications." Web Engineering. Springer Berlin Heidelberg, 2007. 501-505.

[61] Avison, David, and Guy Fitzgerald. Information systems development: methodologies, techniques and tools. McGraw Hill, 2003.

[62] Isakowitz, Tomas, Michael Bieber, and Fabio Vitali. "Web information systems." Communications of the ACM 41.7 (1998): 78-80.

[63] Komiak, Sherrie YX, and Izak Benbasat. "The effects of personalization and familiarity on trust and adoption of recommendation agents." Mis Quarterly(2006): 941-960.

[64] Wood, Jason, Helen Wright, and Ken Brodie. "Collaborative visualization."Visualization'97, Proceedings. IEEE, 1997.

[65] Abbing, Jana, and Kevin Koidl. "Template approach for adaptive learning strategies." (2006).

A Linked Data Approach to Care Coordination

Spyros Kotoulas   Vanessa Lopez   Marco Luca Sbodio

Martin Stephenson   Pierpaolo Tommasi   Pol Mac Aonghusa

{spyros.kotoulas, vanlopez, marco.sbodio, martin_stephenson, ptommasi, aonghusa}@ie.ibm.com
Smarter Cities Technology Centre
IBM Research Ireland

ABSTRACT

The success of a society is often judged by its ability to support the most vulnerable. Supporting the most vulnerable individuals is extremely challenging from an information needs perspective, since it requires data from numerous domains and systems, including Social Care, Healthcare, Public Safety and Juridical systems. Information sharing on this scale gives rise to scientific and technical challenges with regard to data representation, access, integration and retrieval granularity. This is a practice-oriented paper presenting a Linked Data-based approach that is uniquely positioned to access and surface information across domains and data sources using a combination of vulnerability indexes and contextual exploration. We apply this approach on a set of enterprise systems from IBM to develop an information sharing architecture and prototype for Care Coordination with a focus on Social Care and Healthcare. We report on expert feedback and user studies that indicate that our approach indeed reduces the time required to gain some business insight while maintaining the flexibility of a Linked Data-based integration approach.

1. INTRODUCTION

Caring for the most vulnerable individuals bears very high cultural and economic significance. Most concisely expressed by H.H. Humphrey as "The moral test of a government is how it treats those who are at the dawn of life, the children; those who are in the twilight of life, the aged; and those who are in the shadow of life, the sick, the needy, and the handicapped', the number of similar quotes by prominent scholars, politicians and religious leaders testifies to the universality of the above sentiment.

Care spans domains with tremendous *economic impact*: averaged across the OECD, Social Care and Healthcare account to some 21% and 9.3% of the GDP respectively[1]. Pub-

[1] OECD Factbook 2012, figures for 2011

lic Safety, Justice and Education, domains that also have a large economic footprint, directly influence and are influenced by Care. The information relevant to Care is vastly *complex*: For healthcare, Nuance reports that LinkBase®[2] contains more than 1 million concepts. Social care depends on information from a very broad domain, from *numerous* relevant organizations (social service administration, educational institutions, homeless shelters and public safety authorities, etc) and differs across administrative boundaries.

Coordinating care has been identified both as a major pain point and a significant opportunity in modern health and social systems [1]. Several studies have shown that costs can be contained and outcomes improved with a more comprehensive approach to Care [2]. In [3], it is reported that 5% of individuals face complex issues spanning multiple domains and accounting for 50% of the cost. Identifying these individuals early on is key to reducing costs. The impact of social determinants for health dictates that multi-domain information is needed for holistic and individualized care delivery [4]. Furthermore, coordination across care agencies and stakeholders requires an integrated view of the individual, their vulnerabilities and their environment [5]. As a simple motivating example, consider an individual quartered in inappropriate housing while suffering from a relatively minor health issue, aggravated by the housing condition. As a result, the given individual frequently resorts to visiting emergency rooms, resulting in significant cost to the healthcare system and a less effective treatment. By itself, the housing situation does not warrant state intervention. Nevertheless, resolving it would dramatically improve the individual's health situation and lower costs for the health system. A possible conviction for illegally selling prescription medication would strengthen the need to this intervention.

We investigate the unique challenges presented in the Care Coordination domain and propose a novel technical solution to augment applications with cross-domain context, based on Semantic Web technologies. Our approach is novel in that it marries the usability of vulnerability indexes (which in our case are closely related to business rules) with the flexibility of Semantic technologies, specifically for accessing and presenting distributed information across domains. Semantic technologies are well suited because: (a) The distributed nature of RDF allow us to access information and integrate across silos, (b) explicit and global semantics allow

[2] http://www.nuance.com/for-healthcare/resources/clinical-language-understanding/ontology/index.htm

us to ground vulnerability indexes across systems, and (c) the distributed and incremental data integration paradigm as well as the existing wealth of information in Linked Open Data can help giving context to cope with the complexity of the data.

We present a demonstrator of a system that supports two key use-cases for this domain:

- Displaying a view of the combined needs across several dimensions and domains for a given person and people in their social context, based on a set of vulnerability indexes. This allows a social worker to quickly assess the situation of an individual. From a knowledge management perspective, it requires grounding a set of business rules across several ontologies and instance data in several data sources.

- Exploration of the context to surface information not directly covered by the vulnerability indexes. Given the heterogeneity of the domain, the user will most likely need additional information around a given individual, e.g. the vulnerability indexes might capture that a person is suffering from some disease, but the social worker might want information about the nature of the disease, such as "eating disorder", or about complicating factors, from exploring the semi-structured information, including external Linked Data sources.

Our demonstrator is integrated and works in tandem with IBM enterprise systems in the domains of Social Care and Clinical Care, although the approach is applicable to a much wider variety of systems. We expose the information of each system as RDF through relational-to-RDF mappings, integrate this information and query it in a federated manner. We use generic queries representing the vulnerability indexes and augment and adapt the results to make them consumable by the non-expert. Then, we present the contextual information in the user interface of the enterprise application. Although our demonstrator works on top of the actual databases of the enterprise systems, all personal information presented in this paper is fictional. A system based on the work reported in this paper is currently being deployed on the field, with application to eldercare in China.

This work is an extension of work presented as demos or posters [6, 7] with a refinement of Decomposable Vulnerability Indicators to three levels of abstraction, the inclusion of term simplification for cross-domain sharing and user studies for evaluation.

The rest of the paper is structured as follows: In Section 2, we are giving an overview of the domains we are addressing and the relevance of the Semantic Web in each domain. Then, in Section 3, we present two motivational use-cases, from which we elicit a set of challenges. Our general approach is outlined in Section 4 and we go into implementation details for our prototype in Section 5. We conclude with an evaluation, based on user-studies, an analysis of the strengths and weaknesses of our semantic approach and future work.

2. RELATED WORK

In this Section, we are giving an overview of the main characteristics, pain points, research efforts and technologies for the domains targeted in this paper.

Care coordination generally refers to combining information from several domains (the most important ones being Social Care and Healthcare) to improve outcomes and lower costs. Although it is one of the major cornerstones of health reform, it lacks a common definition and is recognized as a modern-day Tower of Babel [5]. For instance, in Camden, New Jersey, 1% of patients account for a third of the city's medical costs [8]. According to Gawande [8], the routinely higher cost and lower quality of care for high cost/high need people are due to lack of integrated health and social services. Taking high-cost situations into coordinated care requires considering multiple sources spanning highly diverse domains. There are two recent examples implementing a patient centric view of care coordination for special high-need patient populations: the *patient-centered Medical Home* in NY [9] - a primary care model to contain healthcare costs by promoting patient-centered care-, and the *Common Grounds organization*, focused on homelessness, veterans' affairs, mental illness, and health care. Common Ground launched a campaign to place chronically homeless people into permanent housing, using vulnerability indexes to prioritize care for the homeless population that faced the greatest risk of dying on the streets [9].

Social Care is usually organized and managed separately from healthcare, and through different legal entities. While healthcare records are deep but narrow, with a wealth of technical and biomedical details, social care records capture a very broad spectrum of information [5], ranging from family relations, vulnerability and risk models, social programs and received benefits to accommodation conditions. Social care programs are not managed in a uniform way across administrative domains and standardization is very limited or non-existent. In the open domain, there are limited resources specifically addressing the domain, the UK Social care online taxonomy[3] being one of them. Nevertheless, since the domain is often not as specialized as healthcare, existing Linked Data sources can be exploited to provide definitions or links to other relevant entities and generalize terms. In addition, large open datasets such as censuses or deprivation indexes provide data on population characteristics (health, housing, employment, transport) and can highlight important social issues for the area where the individual lives (hot spots).

Healthcare is a very complex domain, where numerous organizations are involved during the care providing process: medical institutes, hospitals, pharmaceutical companies, nursing facilities, etc. With the wide adoption of information technology solutions, medical records are scattered among different archives both within and across institutions, often based on proprietary formats. Even within the same hospital, patient records may be stored in different systems such as Electronic Health Records (EHRs) or Hospital Information Systems (HIS) or Laboratory Information Systems (LIS). There have been significant standardization efforts in the field: SNOMED-CT (Systematized Nomenclature Of Medicine Clinical Terms)[4] is a international medical terminology including more than 311,000 concepts, Health Level 7 (HL7[5]) provides standards for the definition of messages between clinical applications, the International Classification

---

[3]http://www.scie-socialcareonline.org.uk
[4]http://www.ihtsdo.org/snomed-ct/
[5]http://www.hl7.org/implement/standards/rim.cfm

of Diseases (ICD-10)[6] provides a system of 141,000 diagnostic codes for classifying diseases, symptoms, abnormal findings etc. Even with these recommendations, clinical information system interoperability still poses a huge challenge for the IT industry, mainly in terms of data integration and complexity. As a result, in many cases, the data that is stored at the point of origin is not available at point-of-care.

Semantic Web-related technologies have gained popularity because they facilitate integration of heterogeneous data using rich explicit semantics and the ability to infer additional information [10]. In [11, 12], information is standardized using ontologies. In [13], they surveyed the feasibility and state of the art for using semantic technology to represent, integrate and analyze knowledge in biomedical networks. Recognizing that a single ontology for Healthcare is not an achievable goal, [14] investigates alignment techniques to better support data integration at scale. In [15], the authors report on large-scale biomedical ontology integration and access, resulting in a very large dataset (300 million triples).

The closest system to our approach is InfoSleuth [16], which provides semantic integration across an open set of sources in the healthcare domain. Unlike InfoSleuth, our approach focuses on making information spanning multiple domains accessible to non-experts.

Compared to the literature described above, our work is different in the following ways: (a) Rather than solely for data integration, we rely on business rules as a navigational aid, (b) we focus on cross-domain information sharing and use Linked Open Data not only to enrich enterprise data, but also to simplify it, (c) instead of focusing on Healthcare, we are applying Semantic Technologies across very diverse domains and focus on information presentation to the non-expert, which brings about additional challenges.

3. USE-CASES AND CHALLENGES

In this Section, we present two motivational use-cases that set the ground for further discussion. The first use-case captures a situation where a social worker wants an overview of the situation of an individual across several dimensions, so as to get insight on their needs and potential vulnerabilities. The second revolves around exploration of the information in order to retrieve specific facts, from an open set, that may be of importance to the social worker.

In the Social Sciences domain, *Vulnerability Indexes* are used as means to systematically define possible risk factors for negative outcomes. Table 1 shows some factors that contribute to the risk that a given individual is at increased morbidity risk [9]. Even for this simple case, one can easily observe that information needs to come from several sources: Data concerning homelessness is likely to be found in the information system of a homeless shelter, data concerning liver cirrhosis is likely to be found in a medical record, etc. A fully-fledged vulnerability index would cover more dimensions and involve hierarchies of contributing factors. Although defining such indexes goes beyond the scope of this paper and would typically be performed by a domain expert, in Section 4, we show an example.

Vulnerability indexes can help users abstract from the volume and domain heterogeneity of information. Nevertheless, in some scenarios, they need to retrieve relevant *facts*, that

are not capture by the business rules. For example, a social worker is looking at the situation of an individual who has early symptoms of Alzheimer, suffers from mobility problems and has no known relatives to help. Although none of the problems listed above is life-threatening by itself, their combination is. A social worker will need to *explore relevant information*, identify the problem, based on their domain experience, and take appropriate measures.

These use-cases bring forth a set of challenge that we believe that they are pervasive in several complex domains beyond the context investigated here.

- **Large volumes of information, siloed across distributed and heterogeneous infrastructures.** Deployments of social care systems rely on multiple-Terabyte databases. Healthcare systems are typically fragmented and rely on several large databases. Infrastructures are also heterogeneous: while some systems rely on relational models, medical records are often modeled using hierarchical structures.

- **Information is highly sensitive.** In effect, this precludes centralizing information due to legal or policy limitations. Organizations are much more likely to provide access to isolated pieces of information rather than providing database dumps.

- **Models are complex and span multiple domains.** Creating a model for a single addressed domain is a very challenging task (take HL7, for example). A model encapsulating all relevant domains would be difficult to develop, use and maintain.

- **Data consumability is challenging.** Traditional UI techniques do not cope well with schema heterogeneity while generic semantic browsing does not cope well with accessibility to non-expert users. In addition, users with various roles require information at a different granularity: while a medical professional needs exact information about a disease, a social worker only needs to know about complicating environmental of psychological factors.

4. APPROACH

In this Section, we describe at a high-level an approach, based on *Decomposable Vulnerability Indicators* and contextual exploration, addressing the challenges presented in Section 3, consisting of the following main elements:

- To abstract from the infrastructure of each source, and to allow enforcement of policies defined by each organization, we use a *semantic data management* layer.

- To abstract from the complexity of each source, and to allow incremental integration, we use a set of *reference ontologies* to partially map our data against.

- To abstract from the particular structure of each source, and our reference ontologies, we use a *contextual information access* layer.

4.1 Reference ontologies.

A reference ontology usually represents knowledge about a particular domain, independently from specific objectives [17]. We use an extensible set of reference ontologies for defining

[6]http://www.who.int/classifications/icd/en/

if:	an individual has been homeless in the last 6 months
and one of:	
	more than three hospitalizations or emergency room visits in a year
	more than three emergency room visits in the previous three months
	aged 60 or older
	cirrhosis of the liver, end-stage renal disease
	history of frostbite, immersion foot, or hypothermia
	HIV+/AIDS
	tri-morbidity: co-occurring psychiatric, substance abuse, and chronic medical condition
then:	they have a 40% chance of dying prematurely

Table 1: Example factors that put individuals at high morbidity risk.

mappings from heterogeneous data sources to RDF. Most integration is done using these ontologies. Although, on a more general view, aligning these ontologies might be necessary, in this paper, since the ontologies cover different domains, we only had to do limited linking between concepts in the ontologies.

4.2 Semantic Data Management.

The semantic layer provides a *virtualized global repository* over the underlying store(s). That is, the semantic layer hides the distribution and heterogeneity of the underlying store(s) by allowing applications to formulate queries guided by the reference ontologies. This global schema only covers part of the information in these sources. In addition, the size of the databases is very large and the information stored therein highly sensitive. Thus, we are federating data on-demand, i.e. we are only exposing as RDF the data that is aligned and is needed in our scenarios. To this end, we are using a federated querying architecture. The information at each source is physically stored in the application and we map it to RDF at runtime. Management and linking information is stored centrally using a high-performance RDF store.

4.3 Contextual Information Access.

Context is defined as any information that can be used to characterize the situation of an entity [18]. A system is context-aware if it uses context to provide relevant information and/or services to the user, where relevance depends on the user's task [18]. Task-dependence is particularly important in Care Coordination. In this light, generic semantic browsing does not cope well since it does not take any formal description of the task at hand into consideration. We are using vulnerability indexes as task descriptions, summarization techniques and navigational aids for context. Therefore, we use *views* to instantiate or compute them and *contextual retrieval* to explore beyond the data points touched by the views.

4.4 Decomposable Vulnerability Indicators

Contextual Information access is mainly realized through *Decomposable Vulnerability Indicators (DVIs)*, which are generic navigational structures with the following characteristics:

- *Formalization:* Contributing factors are formaly represented by grounding them on OWL ontologies. This allows abstracting from the data representation and makes DVIs *transferable* across systems.

- *Decomposability:* DVIs are decomposable into contribut-

ing factors represented as a an acyclic graph. Each node in the graph represents a (potentially composite) factor. The incoming edges on the nodes for composite factors are used to calculate the values for the former using arbitrary functions. Factors with no incoming edges are grounded with terms from an ontology.

- *Computability:* DVIs are computable based on their formal semantics and their acyclic graph structure.

Figure 1 shows a DVI, based on (but not equivalent to) the vulnerability index in Table 1. This DVI (and its instantiation) is a fragment of the one shown in Figure 3, along with some example data.

- At the top level, one can see the definition of the DVI. The "Vulnerability" node is providing a high-level representation of the risk associated with an individual. The total score for vulnerability depends on a series of factors. In this example, it is composed from the weighted sum of vulnerabilities regarding Health, Shelter, Education etc. The node for Health can be further decomposed into the sum of some constituent factors: The number of emergency room visits, the age of the person, when over a given threshold, and the presence of some medical conditions. The figure indicates various features in DVIs such as sums, existence of conditions, counts, logical AND etc.

- At the semantic level, DVI definitions are always grounded on ontologies. For example, Liver Cirrhosis is mapped to the concept for liver cirrhosis in the Human Disease Ontology [7]. Similarly, unemployment is mapped to the relevant concept from the Social Care Reference Taxonomy [8]. Using this design, DVI definitions are portable (assuming sufficient overlap between used ontologies) and can span an arbitrary number of domains and ontologies. One can see part of the relevant subgraph used for calculating the DVI, capturing some information about Bob. The dotted lines indicate the correspondence between the semantic data and the DVI definition. The oval shapes represent instance data while the rectangles with the rounded corners represent concepts from an ontology (or other external assets). In this particular case, the Human Disease Ontology is used to map the specific medical condition of Bob to a more general one.

---

[7] http://disease-ontology.org/
[8] http://www.scie-socialcareonline.org.uk/topic. asp?guid=362fac89-bca0-11d4-ba18-009027f63525

- In the bottom of the figure, we show a possible logical representation of the data, in a relational format. We are using a set of mappings from relational databases to RDF (shown as curved lines in the figure). Such data is possibly physically distributed across systems.

4.5 Contextual exploration

In some scenarios, a social care worker needs to retrieve relevant *facts* that are not captured in the business rule. While business rules are grounded to the data in different systems to create multi-dimensional views of the citizen, family and community ecosystem, interactive contextual access and exploration gets the relevant information for an entity when the structure is not known in advance - i.e., not modeled through business rules and based on interlinked schemas, without the requirement to come up with a common shared model(s) to suit all parties involved. Following the Linked Data principles, potentially useful data sources are published by populating and extending the existent schemas, and by reusing reference vocabularies that act as common anchors. In this setup, dynamic contextual access allows exploring all the known information for an entity in a given context (e.g., context around mental health), by following the relationships across the data sources, collecting the triples in the vicinity of the search node or between nodes.

Additional sources are used to uncover connections between factors and records. E.g, for factors that are also described as entities in DBpedia, we have added links (owl:sameAs) to the corresponding DBpedia term. In turn, for each topic linked to a DBpedia term, we extract the social care topics that are also mentioned in the descriptions of the corresponding Wikipedia page, so as to add links to commonly co-related factors. These correlations, although do not necessarily imply causality, can be used to uncover and present relevant content for the user to explore and interpret.

Specialized terms inhibit information consumption across domains. External open data sources are used to generalize specialized social and medical terms (e.g., pica disease is an eating disorder, categorizations of various social programs), providing a common vocabulary and meaningful relationships to other relevant entities. Nevertheless, these sources do not give useful information regarding the level at which information should be presented, or the most easily identifiable term for the non-specialist. For example, consider the two fragments of the human disease ontology in Figure 2, part of a hierarchy that includes some 6000 diseases.

Starting from the diagnosis in the medical system (underlined), we need to present this information to a social worker with limited knowledge in the medical domain. For example, the right level of abstraction might be the terms indicated in bold. We observe the following: (a) The more general terms are more likely to be understandable by non-experts. (b) We can not use a fixed number of hops in the hierarchy for all terms. (c) sometimes, the more specialist term might be better understandable than the more general ("skin disease" vs "integumentary system disease").

To overcome these challenges, we are using implicit user feedback. During exploration, we record user behavior to infer what is the most meaningful level of abstraction for a given user group. A prerequisite is that there is reasonable consensus between users regarding which terms are understandable. We show this in our evaluation.

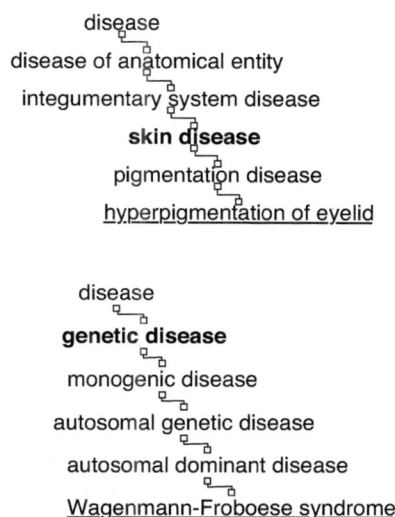

Figure 2: Example disease hierarchies

4.6 Comprehensive example

We describe a DVI and associated contextual exploration capability suitable for a social worker wanting to have a 360-degree view of the vulnerabilities of an individual. The six vulnerabilities that influence care are: Health (known diseases, mental health problems, prescriptions, etc.), Education and Work (degrees, school attendance, time since last employment, etc.), Shelter (homeless, shelter, reasons for eviction, poor housing conditions, number of people living in same household, etc.), Safety (criminal history, crime victims, custodial institutions, etc.), Income (earnings, assets and expenses, such as medical or accommodation expenses) and Food (food vouchers, residential care, etc).

Figure 3 shows the instantiation of this DVI (1) and contextual exploration panel (2) for an example person, *Bob Pugh*. The magnitude of the vulnerability is signified by the size and colour or the circles (red is important), edges signify contributing factors, and the hover-over rectangle displays provenance information and an explanation of the scores. At a glance, the Social Worker can see that there are problems with Bob (root node is large and red). The main reasons for this have to do with Health and Food. It is also possible for the care worker to drill into factors. Clicking on Income, the social worker can see that Bob is receiving income support, and by clicking on the respective node, she can find more detail (e.g., child benefit). In addition, for some conditions (not shown in the figure), the social worker can also see related factors from Open Data sources, which she might want to investigate further. For example, unemployment is related to education, homelessness and human trafficking, according to Wikipedia links.

From a technical perspective, each node is associated to two SPARQL queries. The first one is to calculate the score of a given contributing factor (if present) obtained from a given data source(s) and with a given weight. The second one is a CONSTRUCT query to retrieve the set of triples providing additional context in the ontology(-ies) associated to the data that contributed to the score, as well as further

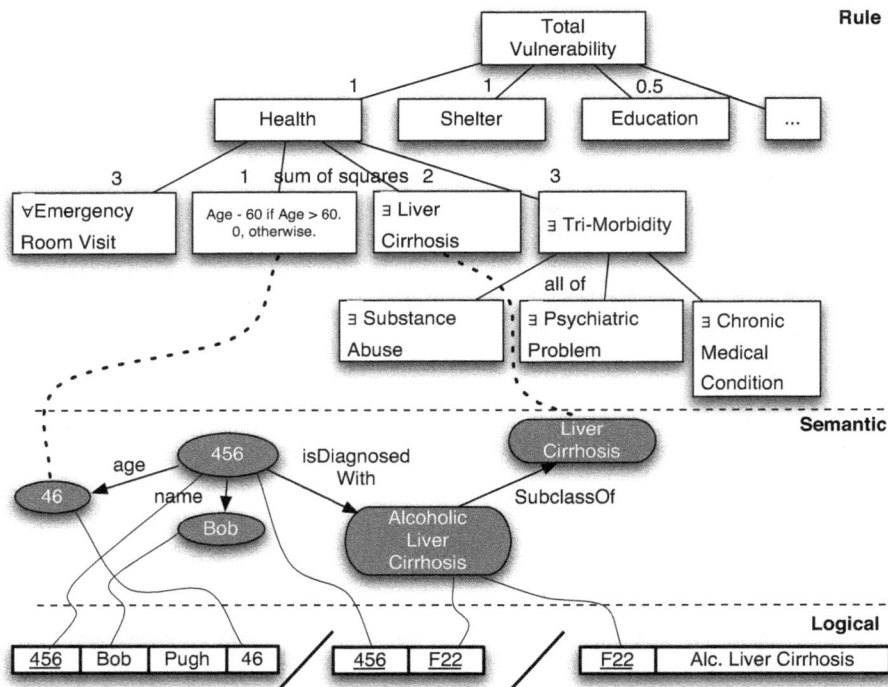

Figure 1: Example Decomposable Vulnerability Indicator

information on the values from which the score was derived. In relation to the DVI in Figure 1, one could consider each node at the rule level (top-level) as pairs of SPARQL queries (one SELECT and one CONSTRUCT), the nodes at the semantic level as RDF nodes (ontologies and instance-level) and the nodes at the logical level as the form in which the data actually resides (in this case, relational).

5. REALISATION

We present an architecture supporting our approach (Figure 4). For conciseness, several components are considered black boxes, not evaluated in this paper. We describe our integration platform and the two enterprise systems from which we are pulling information (PCI and Cúram).

5.1 Platform

Access is controlled using *IBM Tivoli* infrastructure at a global level. Separate access control mechanisms are in place for each source (not shown in Fig. 4). Web-facing services use a set of REST services. These services are running on IBM WebSphere Application Server. The main components for these services are the *Node registry*, which tracks nodes in the distributed data layer, the *View definitions*, that are used to project information out of the graph model for use by analytics widgets and UI elements, the *Provenance tracking component*, which uses PROV-O[9] to track information provenance (for a detailed description see [19]), and the *Linker*, that links information across sources. For performance reasons, we are keeping a set of *Ancillary Indexes*, including full-text Lucene indexes and proprietary

structures for the Linker. All components besides the node registry store their metadata in a single *Metadata Repository*, using the SPARQL extensions of DB2 [20]. In turn, physical indexes for the metadata repository and the ancillary indexes are maintained in a storage area network. *Data Sources* are exposed as virtual RDF, using SeDA (an IBM technology executing D2R mappings, similar to D2RQ[10] and Quest [21]). The virtual RDF Data Sources, the Metadata Repository and the Ancillary Indexes are accessed through the *Federated Query Engine*, providing transparent access to the distributed information. All core components can be clustered, for high availability and performance.

5.2 PCI

IBM Patient Care and Insights[11] supports patient centered care processes. It integrates and analyzes the full breadth of patient information sourced from different care providers. It also enables interactive, secure collaboration between patients, care givers, healthcare providers and payers via personalized electronic care plans. From the perspective of this paper, we are interested in analytics results (e.g. risks for a particular disease), clinical summaries (e.g. previous procedures, prescriptions, lab test results) and care plan data (e.g. care plan goals, associated activities and results).

5.3 Cúram

The IBM Cúram Social Program Management Platform[12] is a business and technology solution that delivers prebuilt

---

[9] http://www.w3.org/TR/prov-o/

[10] http://d2rq.org/
[11] http://www-01.ibm.com/software/ecm/patient-care/
[12] http://www-03.ibm.com/software/products/en/social-programs/

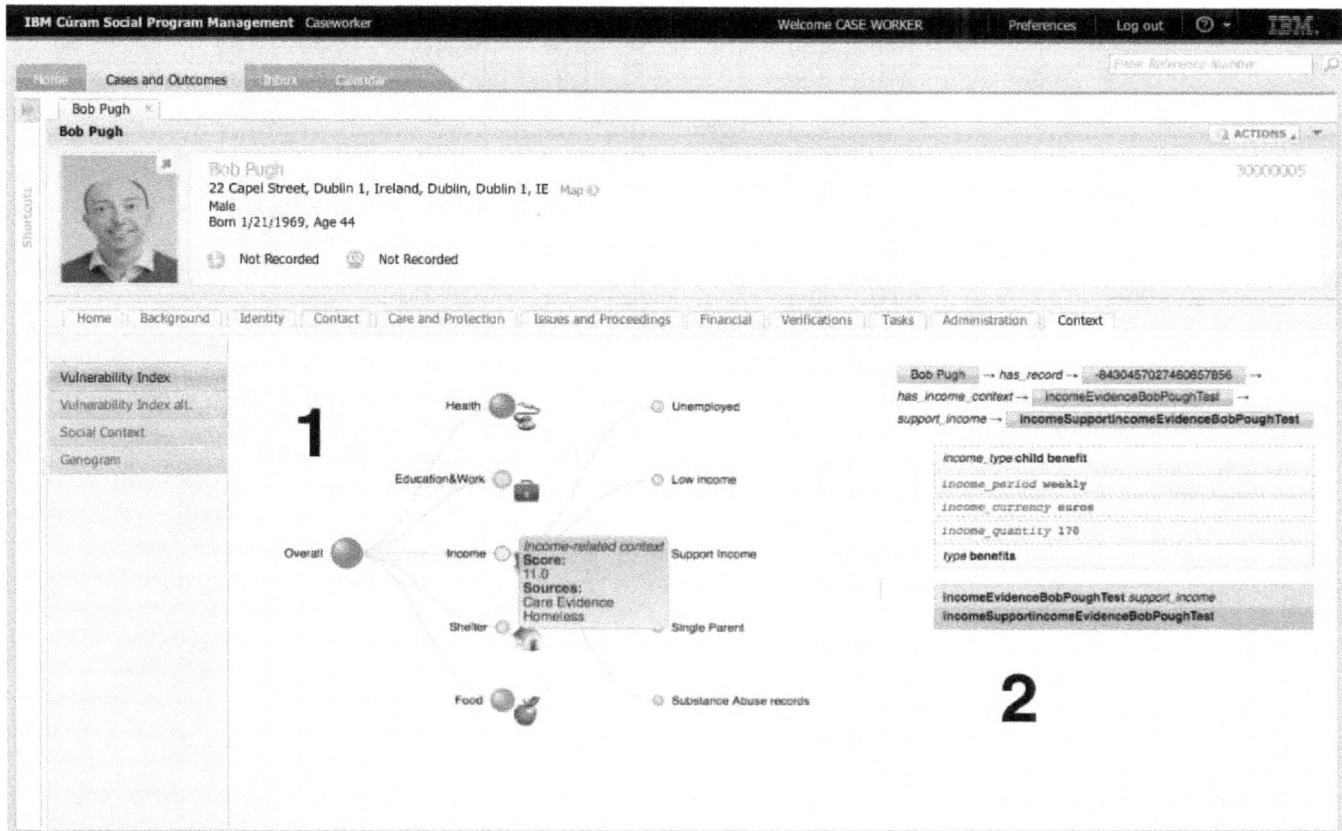

Figure 3: Integration into enterprise system

social program components, business processes, toolsets and interfaces on top of a dynamically configurable architecture. It helps social program organizations provide optimal outcomes for citizens and lower costs for organizations. Cúram manages multiple aspects of social care, with connection to this paper, the information of interest mainly regards social relationships and case evidences, e.g. known problems concerning employment, substance abuse, participation in social assistance programs and information concerning housing, education and safety.

In addition, we have created an additional data source based on data models from homeless shelters. In total, this deployment is using 3 relational databases (some enterprise systems have multiple databases), 1 non-relational database, 1 RDF data source and the ontologies described in the next subsection.

5.4 Ontological modeling

The advantage of using RDF to model the data is the flexibility in retrieving and adapting information within and across sources (compared to traditional Extract-Transform-Load (ETL)). For instance, Cúram supports dynamic configuration of evidence types by the system administrator, in effect, providing an extensible model over a relational infrastructure. E.g., the administrator may define (at any time) a new type shelter evidence for homeless containing info such as number of days in the street, reasons for eviction, last known residence, etc. This means that, in practice, the sys-

tem does not have a fixed model. In practice, the enterprise system is always adapted according to customer needs. The RDF social care model is also extensible with new properties, or new evidence types can be created beyond the aforementioned six (Health, Shelter, Safety, Income, Education and Employment and Food evidences). Through evidence types we also link new data sources with different schemas. For example, if we consider the data coming from 100khomes.org health homes questionnaires, the new schema is linked to the existent social care ontology by creating a new record of type both health and homeless evidence. As such, when exploring the shelter evidence for a given person, data from both Curam and these questionnaires can be retrieved as context.

Table 2 shows the set of ontologies we have used in our deployment. Following best practices, we have aimed for maximizing re-use. Nevertheless, given that some domains have not been traditionally addressed in Semantic Web deployments, we have had to develop some ontologies and adapt existing taxonomies.

6. EVALUATION

6.1 Expert feedback

We have had extensive discussions with domain experts from different divisions within IBM (research, product, sales). At a high-level, given the complexity of the domain, they appreciate the flexibility of Semantic approaches, since de-

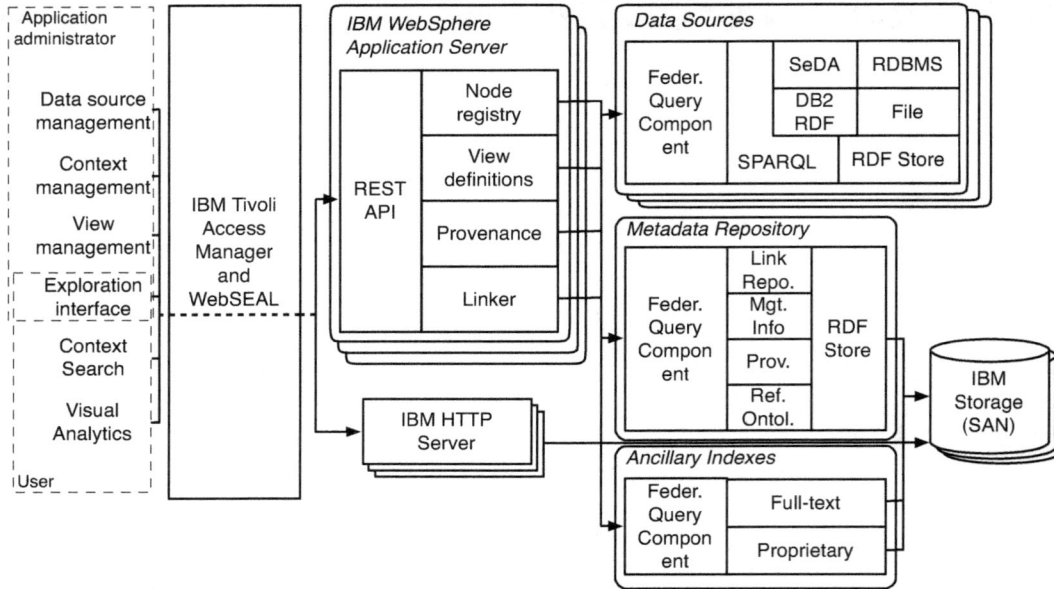

Figure 4: System architecture

Ontology	Description
Clinical	We have developed three ontologies based on HL7 to capture clinical summaries, medical data analytics and care plans
Social Care Reference taxonomy and vocabulary	Partially extracted from the taxonomy of topics in the social care online taxonomy to annotate datatypes and values in all 6 different dimensions for evidences or needs. These values are also manually linked to DBpedia.
Family Ontology	We have extended the family relationships ontology described in [22].
FOAF, VCARD	Personal details and addresses.
Common Ground	Used to model health questionnaires from the 100khomes campaign [9]
WSG84, Time	Representation of geospatial and temporal features.
Human Disease	Representation of diseases.
Social care evidence ontology	To model the relevant contextual data stored in social care systems such as Curam . Captures the core need evidence for applicants to social services.

Table 2: Set of ontologies used in our deployment

ploying a Data Warehouse or a Master Data Management infrastructure is known to be a challenging project, with high start-up costs.

Generic graph-based exploration, typical in many Semantic Web approaches is not attractive from an enterprise application perspective. Use-case specific navigational aids are necessary, hiding the complexity of the graph. On the other hand, ETL-like approaches relying on fixed schemas are insufficient as the number of input systems grows and the complexity of the domain increases. This extends to fixed ontologies. Reconciling user-friendliness, attractive visualizations and flexibility is seen as a major challenge and opportunity. Similarly, as far as analytics are concerned, they should also be domain specific and be semantically informed, while, at the same time allowing for more flexibility than database views.

Web-style exploration is preferred to graph-based visualizations. Our initial prototype for contextual exploration was based on a graph UI. According to the experts, this is not suitable for an enterprise domain. For DVIs, displaying provenance and explanations is imperative. In addition, the ability to abstract is also deemed necessary, given the complexity of the domain.

For the future, suggested areas for improvement include exploring other types of visualizations that show how different causes/evidence are influencing each other and the various KPIs. For instance, using Sankey diagrams to visualize magnitude of flows between vulnerabilities. More generally, it is of interest to investigate and expose how the various contextual information is interconnected.

6.2 User study: Term specialization

We have firstly evaluated the mechanism to simplify specialist terms in isolation. The same 10 users were presented with 21 random terms from the Human Disease Ontology. For each term, the users were called to respond on whether they know the term. If not, they would be presented with the more general term (following the subclassOf relations in the hierarchy). If yes, the currently displayed term as well as the original term would be stored. This experiment

ID	Domain	Question
A1	Employment	When did you last work? (never/in the last x months / over x years)
A2	Education	What is the highest grade of education that you have completed?(primary..)
A3	Income	What type of services is your family receiving?
A4	Housing	What is your current housing situation (homeless/ poor housing / temporary shelter / home ownership / (non)-subsidized rental / ..
A5	Substance abuse	Do you or have you ever had a problem with alcohol or drugs? (yes / no)
A6	Physical health	Do you have any health or medical conditions? (no / yes - list diseases)
B1	Housing	What is your primary reason for homelessness? (eviction / poor housing / domestic violence / release from jail/ natural disaster/ ..)
B2	Housing	How long have you been living on the street (x months/ years)
B3	Child Welfare	Do you currently have children in foster care ?
B4	Mental health	Do you have emotional, personal problems or stress? (no / yes - list)?

Table 3: Intake questions for user study. A1 to A6 refer to the vulnerable individual, B1 to B4 refer to the homeless individual.

simulates the learning behavior of our user interface.

Figure 5 (left) shows the results of our study. The horizontal axis shows the different terms and each bar represents the number of times a user would go to the more general concept (for each user). For 120 out of 210 observations, the users are in exact agreement, for 22 out of 210 observations, the users picked a number of relations one higher than the mean and for 25 out of 210 one lower than the mean. This means that, if we adapt the term, 57% of the users will immediately identify the condition, compared to 21% if we leave the term unchanged. If we also display the terms within one level in the hierarchy, this number would rise to 80%.

6.3 User study: Comparison with generic graph exploration

We have compared the DVI-based user interface to a generic graph exploration approach used as a baseline, on a set of timed tasks. We have simulated an intake scenario, where a social worker is called to gather information about various aspects of somebody's life. Currently, this is done manually, by means of an interview[13]. Our DVI is generic, has been developed without prior knowledge of the questionnaire and has not been adapted in any way to the particular scenario. We have used a subset of the actual intake questions to test the ability of our system to retrieve this information. The set of questions is given in Table 3.

We have asked 10 users to retrieve the answers to the questions in Table 3, using our user-interface and Pubby[14], one of the most commonly-used exploration interfaces for RDF data. The users were not experts in the domain, so as to have a realistic scenario in which they would not be familiar with the terminology. 50% of the users were experts in the Semantic Web field but we observed no significant difference with the other 50%. We note that we have not tuned our approach to correspond to the input questions and our DVIs are generic. For each question, we started a timer once the user was given the question and stopped the timer when the user would give up or report the answer, essentially measuring the time the user needs to get some business insight. Each user used both systems but the order was randomized (i.e. each system was used first in 50% of

the cases). We have used two individuals for all users: a vulnerable one (more general) and a homeless one (specific vulnerability).

The results are reported in Figure 5 (right), as a violin plot. The arrows represent the median values and the two areas represent the value distributions and density. E.g., for A1 and our system, the median is 42 seconds, most values are in the 10-50 range, and there is an outlier at around 157 seconds. The results for one-way ANOVA ($F(1,104)=8.366,p=0.005$) indicate that the difference for the two systems is statistically significant. Our approach required less time to acquire the required information, although, for both systems, there is significant variance. On average, using the baseline system took 54.1% more time than our system. The number of clicks in both systems was comparable. For Pubby, there were 3 cases where users gave up, not being able to find the answer and 3 more cases where the users reported a result that was wrong. In contrast, for our system, users always succeeded in finding the correct answer. Users also commented that navigation with Pubby was sometimes confusing, due to information overload, e.g., users confused property values with descriptions of properties.

Obviously, a user interface tailored to the scenario and the systems used would perform better than our approach. Nevertheless, it would lack generality. With our experiments, we have shown that our approach can address the same information space as a generic exploration tool while reducing the time to reach a business result.

7. DISCUSSION AND CONCLUSIONS

In this section, we discuss the benefits and open problems to create an intelligent user interface, showcased in the care coordination domain, in which, data coming from several heterogeneous and large systems has been accessed and presented in an integrated way and in context, guided by a set of reference ontologies. In this scenario, contextual access consists of providing meaningful views to understand the vulnerabilities and dependencies across particular needs for an individual, and providing additional exploration capability, grounded on these views.

Traditional ETL and data warehousing approaches typically fit data on a global model. While such approaches have shown good performance, the suffer from information loss, since data that does not fit this model is not accessible. A semantic approach is more suitable for situations requiring

---

[13]Questionnaires for self-sufficiency assessment in order to identify barriers preventing a household from self-sufficiency. The results feed into a process to create an outcome plan.

[14]http://wifo5-03.informatik.uni-mannheim.de/pubby/

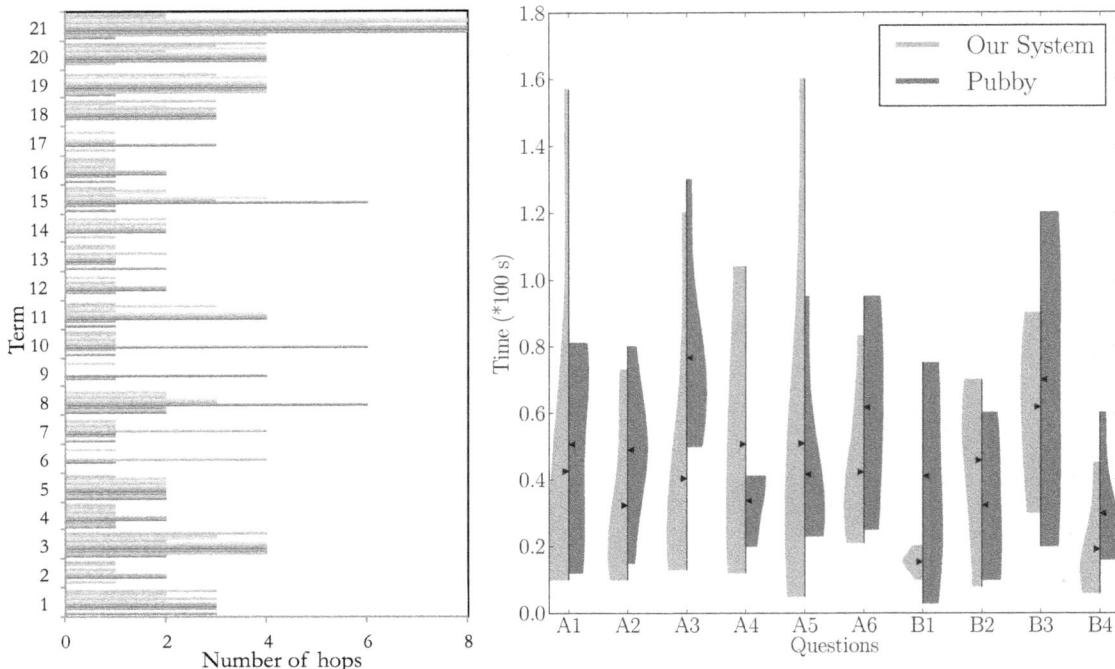

Figure 5: Level of term specialization identifiable by users (left). Comparison with generic graph exploration (right).

partial, dynamic and extensible integration across multiple schemas, models, domains and sources. RDF provides a natural way to implement a consolidated and extended information space within the enterprise, while allowing re-use of assets from the Web, such as ontologies and vocabularies. In some cases, these ontologies and vocabularies facilitate querying and allow displaying information in a more consumable way, through common or related (linked) values - e.g., broader or narrower topics. Nevertheless, a semantic approach also bears significant cost. The lack of a global model raises challenges with regard to user interfaces, since the application can not longer assume a given structure for query results. In our work, we have tried a middle ground between an easy-to-use user interface based on vulnerability indexes and a powerful exploration interface that can access the entire information space.

Our evaluation results show that our approach indeed allows users to get the required insight from the data in less time, while maintaining generality, at least within the given domain. In addition, our user study shows that there is consensus across a given group of users regarding the fitness-for-use of different aggregation levels for specialist terminology, allowing our system to adapt to the user domain knowledge.

A system using the approach described in this paper is currently undergoing field deployment with application to eldercare in China. We hope to provide additional insight based on this deployment.

Privacy is critical in this domain and merits additional research. For example HIPAA regulations[15] put considerable

---
[15]http://www.hhs.gov/ocr/privacy/index.html

limitations on sharing healthcare information. Nevertheless, current practice in care coordination, is that consent is generally managed using an all-or-nothing model, i.e. people going into coordinated care agree to all agencies sharing any of their data. Better privacy models for care coordination is an exciting research direction. Additional future work lies in providing tools for administrators to manage context, performance evaluations and on-the-field experiments with care workers.

We are planning to apply the approach presented in this paper in similar complex domains. Urban planning and public safety are of particular interest. Both domains present similar challenges regarding information sources and domain complexity, but pose additional requirements concerning managing geospatial information.

Acknowledgements. *We would like to thank Wei Jia Shen, Gang Hu and Guo Tong Xie for providing us access to data from PCI and developing the medical ontology, Anastasios Kementsietsidis, Achille Fokoue, M. Mustafa Rafique and Kavitha Srinivas for their work in the federated query component and data management infrastructure, Kevin McAulliffe, Tom Erickson and Jason Ellis for their feedback on the user interfaces and Nuno Lopes for reviewing.*

8. REFERENCES

[1] Rigby, M., Hill, P., Koch, S., Keeling, D.: Social care informatics as an essential part of holistic health care: A call for action. I. J. Medical Informatics **80**(8) (2011) 544–554

[2] Peikes, D., Chen, A., Schore, J., Brown, R.: Effects of care coordination on hospitalization, quality of care, and health care expenditures among medicare beneficiaries. JAMA: the journal of the American Medical Association **301**(6) (2009) 603–618

[3] Conwell, L.J., Cohen, J.W.: Characteristics of persons with high medical expenditures in the US civilian noninstitutionalized population, 2002. Medical Expenditure Panel Survey, Agency for Healthcare Research and Quality (2005)

[4] Marmot, M., Wilkinson, R.: Social determinants of health. Oxford University Press (2009)

[5] Kodner, D.L., Spreeuwenberg, C.: Integrated care: meaning, logic, applications, and implications–a discussion paper. International journal of integrated care **2** (2002)

[6] Kotoulas, S., Lopez, V., Stephenson, M., Tommasi, P., Shen, W., Hu, G., Sbodio, M.L., Bicer, V., Kementsietsidis, A., Rafique, M.M., Ellis, J.B., Erickson, T., Srinivas, K., McAuliffe, K., Xie, G.T., Aonghusa, P.M.: Coordinating social care and healthcare using semantic web technologies. In: International Semantic Web Conference (Posters & Demos). (2013) 169–172

[7] Kotoulas, S., Lopez, V., Tommasi, P., Sbodio, M.L., Stephenson, M., Aonghusa, P.M.: Improving cross-domain information sharing for care coordination using semantic web technologies. In: IUI. (2014)

[8] Gawande, A.: The hot spotters. New Yorker **86** (2011) 41

[9] 100000 Homes Campaign: Vulnerability index, prioritizing the street homeless population by mortality risk. (`http://www.naph.org/Main-Menu-Category/Our-Work/Quality-Overview/100000-Homes-Campaign/Vulnerbility-Index.aspx`) Accessed: 2013-05-01.

[10] Baker, C.J., Cheung, K.H.: Semantic web: Revolutionizing knowledge discovery in the life sciences. Springer (2007)

[11] Cheung, K.H., Prudâ ĂŽhommeaux, E., Wang, Y., Stephens, S.: Semantic web for health care and life sciences: a review of the state of the art. Briefings in bioinformatics **10**(2) (2009) 111–113

[12] Manning, M., Aggarwal, A., Gao, K., Tucker-Kellogg, G.: Scaling the walls of discovery: using semantic metadata for integrative problem solving. Briefings in bioinformatics **10**(2) (2009) 164–176

[13] Chen, H., Ding, L., Wu, Z., Yu, T., Dhanapalan, L., Chen, J.Y.: Semantic web for integrated network analysis in biomedicine. Briefings in bioinformatics **10**(2) (2009) 177–192

[14] Puri, C., Gomadam, K., Jain, P., Yeh, P.Z., Verma, K.: Multiple ontologies in healthcare information technology: Motivations and recommendation for ontology mapping and alignment. In: Proc of the Workshop on Working with Multiple Biomedical Ontologies (at ICBO). Volume 26. (2011)

[15] Salvadores, M., Alexander, P.R., Musen, M.A., Noy, N.F.: Bioportal as a dataset of linked biomedical ontologies and terminologies in rdf. Semantic Web **4**(3) (2013) 277–284

[16] Nodine, M., Hee, A., Ngu, H., Bohrer, W.: Semantic brokering over dynamic heterogeneous data sources in infosleuth. In: Proc. of the 15th Inter. Conference on Data Engineering, IEEE Computer Society (1999) 358–365

[17] Burgun, A., et al.: Desiderata for domain reference ontologies in biomedicine. Journal of biomedical informatics **39**(3) (2006) 307–313

[18] Dey, A.K.: Understanding and using context. Personal and ubiquitous computing **5**(1) (2001) 4–7

[19] Lopez, V., Kotoulas, S., Sbodio, M.L., Stephenson, M., Gkoulalas-Divanis, A., Aonghusa, P.M.: Queriocity: A linked data platform for urban information management. In: ISWC (2). (2012) 148–163

[20] Bornea, M.A., Dolby, J., Kementsietsidis, A., Srinivas, K., Dantressangle, P., Udrea, O., Bhattacharjee, B.: Building an efficient RDF store over a relational database. In: SIGMOD. (2013)

[21] Rodriguez-Muro, M., Hardi, J., Calvanese, D.: Quest: Effcient SPARQL-to-SQL for RDF and OWL. In: International Semantic Web Conference (Posters & Demos). (2012)

[22] Stevens, R., Stevens, M.: A family history knowledge base using OWL 2. In: OWLED. (2008)

Reader Preferences and Behavior on Wikipedia

Janette Lehmann
Universitat Pompeu Fabra
Barcelona, Spain
lehmannj@acm.org

Claudia Müller-Birn
Freie Universität Berlin
Berlin, Germany
clmb@inf.fu-berlin.de

David Laniado
Barcelona Media
Barcelona, Spain
david.laniado@gmail.com

Mounia Lalmas
Yahoo Labs
London, UK
mounia@acm.org

Andreas Kaltenbrunner
Barcelona Media
Barcelona, Spain
kaltenbrunner@gmail.com

ABSTRACT

Wikipedia is a collaboratively-edited online encyclopaedia that relies on thousands of editors to both contribute articles and maintain their quality. Over the last years, research has extensively investigated this group of users while another group of Wikipedia users, the readers, their preferences and their behavior have not been much studied. This paper makes this group and its activities *visible* and *valuable* to Wikipedia's editor community. We carried out a study on two datasets covering a 13-months period to obtain insights on users preferences and reading behavior in Wikipedia. We show that the most read articles do not necessarily correspond to those frequently edited, suggesting some degree of non-alignment between user reading preferences and author editing preferences. We also identified that popular and often edited articles are read according to four main patterns, and that how an article is read may change over time. We illustrate how this information can provide valuable insights to Wikipedia's editor community.

Keywords

Wikipedia; reader; reading behavior; reading interest; article quality; editor; engagement

Categories and Subject Descriptors

H.1.2 [**User/Machine Systems**]: Human information processing; H.5.3 [**Group and Organization Interfaces**]: Computer-supported cooperative work, Organizational design

General Terms

Human Factors; Measurement;

1. INTRODUCTION

Peer-production communities have transformed the way people use and experience the Web. The collective action of these communities usually evolves around a digital artifact, such as an online encyclopedia or a piece of software. Wikipedia is a famous example of a peer-production community, and is the focus of our study.

Wikipedia is a multilingual, web-based, free encyclopedia, written collaboratively by a large number of volunteers. Since its creation in 2001, Wikipedia has grown into one of the most visited websites, attracting 530 million unique visitors monthly (October 2013).[1] As of November 2013, Wikipedia was available in 287 languages and comprised about 30 million articles. The English Wikipedia, the largest language version, had more than 30,653 active contributors[2] working on over 4.5 million articles. It was ranked as the 8th most popular website on the Internet in the US,[3] where popularity is measured by the number of page views.

Scholars have attributed the success of Wikipedia to its *production side*, that is the quality of its articles and authors' participation [12, 22, 32]. Thus, Wikipedia's production side has been the focus of numerous studies. A literature review by Okoli et al. [15] covering 477 research studies on Wikipedia showed that 42% of the studies mostly centered on issues related to participation, i.e. how editors create and edit articles, resolve disputes, or organize their community. Only 20% of the studies related to readers in Wikipedia, the *usage side* of Wikipedia, such as examining the popularity of articles or topics in Wikipedia. Less than 1% of the reviewed studies looked at users' reading preferences and only one study investigated reading behavior [15].

One reason for the limited focus on Wikipedia readers might be how scholars consider the role of passive users, i.e. the readers, in online communities. Readers are often considered to not provide any visible contribution to the community, and have been referred to as "lurkers" or "free-riders" who are "more resource-taking than value-adding" [13]. When scholars showed interests in this user group, it was mostly because reading is often seen as the prerequisite for becoming a contributor [14, 16, 17]. For example, Halfaker et al. [8] carried out several experiments to encourage Wikipedia readers to become contributors.

An exception is the work by Antin et al. [2], who claim that reading can be seen as a form of participation and is therefore valuable: the fact that a user is reading an article and not editing could be interpreted as an indication of an article's quality, such as its reliability [1]. Thus, reading activity – the usage side – can provide valuable insights to editors – the production side.

---

[1] http://reportcard.wmflabs.org/
[2] Registered (and signed in) users who made 5 or more edits in a month.
[3] http://www.comscore.com/Insights (for desktop access). The ranking is 9th when accounting for mobile access.

Other peer-production communities, such as open source software development projects, have included the usage side into their definition of success. They use measures that typically revolve around quantifications of volume related to the number of accesses to a particular project's product or outcome [5, 10].

Inspired by these perspectives, we conjecture that the same paradigm can be used in the context of Wikipedia. Instead of looking exclusively at the production side (the editors), we analyze the usage side (the readers) and discuss how our analysis can inform Wikipedia's production side. We explore *users' reading preference and behavior*, and Wikipedians' *editing preference*, which enables such a connection. Through examples, we demonstrate how readers can provide valuable insights to Wikipedia's editor community and that they are *not* resource-taking *but* value-adding.

But first, we review existing literature on reading preference and reading behavior and show that current knowledge is limited and rather exploratory.

2. RELATED WORK

Few studies about reading preference of users on Wikipedia exist. Spoerri et al. [20] examined readers' interests with respect to the topics they read about. The analysis, based on view count, showed that the most accessed articles were in the areas of entertainment (music, films, TV series), politics/history (politicians such as George W. Bush, historical events such as World War II), and geography (places such as Paris or countries such as USA). This aligns with the study reported by Waller et al. [26], who investigated search queries from Australians to Wikipedia. In general, people are more interested in "lighter" topics such as entertainment than in more "serious" or advanced topics. In this paper, we also show that readers in English Wikipedia have similar interests. However, a survey carried out on university students regarding the specific websites they have in mind when searching for information, reveals that 34% of the students would use Wikipedia for factual information and only 6% indicated thinking about Wikipedia when searching for entertainment related information [24].

Preference for both information searching and entertainment is a shared characteristic of Wikipedia readers and editors according to West et al. [27]. The authors leveraged data from a browser toolbar to investigate differences in Web usage between Wikipedia editors, readers and Internet users who did not access Wikipedia. They found that editors are "information-hungry" and "entertainment-loving", as they spend more time on news and search, but also on YouTube and other entertainment sites; Wikipedia readers' preferences are in a middle ground between those of editors and users not accessing Wikipedia.

A comparison of reading behavior and editing activity in Wikipedia was performed by Reinoso et al. [19]. The authors compared for different language editions of Wikipedia the number of page views and the number of edits performed on them. For languages such as English, German and Spanish, the number of views and edits were highly correlated. This was not the case for Japanese and Dutch.

Reading behavior has been studied by Ratkiewicz et al. [18], who explored the dynamics of the popularity of Wikipedia topics. Popularity was defined as the number of hyperlinks linking to an article and the number of clicks to it. The authors found that almost all articles experience a burst just after their creation and the majority of articles receive little attention thereafter. Only few articles show intermittent bursts later in their lifetime. Ten Thij et al. [25] built a model to explain bursts in reading behavior caused by featuring an article on Wikipedia's main page.

Finally, two studies looked at how readers navigate within Wikipedia. Helic [9] analyzed users' click paths on Wikigame, where users must find the way (clicking links) from one randomly selected Wikipedia article to another. The author showed that users are very efficient at navigating; indeed users easily found short paths between the randomly selected articles. Gyllstrom et al. [7] investigated different browsing patterns on Wikipedia. They found out that users' browsing behavior depends more on the page topic than on the linking structure. They suggested that understanding different browsing strategies can help editors to better present or organize their content.

These studies demonstrate the still limited knowledge on user reading behavior on Wikipedia, in particular in relation to Wikipedia's production side. In the following sections, we carry out an analysis to gain insights on reading preference and behavior in Wikipedia, and discuss how these insights can add value to Wikipedia's peer-production side. We start by describing the datasets used in our work.

3. DATASETS

Our study is based on data collected over a period of 13 months (September 2011 to September 2012) from various sources for the English Wikipedia. In the first part of our analysis (Section 4.1), we use all Wikipedia articles to determine and study the most popular topics. To work on a more homogeneous dataset and avoid the effect of structural differences between different types of articles, we then focus for the rest of our analyses on a specific sub-set of articles – namely biography articles which contain descriptions of persons, such as actors, singers and historical figures. Biography articles form the most popular topic in Wikipedia. This approach was already followed in previous research [6]. To detect biographies, we considered all articles belonging to the Wikipedia category "Living people", as well as to the categories "Births by year" and "Deaths by year" and recursively to their subcategories. We then removed categories that did not contain biographies, and articles that were lists of biographies.

Page view data. As a measure of page popularity we use the *page view* data provided by the Wikimedia Foundation.[4] The dataset contains for each page in any Wikimedia project the number of requests per hour. We used this dataset for our study on reading preferences. For the 13-month period under consideration, we aggregated the hourly views for each month, to have monthly views for each article. The resulting dataset comprises a total of 4.3 million articles. The most visited page is the Main page, with 600 million page requests. Within this dataset we identified 1.02 million biography articles having 460 million page views in total.

Browsing data. Page popularity is only one criterion that can be considered when studying readers in Wikipedia. For example, accounting for the time spent on a page and the pages accessed during a visit on Wikipedia provides additional insights on reading activity. This information can be obtained from activity log data containing the entire navigation trace of users.

Since activity log data are not provided by the Wikimedia Foundation, we collected anonymized activity log data (tuples of browser cookie, URL, referral URL and timestamp) for a sample of users who gave their consent to provide browsing data through the Yahoo toolbar.[5] We identified in these browsing data users who have accessed the English Wikipedia by requesting for the following two types of URLs:

---

[4]http://dumps.wikimedia.org/other/pagecounts-raw/

[5]A toolbar is a browser extension that provides additional functionalities and direct access to selected websites.

where $PAGE$ refers to the title of the page that was viewed. We identified these page titles in Wikipedia and resolved redirects to avoid duplicate entries.[6] We detected 288K biography articles, accessed by 387K users, and a total of 4.5M million clicks for our 13-month sample.

Article characteristics. To characterize Wikipedia articles from the editors' side, we computed their length and edit count. We retrieved these data through the Wikimedia Tool Labs [28]. Depending on the time window of our analysis (we used several), we computed for each article its text length (the size in bytes of the last revision of the article for the given time window) and number of edits (the number of revisions of the article during that time window).

To identify articles that have been considered of high quality by the community through its internal quality assessment system, we checked for each article whether it was included in the Wikipedia lists of Featured [29] or Good articles [30], or assigned as an A-class article [31] at the end of our 13-month period. These articles have been assessed by Wikipedia's editors using a set of pre-defined criteria developed over the course of the Wikipedia project, such as being well-written, comprehensive, and neutral. We found that 0.37% of the 1.02 million biography articles were assessed of high quality. 3% of these articles are A-class articles, 74% are good articles, and 23% are featured. In the rest of this paper, we refer to these articles as high quality articles (HQA).

4. READING PREFERENCE

In the first part of our study we look at the *reading preferences* of users on Wikipedia. First, we identify what are the most read topics on Wikipedia and show that articles belonging to the most popular topics do not necessarily correspond to those frequently edited by Wikipedia editors. In other words, reading preferences do not always align with *editor preferences*. We then characterize the difference between reader and editor preferences using a *preference* matrix. All studies in this section are based on the page view data provided by the Wikimedia Foundation.

4.1 Popular topics

In the first part of our analyses, we study the popularity of topics in Wikipedia. We select the 500 most read articles, measured by the number of article views over our data period.[7] We manually assigned a topic to each article using a three-round process.[8] In the first round, we collaboratively coded the articles (about 50) by using Wikipedia categories as reference point until we obtained an almost stable set of topics for these articles. In the second round, we separately coded the remaining articles. In the third round, we checked the assigned topics and discussed all ambiguous cases. To ensure a shared understanding of the existing topics, the second and third rounds were iterative. Newly introduced topics were cross-validated over the entire dataset. This process resulted into 12 distinct topics listed in the first column of Table 1. A description of the topics is provided in the fourth column.

---

[6] http://en.wikipedia.org/wiki/Wikipedia: Redirect

[7] We selected the 500 most read articles only, as we did not observe significant changes in our results by considering more articles.

[8] The hierarchical and overlapping structure of Wikipedia's category system prevent us to automatically determine the main category (the topic) of an article in a straightforward manner.

Table 1: Article topics, percentages of articles in each topic, and percentage of high quality articles ($\%HQA$) in each topic for the 500 most popular articles (measured using page views).

Topics	%Articles	%HQA	Description
Biography	44.2%	31.2%	*Biographies of persons*
Media personality	18.8%	24.5%	
Musician	11.6%	37.9%	
Sportsperson	6.8%	35.3%	
Historical figure	4.2%	33.3%	
Politic./businessp.	1.8%	33.3%	
Criminal/victim	0.4%	0.0%	
Misc	0.4%	50.0%	
Publisher/writer	0.2%	100.0%	
Entertainment	17.4%	32.2%	*Cinema and TV*
Series	10.8%	22.2%	
Movie	5.4%	55.6%	
Misc	1.2%	16.7%	
List	7.6%	0.0%	*"List of" articles*
Tech	5.0%	12.0%	*Web, software, electronics, etc.*
History	4.4%	22.7%	*Wars, monuments, incidents, etc.*
Misc	3.8%	15.8%	*Further articles*
Health	3.4%	23.5%	*Diseases, medicine, etc.*
Leisure	3.2%	18.8%	*Games, novels, etc.*
Sport	3.0%	66.7%	*Sports, sport events, etc.*
Places	2.8%	21.4%	*Regions, buildings, etc.*
Adult	2.6%	7.7%	*Articles about adult content*
Culture/Belief	2.6%	7.7%	*Religions, festivals, etc.*

From Table 1, we see that a large percentage of users access Wikipedia to read about entertainment-related topics such as TV series, movies, and biographies of actors and singers. Articles related to history, health and tech content (such as web services and software) are also frequently accessed. This is in accordance with previous studies [21, 26].

The third column of Table 1 shows the percentage of high quality articles per topic. The lower the topic popularity, the smaller the number of high quality articles belonging to that topic. Indeed, we observe a Spearman's rank correlation coefficient of $\rho = 0.72$ (*p*-value < 0.01), suggesting a high correlation between topic popularity and the percentage of high quality articles. However, there are some exceptions. For instance, for the topics "Health" and "Sport", although the percentage of articles belonging to these topics is relatively low, many articles are of good or high quality (23.5%, and 66.7%, respectively). On the other hand, the percentage of high quality articles in the "Tech" area is low (12.0%), albeit this being the fourth most popular topic in our dataset.

These observations suggest some degree of non-alignment between *users'* reading preferences and *authors'*[9] editing preferences. To examine this further, we define several measures to characterize these two preferences next.

4.2 Reading and editing preferences

Table 1 provides a first indication of some non-alignment between reading and editing preferences in Wikipedia. In this section, we define various measures to study this.

Measuring reading preferences. In this paper, we define reading preference as the popularity of articles, measured by the number of page views. Previous studies suggest that popularity is a dynamic phenomenon that can partly be characterized by bursty behavior of page views [18, 25]. Our goal is to determine a value that best represents the popularity of an article by filtering out such bursty behavior. Thus, we calculate the monthly article popularity measured by the number of page views in each month from September 2011 to September 2012. Then, we measure the median rank of ar-

---

[9] In this paper, we use author and editor interchangeably.

Table 2: Spearman's rank correlation coefficient ρ between measures capturing reader and editor preferences.

	$ArticleLength_a$	$\#Edits_a$
$Popularity_a$	0.22	0.16

ticle popularity ($Popularity_a$) by their monthly popularity, which is less sensitive to outliers.

Measuring editing preferences. To determine editors' preferences, i.e. the articles they are mostly working on, we use three measures, each indicating a particular angle regarding editors' preferences. First, we employ the number of edits ($\#Edits_a$), a common measure of editing activity. For each article, we calculate the number of revisions over the whole period range. This measure, however, does not provide information about the effect of an edit, such as its informativeness and quality. We therefore propose to use article length ($ArticleLength_a$) as a measure for the informativeness of an article. The fact that an article is long suggests that a number of editors spent time and effort writing about the topic of the article, to make it more informative. We calculate the length of an article for a given time period using the latest version of the article in that period. Finally, editing may lead to the article being identified by the community as good, featured, or A-class (the pinnacle of the editing process). This would happen when the article is considered to provide comprehensive information on a topic.[10] We use the available data provided by Wikipedia – whether an article is a good or featured article, or belongs to the A-class articles (HQA_a) at the end of our data period – as a measure for article quality.

We compare reader and editor preferences by measuring the correlation between the reader preference measure $Popularity_a$ and the editor preference measures $ArticleLength_a$ and $\#Edits_a$. As discussed in Section 3, we focus on biography articles, which form the most popular article topic in Table 1. Table 2 reports the Spearman's rank correlation coefficient ρ for the three metrics. We observe low correlations: 0.22 for $ArticleLength_a$, and 0.16 for $\#Edits_a$. These values suggest some non-alignment between reader and editor preferences. To further investigate this, we built a linear regression model using $ArticleLength_a$, $\#Edits_a$, and HQA_a as features to predict the number of page views of an article. Our model predicted the number of page views with a coefficient of determination of $R^2 = 0.24$ ($R^2 = 1.0$ would represent a perfect fitting model), further indicating that readers and editors preferences diverge in many cases.

Next, we introduce a *preference* matrix, which allows visualizing the differences in reading and editing preferences using the above defined measures.

4.3 Preference matrix

For each article, we calculate its popularity (our reading preference measure) and its length (an editing preference measure).

The distributions of popularity values and article length values indicate whether articles are popular or not, and whether articles are long or short. We determine the upper and lower quartiles of both distributions since we want to identify articles with extreme values. We remove all articles that fall into the interquartile range of the article length or popularity distribution (the middle $25 - 75\%$ of both distributions). This means that we only consider articles that differ significantly from those having an average length or popularity.

---

[10]See criteria for featured articles http://en.wikipedia.org/wiki/Wikipedia:Featured_article_criteria

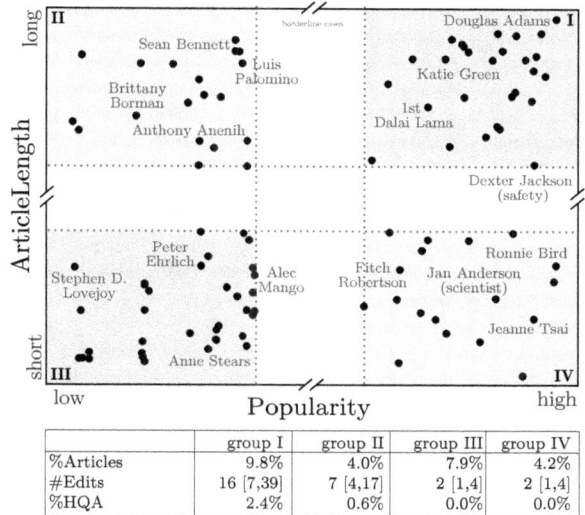

	group I	group II	group III	group IV
%Articles	9.8%	4.0%	7.9%	4.2%
#Edits	16 [7,39]	7 [4,17]	2 [1,4]	2 [1,4]
%HQA	2.4%	0.6%	0.0%	0.0%

Figure 1: (Top) Preference matrix defined by article popularity and length. (Bottom) Percentage of articles belonging to a group (%$Articles$), median and interquartile range of the number of edits per group over the whole data range (#$Edits$), and percentage of high quality articles in each group (%HQA).

This results in the four groups of articles shown in Figure 1. The horizontal axis represents article popularity (the reading preference) and the vertical axis represents article length (one of the measures characterizing editing preference). The values of both measures are transformed into an ordinal scale to overcome scaling issues, i.e. we ranked all values for article popularity and article length. Each dot in the matrix represents an article and the position corresponds to its popularity and length. We only show a random sample of 100 articles in Figure 1 to improve legibility.

Under the preference matrix, we report the percentage of articles belonging to each group, and the other two editing preference measures, namely, the percentage of high quality articles, and the median and interquartile range of the number of edits. We see that featured articles tend to be long, confirming previous work [33] and suggesting a relationship between article length and article quality.

Many articles belong to group I (9.8%) and group III (7.9%). Whereas group I contains very long and often read articles, articles in group III are short and seldom read. In both groups, we have articles for which editing and reading preferences align.

A divergence between reader and editor preferences can be observed for articles belonging to groups II and IV. Group II articles (4% of all articles) tend to be not read very often, even though they are very long (probably very informative). This group also contains a low number of high quality articles. For instance, it contains the biographies of the Nigerian politician "Anthony Anenih" and the American football player "Sean Bennett". We speculate that not many users read these articles because the person in question is not popular nowadays (e.g., former American football player) or is of interest only to a specific user community (e.g., users interested in Nigerian politics). This is further accentuated by the lower edit activity in this group (median of 7 edits) compared to group I (median of 16 edits). In fact, many of the articles forming group II are on topics that were popular in the past and heavily edited during that time.

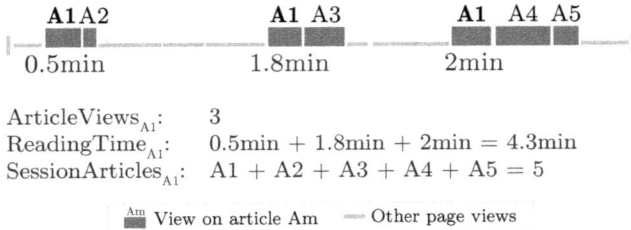

A1 A2   **A1 A3**   **A1 A4 A5**

0.5min   1.8min   2min

$ArticleViews_{A1}$:   3
$ReadingTime_{A1}$:   0.5min + 1.8min + 2min = 4.3min
$SessionArticles_{A1}$:   A1 + A2 + A3 + A4 + A5 = 5

^{Am} View on article Am   — Other page views

Figure 2: Example of a reading session on Wikipedia showing the reading behavior measures for article $A1$.

Finally, 4.2% of all articles belong to group IV. For these articles as well, reader and editor preferences do not align. Even though articles are regularly accessed by readers, they are short (and have seldom been edited) and none of them is of high quality. Taking the examples of "Jan Anderson (scientist)" and "Ronnie Bird", we see that these articles are often viewed, but are short and have hardly been edited during the last 13 months (median of 3 edits per article). Additionally, none of these articles is considered to be of high quality, even though readers access them very often.

To summarize, we observe differences between what readers access and what editors work on. The most edited articles tend to be long (groups I and II) and the number of high quality articles in these groups is higher compared to the other two groups. However, only articles in group I are very popular, suggesting that article quality does not drive popularity.

The opposite can be observed for articles in groups III and IV. These groups contain shorter articles, and fewer high quality articles. Moreover, articles in these groups tend to be edited less. This indicates that editors rarely added content to them in the past, reflecting low interests in these articles. Whereas articles in group III neither meet authors nor readers interests, we can see that readers are interested in articles of group IV despite the scarce attention these receive from editors.

Next, we analyze how users read articles during their browsing sessions, and how this matches with the editing activity.

5. READING BEHAVIOR

Here we study how users read Wikipedia articles. That is, we look at the biographies that users read when *visiting* Wikipedia. We introduce three measures to characterize patterns of reading behavior: $ArticleViews_a$, $ReadingTime_a$ and $SessionArticles_a$.

Reading session. We separated the reading activity of users by sessions, where a session is a sequence of pages visited by a user until he or she goes offline. Following [3], a user is said to have gone offline – meaning that the session has ended – if more than 30 minutes have elapsed between two successive activities of that user. All reading activities of a user on Wikipedia during this session form what we refer to as a *reading session*.

During a reading session, a user spends time reading an article a. We use $ReadingTime_a$ to refer to the time spent on article a. This user may return to article a several times during a session, and visit several other articles. To capture these, we define two additional measures: $ArticleViews_a$ is the number of times the article a was viewed and $SessionArticles_a$ is the number of articles viewed during the reading session where article a was read.

In Figure 2 we show an example of a reading session of a user. The figure depicts how the user visits articles on Wikipedia as well as several other webpages. The starting point on Wikipedia is article $A1$. After reading this article, the user follows a link to article $A2$. Then, he or she probably clicks on an external link to navigate to other websites. After a while, the user returns to article $A1$ and then uses a link to reach article $A3$. This pattern occurs another time during this session. At the bottom of Figure 2 the values for the aforementioned three measures are given.

Data processing. We use the browsing data as it enables us to access the readers' entire navigation traces (Wikipedia articles and other webpages) during their browsing sessions. To have a more homogeneous and robust dataset, we discarded articles with lower values of length or popularity, and focused our analysis on articles belonging to group I of the preference matrix (see Figure 1), which contains the large majority of articles in our browsing data (83.47%). These articles allow for a reliable interpretation of any observed difference between reading interests and editing preferences since their length and popularity are high enough.

We characterize the reading behavior of an article a by calculating per month the average of $ArticleViews_a$, $ReadingTime_a$ and $SessionArticles_a$. We also calculate $Popularity_a$, the popularity measure defined in the previous section. Therefore, for each article a we obtain 13 vectors, one for each month of the 13-month period. We refer to each vector ($ArticleViews_a$, $ReadingTime_a$, $SessionArticles_a$, $Popularity_a$) as a *behavior vector*.

We generate behavior vectors of an article for the months where it was visited in at least 10 reading sessions. This enables us to derive stable values for the three measures calculated based on reading sessions. This results into 9,726 articles and 49,921 behavior vectors. To ensure that the two datasets (page view and browsing data) are comparable, i.e., no strong bias in the browsing data is influencing our results, we ranked the articles according to their overall popularity in both datasets, and found that their rankings correlate (Spearman's rank correlation coefficient was of 0.64).

5.1 Reading patterns

We use the k-means algorithm to cluster the behavior vectors. Since our dataset does not follow a normal distribution, and thus to avoid the extensive influence of heavy outliers, we do not use the value of each measure, but the corresponding article rank. The number of clusters is determined by a minimal cluster size such that each cluster contains at least 20% of the 49,921 behavior vectors. Since the clustering is performed with the behavior vectors of the articles, an article can occur in multiple clusters. This allows us to analyze changes in the reading pattern of an article across the 13-month period; we return to this in Section 5.2.

We obtain four clusters, shown in Figure 3, each corresponding to a pattern of reading behavior. The first row displays the name given to each pattern. The second row contains the cluster centers normalized by the z-score. Each bar corresponds to one measure. The vertical axis shows how many standard deviations a rank value is above or below the mean rank, on average. This means that bars above zero indicate higher ranks for the respective measure whereas bars below zero indicate lower ranks. The third row contains the number of articles and behavior vectors within each cluster. Since the sizes of the clusters are similar, there is no dominant reading pattern. As some subtopics are more predominant (e.g., there are more articles about media personalities and musicians), the fourth row shows the percentage of articles of the various biography subtopics (e.g., musicians, sportspersons) that belong to a given cluster.[11] We only show the subtopics with the largest percentage. The last three rows of Figure 3 report the values

---

[11] For each cluster, we sampled at random a subset of 500 articles, and determined the sub-categories of these articles by using the three-round process described in Section 4.1. We manually catego-

	Focus	Trending	Exploration	Passing
Reading behavior				
	5,278 articles 10,605 behavior vectors	3,876 articles 14,267 behavior vectors	4,826 articles 11,579 behavior vectors	5,684 articles 13,470 behavior vectors

Article topic		CA			CA			CA			CA
	artist/writer	43%		historical fig.	42%		sportsperson	28%		media pers.	27%
	historical fig.	41%		criminal/victim	38%		musician	26%		sportsperson	27%
	polit./businessp.	37%		musican	38%		media pers.	23%		musician	19%

	Focus	Trending	Exploration	Passing
ArtLen	28K [16K,51K]	38K [21K,69K]	26K [15K,45K]	16K [10K,27K]
#Edits	11 [5,23]	20 [9,41]	10 [5,21]	8 [3,18]
%HQA	7.7%	16.9%	10.5%	5.1%

■ Popularity$_a$ ■ ArticleViews$_a$ ▨ ReadingTime$_a$ □ SessionArticles$_a$

CA - Percentage in topic   ArtLen - Article length   #Edits - Number of edits   %HQA - Percentage of high quality articles

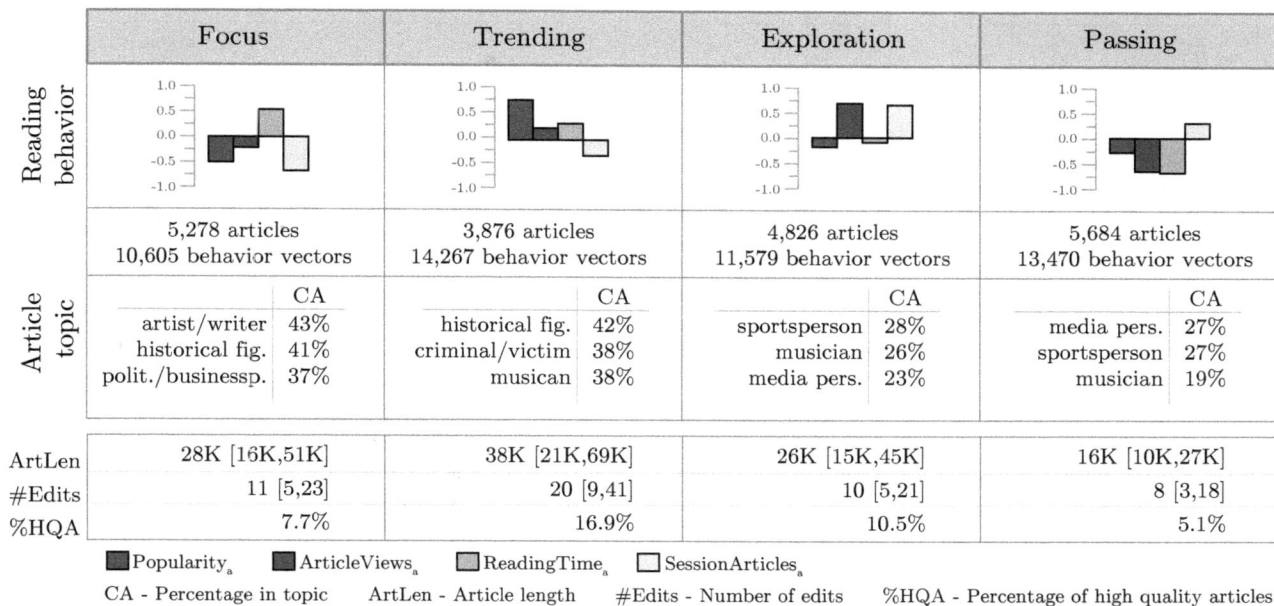

Figure 3: (1st row) Article clusters and reading characteristics. (2nd row) Number of articles and behavior vectors per cluster. (3rd row) Most dominant article topics per cluster. (4th row) Median and interquartile range of the article length ($ArtLen$), number of edits per cluster ($\#Edits$), and percentage of high quality articles in each group ($\%HQA$).

of the three editing preference measures. For each behavior vector, we calculated the length of the corresponding article, using the latest revision of the article for the given month, and the number of edits made during the month (we report median and interquartile range). We also determined the percentage of high quality articles.

We discuss now each of the identified reading patterns and relate them to the editing preferences. The patterns "Focus", "Trending", and "Exploration" are what content portals aspire to: users spending time reading their articles and/or reading many articles.

Focus. Articles following this pattern are characterized by an expected encyclopedic reading behavior: people spend a lot of time reading the article (high $ReadingTime_a$), but access very few other articles (low value of $SessionArticles_a$) within the session. Users have a specific information need (e.g., they want to learn something about "Jacques Cousteau"). Articles in this cluster have a lower than average popularity, and are about artists/writers, historical figures, and politicians/businesspersons.

The high reading time indicates a strong interest in the content of the article. Hence, we would expect many of these articles to be marked as good, featured, or A-class, as the quality of these articles seems important. However, the percentage of high quality articles in "Focus" ($\%HQA = 7.7\%$) is lower than for the "Trending" and "Exploration" clusters. Moreover, although we observe an appropriate article length ($ArtLen = 28K$), the number of edits ($\#Edits = 11$) suggests that editors are not interested in improving these articles. Indeed, the article about "Jacques Cousteau" is long (a median of $30K$ characters), but it is neither featured nor good nor A-class, and the number of edits is low (a median of 5.5 edits per month).

Trending. Many biographies about historical figures, musicians and criminals/victims follow this pattern: articles are visited very often (high $Popularity_c$). Users read only a few other articles

(low $SessionArticles_a$), similarly to the "Focus" reading pattern, but they spend less time reading the articles. This suggests that users are probably "quickly looking up" for information about something that is currently trending or has recently happened. For example, users read about the politician "Ron Paul" when he was a candidate for the presidency of the United States, but only to catch up on any recent news about him.

"Trending" articles exhibit the highest edit activity and the highest percentage of high quality articles compared to the other two clusters ($\#Edits = 20$ and $\%HQA = 16.9\%$). These articles not only attract users to read them but also authors to edit them, which is in accordance with a previous study by Reinoso [19] and also aligns with the work from Keegan et al. [11] about breaking news and current events in Wikipedia. The high percentage of high quality articles suggests that editors do not only work on the articles to increase the quality, but also to "update" information caused by recent or continuous events related to the article topic. Indeed, we saw in our dataset that featured articles are also edited frequently (a median of 19 edits per month). Featured articles are usually only changed in case new information becomes available.

Returning to our previous example, the politician "Ron Paul", we observed a median of 81 edits per months during the time the article was trending (December 2011 until May 2012). In the other months (when "Ron Paul" was not competing for the presidential primaries), the article belonged to the "Focus" cluster and had only 20 edits per month. We return to this later in this section.

Exploration. This pattern primarily contains biographies describing sportspersons, musicians, and media personalities that have an average popularity. The number of articles viewed in a session ($SessionArticles_a$) is the highest compared to the other clusters, indicating that users explore many other articles in a reading session. Looking into the articles that were visited, we saw that articles requested during the same session belong mostly to

rized all articles based on the subtopics of the category biography as shown in Table 1.

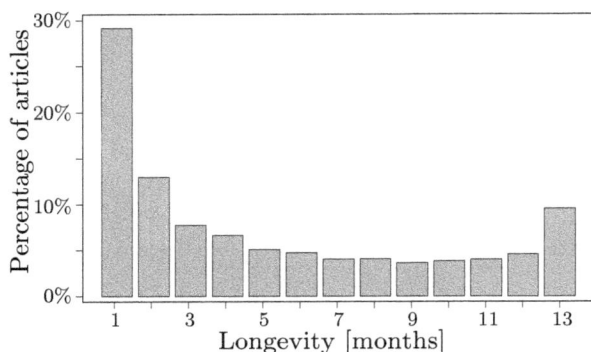

Figure 4: Stability of articles: *longevity* is the number of months in which an article was visited in at least 10 reading sessions. For each longevity value, we plot the percentage of articles with that value.

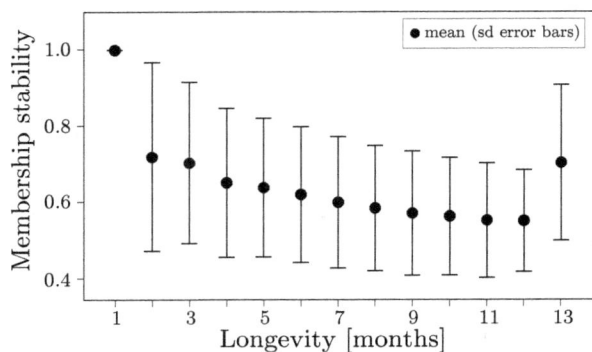

Figure 5: Stability of articles: *membership* is the average fraction of the months of its longevity an article remains in its "home" (i.e. most frequent) cluster. For each longevity value, we plot the mean and standard deviation of the membership values of the articles.

the same topic[12] (e.g., users who read the article about the actor "Al Pacino" also read articles about his movies). The high value of $ArticleViews_a$ indicates that users return regularly to the article under consideration, suggesting that they use it as a basis to navigate to other articles on the same topic. This hypothesis is supported by the low reading time of the focal article.

The editing preferences are comparable to the "Focus" pattern, in terms of number of edits (moderate values of 10 edits per article) and article length. The difference between the "Focus" and the "Exploration" reading patterns may be explained by external factors that influence the consumption of online content by users, such as the death of a famous artist [18].

Passing. Many biography articles about sportspersons, musicians, and media personalities belong to this cluster. The number of articles viewed in a session ($SessionArticles_a$) is above average, suggesting that users read different articles. Users browse many articles in the same session, but in contrast to "Exploration" they seem to only pass through the focal article (low $ReadingTime_a$), and do not return to it (low $ArticleViews_a$).

An example is the article about "Jackie Jackson", member of "The Jackson 5". When users are reading about "The Jacksons", they also view this article, but then quickly move to other related articles. The question is whether users do not spend much time on the article, because they are not interested in reading more about "Jackie Jackson", or because there is not much information provided about her (her article has a median text length of 9K).

Indeed, compared to the other clusters, the "Passing" cluster has a lower percentage of high quality articles ($\%HQA = 5.1\%$), and has shorter articles ($ArtLen = 16K$) and the lowest number of edits per article (a median of 8).

To summarize, we observe that articles exhibit different reading patterns. These seem to be mainly driven by the topics of the articles and therefore the interests of users, and less by their quality. Thereby, users show their interest in an article in different ways, e.g., by exploring also related articles ("Exploration" cluster) or by spending time reading the article ("Focus" cluster). Sometimes, the interest in an article is driven by external factors, as shown with

---

[12]We extracted all wikilinks between the articles in each reading session and found that on average over 76% of the articles visited in a session are connected to one another. This applies even for long reading sessions containing more than 10 articles (the average becomes 70%).

articles belonging to the "Trending" cluster (e.g., users read biographies about currently trending persons). On the other hand, for articles belonging to the "Passing" cluster, the question is whether the reading behavior is partly caused by a lower quality of the articles. In future work, we will investigate this. Overall, our results show that popularity and reading time are not the only factors that should be taken into account when measuring user reading preferences – how often users return to an article and how many other related articles they read provide further information about their reading preferences.

Three out of the four clusters constitute reading patterns where users are interested in the articles they are reading. However, editors seem to focus on articles in mainly one cluster, the "Trending cluster". The editing activity, the article length and the percentage of high quality articles is higher in that cluster, than in the "Focus" and "Exploration" cluster. This shows again a non-alignment between reader and editor preferences.

Finally, as shown in our example of "Ron Paul", an article can be in several clusters, depending on the month under consideration. That is, articles can transition between patterns across the 13-month period. We study this next.

5.2 Changes in reading patterns

The analysis conducted in the previous section used measures calculated on a monthly basis (the behavior vectors) to identify reading patterns. As a result, articles can belong to more than one cluster. In this section, we use this fact to study how articles might move (if they do) between reading patterns, and discuss possible reasons for these transitions. First, we determine how stable articles are in terms of their popularity and the way they are read across the 13-month period. We then look at typical transitions between reading patterns.

Stability. We calculate the number of months in which an article was visited in at least 10 reading sessions. We refer to this as the article *longevity*, denoted $Longevity_a$ for article a. In Figure 4, we plot on the x-axis the longevity values and on the y-axis the percentage of articles for a given longevity value. Almost 30% of the articles (2, 836) have a longevity value of 1, meaning that these articles have been accessed in at least 10 reading sessions only in a single one-month period. Another 13% of the articles (1, 264) have been accessed in at least 10 reading sessions in two different months. This percentage decreases continuously for larger numbers of months, but increases again for 11 and more months. About 10% (928) of articles are read at least 10 times a month over the whole 13-month period. This suggests that there are articles that are frequently accessed over a long time period.

We examine the stability of an article in terms of which clusters it belongs to (i.e., the reading patterns it exhibits). We calculate the number of months an article a remains in its "home" cluster, which is the predominant reading pattern exhibited by the article. Then, we normalize this value by dividing it with the corresponding $Longevity_a$ value. We refer to this as the article *membership* stability, denoted $Membership_a$ for article a. In Figure 5, the y-axis shows the average and standard deviation of the *membership* values for all articles for a given longevity. For example, an article with a longevity of 3 (the article was visited in at least 10 reading sessions during three, not necessarily consecutive, months) has a membership value of 0.7 on average. This means that on average the article was read 70% of its lifetime according to its most frequent reading pattern.

Figure 5 suggests that the higher an article's longevity, the lower its membership stability. This means that the longer - in terms of months - the article is accessed frequently, the higher the probability that its reading pattern changes. However, the average membership stability values are always above 0.5, indicating that many articles remain in their "home" cluster for at least 50% of their lifetime. It is interesting to note that the membership stability increases again for articles with a longevity value of 13. This means that high longevity implies high membership stability.

Next, we look at changes of reading patterns of articles and explore possible reasons behind these changes.

Transitions. We study the most frequent changes, i.e., transitions, between reading patterns (clusters). A $Transition_a$ exists for an article a if one behavior vector of a belongs to cluster C at month m and another behavior vector belongs to cluster D at month $m + 1$, where the clusters represent two distinct reading patterns. We selected two cases to explore transitions. We consider all articles and then only articles with a $Longevity_a$ value of 13 – the set of highly stable articles in terms of their monthly access rate.

In Figure 6, we visualize the transitions between the four clusters by two networks, one for each case. Each vertex represents one cluster (i.e., reading pattern) and the size of a vertex corresponds to the number of articles in that cluster. The undirected edges in the network depict the transitions between the clusters. We use an undirected network since we observed a similar number of transitions in both directions. The largest difference we observed is smaller than 2.0%, which can be explained by the fact that an article usually belongs to one cluster (e.g., "Exploration"), moves to another cluster for a short time (e.g., to "Trending" because something happened with the person under consideration), and then moves back to the original cluster.

Each edge has a weight, which is the percentual amount of transitions between two clusters; for example, an edge weight of 23% means that 23% of all transitions in the network take place between these two clusters.

The complete network (left side of Figure 6) show how external factors, such as recent or continuous events related to a person, drive changes in reading patterns. This is the case for example for the biography article of the Facebook co-founder "Chris Hughes". Before March 2012, users tended to "pass by" this article (when reading about Facebook). However, this changed in March 2012 when Chris Hughes became the owner of the "The New Republic" magazine, attracting some media attention. Users started reading this article in a more "explorative" manner, using it as a starting point to access other articles related to the person.

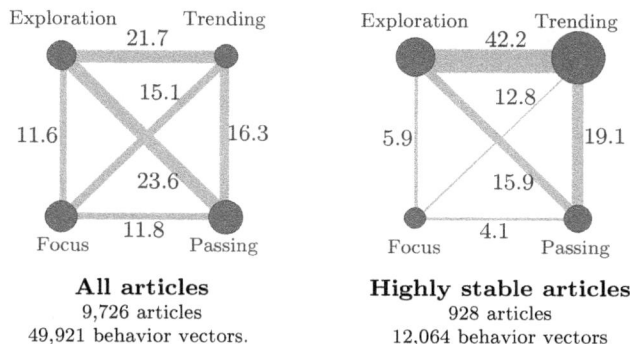

All articles
9,726 articles
49,921 behavior vectors.

Highly stable articles
928 articles
12,064 behavior vectors

Figure 6: Transitions between reading patterns considering all articles (left) and only articles with a high stability (right). The vertex size represents the number of articles that belong to the cluster, and the edge weight represents the percentage of transitions between two clusters.

The edge weights differ a lot in the network. We see a strong connection between the "Passing", "Exploration", and "Trending" clusters, indicating that many articles adopt all three reading patterns and sway between clusters. A transition can be even long-lasting, as in the case of the article "Jacqueline Kennedy Onassis". Until April 2012, the article was in the "Trending" cluster, but then lost its popularity and moved to the "Exploration" cluster. We assume that the article started to trend when her audio tapes, recorded after her husband's assassination, were released.

We observe also that articles belonging to the "Focus" cluster are isolated – the likelihood that an article is moving from or to the "Focus" cluster is low. Articles that are read in this way can be considered as the most stable ones, as their reading behavior hardly varies. An example of such an article is "Franklin D. Roosevelt".

Looking at stable articles only (right side of Figure 6) we see a different pattern. Compared to the network comprising all articles, we observe that "Focus" becomes even more isolated, showing again its special characteristic – a constant reading pattern. The transitions between "Exploration" and "Trending" become stronger, whereas the transitions between "Exploration" and "Passing" become weaker. Returning to Figure 3 we see that the "Exploration" and "Trending" clusters contain the same type of biographies: media personalities, musicians, and sportspersons. We conclude that these two clusters indeed describe reading patterns for the same type of articles.

6. DISCUSSION

We analyzed readers' preferences and reading behavior. We did so by connecting them to editors' preferences, allowing us to relate the usage side of Wikipedia to its production side. Our goal was to provide insights about how the reading experience and the editing process on Wikipedia could be enhanced. We discuss now our main results, position them in light of our goal, and present examples of potential applications.

Using the page view data provided by the Wikimedia Foundation, we studied reading preferences of users on Wikipedia. Our results confirm other works showing the dominance of *entertainment-related topics* among the most read topics on Wikipedia [21, 26]. The encyclopedic character of Wikipedia does not exempt it from following the known prominence of consuming and interacting with entertainement-related content observed on the Web.

We then introduced a preference matrix, which enabled us to differentiate four groups of reading versus editing preferences. These groups provide valuable insights into Wikipedia's quality system, in particular groups II and IV, where the preferences do not align.

Group II articles are often edited but not often read, whereas group IV contains articles that are popular, but hardly looked at by editors. Being aware of these divergences can help Wikipedia editors making an *informed* decision about which articles to focus next. As opposed to tools such as WikiDashboard [23], which allows readers to evaluate article quality on the basis of an author history, the preference matrix can provide editors with a visualization of user reading preferences. This might draw their attention to articles or topics they have not edited before. Moreover, task recommendation services, such as the SuggestBot [4], could use the preference matrix as input to recommending tasks.

In the second part of our work, we studied the reading behavior of users and identified four main reading patterns: "Focus", "Trending", "Exploration" and "Passing". Information about the reading behavior of users can be useful in many ways, such as for the selection of articles for the main page, or the Article Feedback Tool (AFT).[13] Knowing which articles follow, for instance, the "Focus" pattern might help making the Article Feedback Tool more efficient since using this tool over the entire Wikipedia corpus failed. Editors complained about the low quality of the feedback made on articles. The fact that an article is often read and users spent time on it may indicate that users are interested in the article. As such, their feedback (if any) is likely to be more constructive and valuable.

In conformity with the work from Gyllstrom et al. [7], we showed that the reading behavior depends less on the article quality, but more on the article topic and therefore the interests of the reader. The quality of articles does not greatly influence what users choose to read. In general, the editing activity and the quality of articles reflect mostly the authors' interests and not the readers' interests. The exception to this are articles belonging to the "Trending" pattern, which are both accessed by many users and edited by many authors, compared to the three other reading patterns.

Understanding reader preferences and behavior can support editors in their work in several ways. The identified browsing patterns provide information about which articles the readers are interested in and how these and related content are read. If readers are interested in an article topic, they tend to look up information ("Trending"), spend a lot of time in reading the article ("Focus"), or consume the article content, but also related information ("Exploration").

This information can be used to improve the structure and presentation of the article content. For instance, the "Exploration" pattern corresponds to a navigation "way" to consume Wikipedia content. One article is focal, but also acts as a source to explore other articles. Knowing that these articles are consumed in this way, Wikipedia editors may add more links, keeping the users engaged by providing additional and relevant content. From an interface design perspective, navigation tools could be provided to guide users with the aim to enhance their reading experience.

Additionally, reading pattern can help editors to decide which articles to edit next. For instance, for the "Focus" pattern, we observed the highest reading time per article compared to all other patterns, but the proportion of high quality articles is lower than in the "Trending" and "Exploration" cluster. With respect to Wikipedia's production side, articles following the "Focus" pattern may greatly benefit from improvement in their quality, as users are very interested in them.

---

[13] http://en.wikipedia.org/wiki/Wikipedia:
Article_Feedback_Tool

Also articles belonging to the "Passing" cluster may benefit from improvements. We assumed that users are not interested in the article, and therefore only pass through the focal article during their reading session. Another explanation is that these articles are not very informative (they are often short), and have rarely (likely as a consequence) been marked as good or chosen to be featured. In future work, we will investigate this hypothesis.

Finally, we looked at the stability of the reading patterns. We found that many articles are stable (remain in the same cluster), and that changes of the reading patterns are of temporal nature (e.g., in case of an event) or due to the time passing (e.g., interest in the person is decreasing). Studying the transitions between the reading patterns revealed two main findings. First, we observed a strong connection between the "Exploration" and "Trending" clusters, indicating that many articles adopt both reading patterns. Second, we observed that the "Focus" cluster represents a reading pattern that is isolated from the others. Articles in this cluster usually do not change their reading pattern. It indicates that this pattern represents articles with a high stability.

The above observations can inform the Wikipedia editor community in two ways. The stability of articles allows them to make long-lasting decisions for their editorial work. For instance, when adapting an article for explorative reading, these adaptions, such as adding links, are useful for the consumption of that article later on. On the other hand, transitions between reading patterns inform editors about recent trends (e.g., when an article is moving from "Passing" to "Exploration", indicating an increased interest from the reader side). Such articles can be candidates to be placed on the front page to raise awareness.

In future research, we will look more closely into the structural aspects of the article and how these may affect user reading behavior. It will also be important to look at different topics (beyond biographies) and how a specific reading behavior might depend on the topic.

7. CONCLUDING REMARKS

This paper provides new insights about how users consume content on Wikipedia: their reading preferences and behaviour. This paper also attempts to connect Wikipedia's readers (usage side) and Wikipedia's editors (production side). Using several measures to characterize reading preferences and behavior, we learn how users consume Wikipedia content, and illustrate how this information could inform Wikipedia editors about their editing tasks, for instance which articles to prioritize and why.

Identifying how an article is read can be used to determine which articles are more "engaging" than others, for instance, as measured by the average time spent on the article or the number of articles accessed from it. Articles that are more engaging are likely to promote a successful reading experience and even encourage users to return to them or to other articles. Readers that regularly return to Wikipedia are more likely to recognize the effort of Wikipedia's community and might even develop a sense of belonging to that community [17]. This in itself may further engage Wikipedia editors as they feel that their work is recognized and appreciated.

8. ACKNOWLEDGMENTS

This work was partially funded by Grant TIN2012-38741 (Understanding Social Media: An Integrated Data Mining Approach) of the Ministry of Economy and Competitiveness of Spain, and by CENIT program, project CEN-20101037 "Social Media". This work was carried out as part of Janette Lehmann's PhD internship at Yahoo Labs Barcelona.

9. REFERENCES

[1] B. T. Adler, K. Chatterjee, L. de Alfaro, M. Faella, I. Pye, and V. Raman. Assigning trust to Wikipedia content. In *Proc. WikiSym*, 2008.

[2] J. Antin and C. Cheshire. Readers are not free-riders: reading as a form of participation on Wikipedia. In *Proc. CSCW*, 2010.

[3] L. D. Catledge and J. E. Pitkow. Characterizing browsing strategies in the World-Wide Web. In *Proc. WWW*, 1995.

[4] D. Cosley, D. Frankowski, L. Terveen, and J. Riedl. Suggestbot: using intelligent task routing to help people find work in wikipedia. In *Proc. IUI*, 2007.

[5] K. Crowston, H. Annabi, J. Howison, and C. Masango. Towards a portfolio of floss project success measures. In *Proc. ICSE*, 2004.

[6] L. Flekova, O. Ferschke, and I. Gurevych. What Makes a Good Biography? Multidimensional Quality Analysis Based on Wikipedia Article Feedback Data. In *Proc. WWW*, 2014.

[7] K. Gyllstrom and M.-F. Moens. Surfin' Wikipedia: An Analysis of the Wikipedia (Non-random) Surfer's Behavior from Aggregate Access Data. In *Proc. IIIX*, 2012.

[8] A. Halfaker, O. Keyes, and D. Taraborelli. Making Peripheral Participation Legitimate: Reader engagement experiments in Wikipedia. In *Proc. CSCW*, 2013.

[9] D. Helic. Analyzing user click paths in a wikipedia navigation game. In *MIPRO*, pages 374–379, 2012.

[10] A. Iriberri and G. Leroy. A life-cycle perspective on online community success. *ACM Comput. Surv.*, 41(2), 2009.

[11] B. Keegan, D. Gergle, and N. Contractor. Hot Off the Wiki Structures and Dynamics of Wikipedia's Coverage of Breaking News Events. *American Behavioral Scientist*, 57(5):595–622, 2013.

[12] A. Kittur and R. E. Kraut. Harnessing the wisdom of crowds in wikipedia: quality through coordination. In *Proc. CSCW*, 2008.

[13] P. Kollock. The economies of online cooperation: Gifts and public goods in cyberspace. In *Communities in Cyberspace*, pages 220–239. Routledge, 1990.

[14] J. Lave and E. Wenger. *Situated Learning: Legitimate Peripheral Participation (Learning in Doing: Social, Cognitive & Computational Perspectives)*. Cambridge University Press, September 1991.

[15] C. Okoli, M. Mehdi, M. Mesgari, F. Å. Nielsen, and A. Lanamäki. The People's Encyclopedia Under the Gaze of the Sages: A Systematic Review of Scholarly Research on Wikipedia. http://ssrn.com/abstract=2021326, 2012.

[16] J. Preece, B. Nonnecke, and D. Andrews. The top five reasons for lurking: improving community experiences for everyone. *Comp. in Human Behavior*, 20(2), 2004.

[17] J. Preece and B. Shneiderman. The reader-to-leader framework: Motivating technology-mediated social participation. *TOCHI*, 1, 2009.

[18] J. Ratkiewicz, S. Fortunato, A. Flammini, F. Menczer, and A. Vespignani. Characterizing and modeling the dynamics of online popularity. *Phys. Rev. Lett.*, 105:158701, Oct 2010.

[19] A. J. Reinoso. *Temporal and behavioral patterns in the use of Wikipedia*. PhD thesis, Universidad Rey Juan Carlos, 2011.

[20] A. Spoerri. Visualizing the overlap between the 100 most visited pages on Wikipedia for September 2006 to January 2007. *First Monday*, 12(4), 2007.

[21] A. Spoerri. What is popular on wikipedia and why? *First Monday*, 12(4), 2007.

[22] B. Stvilia, M. B. Twidale, L. C. Smith, and L. Gasser. Information Quality Work Organization in Wikipedia. *J. Am. Soc. Inf. Sci. Technol.*, 59(6):983–1001, Apr. 2008.

[23] B. Suh, E. H. Chi, A. Kittur, and B. A. Pendleton. Lifting the veil: improving accountability and social transparency in Wikipedia with wikidashboard. In *Proc. CHI*, 2008.

[24] C. Tann and M. Sanderson. Are web-based informational queries changing? *J. Am. Soc. Inf. Sci. Technol.*, 60(6):1290–1293, 2009.

[25] M. ten Thij, Y. Volkovich, D. Laniado, and A. Kaltenbrunner. Modeling and predicting page-view dynamics on Wikipedia. *CoRR*, abs/1212.5943, 2012.

[26] V. Waller. The search queries that took Australian Internet users to Wikipedia. *Information Research*, 16(2):476, 2011.

[27] R. West, I. Weber, and C. Castillo. Drawing a data-driven portrait of Wikipedia editors. In *Proc. WikiSym*, 2012.

[28] Wikimedia. Tool Labs. https://wikitech.wikimedia.org/wiki/Nova_Resource:Tools/Help.

[29] Wikipedia. List of featured articles. http://en.wikipedia.org/wiki/Wikipedia:Featured_articles.

[30] Wikipedia. List of good articles. http://en.wikipedia.org/wiki/Wikipedia:Good_articles.

[31] Wikipedia. Version 1.0 Editorial Team/Assessment. http://en.wikipedia.org/wiki/Wikipedia:Version_1.0_Editorial_Team/Assessment.

[32] D. Wilkinson and B. Huberman. Assessing the value of cooperation in wikipedia. *First Monday*, 12, 2007.

[33] T. Wöhner and R. Peters. Assessing the quality of Wikipedia articles with lifecycle based metrics. In *Proc. WikiSym*, 2009.

A Study of Age Gaps between Online Friends

Lizi Liao
School of Computer Science
Beijing Institute of Technology
liaolizi.llz@gmail.com

Jing Jiang
School of Information Systems
Singapore Management
University
jingjiang@smu.edu.sg

Ee-Peng Lim
School of Information Systems
Singapore Management
University
eplim@smu.edu.sg

Heyan Huang
School of Computer Science
Beijing Institute of Technology
hhy63@bit.edu.cn

ABSTRACT

User attribute extraction on social media has gain considerable attention, while existing methods are mostly supervised which suffer great difficulty in insufficient gold standard data. In this paper, we validate a strong hypothesis based on homophily and adapt it to ensure the certainty of user attribute we extracted via weakly supervised propagation. Homophily, the theory which states that people who are similar tend to become friends, has been well studied in the setting of online social networks. When we focus on age attribute, based on this theory, online friends tend to have similar age. In this work, we take a step further and study the hypothesis that the age gap between online friends become even smaller in a larger friendship clique. We empirically validate our hypothesis using two real social network data sets. We further design a propagation-based algorithm to predict online users' age, leveraging the clique-based hypothesis. We find that our algorithm can outperform several baselines. We believe that this method could work as a way to enrich sparse data and the hypothesis we validated would shed light on exploring the proximity of other user attributes such as education as well.

Categories and Subject Descriptors

J.4 [**Computer Applications**]: Social and Behavioral Sciences

General Terms

Algorithms, Experimentation

Keywords

Social Network Analysis; Age Prediction; Homophily

1. INTRODUCTION

With the fast adoption of social media, more and more people have moved their social activities online. Large online social networks such as Facebook and Twitter allow users to make friends and form communities beyond the physical boundaries that offline social networks have. To better understand these online social networks, there have been many studies on online user behaviors and properties of online communities, some relating to hypotheses and theories developed from offline social networks. In particular, researchers have studied homophily [17] in the online setting [18, 24]. Homophily is the theory that people similar to each other tend to become friends, or in other words, "birds of a feather flock together." Here similarity between people may be based on various attributes including location, age, education, social status, interest, etc. Researchers have studied to what extent this theory is true in online social networks and whether this theory can be exploited for prediction tasks [15, 4, 22, 19, 1].

In this paper, we are interested in the particular attribute of age of online users and the age gaps between online friends. Based on the notion of homophily, we expect that users of similar age are more likely to become friends than users with a larger age gap. If this hypothesis is true, then presumably we can make use of the friendship links in online social networks and a small number of users' age information to predict other users' age. This age prediction task can be useful for many applications such as user profiling and targeted advertising, especially considering that age information is often unknown for many online users.

While it is not new to leverage the theory of homophily to infer user attributes, including age, in online social networks [18, 24], in this work we focus on a stronger hypothesis than the general notion of homophily. With the huge amount of link information provided by social media, we could obtain useful information about a user's age via his or her friends. At the same time, by observing links between

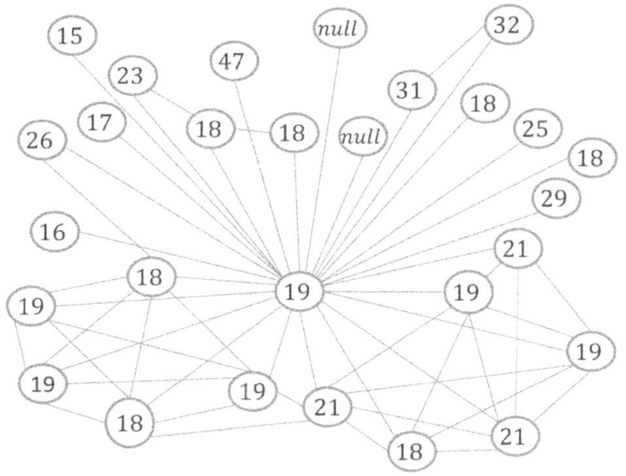

Figure 1: An example of an ego network with age information. There are some public accounts without age information denoted as *null*.

his or her friends, we could further infer the certainty of the information we get. In fact, the friendship links among a user's friends provide latent but precious information (see Figure 1). We hypothesize that users who form a large clique in an online social network (i.e. users who are pairwise friends with each other) are more likely to have similar ages. Using data from two real online social networks, we validate our hypothesis based on various statistics gathered from the data sets. We further propose a maximal clique based age propagation algorithm to predict users' age. Our algorithm is based purely on the topology of the social network and a small percentage of users' age; it does not use any other information such as users' profile, online behavior or user-generated content. We find that our algorithm can perform better age prediction compared with baselines that use random prediction or only immediate friends' age for prediction. On a Twitter network with over 25K of users, by observing about 10% users' age, our algorithm can predict the other users' age (within an error gap of 5) with an accuracy of over 79%. We expect that our clique-based hypothesis can be combined with other age prediction methods to further improve the accuracy of predicting online users' age.

Our work has the following contributions: (1) We propose a new hypothesis that the age gap between online friends is smaller in larger cliques and empirically validate this hypothesis. (2) We design a scalable algorithm to predict a user's age using maximal cliques and label propagation, which could help with the data sparsity problem. (3) We empirically evaluate our algorithm and show that the performance is better than several baselines. (4) Our method could work as a way to enrich sparse data and the hypothesis we validate would shed light on exploring the proximity of other user attributes such as education.

The rest of the paper is organized as follows. We first discuss some related work in Section 2 and provide information about our MG and Twitter data sets in Section 3. We explore the property of homophily in Section 4. In Section 5, we take a step further to validate out stronger hypothesis for the relation between age gap and clique size. The formu-

lation of our task and details of our clique age propagation algorithm are shown in Section 6, followed by the evaluation of our algorithm in Section 7. Finally our work is concluded in Section 8.

2. RELATED WORK

As we aim to profile a user's age attribute accurately via heuristics based on homophily, our work is related to homophily in social networks, user attributes inference and age prediction. We briefly summarize related research below.

2.1 Homophily in Social Networks

The hypothesis that people similar to each other tend to become friends dates back to at least the 70s in the last century. In social science, there is a general expectation that individuals develop friendships with others of approximately the same age [23]. In [16] the authors study the interconnectedness between homogeneous composition of groups and the emergence of homophily. In more recent years, the authors of [12] investigate the origins of homophily in a large university community, using network data in which interactions, attributes and affiliations are all recorded over time. In [8] the authors try to find the role of homophily in online dating choices made by users. Given attributes of some fraction of the users in an online social network, [19] infers the attributes of the remaining users. In [1] the authors leverage the principle of homophily to the inference of three attributes: gender, political orientation and age.

2.2 Inferring User Attributes

Inferring online users' attributes such as location and age has been studied extensively in recent years. Online social networks like Twitter have provided abundant resources. By learning distinguishing attributes of certain classes of users through third-person text, [5] aims to classify users in the analysis of first-person communication. The attribute extraction method is based on [2]. Using the networks and cities of US LiveJournal members, [15] finds that the likelihood of friendship is almost inversely proportional to distance of location. Based on the assumption that people tend to make friends with those having similar geographical location attributes, [4] observes and measures the relationship between geography proximity and friendship on Facebook. In [22] the authors solve two intimately related tasks for online social networks: link and location prediction.

2.3 Age Prediction

There has long been interests concerned with how various morphological, phonological and stylistic aspects of language can vary with a person' age. Early work has an emphasis on predicting author properties based on the usage of function words, parts-of-speech, punctuation and some spelling/grammatical errors [11]. Recently, researchers have focused less on the sociolinguistic implications and more on the tasks themselves, which leads to classifiers with feature representations capturing content in addition to style. These features include function/content words, word classes [13], content word classes [3] and unigrams [20]. There are also applications of simple classifiers to map a sequence of queries into the gender and age of the user issuing the queries [9]. In [21], stacked-SVM-based classification algorithms over a rich set of features are applied to classify several user attributes, such as gender, age, regional origin and political orientation.

However, none of these studies has leveraged information of associations between social network users to predict user age. In fact, social network information has been widely used in tasks like location inference in social media platforms. Sadilek et al. estimate a user's future location through the locations of users in his or her ego network [22]. Their approach requires both users' locations to be known in order to estimate the social relationship. Davis Jr et al. [7] use a user's Twitter follower network to do this task. Although their approach is based on location information in an individual's ego network, it uses location names only and their approach is non-iterative. Backstrom et al. [4] propose a location inference method for the Facebook social network using probabilistic inference to select the location from a user's friends. Our algorithm also predicts users' ages through ages of others in their ego network. However, we incorporate clique heuristics into our proposed propagation algorithm and the algorithm is iterative. Our algorithm is efficient which can run in seconds, and only a small number of initial ages are needed.

3. DATA SETS

In order to study the age gaps between online friends, we need online social networks with users' age information. Our data come from two sources: (1) MG[1], a social network platform for mobile users, and (2) Twitter.

MG is a social network platform developed by an Internet advertising company targeted at mobile users. The platform has attracted millions of users from over 100 countries. The platform allows users to establish friendship links with other users in the network and engage in online as well as offline conversations using mobile phones, in a way similar to the well-known service WhatsApp Messenger. When users sign up for the service, they self-report various personal information such as gender, age and country.

Country	USA	Australia	India	Singapore
all users	173,845	19,116	1,721,295	57,186
users with age	91,094	10,223	805,738	29,279
friend links	107,234	9,604	6,099,372	156,346

Table 1: Statistics of the MG data.

We collected the data from MG before April 2012. This subset of data contains over 6 million users, among which 43.7% specified their date of birth in their profiles. We observe that most users befriend with people from the same country, which is not surprising. To simplify our analysis, we further chose only users from the following four countries to form four subsets of data: USA, Australia, India and Singapore. These countries are among the top-ranked countries in terms of number of subscribed users.

As links in the MG network are mutually established—a friendship invitation has to be verified by the other party first before a link is established—we can directly treat the existing links in the data as friendship links. As for the age information, because age has been self-reported by a large proportion of users, we use the age information of these users as ground truth. We still keep the other users in the network

as they can be used for age propagation in our age prediction algorithm later. Some statistics of the data are given in Table 1. We can see that around half of the users chose to input their age information. To get an idea of the age distribution of these users, in Figure 2 we plot the number of users for each age ranging from 10 to 60. We ignore users who are below 10 or above 60. The number of users is plotted in log scale as there is much difference between the numbers of users in different countries and with different ages. From the figure we can see that most MG users are in their 20s or early 30s. The distributions of the different countries are similar.

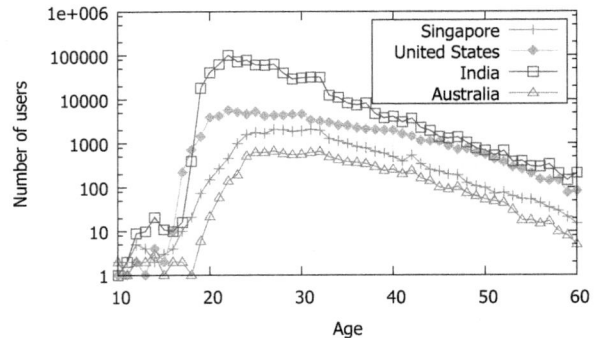

Figure 2: Age distribution of four representative countries in the MG data set.

Twitter is one of the most popular social media platforms for users to post short messages in real time, which are known as "tweets." Twitter users can "follow" other users, i.e. to automatically receive all the tweets published by those users. These following relations are one-directional and usually do not indicate friendships. However, when two users mutually follow each other, there is a strong indication that they are interested in each other's posts and we can loosely regard them as friends [10]. When signing up for the service, Twitter users have the option to reveal their age in their profiles, but most users do not explicitly specify their age or date of birth, making it hard to directly obtain the age information of users. Additionally, Twitter also provides a mechanism for users to specifically reference other users by their usernames (@username) in tweets, which we call "at-mentions." Below we will show how we exploit at-mentions to infer users' age.

We collected a Twitter data set as follows. Starting from a set of 59 seed users in Singapore, we first crawled these users' direct followers and followees and then crawled their followers/followees' followers and followees, i.e. we crawled all users who are either one or two hop(s) away from the seed users. Using features derived from [14] on Twitter bot detection, we filtered out potential spammers, promoters and other automated Twitter accounts so that the remaining data consist primarily of "regular" Twitter users. After these preprocessing steps, we were left with 25,703 users.

We created a friendship link between two users if they mutually follow each other. For age information, we employed the following two strategies to obtain the ground truth. (1) For those users who mentioned either their age or date of birth in their short profile biographies, we used a set of patterns to extract such information. In this way, we obtained more than 700 users with age information after manual correction. (2) Inspired by [24], we observe that many tweets contain the pattern "happy X-th birthday" (where X is a number) together with an at-mention. By extracting these expressions, we can infer the age of the users who were mentioned. With this strategy applied to tweets within a one year span, we were able to obtain the age of a little more than 3000 users, and we found the accuracy of this strategy to be around 87% based on a manual inspection on 200 sample users. For those 87% sample users, the age extracted indeed indicates an age after the human annotator read the corresponding tweet. While there is no way for us to verify whether this age is true because people can always lie in social media, we consider it to be correct. Figure 3 shows the age distribution of all those users with age information. We can see that Twitter has a younger user base with many users between 15 and 20. The figure peaks at age 18. This may come from two possible reasons: (1) Twitter has a younger user base in general. (2) Eighteen is probably a special age that indicates that the person has become an adult, and therefore we see more 18th birthday greetings on Twitter. We do not know which reason dominates, and we are aware that the age labels obtained this way contain bias.

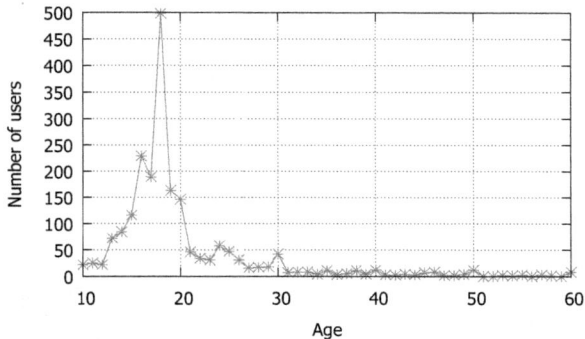

Figure 3: Age distribution of the Twitter data set.

4. AGE GAP BETWEEN ONLINE FRIENDS

In this section we empirically validate the hypothesis that online friends tend to have similar age. Since the age information in the Twitter data set is very sparse, we only plot the number of friendship links versus age gap for the MG data set. It is shown in Figure 4. Here the x-axis is the absolute value of the age difference between a pair of linked users (i.e. friends) and the y-axis is the number of linked user pairs (i.e. friendship links) with that age gap. We can see that most links have a relatively small gap, which demonstrates that users of similar age are more likely to become friends than users with a larger age gap. Later in our experiments we will see that age prediction based on a randomly selected friend's age can achieve a reasonable performance already. However, for a randomly picked age, we could not be sure about its certainty. Furthermore, from Figure 4, we can see that there is still a significant percentage of friendship links with a relatively large age gap. For example, 32.2% of the friendship links have an age gap of 5 or above. If we perform propagation-based age prediction, these links will likely deteriorate the performance.

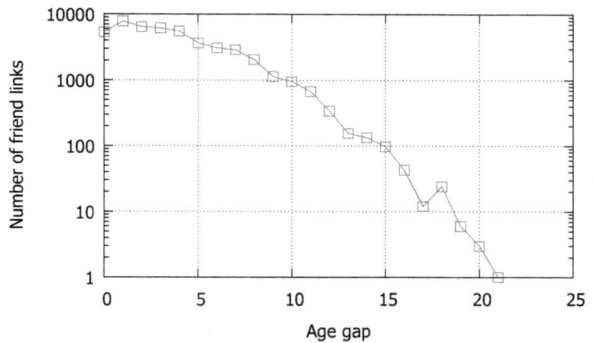

Figure 4: Number of friendship links vs. age gap in the MG data set.

5. AGE GAP IN CLIQUES

As demonstrated in the previous section, there are more friendship links with smaller age gaps than larger age gaps, but the number of friendship links with relatively large age gaps is still significant and should not be ignored totally. However, we hypothesize that chances that several people with very different ages forming a friendship clique are small. Before turning to the validation of our hypothesis, we first revisit a few key concepts in graph theory. Figure 5 gives an simple example. The node in the middle is the ego and the other nodes are her friends. In the right hand side of Figure 5 we have highlighted 3 maximum cliques with a clique size of at least 3. There are 3 other maximum cliques of size 2 that are not highlighted.

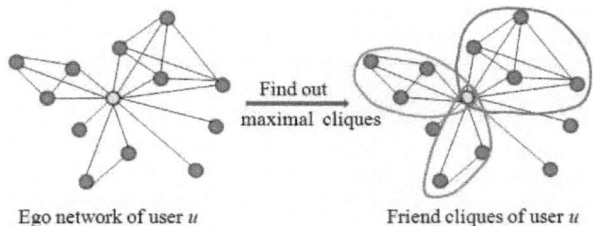

Figure 5: An example of an ego network and the maximum cliques in it.

DEFINITION 1 (CLIQUE). *In an undirected graph, a clique C is a subset of the nodes in the graph such that for every two nodes in C there exists an edge in the graph that connects the two nodes. The subgraph induced by C is complete.*

DEFINITION 2 (MAXIMAL CLIQUE). *In an undirected graph, a maximal clique is a clique that is not contained in any other clique in the graph.*

DEFINITION 3 (MAXIMAL CLIQUE SIZE). *The clique size of the maximal clique C, denoted as $|C|$, is the number of nodes in this clique.*

Our hypothesis can be stated as follows:

When several users in a social network form a clique, they tend to have a small age gap. The larger the clique size is, the smaller the age gap is between users in the clique.

The hypothesis stated above is intuitive. When users form a clique in a social network, they have stronger ties among themselves and are more likely to be similar to each other. For example, a group of classmates are likely to form a clique in a social network, and classmates usually have the same age. For the typical example shown in Figure 1, there are 2 large cliques with a size of 6. The left one is a clique of schoolmates in high school. Apparently they are about the same age. The right one is a clique of college friends. There are some age differences in it but overall the ages are still very close. We also observe that there are quite a lot of smaller cliques in user's ego network. The age gaps within those small cliques are more randomly ranged. Most large gaps occur in those small maximal cliques with a size of 2 or 3. This makes sense, since user might become friends with some random people online while the chances of many random people become pair-wise friends with each other are relatively low.

This is a stronger hypothesis than the one we tested in the previous section. Essentially in the previous section we only looked at all cliques (not necessarily maximal cliques) of size 2. With this new hypothesis, we expect to see the age gap to decrease when clique size increases.

To validate this stronger hypothesis, we processed our data in the following way to obtain some useful statistics. Our main idea is to check for each user whether her age difference from friends in a large maximal clique is generally smaller than her age difference from friends in a smaller maximal clique. To do so, first, we found all maximal cliques from our data sets. Figure 6 shows the numbers of maximal cliques of different sizes in the MG data set. We can see that as expected the number of maximal cliques decreases as the clique size goes up.

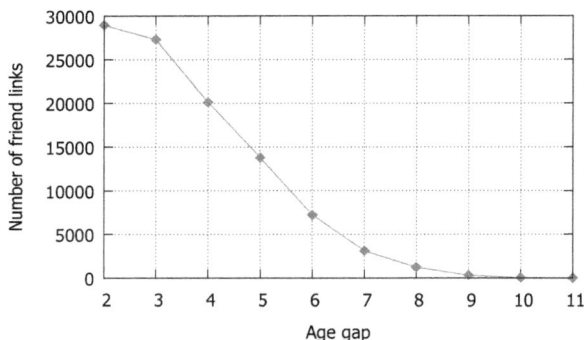

Figure 6: Maximal clique frequency distribution.

We then calculated a measure which we call MAG (mean age gap) for each user with respect to each maximal clique that contains this user. MAG is defined as follows:

$$MAG(u, \mathcal{C}) = \frac{\sum_{u' \in \mathcal{C} \setminus u} |age(u) - age(u')|}{|\mathcal{C}| - 1}, \quad (1)$$

where $\mathcal{C} \setminus u$ is the set of users from $\mathcal{C}$ excluding u, $age(u)$ is the age of user u, and $|\mathcal{C}|$ is the size of $\mathcal{C}$. Essentially $MAG(u, \mathcal{C})$ is the average age gap between u and all other users in $\mathcal{C}$. Our hypothesis is that if $\mathcal{C}$ is large, then this average age gap is small.

Since a user may be inside more than one maximal clique in the social network, we further define $MAG^{(n)}(u)$ as follows:

$$MAG^{(n)}(u) = \frac{1}{|\mathcal{S}_u^{(n)}|} \sum_{\mathcal{C} \in \mathcal{S}_u^{(n)}} MAG(u, \mathcal{C}), \quad (2)$$

where $\mathcal{S}_u^{(n)} = \{\mathcal{C} : |\mathcal{C}| = n \text{ and } u \in \mathcal{C}\}$. Basically $\mathcal{S}_u^{(n)}$ is the set of maximal cliques of size n which contain u, and $MAG^{(n)}(u)$ is the average of $MAG(u, \mathcal{C})$ over all cliques $\mathcal{C}$ of size n which contain u.

Finally, we define $MAG^{(n)}$ to be the average of $MAG^{(n)}(u)$ over all users who are inside at least one maximal clique of size n. We expect that $MAG^{(n)}$ becomes smaller when n becomes larger, i.e. the average age gap in larger maximal cliques tends to be smaller.

We observe that sometimes the extreme age values in a maximal clique may be outliers. To alleviate the impact of these extreme values, we follow the practice of trimmed estimators in statistics and consider three trimmed versions of $MAG^{(n)}$. Specifically, $MAG_{\neg\min}^{(n)}$ is the version where when we compute $MAG(u, \mathcal{C})$ we exclude the friend of u in $\mathcal{C}$ with the minimum age. $MAG_{\neg\max}^{(n)}$ is defined similarly. $MAG_{\neg\min, \max}^{(n)}$ is the version where both the minimum and the maximum ages are excluded when computing $MAG(u, \mathcal{C})$.

Given the definition of $MAG^{(n)}$ above, we can plot the values of $MAG^{(n)}$, $MAG_{\neg\min}^{(n)}$, $MAG_{\neg\max}^{(n)}$ and $MAG_{\neg\min, \max}^{(n)}$ against n. We use the Singapore users from the MG data set to plot these curves. Specifically, we use only maximal cliques in which all users' age values are known. The plots are shown in Figure 7. We can see that indeed as the clique size goes up, the mean age gap decreases. When the clique size is 7 and above, the mean age gap is below 5. This empirical analysis gives us the basis for the age prediction algorithm that we will present in the next section.

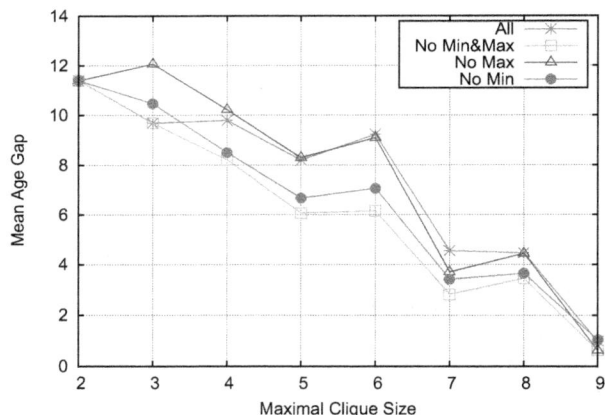

Figure 7: Relationship between mean age gap and maximal clique size.

6. AGE PREDICTION

In the previous section we empirically showed that in large cliques in online social networks, we observe users with small age gaps. This observation inspired our idea of using online cliques to help predict users' age with higher confidence. The assumption is that if two users are friends and they are inside a large clique in the online social network, we can use one user's age to infer the other's age.

First of all, we need a scalable algorithm to find cliques in a large undirected graph. Second, verified age information is still sparse in many social networks such as Twitter, which means prediction based on immediate friends' age would have a low coverage. Third, a user may be inside multiple different maximal cliques, and how to make use of these multiple cliques together to infer this user's age is not clear.

We address the three concerns above in the following way. To find maximal cliques, we make use of the *Bron-Kerbosch* algorithm [6], which is a recursive backtracking algorithm. To tackle the data sparseness problem, we allow predictions using multiple hops of friendship links. And finally since a user can be inside multiple different maximal cliques, we propose an edge weighting function related to clique size to make use of larger maximal cliques.

6.1 Problem Statement and Solution Overview

Let us use $\mathcal{L} = \{(u_1, a_1), \ldots, (u_M, a_M)\}$ to denote a set of labeled users, i.e. users with known age. Here u_i is a user and a_i is her age. We use $\mathcal{U} = \{u_{M+1}, \ldots, u_{M+N}\}$ to denote the unlabeled users. Our goal is to predict the age of the users in $\mathcal{U}$ using $\mathcal{L}$.

We now present our maximal clique based age propagation (MCAP) algorithm. An overview of our algorithm is shown in Figure 8.

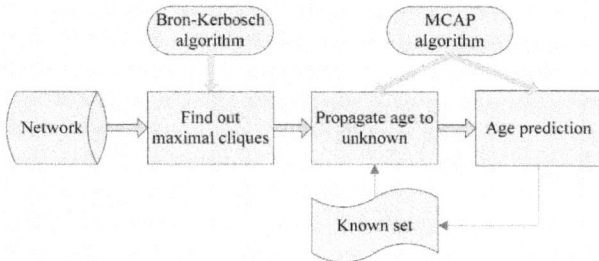

Figure 8: The framework of our age prediction algorithm.

6.2 The MCAP Algorithm

In this section we formally present the maximal clique based age propagation algorithm. We assume that we are able to find all the maximal cliques in a social network. The details of how to find maximal cliques will be given in the next subsection.

The MCAP algorithm is a label propagation algorithm. Label propagation is a type of semi-supervised and iterative algorithms designed to infer labels for items connected in a network [25]. Usually, only a small number of items in the network has known labels, which serve as a source of ground truth information for the estimation of other nodes' labels. Label propagation algorithms usually proceed iteratively where in each iteration some items with unknown labels receive predicted labels based on their neighbors.

Based on our validated hypothesis, we want users who are located in large cliques to have small age gaps. With this goal in mind, in the social network we have, we set the weight between two nodes based on the maximal cliques we have found in the network. Specifically, for two connected users u_i and u_j in the network, we define $w_{i,j}$, the weight for the edge between these two users, to be the size of the largest

maximal clique that contains u_i and u_j. Let $\mathcal{N}(u)$ denote the set of neighbors of user u. We now define a propagation probability from user u_i to user u_j as follows:

$$p(i \rightarrow j) = \frac{w_{ij}}{\sum_{u_k \in \mathcal{N}(u_i)} w_{ik}} \quad (3)$$

Let $\mathbf{p}$ denote the propagation probabilities as defined above for all pairs of connected nodes. We will use these probabilities to propagate the age information.

Algorithm 1 The MCAP algorithm.

1: **MCAP**$(\mathcal{L}, \mathcal{U}, \mathbf{p})$
2: **Input:**
3:   $\mathcal{L}$: A set of users with known age
4:   $\mathcal{U}$: A set of users with unknown age
5:   $\mathbf{p}$: The propagation probabilities, where $p(i \rightarrow j)$ is the probability to propagate u_i's age to u_j
6: **Method:**
7: **while** $\mathcal{U}$ is not $\emptyset$ **do**
8:   **for** each user $u_j \in \mathcal{U}$ **do**
9:     define $\mathcal{A}_j = \emptyset$ for u_j
10:   **end for**
11:   **for** each user $u_i \in \mathcal{L}$ **do**
12:     **for** each user $u_j \in \mathcal{N}(u_i)$ and $u_j \notin \mathcal{L}$ **do**
13:       add the pair $(a_i, p(i \rightarrow j))$ to $\mathcal{A}_j$
14:     **end for**
15:   **end for**
16:   **for** each user $u_j \in \mathcal{U}$ **do**
17:     **if** $\mathcal{A}_j \neq \emptyset$ **then**
18:       $a_j \leftarrow$ age in $\mathcal{A}_j$ with the maximum probability
19:       $\mathcal{L} \leftarrow \mathcal{L} \bigcup \{u_j\}$
20:       $\mathcal{U} \leftarrow \mathcal{U} \setminus \{u_j\}$
21:     **end if**
22:   **end for**
23: **end while**

We outline the MCAP algorithm in Algorithm 1. The algorithm iteratively propagates the age of labeled users to the unlabeled users. In each iteration, an unlabeled user stores the propagated age from her neighbors together with a probability score, which is based on the weights of the edges between her and her neighbors. At the end of each iteration, if an unlabeled user has received some propagated age values, we set the age with the maximum probability to be the age of this user. The user is then added to the labeled set and removed from the unlabeled set. The algorithm continues until all users in the unlabeled set have been labeled and moved to the labeled set.

While the MCAP algorithm may appear very simple, it is also very efficient. In our experiments, we find that for a large social network with around 25% labeled users, we can predict the age of all the unlabeled users within 3 or 4 iterations.

6.3 Finding Maximal Cliques

In this subsection we discuss how we find all maximal cliques inside a social network. As defined, a maximal clique cannot be extended by including one more adjacent node, that is, a clique which does not exist exclusively within the node set of a larger clique. We make use of the *Bron-Kerbosch* algorithm [6] for finding maximal cliques. The basic form of the *Bron-Kerbosch* algorithm is a recursive backtracking algorithm that searches for all maximal cliques in a given graph G. As the *Bron-Kerbosch* algorithm is a well-known existing algorithm, we do not give the details here.

7. EMPIRICAL EVALUATION

In this section, we carry out a set of experiments to evaluate our algorithm. We find that our propagation algorithm is quite efficient. After finding the maximal cliques in a social network, running the MCAP algorithm on our data sets can be finished in seconds when running on a regular laptop machine with a double core 1.80GHz processor and 4GB of memory.

7.1 Evaluation Metrics

We introduce the following metrics to help us evaluate the performance of our proposed algorithm. We compare the predicted age of a user versus her actual age. The first metric we consider is the **Error Gap** which quantifies the gap in years between the actual age of the user $a_{act}(u)$ and the predicted age $a_{pre}(u)$. The **Error Gap** for user u is defined as:

$$\text{ErrGap}(u) = |a_{act}(u) - a_{pre}(u)|. \qquad (4)$$

In order to give a strong insight into the distribution of age prediction errors, the next metric **Accuracy** considers the percentage of users with their **Error Gap** capped within d years:

$$\text{Accuracy}(d, \mathcal{U}) = \frac{|\{u : u \in \mathcal{U} \text{ and } \text{ErrGap}(u) \leqslant d\}|}{|\mathcal{U}|}. \qquad (5)$$

7.2 Experiments on MG

7.2.1 *Leave-One-Out Evaluation*

In the first set of experiments, we want to check when only the test user's age is unknown but all other users' ages are known, how our algorithm can perform. Due to the richness of gold standard data in the MG data set, it can easily meet the requirement of all friends' ages in an ego network being known. As age information is quite sparse in Twitter, this requirement seems too rigorous which will leave us with not enough data. Thus we only carry our this experiment on the MG data. Since the Twitter data we have is restricted in Singapore, this experiment was carried out only on the Singapore MG data to keep consistency with later experiments. In this Leave-One-Out experiment, for each user with known age, we hide her age and run the MCAP algorithm to predict her age. We also consider the following baselines: (1) Random Guess: We randomly assign an age to the user based on a uniform distribution over all the age values. (2) Friend Random: We randomly select a friend of the user and use the friend's age for prediction. (3) Friend Average: We use the average age of the friends to predict the user's age. (4) Friend Median: We use the median age of the friends to predict the user's age. For our own MCAP algorithm, we consider two variations. The first is the standard algorithm and the second, which we refer to as "No Min&Max," is the version where we ignore the minimum and maximum age in a clique. The results are shown in Figure 9.

The figure shows that maximal clique age propagation algorithm as well as its optimized version performs better than

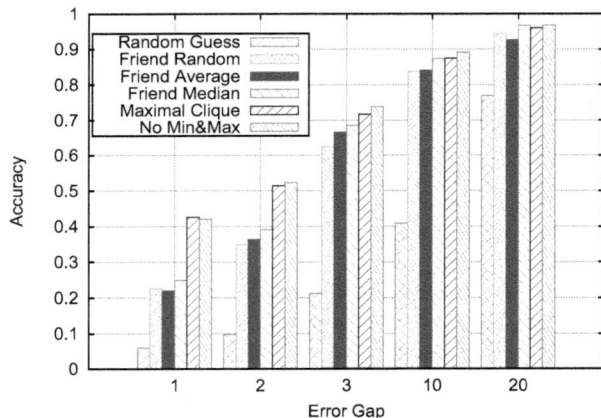

Figure 9: Results for Leave-One-Out for MG.

the four baselines. With **ErrGap** no bigger than 3, the accuracy of the optimized MCAP can reach 73.84%. At the same time, it is worth mentioning that when **ErrGap** is less than 2, our algorithm performs substantially better than the baselines.

7.2.2 *Leave-Many-Out Evaluation*

The Leave-One-Out experiment results are promising but the setting might not be close to real life cases. So we carry out another evaluation method, attempting to recover the ages of many individuals simultaneously. To do this, we first remove the age information from 75% of the individuals who have provided it. We then attempt to recover the age of all other users. Here we keep users with at least one friend remaining in the set with known age. The performance is shown in Figure 10. We can see that overall the performance is worse than Leave-One-Out results, as we now have much less information about the age of a user's friends. Predicting in this way correctly predicts 54.62% of users within 3 years of gap from their actual age after 3 iterations.

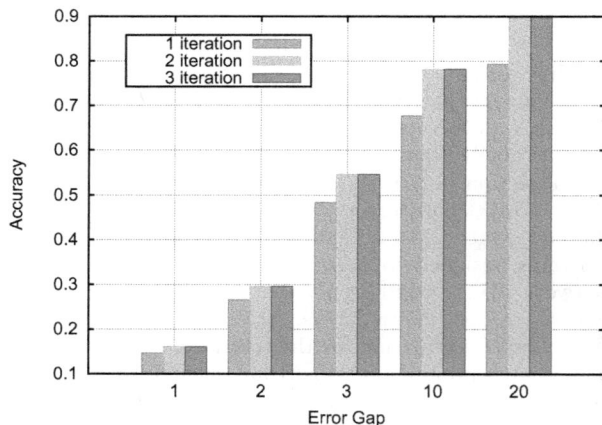

Figure 10: Results for Leave-Many-Out for MG.

In our experiment, we can run our prediction algorithm iteratively, using the newly guessed ages as input as well as the ages provided by the 25% users. Figure 10 shows the performance of such iterative approach. We can see that the

ErrGap	3	5	10	20
MCAP	0.6829	0.7902	0.9258	0.9830
Friend Median	0.4907	0.6830	0.8381	0.9350
Average	0.2573	0.5040	0.8554	0.9496

Table 2: Results for age prediction on Twitter

second iteration is substantially better than the first iteration. For error gap being no bigger than 3, the performance rise to 54.60% from 48.35%. For error gap being no bigger than 10, the performance rises to 78.09% from 67.64%. That is to say, when we are predicting the age of many individuals at once, we can perform better by using the information contained in the links between the individuals whose ages we are trying to predict. In the first pass, we make our prediction based only on the known ages. In subsequent passes, we can use the predicted ages as part of the input, to improve performance. As shown, the results converges quickly.

7.3 Experiments on Twitter

To better understand the portability of the age predictor, we next conduct experiments on the Twitter data set we collected. As mentioned above, gold standard data in Twitter is really rare. For about 25K Twitter users we crawled, after filtering and manual correction, there are only about 2.94% users who have directly stated their age information. Even after the heuristic process of extracting birthday mentions, the rate of gold standard data still remains pretty small (only 13.21%). When doing propagation, users with age information and users without age information are both kept for building graph. When computing the performance, we only look at users with age information. We compare our method with a baseline using the median age of friends (referred to as "Friend Median"). In the case when a user has no friend with age information, we resort to using the average age of all the training users. We also compare with another baseline (referred to as "Average") by assigning the average age of all the training users to our test users.

To address the problem of insufficient data, we divide the ground truth data (manually corrected data) into 10 subsets. Then, we perform 10-fold cross validation. For each round, we hold out one subset, using other subsets as initial labeled data to run the maximal clique based age propagation algorithm. After prediction, we compute the performance based on the held-out subset. The final results are averaged over the 10 rounds. The results are shown in Table 2.

The results in Table 2 are surprisingly good, considering that only 13.21% of users' age information is leveraged and 10% of it has been held out for evaluation. Even in such circumstances, the results are still much better than Leave-Many-Out results on MG. This suggests that the Twitter data set might have a much more concentrated age distribution on cliques, making it easier to do age prediction using maximal cliques.

8. CONCLUSIONS

The social relationships in social media platforms provide strong evidence of an individuals' age information. We validated our hypothesis about the relationship between average age gap and clique size on the MG data set. Based on this hypothesis, we presented a new algorithm, maximal clique-based age propagation (MCAP), that leverages the age distribution of a user's ego network to predict the user's age. We first find out all maximal cliques in the undirected network built on user friendships, and then weight the network based on clique size. We iteratively propagate the ages of the age-known users to infer the age of age-unknown users and add them to the set of age-known users. With a small number of initial age-known users, the age predictor efficiently infers 54.62% of MG users within an error gap of 3 and 79.02% of Twitter users within an error gap of 5 from their actual age.

As a purely social network based approach, we anticipate continued refinement of this approach through incorporating more information. For example, there are not only friendship relations in MG, but also best-friend and blacklist relations. We are also interested in combining this purely relationship-driven approach with some linguistic features to develop more robust predictors.

9. ACKNOWLEDGMENTS

This research is supported in part by the PhD Joint Education grants from Beijing Institute of Technology, Chinese National Program on Key Basic Research Project (Grant No. 2013CB329605). This research is also partially supported by the Singapore National Research Foundation under its International Research Centre@Singapore Funding Initiative and administered by the IDM Programme Office, Media Development Authority (MDA). We thank the anonymous reviewers for providing their valuable comments on the pervious version of this paper.

10. REFERENCES

[1] F. Al Zamal, W. Liu, and D. Ruths. Homophily and latent attribute inference: Inferring latent attributes of twitter users from neighbors. In *ICWSM*, 2012.

[2] E. Alfonseca, M. Pasca, and E. Robledo-Arnuncio. Acquisition of instance attributes via labeled and related instances. In *SIGIR*, pages 58–65, 2010.

[3] S. Argamon, M. Koppel, J. W. Pennebaker, and J. Schler. Mining the blogosphere: Age, gender and the varieties of self-expression. *First Monday*, 12(9), 2007.

[4] L. Backstrom, E. Sun, and C. Marlow. Find me if you can: improving geographical prediction with social and spatial proximity. In *Proceedings of the 19th international conference on World wide web*, pages 61–70. ACM, 2010.

[5] S. Bergsma and B. Van Durme. Using conceptual class attributes to characterize social media users. pages 710–720, 2013.

[6] C. Bron and J. Kerbosch. Algorithm 457: finding all cliques of an undirected graph. *Communications of the ACM*, 16(9):575–577, 1973.

[7] C. A. Davis Jr, G. L. Pappa, D. R. R. de Oliveira, and F. de L Arcanjo. Inferring the location of twitter messages based on user relationships. *Transactions in GIS*, 15(6):735–751, 2011.

[8] A. T. Fiore and J. S. Donath. Homophily in online dating: when do you like someone like yourself? In *CHI'05 Extended Abstracts on Human Factors in Computing Systems*, pages 1371–1374. ACM, 2005.

[9] R. Jones, R. Kumar, B. Pang, and A. Tomkins. I know what you did last summer: query logs and user

privacy. In *Proceedings of the sixteenth ACM conference on Conference on information and knowledge management*, pages 909–914. ACM, 2007.

[10] D. Jurgens. That's what friends are for: Inferring location in online social media platforms based on social relationships. In *Seventh International AAAI Conference on Weblogs and Social Media*, 2013.

[11] M. Koppel, J. Schler, and K. Zigdon. Determining an author's native language by mining a text for errors. In *Proceedings of the eleventh ACM SIGKDD international conference on Knowledge discovery in data mining*, pages 624–628. ACM, 2005.

[12] G. Kossinets and D. J. Watts. Origins of homophily in an evolving social network1. *American Journal of Sociology*, 115(2):405–450, 2009.

[13] J. Schler, M. Koppel, S. Argamon, and J. W. Pennebaker. Effects of age and gender on blogging. In *AAAI Spring Symposium: Computational Approaches to Analyzing Weblogs*, pages 199–205, 2006.

[14] K. Lee, J. Caverlee, and S. Webb. Uncovering social spammers: social honeypots+ machine learning. In *SIGIR*, pages 435–442, 2010.

[15] D. Liben-Nowell, J. Novak, R. Kumar, P. Raghavan, and A. Tomkins. Geographic routing in social networks. *Proceedings of the National Academy of Sciences of the United States of America*, 102(33):11623–11628, 2005.

[16] J. M. McPherson and L. Smith-Lovin. Homophily in voluntary organizations: Status distance and the composition of face-to-face groups. *American sociological review*, pages 370–379, 1987.

[17] M. McPherson, L. Smith-Lovin, and J. M. Cook. Birds of a feather: Homophily in social networks. *Annual Review of Sociology*, 27:415–444, 2001.

[18] A. Mislove, B. Viswanath, K. P. Gummadi, and P. Druschel. You are who you know: Inferring user profiles in online social networks. In *Proceedings of the Third ACM International Conference on Web Search and Data Mining*, pages 251–260, 2010.

[19] A. Mislove, B. Viswanath, K. P. Gummadi, and P. Druschel. You are who you know: inferring user profiles in online social networks. In *Proceedings of the third ACM international conference on Web search and data mining*, pages 251–260. ACM, 2010.

[20] D. Nguyen, R. Gravel, D. Trieschnigg, and T. Meder. "How old do you think i am?" A study of language and age in twitter. In *Seventh International AAAI Conference on Weblogs and Social Media*, 2013.

[21] D. Rao, D. Yarowsky, A. Shreevats, and M. Gupta. Classifying latent user attributes in Twitter. In *Proceedings of the Second International Workshop on Search and Mining User-generated Contents*, pages 37–44, 2010.

[22] A. Sadilek, H. Kautz, and J. P. Bigham. Finding your friends and following them to where you are. In *Proceedings of the fifth ACM international conference on Web search and data mining*, pages 723–732. ACM, 2012.

[23] S. B. Kurth. Friendships and friend relations. *Social Relationships*, pages 136–170, 1970.

[24] F. A. Zamal, W. Liu, and D. Ruths. Homophily and latent attribute inference: Inferring latent attributes of Twitter users from neighbors. In *ICWSM*, 2012.

[25] X. Zhu and Z. Ghahramani. Learning from labeled and unlabeled data with label propagation. Technical report, Technical Report CMU-CALD-02-107, Carnegie Mellon University, 2002.

Understanding and Controlling the Filter Bubble through Interactive Visualization: A User Study

Sayooran Nagulendra and Julita Vassileva
Department of Computer Science
University of Saskatchewan,
Saskatoon, Canada
{sayooran.nagulendra, julita.vassileva}@usask.ca

ABSTRACT

The "filter bubble" is a term which refers to people getting encapsulated in streams of data such as news or social network updates that are personalized to their interests. While people need protection from information overload and maybe prefer to see content they feel familiar or agree with, there is the danger that important issues that should be of concern for everyone will get filtered away and people will lack exposure to different views, living in "echo-chambers", blissfully unaware of the reality. We have proposed a design of an interactive visualization, which provides the user of a social networking site with awareness of the personalization mechanism (the semantics and the source of the content that is filtered away), and with means to control the filtering mechanism. The visualization has been implemented in a peer-to-peer social network, called MADMICA, and we present here the results of a large scale lab study with 163 crowd-sourced participants. The results demonstrate that the visualization leads to increased users' awareness of the filter bubble, understandability of the filtering mechanism and to a feeling of control over their data stream.

Categories and Subject Descriptors

D.2.8 [**Information Storage and Retrieval**]: Information Search and Retrieval – *information filtering*

General Terms

Design; Experimentation; Human Factors

Keywords

Visualization; Filter Bubble; Recommender Systems; Online Social Networks

1. INTRODUCTION

Today, social networks provide a global platform for people to share and collaborate with their friends and families. With the growth of mobile and web technologies, these social networks are growing rapidly and millions of users are sharing data with their friends and families. Facebook, Twitter and Google+ are currently the most widely used social networks. As of September 2013, Facebook has 1.15 billion users and 699 million daily active users

[1]. Nearly a quarter (24 %) of the content that is shared on the internet is shared on Facebook [2] and more than 3.5 billion pieces of content are shared each week [3], creating a stream of data that can overload any user. The social data overload problem is commonly solved by filtering out the irrelevant data. Personalized stream filtering mechanisms can reduce information overload by presenting the user with only the content deemed to be the most relevant. Some of the major social media sites, such as Facebook, Digg and YouTube, have already implemented personalized stream filtering.

Paradoxically, the main problem with information filtering algorithms is that they could be "too good". The high level of optimization to the scope of interests of the user, inferred by these algorithms from the user's previous behavior, leads to users becoming encapsulated in the "bubble" of their comfort, seeing only content related to their interests, and being spared of anything else. This is referred as "the filter bubble" problem [4].

We proposed an approach [5] to make the user aware of the filtering mechanism and take control over it. It is based on an interactive visualization that shows the filter bubble and some features of the hidden filtered data (its semantics and origin). The intention is to make the user aware of the user model that the recommender system has developed, so that the user can consciously decide to explore items that are filtered away by manipulating the visualization. Yet showing what is hidden and filtered away from the stream can bring back the social data overload problem. Therefore, the main challenge is to find an effective visualization technique that can be seamlessly integrated into the activity stream, and presents the right amount of detail about the hidden filtered social data, without contributing additionally to the social data overload.

In this paper we present a quantitative evaluation of an interactive visualization which metaphorically visualizes the filter bubble and provides awareness, understanding and control of personalized filtering to alleviate the filter bubble problem. The paper is organized as follows. Section 2 reviews related work on open learner modeling, explanation and visualization of recommendations, as well as on the filter bubble problem and some previous approaches to address it. Section 3 presents the visualization design, section 4 – a large study of the usability and understandability of the visualization using a crowd-sourced lab experiment. Section 4 discusses the results and Section 5 concludes the paper.

2. RELATED WORK

Recommender Systems (RSs) are software tools and techniques which adapt to the needs of an individual user and provide personalized suggestions of the most relevant information [6]. The personalized suggestions help users to make decisions about consuming various types of items, such as what news items are interesting, what books to read or buy, what movie to watch and so on. Information filtering systems are a type of recommender systems, which select from a time-ordered stream of data (containing, for example, news, events, social updates, etc.) those that fit the scope of interest of the user. The difference between filtering and recommendation is that in filtering the irrelevant data is simply not displayed, i.e. remains hidden from the users, while in recommendation the most relevant data is highlighted in some way (e.g. shown first in a list of search results as in Goolge search, highlighted in a stream of data, etc.), but the irrelevant data is still available for the user to see.

Many researchers have worked on developing new RSs and improving the accuracy of their filtering algorithms. However the ultimate measure of success in this area is the user acceptance and trust of the recommendations [7]. The way recommendations are presented is critical for the user acceptance of recommender systems. Visualization techniques can be deployed to provide an intuitive "at a glance" explanation for recommendations and can also motivate the user to accept the recommendation. Presenting the recommendations in a ranked list according to their recommendation score is the most simple and commonly used visualization technique. Features like colour and font-size can be used to emphasize recommended items in a stream or list or items [8].

Previous work in the area of visualizing recommendations can be found in two communities – student modeling and recommender systems. In the AI and education / student modeling community, the idea dates back to the pioneering work by Kay and co-authors [9] on scrutable user models. Work by Bull et al. [10], Dimitrova [11], and Zapata-Rivera and Greer [12] on open learner modeling falls into this stream and more recently, work by Bakalov et al. [13]. More recently, Bakalov et al. [14], and Parra et al. [15] have expanded this work into the area of recommender system by visualizing user models and allowing users to manipulate them and control the system recommendation process.

A different stream of work on interactive visualizations of recommendations is motivated by the need to explain recommendations identified by Herlocker et al. [16] and elaborated by Tintarev & Masthoff [17]. An early attempt, by Webster & Vassileva [18] proposed an interactive visualization of a collaborative filtering recommender that allows the user viewer to see the other users in her "neighborhood", who are similar to her, and also to change manually to degree of influence that any of the other users can have on the recommendations of the viewer. Much more elaborate approach of visualizing hybrid recommendation was proposed by Bostandjiev et al. [19].

Yet all these approaches focus on explaining to the user why she receives certain recommendations an on providing visual tools to change the recommendations. None of them shows the not-recommended items; they remain hidden. Two works take the approach of visually emphasizing items among all other non recommended items. iBlogViz [20] is a system that visualizes blog archives. It uses many visual cues to represent the blog content and social interaction history with the blog entry which help to navigate the blog archive quickly and easily. Particularly, visual cues about the social response (comments) to the news can be used to help users navigate stream data quickly to find interesting news. Rings (http://rings.usask.ca) [21] is a visualization of the Facebook social data stream, organized around the people who post in the user's Facebook stream. It helps the users of OSN to browse social data efficiently focusing

on the active and influential friends and seeing the hidden time pattern of their social updates, without any filtering. In fact most of the users of Rings used the system to counter-act the Facebook filtering approach and to discover all the posts of their friends that they can't normally see on their stream. This is an anecdotal evidence that some users in social networks realize that the social updates they see have been selected by Facebook, i.e. that they are in a "filter bubble" - a term introduced by Eli Pariser [4] to denote a limited scope of information defined by the user's interests and isolated from anything that doesn't belong to this scope.

Isolating the user in a filter bubble has its advantages and disadvantages. The main advantage is that it can help users get relevant information a lot faster while not causing social data overload. On the other hand, there are number of problems [4]. The first one is the problem of distortion of the content posted on the site or by the user's friends and the user does not know in what way the way is biased. Users become less likely to be recommended information that is important, but not "likeable". The second problem the filter bubble brings is the information equivalent of obesity. Because of the users' tendency to give positive feedback, they will give feedback only to information items they are most compulsively attracted to. Using an analogy from food, users will be eating candy all the time, and the filter bubble leaves users locked in a world consisting of information junk food. As a result the users are increasingly surrounded by the ideas with which they are already familiar and agree, while being protected from surprising information, or information that challenges their views, makes them think or learn. Psychologist Lowenstein mentions that the "curiosity is aroused when we are presented with an 'information gap'" and Pariser suggests that the existence of curiosity, is based on the awareness that something exists that is hidden or unknown [4]. The third problem is the matter of control, since the growth of user knowledge will be greatly influenced by the algorithms and systems giving excessive power to the computer scientists who develop the personalization techniques.

The importance of these three problems increases rapidly, as an increasing proportion of users are using OSN to get all their information and news; and nearly all OSN deploy information filtering to personalize their streams to users. Recommendation techniques have been applied to personalize the streams in online social networks such as Facebook, Google+ and Twitter [22, 23]. Facebook's edge rank algorithm is one such filtering technique which presents a personalized stream of news and friends' status updates to the user by ranking every interaction on the site [24]. Yet the algorithms used for filtering are not revealed by the companies and it is not possible to experiment with them or work to improve them. Moreover, most of the personalization systems do not create awareness about what is being hidden from the user.

Resnick et al. [25] outline some strategies for promoting diverse exposure. They discuss two approaches: the first one is to build diversity aware recommender systems and filtering mechanisms. As an example of this approach, Tandukar and Vassileva [26] developed an interest-based stream filtering technique, which allows for diversity exposure by allowing popular items to pass through the filter to ensure some serendipity. The second approach is to provide tools and techniques that encourage users to consider themselves searching for diverse exposure. Munson has implemented a browser extension which displays the bias in a user's online news reading over time, which encourages users to seek the diverse exposure of news [27].

Though algorithmic personalization approaches can certainly find the most relevant content related to what users are already interested in a more efficient manner human curators and especially the user herself is probably the most appropriate agent to take the responsibility for ensuring a diverse exposure, to address the third problem outlined by Pariser. This means enabling the users to select what they want to see as well as what they do not want to see over the personalization presented by the algorithms. To enable them to do this, it is necessary first to make them aware of their filter bubble, as well as understanding of how they got inside it, and how they can control it to let different kind of information in and out, enlarge it or make it smaller. To our best knowledge there is currently no existing work that aims to create this kind of awareness and control in users. This is the aim of our work.

3. VISUALIZATION DESIGN

The first question when designing the visualization was to select a platform in which it would be possible to evaluate it. Currently, most of the popular OSN are centralized. Our previous experience with Rings [21] showed how difficult it is to do research on a live platform, which changes constantly the API and imposes access restrictions. Having no control or even detailed knowledge about the existing filtering mechanism makes it very hard to make convincing visualizations of the filtered data. That is why we decided to use our own OSN, called MADMICA [28] (available online at http://madmica.usask.ca), an implementation of a privacy-aware decentralized (peer-to-peer) OSN using the Friendica open source framework [29]. MADMICA uses a personalized stream filtering mechanism, developed by Tandukar

& Vassileva [30], which was developed and evaluated in a simulation [26]. This is a decentralized, content-based filtering algorithm, which enables each peer to learn the user's interests in discrete semantic categories, and to filter away messages received from the user's friends depending on the similarity of their interests. In essence, the filtering approach is based on a model of the user's interest in a finite set of categories of social data that is overlaid with a model of the strength of user interpersonal relationships (over each category), The intuition behind the filtering approach is that two people can be friends, but may not share the same level of interest in different topics or categories and may not trust each other's judgment or "likes" with regard to these categories.

The goals of the visualization are to create:

> 1) awareness,
> 2) understanding,
> 3) control of personalized stream filtering in an OSN to alleviate the filter bubble problem, and to
> 4) increase the users' trust in the system.

The visualization design is based on a bubble metaphor to make the effect of the personalized stream filtering in OSNs more understandable for the users (see Figure 1 and Figure 2).

It divides the space of the screen in two parts - outside and inside the bubble. The items that are inside the bubble are visible for the user, those outside the bubble are those that have been filtered away and are invisible in the stream (but they are shown in the visualization).

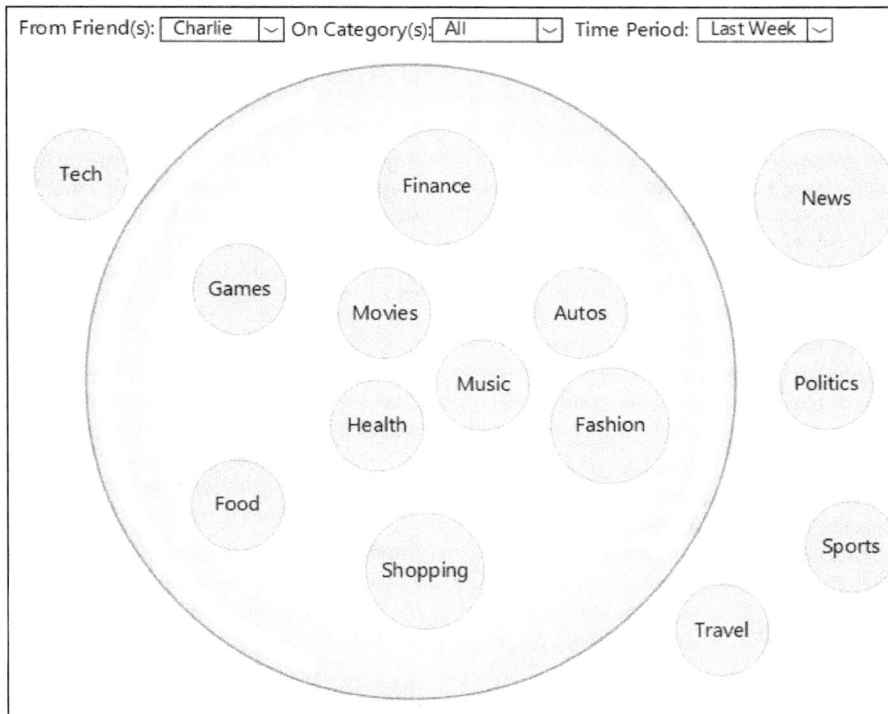

Figure 1. Anna's "category view" of her filter bubble related to Charlie's posts

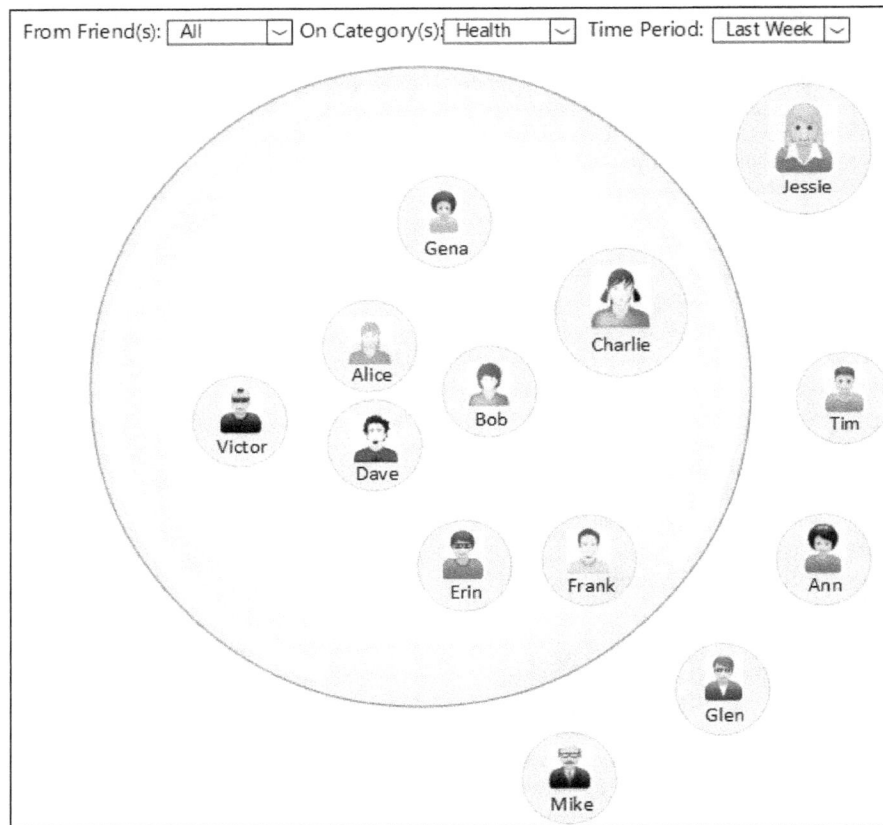

Figure 2. Anna's "friends view" of her filter bubble related to a certain category of posts ("health")

The visualization is personalized to the user viewing it (let's say Anna), and provides two alternative points of view: one focusing on the user's (Anna's) friends (see Figure 2) and one focusing on the semantic categories of the social data originating from them in the OSN (see Figure 1). We assume that there is a finite set of discrete semantic categories in which the content can be classified. For practical reasons, we consider categories of higher level of generality, e.g. "news", "technology", "health", "sport", similar to the categorization used by news websites, Google, Yahoo, etc., rather than user-generated tags, which can be too many, partially overlapping or redundant.

The category view shown in Figure 1 represents Anna's "Category view" - all the categories of the posts shared by Anna's friend Charlie during the last week that were shown in Anna's newsfeed (inside the bubble) or filtered out by the system (outside the bubble). All the category circles inside the bubble represent the categories of posts that are shown in Anna's newsfeed; they represent the categories of shared interests between Anna and her friend Charlie. But Charlie has more interests – those shown outside Anna's filter bubble. Anna is not interested in these categories or doesn't share Charlie's views, and therefore posts related to these categories are being filtered out by the filtering mechanism. The filtering mechanism decides which categories are of shared interest between Anna and Charlie based on the past history of actions that Anna performed on the posts shared by Charlie in the category "health" (actions, such as "like", "share", "comment").

The "Friends view" of Anna's bubble visualization is shown in Figure 2. It represents all the friends who shared some posts in a given category (here, "health") during the last week that were shown in Anna's newsfeed or filtered out by the system. The position of each friend's circle relative to the big bubble is intended to create awareness about the filtering mechanism, i.e. whose posts related to the selected category, the user (Anna) can see in her newsfeed. For example, Anna receives all posts related to the category "health" from her friends Gena, Charlie, Alice, Bob, etc., but does not receive the health-related posts of Mike, Glen, Ann, Tim and Jessie. The filter bubble shape itself metaphorically creates the awareness that the user is encapsulated in a bubble and that there are friends outside of the bubble who have posted on the topic but the user has not seen these posts. Thus user awareness is achieved.

Providing some understanding about the personalized stream filtering is the second goal of this visualization. Organizing posts by categories and friends gives some understanding about the principles of the personalized filtering: that it is based on the categories of posts and the post origin (the friends who shared them). In addition to that, it visualizes the common interests between user and each of her friends – by selecting the "Category view" and a particular friend from the drop-down menu, the user can see inside the big bubble are common interests between her and the selected friend. It also visualizes the interest-based communities of the user – by selecting the "Friend view" and a particular category of interest, the user can see in the big bubble all friends who share interest in this category with the user.

Providing control of the personalized stream filtering to the users i.e. allowing users to manually override the filtering system is the third main goal of this visualization. User control is achieved by allowing users to drag and drop the circles in and out of the big bubble in either of the two views. For example, if Anna drags and drops the circle representing the "games" category in the "Category view" (see in Figure 1) from inside the big bubble to its outside the user effectively tells the system that she does not like to see that category of posts from the selected friend in her newsfeed in the future. Similarly, the user could drag and drop a friend from within her "Friends view" bubble to the outside and it signals the system to filter out the posts shared by that friend about the selected category in the future. In the reverse situation, when the user realizes that she is interested in posts in category "health" shared by a friend (say, Glen), who is outside her "friends-view" bubble in Figure 2 and wants to see his posts in her newsfeed homepage in the future, she will drag and drop that particular friend inside the big bubble. Actually, this action is allows Anna to come out of her filter bubble and explore new interests. The visualization allows to apply the same action across all friends (in Category view) and across all categories (in the Friends view). For example, if Anna wants to see all posts by Glen in any category, she will select the "Friends view" and the generic category "All" from the "Categories" menu and then she will drag Glen in her bubble.

We presented in [5] a detailed justification of the visualization design decisions and a pilot user study to evaluate the usability and user acceptance of the visualization and whether it achieves its goals of providing awareness, control and trust in the filtering mechanism in MADMICA. Eleven (11) graduate students from the MADMUC research lab used the MADMICA system with the filter bubble visualization instead of Facebook and shared interesting and research-related links over a period of three weeks in March 2013. The results of the study showed that the filter bubble visualization made the users aware of the filtering mechanism, engaged them in actions to correct and change it, and as a result, increased the users' trust in the system [5]. In order to gain a deeper understanding of the ways users perceive and understand the visualization, we carried out a large scale quantitative study with 163 Mechanical Turk participants, described in the next section.

4. EVALUATION

A quantitative study was carried out to evaluate the understandability of the visualization and whether the users understand that the visualization provides awareness, understanding and control of filtering and the filter bubble. The study was conducted as an online survey on a crowd-sourcing platform and required them to interact with the visualization, but not with MADMICA, as recruiting all participants to use our OSN would have been unrealistic.

4.1 Hypotheses

The goal of this user study was to find out if the visualization is understandable, if it creates awareness and understanding of the personalized stream filtering mechanism and ability to control it to alleviate the filter bubble. So the evaluation aims at testing the following hypotheses.

1. Users understand that the visualization provides *awareness* of the filtering and the filter bubble.
2. Users understand that visualization provides *understanding* of the filtering and the filter bubble.
3. Users understand that visualization provides *control* of the filtering and the filter bubble.
4. Users understand the visualization and its functions.

4.2 Experimental Setup

The study was carried out as an online survey. Unlike the conventional online surveys, this survey had the interactive visualization embedded into the survey so that users could explore it and get some hands-on experience with it before answering the survey. First, the participants were given some introduction about the MADMICA social network and the filter bubble problem in general. Then a sample newsfeed homepage was displayed in the survey so that users could actually browse through the newsfeed without leaving the survey page. The sample newsfeed contained around 15 newsfeed items on 5 different categories such as Health, News, Movies, Music and Sports from five different hypothetical friends named Alice, Bob, Charlie, Dave and Frank. The participants were given instructions to assume that the aforementioned people are their friends in MADMICA and to browse through the newsfeed homepage as they would do in Facebook. In addition to this, 7 posts from different friends and in different categories were hidden from the newsfeed as a result of the personalization algorithm. Then the users were presented with the interactive visualization exactly as in the MADMICA system and were instructed to explore the visualization. Then they were directed to the questionnaire to answer the questions.

4.3 Method

The online survey was conducted using Amazon Mechanical Turk (MTurk) which is a popular crowd-sourced participant pool. We ensured the data quality by placing attention check questions (ACQs) and restricting participation to MTurk workers with certain qualifications [30].

The suggested qualification among researchers to ensure data quality was to allow participants who have the HIT Approval Rate (%) for all Requesters' HITs greater than or equal to 95 [30]. But we set even higher qualification to ensure the high data quality as follows: HIT Approval Rate (%) for all Requesters' HITs greater than or equal to 98% AND Number of HITs Approved greater than or equal to 5000. The data collection continued for 1 week and reached our target sample of 230 participants. Then we analyzed the data and checked the ACQ for validity and as a result, 163 valid responses were collected. For each participant with a valid response, we paid a compensation of 1$, which is a good rate for an approximately 30-45 min. long study on MTurk.

The 25 questions were grouped according to the metrics which they intend to measure. The metrics for understandability of the visualization are adapted based on the International Standards for Software Quality Evaluation [31]. Table 2 summarizes the metrics chosen for the understandability of the visualization [31].

Table 2. Understandability Metrics

Metric Name	Purpose	Formula	Interpretation of measured value
Evident Functions	What proportions of functions users were able to identify by exploring the visualization	X = A / B A = Number of functions identified by the user B = Total number of actual functions	$0 <= X <= 1$ The closer to 1.0 is the better.
Function understandability	What proportions of functions users were able to understand correctly by exploring the visualization	X= A / B A= Number of functions whose purpose is correctly described by the user B= Number of functions available	$0 <= X <= 1$ The closer to 1.0 is the better.
Understandable input and output	Can users understand what is required as input data and what is provided as output by the visualization?	X= A / B A= Number of input and output data items which user successfully understands B= Number of input and output data items available from the visualization	$0 <= X <= 1$ The closer to 1.0 is the better

Table 3. Statistical Hypotheses

Test	H0 (null)	H1 (alternative)
1	$\mu_{Awareness} \leq 0.5$	$\mu_{Awareness} > 0.5$
2	$\mu_{Understanding} \leq 0.5$	$\mu_{Understanding} > 0.5$
3	$\mu_{Control} \leq 0.5$	$\mu_{Control} > 0.5$
4	$\mu_{Understandability} \leq 0.5$	$\mu_{Understandability} > 0.5$

Table 4. Hypothesis Analysis

Test	Variable	Mean	2-tailed t	Degree of freedom (df)	1-tailed Critical t	1-tailed t < 2-tailed t	Means are in correct order	Alternative Hypothesis Accepted
1	Awareness	.7117	11.358	162	1.6543	YES	YES	YES
2	Understanding	.6176	6.953	162	1.6543	YES	YES	YES
3	Control	.7607	14.824	162	1.6543	YES	YES	YES
4	Understandability	.6967	13.884	162	1.6543	YES	YES	YES

There are 3 independent variables to assess the understandability of the visualization: awareness, understanding and control. Each of the independent variables was evaluated using the metrics given in Table 2 i.e. understandability of each independent variable was calculated. In addition to that, the overall understandability (referred as understandability hereafter) was also calculated using the understandability metrics. Six (6) questions (2 Yes/No and 4 Multiple Choice Questions) were used to evaluate each of the independent variables. Altogether, 18 questions were used to evaluate the overall understandability with 6 questions for each metric. Our original hypotheses were converted into the statistical form with the corresponding null hypothesis (see Table 3).

As shown in Table 3, we considered the mean value of understandability for our hypothesis testing. The mean value is 0.5 according to the scale of metrics used to measure the understandability. We set the null hypothesis as the mean value of understandability is less than or equal to 0.5, i.e. the participants do not have a clear understanding about the visualization. Our research hypothesis is the mean value is greater than 0.5, i.e. the participants do have clear understanding about the visualization. As mentioned in the metrics Table 2, the closer this mean value to 1.0 is, the better the understanding.

4.4 Results

The internal consistency (reliability) of question items was measured using the Cronbach's alpha. The acceptable value of Cronbach's Alpha should be the range of 0.70 to 0.95 [32]. The measured value for the Cronbach's alpha is 0.7 for our questionnaire. This value is in the acceptable range [33].

4.4.1 Test on the Four Hypotheses

One-sample t-test was used to determine whether the mean of a particular data set is different from the particular value. Before doing the t-tests, tests were carried out to verify that the following 4 conditions were met: understandability is measured at the ratio level, the collected data are independent which means that there is no relationship between the observations, there are no significant outliers in the data, and the understandability is approximately normally distributed [34, 35]. Then the t-tests were conducted for the 4 hypothesis tests and the results are summarized in Table 4.

The first t-test was conducted for the hypothesis 1 defined in section 4.2.1. The Mean understandability of awareness (M = 0.7117, SD = 0.2379) was higher than the tested understandability value of 0.5, a statistically significant mean difference of 0.21, 95% CI [0.18 to 0.25], t (162) = 11.358, p < .001.

Similarly, the t-tests for hypothesis 2, 3, 4 were conducted and the results follow. The Mean understandability of *understanding* the filtering (M = 0.6176, SD = 0.2159) was higher than the tested understandability value of 0.5, a statistically significant mean difference of 0.12, 95% CI [0.08 to 0.15], t (162) = 6.953, p < .001. The Mean understandability of *control* (M = 0.7607, SD = 0.2246) was higher than the tested understandability value of 0.5, a statistically significant mean difference of 0.26, 95% CI [0.23 to 0.30], t (162) = 14.824, p < .001.

Finally, the Mean *understandability of visualization* (M = 0.6967, SD = 0.1808) was higher than the tested understandability value of 0.5, a statistically significant mean difference of 0.20, 95% CI [0.17 to 0.23], t (162) = 13.884, p < .001. In all four tests, there were a statistically significant difference between means (p < .001) and, therefore, we can reject the null hypotheses defined in Table 3, and accept the alternative hypotheses.

4.4.2 Additional Test on Graphical Language

The key graphical language constructs of this visualization are:

1. The relative position of user's circles to the bubble (inside / outside)

2. The size of the users' circles (larger - more posts)

3. Dragging user circles in and out (showing / filtering away)

In addition to the above 3 constructs, we identified another potential construct from the qualitative study as follows: the relative position of circles inside the bubble (closer to the center or to the periphery). All the 3 other constructs were as part of each function of the visualization (providing awareness, providing understanding, and providing control) and were tested for statistical significance. In order to test whether users interpret this fourth construct or not, we included the answers based on this construct for two of the questions in the survey. During the analysis, we created a score for users based on how many out of the 2 questions they did not select this construct as an answer. Then the hypotheses were formed as follows: H0: μ Score ≤ 0.5, H1: μ Score > 0.5. One sample t-test was conducted and the results are as follows: the Mean score for not selecting the graphical construct (M = 0.9571, SD = 0.1405) was much higher than the test score value of 0.5, a statistically significant mean difference

of 0.46, 95% CI [0.44 to 0.49], t (162) = 41.523, p < .001. There were a statistically significant difference between means (p < .001) and, therefore, we can reject the null hypothesis, and accept the alternative hypothesis.

4.4.3 Discussion

The results of the study suggest that overall the participants had a good understanding about the visualization. By comparing the means of variables Awareness, Understanding, and Control, we can see that users have a good understanding (0.7607) about the control of filtering and the filter bubble provided by the visualization. This can be linked with the drag and drop feature of the visualization, which is very popular and commonly used action in many user interfaces. On the other side, the users' understanding about the visualization providing understanding to the filtering and the filter bubble has the lower value (0.6176). Though it is higher than 0.5, it clearly shows that the visualization has to be improved on this aspect. A possible improvement could be to provide some context sensitive help to the visual cues in the visualization. The overall understandability value of the visualization (0.6967) shows that the users had good understanding about the visualization after exploring it for a short time and it could be considered as an intuitive visualization. But it can be envisioned that the users will better understand if there is a context sensitive help provided with the visualization.

Analyzing the t-test values gives us more insight into the understandability measures. As mentioned earlier, the understandability of visualization is calculated using the three variables awareness, understanding and control. These three variables are understandability variables and are measured using the metrics presented in Table 2. The variables awareness, understanding and control obtained a high 2-tailed value respectively 11.358, 6.953, and 14.824. These values are comparatively very high when compared with their relevant one-tailed t-test value, which is 1.65. This indicates that these three variables are a very good measure for the understandability of this visualization.

The additional test on graphical language results suggest that the users very rarely interpreted the position of circles inside the bubble (closer to the center or to the periphery). A possible reason for this might be the nature of the question; the users might have only focused on the first 3 graphical constructs which are intuitive and obvious. Yet, the position of circles inside the bubble seems a useful construct and could be added as an improvement to the visualization in future.

5. CONCLUSIONS

This paper presented an interactive visualization of the information filter bubble that can help users understand how information filtering works in an online social network, and empowers them to control the algorithms by manipulating the visualization to "escape" the bubble. This is a novel contribution since no previously existing approaches to visualizing recommendations have focused specifically on the filter bubble problem. The results of a crowd sourced lab study with 163 participants demonstrates that the visualization leads to increased users' awareness of the filter bubble, understandability of the filtering mechanism and to a feeling of control over the data stream they are seeing. Future work directions include conducting a study of evaluating the intuitiveness of the visualization by comparing it to the same interactive visualization provided with guided help.

6. ACKNOWLEDGEMENT

This work has been supported by the NSERC Discovery Grant of the second author.

7. REFERENCES

[1] Facebook Investors, Available online at: http://investor.fb.com/releasedetail.cfm?ReleaseID=780093. (accessed 4 Aug 2013)

[2] Chart of the day: How People Share Content on the Web, Available online at: http://www.businessinsider.com/chart-of-the-day-social-networking-sites-dominate-sharing-2009-7. (accessed 4 Aug 2013)

[3] An Infographic: The Biggest Shift since the Industrial Revolution | TechnoBuffalo, Available online at: http://www.technobuffalo.com/2010/06/01/an-infographic-the-biggest-shift-since-the-industrial-revolution/. (accessed 5 Sept 2013)

[4] Pariser, E.: The Filter Bubble: What the Internet Is Hiding from You. Penguin Press HC (2011)

[5] Nagulendra, S., Vassileva, J.: Providing Awareness, Understanding and Control of Personalized Stream Filtering in a P2P Social Network. 19th International Conference, CRIWG 2013. pp. 61–76 Springer Berlin Heidelberg (2013).

[6] Resnick, P., Varian, H.R.: Recommender systems. Communications of the ACM. 40, 3, 56–58 (1997)

[7] Konstan, J.A., Riedl, J.: Recommender systems: from algorithms to user experience. User Modeling and User-Adapted Interaction. 22, 1-2, 101–123 (2012)

[8] Webster, A., Vassileva, J.: Visualizing personal relations in online communities. Proceedings of the adaptive hypermedia and adaptive web-based systems (AH'2006), June 21–23, pp. 223–233, Springer LNCS 4018, Dublin (2006)

[9] Cook, R., and Kay, J. The Justified User Model: A Viewable, Explained User Model. In Proc. of the 4th Int. Conf. on User Modeling (1994)

[10] Bull, S., Pain, H. & Brna, P. (1995). Mr. Collins: A Collaboratively Constructed, Inspectable Student Model for Intelligent Computer Assisted Language Learning, Instructional Science 23(1-3), 65-87.

[11] Dimitrova, V.: STyLE-OLM: Interactive open learner modelling. International Journal of Artificial Intelligence in Education 17(2), 35–78 (2003)

[12] Zapata-Rivera, J. D., & Greer, J. (2004) Interacting with Bayesian student models. *International Journal of Artificial Intelligence in Education.* 14(2), 127-163.

[13] Bakalov F., König-Ries B., Nauerz A., and Welsch M: IntrospectiveViews: An Interface for Scrutinizing Semantic User Models. UMAP 2010: 219-230.

[14] Bakalov F., Meurs M.-J., König-Ries B., Sateli B., Witte R., Butler B., Tsang A.: An approach to controlling user models and personalization effects in recommender systems. IUI 2013: 49-56

[15] Parra D., Brusilovsky P., Trattner Ch.: See what you want to see: visual user-driven approach for hybrid recommendation.IUI 2014: 235-240

[16] Herlocker J. L., Konstan J. A., and Riedl J.: Explaining collaborative filtering recommendations. In Proceedings of ACM CSCW'00 Conference on Computer-Supported Cooperative Work, 2000.

[17] Tintarev N.and Masthoff J.: A survey of explanations in recommender systems. In Data Engineering Workshop, IEEE 23rd International Conference, 801 –810, 2007.

[18] Webster, A., Vassileva, J.: The KeepUP Recommender System. Proc. 2007 ACM Conference on Recommender Systems RecSys '07. pp. 173–176 ACM, Minneapolis, Minnesota, USA. (2007)

[19] Bostandjiev S., O'Donovan J., and Höllerer T.: TasteWeights: A Visual Interactive Hybrid Recommender System . In ACM Recommender Systems: 2012

[20] Indratmo, Vassileva, J., Gutwin, C.: Exploring blog archives with interactive visualization. In: International conference on Advanced Visual Interfaces (2008)

[21] Shi, S.: Keeping Up with the Information Glut by Visualizing Patterns of Posting by Friends on Facebook, http://hdl.handle.net/10388/ETD-2011-09-139, (accessed 11 Feb 2013)

[22] Kywe, S.M. et al.: A Survey of Recommender Systems in Twitter. Proc. 4th International Conference, SocInfo 2012, Lausanne, Switzerland, December 5-7, 2012. pp. 420–433 (2012)

[23] Manish, A. et al.: An Online News Recommender System for Social Networks. SIGIR-SSM. (2009)

[24] Kincaid, J.: EdgeRank: The Secret Sauce That Makes Facebook's News Feed Tick | TechCrunch, Available online at: http://techcrunch.com/2010/04/22/facebook-edgerank/. (accessed 6 July 2013)

[25] Resnick, P., A. Munson, S., Garrett, R.K., Stroud, N.J., Kriplean, T.: Bursting Your (Filter) Bubble: Strategies for Promoting Diverse Exposure. Proc. Conference on Computer supported Cooperative Work CSCW 2013 Companion proc. pp. 95–100 ACM (2013)

[26] Tandukar U., Vassileva J.: Ensuring Relevant and Serendipitous Information Flow in Decentralized Online Social Network. Proc. AIMSA'2012, 15th biennial conference on AI Methods Systems, Applications, Springer Verlag, LNAI 7557, pp. 79-88. (2012)

[27] Munson, S.A., Resnick, P.: Presenting diverse political opinions. Proc. 28th international conference on Human factors in computing systems - CHI '10. p. 1457 ACM Press, New York, New York, USA (2010)

[28] Nagulendra, S., Vassileva, J.: Minimizing Social Data Overload through Interest- Based Stream Filtering in a P2P Social Network, Proc. IEEE International Conference on Social Computing, SocialCom'2013 (2013)

[29] Macgirvin, M.: DFRN – the Distributed Friends & Relations Network, Available online at: https://macgirvin.com/spec/dfrn2.pdf. (accessed 2 Aug 2012)

[30] Paolacci, G., Chandler, J.: Running experiments on Amazon Mechanical Turk. 5, 5, 1–14 (2014).

[30] Tandukar, U., Vassileva, J.: Selective Propagation of Social Data in Decentralized Online Social Network. Proc. UMAP 2011 Workshops, LNCS 7138. pp. 213–224 Springer-Verlag Berlin Heidelberg (2012)

[31] ISO/IEC TR 9126-2:2003 – Product Quality – External Metrics, Available online at:

http://www.iso.org/iso/iso_catalogue/catalogue_tc/catalogue_detail.htm?csnumber=22750. (accessed 2 Feb 2014)

[32] Bland, J. M., Altman, D. G.: "Statistics notes: Cronbach's alpha," pp. 570-572 (1997)

[33] George, D., Mallery, P., SPSS for Windows step by step: A simple guide and reference. 11.0 update (4th ed.), Boston: Allyn & Bacon (2003)

[34] Testing for Normality using SPSS, Available online at: https://statistics.laerd.com/spss-tutorials/testing-for-normality-using-spss-statistics.php. (Accessed 2 Mar 2014)

[35] One-Sample T-Test using SPSS, Available online at: https://statistics.laerd.com/spss-tutorials/one-sample-t-test-using-spss-statistics.php. (Accessed 2 Mar 2014)

The Shortest Path to Happiness: Recommending Beautiful, Quiet, and Happy Routes in the City

Daniele Quercia
Yahoo Labs
Barcelona, Spain
dquercia@yahoo-inc.com

Rossano Schifanella[*]
University of Torino
Torino, Italy
schifane@di.unito.it

Luca Maria Aiello
Yahoo Labs
Barcelona, Spain
alucca@yahoo-inc.com

ABSTRACT

When providing directions to a place, web and mobile mapping services are all able to suggest the shortest route. The goal of this work is to automatically suggest routes that are not only short but also emotionally pleasant. To quantify the extent to which urban locations are pleasant, we use data from a crowd-sourcing platform that shows two street scenes in London (out of hundreds), and a user votes on which one looks more beautiful, quiet, and happy. We consider votes from more than 3.3K individuals and translate them into quantitative measures of location perceptions. We arrange those locations into a graph upon which we learn pleasant routes. Based on a quantitative validation, we find that, compared to the shortest routes, the recommended ones add just a few extra walking minutes and are indeed perceived to be more beautiful, quiet, and happy. To test the generality of our approach, we consider Flickr metadata of more than 3.7M pictures in London and 1.3M in Boston, compute proxies for the crowdsourced beauty dimension (the one for which we have collected the most votes), and evaluate those proxies with 30 participants in London and 54 in Boston. These participants have not only rated our recommendations but have also carefully motivated their choices, providing insights for future work.

Categories and Subject Descriptors

H.4 [**Information Systems Applications**]: Miscellaneous

General Terms

Human Factors, Design, Measurement.

[*]This work has been done while the author was visiting Yahoo Labs, Barcelona, within the framework of the Faculty Research and Engagement Program.

Keywords

Social Media; Urban Informatics; Derives

1. INTRODUCTION

At times, we do not take the fastest route but enjoy alternatives that offer beautiful sceneries. When walking, we generally prefer tiny streets with trees over large avenues with cars. However, Web and mobile mapping services currently fail to offer that experience as they are able to recommend only shortest routes.

To capture which routes people find interesting and enjoyable, researchers have started to analyze the digital traces left behind by users of online services like Flickr or Foursquare. Previous work has, however, not considered the role of emotions in the urban context when recommending routes. Yet, there exists the concept of psychogeography, which dates back to 1955. This was defined as "the study of the precise laws and specific effects of the geographical environment, consciously organized or not, on the emotions and behavior of individuals" [9]. The psychogeographer "is able both to identify and to distill the varied ambiances of the urban environment. Emotional zones that cannot be determined simply by architectural or economic conditions must be determined by following the aimless stroll (*derive*)" [6]. Mobile applications have been recently proposed to ease making *derives* (i.e., detours in the city): these include Derive app[1], Serendipitor[2], Drift[3], and Random GPS.[4] The goal of our work is to go beyond supporting *derives* and to propose ways of automatically generating routes that are not only short but also emotionally pleasant. This goal is not algorithmic but is experimental. We rely on crowdsourced measurements of people's emotional experience of the city and use those measurements to propose new ways of recommending urban routes. Despite emotional responses being subjective and difficult to quantify, urban studies have repeatedly shown that specific visual cues in the city context are consistently associated with the same fuzzy concept (e.g., with beauty) [7, 23, 25, 28]. For example, previous work has found that green spaces and Victorian houses are mostly associated with beauty, while trash and broken windows with ugliness.

[1] http://deriveapp.com/s/v2/
[2] http://serendipitor.net/site/
[3] http://www.brokencitylab.org/drift/
[4] http://nogovoyages.com/random_gps.html

To meet our research goal, we make three main contributions:

- We build a graph whose nodes are locations and whose edges connect geographic neighbors (§3.1). With this graph, we rank locations based on whether they are emotionally pleasant. The emotion scores come from a crowd-sourcing platform that shows two street scenes in London (out of hundreds), and a user votes on which one looks more beautiful, quiet, and happy (§3.2).

- We quantitatively validate the extent to which our proposal recommends paths that are not only short but also emotionally-pleasing (§4). We then qualitatively evaluate the recommendations by conducting a user study involving 30 participants in London.

- We finally test the generalizability of our proposal by: a) presenting a way of predicting the beauty scores from Flickr metadata; and b) testing the beauty-derived paths with our 30 participants in London and with a new group of 54 participants in Boston (§5).

2. RELATED WORK

Early research on route recommendation focused on finding the most *efficient* routes. For example, Chang *et al.* ([2]) used a backtracking algorithm to recommend *car* routes that deviate from a user's familiar/past trajectories. Ludwig *et al.* ([16]) used an adaptive A*-like algorithm to recommend *public transport* routes that afford both short walks and little waiting times. More recently, tools for recommending the safest or smoothest *cycle* paths in the city have also been proposed [24].

In addition to ways of recommending efficient paths, researchers have also investigated the problem of recommending *distinctive* and *interesting* urban routes [22, 31]. The idea behind this line of work is to use geo-referenced online content (e.g., Flickr pictures) to learn and recommend popular trajectories [1, 34, 35]. De Choundry *et al.* ([8]) and El Ali *et al.* ([10]) both used Flickr data to mine popular spatio-temporal sequences of picture uploads and to then recommend the corresponding urban routes. De Choundry *et al.* identified the movements of individual tourists by tracking when and where they were uploading photos and by then using the resulting trajectories to connect points of interests in a graph. By embedding location information such as average time spent at a location and location popularity, they were able to use an orienteering algorithm on the graph to compute the optimal number of interesting locations to visit given a time budget. El Ali *et al.* followed a similar idea: by clustering sequences of pictures uploaded at similar times, they used a sequence alignment algorithm borrowed from biology to produce trajectories containing interesting locations.

In addition to using geo-located pictures, one could exploit GPS traces. As opposed to social media, mobile phones enjoy high penetration rates and, as such, GPS traces can help identify interesting places not only in cities but also in suburban regions [32]. Zheng *et al.* ([36]) mined such traces by arranging both visited places and mobile users in a bipartite graph, and then ranking places by graph centrality to extract top interesting regions. Their focus was on spotting interesting locations rather than routes.

All this line of work has been tailored to touristic use cases where paths can be considerably longer than the shortest ones [29], and where recommending frequently visited locations is a reasonable choice.

More recently, given the popularity of mobile social networking applications, researchers have been able to explore personalization strategies for tourists and residents alike. Meng *et al.* ([18]) leveraged traces from Foursquare to plan itineraries that need to pass through different types of locations (e.g., restaurants, gas stations) and, given a user demand for some location types, they computed paths using an ant colony optimization algorithm. Cheng *et al.* ([3]) annotated historical data of traveled paths with demographic information and used a Baeysian learning model to generate personalized travel recommendations based on demographic segmentation. Kurashima *et al.* ([15]) addressed a somewhat similar problem - they profiled users according to their past travel histories. These approaches output sequences of locations according to different criteria but do not focus on the nature of the paths connecting those locations.

To date, there has not been any work that considers people's emotional perceptions of urban spaces when recommending routes to them. We thus set out to do such a work by collecting reliable perceptions of urban scenes, incorporating them into algorithmic solutions, and quantitatively and qualitatively evaluating those solutions.

3. OUR PROPOSAL

Our goal is to suggest users a short and pleasant path between their current location s and destination d. We meet this goal in four steps:

1. Build a graph whose nodes are all locations in the city under study (§3.1).

2. Crowdsource people's perceptions of those locations along three dimensions: *beautiful*, *quiet*, and *happy* (§3.2).

3. Assign scores to locations along each of the three (§3.3).

4. Select the path between nodes s and d that strikes the right balance between being short and being pleasant (§3.4).

3.1 Building Location Graph

We divide the bounding box of central London (travel zone 1[5]) into 532 walkable cells, each of which is 200x200 meters in size. Previous research has established that 200m tends to be the threshold of walkable distance in urban areas [20, 4]. In dense parts of London, such a distance would typically correspond to two blocks that could be covered by a 2.5-minute walk. Having those cells at hand, we make them be nodes in a location graph. Each node is a location and links to its eight geographic neighbors.[6] To quantify the extent to which a node reflects a pleasant location, we need to capture the way people perceive that location, and we do so next.

3.2 Crowdsourcing Perceptions

We rely on the data gathered from a crowdsourcing web site to assess the extent to which different city's locations are

---

[5] http://visitorshop.tfl.gov.uk/help-centre/about-travel-zones.html

[6] Since a boundary cell would have less than eight neighbors, we link it to a number of additional closest cells within the grid such that, as a result, it would link to eight nodes in total.

perceived to be beautiful, quiet and make people happy [25]. Available under `UrbanGems.org`, the site picks up two random urban scenes and ask users which one of the two is more beautiful, quiet, or happy. As for scenes, the site does not use Flickr images, as they considerably vary in quality, but taps into two image sources that offer pictures of comparable quality: Google Street View pictures captured by camera-mounted cars, and Geograph[7] pictures provided by volunteers. To control for image bias, we perform two main steps. First, we make sure that multiple images from the two sources are available at *each* location. Second, we check whether user ratings are not correlated with objective measures of image quality, and we indeed find that there is no correlation between images' ratings and two commonly used proxies for quality (i.e., sharpness and contrast levels [33]).

At each game round, users should either click on one of the two scenes or opt for "Can't Tell", if undecided on which picture to click on. With each selection, the user is asked to guess the percentage of other people who shared their views, scoring points for correct guesses. Those points can then be shared through the social media sites of Facebook and Twitter. To avoid the sparsity problem (too few answers per picture), a random scene is selected within a 300-meter radius from a subway station and within the bounding boxes of census areas. This results into 258 Google Street views and 310 Geograph images, all of which have ratings that are roughly normally distributed [25]. We use multiple images from the two sources at each location. By collecting a large number of responses across a large number of participants, we are now able to determine which urban scenes are perceived in which ways along the three qualities.

The choice of the three qualities is motivated by their importance in the urban context according to previous studies. Being able to find *quiet* places might "promote 'sonic health' in our cities and offer a public guide for those who crave a retreat from crowds"[8]. As for *beauty*, we are not the first to measure its perceptions. In 1967, Peterson proposed a quantitative analysis of public perceptions of neighborhood visual appearance [23] and found that beauty and safety are approximately collinear. Finally, we choose happiness not least because urban studies in the 1960s tried to systematically relate well-being in the urban environment (i.e., happiness) to the fundamental desire for visual order, beauty, and aesthetics [17]. As a result, well-being or, more informally, happiness has taken centre stage in the scientific discourse for decades.

The platform was released in September 2012 and after 4 months data from as many as 3,301 participants was collected: 36% connecting from London (IP addresses), 35% from the rest of UK, and 29% outside UK. A fraction of those participants (515) specified their personal details: the percentage of male-female for those participants is 66%-34%, the average age is 38.1 years old, and the racial segmentation reflects that of the 2001 UK census.[9] Upon processing 17,261 rounds of annotation (each round requires to annotate at most ten pairs), we rank pictures by their scores for beauty, quiet, and happiness, and those scores are based on the fraction of votes the pictures have received. The ranking is reliable because the number of annotators is $>3K$ and distribution of scores is normal with median as high as 171

---

[7] http://www.geograph.org.uk/
[8] http://www.stereopublic.net/
[9] http://en.wikipedia.org/wiki/Ethnic_groups_in_the_United_Kingdom

Name	Formula
Linear	h_i
Cubic	h_i^3
Exponential	e^{h_i}
Square root	$\sqrt{h_i}$
Sigmoid	$\frac{1}{1+e^{-h_i}}$

Table 1: **Five expressions experimentally used to map crowdsourced scores to probabilities. With a location's crowdsourced scores of happiness, those expressions return the location's likelihoods of being considered happy if one were to visit it.**

for beauty, 12 for quiet, and 16 for happy. The number of answers for the three qualities is different as the default question is that on beauty, which thus preferentially attracts more answers.

We compute the correlations between each pairwise combinations of the three qualities. All correlations are statistically significant (i.e., all p-values are < 0.0001) and are the following: happy-quiet has $r = 0.29$, quiet-beauty $r = 0.33$, and beauty-happy is $r = 0.64$. As one would expect from the literature [7], we find that the strongest affiliation is that between beauty and happiness, so we should expect that the paths we will recommend for beauty and those for happiness might partly overlap at times.

3.3 Scoring Locations

To rank a location, we need to compute the likelihood that it will be visited because it is pleasant. One simple way of expressing that is with $p(go|happy) \propto p(happiness|go)$.

The probability $p(happiness|go)$ captures the idea that individuals visits locations that make them happy. We thus need a way to measure a location's happiness and, to that end, we resort to our crowdsourced scores (§3.2). More specifically, given the crowdsourced happiness score h_i for cell i, we compute the corresponding happiness probability with a curve that is, for example, cubic:

$$p(happiness|go) = k \cdot h_i^3, \text{ where } k = \frac{1}{max\{h_i^3\}\forall_i} \quad (1)$$

Thus, the higher a location's crowdsourced score, the happier it is likely to be. By substituting h_i^3 with any of the expressions in Table 1, we obtain the alternative happiness scoring functions. We apply those scoring functions to the two remaining scores of quiet and beauty too. We do so by simply substituting h_i with q_i (location i's quietness score) and with b_i (i's beauty score). Next, for brevity, we will report only the results for the cubic curve for which our experiments have shown the highest percentage improvements.

3.4 Selecting Best Path

Upon the location graph and having the likelihood of visiting each location, we now select the best path from source s to destination d in four steps:

Step 1. Identify M shortest paths between s and d. To identify them, we run Eppstein's algorithm [11] and find the M shortest paths connecting each pair of nodes s and d. To be sufficiently "exhaustive", we initially set M to be as high as 10^6. This choice makes it possible to explore the full set

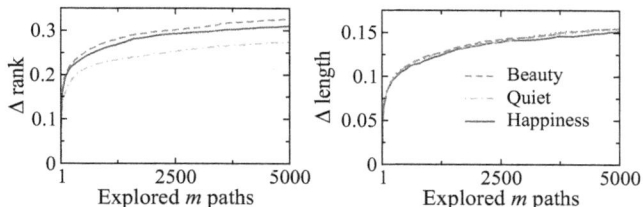

Figure 2: Δrank and Δlength for different exploration levels m (left panel). Respectively, these represent improvements in beauty/quiet/happiness ranks (left panel) and demand for extra walking time if only the first m shortest paths are considered (right).

Path recommended for	ΔBeauty	ΔQuiet	ΔHappy
Beauty	**30%**	6%	22%
Quiet	10%	**26%**	5%
Happy	24%	2%	**30%**

Table 2: Percentage improvements for beauty, quiet, and happiness in the recommended paths over the shortest ones (results averaged across 190 paths).

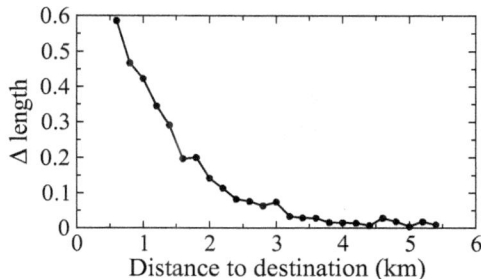

Figure 3: Additional distance (% over shortest paths) required to recommend pleasant paths for destinations at different distances (km). As expected, for closer destinations, the additional cost is larger than that for farthest destinations.

of solutions, including any of the solution that alternative approaches might return (e.g., orienteering algorithms).

Step 2. Compute the *average* rank for all locations in each of the first m paths (with $m \leq M$). For computational tractability, we do not consider all the M paths at once but iteratively explore the first m paths. At each exploration, we record the path with the lowest (best) average rank. Such a path exploration has, of course, diminishing returns (Figure 2, left panel): the more paths we consider (the higher m), the less likely the best value for rank will change. This suggests that it is not necessary to explore all M paths but we can explore a tiny subset of them without loss of performance, and that is what the next step does.

Step 3. Terminate when the average rank improves less than ϵ. To select ϵ, we use The Marginal Value Theorem (MVT). This is an analytical tool for optimizing the trade-off between benefit (rank improvement Δrank) and cost (exploration of the first m paths). One can show analytically that, for the function of rank vs. m, it is best to keep increasing m only until $\frac{\Delta \text{rank}}{\Delta m}$ equals $\frac{\text{rank}}{m}$; after that, one should terminate and take the path among those considered that has the best average rank.

Step 4. Select the path that has so far been found to have the best rank.

By repeating these steps for each of the three ranks (beauty, quiet, and happiness), we obtain three paths between s and d in addition to the shortest one (to the baseline).

4. EVALUATION

The goal of our proposal is to recommend paths that are not only short but also pleasant. To ascertain the effectiveness of our proposal at meeting this goal, our evaluation ought to answer three main questions:

(Validation) Is our proposal able to recommend paths that are pleasant? (§4.1)

(Length trade-off) Are pleasant paths considerably longer than shortest ones? (§4.2)

(User assessment) Do people find the recommended paths to be actually beautiful, quiet, and happy? (§4.3)

4.1 Validation

We compare how our recommended paths differ from the shortest ones in terms of average beauty, quiet and happy scores. We choose shortest path as baseline since it reproduces existing approaches that focus on time efficiency. To make this comparison computationally tractable, we con-

sider twenty nodes that correspond to popular landmarks and cover the entire central part of the city under study. We analyze the 190 paths resulting from each node pair. As one expects, the paths recommended for beauty, quietness, and happiness all show a percentage increase in the corresponding dimension (Table 2). More specifically, compared to the shortest paths, beautiful ones are, on average, 30% more beautiful (and are happier as well); quiet paths are 26% quieter; and happy paths are, again, 30% happier (and are also more beautiful). From these results, we conclude that not only our proposal effectively biases paths in the way we expect (which should be the case for any working solution) but also it does so to a considerable extent: with an increase that goes from 26% to 30%. Now the question is whether this bias comes at the price of considerable longer paths.

4.2 Length Trade-off

We test whether the recommended paths are considerably longer than the shortest ones. We find that, on average, the recommended paths are only 12% longer. This is a good result for two main reasons. First, it is far lower than what previous work reported, which admittedly focused on different contexts such as tourism or entertainment. For example, paths recommending touristic attractions tended to be half-a-day touristic experiences (twelve hours) [8], and those capturing people's salient experiences tended to be 60% longer than the shortest paths [10]. Second, the increase of 12% in length practically translates into about 2 and a half additional cells, which correspond to roughly 7 and a half additional minutes. These numbers are all average values and, as such, they collate both long and short paths together. To break down those results, we plot the extra length required for recommending pleasant paths (over shortest) for destinations at increasing distances (Figure 3). We expect

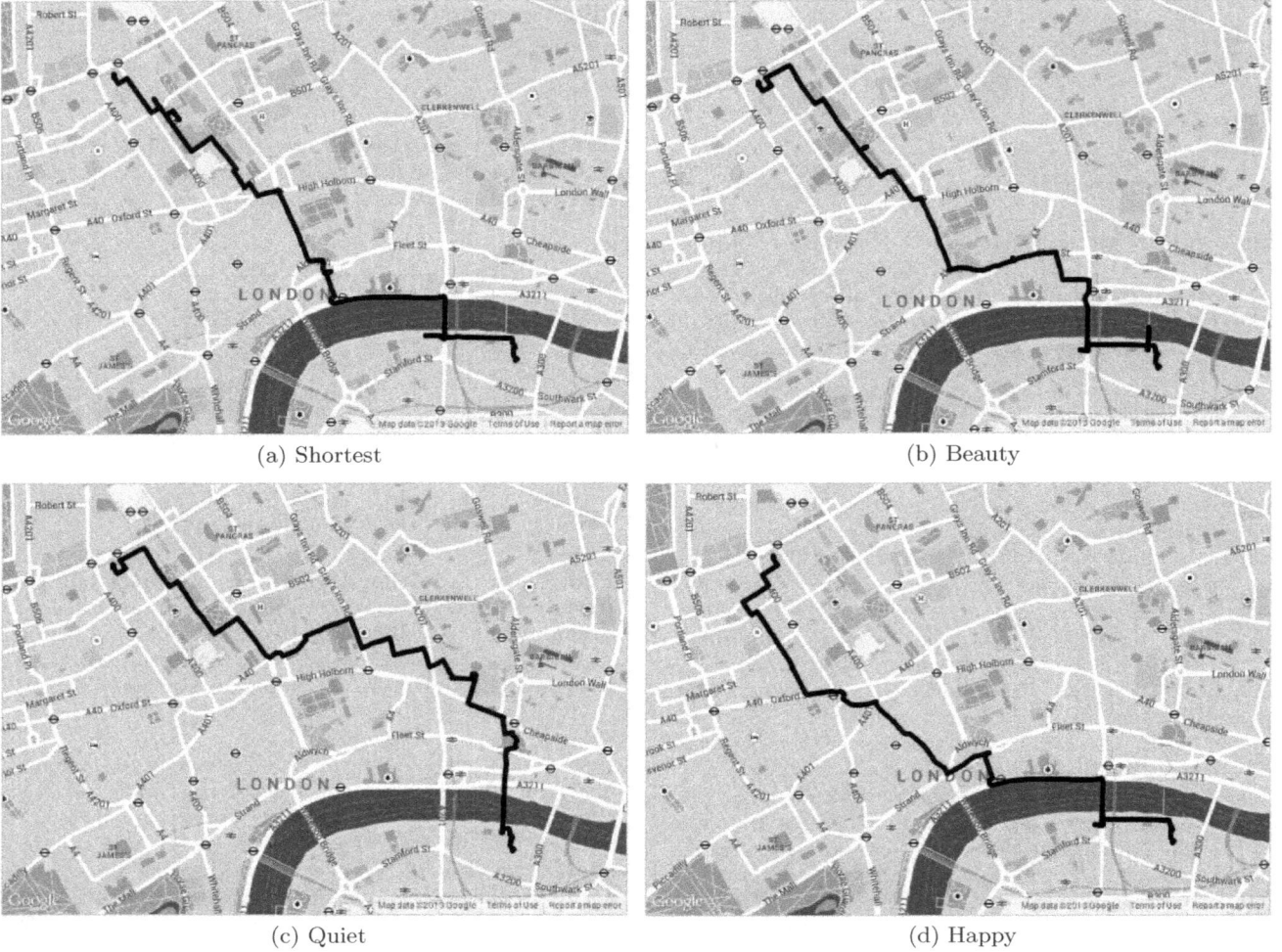

(a) Shortest   (b) Beauty

(c) Quiet   (d) Happy

Figure 1: Maps showing the different paths between Euston Square and Tate Modern.

that the farther the destination, the lower the extra time required by our recommendation over the shortest paths. We find that, for 1km (x-axis), paths tend to be 40% longer (y-axis), and, more importantly, that extra cost indeed decreases exponentially. That is because, to identify pleasant sceneries, the shorter a path, the more deviations (and extra walking time) are required; by contrast, in a longer path, there is plenty of room for finding pleasant sceneries without imposing any additional walking overhead.

4.3 User Assessment

To evaluate whether our recommendations are perceived by individuals as desirable alternatives to current shortest route planners, we resort to a mixed-method user study in which both quantitative and qualitative measures are extracted. The goal of the study is to test four paths - shortest, beautiful, quiet, and happy - between the same source and destination. We have to keep the two end points fixed to avoid rating sparsity.

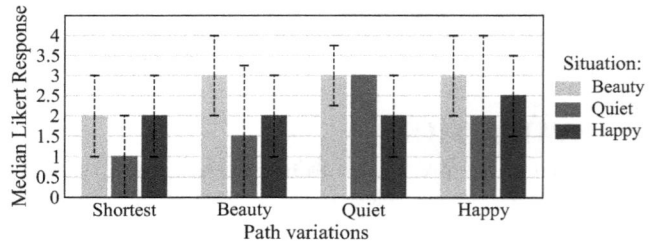

Figure 4: Median of Likert responses for four path variations (shortest, beauty, quiet, and happy) in the three scenarios. Error bars reflect the range across quartile, which measures dispersion. All results are statistically significant.

4.3.1 Experimental Setup and Execution

Our participants will see the four paths, like the ones shown in Figure 1, on a web page but do not know which one is what. The two end points of the paths are Euston Square and Tate Modern. We chose those two specific points because the resulting paths: 1) are between two locations well-known to Londoners; 2) are in central London, and that increases the chance participants will know them; 3) are at walking distance; and 4) go across the River Thames, allowing us to test any potential effect of the mental divide between North and South London [26].

To begin with, we ask each of our participants to read a consent form and optionally provide age, gender, years living in London, and email address. They are also asked to tell us the extent to which they are familiar with the five paths using a Likert scale (i.e., they have to choose among Strongly disagree, Disagree, Neither agree nor disagree, Agree, and Strongly agree). After this initial step, we test the four routes in three different scenarios, each of which corresponds to one of the three fuzzy qualities - beauty, quietness, and happiness - and is meant to emulate a realistic use of a navigation service. For the *happy scenario*, a participant has to imagine to be in the company of a friend who is a bit down. Given that, the participant decides to bring the friend to the Tate Gallery and has to assess which of the five paths would make this friend happier using, again, a Likert scale. For the *quiet scenario*, the participant wishes to go to the Tate. Today (s)he has been exposed to many people and lots of car traffic in central London, and thus (s)he wishes to find a quiet path to get there. The participants has to assess the extent to which each of the five paths is expected to be quiet on a Likert scale. Finally, for the *beauty scenario*, the participant has to imagine that his/her best friend is visiting from Italy, and this friend loves beautiful things. The participant has to say which of the five paths is expected to offer beautiful views. After answering each of the 5x3 questions, our participants can motivate each of their answers under a free-text box.

4.3.2 Demographics of Participants

Among our 30 participants in London, the percentage of male-female is 58%-42%. The most common age band is that of 30-35, which includes half of our participants; by contrast, only 5% are below 23 years old, and 10% above 48. As for familiarity with London, our respondents have lived in London, on average, for two and a half years. Since this sample of users relates only to specific social groups, it would be interesting to compare their demographics to those of social media users. From the latest Ignite report on social media [14], Foursquare and Twitter users tend to be university educated 25-34 year old women (66% women for Foursquare and 61% for Twitter), while Flickr users tend to be university educated 35-44 year old women (54% women). The demographics of our respondents thus show a skew towards 30-35 year old men (58% men). As such, compared to social media users, our respondents reflect a slightly older age group and are more likely to be men.

4.3.3 Quantitative and Qualitative Results

As typically done, we treat our Likert responses as ordinal data and collate them into bar charts. We summarize the central tendency by the median and the dispersion by the range across quartiles (error bars), and show the results in Figure 4. We will present the results that are statistically significant. We find that across the three scenarios, the shortest path performs worst, with median from 1.5 to 2 and dispersion ± 1. The best performing variation across the three scenarios is the happy variation with median as high

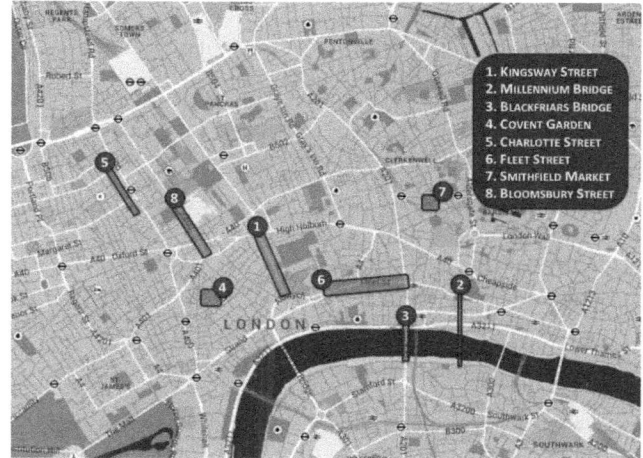

Figure 5: Map of London with eight frequently mentioned places.

as 3. Finally, the clear-cut scenario is that of quiet, in which the quiet variation is indeed the one most preferred by our respondents whose ratings have, in this case, no dispersion: for the quiet path, we find a median score 3 ± 0 as opposed to 1 ± 1 for the shortest path, 1 ± 1.75 for the beauty variation, and 3 ± 2 for the happy variation. These results suggest that, without telling which path is what, our participants readily associate the path to the intended quality of quiet, beauty, or happiness.

To gain further insights into their choices, we have asked the participants to motivate their ratings (the map in Figure 5 marks the places they frequently mentioned). All the respondents do not perceive any extra walking time for the quiet/beautiful/happy paths. Both beautiful and happy paths are associated with *peaceful* places (e.g., back streets around St Paul's cathedral, the walkable Millenium Bridge as opposed to the car-infested Blackfriars Bridge). By contrast, *busy* places make people unhappy. By busy, our participants mean streets full of cars. For example, they consider the shortest path unpleasant because it was going through Kingsway, which is a heavily trafficked road in central London. However, at times, by busy, they also mean a street full of people. One participant considers a path undesirable because it goes through Kingsway and Fleet street: "Kingsway is always busy with cars, and Fleet street with pedestrians". Also, beautiful and happy paths are positively associated with *historical* places (e.g., the Bloomsbury area). Interestingly, places that mix the two contrasting qualities of being *historical yet busy* lead to controversial feedbacks. Most of our respondents consider Covent Garden and Charlotte street in extremely positive ways: "There is certainly colour in Charlotte street and some beautiful shops and events happening though Covent Garden"; "Charlotte street is funky"; "I am very fond of Charlotte Street and Endell Street: they contain exciting and charming cafes and shops". Yet, at times, the same very street acquires negative connotations: "I would not think a busy Charlotte street would make the friend happier". Overall, we note that the presence of charming shops and historical elements balances the otherwise negative perceptions of busy places. Indeed the respondent who thought that Charlotte street would not make the friend happier adds: "...However the presence of people on a street packed with businesses might contribute to happiness". Also, places offering distinctive experiences are considered happy. So is considered Soho: it "offers a different view of London"; another respondent adds "I like Soho and the area around Covent Garden. I think that walking in these areas would make my friend happier". The concept of happiness also captures hard-to-quantify contextual aspects of urban life such as smell. As for unhappy places recommended by the shortest path, one respondent recalls that "Southampton row is smelly" and should not be recommended. Our respondents also point out that the experiences of a place might change during the course of a day: "Fleet street is beautiful because of its history. However, depending on the time of day, it can be colourless and busy leading to the opposite results". Finally, the urban quality among the three that results in the least controversial feedback is that of quiet as it is readily associated with parks and back roads. To sum up, a desirable place tends to be peaceful, historical, and distinctive, whilst avoiding being too busy. Interestingly, places that either mix contrasting qualities (e.g., historical/charming *vs.* busy) or experience drastic changes over time (e.g., busy during the week, and lovely in the weekend) yield mixed results.

5. CROWDSOURCING AND LONDON

Critics might rightly claim that this work suffers from two main drawbacks. First, it relies on crowsourced ratings whose collection requires intense user involvement. Second, our evaluation has so far focused on a single city. To partly address those two concerns, in this section, we present a way of predicting the beauty scores from Flickr metadata (§5.1) and test these predictions not only in London but also in the city of Boston (§5.2).

5.1 Beyond Crowdsourcing: Flickr

We test whether one can predict beauty scores out of Flickr metadata. We choose beauty over quiet or over happiness since, being the default question, it has received the highest number of votes. We gather a random sample of 7M geo-referenced Flickr pictures within our bounding box of London, 5.1M of which have at least one tag and, as we shall see, 3.7M can be used for our purposes. For each of our locations (cells), we gather these statistics: number of pictures (density), number of views, of favorites, of comments, and of tags received by those pictures. We also get hold of the actual tags, clean them (i.e., convert them to lowercase and remove those that are stop-words), and process them using a dictionary called "Linguistic Inquiry Word Count" [21]. LIWC is a standard dictionary of 2,300 English words that capture 80% of the words used in everyday conversations and reflect people's emotional and cognitive perceptions. These words fall into 72 categories, such as positive and negative emotional words, and words about work, school, money. Rather than grouping words based on their material subject matter (e.g., 'sports', 'technology'), LIWC categories are generally abstract, and are based on linguistic and psychological processes. For example, there exist categories for cognitive processes (such as 'insight' and 'certainty'), psychological constructs (e.g., affect, cognition), as well as personal concerns (e.g., work, home, leisure activities). Each word may thus belong to multiple categories; for example, the prefix entry 'hostil*' belongs to the categories

Category	Example words	Description
posemo	happy, pretty, good	Express pos. emotions
negemo	hate, worthless	Express neg. emotions
swear	c**t, f**k	Swear words
anx	afraid, scare	Express anxiety
sad	cried, deprived	Express sadness
anger	abusive, disgusting	Express anger

Table 3: Categories that reflect the use of language and whose presence in Flickr tags correlates with the beauty scores.

'affect' (affective processes), 'negemo' (negative emotions) and 'anger'. Having this dictionary at hand, we count the number of tags matching the 72 categories, and, after doing so, we are left with 3.7M pictures that have at least one classified tag. For each location (cell), we compute the *normalized count* for each LIWC category c:

$$f_c = \frac{w_c - \mu_c}{\sigma_c} \qquad (2)$$

where w_c is the fraction of tags classified in category c (over the total number of classified tags) for the location; μ_c is the fraction of tags in category c, averaged across all locations; and σ_c is the corresponding standard deviation.

Out of the Flickr features and LIWC categories, those that are significantly correlated with beauty scores are density (number of pictures in a cell), 'posemo', 'negemo', 'swear', 'anx' (anxiety), 'sad', and 'anger'. We thus use the presence of those categories as predictors in a linear regression whose dependent variable is the beauty score. We find the following coefficients:

$$beauty' = 0.37 + 0.03 \cdot log(density) + 0.20 \cdot f_p - 0.21 \cdot f_n \quad (3)$$

where f_p is the fraction of tags containing positive emotions, and f_n is the fraction of tags containing emotions in the categories 'negemo', 'swear', 'anx', 'sad', and 'anger'. We should concede that statistical models more sophisticated than a linear regression could have been used: for example, one might well decide to exploit the spatial autocorrelations of the beauty scores. However, given that our goal is to carry out a preliminary study on Flickr, we opt for a linear regression, not least because it yields predictions that are easy to explain (as opposed to black-box machine learning approaches) and that are reasonably accurate. The R^2 of the regression is indeed 0.31, which means that as much as 31% of the variability of the beauty score can be solely explained by the presence of Flickr tags.

5.1.1 Results

To build paths from Flickr metadata, we use the Flickr-derived beauty scores and run the steps described in Section 3.4. We find that the resulting beautiful paths are, on average, 28% more beautiful than the shortest ones. To see how users perceive a Flickr-derived path, during our user study in London (Section 4.3), we had added a fifth path (in addition to the four we have already presented): a Flickr-derived beautiful path between Euston Square and Tate Modern (Figure 6(a)). Our 30 respondents rate this path with neutral answers (median 2) but little uncertainty (0 dispersion). That is, our respondents do not feel strongly

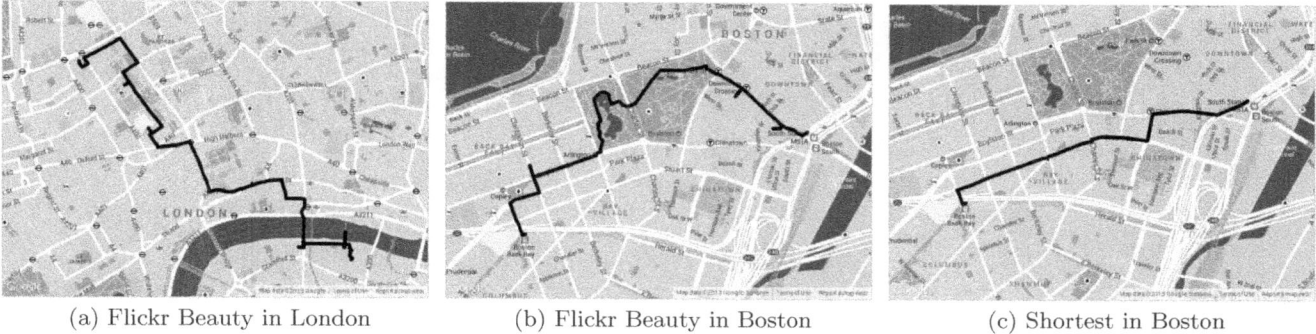

| (a) Flickr Beauty in London | (b) Flickr Beauty in Boston | (c) Shortest in Boston |

Figure 6: Maps showing the different paths with beauty scores predicted from Flickr's metadata.

about the recommendation based on Flickr but agree with each other when judging it, suggesting that Flickr-derived recommendations can be used as general-purpose suggestions when personalization is not possible (e.g., in cold-start situations). However, by comparing those who rated the Flickr variation above the median and those who rated it below, we find that these two classes of individuals differ. The Flickr variation is preferred by:

Women. The percentage of male-female is 25%-75% for above-median raters, and 60%-40% for those below;

Short-term residents. The average number of years living in London is 2 and a half for those above, and 3 and a half for those below.

5.2 Beyond London: Boston

London is in itself quite a peculiar city: from a geo-demographic perspective, London is by far the largest city in the EU (the most densely populated within city limits), with a diverse range of people and cultures spread all over its area. To complement our London study, we present in this section a brief study in the city of Boston, chosen for their very different characteristics. From a geo-demographic perspective, we scale both population density and area size of a factor down with respect to London. From a Flickr perspective, picture density is slightly higher in Boston (1.1 more pictures per m^2 than in London), while engagement with content is slightly lower (a London picture has, on average, 0.8 more tags than one in Boston).

5.2.1 Quantitative Results

By running the steps in §3.4 on the metadata in Boston, we find that the Flickr-derived beautiful paths are, on average, 35% more beautiful than the shortest paths. This is higher than any improvement we have experienced for any of the three qualities in London, suggesting that routing through beautiful sceneries (and, accordingly, avoiding ugly ones) is easier in Boston than it was in London. Indeed, American cities (including Boston) tend to offer urban situations far more diverse in terms of safety and beauty than what European cities do [28], and, for the routing algorithm, diversity translates into more options to choose from.

In Boston, we repeated the London's user study (§4.3.1): we were able to recruit as many as 54 participants who compared a Flickr-derived beautiful path (Figure 6(b)) with the shortest one (Figure 6(c)) using, again, a Likert scale. These

two paths go from Back Bay Station to South Station, and the Flickr-derived is chosen to be the one that has the highest improvement in average beauty.

The percentage of male-female participants overall is 57%-43%. Also, the most common age band is that of 30-35, which includes 43% our participants; by contrast, 32% are below 30 years old, and only 17% above 42. As for familiarity with Boston, our respondents have lived in the city, on average, for four and half years.

From our respondents' ratings, we find that, again, the shortest path performs worst, with a median of 1 and dispersion ± 1. Thus the best performing is the Flickr-defined path with median as high as 3 ± 1, and the median increases to 4 if we consider people younger than 30 years old. These results confirm once again the ease with which our algorithm can find beautiful alternatives.

5.2.2 Qualitative Results

Our respondents see the Flickr-derived beautiful path positively. To ease illustration, the map in Figure 7 shows the places our participants frequently mentioned. The most positive feedback for the beautiful path is: "You will see almost the entire city of Boston in shorter period of time". By contrast, the shortest path receives negative and neutral feedbacks. The most negative one mentions that a specific segment "is gross and no one needs to see it", while the most positive feedback is neutral at best: "It's an interesting and attractive walk . . . but I wouldn't use the word beautiful". What is considered positive/negative in Boston is similar to what we found in London. On the positive side, respondents repeatedly mention green spaces: "Boylston is really nice and they have a lot of shopping. The park is also gorgeous", and another respondent adds "green space, manicure landscaping, public activities obviously all carefully designed to appeal to visitors as well as residents". As for negative qualities, respondents cite the presence of cars ("It is heavily trafficked by cars in some areas") and that of dirt ("Some places between South Station and Stuart are also rather dirty"). In a way similar to London, we also have mixed results for few locations: those are the ones that tend to be used quite differently from day to night.

6. DISCUSSION

We are now ready to wrap up this work by discussing some open questions.

Scalability. The two main steps of our approach are: 1) building the location graph with nodes and corresponding

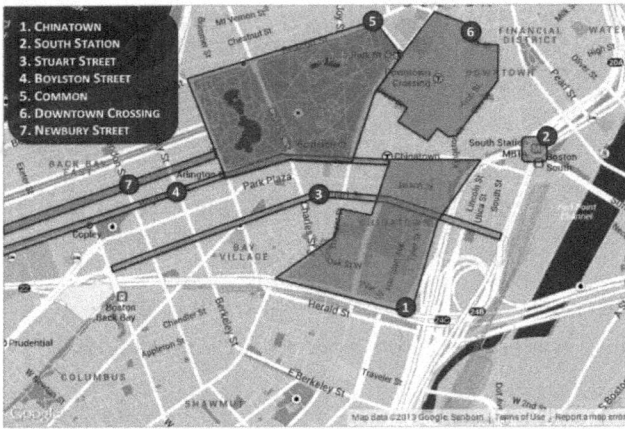

Figure 7: Map of Boston with seven frequently mentioned places.

scores; and 2) finding the best path between source to destination in the graph. The complexity for the creation of the graph is negligible: it is linear with the number of nodes and has to be computed just once for every city (even offline). The second step mainly consists of the Eppstein's algorithm, which is efficient as its complexity for computing a single path from source to destination is $O(e + n \cdot log(n) + m \cdot log(m))$, where n is the number of nodes, e is the number of edges, and m is the number of paths that are explored (e.g., in Boston our m was just 700). More practically, a 24-core Intel server running Red Hat takes 51 millisecond to compute the best path.

Personalization. Perceptions of urban qualities such as happiness might well differ from one individual to another. In our user study, some respondents were happy to visit streets full of shops, while others cringed at the idea of facing a human mob of shoppers. Walking can be monitored and mapped, but as psycho-geographers observed, "[walks on a map] can, in itself, never capture the personal histories that underlie them... A map can never accurately capture the lives of those individuals whose journeys it sets out to trace, for in the process individuality is inevitably flattened out and reduced to points on a chart" [6]. Personalization approaches might partly account for the subjectivity of urban experiences by, for example, tailoring recommended paths to a user's past visits [19, 27].

Limited Spatial Representation. To make our problem computationally tractable, we had to model the city's spatial configuration in simple ways. We opted for dividing the city grid into several cells, and those cells then represented nodes of our location graph. The finest unit of analysis consequently became the cell or, more specifically, its centroid. This means that we can capture neither whatever happens inside a cell (e.g., presence of a crime-infested council estate) nor the nature of the link that connects the centroids of two neighboring cells (e.g., crossing a large street full of cars). More effective spatial representations are thus in order. One could, for example, resort to Space Syntax [13], a set of techniques for describing the spatial patterns produced

by buildings and towns. These techniques would account for aspects we have so far left out from our analysis, including walkability, which is considered to be one of the most salient factors that make urban life thrive [30].

Salient City Pictures. Our predictive models work on input of metadata associated with Flickr pictures. As we have not done any particular filtering, not all pictures are salient representations of the places in which they have been geographically tagged. Thus it might be useful to use existing techniques (e.g., computer vision algorithms) to determine the extent to which a picture represents its associated urban location.

Limited Contextual Representation. Our study participants gave feedbacks that could be explored in future work. They, for example, had fascinating insights related to weather conditions and temporal aspects. One said: "The area around St Paul's can be very lovely. It depends rather on the time of day. At weekends when the City is quiet this will be nice. At busier times it could be manic". Future work might go into studying temporal dynamics at different levels: time of the day (day *vs.* night), day of the week (e.g., Saturday *vs.* Monday), time of the year (e.g., different seasons). It would be also interesting to see how those dynamics change depending on, for example, weather conditions.

Beyond route recommendations. To offer an engaging user experience, designers have to build applications that go beyond just showing paths on a map. They could, for example, show the main points of interest along the path [8, 10]. Our survey respondents mentioned that historical elements contribute to a pleasant urban experience. A mobile app called "NYPL Time Traveller" has recently integrated the historical photographic collection of the New York Public Library with Foursquare, displaying historical NYC pictures related to the places in which they check in [12]. Also, our respondents associated the concept of happiness not only with historical memories but also with their own personal stories. A respondent said: "I would have a lot to say on the way about buildings, history, events and people I met along this path". Therefore, one could also allow individuals to record their memories associated with a specific place and to show these memories back to them when physically revisiting that place, in a way similar to StoryPlace.me or to the artistic project behind "Map your Manhattan" [5].

7. CONCLUSION

Our goal has been to propose ways of recommending emotionally pleasing routes in the city. We have ascertained whether we met that goal in two steps: validation and evaluation. First, we have validated that our proposed route variations actually recommend what they are meant to (e.g., paths with highest perceived happiness), and they do so adding just a few extra walking minutes compared to the shortest routes.

A user study involving 30 participants in London has shown that people perceive those recommendations the way we expect them to. Their quantitative assessments and qualitative insights all confirmed the results learned in the validation step.

Finally, we have shown that we do not necessarily need to collect crowd-sourced ratings for every new city. Reasonable proxies can be computed from Flickr metadata. We did so for the city of Boston and ascertained its effectiveness with as many as 54 participants.

Viewing a path (no matter how familiar it is) does not capture the full affective experience of 'being there'. In the future, we will build upon the analysis presented here by designing a mobile application and testing it in the wild across different cities in Europe and USA.

8. ACKNOWLEDGMENTS

We thank Adam Barwell for his important role in building the crowdsourcing site; Jon Crowcroft of Cambridge and the whole NetOS for continuous support; Abdo El Ali for his feedbacks on earlier versions of the user evaluation; friends at MIT, Northeastern, and Harvard who helped with the survey; and Henriette Cramer, Giovanni Quattrone, and Olivier Van Laere for their useful feedbacks. This work is supported by the SocialSensor FP7 project, partially funded by the EC under contract number 287975.

9. REFERENCES

[1] R. Baraglia, C. I. Muntean, F. M. Nardini, and F. Silvestri. LearNext: learning to predict tourists movements. In *CIKM*, 2013.

[2] K.-P. Chang, L.-Y. Wei, M.-Y. Yeh, and W.-C. Peng. Discovering personalized routes from trajectories. In *Proc. of the 3rd ACM SIGSPATIAL Int. Workshop on Location-Based Social Networks (LBSN)*, 2011.

[3] A.-J. Cheng, Y.-Y. Chen, Y.-T. Huang, W. H. Hsu, and H.-Y. M. Liao. Personalized travel recommendation by mining people attributes from community-contributed photos. In *Proc. of the 19th ACM Int. Conference on Multimedia (MM)*, 2011.

[4] P. C.L. and TfL. Legible London wayfinding study. In *TfL*, 2006.

[5] B. Cooper and A. Gopnik. *Mapping Manhattan: A Love (and Sometimes Hate) Story in Maps by 75 New Yorkers.* Harry N. Abrams, 2013.

[6] M. Coverley. *Psychogeography.* Pocket Essentials, 2006.

[7] A. De Botton. *The Architecture of Happiness.* Vintage Series. Knopf Doubleday Publishing Group, 2008.

[8] M. De Choudhury, M. Feldman, S. Amer-Yahia, N. Golbandi, R. Lempel, and C. Yu. Automatic construction of travel itineraries using social breadcrumbs. In *Proceedings of the 21st ACM Conference on HyperText (HT)*, 2010.

[9] G. Debord. Introduction to a Critique of Urban Geography. 1955.

[10] A. El Ali, S. N. van Sas, and F. Nack. Photographer paths: sequence alignment of geotagged photos for exploration-based route planning. In *Proc. of the ACM Conference on Computer Supported Cooperative Work (CSCW)*, 2013.

[11] D. Eppstein. Finding the k Shortest Paths. *SIAM Journal on Computing*, 28(2), 1999.

[12] Foursquare. A different kind of time travel - go back to the New York of 100+ years ago. *Official Blog*, June 2013.

[13] B. Hillier and J. Hanson. *The Social Logic of Space.* Cambridge University Press, 1989.

[14] Ignite. 2012 Social Network Analysis Report. In *Social Media*, 2012.

[15] T. Kurashima, T. Iwata, G. Irie, and K. Fujimura. Travel route recommendation using geotags in photo sharing sites. In *Proc. of the 19th ACM Conference on Information and Knowledge Management (CIKM)*, 2010.

[16] B. Ludwig, B. Zenker, and J. Schrader. Recommendation of personalized routes with public transport connections.

[17] K. Lynch. *The Image of the City.* Urban Studies. MIT Press, 1960.

[18] X. Meng, X. Lin, and X. Wang. Intention oriented itinerary recommendation by bridging physical trajectories and online social networks. In *Proc. of the ACM SIGKDD Int. Workshop on Urban Computing (UrbComp)*, 2012.

[19] A. Noulas, S. Scellato, N. Lathia, and C. Mascolo. A Random Walk around the City: New Venue Recommendation in Location-Based Social Networks. In *Proc. of the IEEE Conference on Social Computing (SocialCom)*, 2012.

[20] S. O'Sullivan and J. Morrall. *Walking Distances to and from Light Rail Transit Stations.* Transportation Research Board, 1996.

[21] J. Pennebaker. *The Secret Life of Pronouns: What Our Words Say About Us.* Bloomsbury, 2013.

[22] F. S. Peregrino, D. Tomas, P. Clough, and F. Llopis. Mapping routes of sentiments. In *Spanish Conference on Information Retrieval*, 2012.

[23] G. L. Peterson. A Model of Preference: Quantitative Analysis of the Perception of the Visual Appearance of Residential Neighborhoods. *Journal of Regional Science*, 7(1):19–31, 1967.

[24] M. Quaggiotto, S. Scacchetti, and D. Bloise. BikeDistrict Milano. 2012.

[25] D. Quercia, N. Ohare, and H. Cramer. Aesthetic Capital: What Makes London Look Beautiful, Quiet, and Happy? In *Proc. of ACM Int. Conference on Computer-Supported Cooperative Work (CSCW)*, 2014.

[26] D. Quercia, J. P. Pesce, V. Almeida, and J. Crowcroft. Psychological maps 2.0: a web engagement enterprise starting in London. In *Proc. of the 22nd Int. Conference on World Wide Web (WWW)*, 2013.

[27] D. Saez-Trumper, D. Quercia, and J. Crowcroft. Ads and the city: considering geographic distance goes a long way. In *ACM Conference in Recommender Systems (RecSys)*, 2012.

[28] P. Salesses, K. Schechtner, and C. Hidalgo. The Collaborative Image of The City: Mapping the Inequality of Urban Perception. *PLoS ONE*, July 2013.

[29] J. Schöning, B. Hecht, and N. Starosielski. Evaluating automatically generated location-based stories for tourists. In *Proc. of the Conference on Human Factors in Computing Systems - Extended Abstracts (CHI)*, 2008.

[30] J. Speck. *Walkable City: How Downtown Can Save America, One Step at a Time.* Farrar, Straus and Giroux, 2012.

[31] S. Van Canneyt, S. Schockaert, O. Van Laere, and B. Dhoedt. Time-dependent recommendation of tourist attractions using Flickr. In *Proc. of the Belgian/Netherlands Artificial Intelligence Conference (BNAIC)*, 2011.

[32] L.-Y. Wei, W.-C. Peng, and W.-C. Lee. Exploring pattern-aware travel routes for trajectory search. *ACM Transactions on Intelligent System Technologies*, 4(3):1–25, July 2013.

[33] C.-H. Yeh, Y.-C. Ho, B. A. Barsky, and M. Ouhyoung. Personalized photograph ranking and selection system. In *Proc. of the Int. Conference on Multimedia (MM)*, 2010.

[34] H. Yoon, Y. Zheng, X. Xie, and W. Woo. Smart itinerary recommendation based on user-generated GPS trajectories. In *Proc. of the 7th Conference on Ubiquitous Intelligence and Computing (UIC)*, 2010.

[35] H. Yoon, Y. Zheng, X. Xie, and W. Woo. Social itinerary recommendation from user-generated digital trails. *Personal and Ubiquitous Computing*, 16(5), 2012.

[36] Y. Zheng, L. Zhang, X. Xie, and W.-Y. Ma. Mining interesting locations and travel sequences from GPS trajectories. In *Proc. of the 18th ACM Conference on World Wide Web (WWW)*, 2009.

Communications in Computer and Information Science, 53, 2009.

Comparing the Pulses of Categorical Hot Events in Twitter and Weibo

Xin Shuai
Dept. of Informatics
Indiana University
Bloomington
xshuai@indiana.edu

Xiaozhong Liu
Dept. of Information and
Library Science
Indiana University
Bloomington
liu237@indiana.edu

Tian Xia
Dept. of Information Resource
Management
Renmin University of China
xiatian1119@gmail.com

Yuqing Wu
Dept. of Computer Science
Indiana University
Bloomington
yuqwu@indiana.edu

Chun Guo
Dept. of Information and
Library Science
Indiana University
Bloomington
chunguo@indiana.edu

ABSTRACT

The fragility and interconnectivity of the planet argue compellingly for a greater understanding of how different communities make sense of their world. One of such critical demands relies on comparing the Chinese and the rest of the world (e.g., Americans), where communities' ideological and cultural backgrounds can be significantly different. While traditional studies aim to learn the similarities and differences between these communities via high-cost user studies, in this paper we propose a much more efficient method to compare different communities by utilizing social media. Specifically, Weibo and Twitter, the two largest microblogging systems, are employed to represent the target communities, i.e. China and the Western world (mainly United States), respectively. Meanwhile, through the analysis of the Wikipedia page-click log, we identify a set of categorical 'hot events' for one month in 2012 and search those hot events in Weibo and Twitter corpora along with timestamps via information retrieval methods. We further quantitatively and qualitatively compare users' responses to those events in Twitter and Weibo in terms of three aspects: popularity, temporal dynamic, and information diffusion. The comparative results show that although the popularity ranking of those events are very similar, the patterns of temporal dynamics and information diffusion can be quite different.

Categories and Subject Descriptors

J.4 [**Social and Behavioral Sciences**]: Sociology; H.3.3 [**Information Storage and Retrieval**]: Information Search and Retrieval

General Terms

Measurement

HT'14, September 1–4, 2014, Santiago, Chile.
Copyright 2014 ACM 978-1-4503-2954-5/14/09 ...$15.00.
http://dx.doi.org/10.1145/2631775.2631810.

Keywords

Social Media; Information Retrieval; Community Comparison; Twitter; Weibo; Wikipedia; Click Log Mining; Information Diffusion

1. INTRODUCTION

The way people perceive and exploit their cultural environments through the social media has been observed and well documented [6, 13, 21], including sentiment analysis [1, 15], the potential role of the Internet in China [3], comparisons of decision-making in face-to-face versus computer-mediated communication, network influences on social isolation [22], predictions about the role of media on society [21], as well as instrumental uses of Twitter as a communication tool [7]. However, to the best of our knowledge, few scholarly studies ever conducted comprehensive comparisons of users' behavior in social media in China and the Western world (mainly United States), especially during the periods of hot events. For social scientists, such comparisons are becoming increasingly crucial and intriguing, because the responses of users from the two types of social media are quite representative of Chinese and Americans, respectively. With a new, compelling global landscape being cultivated world-wide [24] due to the growth of China in economic, political, and cultural aspects, mining and comparing large scale datasets from China and United States can help us better understand the ideological and cultural differences between the two of the world's powers.

Social media, especially microblogging systems, can efficiently and effectively reflect real world events [1], which provide good dynamic recourses for researchers to conduct various studies of the large scale of users or communities at a low cost, including information diffusion [17], information ranking [11, 12], sentiment analysis [15], and social networks analysis [8]. Motivated by these findings, in order to compare two of the largest microblogging user groups in the world, we collect massive Twitter and Weibo corpora for comparative studies with a number of innovative indicators. Although Twitter and Weibo are both microblogging platforms with very similar functionalities, they are consumed by totally different users: One, the default languages of Twitter and Weibo are English and Chinese, respectively; Two, Twitter access is strictly forbidden in mainland China due to political reasons [23], while, theoretically, the whole world can access to the Weibo platform. However, as Weibo's default language is Chinese, the primary users are people of Chinese heritage, even though they may physically reside anywhere in the world.

Although accessing Twitter is an impossible mission in China, an increasing number of Chinese users began to seek the real-time information from the rest of the word via other channels, like news, search engines, and other websites. With a very different cultural and ideological background, Chinese users' reaction and interest toward the same event or topic could be different (or similar) from the rest of the world (e.g., US). Fortunately, Twitter and Weibo provide us a good opportunity to investigate and compare the two groups of users by analyzing their textual messages published on the two microblogging platforms.

The main goal of this paper is to compare the similarities and differences in response to hot events between Twitter and Weibo users from textual and social network perspectives. The contributions of this paper are twofold:

- One, we identify a set of "Hot Events" via peak detection and trend analysis from Wikipedia click log. In addition, based on Wikipedia category metadata, we group all the hot events into different categories, such as Science, Politics, and Sports, etc. We, then, trace the temporal pulses of categorical hot events in both Twitter and Weibo corpora utilizing information retrieval methods. Especially, Wikipedia offers both Chinese and English content and metadata for each candidate event, which enables cross-language search and mining for both Twitter and Weibo corpora.

- Two, from textual and social network perspectives, we propose several indicators to compare Weibo and Twitter response towards the same set of categorical hot events. We apply statistical analysis and case study methods to both quantitatively and qualitatively compare the two communities.

Experiment result shows that, while Twitter and Weibo communities share similar interests from the event popularity perspective, temporal analysis and information diffusion modeling reveal that Twitter and Weibo users are different in consuming those hot events. Especially, we find Weibo and Twitter users are more similar when they are contagious to the hot events in Science and Technology categories. On the contrary, some other categories, i.e., Arts and Politics, distinguish Twitter from Weibo users.

In the remainder of this paper, Section 2 reviews relevant literature and methodology for social media mining and comparison, Section 3 proposes our novel method for comparing Twitter and Weibo communities, Section 4 describes the experiment setting and evaluation results, and Section 5 discusses the findings and limitations of the study and identifies subsequent research steps.

2. LITERATURE REVIEW

Information retrieval and text mining algorithms are used by scholars to analyze and compare large textual corpora, especially to investigate users' interest [11] via sentiment analysis [15]. In this context, Twitter and Weibo, the most popular microblogging systems, have been successfully used to represent and investigate Western (mainly US) and Chinese communities, respectively. For instance, Baucom et al. [1] used Twitter to mirror real world events and found that Twitter sentiment along with geo-location information can be used to estimate very dynamic real world events, e.g., score changes in athletic events. Similar studies [2,15,18] also verify the close relatedness between real-world events and chronological Twitter data. It is clear that massive Twitter data can be used to

characterize and predict the real-world events, which has been successfully applied to a number of data mining tasks, i.e., information retrieval [19], information diffusion [17], and event prediction [16].

In the past few years, the number of Chinese Internet users is growing very fast. So far, more than 20% of Internet users come from China, thus investigating the behavior of Chinese Internet users becomes increasingly important [3, 24]. While using Twitter to characterize real world events is well documented, Weibo is becoming an important means to understand the Chinese community. For instance, Zhao et al., [25] employed Weibo data to investigate event discussion by using term-message-user network. They used random-walk algorithms to study the temporal event information diffusion, and the event is pre-defined by domain expert. Similarly, Guan et al., [5] studied 21 (expert pre-defined) hot events of Weibo by utilizing 32 prestigious users (influential users).

Unfortunately, due to the language and political barriers, most users from each community can only access one system exclusively. While most previous studies treat Twitter and Weibo as the same kind of social media except for language, some other researchers [4, 10] found that Chinese Weibo may have some unique features. Not until recently, some researchers became aware of the importance of comparing the Weibo and Twitter corpora. For instance, Gao et al., [4] compared Twitter and Weibo corpora from sentiment, entity, system access perspectives. A list of comparison indicators were listed in the Table 1.

Table 1: Twitter and Weibo comparison in previous studies

Comparison Indicator	Previous Studies	Findings
HashTag distribution	[4, 10]	Weibo users are interested in entertainment and sports topics, and Weibo users like more joke related content comparing with Twitter users.
URL distribution	[4]	Weibo users post less URLs compared with Twitter users.
Forward distribution	[10]	Weibo users forward message slower than Twitter.
Follow distribution	[10]	Twitter users number of actions will have a more significant effectiveness on the number of "Followers" than that of Weibo.
Gender distribution (for 32 users)	[5]	Male users are more likely to be involved.
Picture distribution (for 32 users)	[5]	Messages containing pictures are more likely to be posted.
Sentiment distribution	[4]	Weibo users post more positive messages comparing with Twitter users.
System access distribution	[4]	On Twitter, more than 95% of the users use more than one client application while on Sina Weibo around 65% of the users switch between different clients.
Entity distribution	[4]	Weibo users post more entity information than Twitter users.

All of these comparative studies are inherently similar; they all focus on comparing some statistical properties of microblogging features, like HashTag, forwarding linkage, following linkage, etc. While those are all very interesting findings, they provide very limited knowledge about the differences and similarities between China and United States in the real world. To be specific, no prior study ever investigated topical or categorical Twitter and Weibo comparison during hot events, which is important; the nature of Weibo (or Twitter) users' responses to e.g. *Political* news can be very different from that of *Science*.

Different from these studies, this paper paves a new way to investigate the similarity and difference between Weibo and Twitter at the topical level, exploring the categorical hot events extracted from the Wikipedia page click log. We propose multiple indicators to compare Twitter and Weibo communities. Meanwhile, information diffusion techniques [14, 17] are used in this study for social network-based comparison.

3. RESEARCH METHODS

The overall framework of our study is shown in Figure 1 and can be decomposed into four steps: First, the pre-processing of textual messages in Twitter and Weibo in different languages; Second, the identification of categorical hot events from the Wikipedia dump and click logs; Third, the tracing of hot event pulses in Twitter and Weibo corpora via information retrieval; Fourth, the comparison of Twitter and Weibo hot event pulses in terms of event category and a number of other indicators.

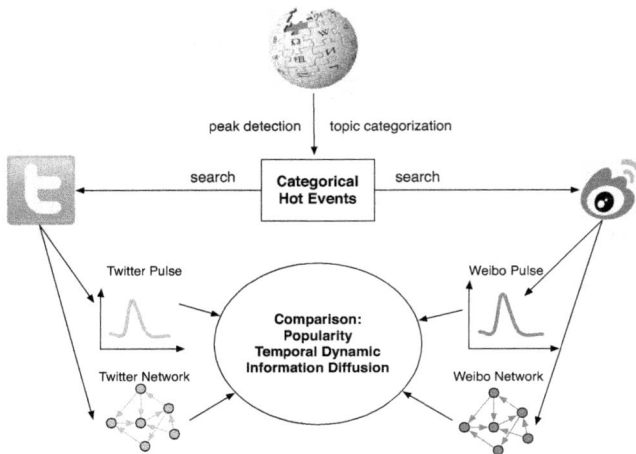

Figure 1: Twitter and Weibo comparison via Wikipedia categorical hot events.

3.1 Twitter and Weibo pre-processing

To pre-process the textual messages from Twitter and Weibo is to index all those messages to support full-text search. Specifically, we index the following fields for each message: id, creator, timestamp, content, and hashtags. The most important step in indexing is word tokenization. Since the English and Chinese languages are totally different, we apply different tokenization techniques to Twitter and Weibo, respectively.

For Twitter, we split the sentence into word tokens at white spaces and punctuation symbols, remove all stop words according to [9], and convert all tokens into lowercase. In addition, we apply stemming techniques to normalize the form of tokens.

For Weibo, since the Chinese language contains both simplified and traditional versions and does not delimit words by white spaces, tokenization is more challenging than in Twitter. We first normalize the words by converting all traditional characters into simplified characters, then apply the CRF model [20] to segment Chinese sentences into tokens.

3.2 Hot Event Identification via Wikipedia Click Log

In order to compare the responses of Twitter and Weibo communities to hot events, we first identify a set of candidate hot events. In this study, we discover hot events from Wikipedia. As the largest online encyclopedia, Wikipedia has become the most common online resources to gain knowledge and information about the world for people around the globe. When some hot events occur, people

tend to view the Wikipedia pages relevant to those events, thus generating a traffic spike in the click logs of those pages. Therefore, we can utilize Wikipedia as a proxy to sense what happens in the real world, and estimate the start and end time of hot events based on when traffic spikes occur. In particular, Wikipedia provides multilanguage versions (e.g., English and Chinese) of the same page to facilitate the access of users from different countries. In addition, each Wikipedia page contains category metadata defined by page editors, so we're able to categorize events by analyzing the Wikipedia page category.

3.2.1 Peak Detection in Wikipedia Click Log

Wikipedia page view statistics provide the number of times a particular page has been viewed (i.e. clicked). Wikipedia provides hourly page view statistics about how many times each Wikipedia page has been clicked for each hour. We can easily aggregate the hourly click statistics to obtain daily click statistics for each page.

Some Wikipedia pages related to some real world events are likely to be viewed much more frequently during the time when those events receive media coverage than the time when they are little discussed by the public. This sometimes explains spikes in the click log statistics during periods of time when such events are taking place and receiving public attention. For example, those pages regarding to athletes who attend Olympics will be clicked more frequently during the Olympics than other times; Articles on topics pertaining to a particular holiday may get more hits around the time of year when the holiday takes place; During an election year, anything somehow related to that election may be viewed more than at other times.

Given a Wikipedia page p and a date range $[d_0, d_n]$, we use $T(p, d)$ to denote the number of clicks Wikipedia page p received on date d. To detect a peak in $\{T(p, d) | d \in [d_0, d_n]\}$, We define a threshold as:

$$h_p(d_0, d_n) = \underset{d \in [d_0, d_n]}{mean} T(p, d) + \alpha * \underset{d \in [d_0, d_n]}{std} T(p, d) \quad (1)$$

where $\underset{d \in [d_0, d_n]}{mean} T(p, d)$ and $\underset{d \in [d_0, d_n]}{std} T(p, d)$ is the mean and standard deviation of $T(p, d)$ over $[d_0, d_n]$. The threshold α determines the degree of "peakiness" sufficient to detect an event. We will manually set it based on some some preliminary observations and the tuning of α is left for future work

If we can find $d_p \in [d_0, d_n]$ such that $T(p, d_p) > h_p(d_0, d_n)$, we claim that there exists a spike $T(p, d_p)$ in the click logs of page p occurring on d_p, and some event relevant to page p was occurring during d_0 and d_n. If multiple values of d_p satisfy Equation 1, we choose the d_p such that $T(p, d_p) > T(p, d)$ for any $d \in [d_0, d_n]$ to be the peak.

Once p_d of the hot event is detected, we further determine the start and end date of the event. Specifically, we define the start date d_s and end date d_e as the latest date that satisfies $T(p, d_s) \leq \underset{d \in [d_0, d_n]}{mean} T(p, d)$, and the earliest date that satisfies $T(p, d_e) \leq \underset{d \in [d_0, d_n]}{mean} T(p, d)$, respectively. To fully capture the whole period of the event, we empirically apply three days offset before d_s, and after d_e. Finally, we obtain an event $E_p(d_s, d_p, d_e)$ related to Wikipedia page p, starting from d_s and ending at d_e with a peak on d_p. Note that the optimal selection of the number of offset days is left for future work.

3.2.2 Event Categorization

After identifying all $E_p(d_p, d_s, d_e)$, we categorize them into different topics. Since each event corresponds to a Wikipedia page, we can easily categorize those events by categorizing those pages. The category system of Wikipedia is organized as an overlapping 'tree', formed by linking related categories in a hierarchy. Any category may branch into subcategories, and it is possible for a category to be a subcategory of more than one 'parent' category (A is said to be a parent category of B when B is a subcategory of A).

At the bottom of each Wikipedia page, a set of category names are provided. The page editor either uses existing category names, or creates a new category name and links that category to one of the existing category names. Generally, those user-defined categories are either too vague or too specific to serve as feasible options for the topical classifications as we need. Fortunately, Wikipedia has already identified 25 categories as the main topic classifications for all Wikipedia pages.[1] The overall category structure in Wikipedia is shown in Figure 2.

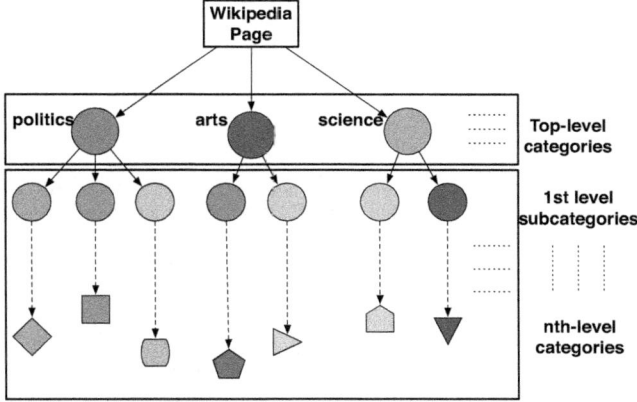

Figure 2: Wikipedia category hierarchy.

To categorize all Wikipedia page into one of the 25 categories, we create a vector with 25 dimensions for each page, with every dimension corresponding to one category. Then we take two steps to fill the values of the vector per dimension for each page. First, for each user-defined category we find at the bottom of the page, we trace it back in the tree-like category structure (see Figure 2) to find its corresponding top-level category; Second, we calculate TF-IDF score for each dimension of the vector. Finally, we pick the corresponding category with the highest TF-IDF score, as the most representative category for that page.

Table 2 outlines nine most important and representative categories (with event count) from the 25 categories. We conduct comparison analysis and illustrate experimental results based on these nine selected categories.

Table 2: Event category descriptions

Category	Exemplar Wikipedia pages	Counts
Agriculture(AGR)	Spinach, Cranberry, Royal jelly	63
Arts(ART)	Russell Crowe, Breaking Dawn, Yo-Yo Ma	114
Business(BUS)	Citigroup, McAfee, Loan	45
Culture(CUL)	Nobel Prize, Divine Comedy, Kung fu	93
Geography(GEO)	Times Square, Hawaii, Taipei	60
Politics(POL)	Iran, Barack Obama, Communist Party	181
Science(SCI)	Marie Curie, Atkins diet, Tsunami	95
Sports(SPO)	Table tennis, Miami Heat, FIFA World Cup	40
Technology(TEC)	Laser, 5G, Xbox	42

---

[1]http://en.wikipedia.org/wiki/Category:Main_topic_classifications

3.3 Tracing Hot Event via Information Retrieval

After locating categorical hot events from the Wikipedia corpus, we trace the hot event pulses from both the Twitter and Weibo corpora. Note that each Wikipedia page (we selected) has both Chinese and English titles provided by Wikipedia editors. For this study, we apply information retrieval techniques to search the Wikipedia title (English or Chinese) in the Twitter and Weibo indexes we built. In order to find accurate and comprehensive relevant messages from both indexes, we use title content exact match (some very short and ambiguous titles are removed). Unlike other information retrieval studies, ranking in this study is not important, since we care more about the daily total number of relevant messages, which indicates the hot event pulse (event mention probability) in Twitter or Weibo. However, there is one limitation to this approach: Wikipedia and Twitter or Weibo are written in different styles. For instance, both Weibo and Twitter limit the total length of messages, and users are more likely to use abbreviations or spoken language to represent the target event or topic. Therefore, only using Wikipedia titles to query relevant messages from Twitter and Weibo will result in low recall value.

To cope with this problem, for each Wikipedia page we expand the search query by incorporating all relevant redirect pages (in Chinese and English). For instance, for the Wikipedia page "Patient Protection and Affordable Care Act" we also use the titles of its redirected Wikipedia pages as the search queries, i.e., "Obamacare". Most of the time, users will write "obamacare" in the Twitter message, instead of "Patient Protection and Affordable Care Act". So, for each hot event, we send the following boolean query:

$$("Page\ Title"\ OR\ "Redirect\ Page\ Titles")$$
$$AND$$
$$(Date\ ranging\ from\ Event\ Start\ Date\ to\ Event\ End\ Date)$$
$$(2)$$

The query indicates that all the relevant messages, in either Twitter or Weibo, should match at least one Wikipedia page title in the collection of event Wikipedia pages or any related redirected Wikipedia pages. Meanwhile, all the relevant messages should fall between event start and end dates.

After querying the Wikipedia page title plus redirected titles relevant to event $E_p(d_s, d_p, d_e)$, we come up with three types of temporal pulses: Wikipedia pulse, Twitter pulse and Weibo pulse. Specifically, given the same event, Wikipedia pulse represents the general public's attitude, Weibo pulse represents the Chinese attitude, while Twitter represents the American attitude (although people from most countries can get access to Twitter, the dominant users are still Americans). We use three time-series vectors with the same length to denote three types of temporal pulses given event $E_p(d_s, d_p, d_e)$: $T_{E_p}^{Wiki}$, $T_{E_p}^{Twitter}$ and $T_{E_p}^{Weibo}$. To be specific, $T_{E_p}^{Wiki}(d)$, $T_{E_p}^{Twitter}(d)$ and $T_{E_p}^{Weibo}(d)$ denote the number of Wikipedia clicks, Twitter messages, and Weibo messages, respectively, related to E_p on date d. Figure 3 is a visual example of the three time-series vectors for *Obama Barack*.

3.4 Twitter and Weibo Comparison

The goal of this paper is to compare the differences in responses to a set of commonly interesting hot events shared between two distinct communities: Twitter and Weibo users. We propose difference indicators to compare both responses in three aspects: the degree of popularity, the temporal dynamic, and the information diffusion pattern. In the following statements, we use X to represent Twitter or Weibo community.

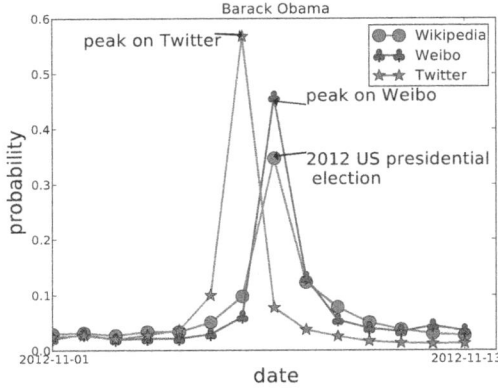

Figure 3: The Wikipedia, Twitter and Weibo response towards _Barack Obama_. All three vectors are normalized.

3.4.1 Popularity

The popularity of an event represents the degree of collective attention towards the event, which can be measured by the sum of daily probabilities that this event is mentioned on Twitter or Weibo during the time period of the event. To be specific, the popularity of event E_p is computed as:

$$P^X(E_p) = \sum_{d=d_s}^{d_e} \frac{T_{E_p}^X(d)}{N^X(d)} \tag{3}$$

where $T_{E_p}^X(d)$ is the number of messages in microblogging platform X related to E_p on d, and $N^X(d)$ is the total number of messages posted on d. We can further obtain the categorical popularity $P^X(C)$ for category C by averaging the values of $P(E_p)$ for all $E_p \in C$.

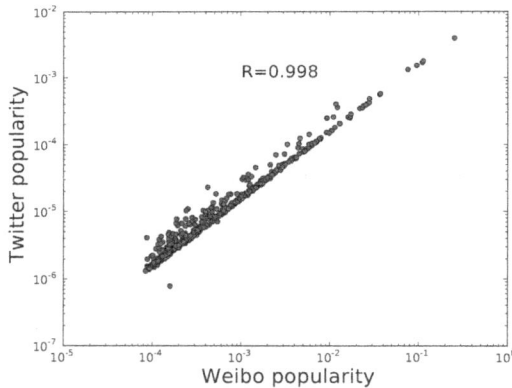

Figure 4: The correlation between Weibo popularity and Twitter popularity. The two popularity scores are highly correlated

3.4.2 Temporal Dynamic

We use d_p to denote the peak date of event E_p detected from Wikipedia click data. We are interested in when the discussion of E_p reaches the maximum degree on Twitter and Weibo and how the spiky discussion date is temporally related to d_p. Therefore, we

compute the peak temporal delay as:

$$Delta^X(E_p) = d_p^X - d_p \tag{4}$$

where d_p^X denotes the dates when the volume of messages reaches the maximum on Weibo or Twitter. Similarly we can obtain the categorical peak delay $Delta^X(C)$ for category C by averaging the values of $Delta^X(E_p)$ for all $E_p \in C$.

To better understand the temporal dynamic between $T_{E_p}^{Twitter}$ and $T_{E_p}^{Weibo}$, we utilize KL- divergence, which is a non-symmetric measure of the difference between two probability distributions. After normalizing $T_{E_p}^{Twitter}$, $T_{E_p}^{Weibo}$ and $T_{E_p}^{Wiki}$, we calculate the KL-divergence as:

$$D_{kl}^X(T_{E_p}^X || T_{E_p}^{Wiki}) = \sum_{d=d_s}^{d_e} ln \frac{T_{E_p}^X(d)}{T_{E_p}^{Wiki}(d)} * T_{E_p}^X(d) \tag{5}$$

Again, we obtain the categorical KL-divergence $D_{kl}^X(C)$ for category C by averaging the value of $D_{kl}^X(T_{E_p}^X || T_{E_p}^{Wiki})$ for all $E_p \in C$.

3.4.3 Information Diffusion Pattern

Microblogging users access information via two types of ways: propagation through social network (internal information diffusion) or exposure to other channels (external information infection) [14]. In this study, we compare the dynamics of information diffusion in the social network environments of Weibo and Twitter. Specifically, we are trying to answer the following research question: Given an event E_p, what is the probability that a user is infected (i.e. discuss E_p) before the event peak d_p, denoted as $Pr^X(E_p, K)$, given that a number of neighbors (i.e. K neighbors) of the user in the social network, have already mentioned this event on the start date d_s of this event?

To construct social networks, we collect a large number of Weibo and Twitter messages and extract three types of relationships: forwarding, replying, and mentioning. For example, if u_i forwards to, replies to, or mentions u_j more than t times in historical data, we create a directed edge $u_i \rightarrow u_j$ on the social network.

Consequently, we obtain a directed social network $G(V, E)$ where V is the set of users and E the set of edges ($u_i \rightarrow u_j$) indicating that u_i previously forwarded, replied to, or mentioned u_j. Given an event E_p and value K, we define a *K-diffusion network*, which is a subgraph $G'_{E_p}(V', E')$, where $V' \subset V$ and $E' \subset E$. Specifically, $V' = S \cup N$ where S is the set of nodes in V representing the users who initiate the discussion of E_p before E_p starts (also called "seed users set"), and N is the set of nodes in V who are directly linked to K nodes in S; and $E' = \{(u'_i, u'_j) | u'_i \in N, u'_j \in S, u'_i \rightarrow u'_j\}$. We compute the diffusion probability $Pr^X(E_p, K)$ on $G'(V', E')$ as the fraction of users in N who also discussed E_p, after E_p starts until reaching the peak. (A similar method is introduced in [17].)

Again, we obtain the categorical diffusion probability curve $Pr(C, K)$ for category C by averaging the values of $Pr^X(E_p, K)$ for all $E_p \in C$.

4. EXPERIMENT

4.1 Data preparation

We dump a total of 3.4 million Wikipedia article pages (in the English version) and collect their click log statistics from Oct 15, 2012 to Nov 15, 2012. Then we rank those pages based on their aggregated daily click numbers during that time period and select the top 1% (i.e. 3.4 thousand) pages. We drop the other 99% pages since we only care about extremely hot events in our papers. After

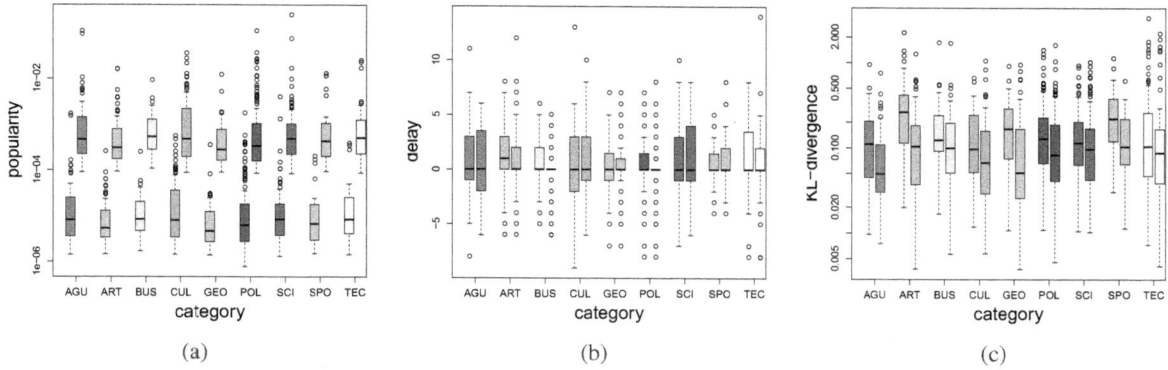

Figure 5: The distribution of (a) popularity, (b) delay, and (c) KL-divergence for nine categories in Weibo and Twitter. For each category, the left box represents the distribution for Weibo while the right box represents the distribution for Twitter. Overall, Weibo and Twitter are similar in terms of relative popularity ranking but different in terms of temporal dynamic patterns.

applying the peak detection algorithm in Equation 1 (we empirically set the value of α to four) to the 3.4 thousand pages, around six thousand pages with daily click peaks are detected. After filtering out the pages without Chinese version, over three thousand pages with both Chinese and English version are left.

Next, we query the title of those Wikipedia pages in both Twitter and Weibo using methods proposed in Section 3. Based on the retrieval results, those pages with more than 50 hits returned from both Twitter and Weibo search index are selected. Furthermore, we classify these hot events into one of the 25 top categories defined in Wikipedia and pick the nine most representative categories. The category names, sample Wikipedia pages, as well as the page counts in each of the nine categories, are listed in Table 2.

In addition, to conduct the information diffusion analysis, we build up $G^X(V, E)$ by collecting the user's forwarding, replying and mentioning relationships (the threshold of communication frequency t is set to one) from Sep 15, 2012 to Oct 15, 2012, on both Twitter and Weibo. Consequently, $G^{Twitter}(V, E)$ contains 28 million nodes and 140 million edges, while $G^{Weibo}(V, E)$ contains 1 million nodes and 3.8 million edges. We can see that the size of $G^{Weibo}(V, E)$ is much smaller than $G^{Twitter}(V, E)$. Moreover, to construct seed users set S, for each event E_p, we search users who mentioned E_p during the period of $[d_s - 3, d_s - 1]$. Here we pick up a three-day pre-start period to find seed users with regards to E_p and we will investigate how to better select the period in our future work.

4.2 Popularity

After calculating the popularity scores for all hot events discussed in Weibo and Twitter, we compute the Pearson's correlation between Weibo popularity and Twitter popularity. Figure 4 shows that these two popularity scores are highly correlated, indicating that the degree of popularity of the selected hot events are very similar in Twitter and Weibo. In other words, if some event is popular in Twitter, it is likely that the same event is also popular in Weibo, vise versa.

The distribution of popularity scores in each category is characterized in Figure 5(a). Overall, those events are more popular in Twitter than Weibo, for all categories. It is because that those detected hot events are more favorable to Twitter user than Weibo users, as Twitter users are more likely to use Wikipedia than Weibo users (in China, the most popular online encyclopedia is Baidu

Baike[2]). However, with regards to the relative categorical popularity, both Weibo and Twitter share almost the same ranking, again demonstrating that the event popularity scores are highly corrected between Weibo and Twitter. In particular, for both Weibo and Twitter, users' interests are more focused on *Agriculture*, *Business*, and *Culture* categories, while *Arts* and *Geography* categories are less popular.

4.3 Temporal Dynamic

The temporal dynamic of an event characterizes when and how users' response to the event reaches a peak. Particularly, *peak delay* indicates how fast the peak is reached, while *KL-divergence* depicts how diverse the pulses are between Weibo and Twitter. In either metrics, the pulse of the click log of Wikipedia servers as the baseline community response to certain event.

4.3.1 Peak delay

Figure 5(b) demonstrates the distribution of peak delay for all categories. Overall, both Weibo and Twitter users respond to hot events very fast (although Twitter response seems faster), with less than one day of delay on average. In particular, in *Politics* and *Business*, the delay is almost negligible on Twitter compared to Weibo.

Figure 3 is a case from *Politics* to illustrate the peak delay difference between Weibo and Twitter. Obviously, both Chinese and Americans show enormous attention towards the status of *Obama* during the 2012 US presidential election. However, the discussion about *Obama* reached its maximum on Twitter only one day after the election was held on Nov 6, 2012. By contrast, Weibo discussion and Wikipedia clicks about *Obama* reached the maximum one day behind the Twitter peak day. This demonstrates the potential use of Twitter as a predictive tool for political elections. Figure 6(a) shows another example from *Business*. The *Tommy Hilfiger* Corporation announced its deals for Black Friday 2012 around Oct 22, 2012, but the related discussion on Twitter reached its peak as early as almost one week before the announcement. Another interesting observation is the spot of the Weibo peak after the announcement day, even though it seems that Chinese users are irrelevant to Black Friday. The signal may be generated by some Chinese economists who are interested in American markets.

---

[2]http://baike.baidu.com/

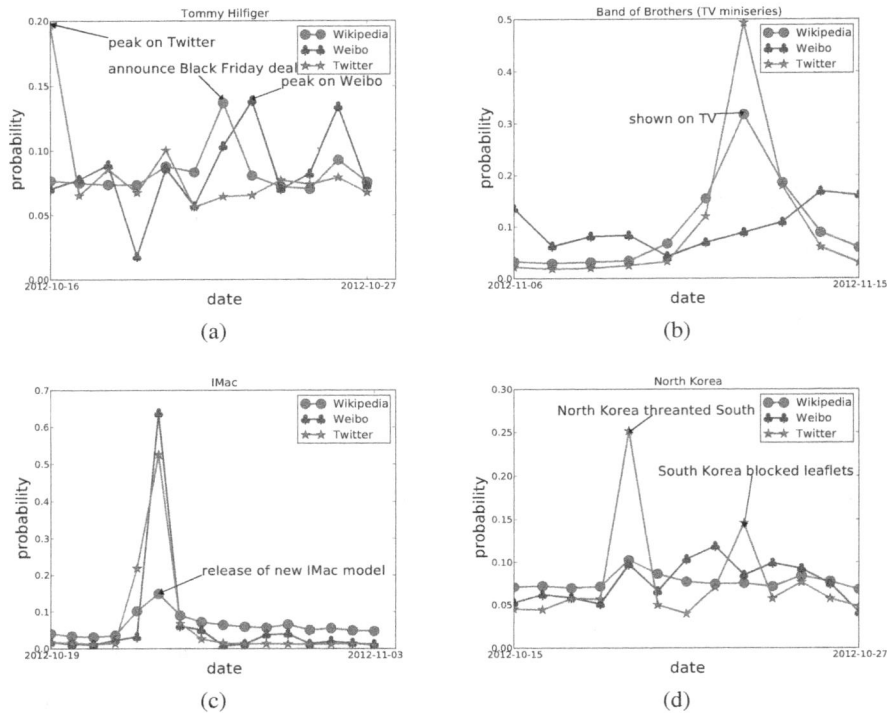

Figure 6: The temporal dynamic of users response curves shown for (a) Tommy Hilfiger (*Business*), (b) Band of Brothers (*Arts*) (c) IMac (*Technology*) and (d) North Korea (*Politics*). All are typical examples to illustrate the similarity ((c)) and differences ((a),(b),(d)) between Weibo and Twitter.

4.3.2 KL-divergence

Peak delay analysis only gives a one-point comparison (i.e. peak day) in the temporal response. To better investigate the difference in the whole process of users responses between Weibo and Twitter, we utilize KL-diverence to compare the overall temporal pulses between Weibo and Twitter during the time period of some event. Figure 5(c) shows KL-divergence distribution for all categories. Overall, the Weibo pulse follows Wikipedia pulse more closely than Twitter, implying that Twitter users' response is closer to Wikipedia users' response. Again, it is because that Twitter users are more likely to use Wikipedia than Weibo users.

Nevertheless, the degrees of difference in KL-divergence are not in the same level for all categories. In particular, Weibo and Twitter users' responses exhibit large gaps in *Arts*, *Culture* and *Geography*, while relatively similar trends in *Science* and *Technology* comparing with other categories. The reason of the categorical difference, we hypothesize, is that China and the Western world are quite different in cultural background and geographical location, but the people from the two communities have almost equal chance to get access to scientific and technological information through the Internet.

To better illustrate the temporal dynamic differences between Weibo and Twitter, we particularly select several instances from multiple categories. Figure 6(b) shows the users responses to *Band of Brothers* (belonging to *Arts*), a very popular TV show in the US. When it was shown on Spike TV on November 12, 2012, hot discussion was triggered on Twitter but not on Weibo, although this TV show is also well-known in China. Figure 6(c) demonstrates temporal pulses of *iMac* (belonging to *Technology*) when Apple released its new iMac model on October 23, 2012. We can see

that Weibo and Twitter users respond to the technology news in an almost synchronized manner, with only small differences in the degree of peakiness. Figure 6(d) shows the difference between Weibo and Twitter users responses to the news about North Korea threatening South over propaganda balloons on Oct 19, 2012 by Reuters. The relationship between North and South Korea is always a political focus for both China and the the Western world. We can see that Twitter users respond much more intensely to this event than Weibo users. Moreover, there's even another Twitter spike spotted when South Korea claimed to block leaflets from the North on Oct 23, 2012. The difference between China and the Western world with regards to their political backgrounds and attitudes towards North and South Korea, may affect the media coverage and opinions about the same event, thus leading to different public attentions.

Finally, we list another two closely related examples to further illustrate the users responses difference between Weibo and Twitter from different categories. Figure 7 shows the collective attention towards the 2012 Nobel prize winner *Mo Yan* in literature (belonging to *Arts*) and *Lloyd Shapley* in economics (belonging to *Science*). When the announcement of *Mo Yan* winning the 2012 Nobel prize in literature was released on Oct 11, 2012, it was breaking news in China, because he is the first recognized Chinese person who ever won Nobel prize. Correspondingly, there's an obvious spike in Weibo response around Oct 11, 2012 (Figure 7(a) does not clearly show this spike since we cut off our data on Oct 15, 2012) and gradually the spiky discussion faded out. Such a spiky trend is not clearly seen on Twitter, even though people outside of China also paid attention to *Mo Yan* and kept steady attention. On the contrary, the news that American economist *Lloyd Shapley* won the

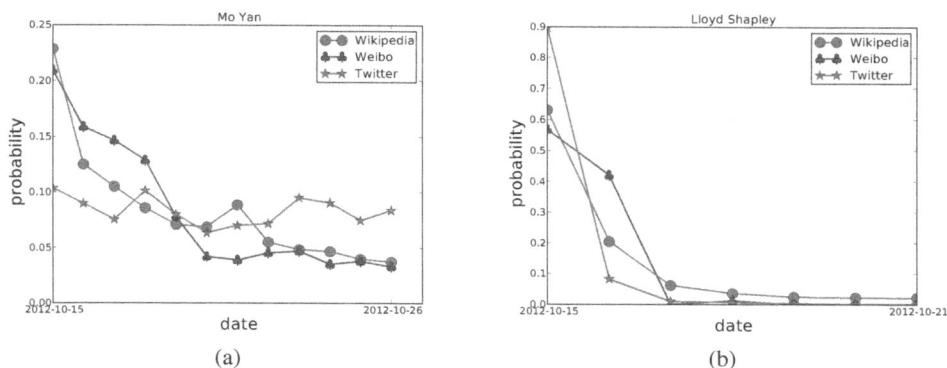

Figure 7: The difference between Weibo and Twitter response towards 2012 Nobel prize winners (a) *Mo Yan* in literature (belonging to *Arts*) and (b) *Lloyd Shapley* in economics (belonging to *Science*). Weibo users paid more attention to *Mo Yan*'s news in literature while Weibo and Twitter users respond similarly to *Lloyd Shapley*'s news.

Nobel prize in Economic Sciences on Oct 15, 2012, aroused both spiky discussion on Twitter and Weibo users around that day, and then both trends went down sharply.

4.4 Information Diffusion Pattern

We have already compared the users' responses in Weibo and Twitter in terms of popularity and temporal dynamic, now we focus on how the underlying social networks structure can affect the users response. To be specific, we investigate whether the probability that a user will respond to some hot event (i.e. diffusion probability) is affected by the number of the user's neighbors who have already responded to the same event,

Figure 8 depicts the diffusion probability curve against different K on Twitter network for four different categories of events: *Arts*, *Politics*, *Science*, and *Technology*. Overall, the diffusion probability increases consistently when K increases (except for the *Technology* category, which stops increasing after some K value), which indicates a complex contagion phenomenon. In other words, a user is more contagious to the infection of an hot event when more of his/her neighbors have already responded to it earlier. Therefore, the social network in Twitter does play a role to facilitate information diffusion around those selected hot events. Moreover, there exist differences in the diffusion patterns among various categories. Specifically, the trend increase in *Arts* and *Politics* is faster than *Science* and *Technology* (while K increases), which implies that Twitter users are more likely to be affected by their neighbors by the infection events in *Arts* and *Politics* categories than *Science* and *Technology* categories. Social media users tend to be subjective about evens in *Arts* and *Politics* and more easily to be emotionally influenced by their neighbors; On the contrast, users generally hold objective opinions about events in *Science* and *Technology*, therefor less likely to be affected by their neighbors.

By contrast, on Weibo, we find the diffusion probability is significantly lower than that on Twitter, for all the categories. We can interpret this finding in two ways. First, compared with Twitter, Weibo users are less likely to be contagious to the target infection hot event via internal social networks (they might choose the external channels, i.e., news and other websites, to access the hot event). Second, as mentioned before, Twitter users are more likely to use Wikipedia than Weibo users. Specifically, those hot events sampled from Wikipedia, are not necessarily the 'global tast'. For instance, we find a large number of American musicians, artists, politicians, and athletes in the hot events extracted from Wikipedia query log,

of whom Chinese Weibo users may have limited knowledge. This could be the reason that Weibo users are less likely to be contagious via the Weibo network.

Meanwhile, for the Weibo network, it is rare to find the diffusion phenomenon through social networks, when K is larger than three. We plot distribution of diffusion probability for all categories on Weibo in Figure 8(b) when $K = 1, 2, 3$. We can see that there's a huge increase in the diffusion probability when K increases from 1 to 2. Specifically, except for *Technology*, the diffusion probability increases more than twice over all other categories. Especially, in *Arts* and *Business*, the probability increases almost more than ten times more. There's a dip when K changes from 2 to 3, possibly due to the data sparsity problem. When $K > 3$, we hardly find events that diffuse through the Weibo network. This finding verifies our earlier assumption that Weibo users access (Wikipedia) hot events more randomly, instead of through Weibo social network.

5. CONCLUSION AND FUTURE WORK

In this paper, we compared how users of each respond to external hot events Twitter and Weibo, the two largest social media communities in the world. We employed Wikipedia as the research vehicle for hot event discovery, categorical aggregation, and English→Chinese translation, and proposed a set of static and dynamic indicators to compare Twitter and Weibo from three perspectives: popularity, temporal dynamic, and information diffusion. We want to share the following observations, drawn from our extensive evaluation on Twitter and Weibo data:

1. Based on the study of event popularity, we observed that Weibo and Twitter users share similar degree of interests towards a set of commonly interesting events between the two communities.

2. Based on the study of peak delay, we observed that both Weibo and Twitter users respond quickly to hot events, with less than one day delay from the peak of Wiki searches for most events. In addition, we observed that Twitter users respond faster than Weibo users on *Politics* and *Business* events. Our heuristics is that this is due to the ideological difference of the user base and/or information blockade in Mainland China.

3. Based on the study of KL-divergence, we observed that Twitter and Wikipedia temporal pulses are relatively similar com-

paring with Twitter, which we attribute to the significant overlapping between Twitter and Wikipedia communities. We also observed that Weibo and Twitter users demonstrate very similar responses to *Science* and *Technology* events while the two communities' responses to events in *Arts*, *Sports*, *Politics* and *Culture* display larger gaps.

4. Based on the study of information diffusion, we observed that while Twitter users are more likely to be infected by hot events via Twitter social network (internal exposure), Weibo users access hot events more likely via other channels (external exposure).

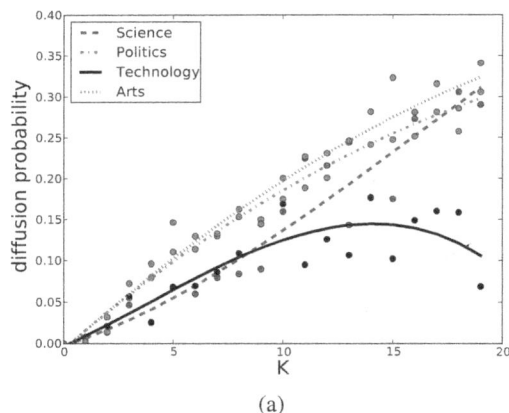

(a)

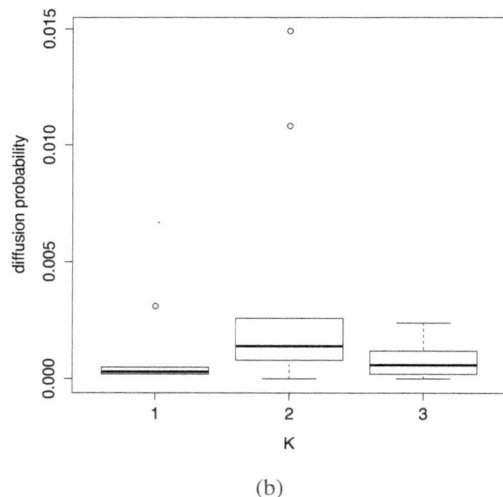

(b)

Figure 8: The diffusion pattern of hot events through social networks in (a) Twitter and (b) Weibo. Specifically, (a) shows the diffusion probability curves of four categories and (b) shows the diffusion probability distribution when K=1,2,3

While interesting observations were discovered in the study described in this paper, the results are far from conclusive. We are aware of two important limitations of this study: (1) the language variation in Chinese, such as the use of homophone and metaphor to discuss certain hot (sensitive) events negatively affected the search in Weibo corpus, yielding fewer results than desired; (2) the purposive sampling method used in this study, e.g. using categori-

cal cross-language event metadata offered by Wikipedia, may lead to bias as the overlapping between Twitter and Wikipedia communities is significantly larger than that between the Weibo and Wikipedia communities.

Our immediate next step is to address the limitations listed above. To address limitation (1), we will use more sophisticated text mining and natural language processing algorithms to find the latent semantic match results, instead of just focusing on explicit word search (statistical match). To address limitation (2), we will distinguish events that are *global* and *regional*, and compare Twitter and Weibo on these two types of events separately.

In summary, this is a pilot study that opens the door for more in-depth analysis of the social phenomenon boosted by blogging and instant messaging. We are looking forward to working with social scientist to further analyze the results for more insightful discoveries.

6. ACKNOWLEDGMENTS

Xin Shuai thanks the National Science Foundation for its support of his PhD research under grant SBE #0914939; Tian Xia thanks the Beijing Higher Education Young Elite Teacher Project for its support of his work.

7. REFERENCES

[1] Eric Baucom, Azade Sanjari, Xiaozhong Liu, and Miao Chen. Mirroring the real world in social media: twitter, geolocation, and sentiment analysis. In *Proceedings of the 2013 international workshop on Mining unstructured big data using natural language processing*, pages 61–68. ACM, 2013.

[2] Johan Bollen, Huina Mao, and Alberto Pepe. Modeling public mood and emotion: Twitter sentiment and socio-economic phenomena. In *The International AAAI Conference on Weblogs and Social Media*, 2011.

[3] Surajit Chaudhuri, Raghu Ramakrishnan, and Gerhard Weikum. Integrating db and ir technologies: What is the sound of one hand clapping? In *Conference on Innovative Data Systems Research*, pages 1–12, 2005.

[4] Qi Gao, Fabian Abel, Geert-Jan Houben, and Yong Yu. A comparative study of users' microblogging behavior on sina weibo and twitter. In *User Modeling, Adaptation, and Personalization*, pages 88–101. Springer, 2012.

[5] Wanqiu Guan, Haoyu Gao, Mingmin Yang, Yuan Li, Haixin Ma, Weining Qian, Zhigang Cao, and Xiaoguang Yang. Analyzing user behavior of the micro-blogging website sina weibo during hot social events. *Physica A: Statistical Mechanics and its Applications*, 395:340–351, 2014.

[6] Bernard J Jansen, Mimi Zhang, Kate Sobel, and Abdur Chowdury. Twitter power: Tweets as electronic word of mouth. *Journal of the American society for information science and technology*, 60(11):2169–2188, 2009.

[7] Akshay Java, Xiaodan Song, Tim Finin, and Belle Tseng. Why we twitter: understanding microblogging usage and communities. In *Proceedings of the 9th WebKDD and 1st SNA-KDD 2007 workshop on Web mining and social network analysis*, pages 56–65. ACM, 2007.

[8] Haewoon Kwak, Changhyun Lee, Hosung Park, and Sue Moon. What is twitter, a social network or a news media? In *Proceedings of the 19th international conference on World wide web*, pages 591–600. ACM, 2010.

[9] David D. Lewis, Yiming Yang, Tony G. Rose, and Fan Li. English stop word list, 2004. [Online; accessed 2014-02-07].

[10] Daifeng Li, Jingwei Zhang, Gordon Guo-zheng Sun, Jie Tang, Ying Ding, and Zhipeng Luo. What is the nature of chinese microblogging: Unveiling the unique features of tencent weibo. *arXiv preprint arXiv:1211.2197*, 2012.

[11] Xiaozhong Liu and Howard Turtle. Real-time user interest modeling for real-time ranking. *Journal of the American Society for Information Science and Technology*, 64(8):1557–1576, 2013.

[12] Xiaozhong Liu and Vadim von Brzeski. Computational community interest for ranking. In *Proceedings of the 18th ACM conference on Information and knowledge management*, pages 245–254. ACM, 2009.

[13] Evgeny Morozov. *The net delusion: The dark side of Internet freedom*. PublicAffairs Store, 2012.

[14] Seth A Myers, Chenguang Zhu, and Jure Leskovec. Information diffusion and external influence in networks. In *Proceedings of the 18th ACM SIGKDD international conference on Knowledge discovery and data mining*, pages 33–41. ACM, 2012.

[15] Alexander Pak and Patrick Paroubek. Twitter as a corpus for sentiment analysis and opinion mining. In *The International Conference on Language Resources and Evaluation*, 2010.

[16] Joshua Ritterman, Miles Osborne, and Ewan Klein. Using prediction markets and twitter to predict a swine flu pandemic. In *1st international workshop on mining social media*, 2009.

[17] Daniel M Romero, Brendan Meeder, and Jon Kleinberg. Differences in the mechanics of information diffusion across topics: idioms, political hashtags, and complex contagion on twitter. In *Proceedings of the 20th international conference on World wide web*, pages 695–704. ACM, 2011.

[18] Takeshi Sakaki, Makoto Okazaki, and Yutaka Matsuo. Earthquake shakes twitter users: real-time event detection by social sensors. In *Proceedings of the 19th international conference on World wide web*, pages 851–860. ACM, 2010.

[19] Xin Shuai, Xiaozhong Liu, and Johan Bollen. Improving news ranking by community tweets. In *Proceedings of the 21st international conference companion on World Wide Web*, pages 1227–1232. ACM, 2012.

[20] Jian Sun. Ansj-seg chinese segmenter. [Online; accessed 2014-02-07].

[21] Sherry Turkle. *Alone together: Why we expect more from technology and less from each other*. Basic Books, 2012.

[22] Sebastián Valenzuela, Namsu Park, and Kerk F Kee. Is there social capital in a social network site?: Facebook use and college students' life satisfaction, trust, and participation1. *Journal of Computer-Mediated Communication*, 14(4):875–901, 2009.

[23] Wikipedia. List of websites blocked in china, 2014. [Online; accessed 2014-02-07].

[24] Fareed Zakaria. *The post-American world: release 2.0*. WW Norton & Company, 2011.

[25] Bin Zhao, Zhao Zhang, Yanhui Gu, Xueqing Gong, Weining Qian, and Aoying Zhou. Discovering collective viewpoints on micro-blogging events based on community and temporal aspects. In *Advanced Data Mining and Applications*, pages 270–284. Springer, 2011.

Analyzing Images' Privacy for the Modern Web

Anna Cinzia Squicciarini
College of Information
Sciences and Technology
Pennsylvania State University
asquicciarini@ist.psu.edu
University Park, PA
United States

Cornelia Caragea
Computer Science and
Engineering
University of North Texas
ccaragea@unt.edu
Denton, Tx
United States

Rahul Balakavi
Computer Science and
Engineering
Pennsylvania State University
rmb347@psu.edu
University Park, PA
United States

ABSTRACT

Images are now one of the most common form of content shared in online user-contributed sites and social Web 2.0 applications. In this paper, we present an extensive study exploring privacy and sharing needs of users' uploaded images. We develop learning models to estimate adequate privacy settings for newly uploaded images, based on carefully selected image-specific features. We focus on a set of visual-content features and on tags. We identify the smallest set of features, that by themselves or combined together with others, can perform well in properly predicting the degree of sensitivity of users' images. We consider both the case of binary privacy settings (i.e. public, private), as well as the case of more complex privacy options, characterized by multiple sharing options. Our results show that with few carefully selected features, one may achieve extremely high accuracy, especially when high-quality tags are available.

Categories and Subject Descriptors

I.O [**Computing Methodologies**]: General

1. INTRODUCTION

Images are now one of the most common forms of content shared in online user-contributed sites and social Web 2.0 applications. Sharing takes place both among previously established groups of known people or social circles (e.g., Google+, Flickr or Picasa), and also increasingly with people outside the user's social circles, for purposes of social discovery [6]- to help them identify new peers and learn about peers' interests and social surroundings. For example, people on Flickr or Pinterest can upload their images to find social groups that share the same interests [6, 50]. However, semantically rich images may reveal content-sensitive information [2, 38, 49]. Consider a photo of a student's 2013 New Years' public ceremony, for example. It could be shared within a Google+ circle or Flickr group, or it could be used to discover 2013 awardees. Here, the image content may not only reveal the users' location and personal habits,

but may unnecessarily expose the image owner's friends and acquaintances.

Sharing images within online content sharing sites, therefore, may quickly lead to unwanted disclosure and privacy violations [10, 2, 5]. Malicious attackers can take advantage of these unnecessary leaks to launch context-aware attacks or even impersonation attacks [22], as demonstrated by a proliferating number of cases of privacy abuse and unwarranted access.

To this date, online image privacy has not been thoroughly studied, as most of recent work has been devoted to protecting generic textual users' online personal data, with no emphasis on the unique privacy challenges associated with image sharing [25, 20]. Further, work on image analysis has not considered issues of privacy, but focused on semantic meaning of images or similarity analysis for retrieval and classification (e.g. [11, 36, 29, 17, 16]). Only some recent work has started to explore simple classification models of image privacy [38, 49].

In this work, we carry out an extensive study aiming at exploring the main privacy and sharing needs of users' uploaded images. Our goal is to develop learning models to estimate adequate privacy settings for newly uploaded images, based on carefully selected image-specific features. To achieve this goal without introducing unneeded overhead and data processing, we focus on two types of image features: visual-content images and metadata. Within these feature types, we aim to identify the smallest set of features, that by themselves or combined together with others, can perform well in properly predicting the degree of sensitivity of users' images.

To achieve this goal, we develop and contrast various learning models, that combine an increasingly large number of features using both combined and ensemble classification methods. Our analysis shows some interesting performance variability among all the analyzed features, demonstrating that while models for images' privacy can be well captured using a large amount of features, only some of them have a high discriminative power.

We specifically identified SIFT (Scale-Invariant Feature Transformation) and TAGS (image metadata) as the best performing features in a variety of classification models. We achieve a prediction accuracy of 90% and a Break Even Point (BEP) of 0.89 using these features in combination.

Furthermore, we analyze privacy needs of images on a multi-level scale, consistent with current privacy options offered by most popular Web 2.0 sharing sites and applications. We adopt a five-level privacy model, where image disclosure can range from open access to disclosure to the owner only. In addition to the five-privacy levels, we also introduce new degrees of disclosure for each image, to model the different ways an image can be made available online. These degrees of disclosure are *View, Comment, Download.* According to this multi-level, multi-class privacy framework, we build models to estimate adequate privacy settings, using the best combination of features obtained in our privacy prediction models for binary classification. In these new models, we account for the inter-relations between different privacy classes. An example for such an inter-relation is the following: an image can be downloadable only if it can be viewed. To model these inherent inter-relations, we used Chained classifier [33] models, where predicted class labels are used to predict new class labels. Our experiments confirm that these models, executed using features such as Edge, SIFT, TAGS, and their assembled combinations, consistently outperformed strong baseline models.

To the best of our knowledge, this is the first and most comprehensive study carried out to date on large-scale image privacy classification, that includes not only simple privacy classification based on binary labels, but also models for more complex, multi-facet privacy settings.

The rest of the paper is organized as follows. We discuss prior research in Section 2. In Section 3 we elaborate our problem statement, whereas in Section 4 we discuss different image-based features that we explored. In Section 5 we analyze the patterns of visual and textual features in public and private images. In Section 6, we introduce the multi-class model. We finish our analysis in Section 7, where we discuss pointers to future works and conclude the paper.

2. RELATED WORK

A number of recent studies have analyzed sharing patterns and social discovery in image sharing sites like Flickr [15, 4, 28, 50]. Among other interesting findings, scholars have determined that images are often used for self and social disclosure. In particular, tags associated with images are used to convey contextual or social information to those viewing the photo [35, 30, 14, 4], motivating our hypothesis of using metadata as one among other features for privacy extraction.

Miller and Edwards [28] further confirm that people who share their photos maintain social bonds through tagging together with online messaging, commenting, etc. They also identify two different types of users (normal and power users), indicating the importance of interpersonal differences, users may have different levels of privacy concerns depending on their individual level of privacy awareness and the image content.

Ahern et al. [2] analyzed effectiveness of tags as well as location information in predicting privacy settings of the photos. Further, they conducted an early study to establish whether content (as expressed by image descriptors) is relevant to image's privacy settings. Based on their user studies, content is one of the discriminatory factors affecting image privacy, especially for images depicting people. This supports the core idea underlying our work: that particular categories of image content are pivotal in establishing users' images sharing decisions. Jones and colleagues [23] later reinforced the role of privacy-relevant image concepts. For instance, they determined that people are more reluctant to share photos capturing social relationships than photos

taken for functional purposes; certain settings such as work, bars, concerts cause users to share less. These studies also revealed significant individual differences within the same type of image, based on some explanatory variables relating to the identity of the contacts and the context of photo capture, providing insights into the need for customized, subjective models for privacy patterns. Zerr and colleagues recently developed PiCAlert [49], which carries out content analysis for image private search and detection of private images.

Along the same theme, Besner et al. [5] pointed out that users want to regain control over their shared content but meanwhile, they feel that configuring proper privacy settings for each image is a burden. Similarly, related work suggests sharing decisions may be governed by the difficulty of setting and updating policies, reinforcing the idea that users must be able to easily set up access control policies [3, 42, 13, 38, 20, 25]. Some notable recent efforts to tackle these problems have been conducted in the context of tag-based access control policies for images [46, 24, 42], showing some initial success in tying tags with access control rules. However, the scarcity of tags for many online images [40], and the workload associated with user-defined tags precludes accurate analysis of the images' sensitivity based on this dimension only. Other work [19, 13, 3, 8, 7, 20] has focused on generic users' profile elements, and typically leveraged social context, rather users' individual content-specific patterns.

A loosely related body of work is on recommendation of tags for social discovery [35, 30, 47, 14] and for image classification [34, 48, 14] in photo sharing websites like Flickr. In these works, the typical approach is for authors to firstly collect adequate images and then classify images according to visual and context-related features. After users upload their images, the server extracts features, then classifies and recommends relevant tags and groups.

Finally, there is a large body of work on image content analysis, for classification and interpretation (e.g., [11, 36, 29, 41, 51, 43, 18]), retrieval ([17, 16, 21, 12] are just some examples), and photo ranking [39, 45], also in the context of online photo sharing sites, such as Flickr [34, 48, 14, 40, 31, 32, 15]. This previous work is useful in identifying meaningful content-based features for effective image content extraction, discussed in Section 4.

3. PROBLEM STATEMENT

The objective of our work is to explore the main characteristics of users' uploaded images, and leverage them to automatically determine images adequate privacy settings. Our goal is two-fold: (1) We aim to identify a variety of features that can be informative in profiling images' privacy needs. (2) Among the identified features, wish to determine the smallest set of features, that by themselves or combined together with others, can perform well in properly defining the degree of sensitivity of users' images.

To meet these goals, we analyze images based on visual content features and their associated metadata. The intuition underlying content-based features is that, as demonstrated in recent work (e.g. [5]) although privacy is a subjective decision, certain visual content is likely personal or too sensitive to be disclosed to a public online audience. Hence, we expect that certain visual elements of an image, like the presence of edges, its color, its predominant elements, or the presence of faces, may give some insights about its degree of privacy. Metadata, typically defined in terms of keywords extracted from tags or captions, can provide insights on the image's context, i.e. where it was taken, what it represents to the labeler (e.g. the image owner) what feelings it evokes, etc.

Additional dimensions are purposely not considered for the purpose of this study. For instance, we do not consider any of the additional social networking or personal information about the photo owners and the site where the image is originally posted, as we aim to leverage to the extent possible the content carried by the image itself. Further, information about a photo poster and his online social network activities may not be available or easily accessible.

Our learning models try to address the stated goals using a blend of visual and metadata features using two alternative privacy models. First is a binary model, and accounts for the case of an image which is either to be disclosed or not (public vs. private). The second privacy model accounts for the more complex case of an image to be placed in a social networking site, where users may have more sophisticated options to choose from (i.e. should friend view the images? should they be allowed to download it? should family members be allowed to view and or comment on the image?). In this case, privacy settings will be defined by multi-option privacy privileges and various disclosure options.

4. IMAGE RELEVANT FEATURES

In this section, we discuss the image features considered for our analysis.

4.1 Visual Features

We are interested in identifying few pivotal features that can serve useful for image classification with respect to privacy. We next describe our selected visual features, and provide some observations from the use of the features for privacy models.

- *SIFT* or Scale Invariant Feature Transform [27]. As images privacy level may be determined by the presence of one or more specific objects, rather than the whole visual content itself (e.g. think about an image with somebody carrying a gun and the same image with the person holding flowers instead), features able to detect interesting points of images are needed. SIFT, being one of the most widely used features for image analysis in computer vision, is such a feature. It detects stable key point locations in scale space of an image. In simple terms, the SIFT approach is to take an image and transforms it into a "large collection of local feature vectors" [26]. Each of these feature vectors is invariant to any scaling, rotation or translation of the image. We extract a image profile based on the state-of-the-art model called Bag-of-visual-words (BoW) [37, 44], which can effectively evaluate the image similarity, and is widely used in image similarity search, image retrieval and even content-based social discovery [35]. The image BoW vector is first obtained by extracting the features of preferred images, then clustering them into the visual word vocabulary $\triangle$, where each element is the distinct word occurrence. Features are extracted for each image and each element of the feature vector is mapped onto one of the bag of words and once all the elements are checked,

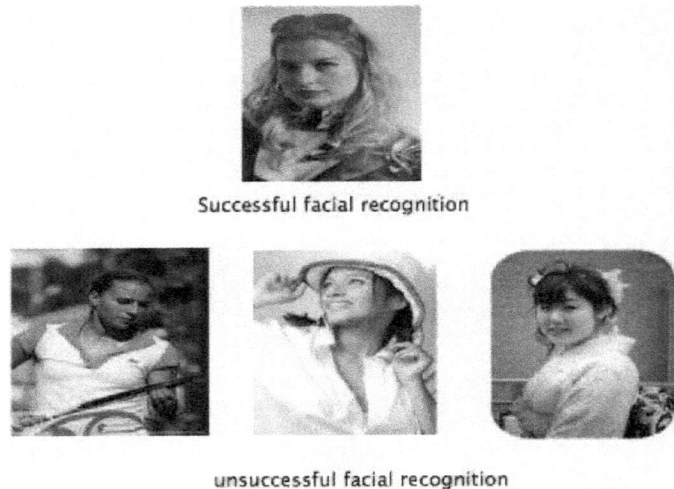

Successful facial recognition

unsuccessful facial recognition

Figure 1: Facial recognition examples

we get a sequence of numbers whose length is equal to the length of the Bag-of-visual-words . Each number represents the number of elements in the original SIFT feature vector, which have been mapped onto the corresponding visual word. As a result, an image profile is created $S = \{s_1, \ldots, s_m\}$, where s_i reflects the strength of image's preference on word w_i and m is the size of $\triangle$.

- *RGB* or Red Green Blue. Images with a given color and texture patterns can be mapped into certain classes, based on what is learnt from the training set. For example, instances with a pattern of green and blue may be mapped to public images, being indicative of nature. Accordingly, we include RGB feature to extract these potentially useful patterns. RGB is a content-based feature which detects six different components from an image. These components are Red, Green, Blue, Hue, Saturation and Brightness. Values corresponding to each of the variables are extracted from an image, and each feature is encoded into a 256 byte length array. This array is serialized in sparse format where each instance corresponds to the feature vector of an image.

- *Facial recognition* Images revealing one's identity are more likely to be considered private [2], although this is subjective to the specific event and situation wherein the image was taken. Henceforth, to discriminate to the extent possible between purely public events with people and other images involving various individuals, we detect the ratio that the area of faces take in the image, to identify whether they are or not prevalent elements in the image.

We extract facial keypoints using the FKEFaceDetector framework. Information about presence of faces is encoded in two attributes for each image similar to [49]. One attribute represents the number of faces found in the image and the second attribute indicates the amount of area occupied by faces in the image.

Tags : ocean, boy, summer, vacation, lighthouse, beach, water, boat, vintagecolors

Figure 2: Example of a Flickr image and its tags

The framework detects faces which are straight-up and clearly visible. In some images, though there are faces visible, due to various factors the faces couldn't be detected. Images with faces not clearly visible, images in dark background, images which show faces from acute angles are few factors which can result in faces not being detected by the API. We show two sets of images where facial recognition is successful and where it fails in Figure 1.

- *Edge Direction Coherence.* As more and more users enjoy the pervasiveness of cameras and smart devices the number of online images that include some "artistic" content (landscapes, sceneries etc) is also increasing. Hence, we would like to include a feature that can help with capturing similarities in landscape images. One such feature, that has shown useful for models on landscape images, is Edge Direction Coherence, which uses Edge Direction Histograms to define the texture in an image. The feature stores the number of edge pixels that are coherent and non-coherent. A division of coherence and non-coherence is established by a threshold on the size of the connected component edges. This feature uses 72 bins to represent coherent pixels and one bin for non-coherent pixels. After separating out non-coherent pixels, we back track from a random coherent pixel to another and check if its within 5 degrees and then update the corresponding coherent bins [41].

4.2 MetaData

Annotation of online images is now common practice, and it is used to describe images, as well as to allow image classification and search by others. Users can tag an image by adding descriptive keywords of the images content, for purposes including organization, search, description, and communication. For instance, each image in Flickr has associated one or more user-added tags. We created a feature vector for each image accordingly. We create a dictionary of words from all images in the training set such that there are no duplicates (in the dictionary). Once we have the dictionary ready, each feature vector is represented in sparse

format, where an entry of the vector corresponds to a word. Each unique word that is a tag for an image, has an entry in the vector. This sparse representation allows compact feature vector for each instance, removing unnecessary information about absence of keywords which are in the dictionary and not in the image.

Accordingly, we try to correlate images by using the feature vector to capture usage of the same tags. We observe that most of the images which show similar descriptive patterns have extensive word usage which are similar. An example of tags usage in Flickr is given in Figure 2. For this image, the associated words are beach, water and ocean, which all have a high degree of similarity. Similar findings are reported for other images, where tags appear extremely useful: As we further elaborate in Section 5.2.3, tags are a predominant feature for privacy classification purposes, although acceptable results are found even in absence of available metadata .

5. PRIVATE VERSUS PUBLIC IMAGES: EMPIRICAL ANALYSIS

Our analysis includes two key steps. First, we analyze a large labeled dataset of images posted online, by means of unsupervised methods, to identify the main distinctions between private and public images. Second, we investigate privacy images classification models, taking into account the results of our clustering analysis and the features discussed in the previous section.

We employ two datasets for our analysis. For the first dataset, we took a sample of Flickr images from the PiCalert dataset [49]. The PiCalert dataset includes randomly chosen Flickr images on various subjects and different privacy sensitivity. Each image in the dataset is labeled using private and public labels by randomly selected users. We focus on about 6000 images randomly sampled from the original dataset, to include actual online images (i.e. still on the site) with associated keywords. The dataset includes public and private images in the ratio of 2:3. The second dataset, was sampled from the Visual Sentiment Ontology repository [9]. The repository has a good blend of landscape images, animals, artwork, people etc. About 4000 Flickr URLs were randomly sampled from the dataset. The associated keywords were extracted from the Flickr site directly.

Some of the privacy labels were already part of the first dataset, whereas we use crowdsourcing methods (i.e. Amazon Mechanical Turk) for labeling the additional datasets and complement existing labels with more complex settings (see Section 6).

Of course, similar to [49], the adopted privacy labels only capture an aggregated community perception of privacy, rather a highly subjective, personal representation. We argue that the provided representation is is correlated to textual and visual features in a plausible way, and can be predicted using carefully crafted classification models.

5.1 Characteristics of private and public images

To understand what makes images private or public, we first explored some of the consistent characteristics among each of these two classes, considering both visual and metadata elements.

139

public image clusters

private image clusters

Figure 3: Public and private images

5.1.1 Visual differences between public and private Images

We first explored whether there are any consistent types of images, or image content that can help define private versus public images.

Our approach to identify these characteristics is to group images by content similarity, to explore what are the visual similarities that define the clusters. To this end, we used unsupervised learning methods. In particular, we applied Content Based Image Retrieval (CBIR) [1] method to identify clusters among public and private images, respectively. Content Based Image Retrieval uses wavelet-based color histogram analysis and enhancements provided by Haar wavelet transformation. With Color histograms, the image under consideration is divided into sub-areas and color distribution histograms are calculated for each of the divided areas. The wavelet transformation is used to capture texture patterns and local characteristics of an image. A progressive image retrieval algorithm is used for image retrieval based on similarity.

Upon running CBICR, we observed similarity patterns among images in different sets that were clustered. Figure 3 shows an excerpt of the clustered results of images. Public images are seen on the top and private images are at the bottom. Most public images belong to one of three categories. (1) Women and Children, (2) Symbols, abstract, and black and white images, (3) Artwork. Private images could be mainly grouped into (1) Women and children, (2) Sketches.

As a first observation, we note that not all images of people are private. Our clusters show that images indicative of people's life events, personal stories etc. are considered equally confidential. Second, images with children or humans in general are equally classifiable as private or public, depending on the specific visual representation in the image. These observations confirm that simply considering the presence of people as the only relevant feature may not be sufficient (we provide additional results on this aspect in the

next Section), and that multiple features are needed, both visually (to describe the content in the cluster classes) and through text, to provide some contextual information.

5.1.2 Keywords patterns in public and private images

To further our understanding of the images and their privacy needs, we analyzed the keywords associated with each image. Specifically, we enriched the dataset by adding annotations for each image in the dataset, and extracted these annotations from the Flickr's tagging systems. Each image in Flickr has associated one or more user-added tag, which we crawled directly from Flickr as it was not part of the original dataset. To obtain keyword groups reflective of the most generic topics used to tag and index the images, we clustered images based on keyword similarity.

Precisely, we performed keyword hypernym analysis over all of the keywords associated with the images [38], using Wordnet as reference dictionary. For each keyword t_i, we created a metadata vector listing the hypernyms associated with the word. After extracting all the hypernyms of all the keywords for an image, we identified a hypernym per part of speech. We identified all the nouns, verbs and adjectives in the metadata and store them as metadata vectors $\tau_{noun} = \{t_1, t_2, \ldots, t_i\}$, $\tau_{verb} = \{t_1, t_2, \ldots, t_j\}$ and $\tau_{adj} = \{t_1, t_2, \ldots, t_k\}$, where i, j and k are the total number of nouns, verbs and adjectives respectively. This selection was done by choosing the hypernym which appeared most frequently. In case of ties, we choose the word which is closest to the root or baseline.

We repeated the same procedure over different parts of speech, i.e Noun, Verb and Adjective. For example, consider a metadata vector $\tau = \{$"cousin","first steps", "baby boy"$\}$. We find that "cousin" and "baby boy" have the same hypernym "kid", and "first steps" has a hypernym "initiative". Correspondingly, we obtain the hypernym list $\eta = \{$(kid, 2), (initiative, 1)$\}$. In this list, we select the hypernym with the highest frequency to be the representative hypernym, e.g.,

Table 1: Prominent keywords in private images

Cluster No	Keywords
1	garment, adornment, class, pattern, appearance, representation
2	letter, passage, message, picture, scripture, wittiness, recording, signaling
3	freedom, religion, event, movement, clergyman, activity, ceremonial, gathering, spirit, group, energy
4	region, appearance, segment, ground, line, metal, passage, water, structure, material
5	body, reproduction, people, happening, soul, organism, school,class, period, respiration

Table 2: Prominent keywords in public images

Cluster No	Keywords
1	season, hour, period, decade, leisure, beginning, drib.
2	phenomenon, happening, relation, passage, electricity
3	covering, vesture, case, people,appearance, adornment, lacquerware, piece, attire, beach.
4	curio, artifact, art, crockery, lceremonial, pattern, covering

"kid". In case that there are more than one hypernyms with the same frequency, we consider the hypernym closest to the most relevant baseline class to be the representative hypernym. For example, if we have a hypernym list $\eta = \{$(kid, 2), (cousin, 2), (initiative, 1)$\}$, we will select "kid" to be the representative hypernym since it is closest to the baseline class "kids". Once we computed the representative hypernyms for each instance, the next step was to cluster the instances based on the hypernyms. This was achieved by calculating the edit distance of each existing cluster center with a new instance and the weighted average distance is compared to a threshold value. The new instance is added to a cluster, once the edit distance between the corresponding cluster center and the instance is below the threshold. If the distance from none of the cluster centers falls below the threshold, then the new instance is added as a part of a new cluster and the instance is made the cluster center. In addition, existing clusters keep updating their cluster centers as new instances are added. A cluster center represents a noun, verb and an adjective. These parts of speech are chosen as they are the words with highest frequency amongst the instances of the cluster.

Using the above methodology, we clustered about 6000 keywords. Keywords clustering resulted in four clusters for keywords bound with private images and five clusters for keywords related to public images. On average we observed that there were around 15 hypernyms per cluster.

Table 1 shows the prominent keywords in the clusters obtained by grouping keywords of private images. Each of the five clusters being identified projects a particular aspect or a concept (clusters are numbered for convenience only).

Cluster 1 represents adornment patterns and physical features. Cluster 2 mainly includes words about writing and communication. Cluster 3 hints at religion or a religion event. Cluster 4 indicates physical structures and perceivable entities. Keywords in the final group gravitate around children and also people at large. These results are consistent with the three image types identified by clustering images per visual content. Specifically, two of the keywords clusters (labeled for convenience as 2 and 3) are consistent with the image cluster inclusive of abstract images and images about sketches, whereas the keyword cluster with keywords surrounding children is consistent with the "women and children" cluster previously identified.

Different patterns were observed for keywords of public images. As shown in Table 2, after the clusters were formed, we observed that cluster 1 mainly grouped words related to a time scale or an event that happened in the past or that is set to happen in the future. Cluster 2 has words related to a phenomenon or something that involved movement. Cluster 3 has words which described dressing style or appearance patterns. Cluster 4 described art work or objects with patterns. These patterns shed light on the themes around private and public images. Some of these patterns (e.g. artwork) were already observed while clustering the images based on visual content using Content Based Image Representation. In addition, clustering the images based on hypernyms of the associated keywords uncovered some additional descriptive patterns, like appearance related or movement related images, that were not observed through our analysis based on content-based similarity.

5.2 Image classification models

We investigate privacy images classification models with three objectives. First, we aim to compare visual features versus metadata, to understand which class of features is more informative for privacy considerations. Second, we evaluate the performance of all the individual features used to gain an understanding of which features can be more effective in discriminating private versus public images. Finally, we aim to identify the smallest combination of features that can successfully lead to highly accurate classification.

We adopt supervised learning, based on labeled images (or items) for each category. Both training and test items are represented as multi dimensional feature vectors. Labeled images are used to train classification models. We use linear support vector machines (SVMs) classifiers. SVMs construct a hyperplane that separates the set of positive training examples (photos tagged as "private") from a set of negative examples (photos tagged as "public") with maximum margin.

5.2.1 Individual Features analysis

We begin by studying the performance of individual features. We specifically evaluated the performance of classifiers trained on 4000 labeled images and evaluated them on a test set of 500 images, using one feature per model. Results are reported in Table 3. As can be seen, TAGS is by far the best performing feature. Content-based features have

Features	Accuracy	Precision	Recall	F meas.
Tags	78.2	0.791	0.782	0.784
RGB	56.6	0.576	0.548	0.553
SIFT	59	0.613	0.59	0.594
Facial Feat.	61.2	0.584	0.612	0.514
Edge Dir. Coh.	54.2	0.588	0.542	0.542

Table 3: Individual features' classification models over 4500 images

lower accuracy, with the worst observed for Edge Direction feature, for which accuracy is only 54.2%.

These results provide initial evidence that users' description of images' content through tags is fairly reflective of its content. Differently, visual features by themselves appear not to be sufficient for privacy classification, most likely due to the heterogeneous content of the images being analyzed (e.g. facial features are inaccurate on images with landscape or food only, whereas Edge Direction does not perform well on images with faces). We also observed that most pictures that had people or faces were difficult to classify. This can be attributed to the fact that, just detecting a person on the image is not sufficient to provide an exact representation of the image. For example, a beach photo with family might be regarded as a private image. But, an image shot in a similar setting and background with a celebrity or a holiday advertisement might be regarded as public. This variation is very difficult to capture accurately without the help of user-defined keywords, which contribute to add contextual information to the image.

Hence, a more sophisticated model combining some of these features needs to be carefully designed.

5.2.2 Models combination

We explored various combinations of supervised learning models for image privacy, using the features listed in Table 3. We were specifically interested in understanding whether the accuracy of visual features, which was low for single-feature models, could be improved by combining them into a single classifier. The intuition is that given that these visual features seem to work best on certain types of images, we aimed to test whether when combined together, they would complement one another, reaching a higher degree of accuracy.

We tested combinations of models for a fixed set of images, increasing the size of the training data, ranging from 1000 to 3700, keeping 500 as the size of test data. To combine the models, we linearly combined the vectors of data of individual features into a single vector. Our results, reported in Figure 4 for two-features combinations, show an overall consistent increase in the accuracy of prediction across most of the combinations with the increasing size of training data. The exception to this pattern is for combinations which involved Facial features, where the peak accuracy is observed when the dataset size is in the 2500-3000 interval, followed by a decrease in the prediction accuracy after the dataset size exceeded 3000 instances landmark.

In Figure 5 and Fig. 6, we report the results for models combining three and four or more features, respectively. Some interesting observations are as follows:

• All combinations, except the FACE,RGB,SIFT combo (which is much lower) have an accuracy ranging from 65% to 74%, therefore achieving sub-optimal accuracy.

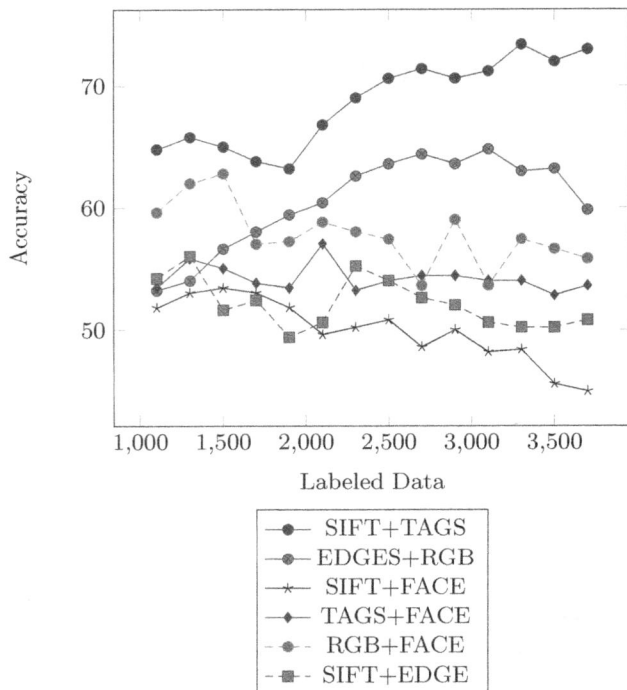

Figure 4: Accuracy analysis of combined classifiers with two features

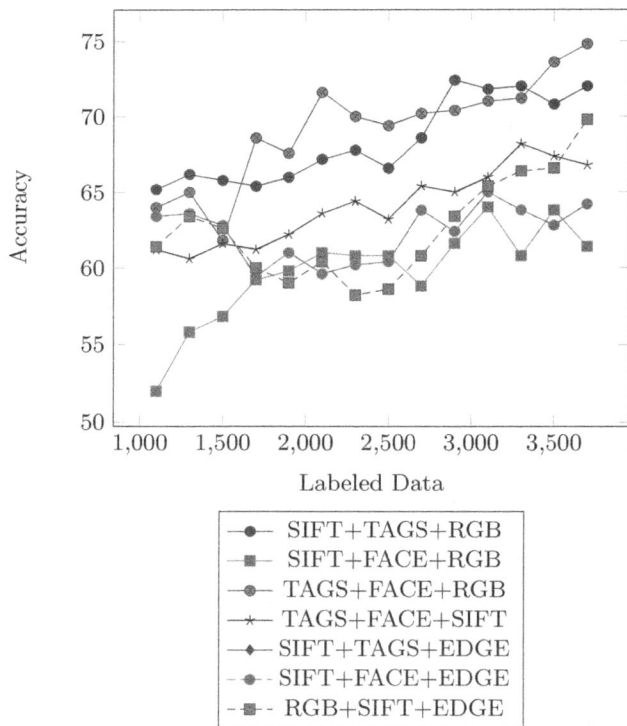

Figure 5: Accuracy analysis of combined classifiers with three features

- When TAGS are in any combined classifier we obtain a better model than the same model with no TAGS as a feature, validating the role of metadata to complement visual information extracted through content-specific features. This observation is valid also for two-feature models (see Figure 4), where the best accuracy is obtained with SIFT+TAGs on a labeled dataset of 3300 training instances, followed by Edge+TAGS.

- SIFT and TAGS appears to be strongest combination, for both two features and three features models. Intuitively, SIFT captured all the visual key points of the images, hence their core, discriminating visual patterns. TAGS on the other hand, gave an indication of the overall context of where the images were taken.

- When we disregard TAGS as a feature and use only visual features for prediction we reach a performance of of 70% over a dataset of size 4500 for SIFT, EDGE and RGB combined together. The combined classifier of SIFT, RGB and EDGE resulted in a BEP of 0.667.

- Finally, it appears evident that simply adding features is not always a recipe for improved accuracy: combining the visual content with metadata leads to a decreased accuracy of the metadata classifier alone (see Figure 6 for the performance of all features combination). For instance, SIFT+FACE+RGB overall perform worse than their individual features.

5.2.3 Tags and Visual models

In this feature study, we explore how TAGS may complement another visual feature to accurately determining adequate image privacy. We adopt a different modeling approach in an attempt to improve the prediction accuracy, and use an ensemble of classifiers, in which two classifiers are individually used to predict the outcome for a particular instance. Based on the prediction data and the confidence of prediction, the ensemble outputs a final classification result which is computed in consideration of both learning models.

In particular, in our case, an ensemble of classifiers is a collection of classifiers, each trained on a different feature type, e.g., SIFT and TAGS. The prediction of the ensemble is computed from the predictions of the individual classifiers. That is, during classification, for a new unlabeled image $\mathbf{x}_{test}$, each individual classifier returns a probability $P_j(y_i|\mathbf{x}_{test})$ that $\mathbf{x}_{test}$ belongs to a particular class $y_i \in \{private, public\}$, where $j = 1, 2$. The ensemble estimated probability, $P_{ens}(y_i|\mathbf{x}_{test})$ is obtained by:

$$P_{ens}(y_i|\mathbf{x}_{test}) = \frac{1}{2} \sum_{j=1}^{2} P_j(y_i|\mathbf{x}_{test}).$$

In experiments, we used the option `buildLogisticModel` of Weka to turn the SVM output into probabilities.

Using an ensemble of classifiers, an image that cannot be classified with good confidence by one classifier, can be helped by another classifier in the ensemble which might be more confident in classifying an image as public or private. We identified that TAGS and all the visual features can be these complementary classifiers: TAGS are collected from the keywords that a user adds to represent the image. Visual features extract the visual patterns from the image itself.

Performance metrics, obtained from a dataset of 4500 images (4000 training, 500 tests) reported in Table 4 confirm this intuition. We particularly observe a peak in the performance when SIFT and EDGE are combined together, along with ensemble of SIFT and TAGS. The latter represents the best performing combination, confirming and improving on the trend and observations made in our combination models (see Section 5.2.2). We note that (although not reported in detail) other ensemble classifiers which did not include TAGS do not reach interesting performance. We speculate

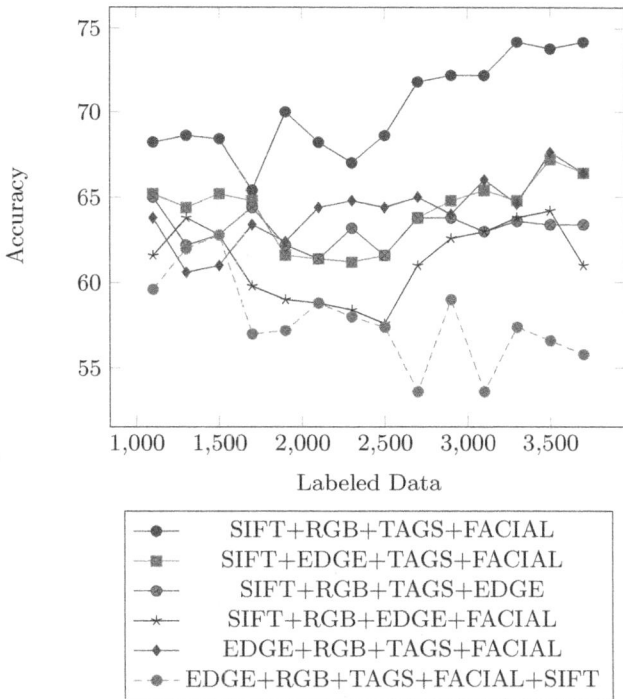

Figure 6: Accuracy analysis of combined classifiers with four or more features

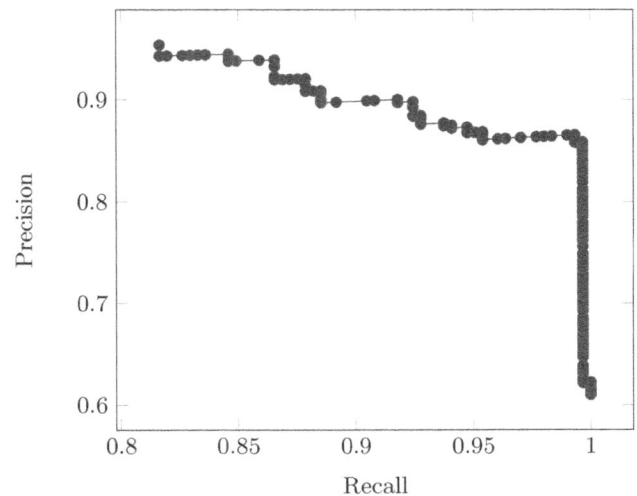

Figure 7: Precision Vs. Recall for SIFT & TAGS ensemble models

Features	Accuracy	Precision	Recall
Tags	82.4	0.859	0.824
Tags and RGB	60.4	0.605	0.604
Tags and SIFT	**90.4**	0.904	0.904
Tags and Facial	50.2	0.498	0.502
Tags and Edges	84.3	0.844	0.843

Table 4: Performance of ensemble models combining TAGS with one content feature

that this is due to the very nature of the features, that fail to complement one another in the ensemble model.

In Figure 7 we show the precision vs recall graph for this classifier of SIFT and TAGS. Accordingly, the BEP (Break Even Point), the point where the value of precision is equal to that of recall, stands at 0.89. Compared to the Picalert framework [49] which presented a BEP of 0.80 after combining textual and a larger number of visual features, the ensembles classifier of SIFT and TAGS shows a stronger performance. In short, these results demonstrate that the ensemble of classifiers can capture different aspects of images that are important for discriminating images as private vs. public, with a small set of features. Note that these experiments also confirm the poor performance of Facial features, which achieve very low precision and recall, showing how the choice of visual features is to be carefully made.

5.2.4 Secondary dataset experiments

To ensure that our models were not bound to a specific dataset, we sampled a new set of images from the Visual Sentiment Ontology [9] repository. The sampling was done by randomly selecting a URL form the complete list of about 45000 images. Using the sampled set, we tested our best classifier, ensemble of SIFT and TAGS, to verify whether its performance would be similar to the performance observed on the tests carried out using the Picalert dataset. In the experiment, we varied the size of the training dataset from 1100 to 2500. Figure 8 shows the models' prediction accuracy, computed using TAGS and ensemble of TAGS and SIFT, across both (Picalert and Visual Sentiment Ontology) the datasets. We make the following observations:

- The obtained accuracy is comparable with the accuracy observed for the models against the PiCalert dataset.

- TAGS performed slightly better on the Picalert dataset, whereas the ensembles combination of SIFT and TAGS performed slightly better on the VSO dataset. This is likely due to the larger availability of high quality tags available in the first dataset. Nevertheless, we note that the final prediction accuracies across different sizes of dataset are within a range of 2-3% when we compare the results from the two datasets.

- We also observed that the pattern of increase and decrease in predication accuracy with change in size of the training set was consistent across both the datasets.

6. MULTI-OPTION PRIVACY SETTINGS

In many online sharing sites (Facebook, Flickr etc), users create a web space wherein they can control the audience visiting it, distinguishing among friends, family members or

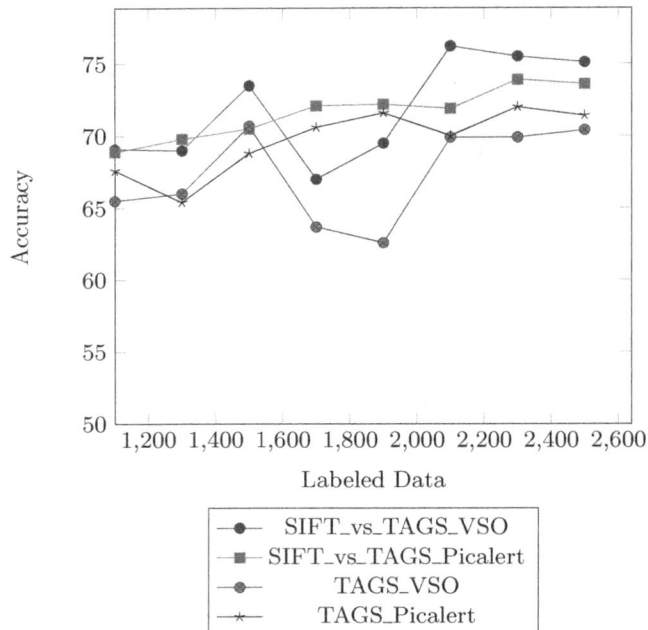

Figure 8: Comparison between performance for models on Picalert and Visual Sentiment Ontology dataset

other custom-social groups, and within these groups, distinguishing the possible access privileges. Accordingly, upon analyzing image privacy using a binary classification model for "public" or "private", we investigate complex multi-label, multi-class classification models, specifically after the options offered to Flickr users, who may distinguish among multiple classes of users and sharing options (view, comment, download).

6.1 Learning models

Our current problem can be mapped into a multi-label, multi-class problem. We have three classifications to perform, and each of them includes five possible labels, ranging from "Only You" to "Everyone". Precisely, the labels are "Only You", "Family", "Friends", "SocialNetwork" and "Everyone". Each classification is indicative of one sharing privilege, and includes "view", "comment" and "Download" access controls for each image.

Our model is based on supervised learning, and both training and test items, are represented as multi dimensional feature vectors. Labeled images, selected at random from the dataset, are used to train classification models. As mentioned, we added three categories for each image, and each category could be classified into one of the five privacy labels above. We noticed that in most of the cases the privacy levels set by users for the three categories are related. For example, if a user wants to make an image comment-able and download-able, it would be possible only if the image is view-able to the users in the same level of privacy. To account for these types of inter-relations of categories for classifying unlabeled images, we apply Chained Classifiers model [33]. Chained classifiers were developed to capture the dependency between categories in a multi-category dataset. The method enables the predictions that were made on a previous iteration on a category to be utilized in the prediction of the subsequent categories. Each classifier in the chain is a Multiclass - SVM classifier for learning and prediction.

In our context, the Chained Classifiers model [33] involves three transformations - one for each label. In a sense, chained classifier simply uses SVM on each of the labels, but it differs from multi-class SVM in that the attribute space of each label is extended by the predicted label of the previous classifiers. Given a chain of N classifiers, $\{c_1, c_2, ..., c_N\}$, each classifier c_i in the chain learns and predicts the ith label in the attribute space, augmented by all previous label predictions c_1 to c_{i-1}. This chaining process passes information about labels between the classifiers. Although increasing the attribute space might be an overhead, if strong correlations exist between the labels then these attributes immensely help increasing the predictive accuracy. An example of a correlation in our usecase - *comment* label has the predicted value of *view* label in the attribute space. Intuitively, an image can only be commented upon if it can be viewed.

6.2 Experimental Results

We again relied on the Picalert dataset for these experiments. We sampled 4500 images, and used the same features set as in our previous experiments. For labeling purposes, we used Amazon Mechanical Turk (AMT). Quality of workers' was carefully monitored. For instance, we disregarded work from users who assigned the same set of labels for 80% of the images. We also manually checked URLs at random to check for consistency of labels.

For these set of experiments, we used the three features that performed best in our binary classification, namely SIFT, Tags, Edges. We increased the size of the training data, ranging from 2000 to 4000, keeping 500 as the size of test data.

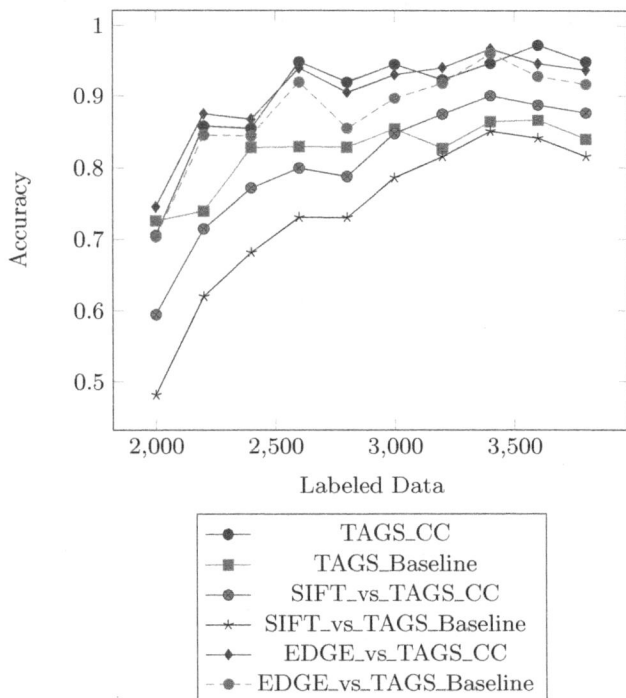

Figure 9: Multi-option privacy settings

We compared the performance of chained classifiers against a baseline classifier model. The baseline model involved running multi-class SVM on each of the three classes separately, using the same set of attributes as opposed to chained classifiers which appends the predicted class label to the attribute list for the current prediction. The two classification models (i.e. chained classifiers and baseline), were used for single-feature analysis as well as for combinations of features. Results are reported in Figure 9.

A few interesting observations can be made. First, our results show the accuracy of prediction across the combinations with the increasing size of training data. Second, we noted that TAGS, as established already in our previous analysis, was the best performing single feature, with extremely high prediction accuracies (up to 94%). Ensemble of features using TAGS & SIFT and TAGS & EDGE also had high prediction accuracy, reaching up to 90%. Finally, we observed that using chained classifiers increases overall performance, regardless of the features used, in comparison to the baseline accuracy achieved using multi-class SVM on each class individually. This result confirms that chained classifiers are useful in capturing the correlation between the class labels and resulted in higher prediction accuracy.

7. CONCLUSION

In this paper, we presented an extensive study investigating privacy needs of online images. We studied the importance of images visual content and user-applied metadata to identify adequate privacy settings. We considered both the case of privacy settings being simple, as well as the case of more complex privacy options, which users may choose from. Our results show that with few carefully selected features, one may achieve extremely high accuracy, especially with the support of metadata.

In the future, we will extend this work along several dimensions. First, given the strong performance of TAGS, we would like to incorporate additional textual metadata in the models, to further the performance of this class of features. Second, we would like to further explore the visual models and their roles in the context of complex privacy settings. Finally, we will implement a recommender system for users to express privacy settings based on their privacy choices.

8. ACKNOWLEDGEMENT

Portion of the work from dr. Squicciarini was supported by a Google Innovation Research Award. Portion of the work from Balakavi was supported by the National Science Foundation under Grant #1353400.

9. REFERENCES

[1] Java content based image retrieval, 2011. https://code.google.com/p/jcbir/.
[2] S. Ahern, D. Eckles, N. S. Good, S. King, M. Naaman, and R. Nair. Over-exposed?: privacy patterns and considerations in online and mobile photo sharing. In *CHI '07: Proceedings of the SIGCHI conference on Human factors in computing systems*, pages 357–366, New York, NY, USA, 2007. ACM.
[3] E. A. Alessandra Mazzia, Kristen LeFevre, April 2011. UM Tech Report #CSE-TR-570-11.
[4] M. Ames and M. Naaman. Why we tag: motivations for annotation in mobile and online media. In

Proceedings of the SIGCHI Conference on Human Factors in Computing Systems, CHI '07, pages 971–980, 2007.

[5] A. Besmer and H. Lipford. Tagged photos: concerns, perceptions, and protections. In *CHI '09: 27th international conference extended abstracts on Human factors in computing systems*, pages 4585–4590, New York, NY, USA, 2009. ACM.

[6] S. D. Blog. Pin or not to pin: An inside look, 2012. http://blog.socialdiscovery.org/tag/statistics/.

[7] J. Bonneau, J. Anderson, and L. Church. Privacy suites: shared privacy for social networks. In *Symposium on Usable Privacy and Security*, 2009.

[8] J. Bonneau, J. Anderson, and G. Danezis. Prying data out of a social network. In *ASONAM: International Conference on Advances in Social Network Analysis and Mining*, pages 249–254, 2009.

[9] D. Borth, R. Ji, T. Chen, T. Breuel, and S.-F. Chang. Large-scale visual sentiment ontology and detectors using adjective noun pairs, 2013. http://www.ee.columbia.edu/ln/dvmm/vso/download/sentibank.html.

[10] Bullguard. Privacy violations, the dark side of social media. http://www.bullguard.com/bullguard-security-center/internet-security/social-media-dangers/privacy-violations-in-social-media.aspx.

[11] O. Chapelle, P. Haffner, and V. Vapnik. Support vector machines for histogram-based image classification. *Neural Networks, IEEE Transactions on*, 10(5):1055–1064, 1999.

[12] S. Chatzichristofis, Y. Boutalis, and M. Lux. Img(rummager): An interactive content based image retrieval system. In *Similarity Search and Applications, 2009. SISAP '09. Second International Workshop on*, pages 151 –153, aug. 2009.

[13] G. P. Cheek and M. Shehab. Policy-by-example for online social networks. In *17th ACM Symposium on Access Control Models and Technologies, SACMAT '12*, pages 23–32, New York, NY, USA, 2012. ACM.

[14] H.-M. Chen, M.-H. Chang, P.-C. Chang, M.-C. Tien, W. H. Hsu, and J.-L. Wu. Sheepdog: group and tag recommendation for flickr photos by automatic search-based learning. In *MM '08: Proceeding of the 16th ACM international conference on Multimedia*, pages 737–740, New York, NY, USA, 2008. ACM.

[15] M. D. Choudhury, H. Sundaram, Y.-R. Lin, A. John, and D. D. Seligmann. Connecting content to community in social media via image content, user tags and user communication. In *Proceedings of the 2009 IEEE International Conference on Multimedia and Expo, ICME 2009*, pages 1238–1241. IEEE, 2009.

[16] R. da Silva Torres and A. Falcão. Content-based image retrieval: Theory and applications. *Revista de Informática Teórica e Aplicada*, 2(13):161–185, 2006.

[17] R. Datta, D. Joshi, J. Li, and J. Wang. Image retrieval: Ideas, influences, and trends of the new age. *ACM Computing Surveys (CSUR)*, 40(2):5, 2008.

[18] J. Deng, A. C. Berg, K. Li, and L. Fei-Fei. What does classifying more than 10,000 image categories tell us? In *Proceedings of the 11th European conference on Computer vision: Part V*, ECCV'10, pages 71–84, Berlin, Heidelberg, 2010. Springer-Verlag.

[19] L. Fang and K. LeFevre. Privacy wizards for social networking sites. In *Proceedings of the 19th international conference on World wide web*, WWW '10, pages 351–360, New York, NY, USA, 2010. ACM.

[20] J. He, W. W. Chu, and Z. Liu. Inferring privacy information from social networks. In *IEEE International Conference on Intelligence and Security Informatics*, 2006.

[21] X. He, W. Ma, O. King, M. Li, and H. Zhang. Learning and inferring a semantic space from user's relevance feedback for image retrieval. In *Proceedings of the tenth ACM international conference on Multimedia*, pages 343–346. ACM, 2002.

[22] K. J. Higgins. Social networks for patients stir privacy, security worries, 2010. Online at http://www.darkreading.com/authentication/167901072/security/privacy/227500908/social-networks-for-patients-stir-privacy-security-w html.

[23] S. Jones and E. O'Neill. Contextual dynamics of group-based sharing decisions. In *Proceedings of the SIGCHI Conference on Human Factors in Computing Systems*, CHI '11, pages 1777–1786. ACM, 2011.

[24] P. F. Klemperer, Y. Liang, M. L. Mazurek, M. Sleeper, B. Ur, L. Bauer, L. F. Cranor, N. Gupta, and M. K. Reiter. Tag, you can see it! Using tags for access control in photo sharing. In *CHI 2012: Conference on Human Factors in Computing Systems*. ACM, May 2012.

[25] K. Liu and E. Terzi. A framework for computing the privacy scores of users in online social networks. *ACM Trans. Knowl. Discov. Data*, 5:6:1–6:30, December 2010.

[26] D. Lowe. Distinctive image features from scale-invariant keypoints. *International journal of computer vision*, 60(2):91–110, 2004.

[27] D. G. Lowe. Distinctive image features from scale-invariant keypoints. *Int. J. Comput. Vision*, 60(2):91–110, Nov. 2004.

[28] A. D. Miller and W. K. Edwards. Give and take: a study of consumer photo-sharing culture and practice. In *CHI '07: SIGCHI conference on Human factors in computing systems*, pages 347–356, New York, NY, USA, 2007. ACM.

[29] W. W. Ng, A. Dorado, D. S. Yeung, W. Pedrycz, and E. Izquierdo. Image classification with the use of radial basis function neural networks and the minimization of the localized generalization error. *Pattern Recognition*, 40(1):19 – 32, 2007.

[30] A. Plangprasopchok and K. Lerman. Exploiting social annotation for automatic resource discovery. *CoRR*, abs/0704.1675, 2007.

[31] M. Rabbath, P. Sandhaus, and S. Boll. Automatic creation of photo books from stories in social media. *ACM Trans. Multimedia Comput. Commun. Appl.*, 7S(1):27:1–27:18, Nov. 2011.

[32] M. Rabbath, P. Sandhaus, and S. Boll. Analysing facebook features to support event detection for photo-based facebook applications. In *Proceedings of the 2nd ACM International Conference on Multimedia Retrieval*, ICMR '12, pages 11:1–11:8, New York, NY, USA, 2012. ACM.

[33] J. Read, B. Pfahringer, G. Holmes, and E. Frank. Classifier chains for multi-label classification, 2011.

[34] J. San Pedro and S. Siersdorfer. Ranking and classifying attractiveness of photos in folksonomies. In *Proceedings of the 18th international conference on World wide web*, WWW '09, pages 771–780, New York, NY, USA, 2009. ACM.

[35] N. Sawant. Modeling tagged photos for automatic image annotation. In *Proceedings of the 19th ACM international conference on Multimedia*, MM '11, pages 865–866, New York, NY, USA, 2011. ACM.

[36] N. Sawant, J. Li, and J. Z. Wang. Automatic image semantic interpretation using social action and tagging data. *Multimedia Tools Appl.*, 51(1):213–246, 2011.

[37] J. Sivic and A. Zisserman. Video google: A text retrieval approach to object matching in videos. In *Proc. of ICCV*, pages 1470–1477, 2003.

[38] A. C. Squicciarini, S. Sundareswaran, D. Lin, and J. Wede. A3P: adaptive policy prediction for shared images over popular content sharing sites. In *22nd ACM Conference on Hypertext and Hypermedia*, pages 261–270. ACM, 2011.

[39] X. Sun, H. Yao, R. Ji, and S. Liu. Photo assessment based on computational visual attention model. In *Proceedings of the 17th ACM international conference on Multimedia*, MM '09, pages 541–544, New York, NY, USA, 2009. ACM.

[40] H. Sundaram, L. Xie, M. De Choudhury, Y. Lin, and A. Natsev. Multimedia semantics: Interactions between content and community. *Proceedings of the IEEE*, 100(9):2737–2758, 2012.

[41] A. Vailaya, A. Jain, and H. J. Zhang. On image classification: City images vs. landscapes. *Pattern Recognition*, 31(12):1921 – 1935, 1998.

[42] N. Vyas, A. C. Squicciarini, C.-C. Chang, and D. Yao. Towards automatic privacy management in web 2.0 with semantic analysis on annotations. In *CollaborateCom*, pages 1–10, 2009.

[43] C. Wang, D. M. Blei, and F.-F. Li. Simultaneous image classification and annotation. In *Computer Society Conference on Computer Vision and Pattern Recognition (CVPR 2009)*, pages 1903–1910. IEEE, 2009.

[44] J. Yang, Y.-G. Jiang, A. G. Hauptmann, and C.-W. Ngo. Evaluating bag-of-visual-words representations in scene classification. In *Proc. of ACM Workshop on Multimedia Information Retrieval*, pages 197–206, 2007.

[45] C.-H. Yeh, Y.-C. Ho, B. A. Barsky, and M. Ouhyoung. Personalized photograph ranking and selection system. In *Proceedings of the international conference on Multimedia*, MM '10, pages 211–220, New York, NY, USA, 2010. ACM.

[46] C. Yeung, L. Kagal, N. Gibbins, and N. Shadbolt. Providing access control to online photo albums based on tags and linked data. *Social Semantic Web: Where Web*, 2, 2009.

[47] J. Yu, X. Jin, J. Han, and J. Luo. Social group suggestion from user image collections. In *Proceedings of the 19th international conference on World wide web*, WWW '10, pages 1215–1216, New York, NY, USA, 2010. ACM.

[48] J. Yu, D. Joshi, and J. Luo. Connecting people in photo-sharing sites by photo content and user annotations. In *Multimedia and Expo, 2009. ICME 2009. IEEE International Conference on*, pages 1464–1467. IEEE, 2009.

[49] S. Zerr, S. Siersdorfer, J. Hare, and E. Demidova. Privacy-aware image classification and search. In *Proceedings of the 35th international ACM SIGIR conference on Research and development in information retrieval*, SIGIR '12, pages 35–44, New York, NY, USA, 2012. ACM.

[50] N. Zheng, Q. Li, S. Liao, and L. Zhang. Which photo groups should I choose? a comparative study of recommendation algorithms in flickr. *J. Inf. Sci.*, 36:733–750, December 2010.

[51] J. Zhuang and S. C. H. Hoi. Non-parametric kernel ranking approach for social image retrieval. In *Proceedings of the ACM International Conference on Image and Video Retrieval*, CIVR '10, pages 26–33, New York, NY, USA, 2010. ACM.

Is Distrust the Negation of Trust?
The Value of Distrust in Social Media

Jiliang Tang, Xia Hu and Huan Liu
Computer Science and Engineering
Arizona State University
Tempe, AZ, USA
{Jiliang.Tang, Xia.Hu, Huan.Liu}@asu.edu

ABSTRACT

Trust plays an important role in helping online users collect reliable information, and has attracted increasing attention in recent years. We learn from social sciences that, as the conceptual counterpart of trust, distrust could be as important as trust. However, little work exists in studying distrust in social media. What is the relationship between trust and distrust? Can we directly apply methodologies from social sciences to study distrust in social media? In this paper, we design two computational tasks by leveraging data mining and machine learning techniques to enable the computational understanding of distrust with social media data. The first task is to predict distrust from only trust, and the second task is to predict trust with distrust. We conduct experiments in real-world social media data. The empirical results of the first task provide concrete evidence to answer the question, "is distrust the negation of trust?" while the results of the second task help us figure out how valuable the use of distrust in trust prediction.

Categories and Subject Descriptors

H3.3 [**Information Storage and Retrieval**]: Information Search and Retrieval—*Information filtering*

General Terms

Algorithms; Design; Experimentation

Keywords

Distrust; The Negation of Trust; A New Dimension of Trust; Added Value of Distrust

1. INTRODUCTION

The pervasion of social media produces a large amount of user generated data, which exacerbates the information overload problem. Trust, which provides information about from whom we should accept information and with whom we should share information [8], plays an important role in helping online users collect reliable information. Therefore trust is extensively studied in social media [36], which encourages many trust related applications such as trust-aware recommendation systems [8, 23], finding high-quality user generated content [21], and viral marketing [30].

Social scientists notice that distrust, the conceptual counterpart of trust, could be as important as trust [31, 18, 3]. For example, both trust and distrust help a decision maker reduce the uncertainty and vulnerability (i.e., risk) associated with decision consequences [3], and distrust may exert a more critical role than trust in consumer decisions [32, 27]. A fundamental problem about distrust is what the relation between trust and distrust is. Some social scientists suggest that distrust is the negation of trust and they are two ends of the same conceptual spectrum [31, 1, 13]. Their theories indicate that low trust is equivalent to high distrust; likewise, the absence of distrust means high trust, and outcomes of high (or low) trust would be identical to those of low (or high) distrust. An alternative understanding is that distrust is a new dimension of trust [18, 15]. There is no consensus answer about the question, which is still considered as the "darker" side of trust by some social scientists [24].

Distrust has attracted increasing attention from social sciences and social scientists investigate distrust from the perspectives of formation mechanisms and constructs [18, 3]. While little work exists in studying distrust in social media and understanding distrust with social media data faces unique challenges. Social media does not provide the necessary information for these perspectives sociologists ascribe in studying distrust, because more often than not, available social media data is from passive observation. This property of social media data not only determines that it is difficult to directly apply methodologies from social sciences but also suggests that we should understand distrust in social media from a new perspective.

In this paper, we study distrust in social media from the computational perspective. The significance of this study is two-fold. First, our work provides the first systematical understanding of distrust in social media. Second, we provide results in social media from the computational perspective, which is complementary to those from social sciences. We first investigate the properties of distrust, and then design two computational tasks by leveraging data mining and machine learning techniques to enable the understanding of distrust with social media data.

- *Task 1:* Predicting distrust from only trust, which is designed to seek an answer for the question of "is dis-

HT'14, September 1–4, 2014, Santiago, Chile.
Copyright 2014 ACM 978-1-4503-2954-5/14/09 ...$15.00.
http://dx.doi.org/10.1145/2631775.2631793 .

Table 1: Statistics of the Epinions.

# of Users	30,455
# of Trust Relations	363,773
# of Distrust Relations	46,196
# of Users Receiving Distrust	9,513
# of Users Creating Distrust	5,324
# of Items	89,270
# of Ratings	562,355
Avg of Rating Score	3.9053

trust the negation of trust?" The intuition of *Task 1* is if distrust is the negation of trust, evidence of low trust can indicate that of distrust, hence, distrust could be predicted by trust.

- *Task 2:* Predicting trust with distrust, which is designed to measure the value of distrust. The intuition of *Task 2* is if distrust has added value over trust, we can potentially predict trust better with distrust.

The rest of paper is organized as follows. Section 2 describes the dataset used in this study and investigates the properties of distrust. Section 3 introduces the details about the first task. We introduce the second task in Section 4. Section 5 presents experimental results and our observations. Section 6 briefly reviews related work. Section 7 concludes this study with future work.

2. PROPERTIES OF DISTRUST

The properties of trust are systematically and extensively studied, and some important properties include transitivity, asymmetry and correlation with similarity [6]. However, the properties of distrust are seldom studied in social media. Can we equally and conversely extend the properties of trust to distrust? In this section, we investigate the properties of distrust analogy to those of trust with real-world social media data.

Before investigations, we first introduce the dataset we used in this work. We collect a dataset from an online social media website Epinions [1] to study distrust. Epinions is a product review site where online users can rate various products with reviews, and establish both trust and distrust relations with other users. We preprocess the data by filtering users without any trust and distrust relations, and the statistics of the dataset are shown in Table 1.

We compute the number of trust and distrust relations each user receives and creates, and these distributions are shown in Figure 1. Note that "In-Trust", "Out-Trust", "In-Distrust" and "Out-Distrust" in the figure denote trust receiving, trust creating, distrust receiving and distrust creating, respectively. The distributions for both trust and distrust suggest a power-law-like distribution that is typical in social networks. With this dataset, we study the properties of distrust in the following subsections.

2.1 Transitivity

Transitivity is a primary property of trust and it describes that trust can be passed between people [13, 6]. For example, if user u_i trusts user u_j, and user u_j trusts user u_k, then transitivity indicates that with a high probability, user

[1] http://www.epinions.com/

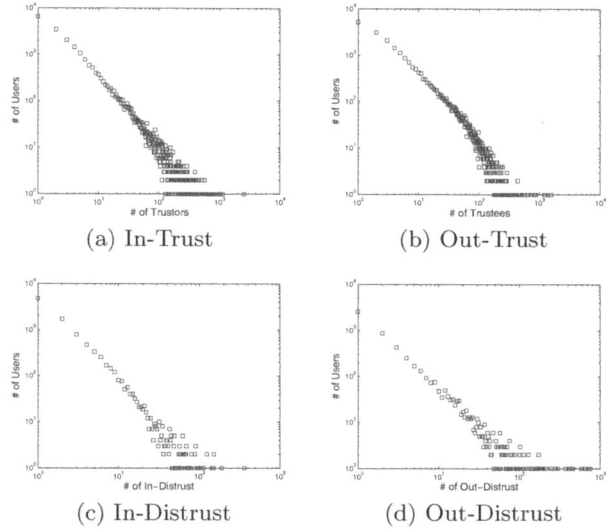

(a) In-Trust   (b) Out-Trust

(c) In-Distrust   (d) Out-Distrust

Figure 1: The Distributions of Trust and Distrust. Note that "In-Trust", "Out-Trust", "In-Distrust" and "Out-Distrust" in the figure denote trust receiving, trust creating, distrust receiving and distrust creating, respectively.

u_i will trust user u_k. In this subsection, we study the property of distrust with respect to transitivity. Note that in this paper, we use x+y, x-y, and x?y to denote the observations of a trust, a distrust and a missing relation from user x to user y, respectively.

To investigate the transitivity property of distrust, we first find all pairs of relations $\langle u_i\text{-}u_j, u_j\text{-}u_k \rangle$, and check whether u_i and u_k are with a trust (u_i+u_k), a distrust (u_i-u_k), or a missing relation ($u_i?u_k$). We conduct a similar process for trust, and the results are demonstrated in Table 3. For the first calculation, we consider all $\langle u_i, u_k \rangle$ pairs (i.e., u_i+u_k, u_i-u_k, and $u_i?u_k$) and use "P1" to denote the percentage of pairs of $\langle u_i, u_k \rangle$ with a trust, a distrust or a missing relation over all pairs. For the second calculation, we only consider $\langle u_i, u_k \rangle$ pairs with observed relations (i.e., trust u_i+u_k and distrust u_i-u_k), and adopt "P2" to represent the percentage of $\langle u_i, u_k \rangle$ with a trust or a distrust relation over pairs with observed relations (i.e., u_i+u_k and u_i-u_k). The results are shown in Table 3.

Golbeck suggests that trust is not perfectly transitive in the mathematical sense and is conditionally transitive [6], which is consistent with our observations - a trust relation u_i+u_k only takes 11.46% (P1) of all pairs of $\langle u_i, u_k \rangle$ for trust. However, among pairs with observed relations, u_i+u_k takes as high as 97.75% (P2), which suggests the transitivity property for trust - if u_i establishes a relation with u_k, it is likely to be a trust relation. For distrust, the percentages of u_i-u_k and u_i+u_k are comparable. u_i-u_k suggests transitivity, while u_i+u_k can be explained by balance theory [2, 12] as "the enemy of your enemy is your friend." These observations are consistent with two possible relations between u_i and u_k suggested by [10]. First, perhaps u_i has concluded that u_j's judgments are simply inferior to u_i's own, and u_j has concluded the same about u_k, therefore u_i

Table 2: Transitivity of Trust and Distrust.

Types		Number	P1	P2
Trust				
$\langle u_i + u_j, u_j + u_k \rangle$,	$u_i?u_k$	25,584,525	88.34%	N.A
$\langle u_i + u_j, u_j + u_k \rangle$,	$u_i + u_k$	3,320,991	11.46%	97.75%
$\langle u_i + u_j, u_j + u_k \rangle$,	$u_i - u_k$	76,613	0.2%	2.25%
Distrust				
$\langle u_i - u_j, u_j - u_k \rangle$,	$u_i?u_k$	716,340	91.70%	N.A
$\langle u_i - u_j, u_j - u_k \rangle$,	$u_i + u_k$	38,729	4.96%	59.73%
$\langle u_i - u_j, u_j - u_k \rangle$,	$u_i - u_k$	26,114	3.34%	40.27%

Table 3: Asymmetry of Trust and Distrust.

	$u_j + u_i(\%)$	$u_j - u_i(\%)$	$u_j?u_i(\%)$
$u_i + u_j$	136,806(37.61)	967(0.27)	226,000(62.13)
$u_i - u_j$	967(2.09)	2,623(5.86)	42,606(92.23)

should strongly distrust u_k as $u_i - u_k$. Second perhaps u_i is expressing the view that u_j's entire value model is so misaligned with u_i's that anyone u_j distrusts is more likely to be trusted by u_i as $u_i + u_k$.

2.2 Asymmetry

The asymmetry of trust is also important and suggests that for two people involved in a relation, trust is not necessarily identical in both directions [7]. For example, if u_i trusts u_j, one cannot infer that u_j trusts u_i. In this subsection, we examine the property of distrust in term of asymmetry.

For each trust relation $u_i + u_j$ (or each distrust relation $u_i - u_j$), we check the possible relations between u_j and u_i, and the results are shown in Table 3. Note that in Table 3 the numbers in parentheses are the percentages of the corresponding relations over all possible relations. We observe 37.71% mutual trust relations, but only 5.86% mutual distrust relations. These results suggest that trust is asymmetric, and distrust is even more asymmetric.

2.3 Correlation with Similarity

Siegler et al. pointed out that there is a strong and significant correlation between trust and similarity [40], and users with trust relations are more similar than those without. In this subsection, we study the similarities of pairs of users with distrust relations. In the context of Epinions, the similarity is calculated as the rating similarity and in this paper we calculate the similarity between u_i and u_j as the number of common items rated by both u_i and u_j. The average similarities for pairs with trust, pairs with distrust and randomly selected pairs are 0.6792, 0.4994 and 0.1247, respectively. Pairs with distrust relations are much more similar than randomly selected pairs, which suggests that distrust may be not a dissimilarity measurement. However, they have much low similarities than pairs with trust relations, which indicates that distrust may not be a similarity measurement as trust.

2.4 Discussion

Through this comparative study of properties of trust and distrust with respect to transitivity, asymmetry and correlation with similarity, we can conclude that the properties

of trust cannot be both equally and conversely extended to distrust. In the following two sections, we leverage data mining and machine learning techniques to design two tasks to enable the computational understanding of distrust with social media data. Before going to the following sections, we would like to first introduce notations used in this paper. Let $\mathcal{U} = \{u_1, u_2, \ldots, u_n\}$ be the user set where n is the number of users. We use $\mathbf{T} \in \mathbb{R}^{n \times n}$ to represent use-user trust relations where $\mathbf{T}_{ij} = 1$ if u_i trusts u_j, zero otherwise. Similarly, we use $\mathbf{D} \in \mathbb{R}^{n \times n}$ to denote user-user distrust relations where $\mathbf{D}_{ij} = 1$ if u_i distrusts u_j, zero otherwise.

3. DISTRUST PREDICTION WITH ONLY TRUST INFORMATION

Some social scientists, who believe distrust as the negation of trust, support that trust and distrust are two ends of the same conceptual spectrum, and distrust can be suggested by low trust [31, 1], which motivates us to design the first task of predicting distrust from only trust. The intuition behind this task is if distrust is the negation of trust, distrust can be suggested for pairs of users with low trust scores. Therefore *distrust prediction problem with only trust information boils down to the problem of predicting low trust with trust information.* Given the propagation of trust, the task of trust prediction is proposed to compute trust scores for any pairs of users in the same trust network [25]. Therefore trust scores of pairs of users in the same trust network can be obtained via trust prediction. For n users, there are totally n^2 pairs of users. Assume that N pairs of users have trust relations; while M pairs of users have distrust relations. The problem of *task 1* is formally stated as:

Given N pairs of users with trust relations, and a trust predictor f, we aim to predict M pairs of users with distrust relations from $n^2 - N$ pairs of users via low trust scores suggested by the trust predictor f.

If distrust is the negation of trust, pairs of users have distrust relations should have low trust among $n^2 - N$ pairs of users; otherwise, distrust is not the negation of trust. The framework of the first task *Task 1* is shown in Algorithm 1. Next we briefly review Algorithm 1. We first choose a trust prediction algorithm f to calculate trust scores for pairs of users without trust relations, and then suggest pairs with low trust scores to distrust. In this paper, we choose two representative trust prediction algorithms - trust propagation [10] and a matrix factorization based method [34] to calculate trust scores.

Algorithm 1 The framework of *Task 1* to predict distrust from only trust

---

Input: User-user trust relation matrix $\mathbf{T}$, a trust prediction algorithm f

Output: Ranking list of pairs of users

1: **for** Each pair of users without trust relations $\langle u_i, u_j \rangle$ **do**
2:     Calculate the score of $\tilde{\mathbf{T}}_{ij}$ that u_i trusts u_j by f
3: **end for**
4: Ranking pairs of users (e.g., $\langle u_i, u_j \rangle$) according to $\tilde{\mathbf{T}}_{ij}$ in an ascending order.

3.1 Trust propagation

In [10], a trust propagation framework is proposed with four atomic propagations - direct propagation, co-citation, transpose trust, and trust coupling as:

- if u_i trusts u_j, and u_j trusts u_k, direct propagation allows us to infer that u_i trusts u_k, and its corresponding operator is $\mathbf{T}$;

- co-citation propagation concludes that u_ℓ should trust u_j if u_i trusts u_j and u_k, and u_ℓ trusts u_k. $\mathbf{T}^\top \mathbf{T}$ is the operator of co-citation propagation;

- in transpose trust, u_i's trust of u_j causes u_j to develop some level of trust towards u_i, and its operator is $\mathbf{T}^\top$;

- trust coupling suggests that u_i and u_j trust u_k, so trusting u_i should imply trusting u_j. $\mathbf{T}\mathbf{T}^\top$ is its operator.

$\mathbf{C}$ is defined as a single combined matrix of all four atomic propagations,

$$\mathbf{C} = \alpha_1 \mathbf{T} + \alpha_2 \mathbf{T}^\top \mathbf{T} + \alpha_3 \mathbf{T}^\top + \alpha_4 \mathbf{T}\mathbf{T}^\top, \qquad (1)$$

where α_1, α_2, α_3, and α_4 control contributions from direct propagation, co-citation, transpose trust and trust coupling, respectively.

Let $\mathbf{C}^k$ be a matrix where $\mathbf{C}^k_{ij}$ denotes the propagation from u_i to u_j after k atomic propagations, and the final estimated matrix representation of the user-user trust relation $\tilde{\mathbf{T}}$ is given by [10],

$$\tilde{\mathbf{T}} = \sum_{k=1}^{K} \gamma^k \mathbf{C}^k \qquad (2)$$

where K is the number of steps of propagation and γ^k is a discount factor to penalize lengthy propagation steps.

3.2 Matrix factorization based method

The low-rank matrix factorization method is widely employed in various applications such as collective filtering [14, 35] and document clustering [39, 5]. A few factors can influence the establishment of trust relations and a user usually establishes trust relations with a small proportion of $\mathcal{U}$, resulting in very sparse and low-rank $\mathbf{T}$; hence, users can have a more compact but accurate representation in a low-rank space [34]. The matrix factorization model seeks a low-rank representation $\mathbf{U} \in \mathbb{R}^{n \times d}$ with $d \ll n$ for $\mathcal{U}$ via solving the following optimization problem,

$$\min_{\mathbf{U}, \mathbf{V}} \quad \|\mathbf{T} - \mathbf{U}\mathbf{V}\mathbf{U}^\top\|_F^2, \qquad (3)$$

where $\|\cdot\|_F$ is the Frobenius norm of a matrix and $\mathbf{V} \in \mathbb{R}^{d \times d}$ captures the correlations among their low-rank representations such as $\mathbf{T}_{ij} = \mathbf{U}_i \mathbf{V} \mathbf{U}_j^\top$. It is easy to verify that Eq. (3) can model the properties of trust such as transitivity and asymmetry [34]. For example, the learned $\mathbf{V}$ is asymmetric, therefore $\mathbf{T}_{ij} = \mathbf{U}_i \mathbf{V} \mathbf{U}_j^\top$ could be unequal to $\mathbf{T}_{ji} = \mathbf{U}_j \mathbf{V} \mathbf{U}_i^\top$.

To avoid over-fitting, we add two smoothness regularizations on $\mathbf{U}$ and $\mathbf{V}$, respectively, into Eq. (3), and then we have,

$$\min_{\mathbf{U}, \mathbf{V}} \quad \|\mathbf{T} - \mathbf{U}\mathbf{V}\mathbf{U}^\top\|_F^2 + \alpha\|\mathbf{U}\|_F^2 + \beta\|\mathbf{V}\|_F^2, \qquad (4)$$

where α and β are non-negative, and are introduced to control the capability of $\mathbf{U}$ and $\mathbf{V}$, respectively. With the learned $\mathbf{U}$ and $\mathbf{V}$, the estimated matrix representation of the user-user trust relation $\tilde{\mathbf{T}}$ is obtained as $\tilde{\mathbf{T}} = \mathbf{U}\mathbf{V}\mathbf{U}^\top$.

4. TRUST PREDICTION WITH DISTRUST INFORMATION

An alternative understanding is that distrust is a new dimension of trust rather than the negation of trust [18, 15]. If distrust is a new dimension of trust, distrust should provide extra information about users, and have potentially added value beyond trust. This intuition motivates us to design the second task to measure the value of distrust. The second task *Task 2* is to predict trust relations among users with distrust information. If distrust has added value over trust, we should predict trust better with distrust information. Assume that $\mathcal{E}$ is the set of pairs of users creating new trust relations after N pairs of users, and then *task 2* is formally stated as,

Given N pairs of users with trust relations, and M pairs of users with distrust relations, we aim to suggest new trust relations to $|\mathcal{E}|$ pairs of users by using information of both N trust relations and M distrust relations.

If distrust is a new dimension of trust and has added value about users beyond trust, using both N trust relations and M distrust relations should obtain better performance than only using N trust relations. Next we will investigate how to exploit distrust in the previously mentioned trust prediction algorithms - trust propagation and the matrix factorization based method.

4.1 Trust propagation with distrust information

The propagation of distrust has attracted increasing attention recently, and two distrust propagation mechanisms are widely investigated [42, 10]. One mechanism assumes that trust and distrust both propagate together, and the single combined matrix of all atomic propagations is defined as,

$$\mathbf{E} = \alpha_1 \mathbf{F} + \alpha_2 \mathbf{F}^\top \mathbf{F} + \alpha_3 \mathbf{F}^\top + \alpha_4 \mathbf{F}\mathbf{F}^\top, \qquad (5)$$

where $\mathbf{F} = \mathbf{T} - \mathbf{D}$ and the estimated user-user trust matrix $\tilde{\mathbf{G}}$ is obtained similarly to Eq. (2) as,

$$\tilde{\mathbf{G}} = \sum_{k=1}^{K} \gamma^k \mathbf{E}^k. \qquad (6)$$

The other assumes if u_i distrusts u_j, u_i will discount all judgments made by u_j, hence, distrust propagates only a single step instead of propagating repeatedly as trust. Under this mechanism, the estimated user-user trust matrix $\tilde{\mathbf{G}}$ is computed as [10],

$$\tilde{\mathbf{G}} = \sum_{k=1}^{K} \gamma^k \mathbf{C}^k (\mathbf{T} - \mathbf{D}) \qquad (7)$$

4.2 The matrix factorization based method with distrust information

A straightforward way to incorporate distrust into the matrix factorization based method is to replace $\mathbf{T}$ in Eq. (4)

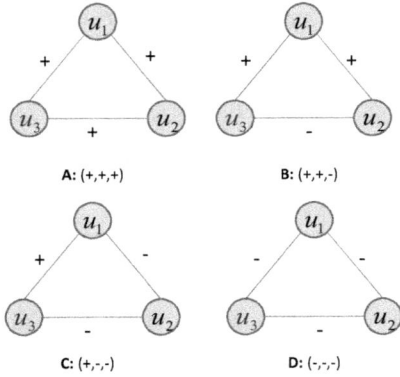

Figure 2: An Illustration of Balance Theory.

with $\mathbf{F} = \mathbf{T} - \mathbf{D}$ as,

$$\min_{\mathbf{U},\mathbf{V}} \quad \|\mathbf{F} - \mathbf{U}\mathbf{V}\mathbf{U}^\top\|_F^2 + \alpha\|\mathbf{U}\|_F^2 + \beta\|\mathbf{V}\|_F^2, \qquad (8)$$

where $\mathbf{F}_{ij}$ is modeled as

$$\mathbf{F}_{ij} = \mathbf{U}_i\mathbf{V}\mathbf{U}_j^\top. \qquad (9)$$

As mentioned above, balance theory paves a way to understand the formation of trust and distrust, and prediction accuracy may be improved by exploiting balance theory. For example, in [17], local-topology-based features based on balance theory are extracted to improve the performance of a logistic regression classifier in signed relation prediction. Next we will investigate how to exploit balance theory under the matrix factorization framework. Note that balance theory is proposed for undirected networks and following a common practice [17], we ignore the directions of relations, and only consider the signs of relations (i.e., trust and distrust) when modeling balance theory.

We use s_{ij} to denote the sign of the relation between u_i and u_j where $s_{ij} = 1$ (or $s_{ij} = -1$) if we observe a trust relation (or a distrust relation) between u_i and u_j. With these notations, balance theory suggests that a triad $\langle u_i, u_j, u_k \rangle$ is balanced if

- $s_{ij} = 1$ and $s_{jk} = 1$, then $s_{ik} = 1$; or

- $s_{ij} = -1$ and $s_{jk} = -1$, then $s_{ik} = 1$.

For a triad $\langle u_i, u_j, u_k \rangle$, there are four possible sign combinations $\mathbf{A}$(+,+,+), $\mathbf{B}$(+,+,-) $\mathbf{C}$(+,-,-) and $\mathbf{D}$(-,-,-) as shown in Figure 2. According to balance theory, only $\mathbf{A}$(+,+,+) and $\mathbf{C}$(+,-,-) are balanced.

There are three major ways to exploit social theories in social media mining including feature engineering, constraint generating, and objective defining [33]. In this work, we choose objective defining to model balance theory. For each user u_i, we introduce a one-dimensional latent factor r_i and we further assume that the trust relation between u_i and u_j due to the effect of balance theory is captured as [37],

$$\mathbf{F}_{ij} = r_i r_j, \qquad (10)$$

It is easy to verify that Eq. (10) can capture balance theory. Combining Eq. (9) and Eq. (10), $\mathbf{F}_{ij}$ can be modeled as

$$\mathbf{F}_{ij} = \mathbf{U}_i\mathbf{V}\mathbf{U}_j^\top + \lambda r_i r_j, \qquad (11)$$

which exploits balance theory under the matrix factorization framework. The parameter λ is introduced to control the contributions from balance theory.

The proposed framework disMF is to solve the following optimization problem,

$$\min_{\mathbf{U},\mathbf{V},\mathbf{r}} \quad \|\mathbf{F} - \mathbf{U}\mathbf{V}\mathbf{U}^\top - \lambda\mathbf{r}\mathbf{r}^\top\|_F^2$$
$$+ \alpha\|\mathbf{U}\|_F^2 + \beta\|\mathbf{V}\|_F^2 + \eta\|\mathbf{r}\|_2^2, \qquad (12)$$

where $\mathbf{r} = [r_1, r_2, \ldots, r_n]^\top$ and the term $\|\mathbf{r}\|_2^2$ is introduced to avoid overfitting. A local minimum of Eq. (12) can be obtained through a gradient decent optimization method.

5. EXPERIMENTS

In this section, we conduct experiments to answer the following questions - (1) is distrust the negation of trust? and (2) does distrust have added value in trust prediction? To answer the first question, we check how accurately we can predict distrust from only trust by evaluating *Task 1*. To answer the second question, we examine whether the performance of trust prediction is improved by exploiting distrust by evaluating *Task 2*. Finally we further probe the effects of distrust in disMF to seek a deep understanding of the value of distrust in trust prediction. Since most of trust prediction algorithms such as trust prediction and matrix factorization methods cannot work well with users with very few trust relations, we further filter users with less than three trust relations and finally we obtain a dataset with $12,353$ users, $322,040$ trust relations and $41,253$ distrust relations for the following evaluations.

5.1 Evaluation of *Task 1*

We first introduce the experimental setting for this evaluation. $\mathcal{A}_T = \{\langle u_i, u_j \rangle | \mathbf{T}_{ij} = 1\}$ is the set of pairs of users with trust relations, and $\mathcal{A}_D = \{\langle u_i, u_j \rangle | \mathbf{D}_{ij} = 1\}$ is the set of pairs of users with distrust relations. The pairs in both $\mathcal{A}_T$ and $\mathcal{A}_D$ are sorted in chronological order in terms of the time when they established relations. We assume that until time t, $x\%$ of pairs in $\mathcal{A}_T$ establish trust relations, denoted as $\mathcal{A}_T^x$, and we use $\mathcal{A}_D^x$ to denote pairs of users in $\mathcal{A}_D$ establishing distrust until time t. x is varied as $\{50, 55, 60, 65, 70, 80, 90, 100\}$. For each x, we repeat the experiments for 10 times and report the average performance since most of predictors can only obtain local optimal solutions. The experimental setting is demonstrated in Figure 3 where N_T^x denotes the set of pairs without trust relations at the time t.

For each x, *Task 1* is to use $\mathcal{A}_T^x$ to predict $\mathcal{A}_D^x$ from N_T^x. We follow the common metric for trust evaluation in [19, 34] to assess the prediction performance. In detail, each predictor ranks pairs in N_T^x in **ascending** order of confidence and we take the first $|\mathcal{A}_D^x|$ pairs as the set of predicted distrust relations, denoting $\mathcal{A}_D^p$. Then the performance of *Task 1* is computed as,

$$M_1 = \frac{|\mathcal{A}_D^x \cap \mathcal{A}_D^p|}{|\mathcal{A}_D^x|} \qquad (13)$$

where $|\cdot|$ denotes the size of a set. The results are shown in the Table 4. "dTP", "dMF", and "dTP-MF" and "Random" in the table are defined as follows:

- *dTP:* this distrust predictor uses the trust propagation algorithm to obtain trust scores for pairs of users and

Table 4: Performance of Different Predictors for *Task 1*. **The magnitude of all numbers in the table is** 10^{-5}.

x (%)	dTP ($\times 10^{-5}$)	dMF($\times 10^{-5}$)	dTP-MF($\times 10^{-5}$)	Random($\times 10^{-5}$)
50	4.8941	4.8941	4.8941	5.6824
55	5.6236	5.6236	5.6236	8.1182
60	7.1885	7.1885	7.1885	15.814
65	11.985	11.985	11.985	19.717
70	13.532	13.532	13.532	18.826
80	10.844	10.844	10.844	16.266
90	12.720	12.720	12.720	25.457
100	14.237	14.237	14.237	29.904

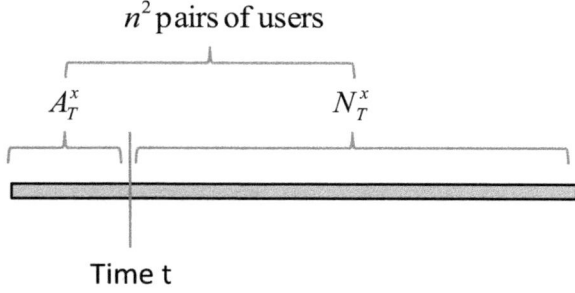

n^2 pairs of users

A_T^x N_T^x

Time t

Figure 3: Experimental Settings for the Evaluation of *Task 1*.

then suggests distrust relations for pairs with low trust scores;

- *dMF*: this distrust predictor adopts the matrix factorization algorithm to compute trust scores for pairs of users and then predict pairs with low trust scores as distrust relations;

- *dTP-MF*: this distrust predictor combines trust scores inferred by dTP and dMF to infer distrust relations; and

- *Random*: this distrust predictor randomly guesses pairs of users with distrust relations.

All parameters in above predictors are determined through cross-validation and the magnitude of all numbers in the table is 10^{-5}.

If distrust is the negation of trust, low trust scores should accurately indicate distrust. However, we observe that the performance of dTP, dMF and dTP-MF is consistently worse than that of the randomly guessing (Random). These results suggest that low trust scores cannot be used to predict distrust; hence distrust is not the negation of trust. Social scientists, who support distrust as a new dimension of trust, argue that pairs of users with untrust can have very low trust scores [24, 9]. This phenomenon is especially true with social media data since users in social media are world-widely distributed and many pairs of users in the trust network do not know each other. As mentioned above, $\mathcal{A}_D^x$ is the set of pairs of users who have distrust relations as ground truth, while $\mathcal{A}_D^p$ is the set of pairs who are predicted with distrust relations (or with low trust scores). The low accuracies in Table 4 also suggest that pairs of users in $\mathcal{A}_D^p$ may also have low distrust.

Let us further examine trust scores for users in $\mathcal{A}_D^x$ and $\mathcal{A}_D^p$ when $x = 70$, since we have similar observations for other values of x. We use $\mathbf{t}_x$ and $\mathbf{t}_p$ to represent the trust score vectors of $\mathcal{A}_D^x$ and $\mathcal{A}_D^p$, respectively. We find that the mean of $\mathbf{t}_x$ 0.0149 is much larger than that of $\mathbf{t}_p$ 5.8634e-7 and its significance is also confirmed by the t-test. These results suggest that pairs of users with distrust relations (or in $\mathcal{A}_D^x$) are unnecessary to have low trust scores.

To sum up, pairs of users with distrust relations are not necessary to have low trust scores and pairs with low trust are not necessary to have distrust relations. These results show strong evidence that using low trust scores fails to predict distrust, and suggest that distrust is not the negation of trust in social media, which correspondingly answer the first question.

5.2 Evaluation of *Task 2*

Before going to the detailed evaluation, we first introduce the experimental setting for this evaluation. We use $\mathcal{O} = \{\langle u_i, u_j \rangle | \mathbf{T}_{ij} \neq 1\}$ to denote the set of pairs of users without trust relations. We choose $x\%$ of $\mathcal{A}_T$ as old trust relations $\mathcal{A}_T^x$, and the remaining $1 - x\%$ as new trust relations $\mathcal{A}_T^n$ to predict. We assume that the last pair of users establishes a trust relation at time t, and we use $\mathcal{A}_D^x$ to denote pairs of users in $\mathcal{A}_D$ establishing distrust until time t. In this paper, we vary x as $\{50, 55, 60, 65, 70, 80, 90\}$. For each x, we also repeat the experiments 10 times and report the average performance. The experimental setting is illustrated in Figure 5 where N_T^x denotes the set of pairs without trust relations at time t.

For each x, *Task 2* uses old trust relations $\mathcal{A}_T^x$ and distrust relations $\mathcal{A}_D^x$ to predict new trust relations $\mathcal{A}_T^n$. We follow a similar evaluation metric for *Task 1* to assess *Task 2*. In particular, each predictor ranks pairs in N_T^x in **decreasing** order of confidence and we take the first $|\mathcal{A}_T^n|$ pairs as the set of predicted trust relations, denoting as $\mathcal{A}_T^p$. Then the performance of *Task 2* is computed as,

$$M_2 = \frac{|\mathcal{A}_T^n \cap \mathcal{A}_T^p|}{|\mathcal{A}_T^n|} \quad (14)$$

We use disTP-m and disTP-s to denote performing multiple steps and a single step distrust propagation in trust propagation (TP), and their comparison results are shown in Figure 4. disMF incorporates distrust into the matrix factorization method (MF) framework, and their comparison results are demonstrated in Figure 6. Parameters for all methods are determined via cross validation. Note that "Random" in figures denotes the performance of randomly guessing.

153

	50%	55%	60%	65%	70%	80%	90%
TP	**0.1376**	0.1354	0.1293	0.1264	0.1201	0.1156	0.1098
disTP-s	**0.1435**	0.1418	0.1372	0.1359	0.1296	0.1207	0.1176
disTP-m	**0.1422**	0.1398	0.1359	0.1355	0.1279	0.1207	0.1173
Random	**0.0023**	0.0023	0.0020	0.0019	0.0018	0.0015	0.0013

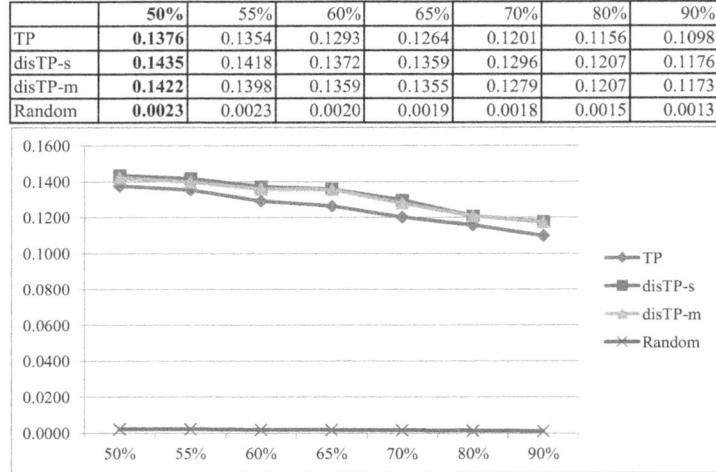

Figure 4: Performance Comparison for Trust Propagation without and with Distrust. The prediction problem becomes more difficult from 50% to 90%.

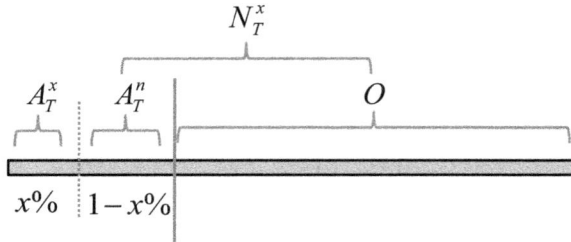

Figure 5: Experimental Setting for the Evaluation of *Task 2*.

Let us first examine the performance comparisons when $x = 50$, which are highlighted in Figure 4 and Figure 6. We make the following observations:

- For the first column results in Figure 4, both disTP-s and disTP-m outperform TP. For example, disTP-s obtains 4.28% relative improvement compared to TP. disTP-s and disTP-m incorporate distrust propagation in the trust propagation, and the improvement is from the distrust propagation. These results support that distrust can improve trust propagation and leads to the performance gain in trust prediction. We also note that most of the time, disTP-s with one-step distrust propagation outperforms disTP-m with multiple step distrust propagation.

- For the first column results in Figure 6, disMF obtains better performance than MF, and gains 8.55% relative improvement over MF. There are two major contributors - (1) factorizing both trust and distrust instead of only trust as MF; and (2) modeling balance theory. We will further investigate the effects of distrust in disMF in the following subsection.

For other values of x, we can have similar observations - distrust can improve the performance of trust prediction.

For example, on average, disTP-s and disMF obtain 6.01% and 10.78% relative improvement over TP and MF, respectively. We also note that with the increase x, the performance of all methods reduces. With the increase of x, the size of $\mathcal{A}_T^n$ $1 - x\%$ decreases. Since the size of $\mathcal{O}$ is fixed, it becomes more and more difficult to predict $\mathcal{A}_T^n$, which is buried in $\mathcal{O}$. This observation is consistent with that in [34].

We perform t-test on all improvement above and the t-test results suggest that all improvement is significant. With the help of distrust, *Task 2* can significantly improve the performance of trust prediction, which supports a positive answer to the second question - distrust has added value over trust. For disTP-s and disTP-m, the improvement is from integrating distrust propagation into trust propagation. While for disMF, there are major two contributors to the improvement - (1) incorporating distrust into trust during the factorization process; (2) capturing balance theory. In the following subsection, we will investigate the effects of these two components on disMF.

5.3 Effects of Distrust in disMF

There are two components in disMF to exploit distrust for disMF. The parameter λ controls their contributions. For example, we can eliminate the effect for the component of balance theory by setting $\lambda = 0$. Therefore we investigate the effects of distrust in disMF by analyzing how the changes of λ affect the performance of disMF. The value of λ is varied as $\{0, 0.001, 0.01, 0.1, 0.5, 1, 5, 10, 100\}$, and the results are depicted in Figure 7. In general, the performance first increases, and then degrades rapidly. In particular, it can be observed,

- when λ is equal to 0, we eliminate the effect of the component of balance theory, and then the only difference between MF and disMF is that disMF is also factorized with distrust in addition to trust. The performance comparison of MF and disMF with $\lambda = 0$ is shown in Table 5. Note that "Imp" denotes the relative performance improvement of disMF with different values of λ compared to "MF". disMF can significantly

	50%	55%	60%	65%	70%	80%	90%
MF	**0.1531**	0.1502	0.1489	0.1444	0.1391	0.1332	0.1277
disMF	**0.1665**	0.1654	0.1639	0.1601	0.1563	0.1498	0.1415
Random	**0.0023**	0.0023	0.0020	0.0019	0.0018	0.0015	0.0013

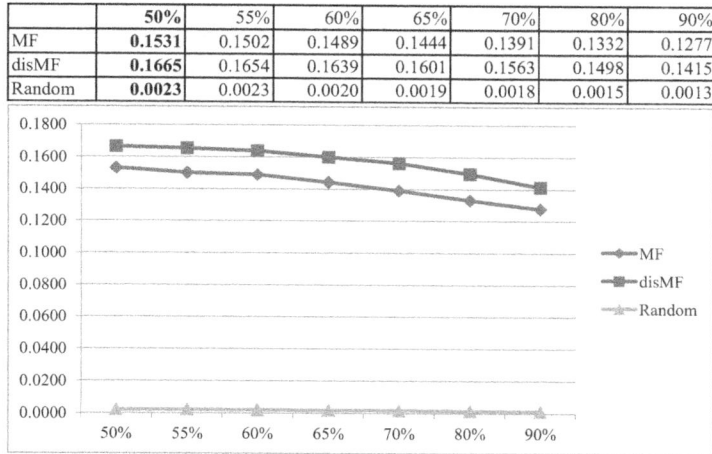

Figure 6: Performance Comparison for the Matrix Factorization based Method without and with Distrust. The prediction problem becomes more difficult from 50% to 90%.

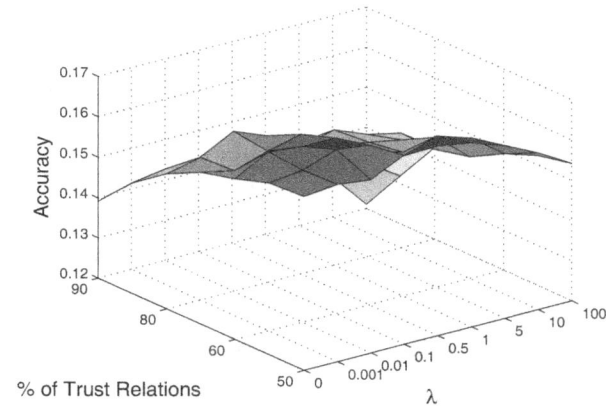

Figure 7: The Effects of Distrust in disMF.

improve the performance of MF by performing factorization on both trust and distrust.

- when λ is increased from 0 to 0.1, the performance improves and details are shown in Table 5, suggesting that the balance theory component for distrust can also improve the performance of trust prediction.

- from $\lambda = 5$ to $\lambda = 100$, the performance decreases rapidly. When λ is very large, balance theory dominates, which will lead to inaccurate estimations of parameters.

In conclusion, by simply adding distrust in the factorization process, disMF ($\lambda = 0$) significantly improves the performance of MF, which can be further improved by modeling balance theory for distrust.

6. RELATED WORK

In social sciences, the conceptual counterpart of trust, distrust, is considered as important and complex as trust [27, 16, 11, 4]. For example, [32, 3] claim that trust and distrust help a decision maker reduce uncertainty and vulnerability (i.e., risk) associated with decision consequences; and [4] indicates that only distrust can irrevocably exclude services from being selected at all. There is an enduring problem about distrust - what is the relation between trust and distrust. Answering this question has its significance. If trust and distrust are the same, lack of distrust research matters little; however, if they are different, the lack of distrust research could be problematic because distrust may have unique impact. Some researchers believe distrust simply means a low level of trust, hence evidence of high trust was always regarded as being that of low distrust, and outcomes of high trust would be identical to those of low distrust [31, 1, 13]. Others believe distrust is a concept entirely separate from trust [18, 15]. Therefore distrust and trust can coexist, and they have different antecedents and consequents [28]. For example, in [18], three reasons are proposed to prove that trust and distrust are separate - (1) they separate empirically; (2) they coexist; and (3) they have different antecedents and consequents. There is still no consensus answer about this problem, and some social scientists consider distrust as the "darker" side of trust [24].

The notion of trust is extensively studied in the online world [36]. The connection between user similarity (such as ratings of movies) and trust is investigated in [40]. A strong and significant correlation is suggested between trust and similarity. The more similar two people are, the greater the trust between them is. A formal framework of trust propagation schemes is developed [10]. By separating trust and distrust matrix, the framework performs operations on them to obtain the transitive trust between two nodes. [29] proposes a method to model and compute the bias or the truthfulness of a user in trust networks, and shows that there are users who have a propensity to trust/distrust other users. In [20], a classification approach is proposed to predict if a user trusts another user using features derived from his/her

Table 5: Performance Comparison. Note that "Imp" denotes the relative performance improvement of disMF with different values of λ compared to "MF".

x (%)	MF (Imp)	disMF ($\lambda = 0$)(Imp)	disMF($\lambda = 0.1$) (Imp)
50	0.1531	0.1614 (+5.42%)	0.1665 (+8.75%)
55	0.1502	0.1610 (+7.19%)	0.1654 (+10.12%)
60	0.1489	0.1600 (+7.45%)	0.1639 (+10.07%)
65	0.1444	0.1557 (+7.83%)	0.1601 (+10.87%)
70	0.1391	0.1525 (+9.63%)	0.1563 (+12.37%)
80	0.1332	0.1465 (+9.98%)	0.1498 (+12.46%)
90	0.1277	0.1381 (+8.14%)	0.1415 (+10.81%)

interactions with the latter as well as from the interactions with other users. The development of trust in social media also encourages many trust online applications. In [22], several approaches are studied to exploit trust networks in recommender systems. The bidirectional effects between trust relations and product ratings are investigated and modeled in [26]. Trust relations are also modeled to help review quality prediction [21].

7. CONCLUSION

As informed by social sciences, distrust could be as important as trust. A fundamental problem about distrust is what the relation between trust and distrust is. Passive observation is the modus operandi to obtain social media data, which lacks necessary information to apply methodologies from social sciences to understand distrust. However, an understanding of distrust with social media data is necessary because if distrust is the negation of trust, lacking distrust study matters little; while if distrust is a new dimension of trust, ignoring distrust in trust study may yield an incomplete and biased estimate of the effects of trust. In this paper, we first investigate the properties of distrust and find that we cannot equally and conversely extend the properties of trust to distrust. Then we then design two tasks by leveraging data mining and machine learning techniques to enable a computational understanding of distrust with social media data. The first task is to predict distrust with only trust information, and the second task is to predict trust with distrust information. We conduct experiments in real-world social media data. The evaluations of the first task suggests that distrust is not the negation of trust, while the results of the second task reveal that distrust has added value over trust.

The computational understanding of distrust in this paper suggests that it is necessary to study distrust in social media and more investigations are needed. First, as suggested by psychology, distrust is an "unwanted" property for online communities and distrust mechanism is rarely implemented by social media services, therefore distrust information is publicly unavailable and we would like to address the data challenge for distrust study. Second, the major computational tasks for trust are well defined including representing trust, measuring trust and applying trust, however, we lack systematical definitions of computational tasks for distrust in social media, and hence we will formally define major computational tasks for distrust. Finally trust information is widely exploited to improve various online applications such as recommender systems, spammer detection, finding high-quality user generated content and viral marketing and

distrust has added value on trust, therefore we will investigate how to exploit distrust to facilitate these applications.

Acknowledgments

The work is, in part, supported by Army Research Office (#025071) and The Office of Naval Research (N000141410095).

8. REFERENCES

[1] B. Barber. *The logic and limits of trust.* Rutgers University Press New Brunswick, NJ, 1983.

[2] D. Cartwright and F. Harary. Structural balance: a generalization of heider's theory. *Psychological Review*, 63(5):277, 1956.

[3] J. Cho. The mechanism of trust and distrust formation and their relational outcomes. *Journal of Retailing*, 82(1):25–35, 2006.

[4] P. Cofta. Distrust. In *ICEC*. ACM, 2006.

[5] C. Ding, T. Li, and M. Jordan. Nonnegative matrix factorization for combinatorial optimization: Spectral clustering, graph matching, and clique finding. In *Data Mining, 2008. ICDM'08. Eighth IEEE International Conference on*, pages 183–192. Ieee, 2008.

[6] J. Golbeck. Computing and applying trust in web-based social networks. *Ph.D. dissertation*, 2005.

[7] J. Golbeck. *Computing with social trust.* Springer Publishing Company, Incorporated, 2008.

[8] J. Golbeck. Trust and nuanced profile similarity in online social networks. *ACM Transactions on the Web*, 3(4):1–33, 2009.

[9] N. Griffiths. A fuzzy approach to reasoning with trust, distrust and insufficient trust. In *Cooperative Information Agents X*, pages 360–374. Springer, 2006.

[10] R. Guha, R. Kumar, P. Raghavan, and A. Tomkins. Propagation of trust and distrust. In *Proceedings of the 13th international conference on World Wide Web*, pages 403–412. ACM, 2004.

[11] R. Hardin. *Distrust: Manifestations and management.* Russell Sage Foundation, 2004.

[12] F. Heider. Attitudes and cognitive organization. *The Journal of psychology*, 1946.

[13] A. Josang, E. Gray, and M. Kinateder. Analysing topologies of transitive trust. In *Proc. of the 1st workshop on Formal Aspects in Security and Trust (FAST2003)*, 2003.

[14] Y. Koren. Factorization meets the neighborhood: a multifaceted collaborative filtering model. In *Proceeding of the 14th ACM SIGKDD international*

conference on Knowledge discovery and data mining, pages 426–434. ACM, 2008.

[15] R. M. Kramer. Trust and distrust in organizations: Emerging perspectives, enduring questions. *Annual review of psychology*, 50(1):569–598, 1999.

[16] D. W. Larson and R. Hardin. Distrust: Prudent, if not always wise. *Distrust*, pages 34–59, 2004.

[17] J. Leskovec, D. Huttenlocher, and J. Kleinberg. Predicting positive and negative links in online social networks. In *Proceedings of the 19th international conference on World wide web*, 2010.

[18] R. J. Lewicki, D. J. McAllister, and R. J. Bies. Trust and distrust: New relationships and realities. *Academy of management Review*, 23(3):438–458, 1998.

[19] D. Liben-Nowell and J. Kleinberg. The link-prediction problem for social networks. *Journal of the American society for information science and technology*, 58(7):1019–1031, 2007.

[20] H. Liu, E. Lim, H. Lauw, M. Le, A. Sun, J. Srivastava, and Y. Kim. Predicting trusts among users of online communities: an epinions case study. In *Proceedings of the 9th ACM Conference on Electronic Commerce*, pages 310–319. ACM, 2008.

[21] Y. Lu, P. Tsaparas, A. Ntoulas, and L. Polanyi. Exploiting social context for review quality prediction. In *Proceedings of the 19th international conference on World wide web*, pages 691–700. ACM, 2010.

[22] H. Ma, H. Yang, M. Lyu, and I. King. Sorec: social recommendation using probabilistic matrix factorization. In *Proceeding of the 17th ACM conference on Information and knowledge management*, pages 931–940. ACM, 2008.

[23] H. Ma, D. Zhou, C. Liu, M. Lyu, and I. King. Recommender systems with social regularization. In *Proceedings of the fourth ACM international conference on Web search and data mining*, pages 287–296. ACM, 2011.

[24] S. Marsh and M. R. Dibben. Trust, untrust, distrust and mistrust–an exploration of the dark (er) side. In *Trust Management*, pages 17–33. Springer, 2005.

[25] P. Massa and P. Avesani. Controversial users demand local trust metrics: An experimental study on epinions. com community. In *Proceedings of the National Conference on artificial Intelligence*, volume 20, page 121. Menlo Park, CA; Cambridge, MA; London; AAAI Press; MIT Press; 1999, 2005.

[26] Y. Matsuo and H. Yamamoto. Community gravity: measuring bidirectional effects by trust and rating on online social networks. In *Proceedings of the 18th international conference on World wide web*, pages 751–760. ACM, 2009.

[27] D. H. McKnight and N. L. Chervany. Trust and distrust definitions: One bite at a time. In *Trust in Cyber-societies*, pages 27–54. Springer, 2001.

[28] D. H. McKnight and V. Choudhury. Distrust and trust in b2c e-commerce: Do they differ? In *ICEC*, pages 482–491. ACM, 2006.

[29] A. Mishra and A. Bhattacharya. Finding the bias and prestige of nodes in networks based on trust scores. In *Proceedings of the 20th international conference on World wide web*, pages 567–576. ACM, 2011.

[30] M. Richardson and P. Domingos. Mining knowledge-sharing sites for viral marketing. In *Proceedings of the eighth ACM SIGKDD international conference on Knowledge discovery and data mining*, pages 61–70. ACM, 2002.

[31] J. B. Rotter. Interpersonal trust, trustworthiness, and gullibility. *American psychologist*, 35(1):1, 1980.

[32] J. Singh and D. Sirdeshmukh. Agency and trust mechanisms in consumer satisfaction and loyalty judgments. *Journal of the Academy of Marketing Science*, 28(1):150–167, 2000.

[33] J. Tang, Y. Chang, and H. Liu. Mining social media with social theories: A survey. *SIGKDD Explorations*, 2014.

[34] J. Tang, H. Gao, X. Hu, and H. Liu. Exploiting homophily effect for trust prediction. In *Proceedings of the sixth ACM international conference on Web search and data mining*, pages 53–62. ACM, 2013.

[35] J. Tang, H. Gao, and H. Liu. mtrust: Discerning multi-faceted trust in a connected world. In *the 5th ACM International Conference on Web Search and Data Mining*, 2012.

[36] J. Tang and H. Liu. Trust in social computing. In *Proceedings of the companion publication of the 23rd international conference on World wide web companion*, pages 207–208, 2014.

[37] S.-H. Yang, A. J. Smola, B. Long, H. Zha, and Y. Chang. Friend or frenemy?: predicting signed ties in social networks. In *Proceedings of the 35th international ACM SIGIR conference on Research and development in information retrieval*, pages 555–564. ACM, 2012.

[38] S. Chang, G. Qi, J. Tang, Q. Tian, Y. Rui and T. Huang. Multimedia LEGO: LEarning structured model by probabilistic loGic Ontology tree. In *IEEE 13th International Conference on Data Mining*, 2013.

[39] S. Zhu, K. Yu, Y. Chi, and Y. Gong. Combining content and link for classification using matrix factorization. In *Proceedings of the 30th annual international ACM SIGIR conference on Research and development in information retrieval*, pages 487–494. ACM, 2007.

[40] C. Ziegler and J. Golbeck. Investigating interactions of trust and interest similarity. *Decision Support Systems*, 43(2):460–475, 2007.

[41] Z. Li, S. Chang, F. Liang, T. Huang, L. Cao and J. Smith. Learning Locally-Adaptive Decision Functions for Person Verification. In *IEEE Conference on Computer Vision and Pattern Recognition*, 2013.

[42] C.-N. Ziegler and G. Lausen. Propagation models for trust and distrust in social networks. *Information Systems Frontiers*, 7(4-5):337–358, 2005.

Automatic Discovery of Global and Local Equivalence Relationships in Labeled Geo-Spatial Data

Bart Thomee
Yahoo Labs
San Francisco, CA, USA
bthomee@yahoo-inc.com

Gianmarco De Francisci Morales
Yahoo Labs
Barcelona, Spain
gdfm@yahoo-inc.com

ABSTRACT

We propose a novel algorithmic framework to automatically detect which labels refer to the same concept in labeled spatial data. People often use different words and synonyms when referring to the same concept or location. Furthermore these words and their usage vary across culture, language, and place. Our method analyzes the patterns in the spatial distribution of labels to discover equivalence relationships. We evaluate our proposed technique on a large collection of geo-referenced Flickr photos using a semi-automatically constructed ground truth from an existing ontology. Our approach is able to classify equivalent tags with a high accuracy (AUC of 0.85), as well as providing the geographic extent where the relationship holds.

Categories and Subject Descriptors

H.2.8 [**Database Management**]: Database Applications—*Spatial databases and GIS*; H.3.1 [**Information Storage and Retrieval**]: Content Analysis and Indexing

Keywords

Geotagged data; geo-spatial analysis; folksonomy; relationship discovery; Flickr

1. INTRODUCTION

In recent years, social media and Web applications, such as del.icio.us, have amassed large quantities of user-generated content. Researchers often leverage the "wisdom of the crowd" in order to organize and search this content. In particular, user-supplied *tags*, textual labels assigned to such content, form a powerful and useful feature that has been successfully exploited for this purpose in many different domains.

Tags are free-form, short keywords associated by a user to some content such as a photo, a link, or a blog entry. The categorization system that arises from applying tags is usually called a folksonomy [43]. Unlike ontologies and taxonomies, folksonomies result in unstructured knowledge,

i.e. they are flat and have no predefined semantics. However, their unstructured nature is also their strength. For example, tagging has lower cognitive cost than picking categories from an ontology, it allows for greater flexibility and self-expression, and the folksonomy may naturally evolve to reflect emergent properties of the data [40].

The availability of large quantities of data has prompted researchers to try to automatically extract knowledge from it. Formerly ontologies used to be built manually by experts, however with large amounts of data this process has proved to be expensive and unsustainable. Currently, most state-of-the-art methods to generate ontologies use large large text databases [25] as their imput. Often, they leverage crowd-sourced data and user-generated content. Many approaches mine Wikipedia or the Web to find interesting relationships, for instance DBPedia[1] and Google's Knowledge Graph[2]. The expectation is that the individual interactions of a large number of agents would lead to global effects that can be observed as semantics. Ontologies would thus become an emergent property of the system as opposed to a fixed formalization of knowledge.

While geo-referenced tags are readily available in large quantities, the problem of referencing relationships geographically has received little attention so far. The presence of the spatial dimension allows us to ask new questions about labeled data, such as *"where does this relationship hold?"*, *"is this relationship valid locally or globally?"*, and *"which tag among several equivalents is most prominent here?"*.

Broadly speaking, we are interested in identifying patterns in the distribution of labels over some domain. In this work we describe a general framework for the spatial domain and focus on geographic patterns for evaluation. Specifically, we look at tags from Flickr[3], a popular photo-sharing website that supports tags and geo-referenced photos. Rather than looking at co-occurrences of tags in photos [39], we analyze the spatial patterns that emerge from the usage of tags, and extract structured information from these patterns in the form of equivalence relationships. The equivalence relationships extracted include synonyms, language variants, misspellings, abbreviations, and even nicknames. For example, our algorithm can determine that the Eiffel Tower may interchangeably be referred to by different tags, such as `la tour eiffel`, `toureiffel`, `eiffelturm`, and `la`

---

[1] http://dbpedia.org
[2] http://www.google.com/insidesearch/features/search/knowledge.html
[3] http://www.flickr.com

dame de fer, even if these tags would never occur together in the same photo. We further determine whether the equivalence relationship holds globally or holds only locally. For example, in the city of Paris there is a park officially known as 'Le Jardin du Luxembourg', which may be referred to by people when tagging their photos by using the tag luxembourg or the tag park. In and around this particular park, these two labels can be considered equivalent, and one may be substituted for the other; yet anywhere else in Paris these two labels should not be considered the same, in particular because the label park will likely also occur around all other parks in Paris. Conversely, while there are many parks in the city of Luxembourg, the equivalence relationship between these two tags does not hold there either.

There are several applications for a system that automatically uncovers geo-spatial equivalence relationships; next we provide a few examples.

Tag canonicalization and entity linking. Mapping the tags to known entities, and thus implicitly knowing the relationships between entities, can enrich existing knowledge repositories. Such mapping of tags to their canonical forms, results in (*i*) the compression of the tag vocabulary, since several terms can be mapped to a single representative entry, and (*ii*) more emphasis on relevant terms when, for instance, performing term counting for building language models. In fact, any related term that would be considered individually (and thus would be competing for attention) will be considered as part of a larger group as a result of canonicalization. For recommendation and personalization, the vocabulary compression yields a reduced dimensionality of the tag space that needs to be considered, e.g., for matrix factorization. Furthermore, the spatial aspect can be beneficial for contextualization in hyper-local search. For example, a user in a Spanish-speaking country may issue the query "bamba" when searching for a popular Mexican folk song, while a user in Israel issuing this query is more likely to refer to a particular peanut butter-flavored snack.

Tag suggestion, correction, de-duplication, disambiguation and search. The canonicalization process yields relationships between tags; these relationships can hold globally true or be region or area specific. This knowledge can benefit the tagging process by flagging misspelled tags, suggesting tags that have a strong presence in the area where the photo was taken, de-duplicating tags when they refer to the same canonical tag, and disambiguating tags by using geo-spatial and contextual information to find the intended canonical terms (e.g., a user tagging a photo of an orange with "orange" when it is taken inside Orange County in California). In addition, search results can be improved when the user searches for a tag by expanding the search query to also include all other tags that map to the same canonical term, as well as diversifying the results by highlighting all possible meanings of the query if it is ambiguous.

Several challenges need to be faced to successfully mine relationships from geo-spatial labeled user-generated content. First, data is present at several different scales (street, city, region, country, etc.). Second, people do not always behave and tag rationally. This fact translates in a high volume of noise in the data. Finally, the large amount of the data imposes the use of efficient techniques.

The main contributions of this work are the following:

- We investigate the problem of automatically uncovering equivalence relationships from geo-spatial data;

- We propose an algorithm to find equivalence relationships and evaluate it on a collection of Flickr tags;

- We validate our approach on a ground truth generated semi-automatically from an existing ontology.

The remainder of this paper is organized as follows. We first discuss related work in Section 2. Section 3 then introduces our framework while Section 4 describes its implementation. Section 5 presents its evaluation and Section 6 concludes with final remarks and future outlooks.

2. RELATED WORK

At its core, this work is an application of geo-spatial data mining to geo-referenced folksonomies.

Folksonomy is a portmanteau term from *folk* and *taxonomy* [43]. It refers to a classification system that creates meaning from unstructured and collaborative annotations that are used in a practical real-world system. While ontologies are traditionally crafted by experts, and therefore relatively expensive to create, folksonomies arise from the steady-state tagging behavior of users, or so-called "wisdom of the crowd", and are relatively inexpensive to create. Additionally, while ontologies usually have a hierarchical structure, folksonomies are composed by a collection of tags which are all equal, i.e., the structure of a folksonomy is flat.

Passant [29] proposes a method to improve the quality of folksonomies by using ontologies for tag canonicalization, disambiguation and structuring. Knerr [21] proposes a formalization of folksonomies in terms of linked data to enable interoperability across different folksonomies. In the same spirit, MOAT [30] is a framework that enables machine-readable semantics for tags. Limpens et al. [22] provides a survey of proposals that attempt to bridge ontologies and folksonomies. Gruber [12] tries to clarify the relationship between ontologies and folksonomies, and argues that contrasting them is a "false dichotomy".

Differently from these other works, the method proposed in this paper takes advantage of the data available from folksonomies in order to enrich ontologies by uncovering new relationships. Similarly to this work, Mika [27] and Lux and Dosinger [23] generate semantic relationship starting from folksonomies. However, they focus on the social part of the folksonomies and do not take into account the geo-spatial aspect of the problem, which is our main contribution.

Closely related to our work, Schmitz [36] try to induce an ontology from Flickr tags. The ontologies are represented as trees of tags that constitute a taxonomy, i.e., the edges are subsumptions ("is-a" relationships). The method used by the authors is a simple rule based approach based on co-occurences, which resembles the mining of generalized (hierarchical) association rules. However, the authors do not take into account the spatial nature of the data. Furthermore, our framework uses a supervised learning approach.

Geo-spatial data mining refers to knowledge extraction from data with spatial coordinates. Examples include data from geographic information systems (GIS), GPS data and mobile trajectories.

Discovering geographic regions within spatial data has been an active research topic for many years. A variety of methods can be applied to uncover the hidden spatial structures, most notably techniques such as clustering [9], density estimation [16, 18] and neural networks [15].

In recent years, georeferenced multimedia collections have considerably grown in size, in particular due to the availability of digital cameras with built-in GPS receivers that can automatically attach the geographic location to every photo that is taken. We can therefore find a considerable number of methods in the research literature that try to represent or summarize geographical regions in terms of either the tags associated with the photos in that region [1, 7] or of the photos themselves [2, 5, 17, 19, 35, 44]. For example, language modeling approaches [14, 38, 42] characterize cells that partition the world into discrete units for automatic photo and video geo-localization.

In our work, we make use of geo-spatial areas that describe tags in a folksonomy order to qualify relationships among them. GeoFolk is a bayesian latent topic model that combines tags and geographic coordinates, modeled jointly via a generative process [41]. The authors show its usefulness in the usual contexts of tag recommendation, content classification and clustering. More refined models that can describe non-gaussian distributions have also been proposed more recently [20]. Indeed, these models are one of the possible building blocks that our framework can use to model areas. However, our final goal of finding equivalence relationships is different from what these works address.

Rattenbury et al. [32] extract place and event semantics from Flickr tags. They use patterns in the spatiotemporal distribution of tags to classify them in these two categories. In particular, places exploit spatial patterns, while events use temporal patterns at a given scale. Conversely, we are interested in semantic relationships between tags. Similarly, Zhang et al. [45] try to discover spatiotemporal relationships in collections of tagged photos. However, while their notion of relationship is vague and never explicitly defined, in this work we aim at discovering well-defined semantic relationships. Furthermore, the authors use a fixed coarse grained quantized vector representation of the tag distribution, while we propose a direct estimation of tag distribution from the data, coupled with a dynamic quantization of the distribution based on its spatial extent.

3. ALGORITHMIC FRAMEWORK

In our approach we focus on labeled instances, e.g. tags in the case of online photos, each of which is associated with a location. Our geo-spatial relationship discovery framework employs both unsupervised and supervised learning, and consists of five main steps, namely:

1. **Data representation** – The data distribution of each label is analyzed in order to produce a geo-spatial representation;

2. **Overlap detection** – The data representations of labels are compared to find spatial overlaps that may indicate that a relationship exists between the labels;

3. **Feature generation** – Descriptive features are generated from the geo-spatial representations and their overlapping area;

4. **Relationship classification** – The features are analyzed in order to determine which, if any, relationship holds between overlapping labels and the geo-spatial extent of this relationship;

5. **Relationship aggregation** – The relationships between labels are optionally analyzed to perform relationship aggregation, e.g., detecting transitivity between three or more relationships.

There are several possible implementations for each of these steps, and our framework does not enforce any particular choice, as long as the various pieces form a consistent pipeline (e.g., the feature generation should work on the chosen data representation). We describe the specific instantiation of the framework we experiment with in Section 4.

The final output of our framework is a set of tuples of the form $(\lambda_a, \lambda_b, E_{ab})$ that represent equivalence relationships between labels λ_a and λ_b. Each relationship is associated with a geo-spatial extent E_{ab} that represents the spatial area where the relationship holds. In the remainder of this section we detail each of the aforementioned steps in the framework.

3.1 Data representation

Given a set of labels Λ, we can define the data collection[4] as $\mathbb{D}_\Lambda = \biguplus \mathbb{D}_\lambda \mid \lambda \in \Lambda$, where the $\biguplus$ operator performs a union of the data instances associated with each label $\mathbb{D}_\lambda$. In case a data item has multiple labels, it will be included in $\mathbb{D}_\Lambda$ as many times its labels. We further define $\mathbb{D}_\lambda \triangleq \{d\}$, where d has a label λ and is represented by a tuple (x, y), which contains a location that is expressed by a coordinate x and a coordinate y. In the specific case of geo-referenced data items, a location refers to a geographic coordinate, where x represents the longitude and y the latitude of the coordinate.

Modeling. For each label $\lambda \in \Lambda$, we individually analyze the geo-spatial distribution of its instances by using unsupervised learning. The algorithm detects where the label exhibits a strong presence, and yields one or more clusters that can be represented as closed surfaces. For example, in two dimensions the surface of each obtained cluster would be formed by the convex hull of all points in the cluster. The choice of which clustering algorithm to apply depends on various factors, such as (i) the complexity of the data, (ii) the scale of the data, (iii) the volume of noise in the data, and (iv) the desired degree of accuracy for the modeling.

For example, mean-shift [3], k-means [24] or DBSCAN [8] can be used to separate the data into disjoint clusters, whereas kernel density estimation [34] or Gaussian mixture decomposition [33] can be used to generate probabilistic models of the data. Some clustering methods require pre-setting the number of clusters to detect, while others implicitly perform clustering without requiring to specify the number of clusters [31]; nonetheless, for the former type of clustering methods there exist practical methods (e.g., Bayesian information criterion) to perform model selection, i.e., to choose the best number of clusters.

The union of the detected clusters for a label forms its geo-spatial representation. Similarly to the definition of the data collection, we define the geo-spatial representation of a label as a cluster collection $\mathbb{C}_\Lambda = \biguplus \mathbb{C}_\lambda \mid \lambda \in \Lambda$, where $\mathbb{C}_\lambda \triangleq \{c\}$ and where each cluster c has a label λ and is represented by its geo-spatial surface S.

---

[4]While we describe our data model using two spatial dimensions for clarity, the extension of our model to higher-dimensional spaces is straightforward.

3.2 Overlap detection

After the geo-spatial representations have been determined for each label, we perform pair-wise comparisons between the representations to find overlaps that may indicate the existence of a relationship between the labels. For each pair of labels λ_a and λ_b, we identify all geo-spatial overlaps between their associated clusters $\mathbb{C}_{\lambda_a}$ and $\mathbb{C}_{\lambda_b}$. Each overlap is represented by a tuple $(\lambda_a, C_a, \lambda_b, C_b, E_{ab})$, where $C_a \subseteq \mathbb{C}_{\lambda_a}$ and $C_b \subseteq \mathbb{C}_{\lambda_b}$, and where E_{ab} is the extent of the geo-spatial intersection between the clusters C_a and C_b. By definition, when there are multiple overlaps between a pair of labels, then no cluster of either label is able to participate in more than one overlap. A further filtering step can be applied to the obtained overlaps in order to discard those whose extents are too small to allow for reliably detecting meaningful relationships.

3.3 Feature generation

Once the overlaps have been identified, we generate features from the union of involved clusters $M_a = \bigcup c \mid c \in C_a$ and $M_b = \bigcup c \mid c \in C_b$, as well as from their geo-spatial intersection $M_{ab} = M_a \bigcap M_b$, as exemplified in Figure 1. The features aim at describing the inherent properties of the geo-spatial extents and densities of the overlapping clusters, thus capturing the important aspects which allow a classifier to determine whether a relationship holds between the overlapping clusters of the labels. We identify three kind of features: *overlap*, *extent* and *density*.

Overlap-based features indicate which kind of relationship likely holds between the overlapping clusters. We can differentiate between various types of overlap, e.g., by using qualitative spatial reasoning to express the overlap between the clusters through different region connection calculi [4]. For instance, a non-tangential proper part relationship between M_a and M_b, i.e., all clusters in M_a are completely covered by the clusters in M_b, would suggest a subsumption relationship is likely.

Extent-based features indicate the strength of the relationship between the labels – the larger the extent of the overlap, the more likely an actual relationship to exist – as well as facilitating the decision process when several relationships have been identified as candidates for describing the overlap. For instance, the relative extent of the overlap may enable an equivalence relationship to be distinguished from a subsumption one.

Density-based features capture how similar the distribution of the data within the extents of the overlapping clusters are, in particular the extent the clusters have in common with respect to their overall extents. These features allow to detect relationships that would be hard to find based on just their overlap or size. For example, when a cluster with a large extent overlaps one or more clusters with small extent an equivalence relationship may still be uncovered between their labels when their normalized densities are similar.

After the feature generation step, we end up with features $F_{a,b,ab} = \{F_a, F_b, F_{ab}\}$ describing each overlap.

3.4 Relationship classification

Different kinds of relationships between labels may be present within the data, such as equivalence and subsumption, where the relationship may vary according to its location. In gen-

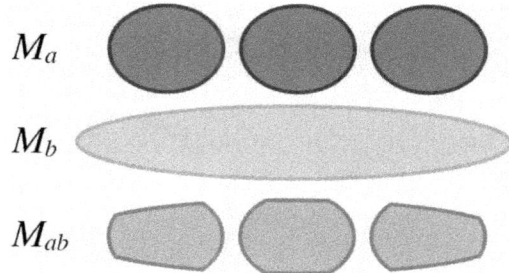

Figure 1: The intersection M_{ab} of clusters M_a and M_b.

eral, each type of relationship can be treated as a different class in a multi-class classifier. Such a classifier takes as input the features $F_{a,b,ab}$ of an overlap between a pair of labels $\{\lambda_a, \lambda_b\}$, and produces as output a decision r that indicates which, if any, relationship holds between the two labels. A classifier need not produce a binary decision, but may rather assign a confidence score to each type of relationship, which would provide the relationship aggregation step with more refined information to better resolve situations when several relationships are possible.

3.5 Relationship aggregation

The final step of our framework optionally performs an aggregation of the relationships detected between each pairs of labels, in order to more accurately deduce which relationships between labels actually hold. For example, if a relationship r is transitive and the output of the classification is as follows:

$$(\lambda_a, \lambda_b, r, E_{ab}), (\lambda_b, \lambda_c, r, E_{bc})$$

we can infer the additional relationship $(\lambda_a, \lambda_c, r, E_{ac})$, where $E_{ac} = E_{ab} \bigcap E_{bc}$, provided that $E_{ac} \neq \emptyset$. Furthermore, if a relationship between two labels holds across n extents, e.g,

$$(\lambda_a, \lambda_b, r, E_{ab}^1), (\lambda_a, \lambda_b, r, E_{ab}^2), \ldots, (\lambda_a, \lambda_b, r, E_{ab}^n)$$

then the relationship also holds on their union $(\lambda_a, \lambda_b, r, E_{ab}^1 \cup E_{ab}^2 \cup \ldots \cup E_{ab}^n)$.

Aggregating the individual relationships for overlaps between pairs of labels provides an opportunity to correct those that have been misclassified. Furthermore adjacent geo-spatial extents may be connected to also cover the extent between them. For instance, the relationship between the labels `holidays` and `vacaciones` may be initially classified as an equivalence relationship that holds in many places in Spanish-speaking countries; these equivalence relationships could be expanded to cover the entire world, even though these labels may have co-occurred in just a few instances.

While our framework is generic in the sense that various types of relationships could be detected with suitable features, classifiers and aggregation, in this paper we solely focus on detecting equivalence relationships between tags, and leave the detection of other relationships to future work.

4. IMPLEMENTATION

In this section we describe one particular instantiation of our algorithmic framework. We discuss the implementation choices of each of the steps of the framework presented in the previous section.

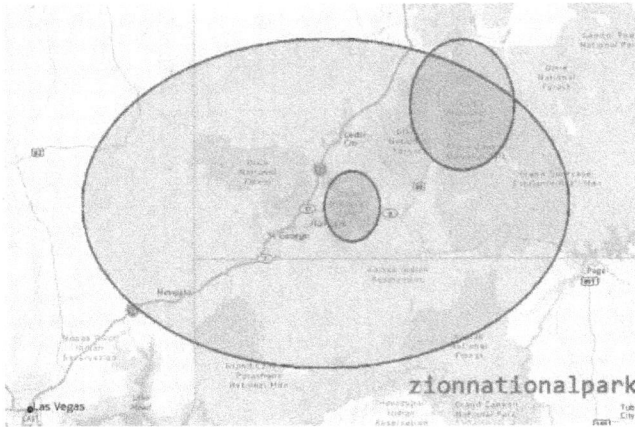

Figure 2: The clusters detected for the tag zionnationalpark ($\epsilon = 0.0001$). The densities within the clusters are not shown. The smallest cluster is centered on Zion National Park and has a large prior of 0.92. The largest cluster is also centered on the park, but has a smaller prior of 0.07. The third cluster is centered on Dixie National Forest, albeit only with a prior of 0.01.

4.1 Data representation

As explained in Section 3.1, there are several ways to generate an intermediate representation of the raw data that is amenable for detecting overlaps and for generating features. In this work, we represent the data via a probabilistic generative model, which allows us to model the data as a probability density function. We adopt the Gaussian mixture model (GMM) [33] to describe the data, in particular because it provides a sound statistical framework for the approximation of unknown distributions that are not necessarily Gaussian themselves [26].

To obtain the spatial representation of a label we first fit a Gaussian mixture model – this can be done for multiple labels in parallel – in order to obtain one or more mixtures. Each mixture component represents a different sub-population within the distribution of the data for a label, and is described by a mean μ, a covariance matrix Σ and a prior α that can be considered the "height" of its underlying Gaussian. To fit the model to the data, we employ the Expectation-Maximization (EM) [6] algorithm. There are various options to choose the hyper-parameter k of the model (the number of mixture components). One approach is to use the Bayesian information criterion (BIC) [37]. For simplicity, we choose a practical iterative approach based on cross-validation as implemented in WEKA [13]. In each iteration, we increase the number of components by one and we compute the log-likelihood of the model on a 10-fold cross-validation. If the log-likelihood increases, we repeat the procedure, otherwise we stop.

In line with our earlier terminology we will refer to mixtures as "clusters" henceforth. The spatial representation of a label $\mathbb{C}_\lambda$ is then the set formed by all of its clusters, i.e. $\mathbb{C}_\lambda \triangleq \{c\}$, where each cluster c has label λ and is represented by the tuple (μ, Σ, α), see Figure 2 for an example.

4.2 Overlap detection

Since the values of the Gaussian function never become zero, any cluster represented as a mixture of Gaussians always

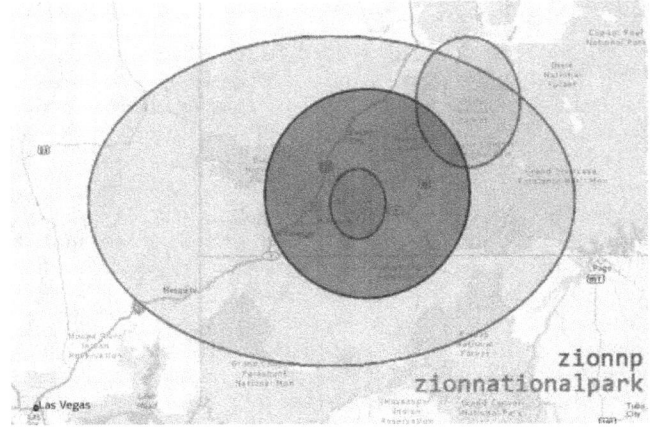

Figure 3: The clusters detected for the tags zionnationalpark and zionnp ($\epsilon = 0.0001$). The densities within the clusters are not shown.

overlaps with every other cluster. However, in practice, the value of the Gaussian function rapidly decreases to zero and becomes negligible a few standard deviations away from the mean. We therefore apply a threshold ϵ to limit the extent of each cluster $c \in \mathbb{C}_\lambda$ to the area bounded by the level curve $L_c = \{(x, y) \mid \mathcal{N}(\mu_c, \Sigma_c) = \epsilon/\alpha_c\}$. This thresholding makes pairwise comparison of distributions feasible by pruning unrelated clusters.

The cluster prior α_c affects the level curve of a cluster, since the level curve will encompass a larger area given a higher prior than the level curve given a lower prior, due to its more influential Gaussian. The level curve of a cluster may be the empty set when all of its densities are below the threshold; such clusters are unlikely to significantly contribute to any kind of relationship and can be filtered out. For each pair of labels λ_a and λ_b we can now determine all geo-spatial overlaps between their associated clusters $\mathbb{C}_{\lambda_a}$ and $\mathbb{C}_{\lambda_b}$ by checking for intersections between the level curves of their clusters, yielding zero or more overlaps. As mentioned earlier, each overlap is represented by a tuple $(\lambda_a, C_a, \lambda_b, C_b, E_{ab})$, where $C_a \subseteq \mathbb{C}_{\lambda_a}$ and $C_b \subseteq \mathbb{C}_{\lambda_b}$, and where E_{ab} is the extent of the intersection between the clusters C_a and C_b, see Figure 3 for an example.

4.3 Feature generation

For each overlap we extract a number of overlap-based, extent-based and density-based features from the union of involved clusters $M_a = \bigcup c \mid c \in C_a$ and $M_b = \bigcup c \mid c \in C_b$, and from their intersection $M_{ab} = M_a \bigcap M_b$.

Overlap-based features. Following the work in the area of qualitative spatial reasoning, we express the overlaps using region connection calculus. The RCC8 model [4] distinguishes between eight different types of region connections that express all possible ways regions can interact with each other, such as partial overlapping or touching as is illustrated in Figure 4; the model can also be applied when multiple regions are involved. Per overlap we first compute the combined level curves L_a from M_a and L_b from M_b beyond which the distributions have value zero, after which we can then compare the areas delineated by the level curves to assign one of the RCC8 region connection types to the overlap.

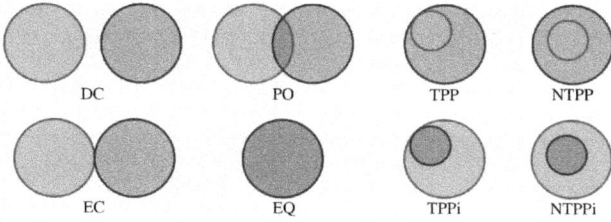

Figure 4: The RCC8 connections. DC = disconnected, EC = externally connected, PO = partially overlapping, EQ = equal, TPP(i) = tangential proper part (inverse), and NTTP(i) = non-tangential proper part (inverse).

Extent-based features. We compute several features from the area covered by M_a, M_b and M_{ab}. In order to do so, we first represent the data for each M_i as a two-dimensional binary histogram $f_i(x, y)$, where a histogram bin is activated when its corresponding location falls inside the area enclosed within the combined level curve. All three histograms $f_a(x, y)$, $f_b(x, y)$ and $f_{ab}(x, y)$ span the same geographic area. For computational reasons we resample the geographic area to fit a histogram with a maximum dimension of 2000 bins, either widthwise or lengthwise depending on the horizontal or vertical orientation of the geographic area. From each of the three histograms we then first compute the second and third order complex translation, rotation and scaling invariant moments [10]. Translation, rotation and scaling invariance allows for a robust description of the shapes of M_a and M_b and their intersection M_{ab} by ignoring their horizontal and vertical displacements, orientational differences and their disparity in size. The second order moments capture the distribution of the mass of each shape with respect to the mean, while the third order moments capture their skewness. In addition to these moments we further calculate the sizes of the areas and compute the Jaccard index, i.e. the area of the intersection M_{ab} divided by the area of the union $M_a \bigcup M_b$.

Density-based features. We compute the same translation, rotation and scaling invariant moments as above, but this time we use the actual densities of the clusters rather than their shapes in the histograms $f_i(x, y)$. We furthermore include the location and value of the maximum density and the average density per histogram cell. Finally, we compute the Jensen-Shannon divergence between M_a and M_b, to capture how similar their density distributions are.

In total, we generate 8 overlap-based features, 28 extent-based features and 40 density-based features, yielding a total of 76 features per overlap, see also Table 1.

4.4 Relationship classification

To find an equivalence relationship, we set up the classification task as a binary classification problem, where the positive class represents the existence of the equivalence relationship and the negative class its absence. While in principle any binary classifier can be used for the task, we choose to use tree-based classifiers to gain insight on the relative importance of the features. In particular, we experiment standard decision trees, with random forests and with gradient boosted decision trees. We use WEKA [13] for the decision trees and the random forests, and an in-house implementation for the gradient boosted decision trees. We present the results of the classification task in Section 5.

4.5 Relationship aggregation

Equivalence is a transitive relationship, thus given the binary relationships uncovered in the previous step, we can compute their transitive closure and therefore discover more relationships, as was also earlier described in Section 3.5. Recall that the aggregated relationship will hold on the union of the intersections of the original extents. Since we evaluate our algorithm on a selection of tags that were in part randomly selected, the number of transitive relationships discovered in this manner is therefore small in our dataset. It is nevertheless valuable to analyze the transitive aggregation from a qualitative point of view; we present examples from our dataset in Section 5.3.

5. EXPERIMENTS

We experiment with our relationship discovery framework and validate it on the specific task of finding *synonyms*. Synonyms represent a very well-defined subset of equivalence relationships, which is easy to assess. However, manually building a ground truth for such a task is a tedious job. For this reason, we devise a procedure to generate it semi-automatically, so that we only need to check the synonyms and non-synonyms identified by the evaluated algorithms for correctness. Before presenting the experimental results, in the next section we describe the dataset used in our experiments and the procedure used to generate the ground truth.

5.1 Dataset

Flickr. Our Flickr dataset contains a sample of over 56 million geo-referenced images uploaded to Flickr before the end of 2010. Each photo is represented by a geographic location, indicated by longitude and latitude, and one or more tags assigned to the photo by the user. We consider each instance of a tag associated with a photo as a label and annotate each label with the location information of its source photo. A single photo may thus generate multiple instances of annotated labels.

We performed sanitization on the data by removing all non-latin characters, reducing all remaining latin characters to their lowercase representation and removing all diacritics, so that tags like España and Gaudí become espana and gaudi respectively. We removed tags that referred to years, such as 2006 and 2007, as well as camera manufacturer names, such as canon and nikon, because these at times get automatically added by capture devices or photo applications and thus are not representative of the tagging behavior of users.

We additionally removed infrequently used tags by ensuring we have at least 50 instances per tag occurring around the world. While infrequently used tags could yield a cluster that characterizes an area, Sigurbjörnsson and van Zwol [39] show that the tag frequency distribution in Flickr follows a power law where the long tail contains words categorized as occurring incidentally, making it unlikely for such tags to generate a good cluster.

Ground truth. To generate the ground truth, we first extracted all (inter-language and intra-language) synonyms from the BabelNet multilingual ontology [28] and applied the same sanitization described above to each synonym. To avoid any ambiguity in interpretation we retained only those terms that were assigned to a single concept. We computed

Table 1: The overlap-based (top), extent-based (middle) and density-based (bottom) features used by our algorithm.

DC	M_a and M_b do not overlap.
EC	M_a and M_b touch each other.
PO	M_a and M_b partially overlap.
EQ	M_a and M_b exactly overlap.
TPP	M_a is a tangential proper part of M_b.
$TPPi$	M_b is a tangential proper part of M_a.
$NTPP$	M_a is a non-tangential proper part of M_b.
$NTPPi$	M_b is a non-tangential proper part of M_a.
$Jaccard$	Jaccard index of M_a and M_b.
$Area_{\{a,b,ab\}}$	Area sizes of the extents of M_a, M_b and of their intersection M_{ab}, respectively.
$\Phi_e(1,1)_{\{r,i\}\{a,b,ab\}}$	Second order invariant (real and complex) moments [10] of the extents of M_a, M_b and M_{ab}.
$\Phi_e(2,0)_{\{r,i\}\{a,b,ab\}}$	Second order invariant (real and complex) moments [10] of the extents of M_a, M_b and M_{ab}.
$\Phi_e(2,1)_{\{r,i\}\{a,b,ab\}}$	Third order invariant (real and complex) moments [10] of the extents of M_a, M_b and M_{ab}.
$\Phi_e(3,0)_{\{r,i\}\{a,b,ab\}}$	Third order invariant (real and complex) moments [10] of the extents of M_a, M_b and M_{ab}.
$JensenShannon$	Jensen-Shannon divergence of M_a and M_b.
$Sum_{\{a,b,ab\}}$	Cumulative densities of M_a, M_b and M_{ab}.
$Avg_{\{a,b,ab\}}$	Average densities of M_a, M_b and M_{ab}.
$MaxX(0,0)_{\{a,b,ab\}}$	Normalized longitude bin $(0-1)$ of maximum density in M_a, M_b and M_{ab}.
$MaxY(0,0)_{\{a,b,ab\}}$	Normalized latitude bin $(0-1)$ of maximum density in M_a, M_b and M_{ab}.
$MaxV(0,0)_{\{a,b,ab\}}$	Maximum density values of M_a, M_b and M_{ab}.
$\Phi_d(1,1)_{\{r,i\}\{a,b,ab\}}$	Second order invariant (real and complex) moments [10] of the densities of M_a, M_b and M_{ab}.
$\Phi_d(2,0)_{\{r,i\}\{a,b,ab\}}$	Second order invariant (real and complex) moments [10] of the densities of M_a, M_b and M_{ab}.
$\Phi_d(2,1)_{\{r,i\}\{a,b,ab\}}$	Third order invariant (real and complex) moments [10] of the densities of M_a, M_b and M_{ab}.
$\Phi_d(3,0)_{\{r,i\}\{a,b,ab\}}$	Third order invariant (real and complex) moments [10] of the densities of M_a, M_b and M_{ab}.

the intersection between the selected terms and the tag vocabulary in Flickr, ensuring that for each concept at least two terms had been used as photo tags. We then manually inspected all terms per concept to validate whether they truly were synonyms and discarded all terms whose meaning was (possibly) ambiguous. For example, `kivu` and `lakekivu` are considered synonyms in BabelNet for the concept "Lake Kivu", even though in reality the former tag describes a much larger region that encompasses the lake; we thus did not consider these two terms as synonyms. Ultimately, we generated 1240 examples. We formed an equal-sized set of non-synonym tags by including a portion of the terms we discarded earlier and by randomly sampling the remainder from the tag vocabulary that were not in the synonym set.

As described in Section 4, we proceeded to fit a Gaussian mixture model to the data instances of each of the synonyms and non-synonyms to obtain one or more clusters per tag, and then detected the overlapping clusters. Whenever the clusters of a pair of tags generated multiple overlaps we only retained the one where the cumulative priors were highest of all clusters that were part of the overlap. Finally, we computed the features for all clusters involved in the remaining overlaps, and we assigned the class `positive` if both tags in the pair were present in BabelNet as a synonym and `negative` otherwise. We determined the overlaps for varying values of the threshold ϵ. In case the pair of tags did not generate overlapping clusters, the overlap-based feature was set to DC and the extent features and density features of the intersection were set to zero.

5.2 Empirical Results

We evaluate three different classifiers on the ground truth for several values of the threshold ϵ: decision tree (DT), random forests (RF) and gradient boosted decision trees (GBDT).

For each classifier and value of ϵ we run a 10-fold cross validation and average results across the folds. For DT we set the minimum number of instances in each leaf to 10 and the confidence factor for pruning to 0.10. For RF we use 50 trees, and for GBDT 20 trees. These settings were chosen empirically in a preliminary test in order to reduce over-fitting. We leave all other settings at their default value.

Table 2 summarizes the results. We report the positive rate (TPR), the false positive rate (FPR) and the area under the ROC curve (AUC). The TPR and FPR are obtained at the optimal point of operation on the ROC curve by giving equal weights to misclassifications. For all three classifiers the AUC is high, where the most powerful classifiers in our evaluation setting is RF, which is able to reach an AUC of 0.85 for $\epsilon = 0.001$. While the GBDT obtains the best TPR, at the same time the FPR is highest, yielding a lower AUC than the RF and one that is comparable to the DT.

When inspecting the generated clusters and their overlaps for different values of ϵ, we observe that higher values lead to fewer and more spatially constrained clusters that less frequently overlap, whereas the reverse is the case for smaller values. Intuitively, the classification performance should increase for higher thresholds of ϵ, since any remaining clusters that do overlap have strong spatial support and similar spatial footprints, and thus are more likely to refer to synonyms than to non-synonyms. Yet, we notice that the performance of the classifiers is relatively stable across all evaluated thresholds ϵ, indicating that the clusters formed for synonymous tags do not always have strong spatial support nor may they necessarily overlap. To this end we investigate which features are more important than others for a correct classification.

Feature importance. By analyzing our model from the GBDT classifier, we can infer which features contribute the

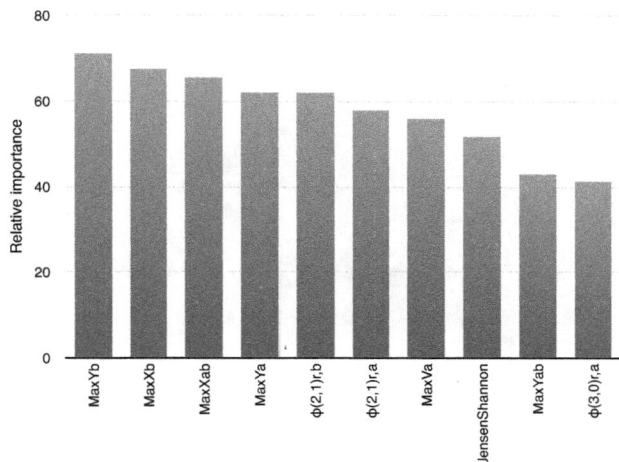

Figure 5: Estimated relative importance of the top-10 features for GBDT.

most to the classification, as described by Friedman [11]. Across all models, all of the features in the top-10 are density based, see Figure 5. Six of these features refer to the relative location and height of the peaks of the clusters and their intersection, one feature refers to the Jensen-Shannon divergence and the remaining three features are second and third order image density moments. Interestingly, when we look beyond the top-10, the overlap-based features from the RCC8 model seem to contribute little to the classification, which may be due to the mismatch between the GMM and the model for which the region connection calculus was originally devised, and deserves further study. Overall our results indicate that the Gaussian mixtures model is very suitable for modeling geo-spatial labeled data and that the features extracted from the clusters and their intersection, primarily the density-based features, are sufficiently informative for the classification task.

Comparison. We implement a baseline based on spatial tag correspondences to place the results of our method into context. Here, we discretize the world by considering it as a large histogram, where each cell has a size of ρ° longitude by ρ° latitude. For example, $\rho = 0.0001$ yields cells of about 10x10m each, while $\rho = 0.01$ yields cells of about 1x1km. We quantize the location of each tag instance to a cell in the histogram, after which we count the number of instances per cell. We then represent the global distribution of non-empty cells for a tag by a sparse feature vector, after which we compare the vectors of pairs of tags using cosine similarity, producing a single feature representing their similarity. We finally evaluate the performance of the baseline, again using the Decision Tree, Random Forest and Gradient Boosted Decision Tree, and report the same metrics as before.

Table 3 summarizes the results. We can see that the baseline achieves worse results in comparison with our method; our method outperforms the baseline for all three classifiers. We notice that the baseline performs particularly badly for the GBDT when ρ is small, although even when ρ is large it still underperforms with respect to the DT and RF; while the GBDT classifier is effective in achieving a low FPR, it is not able to produce a high enough TPR to yield a competitive performance.

Table 2: Evaluation results for our algorithm for the Decision Tree (DT), Random Forest (RF) and Gradient Boosted Decision Tree (GBDT) classifiers. We report the true positive rate (TPR), false positive rate (FPR) and the area under the curve (AUC) for several parameter values ϵ.

ϵ	DT			RF			GBDT		
	TPR	FPR	AUC	TPR	FPR	AUC	TPR	FPR	AUC
0.000001	0.762	0.274	0.759	0.777	0.223	0.832	0.773	0.257	0.737
0.000005	0.746	0.254	0.767	0.763	0.237	0.822	0.808	0.287	0.748
0.00001	0.729	0.271	0.759	0.776	0.224	0.819	0.818	0.318	0.752
0.00005	0.737	0.263	0.773	0.778	0.222	0.823	0.729	0.241	0.721
0.0001	0.733	0.267	0.753	0.770	0.230	0.819	0.829	0.409	0.679
0.0005	0.733	0.267	0.761	0.771	0.229	0.844	0.869	0.313	0.737
0.001	0.762	0.238	0.792	0.787	0.213	0.848	0.848	0.240	0.791

Table 3: Evaluation results for the spatial tag correspondence baseline for the Decision Tree (DT), Random Forest (RF) and Gradient Boosted Decision Tree (GBDT) classifiers. We report the true positive rate (TPR), false positive rate (FPR) and the area under the curve (AUC) for several parameter values ρ.

ρ	DT			RF			GBDT		
	TPR	FPR	AUC	TPR	FPR	AUC	TPR	FPR	AUC
0.0001	0.545	0.455	0.537	0.531	0.469	0.554	0.101	0.014	0.180
0.0005	0.592	0.408	0.602	0.587	0.413	0.611	0.205	0.012	0.290
0.001	0.612	0.388	0.615	0.615	0.385	0.645	0.252	0.025	0.354
0.005	0.663	0.337	0.670	0.658	0.342	0.701	0.350	0.035	0.485
0.01	0.697	0.303	0.675	0.688	0.312	0.747	0.402	0.028	0.559

The baseline is an approach that only considers the occurrences of tags at a global level, and as such it is incapable of detecting equivalence relationships that only hold locally and nowhere else. In contrast, our method only classifies tags as being equivalent in the area spanned by the union of their overlapping clusters, unless the aggregation step expands this area. Furthermore, the size of the cells can considerably influence the accuracy of the classifier, where for very small cells the number of instances per individual cell may be very small and produce many cells per tag, which may result in dissimilar feature vectors for equivalent tags. Conversely, for very large cells the number of instances per individual cell may be very large and produce few cells per tag, which may result in similar feature vectors for non-equivalent tags. In contrast, our method automatically detects the optimal scale at which to represent the tag distribution. The advantage of the baseline over our method, however, is that it is not as complex and is able to detect equivalence relationships that are globally valid.

5.3 Anecdotal Results

In this section we provide several examples of clusters and the obtained classified overlaps to provide a visual illustration of the output of our algorithm and the classifiers. Correctly classified positive examples include the tag pairs baleari – balearics (an archipelago of Spain) and occupylondon – occupylsx (the Occupy London movement), while incorrectly classified positive examples include arcdetriomphe – grandearche (two famous landmarks in Paris, France) and nijocastle – nijojo (a castle located in Kyoto, Japan). Incorrectly classified negative examples also occur, such as the tag pair portknockie – bowfiddlerock (a coastal village town in Scotland and its characteristic landmark). We show a few examples in Figure 6. We observe that positive tag pair examples may be misclassified as a result of so-called

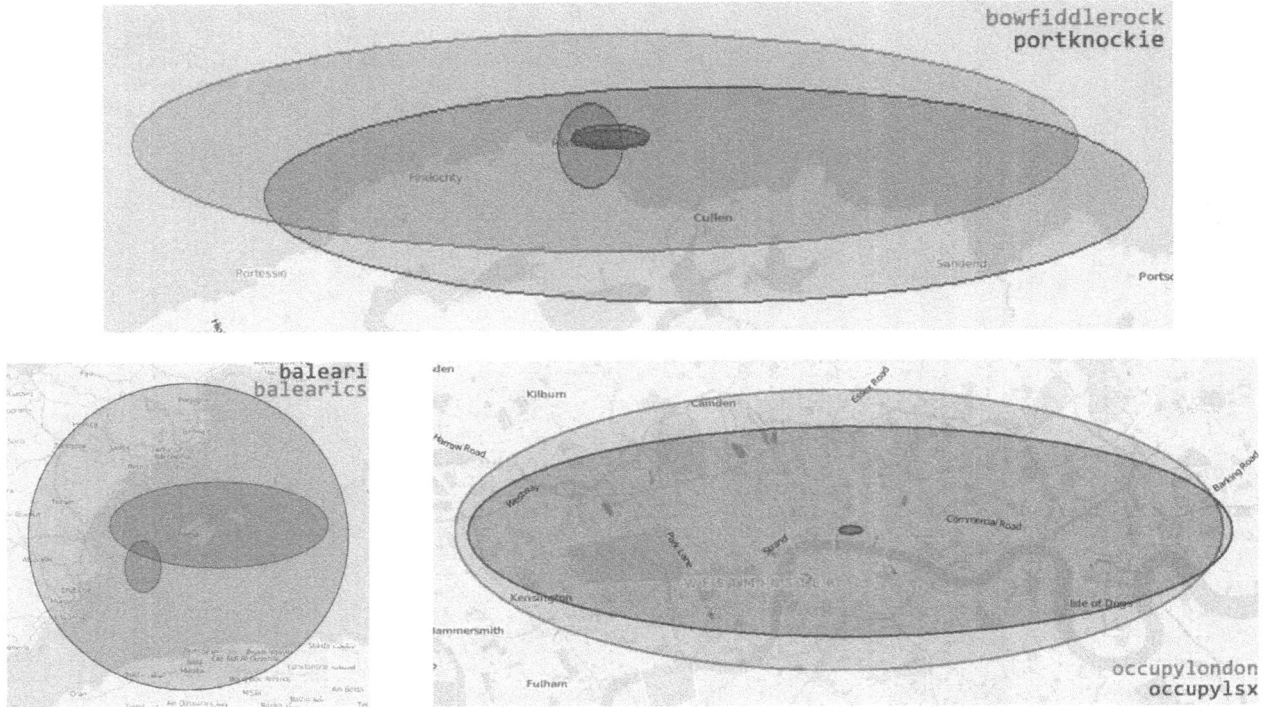

Figure 6: Example overlaps between the tag clusters of portknockie − bowfiddlerock **(top),** baleari − balearics **(bottom-left) and** occupylondon − occupylsx **(bottom-right). The densities within the clusters and overlaps are not shown, but in all three examples the peaks of the densities within the clusters are located in close proximity of each other. The density peaks of** baleari **and** balearics **are principally located on the islands, whereas those of** occupylondon **and** occupylsx **are centered near St. Paul's Cathedral where one of the protester camps of the Occupy London movement was based.**

"bulk tagging" of photos, where people apply the same set of tags to all photos they took that day, while negative tag pair examples are typically misclassified due to subsumption relationships with both having similar tag distributions (e.g. the tags barcelona and spain).

In terms of detecting transitive relationships, the tags louvre − museedulouvre (referring to the famous museum the Louvre in Paris) are positively identified as an equivalence relationship, as were louvremuseum − museedulouvre, both spanning roughly the same geographic area. Thus, we are able to connect the tags louvre − louvremuseum together, whereby their relationship holds in the intersection of their extents.

Interestingly enough our classifiers pointed out mistakes in our ground truth labeling. For example, what we thought to be a negative example, barajas − lemd, is classified as positive; it turns out that the tags refer to the shortened name of Madrid-Barajas Airport and its four-character ICAO airport code.

6. CONCLUSIONS

In this paper we introduced a novel algorithmic framework to automatically discover equivalence relationships in geo-referenced folksonomies. Differently from previous work in the literature, our method is based on the geo-spatial patterns of the tags in the folksonomy, rather than on their co-occurrences in the content. Furthermore, by using a combination of unsupervised and supervised learning, we discover well-defined equivalence relationship rather than generic clusters of related tags as done previously in the literature. Our

method is generic and can be applied to any labeled data with geo-spatial coordinates. We validated our framework on the task of discovering synonyms from their geo-spatial patterns. We built a ground truth semi-automatically by leveraging an existing ontology. Our method is able to correctly classify the synonyms with high accuracy, and the best classifier achieves an AUC of 0.85.

This work can be extended in several directions. On the modeling part, we plan to explore different data representations, such as non-parametric DP-GMM. Furthermore, in this paper we used elliptical Gaussians as the basic mixture. However, by using a diagonal or full covariance matrix, which allows the mixtures to be more freely placed, more complex shapes and more powerful models can be obtained. This characteristic might be useful in discovering relationships different from equivalence.

In this work we mainly focused on validating the approach on a known ground truth, however the capabilities of the framework still need to be evaluated further. We plan to perform a large scale evaluation of the output of the classification. Given the size of the task, crowdsourcing the evaluation of the discovered relationships seems a viable option.

Finally, while in this paper we focused on equivalence relationships, we will expand the relationships that can be discovered to include more different kinds. For example, subsumption relationships are a prime candidate that would require minimal modifications to the framework. Furthermore, by including temporal features in our analysis, we will explore the possibility of uncovering periodic relationships in the data.

7. REFERENCES

[1] S. Ahern, M. Naaman, R. Nair, and J. Yang. World explorer: visualizing aggregate data from unstructured text in geo-referenced collections. In *Proceedings of the 7th ACM/IEEE-CS Joint Conference on Digital Libraries*, pp. 1–10, 2007.

[2] W. Chen, A. Battestini, N. Gelfand, and V. Setlur. Visual summaries of popular landmarks from community photo collections. In *Proceedings of the 43rd Asilomar Conference on Signals, Systems and Computers*, pp. 782–789, 2009.

[3] Y. Cheng. Mean shift, mode seeking, and clustering. *IEEE Transactions on Pattern Analysis and Machine Intelligence*, 17(8):790–799, 1995.

[4] A. Cohn, B. Bennett, J. Gooday, and N. Gotts. Qualitative spatial representation and reasoning with the Region Connection Calculus. *GeoInformatica*, 1 (3):275–316, 1997.

[5] M. Cristani, A. Perina, U. Castellani, and V. Murino. Content visualization and management of geo-located image databases. In *Proceedings of the 26th International Conference on Human Factors in Computing Systems – Extended Abstracts*, pp. 2823–2828, 2008.

[6] A. Dempster, N. Laird, and D. Rubin. Maximum likelihood from incomplete data via the EM algorithm. *Journal of the Royal Statistical Society*, 39(1):1–38, 1977.

[7] D. Deng, T. Chuang, and R. Lemmens. Conceptualization of place via spatial clustering and co-occurrence analysis. In *Proceedings of the 2009 International Workshop on Location Based Social Networks*, pp. 49–56, 2009.

[8] M. Ester, H. Kriegel, J. Sander, and X. Xu. A density-based algorithm for discovering clusters in large spatial databases with noise. In *Proceedings of the 2nd AAAI International Conference on Knowledge Discovery and Data Mining*, pp. 226–231, 1996.

[9] V. Estivill-Castro and I. Lee. AUTOCLUST: automatic clustering via boundary extraction for mining massive point-data sets. In *Proceedings of the 5th International Conference on Geocomputation*, pp. 1–20, 2001.

[10] J. Flusser, T. Suk, and B. Zitova. *Moments and moment invariants in pattern recognition*, chapter 2. John Wiley & Sons, Ltd., 2009.

[11] J. Friedman. Greedy function approximation: a gradient boosting machine. *Annals of Statistics*, 29(5): 1189–1232, 2001.

[12] T. Gruber. Ontology of folksonomy: A mash-up of apples and oranges. *International Journal on Semantic Web and Information Systems*, 3(1):1–11, 2007.

[13] M. Hall, E. Frank, G. Holmes, B. Pfahringer, P. Reutemann, and I. Witten. The WEKA data mining software: an update. *ACM SIGKDD Explorations Newsletter*, 11(1):10–18, 2009.

[14] C. Hauff and G. Houben. Geo-location estimation of Flickr images: social web based enrichment. In *Proceedings of the 34th European Conference on Information Retrieval*, pp. 85–96, 2012.

[15] H. Hotta and M. Hagiwara. A neural-network-based geographic tendency visualization. In *Proceedings of the 2008 IEEE/WIC/ACM International Conference on Web Intelligence and Intelligent Agent Technology*, volume 1, pp. 817–823, 2008.

[16] H. Hotta and M. Hagiwara. Online geovisualization with fast kernel density estimator. In *Proceedings of the 2009 IEEE/WIC/ACM International Conference on Web Intelligence and Intelligent Agent Technology*, volume 1, pp. 622–625, 2009.

[17] A. Jaffe, M. Naaman, T. Tassa, and M. Davis. Generating summaries and visualization for large collections of geo-referenced photographs. In *Proceedings of the 8th ACM International Workshop on Multimedia Information Retrieval*, pp. 89–98, 2006.

[18] C. Jones, R. Purves, P. Clough, and H. Joho. Modelling vague places with knowledge from the Web. *International Journal of Geographical Information Science*, 22(10):1045–1065, 2008.

[19] L. Kennedy and M. Naaman. Generating diverse and representative image search results for landmarks. In *Proceedings of the 17th International Conference on World Wide Web*, pp. 297–306, 2008.

[20] C. Kling, J. Kunegis, S. Sizov, and S. Staab. Detecting non-gaussian geographical topics in tagged photo collections. In *Proceedings of the 7th ACM International Conference on Web Search and Data Mining*, pp. 603–612, 2014.

[21] T. Knerr. Tagging ontology - towards a common ontology for folksonomies. 2006.

[22] F. Limpens, F. Gandon, and M. Buffa. Bridging ontologies and folksonomies to leverage knowledge sharing on the social web: a brief survey. In *Proceedings of the 23rd IEEE/ACM International Conference on Automated Software Engineering – Workshops*, pp. 13–18, 2008.

[23] M. Lux and G. Dosinger. From folksonomies to ontologies: employing wisdom of the crowds to serve learning purposes. *International Journal of Knowledge and Learning*, 3(4):515–528, 2007.

[24] J. MacQueen. Some methods for classification and analysis of multivariate observations. In *Proceedings of the 5th Berkeley Symposium on Mathematical Statistics and Probability*, volume 1, 1967.

[25] A. Maedche and S. Staab. Mining ontologies from text. In *Proceedings of the 12th European Workshop on Knowledge Acquisition, Modeling and Management*, pp. 189–202, 2000.

[26] J. S. Marron and M. P. Wand. Exact mean integrated squared error. *The Annals of Statistics*, 20(2):712–736, 1992.

[27] P. Mika. Ontologies are us: a unified model of social networks and semantics. *Web Semantics: Science, Services and Agents on the World Wide Web*, 5(1): 5–15, 2007.

[28] R. Navigli and S. Ponzetto. BabelNet: the automatic construction, evaluation and application of a wide-coverage multilingual semantic network. *Artificial Intelligence*, 193:217–250, 2012.

[29] A. Passant. Using ontologies to strengthen folksonomies and enrich information retrieval in weblogs. In *Proceedings of the 1st AAAI International Conference on Weblogs and Social Media*, 2007.

[30] A. Passant. Meaning of a tag: a collaborative approach to bridge the gap between tagging and linked data. In *Proceedings of the 2008 Linked Data on the Web Workshop*, 2008.

[31] C. Rasmussen. The infinite Gaussian mixture model. In *Proceedings of the 12th International Conference on Advances in Neural Information Processing Systems*, pp. 554–560, 1999.

[32] T. Rattenbury, N. Good, and M. Naaman. Towards automatic extraction of event and place semantics from Flickr tags. In *Proceedings of the 30th ACM International Conference on Research and Development in Information Retrieval*, pp. 103–110, 2007.

[33] R. Redner and H. Walker. Mixture densities, maximum likelihood and the EM algorithm. *SIAM review*, 26(2):195–239, 1984.

[34] M. Rosenblatt. Remarks on some nonparametric estimates of a density function. *The Annals of Mathematical Statistics*, 27(3):832–837, 1956.

[35] S. Rudinac, A. Hanjalic, and M. Larson. Finding representative and diverse community contributed images to create visual summaries of geographic areas. In *Proceedings of the 19th ACM International Conference on Multimedia*, pp. 1109–1112, 2011.

[36] P. Schmitz. Inducing ontology from Flickr tags. In *Proceedings of the Collaborative Web Tagging Workshop*, 2006.

[37] G. Schwarz. Estimating the dimension of a model. *The annals of statistics*, 6(2):461–464, 1978.

[38] P. Serdyukov, V. Murdock, and R. van Zwol. Placing Flickr photos on a map. In *Proceedings of the 30th ACM International Conference on Research and Development in Information Retrieval*, pp. 484–491, 2009.

[39] B. Sigurbjörnsson and R. van Zwol. Flickr tag recommendation based on collective knowledge. In *Proceedings of the 17th International Conference on World Wide Web*, pp. 327–336, 2008.

[40] R. Sinha. A cognitive analysis of tagging, 2005.

[41] S. Sizov. GeoFolk: latent spatial semantics in Web 2.0 social media. In *Proceedings of the 3rd ACM International Conference on Web Search and Data Mining*, pp. 281–290, 2010.

[42] O. van Laere, S. Schockaert, and B. Dhoedt. Finding locations of Flickr resources using language models and similarity search. In *Proceedings of the 1st ACM International Conference on Multimedia Retrieval*, 2011.

[43] T. Vander Wal. Folksonomy Coinage and Definition, 2007.

[44] K. Yanai, H. Kawakubo, and B. Qiu. A visual analysis of the relationship between word concepts and geographical locations. In *Proceedings of the 8th ACM International Conference on Image and Video Retrieval*, 2009.

[45] H. Zhang, M. Korayem, E. You, and D. Crandall. Beyond co-occurrence: discovering and visualizing tag relationships from geo-spatial and temporal similarities. In *Proceedings of the 5th ACM International Conference on Web Search and Data Mining*, pp. 33–42, 2012.

Evaluating the Helpfulness of Linked Entities to Readers

Ikuya Yamada[1][2][5]
ikuya@ousia.jp

Tomotaka Ito[1]
tomotaka@ousia.jp

Shinnosuke Usami[1][3]
usa@ousia.jp

Shinsuke Takagi[1][4]
shinny@ousia.jp

Hideaki Takeda[5]
takeda@nii.ac.jp

Yoshiyasu Takefuji[2][3]
takefuji@sfc.keio.ac.jp

[1]Studio Ousia Inc., 4489-105-221 Endo, Fujisawa, Kanagawa, Japan
[2]Graduate School of Media and Governance, Keio University, 5322 Endo, Fujisawa, Kanagawa, Japan
[3]Faculty of Environment and Information Studies, Keio University, 5322 Endo, Fujisawa, Kanagawa, Japan
[4]Faculty of Policy Management, Keio University, 5322 Endo, Fujisawa, Kanagawa, Japan
[5]National Institute of Informatics, 2-1-2 Hitotsubashi, Chiyoda, Tokyo, Japan

ABSTRACT

When we encounter an interesting entity (e.g., a person's name or a geographic location) while reading text, we typically search and retrieve relevant information about it. Entity linking (EL) is the task of linking entities in a text to the corresponding entries in a knowledge base, such as Wikipedia. Recently, EL has received considerable attention. EL can be used to enhance a user's text reading experience by streamlining the process of retrieving information on entities. Several EL methods have been proposed, though they tend to extract all of the entities in a document including unnecessary ones for users. Excessive linking of entities can be distracting and degrade the user experience.

In this paper, we propose a new method for evaluating the helpfulness of linking entities to users. We address this task using supervised machine-learning with a broad set of features. Experimental results show that our method significantly outperforms baseline methods by approximately 5.7%-12% F1. In addition, we propose an application, *Linkify*, which enables developers to integrate EL easily into their web sites.

Categories and Subject Descriptors

H.3.3 [**Information Storage and Retrieval**]: Information Search and Retrieval; I.2.7 [**Artificial Intelligence**]: Natural Language Processing—*text analysis*

General Terms

Algorithms, Measurement, Experimentation

Keywords

Entity linking; knowledge base; Wikipedia

Figure 1: Entity mentions in a document are automatically converted into links to improve the user's reading experience.

1. INTRODUCTION

When we read text, such as news articles, weblogs, and web pages, we frequently encounter unfamiliar entities, such as people, organizations, and geographic locations. In such cases, we commonly perform a sequence of time-consuming actions: select the entity, submit a query to a search engine, and typically obtain detailed information using web sites, such as Wikipedia. These actions become especially cumbersome in emerging touchscreen devices, such as smartphones and tablet devices, because merely selecting a text requires multiple actions, such as holding and swiping a finger on the screen.

Entity linking (EL) is the task of linking textual entity mentions in a text to entries in a knowledge base (KB) that contains relevant information regarding the entities. In recent years, EL has received considerable attention [13, 14, 17]. Various open-source EL systems [4, 12, 19, 23] that can easily be integrated into real-world applications have also recently been publicized. Wikipedia is typically used as the KB in EL studies, because it has become one of the largest online encyclopedias, containing over four million entries as of July 2013. In this paper, we use Wikipedia as the KB.

EL can be used to streamline the above-mentioned actions by automatically converting entity mentions in the document into links to relevant web sites. For instance, Figure 1 shows an article in which entity mentions are converted into links. Users can easily acquire detailed information regarding a linked entity by clicking the corresponding link.

Wikipedia contains many entities that are rarely helpful to users. For example, it even contains *A*, *I*, and *You*. Furthermore, general entities, such as *Japanese*, are rarely helpful to users when compared to specific entities, such as *Kyoto City*. Excessive linking can be distracting and typically degrades a user's overall experience.[1] Therefore, we need to ensure the *quality* of links, when we present detected entities to users directly. Unfortunately, this problem has received little attention, since most of the existing EL studies focus on its use as a component of other systems (e.g., web search [24]), rather than on direct usage by users.

In this paper, we propose a novel method for evaluating the helpfulness to users of entities detected by EL systems. We define this task as a post-processing step of EL. We use machine-learning to classify whether an entity is likely to be helpful to users. We use a broad set of features to construct a machine-learning model. Additionally, because we do not introduce any dependencies to EL, our system can be combined easily with the existing EL systems.

We have also developed a dataset to evaluate our proposed method. The dataset is based on the *IITB EL dataset* that is widely used in EL studies. Because the IITB dataset is constructed for EL, we need to create extra annotations that specify whether each of the entities in the dataset is likely to be helpful to users. We add the annotations to the dataset using a crowd-sourcing service. Furthermore, the dataset is publicly available for further studies.

We evaluate our method using the above-mentioned dataset. Experimental results show that our method significantly outperforms the existing baseline methods, i.e., TAGME [7, 8] and Milne and Witten [22]. Furthermore, we consider various machine-learning algorithms to examine the algorithm that is most effective for our task, and we conduct detailed studies using various methods to evaluate the effectiveness of the proposed features.

Finally, we demonstrate that our application, *Linkify*, enables developers to enrich web documents easily by linking entities using EL and our method. The application is publicly available as a web service.

In summary, the main contributions of this paper are as follows:

- **Novel method for detecting entities helpful to users**: We propose a novel method for classifying accurately whether an entity is likely to be helpful to users. We use machine-learning with a broad set of features. Experimental results show that our method significantly outperforms baseline methods.

- **Evaluation of the effectiveness of features**: We conduct several detailed experiments to evaluate the features that are effective for our task.

- **Reusable dataset**: We developed and publicized a dataset. The dataset is based on the IITB EL dataset,

with added manual annotations specifying whether each of the entities is likely to be helpful to users.

- **EL application**: We propose an application, *Linkify*, which enables developers to integrate EL functionality easily into their web documents.

The remainder of this paper is organized as follows. In Section 2, we discuss related work, followed by a description of our method in Section 3. We explain our experimental setup in Section 4 and present the experimental results in Section 5. Finally, we demonstrate an EL application in Section 6 and conclude the paper in Section 7.

2. RELATED WORK

Several applications are capable of enriching a document by automatically linking entities (or more broadly, keywords). Microsoft's *Smart-Tag* service, which was released in 2001, is a representative example. Microsoft implemented it in several of its commercial products including Microsoft Word. In 2005, Google provided a similar feature, *AutoLink*, in its Google Toolbar service. However, both of these features were eventually discontinued and are no longer available to the public. A recent example is Yahoo!'s *Contextual Shortcuts* [26] that automatically converts keywords in the web pages into links and displays the search results, when the user hovers over the link. This tool uses numerous query logs obtained from Yahoo!'s commercial search engine. Similar to this paper, its goal is to detect keywords that are interesting to users. However, its method differs significantly from the one presented here in its dependence on proprietary query logs.

With the recent emergence of large online KBs, such as Wikipedia, DBpedia [1], Freebase [2], and YAGO [25], EL has recently attracted considerable attention [13, 14, 17]. A typical EL system first searches all of the potential entity mentions from a text and resolves each of the mentions to a single entity in KB. The main difficulty of EL is *entity ambiguity*; an entity mention in a text is typically ambiguous, requiring the resolving of an entity to a corresponding KB entry. For example, considering the text, *"Apple was founded by Steve Jobs and Steve Wozniak"*, *"Apple"* must be linked to a computer maker, *Apple Inc.*, not an *apple* for eating. This problem was first addressed by Bunescu and Pasca [3] and has been studied comprehensively [5, 6, 10, 11, 15, 20, 22]. An extensive survey of this problem has recently become available [9]. Additionally, when Wikipedia is used as the KB, EL is often referred to as *wikification*.

Typical EL methods are targeted at obtaining higher recall; in other words, the goal is to extract every entity in the text. This is the ideal behavior for the use of EL as a component of other systems, but is not ideal for direct use by users. Excessive linking of entities results in reduced readability of a document. Therefore, an additional pruning step is typically required when displaying linked entities directly to users. To our knowledge, Wikify! [5, 20] first addressed this problem by adding a preprocessing step to EL. This merely eliminates all entities with a lower *link probability*, the probability that the entity mention appears as a link anchor in KB. Milne and Witten [22] present considerable improvements to this task. In contrast to Wikify!, they address this task by adding a post-processing step and using machine-learning with a handful of features. Following [22],

---

[1]For example, Wikipedia instructs its contributers to insert links only where they are relevant and helpful   http://en.wikipedia.org/wiki/Wikipedia:Manual_of_Style#Wikilinks

TAGME [7, 8] also addresses the task mainly for short texts such as Twitter. We use the systems proposed by Milne and Witten and TAGME as our baseline methods.

3. OUR METHOD

In this section, we describe our proposed method.

3.1 Notation

We first introduce some notation:

- D: A document to be analyzed.

- KB: A knowledge base. In this paper, we use Wikipedia as the KB.

- M: A set of entity mentions in D.

- $m \in M$: An entity mention in M.

- E: A set of KB entities in D.

- $e \in E$: An entity in E.

3.2 Task Definition

Given a document D, EL is a task that consists of two subtasks. First, it extracts mentions $M = \{m_1, m_2, ..., m_n\}$ from D, typically by searching mentions using a predefined mention dictionary generated from titles, redirects, and anchor texts in KB. Then, it disambiguates these mentions to entities $E = \{e_1, e_2, ..., e_n\}$. An entity can be *nil* if an appropriate entity does not exist in KB.

The task addressed in this paper is defined as a post-processing step of EL that selects entities that are likely to be helpful to users from the entities that are successfully resolved in the previous EL ($E^* = \{e^* \mid e^* \in E, e^* \neq nil\}$). We address this task using supervised machine learning. The system decides whether a detected entity is likely to be helpful to users by leveraging a manually annotated training dataset detailed in Section 4.2 and a broad set of features described in the next section.

3.3 Machine-Learning Features

We use a broad set of features in our machine-learning model. Features can be classified into six categories: (1) *link probability*, (2) *entity*, (3) *entity class*, (4) *topical coherence*, (5) *textual*, and (6) *mention occurrence*.

3.3.1 Link Probability Features

$LINK\_PROB(m)$ is the probability that m is used as an anchor text in KB. Let $C_t(m)$ be the set of all KB articles in which m appears and $C_a(m)$ be the set of articles that contain m as an anchor; thus, $LINK\_PROB(m)$ can be determined as follows.

$$LINK\_PROB(m) = \frac{|C_a(m)|}{|C_t(m)|}$$

This feature was first proposed in [20] and has been widely used in EL studies [7, 8, 20, 22]. Wikipedia instructs its contributors to create a link only at the first mention in an article[2]; therefore, the probability should be calculated on an article-by-article basis, rather than on the basis of all m occurrences in KB.

In addition, following [22], we introduce two features based on $LINK\_PROB$, namely, $LINK\_PROB\_MAX(e, M)$ and $LINK\_PROB\_AVG(e, M)$, which represent, respectively, the maximum and average link probabilities of M that are linked to e.

3.3.2 Entity Features

Entity features represent several metrics of e that can be directly derived from KB.

- $GENERALITY(e)$ is defined as the minimum depth at which e is located in KB's category tree. This can be determined by performing a breadth-first search starting from KB's root category. This feature was originally proposed in [22].

- $WIKISTATS(e)$ is the average number of page views of e. We calculate the average number of page views from *October 1, 2013* to *October 30, 2013*.

- $IN\_LINKS(e)$ is the number of KB articles that contain links pointing to e.

- $OUT\_LINKS(e)$ is the number of links pointing to other KB articles in e.

- $CATEGORIES(e)$ is the number of KB categories associated with e.

3.3.3 Entity Class Features

Entity class features are obtained from Linked Data repositories, such as DBpedia[3] and Freebase.[4] In such repositories, an entity is assigned one or multiple classes. For example, *Star Wars* is assigned multiple classes, including *Film Series*, in Freebase. Further, DBpedia provides *schema.org*[5] entity classes.

We use each class of DBpedia, Freebase, and schema.org as an independent machine-learning feature. These are denoted as follows:

- $DBPEDIA_{\{class\}}(e)$

- $FREEBASE_{\{class\}}(e)$

- $SCHEMA\_ORG_{\{class\}}(e)$

Because a significant portion of the entities contained in DBpedia and Freebase are derived from Wikipedia, they have a corresponding entity if it exists in Wikipedia. We extract the classes from the */type/object/type* property of Freebase's JSON API and the *rdf:type* property of DBpedia's RDF.

3.3.4 Topical Coherence Feature

There is only one topical coherence feature, $COHERENCE(e, E)$, which represents how an entity is related to the topics of the document. This can be estimated by measuring how e is related to other entities in E. An in-link-based relatedness measure initially proposed in [21] is typically used to measure the relatedness between two entities in EL studies. This measure is defined as

$$REL(e_1, e_2) = \frac{\log(\max(|c(e_1)|, |c(e_2)|) - \log(|c(e_1) \cap c(e_2)|))}{\log(|KB|) - \log(\min(|c(e_1)|, |c(e_2)|))}$$

---

[2] http://en.wikipedia.org/wiki/Wikipedia:Manual_of_Style/Linking

[3] http://dbpedia.org/

[4] http://www.freebase.com/

[5] http://schema.org/

where $|KB|$ is the total number of articles in KB, and $c(e)$ is the KB articles that have a link to e.

Then, $COHERENCE(e, E)$ is calculated by averaging the relatedness between e and all the other entities in E.

$$COHERENCE(e, E) = \frac{\sum_{e' \in E'} REL(e, e')}{|E'|}$$

where $E' = \{e' \mid e' \in E, e' \neq nil, e' \neq e\}$.

This feature was initially proposed in [22].

3.3.5 Textual Features

Textual features are derived from the textual content of m and the title of e.

- $CAPITALIZED(m)$ indicates whether m is capitalized.

- $MENTION\_LEN(m)$ denotes how many tokens are contained in m.

- $TITLE\_LEN(e)$ denotes how many tokens are contained in the title of e.

- $MENTION\_IN\_TITLE(m, e)$ indicates whether m contains the title of e.

- $TITLE\_IN\_MENTION(m, e)$ indicates whether the title of e contains m.

- $MENTION\_EQ\_TITLE(m, e)$ indicates whether m exactly equals the title of e.

- $EDIT\_DISTANCE(m, e)$ is the similarity between m and the title of e. Similarity is measured using edit distance.

3.3.6 Mention Occurrence Features

Mention occurrence features represent how m appears in D.

- $SPREAD(m, D)$ is the number of tokens between the first occurrence and the last occurrence of m in D.

- $FREQUENCY(m, D)$ is the number of times that m occurs in D.

These features are normalized by the length of D.

4. EXPERIMENTAL SETUP

We designed several experiments. In this section, we detail our experimental setup.

4.1 Knowledge Base

We use the July 2013 English version of Wikipedia, containing *4,172,241 entities* and *1,032,306 categories*, as the KB in our experiments. Note that since Wikipedia contains many general concepts (such as Human and Computer), an entity referred to in this paper may not always correspond to its original definition.

Please note that, although we use Wikipedia as the KB in this paper, our proposed method can be applied to other Wikipedia-based KBs such as DBpedia, Freebase, and YAGO. Freebase and YAGO also contain entities that are not included in Wikipedia; applying our method to such entities remains our future work.

Additionally, we use open-source *Wikipedia Miner Toolkit* [23] for analyzing *Wikipedia backup dumps*.[6] We also obtain the page view data used to calculate $WIKISTATS$ from *Wikimedia downloads*.[7]

4.2 Dataset

To evaluate our method, we developed a dataset based on the public *IITB EL dataset*,[8] widely used in existing EL studies [7, 10, 11, 15, 27]. We had considered using the *TAC2009 EL dataset* [17], also frequently used in EL studies; however, we decided not to adopt it because its entity selection is biased. Ambiguous entities that are difficult to disambiguate, are intentionally selected as the target entities [9]. The *AQUAINT dataset* used in [22] was also considered. However, that dataset contains only 449 items, which is extremely few for use as a dataset for our task.

The IITB EL dataset was constructed by Kulkarni et al. [15]. They manually annotate entities in various news articles obtained from popular news sites, such as Google News and ESPNSTAR. The dataset includes a variety of domains, including sports, entertainment, science and technology, and health.

Because the dataset was initially developed for EL, it does not contain annotations for the task that we address in this paper. Therefore, we add an annotation to each entity in the dataset indicating whether the entity is likely to be helpful to users.

The dataset initially consisted of 19,751 annotations, from which we filtered the *nil* entities (entities that do not exist in KB). In addition, as the dataset was constructed originally from a dump of the August 2008 version of Wikipedia, some of the entities have been changed and removed. We fixed these errors manually, and consequently, 11,189 entities remained.

Here, the problem is that an annotation can be biased by the annotators' perceptions; thus, deciding whether an entity is helpful typically depends on an annotator's subjective judgment. In order to avoid this, we used various online annotators through a crowd-sourcing service called *Amazon Mechanical Turk*.[9] The service enables us to perform labor-intensive tasks instantly by offering the tasks to thousands of online workers.

We posed the following question to the annotators.

> "Do you think converting the highlighted keyword into a link is sufficiently helpful to readers of this document and could it improve the readers' overall user experience?"

The annotators were given the following options to specify whether linking the entity is helpful.

- **Very helpful**: Converting this keyword into a link is highly helpful to readers.

- **Helpful**: Converting this keyword into a link might be helpful to some readers.

- **Rarely helpful**: Converting this keyword into a link is rarely helpful to readers.

---

[6] http://dumps.wikimedia.org/enwiki/
[7] http://dumps.wikimedia.org/other/pagecounts-raw/
[8] http://www.cse.iitb.ac.in/soumen/doc/CSAW/
[9] https://www.mturk.com/mturk/

Link probability features	
$LINK\_PROB(m)$	The probability that m appears as an anchor text in KB
$LINK\_PROB\_MAX(e, M)$	The maximum $LINK\_PROB(m)$ of mentions that link to e
$LINK\_PROB\_AVG(e, M)$	The average $LINK\_PROB(m)$ of mentions that link to e
Entity features	
$GENERALITY(e)$	The minimum depth of e from the root in the category structure of KB
$WIKISTATS(e)$	The average number of page views of e
$IN\_LINKS(e)$	The number of KB articles that have a link to e
$OUT\_LINKS(e)$	The number of links pointing to other KB articles in e
$CATEGORIES(e)$	The number of categories assigned to e
Entity class features	
$FREEBASE\_\{class\}(e)$	Is e assigned a class named *class* in Freebase?
$DBPEDIA\_\{class\}(e)$	Is e assigned a class named *class* in DBpedia?
$SCHEMA\_ORG\_\{class\}(e)$	Is e assigned a class named *class* in Schema.org?
Topical coherence feature	
$COHERENCE(e, E)$	Representing how e is related to the central topics of D
Textual features	
$CAPITALIZED(m)$	Is m capitalized?
$MENTION\_LEN(m)$	The number of tokens in m
$TITLE\_LEN(e)$	The number of tokens in e's title
$MENTION\_IN\_TITLE(m, e)$	Does e's title contain m?
$TITLE\_IN\_MENTION(m, e)$	Does m contain e's title?
$MENTION\_EQ\_TITLE(m, e)$	Does e's title exactly equal m?
$EDIT\_DISTANCE(m, e)$	The similarity between m and e's title
Mention occurrence features	
$SPREAD(m, D)$	The number of tokens between the first and last m occurrences in D
$FREQUENCY(m, D)$	The number of times m appears in D

Table 1: List of features. More details in Section 3.3.

- **Not helpful**: Converting this keyword into a link is not helpful to readers.

Note that we intentionally use *keyword*, rather than *entity*, because the annotators can not possibly understand the exact meaning of entity.

Figure 2 shows the actual screen presented to the annotators. We display the question with the title and the body text of the document, the link, and a short description of the target Wikipedia article, along with options for the above-mentioned answers. Further, the corresponding mention string of the target entity is highlighted in red. We also explain to the annotators that this dataset is intended to be used for improving the user's reading experience by linking entities, and we ask annotators to imagine themselves as actual readers of the document.

We require an Amazon Mechanical Turk *Masters Qualification* for annotators and pay three cents as payment for an annotation. In addition, we assign each annotation task to three individual annotators. As a result, we successfully obtained 33,567 annotations, detailed in Table 2, from 60 individual annotators. In addition, annotators processed an average of 559 tasks and a maximum of 5,793 tasks.

In this paper, we treat the answers *Very helpful* and *Helpful* as positive answers, and *Rarely helpful* and *Not helpful* as negative answers in order to address the task simply as a binary classification problem. Furthermore, we derive the ground-truth answers from counting votes for the corresponding three answers.

The dataset is publicly available[10] for further studies.

----

[10] http://www.github.com/studio-ousia/
el-helpfulness-dataset

Answer	Annotations
Very helpful	4,798
Helpful	5,977
Rarely helpful	6,472
Not helpful	16,320
Total	33,567

Table 2: Detailed number of annotations obtained from Amazon Mechanical Turk.

4.3 Evaluation Criteria

This paper uses *precision*, *recall*, and *F1*, popular in EL studies [7, 10, 15, 20, 22], as performance metrics. F1 is a harmonic mean of precision and recall, defined as:

$$F1 = \frac{2 * Precision * Recall}{Precision + Recall}$$

In this paper, we use F1 as the primary metric.

4.4 Machine-Learning Algorithms

We experiment with various machine-learning algorithms to find the one that performs best. Following the algorithms used in [22], we adopt *support vector machine (SVM)* and *C4.5*. With regard to SVM, we experiment with the non-linear RBF kernel (denoted as SVM_{RBF}) and the linear kernel (denoted as SVM_{LINEAR}). In addition, we add recent ensemble machine-learning algorithms, including *AdaBoost* and *Random Forest*, because ensemble-based algorithms were reported to yield better performance in recent EL studies [13, 18].

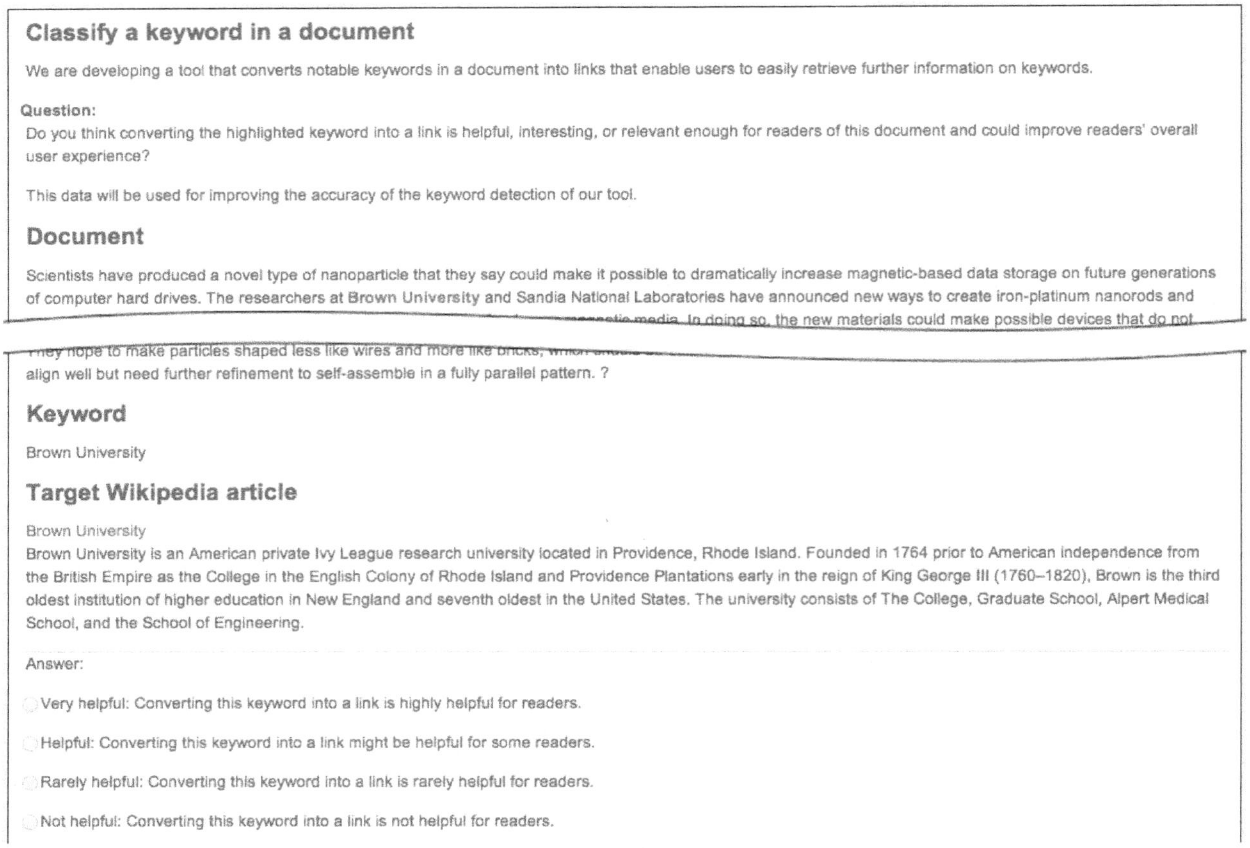

Classify a keyword in a document

We are developing a tool that converts notable keywords in a document into links that enable users to easily retrieve further information on keywords.

Question:

Do you think converting the highlighted keyword into a link is helpful, interesting, or relevant enough for readers of this document and could improve readers' overall user experience?

This data will be used for improving the accuracy of the keyword detection of our tool.

Document

Scientists have produced a novel type of nanoparticle that they say could make it possible to dramatically increase magnetic-based data storage on future generations of computer hard drives. The researchers at Brown University and Sandia National Laboratories have announced new ways to create iron-platinum nanorods and magnetic media. In doing so, the new materials could make possible devices that do not ... They hope to make particles shaped less like wires and more like bricks, which should align well but need further refinement to self-assemble in a fully parallel pattern. ?

Keyword

Brown University

Target Wikipedia article

Brown University
Brown University is an American private Ivy League research university located in Providence, Rhode Island. Founded in 1764 prior to American independence from the British Empire as the College in the English Colony of Rhode Island and Providence Plantations early in the reign of King George III (1760–1820), Brown is the third oldest institution of higher education in New England and seventh oldest in the United States. The university consists of The College, Graduate School, Alpert Medical School, and the School of Engineering.

Answer:

◯ Very helpful: Converting this keyword into a link is highly helpful for readers.

◯ Helpful: Converting this keyword into a link might be helpful for some readers.

◯ Rarely helpful: Converting this keyword into a link is rarely helpful for readers.

◯ Not helpful: Converting this keyword into a link is not helpful for readers.

Figure 2: Annotation screen displayed to the annotators of Amazon Mechanical Turk.

AdaBoost can be configured according to the number of instances used in the model. In this paper, we adopt 1,000 instances. Random Forest can also be parameterized by (1) the number of instances contained in the model (denoted by num_trees) and (2) the number of features used in each instance (denoted by $num\_features$). In this paper, we use $num\_trees = 1,000$ and $num\_features = 3$. We also provide an evaluation when varying num_trees in Section 5.3.4.

4.5 Baselines

In this section, we introduce three baseline methods, $LinkProb$, $TAGME$, and $Milne\&Witten$.

4.5.1 LinkProb

The first baseline is a model that uses only one feature, $LINK\_PROB$. We simply eliminate entities that have link probabilities lower than a threshold. We estimate that the best threshold in our dataset is approximately 10.6%.

Note that this baseline is extremely similar to the method of Wikify! [5, 20]. The system extracts the top 6%[11] of entities in the document based on $LINK\_PROB$.

4.5.2 TAGME

$TAGME$ [7, 8] proposes a method using only two features, $LINK\_PROB$ and $COHERENCE$. We use $C4.5$ to com-

bine these features, because it is reported in the full-paper version[12] of the paper to be the best performing algorithm.

4.5.3 Milne & Witten

$Milne\ and\ Witten$ [22] propose a method using machine-learning with a handful of features, including

- $LINK\_PROB\_MAX$
- $LINK\_PROB\_AVG$
- $COHERENCE$
- $GENERALITY$
- $SPREAD$
- $FREQUENCY$

They also use features based on the locations of the mention in the document, which we eliminated from our feature set in our feature selection process. These features are included in this baseline method.

The system also uses the confidence score assigned by its proposed EL method. Since most of the EL methods do not provide the confidence scores, and we do not want to introduce dependencies to a specific EL method, we eliminate this feature from the feature set of this baseline method.

---

[11]The probability (6%) is estimated by calculating the average of the probability of a word appearing as a link in Wikipedia.

[12]http://arxiv.org/pdf/1006.3498v2.pdf

	Precision	Recall	F1
$C4.5$	0.8281	0.8069	0.8173
SVM_{LINEAR}	0.8581	0.7892	0.8221
SVM_{RBF}	0.8676	0.7806	0.8217
$AdaBoost$	0.8484	0.8383	0.8433
$RandomForest$	**0.8697**	**0.8419**	**0.8554**

Table 3: Results of various machine-learning algorithms.

	Precision	Recall	F1
$LinkProb$	0.6980	0.7761	0.7349
$TAGME$	0.7936	0.7782	0.7857
$Milne\&Witten$	0.8079	0.7904	0.7989
$OurMethod$	**0.8697**	**0.8419**	**0.8554**

Table 4: Results of our method with the baseline methods.

Therefore, the method used in this paper is slightly different from the original. Additionally, C4.5 is used to combine these features.

5. EXPERIMENTAL RESULTS

In this section, we show our experimental results. For all machine-learning algorithms, we perform five-fold cross validation, and scores are averaged over all folds.

5.1 Machine-Learning Methods

As mentioned in Section 4.4, we use our method experimentally with various machine-learning algorithms to investigate which algorithm is the most effective for our task.

Table 3 shows the results of several machine-learning algorithms. First, Random Forest has the highest performance in all metrics. Therefore, we use Random Forest as our machine-learning algorithm in the reminder of this paper.

With regard to the other algorithms, AdaBoost performs competitively with Random Forest. Surprisingly, C4.5 obtains an F1 competitive with the more sophisticated SVM. SVM performs relatively better in precision, though it is worse in recall. In addition, the performance of SVM is not improved on using the RBF-based non-linear kernel instead of the linear kernel.

5.2 Baselines

Table 4 contains the results of our method and the baseline methods. It shows clearly that our method outperforms the baseline methods significantly by approximately *5.7%-12% F1*. *Milne&Witten* achieves the highest scores on all metrics in the baseline methods and *TAGME* follows it. In addition, both of those baseline results are significantly better than those of *LinkProb*, which naively depends on a simple heuristic.

5.3 Feature Analysis

In this section, we evaluate how each of the proposed features contributes to performance.

5.3.1 Effectiveness of Each Feature

First, we evaluate the contribution of each feature separately. Table 5 shows the 15 most effective features measured using the information gain averaged over all instances

Feature name	F1	ΔF1
$LINK\_PROB\_AVG\,(LP)$		
$LINK\_PROB\_MAX\,(LP)$		
$LINK\_PROB\,(LP)$	0.8158	
$COHERENCE\,(TC)$	0.8201	0.43%
$SPREAD\,(MO)$	0.8243	0.43%
$IN\_LINKS\,(ENT)$	0.8314	0.70%
$TITLE\_LEN\,(TXT)$	0.8353	0.39%
$WIKISTATS\,(ENT)$	0.8346	-0.07%
$CATEGORIES\,(ENT)$	0.8449	1.03%
$OUT\_LINKS\,(ENT)$	0.8427	-0.22%
$FREQUENCY\,(MO)$	0.8438	0.11%
$CAPITALIZED\,(TXT)$	0.8461	0.23%
$GENERALITY\,(ENT)$	0.8459	-0.03%
$MENTION\_LEN\,(TXT)$	0.8482	0.24%
$EDIT\_DISTANCE\,(TXT)$	0.8488	0.06%

Table 5: The 15 most effective features. F1 scores are calculated by incrementally adding each feature to the model.

in the Random Forest model. In order to investigate the contribution of each of the listed features further, we add each of them incrementally to the feature set, beginning with the features possessing the highest values, and evaluate how F1 is improved. As explained in Section 4.4, we use $num\_features = 3$; consequently, we need at least three features to construct the initial model.

The link probability features $LINK\_PROB\_AVG$, $LINK\_PROB\_MAX$, and $LINK\_PROB$ are observed to be the three most effective features. Applying Random Forest using only these features obtains approximately *81.58% F1*, which is even better than all of the baseline methods. This indicates that entities that are likely to appear as link anchors in KB are also likely to be helpful to users.

$COHERENCE$ and $SPREAD$ also appear to be highly discriminative. Recall that $COHERENCE$ represents the average relatedness among entities in the document. Similar to $COHERENCE$, $SPREAD$ can be recognized as a representation of an entity's relatedness to the document topics, because an entity spread across the document is likely to be more related than an entity occurring only in the narrower part of the document. Therefore, we consider that there is a strong correlation between an entity's relatedness to the document and its helpfulness to a user.

Finally, the entity features IN_LINKS and $CATEGORIES$ improve the performance effectively. They can be recognized as representations of the *popularity* and *specificity* of an entity in KB, which seem to have strong correlations to the helpfulness of the entity to a user.

Additionally, the ranked list contains all three link probability features (LP), all five entity features (ENT), the one topical coherence feature (TC), four of the seven textual features (TXT), and both of the two mention occurrence features (MO). In addition, no entity class feature (EC) is contained in the list. We examine the effectiveness of entity class features in the following section.

5.3.2 Effectiveness of Features by Categories

Next, we evaluate the effectiveness of each category of features separately. Since the three most effective features in the previous experiment are link probability features, we consider that these features play the most essential role in

Feature types	Precision	Recall	F1	ΔF1
LP Only	0.8228	0.8093	0.8158	
LP+ENT	**0.8511**	0.8266	0.8385	2.27%
LP+EC	0.8487	**0.8341**	**0.8412**	2.54%
LP+TC	0.8281	0.8117	0.8197	0.39%
LP+TXT	0.8268	0.8266	0.8266	1.08%
LP+MO	0.8279	0.8117	0.8196	0.38%

Table 6: Effectiveness of features by their categories.

our feature set. Therefore, we start building an initial model using only link probability features and measure the effectiveness of other feature categories by adding each category of features separately to the initial model.

Table 6 shows the results. We can observe that all of the categories contribute to the performance. In particular, entity class features increase F1 significantly by 2.54%, although they are not listed in Table 5. This is probably because entity class features are highly sparse in our dataset, and consequently, their averaged information gains are lower than those of other features. Notably, entity class features contribute to recall. We further investigate the entity class features in the next section. Additionally, entity features also contribute effectively to performance and particularly improve precision.

5.3.3 Effectiveness of Entity Class Features

As shown in the previous section, entity class features contribute significantly to performance. To investigate specifically what entity classes are effective for our task, we separately extract top-ranked entity class features from the ranked feature list generated in Section 5.3.1. The 15 most effective features are shown below.

- $DBPEDIA_{/ontology/Agent}$
- $FREEBASE_{/people/person}$
- $FREEBASE_{/business/employer}$
- $FREEBASE_{/organization/organization}$
- $SCHEMA\_ORG_{/Person}$
- $DBPEDIA_{/ontology/Person}$
- $FREEBASE_{/book/book\_subject}$
- $DBPEDIA_{/ontology/Disease}$
- $FREEBASE_{/business/business\_operation}$
- $SCHEMA\_ORG_{/Organization}$
- $DBPEDIA_{/ontology/Organization}$
- $FREEBASE_{/sports/pro\_athlete}$
- $FREEBASE_{/location/location}$
- $DBPEDIA_{/ontology/Athlete}$
- $DBPEDIA_{/base/consumermedical/medical\_term}$

We observe that classes that indicate the entity is a *named entity*, such as *agent*, *person*, *organization*, and *location*, are highly ranked. Interestingly, some specific classes, such as *disease*, *medical_term*, and *athlete* are also effective. This is probably because our dataset contains articles on sports, science and technology, and health.

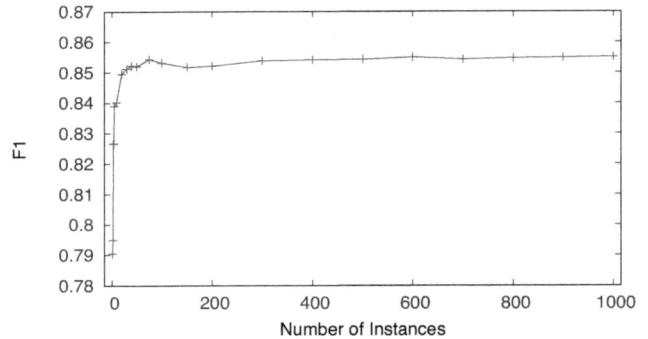

Figure 3: The F1 score results obtained by varying the number of instances in the Random Forest model.

5.3.4 Parameter Settings

Last, we consider the best parameter associated with our Random Forest model. As explained in Section 4.4, Random Forest can be configured according to the number of instances (*num_trees*) in the model. Figure 3 shows how varying *num_trees* affects the F1 score.

F1 reaches its optimum score at approximately 100 instances. The algorithm also performs consistently, when it has more than 250 instances. As explained in Section 4.4, we use *num_trees* = 1,000, which also achieves the best score in this evaluation.

6. ENTITY LINKING APPLICATION

Finally, we demonstrate an application called *Linkify*, a tool that enables developers to enrich their web pages easily by integrating EL functionality into their web sites. Since the tool is implemented as a short JavaScript that runs on the web browser, it can be integrated instantly into any web page by inserting its script tag.

When the script is added to a web page, it converts entity mentions into links automatically by inserting anchor tags. One unique aspect of our system is that the generated link is not just a link to a KB article. On encountering an interesting entity while reading a document, a user probably wants to use the entity to submit a query to a search engine rather than opening it in KB. Therefore, the tool displays a small widget (Figure 4) containing relevant search links such as *Google*, *Twitter*, and *YouTube*. Entity search accounts for a significant portion of the traffic in search engines [16], so streamlining entity search is considered to be extremely significant for improving the user experience. Additionally, the widget initially appears small and can be expanded to show further links by clicking the expand button.

The system also includes our own server-side system that contains our EL implementation and a slightly modified version of the method proposed in this paper. The system is publicly available at `http://linkify.mobi`.

7. CONCLUSION AND FUTURE WORK

In this paper, we proposed a novel method for accurately evaluating user helpfulness of entities in a document. Although there already exist several works that address this problem, we demonstrated that performance can be im-

Figure 4: When the user clicks on the link, a small widget is displayed. The widget appears small initially and can be expanded to show further links.

proved significantly using supervised machine-learning with a broad set of proposed features. We found that *link probability features*, which represent the probability of an entity appearing as a link anchor in KB, are highly effective so that the model that uses only these features can achieve comparable performance to existing methods. However, performance can be significantly improved by introducing the novel features that we proposed in this paper. Most notably, *entity class features*, which represent the class of an entity (e.g., film, actor, organization) improve performance remarkably. In addition, *entity features*, which represent the knowledge of an entity, such as its *popularity* and *specificity*, significantly contribute to performance. We also evaluated several machine-learning methods and found that *Random Forest* performs most effectively for our task. Finally, we proposed an application, *Linkify*, which allows developers to integrate EL functionality into their web sites easily.

For future work, we would like to attempt to improve our model by using actual click-through data obtained from our proposed application. In addition, as the dataset used in our experiments consists mainly of news articles, we intend to apply our proposed method to different kinds of corpus, such as tweets.

References

[1] S. Auer, C. Bizer, G. Kobilarov, J. Lehmann, R. Cyganiak, and Z. Ives. DBpedia: a nucleus for a web of open data. *The semantic web*, pages 722–735, 2007.

[2] K. Bollacker, C. Evans, P. Paritosh, T. Sturge, and J. Taylor. Freebase: a collaboratively created graph database for structuring human knowledge. In *Proceedings of the 2008 ACM SIGMOD International Conference on Management of Data (SIGMOD '08)*, pages 1247–1250, 2008.

[3] R. Bunescu and M. Pasca. Using encyclopedic knowledge for named entity disambiguation. In *Proceedings of the 11th Conference of the European Chapter of the Association for Computational Linguistics (EACL-06)*, pages 9–16, 2006.

[4] D. Ceccarelli, C. Lucchese, S. Orlando, R. Perego, and S. Trani. Dexter: an open source framework for entity linking. In *Proceedings of the Sixth International Workshop on Exploiting Semantic Annotations in Information Retrieval (ESAIR '13)*, pages 17–20, 2013.

[5] A. Csomai and R. Mihalcea. Linking documents to encyclopedic knowledge. *Intelligent Systems, IEEE*, 23(5):34–41, 2008.

[6] S. Cucerzan. Large-scale named entity disambiguation based on Wikipedia data. In *Proceedings of the 2007 Joint Conference on Empirical Methods in Natural Language Processing and Computational Natural Language Learning (EMNLP-CoNLL)*, pages 708–716, 2007.

[7] P. Ferragina and U. Scaiella. TAGME: on-the-fly annotation of short text fragments (by wikipedia entities). In *Proceedings of the 19th ACM International Conference on Information and Knowledge Management (CIKM '10)*, pages 1625–1628, 2010.

[8] P. Ferragina and U. Scaiella. Fast and accurate annotation of short texts with Wikipedia pages. *Software, IEEE*, 29(1):70–75, 2012.

[9] B. Hachey, W. Radford, J. Nothman, M. Honnibal, and J. R. Curran. Evaluating entity linking with Wikipedia. *Artificial Intelligence*, 194:130–150, 2012.

[10] X. Han and L. Sun. An entity-topic model for entity linking. In *Proceedings of the 2012 Joint Conference on Empirical Methods in Natural Language Processing and Computational Natural Language Learning (EMNLP-CoNLL '12)*, pages 105–115, 2012.

[11] X. Han, L. Sun, and J. Zhao. Collective entity linking in web text: a graph-based method. In *Proceedings of the 34th International ACM SIGIR Conference on Research and Development in Information Retrieval (SIGIR '11)*, pages 765–774, 2011.

[12] J. Hoffart, M. A. Yosef, I. Bordino, H. Fürstenau, M. Pinkal, M. Spaniol, B. Taneva, S. Thater, and G. Weikum. Robust disambiguation of named entities in text. In *Proceedings of the Conference on Empirical Methods in Natural Language Processing (EMNLP '11)*, pages 782–792, 2011.

[13] H. Ji, R. Grishman, and H. T. Dang. Overview of the TAC2011 knowledge base population track. In *Proceeding of Text Analysis Conference (TAC)*, 2011.

[14] H. Ji, R. Grishman, H. T. Dang, K. Griffitt, and J. Ellis. Overview of the TAC 2010 knowledge base population track. In *Proceeding of Text Analytics Conference (TAC)*, 2010.

[15] S. Kulkarni, A. Singh, G. Ramakrishnan, and S. Chakrabarti. Collective annotation of Wikipedia

entities in web text. In *Proceedings of the 15th ACM SIGKDD International Conference on Knowledge Discovery and Data Mining (KDD '09)*, pages 457–466, 2009.

[16] T. Lin, P. Pantel, M. Gamon, A. Kannan, and A. Fuxman. Active objects: actions for entity-centric search. In *Proceedings of the 21st International Conference on World Wide Web (WWW '12)*, pages 589–598, 2012.

[17] P. McNamee and H. Dang. Overview of the TAC 2009 knowledge base population track. *Proceeding of Text Analysis Conference (TAC)*, 2009.

[18] E. Meij, W. Weerkamp, and M. de Rijke. Adding semantics to microblog posts. In *Proceedings of the Fifth ACM International Conference on Web Search and Data Mining (WSDM '12)*, pages 563–572, 2012.

[19] P. N. Mendes, M. Jakob, A. García-Silva, and C. Bizer. DBpedia Spotlight: shedding light on the web of documents. In *Proceedings of the 7th International Conference on Semantic Systems (I-Semantics '11)*, pages 1–8, 2011.

[20] R. Mihalcea and A. Csomai. Wikify!: linking documents to encyclopedic knowledge. In *Proceedings of the Sixteenth ACM Conference on Information and Knowledge Management (CIKM '07)*, pages 233–242, 2007.

[21] D. Milne and I. H. Witten. An effective, low-cost measure of semantic relatedness obtained from Wikipedia links. In *Proceedings of the First AAAI Workshop on Wikipedia and Artificial Intelligence (WIKIAI'08)*, 2008.

[22] D. Milne and I. H. Witten. Learning to link with Wikipedia. In *Proceeding of the 17th ACM Conference on Information and Knowledge Management (CIKM '08)*, pages 509–518, 2008.

[23] D. Milne and I. H. Witten. An open-source toolkit for mining Wikipedia. *Artificial Intelligence*, 194:222–239, 2013.

[24] P. Pantel and A. Fuxman. Jigs and lures: associating web queries with structured entities. In *Proceedings of the 49th Annual Meeting of the Association for Computational Linguistics: Human Language Technologies (HLT '11)*, volume 1, pages 83–92, 2011.

[25] F. M. Suchanek, G. Kasneci, and G. Weikum. Yago: a core of semantic knowledge. In *Proceedings of the 16th International Conference on World Wide Web (WWW '07)*, pages 697–706, 2007.

[26] V. von Brzeski, U. Irmak, and R. Kraft. Leveraging context in user-centric entity detection systems. In *Proceedings of the Sixteenth ACM Conference on Information and Knowledge Management (CIKM '07)*, pages 691–700, 2007.

[27] Z. Zheng, F. Li, M. Huang, and X. Zhu. Learning to link entities with knowledge base. In *Proceedings of the 2010 Annual Conference of the North American Chapter of the Association for Computational Linguistics (NAACL HLT '13)*, pages 483–491, 2010.

Asking the Right Question in Collaborative Q&A systems

Jie Yang, Claudia Hauff, Alessandro Bozzon, Geert-Jan Houben
Delft University of Technology
Mekelweg 4, 2628 CD
Delft, The Netherlands
{j.yang-3, c.hauff, a.bozzon, g.j.p.m.houben}@tudelft.nl

ABSTRACT

Collaborative Question Answering (cQA) platforms are a very popular repository of crowd-generated knowledge. By formulating questions, users express needs that other members of the cQA community try to collaboratively satisfy. Poorly formulated questions are less likely to receive useful responses, thus hindering the overall knowledge generation process. Users are often asked to reformulate their needs, adding specific details, providing examples, or simply clarifying the context of their requests. Formulating a good question is a task that might require several interactions between the asker and other community members, thus delaying the actual answering and, possibly, decreasing the interest of the community in the issue. This paper contributes new insights to the study of cQA platforms by investigating the editing behaviour of users. We identify a number of editing actions, and provide a two-step approach for the automatic suggestion of the most likely editing actions to be performed for a newly created question. We evaluated our approach in the context of the Stack Overflow cQA system, demonstrating how, for given types of editing actions, it is possible to provide accurate reformulation suggestions.

Categories and Subject Descriptors: H.3.3 Information Storage and Retrieval: Information Search and Retrieval
General Terms: Experimentation
Keywords: Collaborative Question Answering; Classification; Stack Overflow

1. INTRODUCTION

Collaborative Question Answering (cQA) systems are highly popular Web portals where everyone can ask questions, and (self-appointed) experts jointly contribute to the creation of evolving, crowdsourced, and peer-assessed knowledge bases [5][19], often in a reliable, quick and detailed fashion. Examples of such portals are Yahoo! Answers[1] (for all kinds of

---

[1] http://answers.yahoo.com/

questions) and Stack Exchange[2], which consists of a number of sub portals, each dedicated to a particular topic, such as travelling, mathematics or programming.

In cQA systems users (*askers*) post questions, and rely on other community members to provide a suitable solution to their information need. Potential *answerers* (users that answer questions) look through the list of existing questions, typically ordered by recency, and decide whether or not to contribute to ongoing discussions. Such decisions are influenced by a multitude of factors, including time constraints, quality and difficulty of the question, and the knowledge of the answerer. Users can often also *comment* or *vote* on existing questions and answers. Commonly, when satisfied, an *asker* can mark an answer as *accepted*, thus declaring her need satisfied. Incentives to answer are often based on gamification features of a platform, such as reputation points [3].

Although the median time until a first answer is posted in response to a question can be in the order of a few minutes (as shown for instance for Stack Overflow [16]), more and more questions [4] remain ignored or without an accepted answer. Questions are unanswered when their meaning is not clear to the community members, or when it is not possible, given the available information, to understand the nature of the problem (e.g. the source code that produces a compiling error is missing). A good question should have enough details (but not too much), enough depth (without drifting from the core subject), examples (if applicable) as well as avenues already investigated by the asker [17]. Well-formed questions attract more high-quality answers than poorly formed questions, as subject experts are more likely to help users that already put some effort into finding an answer themselves [4, 16, 21].

We focus on Stack Overflow[3], a cQA platform covering a large variety of topics related to the software development domain. Introduced in 2008, Stack Overflow features more than 5 million questions, and 10 million answers provided by more than 2 million users[4]. To manage and increase the likelihood of good and useful answers, users are provided with editing functionality, which allows the improvement of questions based on the feedback from other community members. Edits usually happen in response to comments or answers, a process which might require several interactions (asker waits for comments or answers, adapts the question, waits again,

---

[2] http://stackexchange.com/
[3] http://stackoverflow.com/
[4] These numbers are based on the Stack Overflow data released in September 2013.

etc.) and, ultimately, might cause the question to sink in the list of open issues.

Our work contributes a novel approach to improve the question formulation process. We envision a system that upon question submission, provides askers with feedback about the aspects of the question they need to change (improve) in order to phrase their needs in the *right* way. This in turn is more likely to attract the *right* answerers.

Here, we perform a first study to investigate the feasibility of this idea. In particular, we propose and evaluate the following two-step approach:

1. Determine whether the question is of high quality or whether it requires an *edit* (**Question Editing Prediction**).

2. When an edit is required, identify which aspect(s) of the question need(s) to be improved to turn it into a high quality question (**Edit Type Prediction**).

In the process, we address the following research questions:

- **RQ1**: To what extent are traces of question edits (and the lack of edits) indicative of well or poorly formed questions?

- **RQ2**: Given sets of properly/poorly formed questions, is it possible to automatically detect which category the question belongs to?

- **RQ3**: Is it possible to predict the type of action required to make a question "better", i.e. improve its quality?

Our results show that:

1. The need for edits is indeed indicative of a question's quality.

2. The need for a question to be edited can be predicted with high accuracy.

3. The identification of the type of required edit is much more difficult to predict: we classified edit types in three categories, and found that only one of them can be accurately predicted.

In the remainder of this paper we first briefly cover related work in Section 2. Then, in Section 3 we present our methodology and developed hypotheses. The experimental setup and the experiments are presented in Sections 4 and 5 respectively. Finally, we discuss our findings and present future work in Section 6.

2. RELATED WORK

Collaborative question answering systems have been emerging as important collective intelligence platforms. Domain specific cQA platforms such as Stack Overflow are transforming the way people share experience, create knowledge and, ultimately, contribute to the evolution of a given field [22, 23].

Several works focused on the issue of question and answers quality in cQA systems, providing a solid scientific support to the premises of our work. Burns and Kotval [6] describe thirteen dimensions that can be used to distinguish questions, including answer factuality, complexity, and depth of answer needed. Dearman and Truong [7] surveyed 135 active members of the Yahoo! Answers platform, identifying the composition of the question as one of the main factors leading to its consideration by the community. Harper et al. [10] investigated predictors of answer quality in several cQA sites, identifying as relevant dimensions the question topic, type (e.g. factual, opinion), and prior effort (i.e. the requester clearly indicated a previous attempt to solve the problem). On a higher abstraction level, an investigation into Stack Overflow identified four main types of questions [17]: *Need-To-Known, Debug/Corrective, How-To-Do-It*, and *Seeking-Different-Solution*. Recent work has also considered the evolution of user behaviour over time: Ahn et al. [1] studied whether users learn to be better question askers over time, by correlating past actions (e.g. receiving upvotes or comments, accepting answers, etc.) with the quality of the subsequent ones. Past work has also investigated the nature of unanswered questions on Stack Overflow [4, 16, 21] - two of the main reasons behind a question remaining unanswered are the lack of clarity and the lack of required information (source code, etc.).

Previous work has also focused on a variety of prediction tasks, including question difficulty prediction [9], question longevity, user expertise estimation and question recommendation. Anderson et al. [2] studied the factors that contribute to the long-lasting value of questions in Stack Overflow. Liu et al. [13] proposed a competition-based model for estimating question difficulty by leveraging pairwise comparisons between questions and users. Another area related to our work is the estimation of user expertise in cQA systems. In [24] it was found that the expertise networks in cQA systems possess different characteristics from traditional social networks, and based on this finding an expertise metric was proposed. Similar aspects were also studied in [12, 19]. Relevant examples of contributions addressing the problem of routing questions to the right answerer can be found in [14, 15] and [25].

To the best of our knowledge, no previous work has targeted the problem of question editing in cQA systems. Iba et al. [11] analysed editing patterns of Wikipedia contributors using dynamic social network analysis; although several observations are related to our setting, the nature and purpose of wikis is different from the one of cQAs. The type and nature of collaborative acts was studied in [20] on the specific example of users proposing novel mathematical problems, or contributing to their solutions. While providing important insights, [20] focused on a qualitative assessment of the collaboration problem. The application of those insights, e.g. by means of automatic analysis methods, was not investigated.

3. METHODOLOGY

This section describes our experimental methodology. We first discuss and present the types of question edits typically encountered on Stack Overflow. Publicly available data dumps[5] contain the entire history of all questions posted to Stack Overflow. Every revision of a question includes information about the editor (the asker or another user) and the time of the edit. We considered only questions whose question body was edited, thus ignoring changes in the title or in the tags.

---

[5]https://archive.org/details/stackexchange

Then, we discuss how we approached the *edit prediction task* as well as the *edit type prediction task* (Section 3.2). Finally, Section 3.3 presents a number of hypotheses, derived from our research questions of Section 1.

3.1 Common Question Edits

We first need to define when we consider a question to be of high and of low quality respectively.

A question is of high quality and thus **well formed** if:

1. it has not been edited in the past; and,

2. it has received at least two answers (the median number of answers for questions on Stack Overflow).

Previous work [18] relies on the number of positive preferences (upvotes) as question quality indicator. Due to the significant correlation between upvotes and number of answers[6] we settled on the number of answers as indicator.

In contrast, we hypothesise that a question might be initially of **poor quality** if it does not receive an answer within 12 minutes after its publication (the median answer time on Stack Overflow), or if it is edited one or more times before it receives the first answer.

However, not all edits are equal: a question may be edited by the asker herself or by a different Stack Overflow user[7]; an edit can lead to a major change in semantics or be simply a correction of a spelling error or a re-formatting of the question.

In order to gain qualitative insights, we first conducted a small-scale study aimed at eliciting the most important edit categories on Stack Overflow. We define as *important* the first edit (in the sequence of edits) that is temporally followed by one or more answers.

We randomly selected 600 (*question,important edit*) pairs, and had three trusted annotators describing the nature of the observed changes. We found that most of our edits fall into one (or more) of the following eight categories:

- **Source code refinement**: the provided source code is modified; additions are more frequent than removal or truncation.

- **Context**: the asker provides additional context and clarifies what she wants to do/achieve, as well as information about the "bigger picture" of this question.

- **HW/SW details**: inclusion of additional details about the hardware and/or software used (software version, processor specification, etc.).

- **Example**: the asker provides examples of inputs, or describes the expected results.

- **Problem statement**: the asker clarifies the technical nature of the problem by posting an error message, stack traces or log messages.

- **Attempt**: the asker details the attempts she already made in order to solve the problem, either before posing the question or in response to comments or posted answers.

---

[6]In our dataset with 5M questions, we observed a linear correlation coefficient of 0.25, p-value<0.001.
[7]Stack Overflow users are allowed to edit other users' questions after they reach a particular reputation level.

- **Solution**: the asker adds/comments on the solution found for the question. The Stack Overflow community explicitly encourages contributions where the user asking the question also provides the final answer. Some askers append their solutions, others create an answer in the discussion.

- **Formatting**: the asker fixes small issues including spelling errors and code formatting.

Table 1 provides an example of each edit type found in our data set (described in detail in Section 4), apart from the *formatting* category. This initial study shows that the most important edit types are related to question clarification as well as to the description of attempts made to solve the problem - including the working solution. We therefore decided to not further consider the *formatting* category.

3.2 Predicting Edits and Edit Types

Extracting Useful Question Edits.

The purpose of this step is to create the training and test data sets for our experiments. Our goal is to create a data set characterised by the presence of two distinct classes of questions, which will be used to train a classifier able to properly identify *edited questions* from *non-edited questions*.

Edited questions were selected as follows. Let there be n edits of question Q_i expressed as revisions $R_{t_{a_1}}^{i_1}, ..., R_{t_{a_n}}^{i_n}$. Here, Q_i can also be considered as $R_{t_{a_0}}^{i_0}$, i.e. the original question posted at time t_{a_0}. Revision IDs are sorted according to time, each subsequent revision is an edit of the previous revision.

Users (the asker as well as anybody else) can also *comment* on a question or *answer* it. Let $C_{t_j}^i$ be a comment on question Q_i or any of its revisions at time t_j. Similarly, let $A_{t_k}^i$ be an answer to question Q_i (or any of its revisions) at time t_k. Which revision the comment or answer are referring to, depends on the timestamp of the comment or answer. We exploit these comments and answers and extract all pairs of original & edited question, with the following sequence characteristics:

$$R_{t_{a_0}}^{i_0} \rightarrow C_{t_j}^i \rightarrow R_{t_{a_1}}^{i_1} \rightarrow A_{t_k}^i \qquad (1)$$

where $t_{a_0} < t_j < t_{a_1} < t_k$. The idea is to be able to automatically catch edits stimulated by discussions with the community.

Intuitively, we consider edits that:

- have been made potentially in response to a first comment; and

- after the edit, triggered the posting of an answer.

To further ensure that the edits occurred in response to the posted comment, we only consider those pairs of original and edited questions where there is some overlap in terms between the comment and the added text in the edit.

As an example, in response to a comment:

"Please add some source code"

a user might edit a question and add:

"My code: [actual code]*."*

Edit Category	Post ID	Added Text (Excerpt)
Attempt (1st edit)	9943644	Update 1: I've tested the application with NHProf without much added value: NHProf shows that the executed SQL is ...
HW/SW details (1st edit)	7473762	I'm running OS 10.6.8

Source code refinement (1st edit)	13318757	Here is the code:
		
		`import android.content.Context;`
		`import android.graphics.Matrix;`
		`...`

Problem statement (1st edit)	7500461	The Error:
		`Exception in thread "AWT-EventQueue-0"`
		`com.google.gson.JsonParseException: The JsonDeserializer`
		`com.google.gson.DefaultTypeAdapters$CollectionTypeAdapter@4e76fba0`
		`failed to deserialize json object ....`

Example (1st edit)	11875006	I have a list of numbers like this in PHP array, and I just want to make this list a little bit smaller. `2000:   3 6 7 11 15 17 25 36 42 43 45 ...`
Context (1st edit)	13923053	EDIT: I have 'jquery-1.8.3.min.js' included first, then I have the line $.noConflict();. Then I have includes for external files using the prototype framework. then I include my user defined function and finally call it. But, I figured ...

Solution (2nd edit)	9215463	**EDIT 2: **Okay that's done the trick. Using @Dervall 's advice I replaced the MessageBox line with a hidden window like this:
		
		`MSG msg;`
		`HWND hwnd;`
		`WNDCLASSEX wcx;`

Table 1: **Each edit type example shows part of the text added in the first or second edit respectively. The *Post ID* is the Stack Overflow ID. Note that revisions of post with ID postID can be accessed via** *http://stackoverflow.com/posts/*postID*/revisions.*

With this basic filtering step we were able to capture around 170K quality-enhancing edits. The resulting question-edit pairs were then ranked according to the amount of editing, measured by the number of characters changed in the edited and original version of the question.

Our *non-edited questions* were selected from among all questions that were never edited and have received at least one answer. We ranked the non-edited questions according to their number of received answers – intuitively, the more answers a question receives, the higher is the engagement of community members with the question.

Extracting Edit Types.

Based on the categories identified in Section 3.1, we conducted a follow-up annotation study on 1000 *edited* questions randomly selected from the 25K most edited questions (i.e. those with the longest edits), with the purpose to derive labelled data for our edit types classifiers.

We collected annotations[8] for the questions according to four categories derived from our initial findings presented in Section 3.1: *Code*, *SEC* (merging the categories *Prob-* *lem Statement*, *Example* and *Context*), *Attempt* (merging the *Solution* and *Attempt* categories) and *Detail*. The decision to group the categories as presented was taken due to the practical difficulties the annotators encountered deciding between them. In later stages, we discarded the *Detail* category due to the small number of annotated instances. Edits which do not fall into one of our categories were labelled as a "null edit".

We note, that for every question to be annotated, *all* edits of that question were labelled, i.e. $R^i_{t_j}$ for $j = 1...n$.

The annotations were then used to train three binary classifiers aimed at providing suggestions about the type of edit to be performed, for those questions that were deemed as in need for edits.

3.3 Hypotheses

This section presents the research hypotheses, based on the research questions posed in Section 1, we investigate in our work.

- **Hypothesis 1**: Communities attracting beginner's programmers (e.g. Android programming, Web design) receive a larger number of edited questions than communities which require more in-depth knowledge

---

[8]We describe the annotation process in greater detail in Section 4.2.

(e.g. Assembler programming, functional programming).

- **Hypothesis 2**: Users new to Stack Overflow post questions in need of refinement. Over time, users learn how to post good quality questions.

- **Hypothesis 3**: Not only the time a user has spent on the portal is important, but also the amount of knowledge the user already has about a particular topic. We posit that users with substantial knowledge on a particular topic are less likely to post questions which require a substantial edit.

- **Hypothesis 4**: As the Stack Overflow platform gained popularity, less and less questions requiring a substantial edit have been posted. Users read the guidelines and "learn" from different forums/portals how to properly ask questions.

- **Hypothesis 5**: New users are most likely to "forget" to add source code and previous attempts to their questions.

4. EXPERIMENTAL SETUP

We use the public Stack Overflow dump[9]. Manual annotations, training and test data used in ours experiments are available for download at `https://github.com/WISDelft/WIS_HT_2014`. We consider, for training purposes, all questions posted up to and including December 31, 2012; the test set includes all questions posted between January 1, 2013 and September 6, 2013. We use a logistic regression-based classifier[10]. The feature set is composed of unigrams (terms) extracted from the dataset, an approach that has been shown to perform well for different prediction tasks in the past. The chosen classifier, though likely to not yield the best possible accuracy, allows us to gain valuable insights into the importance of different features.

4.1 Edit Prediction

The training and evaluation of the edit prediction classifier has been performed using the ranked list of edited and non-edited questions described in Section 3.2.

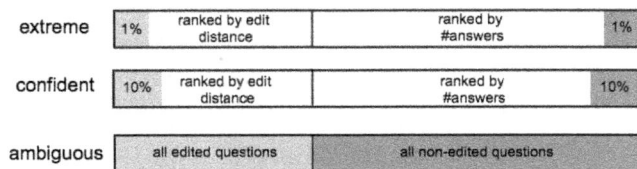

Figure 1: Both the training and test data were partitioned in three ways. The edit prediction classifier was trained on the *Extreme* set of the training data. The evaluation was performed on all data partitions of the test data.

Given these two rankings of the questions in the positive (*edited*) and negative (*non-edited*) class, we create three different data partitions, presented in Figure 1.

[9]Available online at `https://archive.org/details/stackexchange`
[10]Implemented in sklearn `http://scikit-learn.org`

- The **Extreme** set contains the top 1% of positive and negative samples.

- The **Confident** set contains the 10% highest ranked edited and non-edited questions respectively.

- The **Ambiguous** set contains all edited as well as all non-edited questions.

We derive this partitioning of the data separately for our training and test data. We train our edit prediction classifier on the *Extreme* data partition of the training data (i.e. questions posted until the end of the year 2012) and evaluate the performance of the classifier on the *Extreme, Confident* and *Ambiguous* data partitions of our test data (questions posted in 2013).

For training purposes, due to the skewedness of the class distribution (there are more non-edited than edited questions), we randomly sample from the negative class until we have reached the same number of samples as exist in the positive class. A similar sampling process is also used for the test data, with the exception of the *Ambiguous* set, which includes all test questions.

The reason for experimenting with different data partitions is the nature of the task. Our overall goal is to predict for each and every question in our test set whether or not it requires an edit. Due to the nature of the questions, we expect that questions in the *Extreme* test set can be classified with a higher accuracy than questions in the *Ambiguous* test set.

Table 2 contains an overview of the total number of questions used for training and test purposes. We train on nearly 36,000 questions and test our pipeline on up to 1.8 million questions.

4.2 Predicting the Edit Type

Given a question which has been flagged as "to edit" in the first step, this processing step determines which aspect(s) of the question require an edit.

The 1000 annotated questions feature an average of 3.05 ± 1.84 edits. Three trusted annotators evaluated disjoint sets of 300 questions each. Additionally, a common set of 100 questions were labelled by all three annotators to test the agreement. The inter-annotator agreements for the four edit categories are shown in Table 3.

Edit Type	Code	SEC	Detail	Attempt
Kappa	0.67	0.59	0.19	0.65

Table 3: Inter-annotator agreement of edit category annotation, measured by Fleiss' Kappa.

The number of questions belonging to each category are reported in Figure 2. We used a majority consensus approach to determine the category of the 100 overlapping questions. Recall, that we annotate every edit of a question, and thus the total number of items shown in Figure 2 exceeds 1000. Of all edits, 30.75% could not be assigned to any of the four categories. We did not observe significant differences between the edit type distribution at different edit iterations (i.e. first edits are similarly distributed to second or third order edits).

We observe that *Code*, *SEC* and *Attempt* are often occurring categories, indeed more than half of the questions

	#Questions Overall	#Edited Questions	#Non-edited Questions
Test: Extreme	14,920	7,460	7,460
Test: Confident	85,072	42,536	42,536
Test: Ambiguous	1,772,649	522,874	1,249,775
Training: Extreme	35,892	17,946	17,946

Table 2: Basic statistics of our training and test data for the edit prediction task. Since more non-edited than edited questions exist, for the *Extreme* and *Confident* partitions, the number of non-edited questions was matched to the number of edited questions by sampling a subset of all questions in the respective dataset.

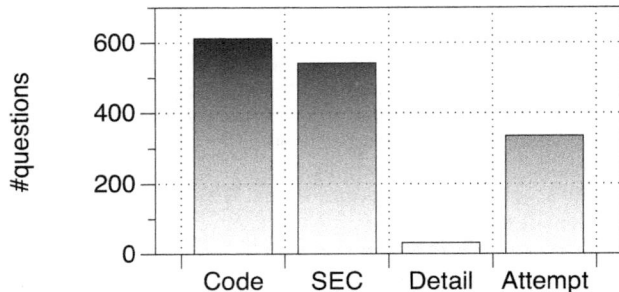

Figure 2: Annotation study results: number of questions with an edit from a particular category. The SEC category captures the problem Statement, Examples and the Context.

have at least one *Code* edit (it is also not uncommon to have several). For these three categories the inter-annotator agreement is also moderate to high (0.59 or higher). In contrast, the category *Detail* suffers both from very low inter-annotator agreement and few positive annotation results.

We train three binary classifiers, dropping the *Detail* category from further experiments due to the annotator disagreement and the small sample size. All questions with a particular edit type belong to the positive class for that edit type classifier, the remaining questions of our annotation set form the negative class. The classifier training follows a similar setup to step one. We derive features from the original question and include it in the training set for a classifier if at least one of the question's edit was annotated as belonging to the classifier's category. Due to the small size of the training data though we cannot rely on word unigrams as features. To avoid overfitting, we employ Latent Semantic Analysis [8] and rely on the 100 most significant dimensions as features. To evaluate the edit type prediction task, we use 5-fold cross validation.

5. EXPERIMENTS

We first present the results of our edit and edit type prediction tasks. Subsequently we present an analysis of a number of user-dependent factors that we hypothesise to influence the likelihood of a posted question requiring an edit (based on the hypotheses presented in Section 3.3).

5.1 Edit Prediction

The performance of our classifier on our test sets is presented in Table 4. As expected, the best results are achieved

for the *Extreme* test set with an F1 score of 0.7. The recall of 0.78 implies that most questions which require an edit are classified as such by our approach, thus clearly demonstrating its feasibility. The classifier is trained on a feature set with a total of 7,206 features.

Test type	Precision	Recall	F1
Extreme	0.63	0.78	0.70
Confident	0.58	0.69	0.63
Ambiguous	0.51	0.65	0.57

Table 4: Classifier performance on the edit prediction task across our three test sets.

When comparing the performance of *Extreme* and *Ambiguous*, the impact of the test set generation process becomes evident. For the *Ambiguous* test set the performance of all three measures drops significantly. This is not surprising, as the middle ground questions (containing small edits or being poorly phrased but remaining unedited) are the most difficult for a classifier to identify correctly. We conclude that our proposed classifier, if employed on the stream of new Stack Overflow questions, would be able to spot the most severe cases of questions requiring an edit with high accuracy. We leave the exploitation of more advanced machine learning models and additional features for future work.

Important Features.
One of the benefits of a regression-based classifier is the ability to gain insights about the importance of different features based on the feature coefficients. In Table 5 we list the features (unigrams) with the highest and lowest coefficients respectively (after feature normalization). For instance, the term *microsoft* is an important feature for to-be-edited questions, while *lexer* is negatively associated with question edits, presumably because users discussing lexers have specific problems and a relatively deep understanding of their topic.

5.2 Edit Type Prediction

We now consider step 2 of our pipeline - the prediction of the type of edit(s) required to create a well-formed question. The results are shown in Table 6, rows one to three.

While the edits of *Code* and *SEC* can be predicted with moderate to high accuracy, the prediction of the *Attempt* category is essentially random.

Automatically Augmenting the Training Data.
Having so far relied on our manually annotated data only, we now turn to an automatic approach to augment the training data (the test data is fixed to our manually annotated

Strategy	Edit category	Nr. positive	Nr. negative	Precision	Recall	F1
No augmentation	Code	612	388	0.63	0.83	0.71
	SEC	542	458	0.57	0.62	**0.59**
	Attempt	336	664	0.39	0.45	0.40
Positive augmentation	Code	8157	338	0.63	0.92	0.75
	SEC	542	458	0.57	0.62	0.59
	Attempt	2387	664	0.40	0.49	0.44
Positive+ negative augmentation	Code	8157	8157	0.63	0.95	**0.76**
	SEC	542	542	0.55	0.49	0.52
	Attempt	2387	2369	0.38	0.56	**0.45**

Table 6: **Classifier performance on the edit type prediction task. Numbers underlined are the ones higher than previous classification version. The best F1 scores in all edit type prediction tasks are highlighted in bold. Note that Nr. positive and Nr. negative only indicates the number of questions that affect training of the classifier. Precison, Recall and F1 are calculated based on the 1000 annotated questions.**

Unigram	Coef.	Unigram	Coef.
dbcontext	0.88	mental	-0.29
microsoft	0.57	nicer	-0.31
xx	0.57	understood	-0.31
com	0.55	pre-compil	-0.34
tick	0.47	lexer	-0.41
neater	0.46	c/c++	-0.42
byte	0.45	firstnam	-0.47
inbuilt	0.44	testabl	-0.53
socket	0.42	string	-18.48
reproduc	0.39	archiv	-19.94

Table 5: **Regression coefficients of the most positively and negatively weighted features (unigrams) for the edit predictiont ask.**

questions). The goal is to provide sounder evidence on the performance of our predictors. We test two augmentation strategies:

1. **Positive augmentation**: we assume that questions with the term `code` appearing in the edited version while not in the original version have a big chance to be a positive question of edit type *Code*; this is verified in our annotated dataset where this is true for more than 38% of the questions in the edit type *Code* category. We use this strategy to collect additional training data from the *Extreme* training set; for the edit type *Code* we identified nearly 7000 additional questions. We followed the same approach for the *Attempt* category, relying on the term `tried` (this assumption holds true for 21% of our annotated data set). No augmentation was performed for category *SEC*, as no indicative terms could be determined.

2. **Negative augmentation**: We consider non-edited question in the *Extreme* training set as well-formed questions, and include similar number as edited questions to be the instances of the negative class.

To ensure that the classification results are not influenced by our selection criteria, the features `code` and `tried` are removed in the training phase.

The classifier performance with both types of enlarged training data are reported in Table 6, rows four to nine.

In the case of positive augmentation it can be observed that both the *Code* and *Attempt* prediction performances increase. The improvements in F1 stem from an increase in recall. This is natural since the augmented training data contains only positive questions.

After negative questions were added as well, the edit type predictions *Code* and *Attempt* are very slightly enhanced. This indicates that the negative questions does not contain much information of each other. For type *SEC* the classifier performs as poorly as a random baseline.

To summarise, we have found that the edit prediction task can be solved with high accuracy, while the edit type prediction task is more difficult to solve. We have presented strategies to semi-automatically enlarge the training data which have been shown to be beneficial for the *Code* and *Attempt* categories.

5.3 Hypotheses Testing

We now turn to an analysis of our hypotheses presented in Section 3.3.

Up to now we have only considered the question content in edit and edit type prediction. We now explore the impact that different factors can have on the quality of a question. Such factors include the topic of a question, the user's prior experience on Stack Overflow, user knowledge on the question's topic, and the temporal influence of Stack Overflow. We first test our **hypotheses H1-H5**, then add related features for the prediction tasks to our classifier to investigate whether they can make a difference.

5.3.1 Topical Influence

We investigate **hypothesis H1**, i.e. if questions about particular frameworks or languages (e.g. `JavaScript`, `Java`), in particular those often used by programming beginners, are more prone to requiring an edit than questions related to more advanced topics such as software engineering (e.g. `design-patterns` or `compilers`).

For simplicity, we consider the tags assigned to each question as indicator of a question's topic. To avoid the influence of insignificant edits, we consider all questions of the *Confident* datasets (both training and test). Since a question may be assigned multiple tags, a question may appear in multiple tag sets. We rank the tags according to:

$$\frac{\#questions\ with\ substantial\ edits}{\#questions\ without\ an\ edit} \qquad (2)$$

filtering out all those tags that appear too infrequently in the data set. We consider this ranking to provide us with an indication of a community's amount of beginners.

Rank	Tag	Ratio	#Questions in *Confident*
1	`asp.net-mvc-4`	6.16	505
2	`jsf`	6.02	615
3	`symfony2`	5.57	338
4	`r`	4.34	2,067
5	`opencv`	4.10	402
6	`matlab`	4.02	981
7	`core-data`	3.91	446
8	`angularjs`	3.67	288
9	`mod-rewrite`	3.52	297
10	`asp.net-mvc-3`	3.50	1,443
	....		
192	`vim`	0.52	746
193	`visual-studio-2008`	0.50	921
194	`web-applications`	0.49	774
195	`oop`	0.45	2,711
196	`database-design`	0.45	1,220
197	`unit-testing`	0.44	1,526
198	`logging`	0.44	624
199	`testing`	0.41	849
200	`design`	0.34	1,386
201	`svn`	0.27	1,186

Table 7: Overview of the topics (tags) which contain the most and least edited questions. All available data was used to generate the rank and ratios. The last column shows the number of questions in the *Confident* data set.

Table 7 provides an overview of the ten most and least edited topics (identified by their tags) in our data set. As hypothesised, the top-ranking topics are those more framework or language related, while low-ranking topics are more generic or advanced. For instance, `asp.net` questions usually require a lot of edits. In contrast, topics like `design` or `testing` require edits with a considerably lower likelihood.

We also report the number of questions a tag is assigned to in the *Confident* data set. It can be observed that the tags of most edited questions usually occur less than the non-edited ones (except the `r` tag). This indicates that not the large number of beginners leads to poorly phrased questions. It is more likely that these questions need to be edited because they are more complex and require more clarifications.

5.3.2 User Influence

Hypothesis H2 is concerned with the user effect - how does a user's familiarity with the portal Stack Overflow affect the probability of an edit? If **hypothesis H2** holds, we expect that the probability of a substantial edit decreases with increasing user experience with the platform. Such experience can be implied based on different types of user actions such as posting questions, answering, commenting or voting on postings.

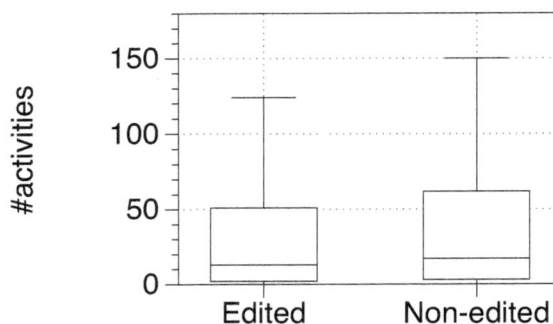

Figure 3: Influence of user experience on posting a question which requires an edit.

We use the *Confident* data set (training & test), which contains a total of 151,762 users – (16.4%) of all Stack Overflow askers. For each question, we determine the number of questions and answers in the entire data set (not limited to *Confident*) the asker has posted previously, then bin them into two groups: edited vs. non-edited questions. The comparison of these two groups is shown in Figure 3 in the form of a box plot. The number of past activities of a user is - as hypothesised - a significant indicator for the likelihood of a question edit. Users with fewer activities are more likely to edit their questions than more experienced users (to a statistical significant degree, p-value<0.001 by a Mann-Whitney test).

5.3.3 Knowledge Influence

Hypothesis H3 considers not only the activity of a user in the past (regardless of the topic), but also the knowledge of a user on a topic. In particular, we hypothesise that the number of questions requiring an edit decreases as a user gathers more experience on the topic (as she becomes more familiar with the terminology, etc.).

To evaluate this hypothesis, for each asker in the *Confident* data set (training+test) we plot the number of days since registering on Stack Overflow vs. the number of specific topic-related questions that require a substantial edit asked on this topic. As before, we use tags as topic indicator.

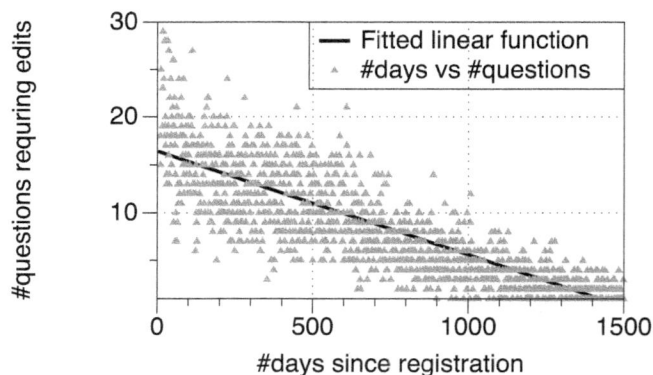

Figure 4: Influence of user knowledge on question edits. Results shown for topic (tag) C#.

Our analysis shows that these two variables are highly negatively correlated, with a Spearman correlation of -0.72 (p-value<0.001). We remove all users with a registration date older than 1500 days, and denote the activity of a user by a vector $(a_1, \ldots, a_{1500})$ where a_i denotes the number of questions and answers posted by this user at day i since his registration. Figure 4 shows the cumulative vector for all users involved in the topic C#. It can be observed that as time passes, a user asks less questions that require substantial edits. Though we only present the results for C#, we note that we observe the same trends for the top 20 topics (tags) on Stack Overflow, which include Java, iOS and Python.

5.3.4 Temporal Influence

Similarly to **hypotheses H2** and **H3**, we can also evaluate **H4** by considering all questions posted in a particular year. If **H4** holds, we expect to see a decreasing trend in questions requiring an edit. There is an influential factor, though, which will lead to more questions that require edits: new users registering and asking questions. Figure 5 plots:

$$E = \#edited\ questions - \#non\text{-}edited\ questions$$

in the *Confident* data partition over time, while Figure 6 depicts the evolution of user registrations in the same time period.

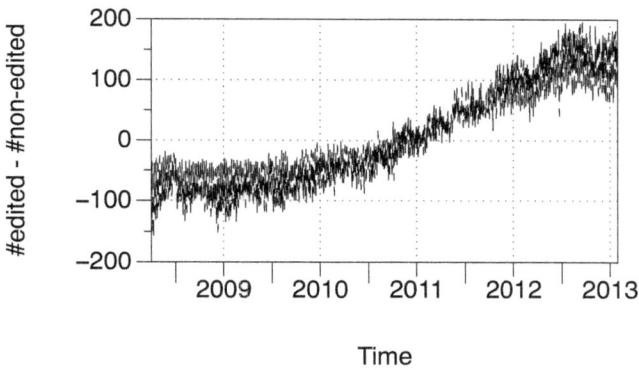

Figure 5: Overview of the gradual increase in edited questions on Stack Overflow over time.

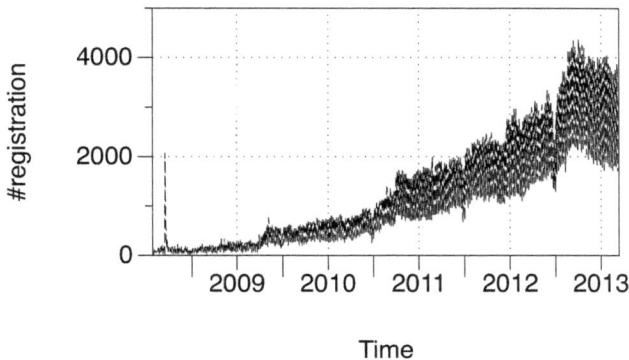

Figure 6: User registration over time.

The Spearman correlation between E and the number of user registrations is 0.79 with a p-value<0.001. This result provides additional support to the motivations of our work, as it shows that, despite the fact that an individual user asks fewer questions when he stays longer on Stack Overflow, the increasing popularity of the platform leads to the creation of several more questions that could benefit from a systematic assessment of their quality.

5.3.5 Influence of User "Age" on Edit Type

Hypothesis 5 is concerned with the role that user seniority plays in influencing the types of information (*Code*, *Attempt*, or *SEC*) that are (not) initially included in the questions.

For each of the 1000 annotated questions, we calculate the age of the question as the difference between its posting date and the registration date, in Stack Overflow, of its asker.

Figure 7 depicts the difference, in terms of age, of edited and non-edited questions in the context of the *Code* edit type: we observe that this type of edits is significantly (p-value<0.001 by a Mann-Whitney test) more likely to occur in the early days of a user's activity on the platform; *SEC* and *Attempt* edits do not show significant differences.

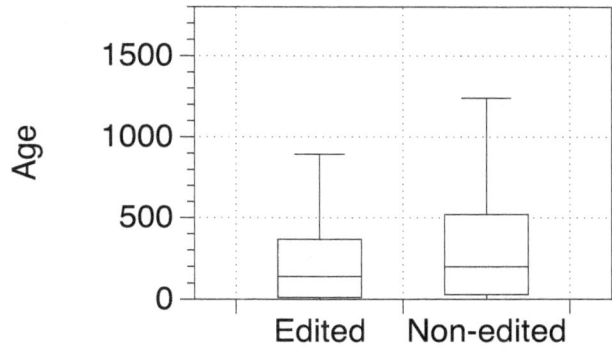

Figure 7: Influence of user age on posting a question which requires a *Code* type edit.

5.3.6 Influence on Prediction

In a final experiment, we created additional features for edit and edit type prediction based on the results of the investigated hypotheses. The following features were added to the existing feature set: 1) tags of a question, 2) #activities of the asker, 3) #days between the registration of the asker and the time she posted the question, and, 4) #days between a question was posted and the time Stack Overflow was launched.

In our experiments we did not observe substantial differences in F1 when adding those features to our original (unigram-based) feature set. This indicates that the content, i.e., the terms in a question, are more important that contextual factors for predicting the question (type) edit.

6. CONCLUSIONS

As cQA systems grow in popularity and adoption, the ability to provide automated quality enhancement tools is a key factor to guarantee usability, reliability, and high knowledge creation quality. In this paper we explored a specific aspect of user contributions: the formulation of well-formulated questions. In order to receive useful answers, a question should feature positive characteristics such as specificity (i.e. provide enough details to understand the nature of the problem), and clarity (i.e. provide examples, or personal experiences).

We analysed the editing behaviour of Stack Overflow users, and identified three main classes of useful editing actions. We then applied machine learning techniques to define an approach for the automatic suggestion of edit types for newly created questions. With respect to the research questions listed in Section 1 we can draw the following conclusions:

- **RQ1**: Question edits are a very good indicator of the quality of a given question, as their presence is also a reflection of several distinct traits of the asker (e.g. being new to a given technology, knowledge in the targeted topic, etc.).

- **RQ2**: Using a simple unigram model, we observe classification accuracies (F1) between 63% and 70%. This is a very promising result which indicates the possibility for significant improvements when adopting more sophisticated techniques.

- **RQ3**: Out of three identified classes of edits, only one (namely *code refinement*) features good prediction performance. The results are encouraging, but suggest that a more in-depth analysis of the different type of editing actions is required, to gain a better understanding of their features.

In addition to improvements to the components of our current question editing suggestion method, future work includes the extension of our analysis to other domains covered by the Stack Exchange platform (e.g. math, literature, etc.), to collect more insights about the editing behaviour of users across different knowledge domains.

Acknowledgements

This publication was supported by the Dutch national program COMMIT. This work was carried out on the Dutch national e-infrastructure with the support of SURF Foundation.

7. REFERENCES

[1] J. Ahn, B. S. Butler, C. Weng, and S. Webster. Learning to be a Better Q'er in Social Q&A Sites: Social Norms and Information Artifacts. *ASIST*, 50(1):1–10, 2013.

[2] A. Anderson, D. Huttenlocher, J. Kleinberg, and J. Leskovec. Discovering Value from Community Activity on Focused Question Answering Sites: A Case Study of Stack Overflow. In *Proceedings of the 18th ACM SIGKDD International Conference on Knowledge Discovery and Data Mining*, KDD '12, pages 850–858, 2012.

[3] A. Anderson, D. Huttenlocher, J. Kleinberg, and J. Leskovec. Steering User Behavior with Badges. In *Proceedings of the 22Nd International Conference on World Wide Web*, WWW '13, pages 95–106, 2013.

[4] M. Asaduzzaman, A. S. Mashiyat, C. K. Roy, and K. A. Schneider. Answering Questions About Unanswered Questions of Stack Overflow. In *Proceedings of the 10th Working Conference on Mining Software Repositories*, MSR '13, pages 97–100, 2013.

[5] M. Bouguessa, B. Dumoulin, and S. Wang. Identifying Authoritative Actors in Question-answering Forums: The Case of Yahoo! Answers. In *Proceedings of the 14th ACM SIGKDD International Conference on Knowledge Discovery and Data Mining*, KDD '08, pages 866–874, 2008.

[6] M. Burns and X. Kotval. Questions About Questions: Investigating How Knowledge Workers Ask and Answer Questions. *Bell Labs Technical Journal*, 17(4):43–61, 2013.

[7] D. Dearman and K. N. Truong. Why Users of Yahoo!: Answers Do Not Answer Questions. In *Proceedings of the SIGCHI Conference on Human Factors in Computing Systems*, CHI '10, pages 329–332, 2010.

[8] S. C. Deerwester, S. T. Dumais, T. K. Landauer, G. W. Furnas, and R. A. Harshman. Indexing by Latent Semantic Analysis. *JASIS*, 41(6):391–407, 1990.

[9] B. V. Hanrahan, G. Convertino, and L. Nelson. Modeling Problem Difficulty and Expertise in Stackoverflow. In *Proceedings of the ACM 2012 Conference on Computer Supported Cooperative Work Companion*, CSCW '12, pages 91–94, 2012.

[10] F. M. Harper, D. Raban, S. Rafaeli, and J. A. Konstan. Predictors of Answer Quality in Online Q&A Sites. In *Proceedings of the SIGCHI Conference on Human Factors in Computing Systems*, CHI '08, pages 865–874, 2008.

[11] T. Iba, K. Nemoto, B. Peters, and P. A. Gloor. Analyzing the Creative Editing Behavior of Wikipedia Editors: Through Dynamic Social Network Analysis. *Procedia - Social and Behavioral Sciences*, 2(4):6441 – 6456, 2010.

[12] P. Jurczyk and E. Agichtein. Discovering authorities in question answer communities by using link analysis. In *Proceedings of the sixteenth ACM Conference on Information and Knowledge Management*, CIKM '07, pages 919–922, 2007.

[13] J. Liu, Q. Wang, C.-Y. Lin, and H.-W. Hon. Question Difficulty Estimation in Community Question Answering Services. In *EMNLP*, pages 85–90, 2013.

[14] X. Liu, W. B. Croft, and M. Koll. Finding experts in community-based question-answering services. In *Proceedings of the 14th ACM International Conference on Information and Knowledge Management*, CIKM '05, pages 315–316, 2005.

[15] D. Ma, D. Schuler, T. Zimmermann, and J. Sillito. Expert recommendation with usage expertise. In *IEEE International Conference on Software Maintenance*, ICSM '09, pages 535–538, 2009.

[16] L. Mamykina, B. Manoim, M. Mittal, G. Hripcsak, and B. Hartmann. Design Lessons from the Fastest Q&a Site in the West. In *Proceedings of the SIGCHI Conference on Human Factors in Computing Systems*, CHI '11, pages 2857–2866, 2011.

[17] S. Nasehi, J. Sillito, F. Maurer, and C. Burns. What makes a good code example?: A study of programming Q&A in Stack Overflow. In *IEEE*

International Conference on Software Maintenance, ICSM '12, pages 25–34, 2012.

[18] A. Pal, S. Chang, and J. A. Konstan. Evolution of Experts in Question Answering Communities. In *Proceedings of the International AAAI Conference on Weblogs and Social Media*, ICWSM '12, pages 274–281, 2012.

[19] A. Pal, F. M. Harper, and J. A. Konstan. Exploring Question Selection Bias to Identify Experts and Potential Experts in Community Question Answering. *ACM Trans. Inf. Syst.*, 30(2):10:1–10:28, 2012.

[20] Y. R. Tausczik, A. Kittur, and R. E. Kraut. Collaborative Problem Solving: A Study of MathOverflow. In *Proceedings of the 17th ACM Conference on Computer Supported Cooperative Work & Social Computing*, CSCW '14, pages 355–367, 2014.

[21] C. Treude, O. Barzilay, and M. Storey. How do programmers ask and answer questions on the web?: NIER track. In *Proceedings of the ACM/IEEE International Conference on Software Engineering*, ICSE '11, pages 804–807, 2011.

[22] B. Vasilescu, A. Serebrenik, P. Devanbu, and V. Filkov. How Social Q&A Sites Are Changing Knowledge Sharing in Open Source Software Communities. In *Proceedings of the 17th ACM Conference on Computer Supported Cooperative Work & Social Computing*, CSCW '14, pages 342–354, 2014.

[23] L. Yang, M. Qiu, S. Gottipati, F. Zhu, J. Jiang, H. Sun, and Z. Chen. CQArank: Jointly Model Topics and Expertise in Community Question Answering. In *Proceedings of the 22nd ACM International Conference on Conference on Information and Knowledge Management*, CIKM '13, pages 99–108, 2013.

[24] J. Zhang, M. S. Ackerman, and L. Adamic. Expertise Networks in Online Communities: Structure and Algorithms. In *Proceedings of the 16th International Conference on World Wide Web*, WWW '07, pages 221–230, 2007.

[25] Y. Zhou, G. Cong, B. Cui, C. S. Jensen, and J. Yao. Routing Questions to the Right Users in Online Communities. In *IEEE 25th International Conference on Data Engineering*, ICDE '09, pages 700–711, 2009.

Empirical Analysis of Implicit Brand Networks on Social Media

Kunpeng Zhang
University of Illinois at Chicago
Department of IDS, College of Business
Administration
Chicago, USA
kzhang6@uic.edu

Siddhartha Bhattacharyya
University of Illinois at Chicago
Department of IDS, College of Business
Administration
Chicago, USA
sidb@uic.edu

Sudha Ram
University of Arizona
Department of MIS, Eller College of
Management
Tucson, USA
ram@eller.arizona.edu

ABSTRACT

This paper investigates characteristics of implicit brand networks extracted from a large dataset of user historical activities on a social media platform. To our knowledge, this is one of the first studies to comprehensively examine brands by incorporating user-generated social content and information about user interactions. This paper makes several important contributions. We build and normalize a weighted, undirected network representing interactions among users and brands. We then explore the structure of this network using modified network measures to understand its characteristics and implications. As a part of this exploration, we address three important research questions: (1) What is the structure of a brand-brand network? (2) Does an influential brand have a large number of fans? (3) Does an influential brand receive more positive or more negative comments from social users? Experiments conducted with Facebook data show that the influence of a brand has (a) high positive correlation with the size of a brand, meaning that an influential brand can attract more fans, and, (b) low negative correlation with the sentiment of comments made by users on that brand, which means that negative comments have a more powerful ability to generate awareness of a brand than positive comments. To process the large-scale datasets and networks, we implement MapReduce-based algorithms.

Categories and Subject Descriptors

H.3 [**INFORMATION STORAGE AND RETRIEVAL**]: Information networks; E.1 [**DATA STRUCTURES**]: Graphs

and networks; H.5.4 [**INFORMATION INTERFACES AND PRESENTATION**]: Hypertext/Hypermedia

General Terms

Algorithms, Experimentation

Keywords

Network analysis; sentiment identification; social media; marketing intelligence; MapReduce

1. INTRODUCTION.

Social media has become one of the most popular communication platforms allowing users to discuss and share topics of interest without necessarily having the same geo-location and time. Information is be generated and managed through computers or mobile devices by one person and consumed by many others. Different people express different opinions on the same topic, and some also express their opinions on multiple topics of interest. A wide variety of topics, ranging from current events and political debate, to sports and entertainment, are being actively discussed on these social forums. For example, Facebook users comment on or 'like' campaigns posted by a company; Twitter users send tweets with a maximum length of 140 characters to instantly share and deliver their opinions on politics, movies, sports, etc. Some e-commerce platforms, such as Amazon.com, allow users to leave their reviews on products. These actions generate a rich data source which can be analyzed to understand the interactions among entities on social media. These networks of interactions may be of two types: explicit or implicit. Explicit networks are formed via "friendship" relationships on Facebook or "following" relationships on Twitter; implicit networks are formed, for example, via reviewing actions of consumers on products from Amazon.com. The networks may also be established when people share common interests, or when brands have overlapping customers. Such networks can be constructed from large datasets of user-generated content, and analyzed to obtain actionable insights to help users or brands make informed decisions.

For example, analysis of large brand-brand networks enables the identification of influential brands, facilitating targeted on-line advertising and eventually leading to product or service purchases.

Analysis of these networks helps in getting a better understanding of brand characteristics and is useful for making intelligent marketing decisions. For example, studying such kinds of networks by incorporating user-generated textual content can help identify influential brands and interactions among brands, which can lead to a better online brand advertising strategy. Most explicit networks are fairly easy to construct; However, they have some shortcomings. They are built based on explicit relationships among brands, which ignores activities between users and brands. In addition, current networking approaches do not consider textual sentiment of social content. In this paper, we attempt to overcome these shortcomings by leveraging user generated social media content including comments, "likes", and posts to build and analyze a new kind of implicit brand-brand network. Unlike regular network analysis ([28]) through users' friend networks, we leverage data on user interactions with brands' "fan" pages to extract networks that capture relationships between different brands. We then use a network analysis approach, together with sentiment analysis, to explore characteristics of the network. In addition, this brand-brand network obtained from a very large dataset of users and their interactions on a social platform requires efficient techniques for construction and analyses via distributed techniques based on Hadoop and MapReduce.

Our empirical study for brand-based networks built from large scale social data makes several contributions in the area of 'big' data on social interactions. The first major contribution is our new approach to build a weighted and undirected brand-brand network representing interactions among users and brands, based on a large amount of social content generated by users on a social media platform. To investigate network properties, we propose a technique for normalizing relationship weights in the network from a global perspective. In addition, we define new structural measures for analyzing the network by modifying traditional measures such as degree, diameter, clustering coefficient, and centrality to incorporate these weights. We then explore the structure of this network to understand its implications. As a part of this exploration, we address three research questions to develop a deeper understanding of brand characteristics from the network perspective coupled with sentiment analysis: (1) What is the structure of a brand network? (2) Does an influential brand have a large number of followers/fans? (3) Does an influential brand receive more positive or more negative comments from social users? Since our datasets and networks are very large, we implement MapReduce-based techniques in a distributed Hadoop[1] environment, for network generation. We collected data from the popular social platform Facebook through their Graph API[2] for an empirical analysis. In addition, we designed some simple but effective rules to filter out spam activities and spam users to improve the data quality.

The rest of this paper is organized as follows. Section 2 reviews all related work and Section 3 describes the overall framework. Section 4 describes the dataset and data cleansing process. Section 5 introduces the brand networks, describes how these are generated and normalized, and lays out important network measures used for analyzing the networks. Section 6 describes our empirical results from analyses of a large Facebook dataset to answer our research questions. We also describe a sentiment identification algorithm in this section. This is followed by conclusions and directions for future work in Section 7.

2. RELATED WORK.

In this section, we describe relevant work in three related areas: brand communities in social networks, network measures, and sentiment analysis on social media content.

Several studies in the marketing literature have examined the spread of influence and behavior across connected consumers; these arise, for example, from product reviews and recommendations, user interactions through comments and likes in social sites, or through participation in brand communities. The potential for word-of-mouth effects in promoting product adoptions, role and influence of early adopters, and broader issues of social contagion in consumer networks have seen much interest ([11, 12, 18]). Diffusion of information over consumer networks has been deemed effective for rapid reach over large online audiences through viral marketing approaches ([3, 1]). Various brands from across industries as well as non-profits are active on social networks for promoting brand image and building brand communities ([30]). 'Fan' pages on Facebook are an example of such communities, and form the basis for our study presented in this paper. Existing research has examined consumer interactions in online communities ([7]), social network based communities for promoting engagement with a brand ([22, 8]), consumer motivations for participation, and effective means for developing consumer-brand relationships ([30]). The topic of brand-brand relationships, however, has not received much attention in the literature - this is the focus of our study, using large-scale data, sentiment analysis and network analysis.

Many different measures exist in literature to quantify and understand network structures. For instance, degree is an important characteristic of a vertex in a network. Based on the degree of the vertices, it is possible to derive many other structural measures for the network. [2] found that a common property of many large networks is that the vertex connectivities follow a scale-free power-law distribution. Such scale free structures occur when networks expand by adding new vertices which attach preferentially to nodes that are already well connected. In addition, there are many studies related to centrality measures. For example, [10] assumed that the interactions in a network follow the shortest paths between two vertices; it is then possible to quantify the importance of a vertex or an edge in terms of its betweenness centrality. [20] proposed a betweenness measure that relaxes this assumption to include contributions from essentially all paths between nodes, although it gives more weight to short paths. It is based on random walks, counting how often a node is traversed by a random walk between two other nodes. [14] presented a novel formulation of centrality for dynamic networks that measures the number of paths in a network.

Sentiment identification has been widely studied in the past. These efforts mainly fall into three major categories. 1) Bag-of-Words approaches produce domain-specific lexi-

---

[1] Apache Hadoop: http://hadoop.apache.org/
[2] The Graph API: https://developers.facebook.com/docs/graph-api/

cons, and there is a vast body of research which attempts to incorporate them as features in machine learning models [32, 21, 9]. 2) Rule-based approaches have also been studied by many researchers. The authors in [4] proposed compositional semantics, based on the assumption that the meaning of a compound expression is a function of the meaning of its parts and of the syntactic rules by which they are combined. They have developed a set of compositional rules to assign sentiments to individual clauses, expressions and sentences. 3) Recently, there has been a wide range of machine learning techniques, which classify the whole opinion document (e.g., a product review) as positive or negative [21, 29, 6, 16]. In [4], the authors viewed such sub-sentential interactions in light of compositional semantics, and presented a novel learning-based approach that incorporates structural inference motivated by compositional semantics into the learning procedure. In [21], authors employed machine learning techniques to classify documents by overall sentiments and results on movie review data show that three machine learning methods they employed (Naïve Bayes, maximum entropy classification, and support vector machines) do not perform as well on sentiment classification as on traditional topic-based categorization. In [19], authors presented a linguistic analysis of conditional sentences, and built some supervised learning models to determine if sentiments expressed on different topics in a conditional sentence are positive, negative or neutral. Several researchers have also studied feature/topic-based sentiment analysis [25, 24, 17, 13, 9]. Their objective is to extract topics or product features in sentences and determine the associated sentiments. In [32], authors used feature-based opinion mining model to identify noun product features that imply opinions. In [15], authors proposed an approach to extract adverb-adjective-noun phrases based on clause structure obtained by parsing sentences into a hierarchical representation. They also proposed a robust general solution for modeling the contribution of adverbials and negation to the score for degree of sentiment. In [26], authors showed that information about social relationships can be used to improve user-level sentiment analysis. In [33, 27], authors considered network context to model the effect of emotions in sentiment. In this paper, we apply state-of-the-art sentiment engine to identify brand sentiment based on user's historical comments on that brand.

3. OVERALL FRAMEWORK.

To understand characteristics of brands on a social media platform, we examine three research questions. **RQ1:** What is the structure of a brand network in terms of various network measures? To answer this question, we build and normalize an implicit brand-brand network based on user historical activities, and then analyze the network using modified network measures incorporating weights. **RQ2:** We also examine if the influence of a brand correlates with the size of a brand. The influence of a brand can be identified by the eigenvector centrality calculated from the brand network. **RQ3:** Since there is a lot of user-generated text (e.g. comments made by users) on social media platforms, the third question we address incorporates such textual information to investigate whether an influential brand attracts more positive or negative comments. The sentiment of comments can be identified by state-of-the-art algorithms described in

Table 1: Description and statistics of raw dataset.

Number of downloaded brands	13,806
Number of unique users	286,862,823
Number of unique countries	122
Number of categories defined by Facebook	172

Section 6.1. Results shown in this paper are obtained from experiments based on a large Facebook dataset.

4. DATA.

We collected a large (approximately 2 TB) dataset from Facebook using their Graph API. All analyses methods proposed and described in the following sections can also be applied to data from other social media platforms, such as Twitter. In this section, we describe the details of the data collection, pre-processing, and cleaning performed to generate a high quality dataset for network analysis.

4.1 Data Collection.

Facebook, the largest and most popular social network platform, has more than 1 billion accounts. Many organizations, and individuals build their own pages on Facebook to share and communicate with their fans. The extensive amount of textual and interaction information generated by users has made it a promising platform for brand analysis. In this work, our focus is on the top social brands as the object of analysis, i.e. the brands with a large number of fans. We used the Facebook Graph API to download all activities on a brand page such as posts initialized by the brand page administrator, as well as posts by users, such as comments, "likes" on posts, and public user profiles (e.g. gender and locale). Each brand may have a number of posts depending on the posting frequency. A post is any information that the brand wants to share and interact with users and may include text, photos, videos, links or a combination of these. For instance, posts may be about a new product release, company annual report filing announcement, special day greetings, surveys, or other important events and activities. Any Facebook user can respond to these posts by liking or making comments on them. While there is no 'dislike' action on Facebook, textual responses to posts can be used to indicate positive, neutral, as well as negative opinions. The dataset (shown in Table 1) used for this work was collected from January 1, 2009 thru January 1, 2013. It contains data from 13,806 brand pages and approximately 280 million users. It covers data from brands in 122 countries in 172 categories as defined by Facebook's classification system.

4.2 Data Cleansing.

Data quality is of paramount importance in any analytics study as it can affect model performance and results. To ensure quality of the dataset we performed a number of cleansing operations. First we removed brands for which most of the posts and comments were not in English, because sentiment identification for non-English text is not well understood and accuracy is not high. To produce robust results we applied a spam filter to remove fake users and their corresponding activities. Our data shows that on average, a user comments on 4 to 5 pages and likes posts on 7 to 8 pages as shown in Figures 1 and 2, respectively.

Users connecting to an extremely large number of brands / pages are likely to be spam users or bots. For example, we found one spam user who appeared on 600+ different brand pages. We also detected one user who "liked" posts across 520 different brand pages. As most users are likely to be interested in a small number of brands, we discarded users making comments on more than 100 brands and those liking posts on more than 150 brands. In addition, we detected other kinds of spam users. For example, there was one user who liked 7,963 posts out of 8,549 posts for a brand. We assume that it is likely to be a spam user if this ratio is very high. We set this threshold to be 90% for every user except the page owner. Lastly, we also removed users who posted many duplicate comments containing URL links. A test on Barack Obama's page, found 209,864 duplicate comments out of 2,987,505 in total. The dataset for our analyses is from the top 2,000 brands, selected as those having the largest numbers of fans on their Facebook page.

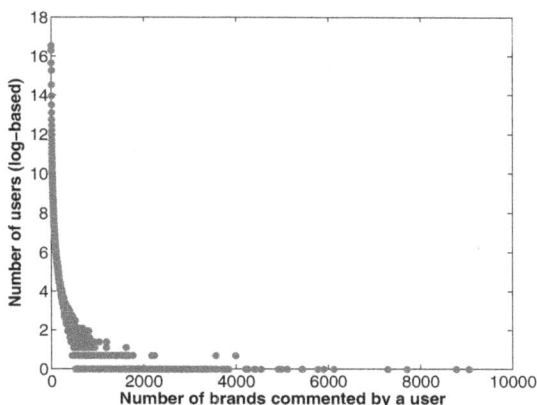

Figure 1: Distribution of individual brands / pages on which users comment. Y-axis is the *log* of number of users. X−axis is the number of brands(pages) on which a user makes comments.

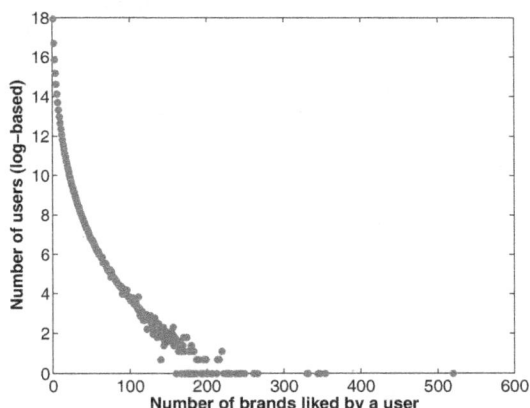

Figure 2: Distribution of individual brands / pages liked by a user. Y-axis is the *log* of number of users. X−axis is the number of brands(pages) liked by a Facebook user.

5. NETWORK ANALYSIS.

From the cleaned dataset, we constructed an implicit brand-brand network based on user historical activities. This is a weighted and undirected network. Link weights in the network were globally normalized. The data is very large, and hence we implemented a MapReduce algorithm (described in algorithm 1) to construct the network using Hadoop. We then modified the standard structural property measures in the network to incorporate weights, and used them to analyze the network. These structural properties include (weighted) degree, density, network diameter, clustering coefficient, and various centrality measures.

5.1 Weighted and Undirected Brand-brand Network.

Each brand has various properties such as a category as defined by the Facebook classification system, number of fans, number of people "talking about it", and a record of users' activities. This information can be used to capture the implicit relationships among brands and extract the brand-brand network. In this network, brands are designated as nodes, and a link between two brands is created if the same user commented on or liked posts made by both brands. Thus, two brands are bridged by common users. The larger the number of common users having activities on two brands, the higher the weight of their interconnecting link. This network represents brand-brand affinity. Formally, we define a weighted and undirected brand network ($\mathbb{B}$) as shown below.

$\mathbb{B} = <\mathbb{V}, \mathbb{E}>$, where $\mathbb{V} = \{b_i \mid b_i$ is a brand. Each b_i has f_i as the number of fans$\}$,

$\mathbb{E} = \{(b_i, b_j) \mid b_i$ has some common users with b_j, the corresponding weight is: $w_{ij} =$ the number of common users$\}$, where $1 \leq i, j \leq N$, N is the total number of brands, $N = 2,000$ in this study.

Alternatively, for the convenience of explaining network measures in the following section, we use the adjacency matrix A defined below to represent the network $\mathbb{B}$ as

$$A_{ij} = \begin{cases} w_{ij} & \text{if node } j \text{ connects to node } i \\ 0 & \text{otherwise} \end{cases}$$

where w_{ij} is the weight between brand i and brand j, which is the number of common users between brand b_i and brand b_j.

Normalization of brand-brand network: ($\mathbb{B} \rightarrow \mathbb{B}_n$)
Well-known brands typically attract more fans and have more common users with other big brands. A comparison across brands in the network requires normalization of the link weights. However, if we normalize the network by using the global maximum weight in the network, we lose global network semantics such as the distribution of connection strength among links of a brand relative to the size of a brand. Consider the case shown in Figure 3a. The connection (b_1, b_3) can be considered relatively stronger than the connection (b_1, b_2), because all (100%) of b_3 users are connected to b_1, while only 10% of b_2 users are interested in b_1. We propose a two step normalization process to characterize the strength of a link in $\mathbb{B}_n$. See example shown in Figure 3b.

The normalization for network $\mathbb{B} \rightarrow \mathbb{B}_n$ is as follows.

- We first normalize each individual link between two brands b_i, b_j by setting $w'_{ij} = \frac{w_{ij}}{f_i * f_j}$.

Table 2: Description and statistics before and after data cleansing. Cleaned dataset containing top 2,000 brands.

After cleaning		After selecting top brands
Number of brands	7,580	2,000
Number of unique users	97,699,832	16,306,977
Number of comments	2,327,635,302	470,742,158
Number of positive comments	651,231,870	179,009,470
Number of negative comments	234,571,177	60,613,968
Number of brand categories	150	118
Number of posts	13,206,402	3,793,941

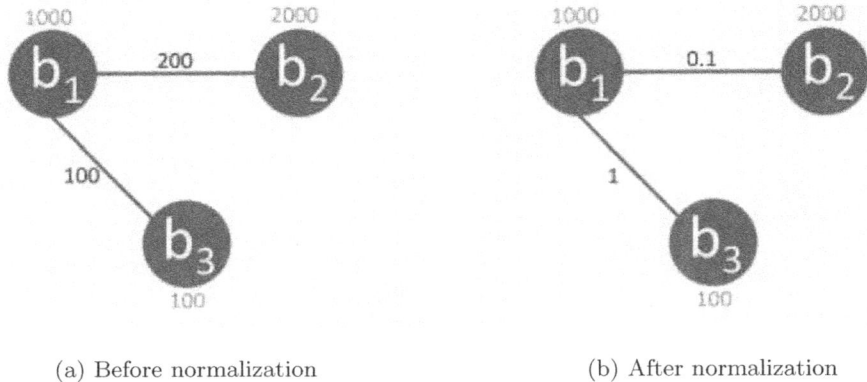

(a) Before normalization

(b) After normalization

Figure 3: An example to show relationship between brands based on common users. Number in red indicates number of fans for that brand. Before the normalization, brand b_1 has 1000 fans. Brand b_2 has 2000 fans, and brand b_3 has 100 fans. The number of common users between b_1 and b_2 is 200. The number of common users between b_1 and b_3 is 100. (b) shows the relative weights after normalization from a global perspective.

- We then normalize all w'_{ij} by setting $w''_{ij} = \frac{w'_{ij}}{max_{\forall(i,j)}\{w'_{ij}\}}$.

where f_i here is the number of fans of brand i.

5.2 Network Generation Using Hadoop.

Having defined all the networks, i.e., the network without normalization $\mathbb{B}$ and the network with normalization $\mathbb{B}_n$, we now focus on the process used to generate a network containing common users between brands. The raw data downloaded from Facebook is in the following format for each brand: $<user_{id}, comment>$ or $<user_{id}, post\ like>$. They are aggregated to generate a large text file consisting of triplets: $<brand_{id}, user_{id}, \#\ of\ activities^3>$. The size of the file is too large to be processed by a single machine. For example, to get common users between two brands b_i and b_j, we need to consider intersections between two sets S_i: {all users having activities in brand b_i} and S_j: {all users having activities in brand b_j}. This consumes enormous processing time because each brand typically has millions of unique users who have activities on its page. We used Hadoop to efficiently generate our network file in the following format of $<b_i, b_j, \#\ of\ common\ users>$. The basic map and reduce functions are shown in the algorithm 1. Without using Hadoop and other distributed computing techniques,

---

[3]Activity implies either making comments or liking posts. # of activities = # of comments + # of post likes.

it would have been impossible to even load such a large dataset (approximately 2 TB) into one single machine.

5.3 Network Measures.

Various structural properties have been defined in literature for networks as a whole and for individual nodes, including node degree, network diameter, network density, clustering coefficient, and centrality. Most of these have been defined in the context of unweighted graphs. In this work, we extend these metrics for weighted graphs ($\mathbb{B}_n$). We first provide formal definitions of each structural property and then report on an analysis of these measures for our extracted networks.

Weighted Node Degree. The simplest yet most frequently used property of a node is its degree, i.e. the number of connections it has to other nodes. The degree of node i (brand b_i) can be easily computed from the adjacency matrix A:

$$k_i = \sum_j A_{ji}$$

In our case, A is a weighted network. Figure 4 shows the degree distribution for our weighted network. The average degree for the weighted network is 0.662 and gives the average connection strength of node neighbors.

Network Density. The density of a network is the ratio of the number of links L that exist in the network to $N(N-1)/2$, to the maximum number of links possible (in an undirected network). Network density is thus determined as:

Algorithm 1 Two MapReduce jobs are chained to generate the brand-brand network.

Input: A text file contains lines of $\langle brand_{id}, user_{id}, \#$ of activities$\rangle$

Output: A text file contains lines of $\langle b_i, b_j, \#$ of common users$\rangle$

```
1:  /* The first job */
2:  input: ⟨brand_id, user_id,# of activities⟩   ▷ //Each line in the
    text file
3:  function MAPPER
4:      output ⟨user_id, brand_id⟩
5:  end function
6:  function REDUCER
7:      for all v ∈ values do
8:          add v→list
9:      end for
10:     for all ⟨b_i, b_j⟩, b_i, b_j ∈ list do      ▷ //(b_i, b_j) = (b_j, b_i).
    Either one is used
11:         ⟨k2, v2⟩ ← ⟨(b_i, b_j), 1⟩
12:     end for
13:     output ⟨k2, v2⟩
14: end function
15:
16: /* The second job */
17: function IDENTITY MAPPER    ▷ //Output is the same as
    input
18: end function
19: function REDUCER
20:     for all v ∈ values do
21:         sum += v    ▷ For the same key, sum over all values
22:     end for
23:     output ⟨key, sum⟩
24: end function
```

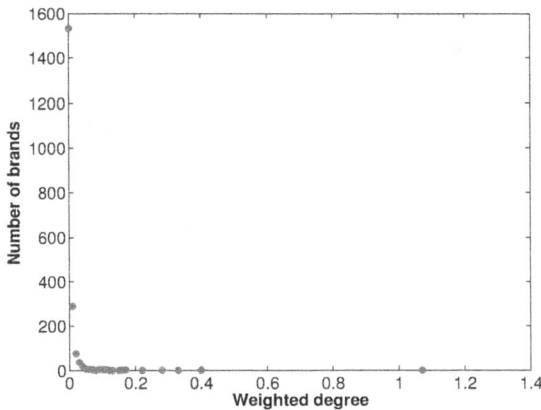

Figure 4: Degree distribution for the weighted brand-brand network. X−axis is the degree value. Y−axis is the number of brands. The weighted network shows the connection strength of each node to its neighbors. We eliminated brands with weighted degree less than 0.01. This is similar to common scale-free networks.

$$\rho = \frac{2L}{N(N-1)} = \frac{\sum_i k_i}{N(N-1)} = \frac{\langle k \rangle}{N-1} \approx \frac{\langle k \rangle}{N},$$

where $\langle k \rangle = \frac{1}{N} \sum_i k_i$ is the average node degree of the entire network.

Network density can also be interpreted as the fraction of links a node has on average normalized by the potential number of neighbors. It shows how densely nodes are connected to others. We consider all weights $w_{ij} > 0$ to be 1 when we compute the density of a network.

Network Diameter. Obviously, there are many paths between any two nodes i and j. The set of all such paths is ϕ_{ij}. We define a subset of these as shortest paths, i.e., those paths that have the minimal number of steps or geodesic distance. Geodesic distance is used to define the diameter of a network. The network diameter D_0 is defined as the longest of all the calculated shortest paths in the entire network. It is representative of the linear size of a network. It also reflects how fast information can be transmitted from one node to another in the network, and is expressed as $D_0 = max(\phi)$, where $\phi = \cup_{i,j} \phi_{ij}$ is the collection of all paths between all pairs of nodes.

Clustering Coefficient. The clustering coefficient can be interpreted as a measure of an "all-my-friends-know-each-other" property. It provides a mechanism for measuring transitivity of an undirected network by the fraction of triangles that exist in the network as compared to all combinations of triples. It is a measure of the extent to which nodes in a graph tend to cluster together. The clustering coefficient of a node is the ratio of existing links from a node's neighbors to each other to the maximum possible number of such links. The clustering coefficient for the entire network is the average of clustering coefficient of all the nodes. A high clustering coefficient for a network is another indication of a small world. Mathematically, it can be defined as below.

The clustering coefficient of the ith node in a network N is:

$$CC_i = \frac{2e_i}{k_i(k_i-1)},$$

where k_i is the number of neighbors of the ith node, and e_i is the number of connections between these neighbors. The maximum possible number of connections between neighbors is,

$$\binom{k_i}{2} = \frac{k_i(k_i-1)}{2}$$

Thus, $CC_N = \frac{1}{n} \sum_{i=1}^{n} CC_i$, where n is the number of nodes in the network N. More detailed description of clustering coefficient can be found in Appendix A.

Centrality. In a network, there are four main measures of centrality: degree, betweenness, closeness, and eigenvector.

(1). *Degree centrality* is the same as the degree of a node. It measures the connectivity of a node.

(2). *Closeness centrality* is defined as the reverse of the length of the average of all shortest path from node i to the rest of the network. $x_i = \frac{1}{\langle l(i) \rangle}$, where $\langle l(i) \rangle = \frac{1}{N-1} \sum_j l_{ij}$ and l_{ij} is a shortest path from i to j. The distance in a weighted network is defined as $d(i,j) = \frac{1}{w_{ij}}$. A small value of x_i indicates that the node is far away from the rest of the network; if it is large, then the node is close to the center.

(3). *Betweenness centrality* is the fraction of shortest paths that pass through a node. It quantifies the number

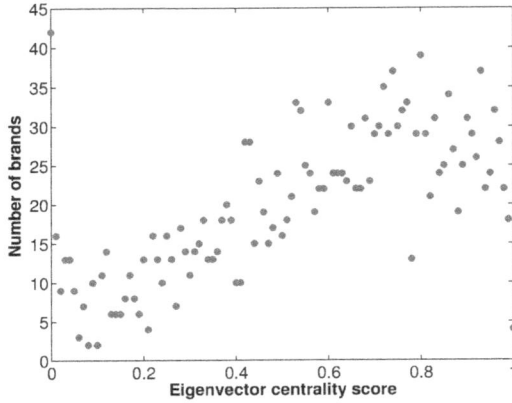

Figure 5: The eigenvector centrality distribution for the brand-brand network $\mathbb{B}_n$. X−axis is the eigenvector centrality score for each brand; Y−axis is the number of nodes in the network. Centrality score of 0 indicates isolated nodes i.e., without any connections to others. All eigenvector centrality scores are rounded to two decimal places.

of times a node acts as a conduit along the shortest path between two other nodes.

(4). *Eigenvector centrality* is widely used to measure the influence of a node in a network. It is based on topological features alone and takes into account only information in the neighborhood of a node. It assigns relative scores to all nodes in the network based on the idea that connections to more important nodes contribute more to the importance of the node in question, than connections to less important nodes. Since our brand-brand network $\mathbb{B}_n$ is weighted, we modify the original eigenvector centrality measure. For the given network $\mathbb{B}_n = (V, E)$ and adjacency matrix $A = (w_{ij})$, the eigenvector centrality score c_i of each brand i can be defined as:

$$c_i = \frac{1}{\lambda} \sum_{j \in N(i)} c_j = \frac{1}{\lambda} \sum_{j \in \mathbb{B}_n} w_{ij} c_j$$

where $N(i)$ is a set of the neighbors for brand i and λ is a constant. This calculation can be rewritten in vector notation with a small mathematical rearrangement as the eigenvector equation: $Ac = \lambda c$.

In general, there will be many different eigenvalues λ for which an eigenvector solution exists. Based on the **Perror-Frobenius theorem** ([23]), the requirement that all entries in the eigenvector be positive implies that only the greatest eigenvalue results in the desired centrality measure. Power iteration is one of the most commonly used eigenvalue algorithms to find the dominant eigenvector.

The eigenvector centrality distribution for our brand-brand network $\mathbb{B}_n$ as shown in Figure 5, reveals that brands in the network $\mathbb{B}_n$ have different influence scores and they are distributed widely in $(0, 1)$. There are around 30 isolated brands in the network, as indicated by the point at the upper left corner in the graph. The rest of the brands have eigenvector centrality scores between 0 and 1, meaning that they have either multiple strong connections or few weak connections to other brands. This centrality measure is useful for ranking brands in terms of influence.

Each brand has a category defined by Facebook, these include sports, politician, food/ beverages, clothing, and TV

Table 3: Top 10 influential brands and their categories.

Rank	Top 10 influential brands	Category
1	Barack Obama	Politician
2	CNN	Media news publishing
3	Starbucks	Food beverages
4	Coca Cola	Food beverages
5	Victoria's Secret	Clothing
6	True Blood	TV show
7	Dexter	TV show
8	Taco Bell	Food beverages
9	Lady Gaga	Musician band
10	Pepsi	Food beverages

Table 4: Different properties of undirected and weighted normalized brand-brand network $\mathbb{B}_n$.

Property	Network $\mathbb{B}_n$
Number of nodes	2,000
Number of links	965,605
Average weighted degree	0.662
Network density	0.483
Network diameter	4
Average clustering coefficient	0.785
Average weighted clustering coefficient	0.882
Average path length	1.503

show. Table 3 shows top 10 influential brands and their associated categories. Among top 100 influential brands, **31 brands are categorized as TV shows, 12 as food beverages, and 9 as musician bands.** A detailed distribution is shown in Figure 6.

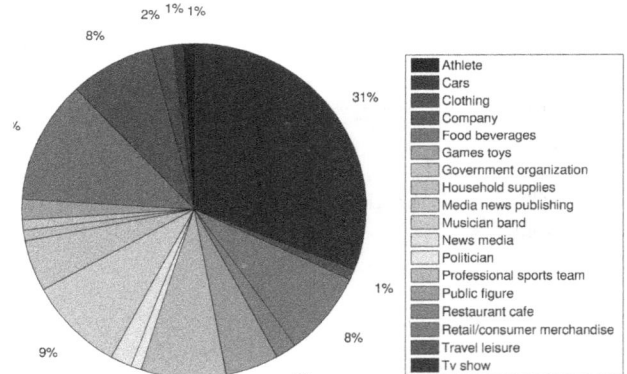

Figure 6: Category distribution of top 100 influential brands.

To summarize, we list the basic properties of our weighted and undirected normalized brand-brand network $\mathbb{B}_n$ in Table 4.

6. IMPLICATIONS OF BRAND-BRAND NETWORK.

Our network analysis provided insights into the properties of the brand-brand network. In this section, we will answer two remaining research questions: **RQ2** and **RQ3**. For this, we first introduce the notion of sentiment of a brand based on all comments made by users on the brand (after data cleansing).

6.1 Brand Sentiment Identification.

Users tend to express their opinions positively, neutrally, or negatively through their comments. Many easy-going or optimistic users tend to make non-negative comments or "like" other's posts, while some tough or pessimistic users like to leave non-positive comments. Previous researchers have developed ways to identify brand sentiment based on user activities on social media platforms [31]. In this work, we use a simple technique to identify brand sentiment, by calculating the positive ratio of all historical comments made by users on that brand. Since we already eliminated spam comments during the data cleansing process, this technique works well and generates good results. Sentiment of a brand b is defined as:

$$\text{SENT}_b = \frac{\# \text{ of positive comments}}{\# \text{ of positive comments} + \# \text{ of negative comments}}$$

We ignore neutral comments here because they do not express any opinions but just state facts.

The textual sentiment algorithm we use in this paper is explained here. We consider three types of values: positive, negative, and neutral. Our textual sentiment identification algorithm integrates the following three different individual components. The first is a rule-based method extended from the basic compositional semantic rules which include twelve semantic rules and two compose functions ([5]). For instance, Rule A is: If a sentence contains the key word "but", then consider only the sentiment of the "but" clause. According to this rule, the following statement is considered positive: *"I've never liked that director and major actors, but I loved the story shown in this movie."* Compose functions generate integers from -5 to $+5$ as output to represent sentiment scores. The second component is a frequency-based method. We argue that rather than simply being classified as positive, negative, or objective, the sentiment should be given a continuous numerical score (e.g., -5 to $+5$) to reflect the sentiment strength. The strength of a sentiment is expressed by the adjective and adverb used in the sentence. We consider two kinds of phrases that derive numerical scores: the phrases in the forms of Adverb-Adjective-Noun (abbreviated as AAN) and Verb-Adverb (VA). Scores were calculated for key words based on a large collection of customer reviews, each of which is associated with a rating. The details of the score calculation can be found in our previous work [31]. Here, we present a few examples. "Easy" has a score of 4.1, "best" 5.0, "never" -2.0, and "a bit" 0.03. Furthermore, the third bag-of-word component considers special characters commonly used in social media text, such as emoticons, negation words and their corresponding positions, and domain-specific words. For example, ":-)" is a positive sentiment and ":-(" a negative sentiment. Some words and phrases express positive opinions like "1st", "Thank you, Obama", "Go bulls", "Thumbs up". Some domain specific words are also included, like "Yum, Yummy" for food related brands. Finally, a random forest machine learning model is applied to the features generated from the output of the three components. The out- puts are represented as three basic features (TS_1 , TS_2 , TS_3) and two derived features ($TS_1 + TS_2$, TS_1 - TS_2). Our sentiment identification algorithm is trained on manually labeled Facebook

Table 5: Spearman rank correlation between the eigenvector centrality of a brand and the size of a brand, the sentiment of a brand, respectively. "EC": Eigenvector Centrality; "SRC": Spearman Rank Correlation; "sent": sentiment.

SRC(EC vs. size)	SRC(EC vs. sent)
0.676	−0.282

comments ($2,000$) and Twitter text($2,000$) using 4 different learning algorithms (decision tree, neural network, logistic regression, and random forest). The random forest learning algorithm was found to achieve the best accuracy of 86%.

6.2 Network Analyses Implications.

Each brand has a number of followers (also called fans) on Facebook. The number of fans can represent the size of a brand, in that a big brand has a strong ability to attract more fans. However, the question that arises is, ÒIs a big brand also more influential/importantÓ? To answer this question, we calculate the Spearman rank correlation between eigenvector centrality and the number of fans. The Spearman correlation coefficient is defined as the Pearson correlation coefficient between the ranked variables. For a sample of size n, the n raw scores X_i, Y_i are converted to ranks x_i, y_i, and ρ is computed using the following equation:

$$\rho = \frac{\sum_i (x_i - \bar{x})(y_i - \bar{y})}{\sqrt{\sum_i (x_i - \bar{x})^2 (y_i - \bar{y})^2}}$$

The correlation value (SRC(EC vs. size)) between eigenvector centrality and the size of a brand in Table 5 tells us that **the size of a brand has a highly positive correlation with the influence of a brand, which means that a big brand is likely to influence other brands in the network.**

For each brand in the network, we collected all comments made by fans across various topics and calculated its sentiment using the sentiment identification algorithm described earlier. To determine if an influential brand receives more positive or negative comments we calculated the Spearman rank correlation between eigenvector centrality and the sentiment of a brand. Surprisingly, the value of SRC(EC vs. sent) in Table 5 demonstrates that **the influence/importance of a brand within the network has a low but negative correlation with its sentiment. This also implies that negative comments on brands are likely to propagate much faster and get more attention than positive comments.**

7. CONCLUSION AND FUTURE WORK.

This paper described a network analysis approach to analyze large dataset containing user historical activities on a social media platform to study characteristics of brands. It is based on an implicit brand-brand network extracted from user interests expressed in brand communities. To our knowledge, it is one of the first studies that develop networks showing relationships between brands based on a large social media dataset.

We proposed a framework for an empirical analysis of network characteristics which includes three components: the first is constructing and normalizing a brand-brand network. Second, we analyzed the network using modified network measures, including weighted degree, density, network diameter, clustering coefficient, and centrality to answer the first research question mentioned earlier; eigenvector centrality reveals brand importance/influence in the network. Third, we addressed two additional research questions. Our findings show that an influential brand has a highly positive correlation with the size of a brand, but a low negative correlation with the sentiment of a brand.

We conducted our experiments on a dataset collected from Facebook. Some simple but effective rules were designed to remove spam activities and users to improve data quality, which is an important consideration when using noisy social media datasets. Given the large data volume, we implemented the network generation algorithm using a MapReduce-based technique in a Hadoop environment; this ensures scalability needed for analysis of large networks.

The brand-brand network developed here is based on user historical activities, but not the content of these activities (except the sentiment of brands determined from comments). Incorporating content analysis can provide a deeper understanding of user activities and interactions and is a topic for continued research. The brand-brand network that our work develops provides a unique view of relationships between brands from the aggregation of consumers' overlapping interests. Such brand networks can be significant for exploring inter-relationships among brands, and related brand communities. Analyses of the undirected and weighted brand network using network measures, such as, centrality can help identify influential brands. Such brand networks can be of much interest for marketing and for obtaining broader understanding of social influence and communication through social media.

References

[1] S. Aral and D. Walker. Creating social contagion through viral product design: A randomized trial of peer influence in networks. *Manage. Sci.*, 57(9):1623–1639, Sept. 2011.

[2] A.-L. BarabÃ§si and R. Albert. Emergence of scaling in random networks. *Science*, 286(5439):509–512, 1999.

[3] A. D. Bruyn and G. L. Lilien. A multi-stage model of word-of-mouth influence through viral marketing. *International Journal of Research in Marketing*, 25(3):151 – 163, 2008.

[4] Y. Choi and C. Cardie. Learning with compositional semantics as structural inference for subsentential sentiment analysis. In *Proceedings of the Conference on Empirical Methods in Natural Language Processing*, EMNLP '08, pages 793–801, Stroudsburg, PA, USA, 2008. Association for Computational Linguistics.

[5] Y. Choi and C. Cardie. Learning with compositional semantics as structural inference for subsentential sentiment analysis. In *Proceedings of the Conference on Empirical Methods in Natural Language Processing*, EMNLP '08, pages 793–801, Stroudsburg, PA, USA, 2008. Association for Computational Linguistics.

[6] K. Dave, S. Lawrence, and D. M. Pennock. Mining the peanut gallery: opinion extraction and semantic classification of product reviews. In *Proceedings of the 12th international conference on World Wide Web*, WWW '03, pages 519–528, New York, NY, USA, 2003. ACM.

[7] K. de Valck, G. H. van Bruggen, and B. Wierenga. Virtual communities: A marketing perspective. *Decis. Support Syst.*, 47(3):185–203, June 2009.

[8] L. de Vries, S. Gensler, and P. S. Leeflang. Popularity of brand posts on brand fan pages: An investigation of the effects of social media marketing. *Journal of Interactive Marketing*, 26(2):83 – 91, 2012.

[9] X. Ding, B. Liu, and P. S. Yu. A holistic lexicon-based approach to opinion mining. In *Proceedings of the 2008 International Conference on Web Search and Data Mining*, WSDM '08, pages 231–240, New York, NY, USA, 2008. ACM.

[10] L. C. Freeman. A set of measures of centrality based on betweenness. *Sociometry*, 40(1):35–41, Mar. 1977.

[11] S. Hill, F. Provost, and C. Volinsky. Network-based marketing: Identifying likely adopters via consumer networks. *Statistical Science*, 22(2):256–275, 2006.

[12] R. Iyengar, C. Van den Bulte, and T. W. Valente. Opinion leadership and social contagion in new product diffusion. *Marketing Science*, 30(2):195–212, Mar. 2011.

[13] L. Ku, Y. Liang, and H. Chen. Opinion extraction, summarization and tracking in news and blog corpora. In *AAAI Spring Symposium: Computational Approaches to Analyzing Weblogs'06*, pages 100–107, 2006.

[14] K. Lerman, R. Ghosh, and J. H. Kang. Centrality metric for dynamic networks. In *Proceedings of the Eighth Workshop on Mining and Learning with Graphs*, MLG '10, pages 70–77, New York, NY, USA, 2010. ACM.

[15] J. Liu and S. Seneff. Review sentiment scoring via a parse-and-paraphrase paradigm. In *Proceedings of the 2009 Conference on Empirical Methods in Natural Language Processing: Volume 1*, EMNLP '09, pages 161–169, Stroudsburg, PA, USA, 2009. Association for Computational Linguistics.

[16] R. Mcdonald, K. Hannan, T. Neylon, M. Wells, and J. Reynar. Structured models for fine-to-coarse sentiment analysis. In *Proceedings of the 45th Annual Meeting of the Association of Computational Linguistics*, 2007.

[17] Q. Mei, X. Ling, M. Wondra, H. Su, and C. Zhai. Topic sentiment mixture: modeling facets and opinions in weblogs. In *Proceedings of the 16th international conference on World Wide Web*, WWW '07, pages 171–180, New York, NY, USA, 2007. ACM.

[18] S. Nam, P. Manchanda, and P. K. Chintagunta. The effect of signal quality and contiguous word of mouth on customer acquisition for a video-on-demand service. *Marketing Science*, 29(4):690–700, 2010.

[19] R. Narayanan, B. Liu, and A. Choudhary. Sentiment analysis of conditional sentences. In *Proceedings of the 2009 Conference on Empirical Methods in Natural Language Processing: Volume 1*, EMNLP '09, pages 180–189, Stroudsburg, PA, USA, 2009. Association for Computational Linguistics.

[20] M. J. Newman. A measure of betweenness centrality based on random walks. *Social Networks*, 27(1):39 – 54, 2005.

[21] B. Pang, L. Lee, and S. Vaithyanathan. Thumbs up?: sentiment classification using machine learning techniques. In *Proceedings of the ACL-02 conference on Empirical methods in natural language processing - Volume 10*, EMNLP '02, pages 79–86, Stroudsburg, PA, USA, 2002. Association for Computational Linguistics.

[22] N. J. Patterson, M. J. Sadler, and J. M. Cooper. Consumer understanding of sugars claims on food and drink products. *Nutrition Bulletin*, 37(2):121–130, 2012.

[23] O. Perron. Zur theorie der matrices. *Mathematische Annalen*, 64(2):248–263, 1907.

[24] A.-M. Popescu and O. Etzioni. Extracting product features and opinions from reviews. In *Proceedings of the conference on Human Language Technology and Empirical Methods in Natural Language Processing*, HLT '05, pages 339–346, Stroudsburg, PA, USA, 2005. Association for Computational Linguistics.

[25] V. Stoyanov and C. Cardie. Topic identification for fine-grained opinion analysis. In *Proceedings of the 22nd International Conference on Computational Linguistics - Volume 1*, COLING '08, pages 817–824, Stroudsburg, PA, USA, 2008. Association for Computational Linguistics.

[26] C. Tan, L. Lee, J. Tang, L. Jiang, M. Zhou, and P. Li. User-level sentiment analysis incorporating social networks. In *Proceedings of the 17th ACM SIGKDD international conference on Knowledge discovery and data mining*, KDD '11, pages 1397–1405, New York, NY, USA, 2011. ACM.

[27] J. Tang, Y. Zhang, J. Sun, J. Rao, W. Yu, Y. Chen, and A. C. M. Fong. Quantitative study of individual emotional states in social networks. *Affective Computing, IEEE Transactions on*, 3(2):132–144, April 2012.

[28] C. Tucker. Social advertising. *SSRN: http: // ssrn. com/ abstract= 1975897*, 2012.

[29] P. D. Turney. Thumbs up or thumbs down?: semantic orientation applied to unsupervised classification of reviews. In *Proceedings of the 40th Annual Meeting on Association for Computational Linguistics*, ACL '02, pages 417–424, Stroudsburg, PA, USA, 2002. Association for Computational Linguistics.

[30] A. M. Turri, K. H. Smith, and E. Kemp. Developing Affective Brand Commitment Through Social Media. *Journal of Electronic Commerce Research*, 14(3):201–214, 2013.

[31] K. Zhang, Y. Cheng, Y. Xie, D. Honbo, A. Agrawal, D. Palsetia, K. Lee, W. keng Liao, and A. N. Choudhary. Ses: Sentiment elicitation system for social media data. In *ICDM Workshops'11*, pages 129–136, 2011.

[32] L. Zhang and B. Liu. Identifying noun product features that imply opinions. In *Proceedings of the 49th Annual Meeting of the Association for Computational Linguistics: Human Language Technologies: short papers - Volume 2*, HLT '11, pages 575–580, Stroudsburg, PA, USA, 2011. Association for Computational Linguistics.

[33] Y. Zhang, J. Tang, J. Sun, Y. Chen, and J. Rao. Moodcast: Emotion prediction via dynamic continuous factor graph model. In *Data Mining (ICDM), 2010 IEEE 10th International Conference on*, pages 1193–1198, Dec 2010.

APPENDIX

A. CLUSTERING COEFFICIENT.

The basic idea behind transitivity is how reliably we can say that if nodes i and j and node i and k are connected whether j and k are connected as well. If that is the case then we have a triangle. In general, if $A_{ij} = 1$ and $A_{ik} = 1$, then the nodes i, j, k form a triplet. There are only two types of triplets: triangles and non-triangles. Triangles contain 6 paths of length 3 whereas non-triangles, regular triplets, contain two paths of length 2. Particularly in social networks a large fraction of triplets are triangles, which means if X is friends with Y and Z then with a high probability Y and Z are also friends. It can be also applied and explained in our brand-brand network. Thus, one way of measuring the strength of transitivity of an undirected unweighted network is by the fraction of triangles with respect to the entire set of triplets.

$$C = \frac{3*\# \ triangles}{\# \ triplets} = \frac{6*\# \ triangles}{\# \ paths \ of \ length \ 2}$$

The number of triangles is given by:

$$n_\triangle = \frac{1}{6} Tr A^3$$

The number of paths of length 2 between two given nodes is given by:

$$n_2(i,j) = \sum_k A_{ik} A_{kj} = (A^2)_{ij}$$

The total amount of paths of length 2 is:

$$n_2 = \| A^2 \| - Tr A^2$$

where $\| \cdot \|$ means summing over all matrix elements. The trace of matrix A means

$Tr A = A_{11} = A_{22} + \cdots + A_{nn} = \sum_i^n A_{ii}$. Finally, we obtain:

$$C = \frac{Tr A^3}{\|A^2\| - Tr A^2}$$

This also called clustering coefficient.

Am I More Similar to My Followers or Followees? Analyzing Homophily Effect in Directed Social Networks

Mohammad Ali Abbasi, Reza Zafarani, Jiliang Tang, and Huan Liu
Computer Science and Engineering, Arizona State University
Tempe, AZ, USA
{Ali.Abbasi, Reza, Jiliang.Tang, Huan.Liu}@asu.edu

ABSTRACT

Homophily is the theory behind the formation of social ties between individuals with similar characteristics or interests. Based on homophily, in a social network it is expected to observe a higher degree of homogeneity among connected than disconnected people. Many researchers use this simple yet effective principal to infer users' missing information and interests based on the information provided by their neighbors. In a directed social network, the neighbors can be further divided into followers and followees. In this work, we investigate the homophily effect in a directed network. To explore the homophily effect in a directed network, we study if a user's personal preferences can be inferred from those of users connected to her (followers or followees). We also study the effectiveness of each of these two groups on prediction one's preferences.

Categories and Subject Descriptors

H.4 [**Database Applications**]: Data mining; D.2.8 [**Software Engineering**]: Metrics—*Complexity measures, Performance measures*

General Terms

Algorithms, Theory

Keywords

Social Media Mining; Preference Prediction; Relational Learning; Homophily

INTRODUCTION

Individuals extensively use online social networks to connect to other users, share information, express themselves, and benefit from the information provided by other users. In social networks, users often connect to those who have similar characteristics or similar interests. As a result, social networks are homogeneous with regards to many personal or behavioral characteristics [11]. *Homophily* is the tendency of similar individuals to form connections. The effect of this phenomena is a network in which connected users

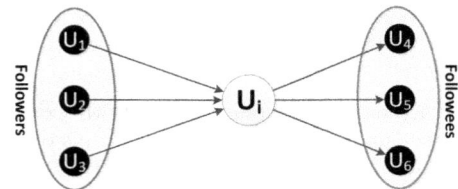

Figure 1: Neighbors in directed social networks can be grouped into *followers* and *followees*.

are more likely to share similar attributes and interests than disconnected users [18]. Homophily has its roots in undirected social networks, in which the two sides of the interaction are equally responsible to create and maintain the relation. Forming a real-world friendship is an example for this type of behavior. There is another type of connection that mostly appears in traditional mass media as well as online directed social networks. In this type of relation, only one party is responsible for the creation of the connection. Becoming a fan of an author or following a user on Twitter are examples of directed relation. In the example of an author and the group of her fans, the connection between the fans and the author is different from a regular friendship. The author has no control over these connections or does not even know many of her fans. Though the fans find themselves similar to the author, it cannot concluded that the author also will find herself similar to the her fans. In this example, the relation is formed and maintained solely by one of the parties involved in the relation. How can we measure the homophily effect in a directed social network? If the fans find themselves similar to the author, does this imply that the author will also reach the same conclusion?

A similar situation can be observed in many online social networks. In many networks, such as Facebook, the relation is bidirectional, where two connected users have to show their willingness for the relation to form. For instance, to form friendships on Facebook, one should initiate a friend request and the other user should accept it. However, in many social networks, the relations is directed. A directed connection, such as *following* on Twitter or *liking* on Facebook, is the result of only one user's action and there is often no need for the consent from the other user to get her involved in the relation.

In this work, we study homophily in directed social networks. To analyze homophily in directed networks, we study if a user's personal preferences can be inferred from her neighbors. Our goal is to determine which group (followers or followees) is more effective in inferring users' personal preferences. We conduct our experiments by using a set of more than 5 million Facebook fan pages to infer users' political orientation.

LITERATURE REVIEW

Predicting individuals' characteristics in the real-world has a long history. One often employs different types of information provided by the individuals such as their content, interactions with others, the products and services that they use, and the locations they visit [5, 1, 2] to infer users' characteristics and preferences. Similarly, in online social media, prediction techniques often use *content, user's interaction information*, or *network information* to infer user's profile attributes and preferences.

Content-based methods use user-generated content as a source to infer profile attributes information. By constructing features from the content and utilizing machine learning techniques such as Support Vector Machines (SVM) [16], Latent Dirichlet Allocation (LDA) [4], or boosted decision trees profile attributes can be predicted. *Interaction-based methods* utilize the interactions among users in online social networks to predict their profile attributes. Interactions include but are not limited to sharing contents of other users, commenting, retweeting, tagging, mentioning, or liking other users or their content [14]. *Network-based methods* use the network connections (links) to infer missing attributes. Recent studies show that it is possible to use information available from connected users in social networking sites to infer missing attributes and preferences with high accuracy [12, 13, 9, 10, 3, 6].

Tan et al. [17] used Twitter mention (@) data to construct a network and showed that users who mention each other in their tweets are more likely to hold similar opinions. Hu et al. [6] showed that connected people are more likely to be similar than randomly chosen disconnected people. Conover et al. [4] reported an accuracy of up to 95% when predicting users' political orientation by employing users' network information on Twitter. Mislove et al. [12] showed that it is possible to use only about 20% of the users providing attributes to infer the attributes for the rest of the network by an accuracy of over 80%. Carter et al. in [7] used the network structure and users' positions within a friendship network on Facebook to accurately predict users' sexual orientation. In a recent study by Kosinski et al. [8], the authors utilized Facebook data to show the degree to which relatively basic digital records of social media users' behavior can be used to accurately predict a wide range of personal attributes. They use Facebook *likes* to extract users' positive association with online content, such as photos, videos, Facebook pages of products, businesses, people, books, places, and websites.

In this study, we focus on network-based approaches, where we infer a user's missing attributes from the attribute information provided by other users in the network. Based on *homophily*, connected users more likely hold similar interests and attributes than those are not connected. This introduces a basic strategy to infer one's missing information based on the information of those connected users who revealed their attributes [15]. In its simplest form, one can use the user's neighbors to infer the user's missing information as well as her interests. This is a well-defined problem in undirected networks; however, it is not clear how one can use a user's neighbors to effectively infer missing information in directed networks.

HOMOPHILY-BASED PREDICTION OF USER'S PREFERENCES

In this section, we introduce our homophily-based approach for predicting user's preferences. We evaluate the predictive power of followers and followees for predicting users' profile attributes. We follow a two-step approach: first, we determine the level of homophily between users and their followers and users and their fol-

lowees. Then we use followers and followees as independent sources to predict users' profile attributes.

Measuring Homophily

To measure homophily, one requires a method to compute homogeneity between users and their followees and followers. We employ a similar measure to the one outlined by Mislove et al. [12] to calculate the homophily among the users. Let a_i denote the value for attribute a for user u_i. We calculate the similarity among the user u_i and her neighbors $u_j \in N(u_i)$ on attribute a as

$$S_a = \frac{\sum_{u_j \in N(u_i)} \sigma(a_i, a_j)}{|N(u_i)|} \qquad (1)$$

where $N(u_i)$ is a set of u_i's neighbors, and $\sigma(a_i, a_j)$ is the Kronecker delta function that returns 1 if the value of attribute a is equal for the two users and 0, otherwise.

$$\sigma(a_i, a_j) = \begin{cases} 1 & \text{if } a_i = a_j \\ 0 & \text{otherwise,} \end{cases}$$

$N(u_i)$ can be either u_i's followers or followees. For every user, we run the algorithm twice; first we use followers and then we use followees. In Equation 1, the value of S_a represents the fraction of the nodes with similar attribute values for the given attribute a.

To measure the statistical significance of S_a, we divide S_a by the expected value E_a when two users are chosen at random. Assume that attribute a can take k attribute values. Let A_i, denote the number of users that take the ith, $1 \le i \le k$ possible value for attribute a. Let $U = \sum_{i=1}^{k} A_i$ denote the total number of users. Then E_a can be computed as

$$E_a = \frac{\sum_{i=1}^{k} A_i(A_i - 1)}{|U|(|U| - 1)} \qquad (2)$$

Let $H_a = \frac{S_i}{E_i}$ denote the degree of homophily between the user and her neighbors. When H_a is 1, there is no correlation between the attribute values. When it is less than 1, there is a negative correlation, and when it is greater than 1, it indicates a positive correlation between the attribute a's value of the user and the neighbors. Higher H_a indicates higher correlation between the attribute values of the user and that of the neighbors.

Predicting the Profile Attribute Values

The algorithm infers the given node's missing information by using the node's neighbors as the source of information. In this study, we use weighted majority vote to infer the user's profile attributes. To predict the value of attribute a for user u_i, we take the majority vote from u_i's neighbors regarding this attribute and assign the value with the highest number of votes.

EXPERIMENTS

As we described earlier, social media users decide whom to follow, however, they have no control on selecting their followers. Thus, we expect a higher degree of similarity between users and their followees than the users and their followers. We conduct two sets of experiments to evaluate the effect of homophily in directed social networks.

- *Observing the homophily*, to investigate the existence of homophily in directed networks, we measure and compare the similarity between users and their followees and users and their followers.

Table 1: Facebook Fan Pages Dataset Statistics

Total number of pages	5,856,000
Number of personal pages	764 K
Number of links	19,646,000
Revealed political orientation	25,129 (0.43%)

Table 2: Popular Categories of Facebook Pages and their Popularity Level in our Dataset

Rank	Category	Fraction of pages
1	Community	16.8%
2	Musician/Band	7.4%
3	Non-Profit Organizations	4.1%
4	Public figure	3.8%
39	Politician	0.4%
49	Political Organization	0.3%
81	Political Party	0.2%

Table 3: Political Orientation Consistency between Users, Their Followees, and Their Followers with Respect to Different Levels of User Popularity

Neighbors	All	$\leq 1K$	$\geq 10K$	≤ 100	$\geq 1M$
Followees	74%	75%	75%	73%	73%
Followers	73.5%	73%	74%	76%	74%
Fe + Fr	72%	72%	73%	73%	72%

- *Investigating the prediction power or followers and followees*, we try to predict users' attributes, by using their followers and their followees and compare the results of two sources.

Dataset

In this study, we use *Facebook fan pages* to construct the directed social network. On Facebook, users can create regular user accounts or fan pages. Despite the regular user accounts on Facebook that form an undirected network, the fan pages' network is directed. To connect to a page, users (and pages) have to like the target page. This is similar to *following* behavior on Twitter. Each page can *like* or *be liked* by other pages and users. In the network, each page is a node and liking another page creates a link from the source node to the target node. There is no limit on the number of users that can like a Facebook fan page. The number of likes is a public property of the page and in our experiments is used to measure the popularity of the pages.

Data collection process.

Table 1 represents the statistics of our Facebook dataset. The dataset is collected by crawling Facebook through the site's public web interface. We start with a small set of seeds from the United States politicians, whose pages are publicly available on Facebook. We expand the set of seed nodes by following a *breadth first search (BFS)*. Thus, after we crawl all of the seed pages, we continue with the pages liked (followed) by the seeds, and this process is iterated until all the possible pages are collected. For every page, we collect the following publicly available attributes: *title, number of likes, political orientation, political party, category, gender,* and *list of liked pages.* Political orientation is an attribute with nominal values. The values and their distributions in our dataset are as follows: *Conservative* (23%), *Other* (20%), *Moderate* (19%), *Liberal* (18%), *Very Liberal* (7%), *Libertarian* (7%), *Very Conservative* (4%), and *Apathetic* (2%). In every step of the crawling task, we use *page category* to filter out pages that are not related to the US politics. Some of the relevant categories are *Politicians* and *Public Figures.* Every page has a category and most of the categories are chosen from a given list with predefined values. Frequency of categories follows a power-law distribution in which 19.8% of all pages belong to one category and 46% of them are in top 10 categories. Even when considering 90% of the pages, they belong to 160 categories. Table 2 shows a list of popular categories from our dataset. We use the category information to filter out pages do nor belong to persons. Therefore, in our final dataset that we use for experiments, every page belongs to a person such as a politician or a public figure.

Homophily in Directed Networks

Our goal in this experiment is to show whether a user is more similar to her followees or her followers and to verify if there is any significant difference between the two. We use the technique described in previous section to measure homophily and to evaluate the results. We use *political orientation* and *page category,* as the attributes for measuring homophily.

The experiments show that in more than 72% of cases, users have similar political orientation with their immediate neighbors, including followees and followers. In our dataset, the probability of holding the same political orientation for randomly chosen pairs of users is 25%. Next, we cluster the neighbors into two groups, including followers and followees. We observe a similarity of 73.5% between users and their followers, which is slightly higher than their 74% similarity with their followees. There is a slightly higher similarity between the user and her followees than the user and her followers. However the difference between these two results are not significant. There is a possibility that users' popularity influences our results. To investigate this possibility, we divide the users into two groups based on their popularity. A user is considered popular if she has more than 10,000 likes and non-popular if she has less than 1,000 likes. As we can see in Table 3, popular users are more politically aligned with their followees than non-popular users. In contrast, non-popular users are more likely to hold the same political orientation as their followers. One explanation for this observation is that popular and non-popular users' liking behavior could be different. Popular users, comparing to the number of followers, often have much smaller number of followees that are chosen very carefully. Therefore, we expect to observe a higher degree of similarity between a popular user and her followees. Popular users have too many followers and these followers might have reasons other than holding the same political orientation for following the popular individual. Non-popular users, on the other hand, are more eager to attract more followers, therefore they follow other users hoping that these users would follow them back. These users, usually have diverse attribute which lead to poor prediction accuracy. Therefore, non-popular users are less likely to share similar attributes with their followees. On the other hand, the small set of followers of non-popular users should have a good reason to follow them. Therefore, there is a higher chance that a non-popular user and her followers share similar interests or attributes, such as a political orientation.

Page Category.

We run the same set of experiments for measuring homophily, but instead of the *political orientation* attribute, we use the *page category.* Table 4 shows the results. On average, 35% of the connected users belong to a similar category. Users in 39% of cases have a similar category with their followees and in 37% of the cases with their followers, which in both cases is higher than using a combination of followers and followees.

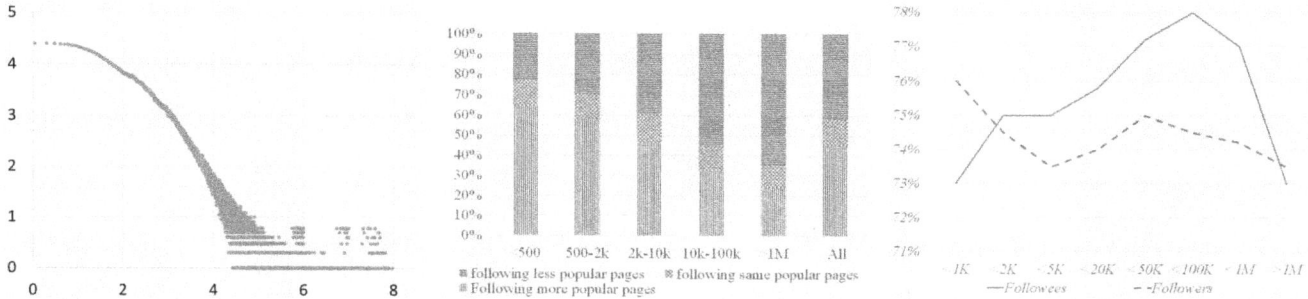

Figure 2: a) User popularity distribution, x-axis is popularity (logarithm of number of page likes) and y-axis is the frequency of pages holding that popularity. b) More than 62% of Facebook pages like pages that are more popular than or equally popular as the page. c) The effect of pages' popularity on liking similar pages. The graph shows the similarity between a page's political orientation with her followees and followers. X-axis is the page's number of likes

The Effect of Popularity on Homophily

Popularity is an attribute that is correlated with the page's number of likes. As popularity follows a power-law distribution, we compute the logarithm of the number of user's likes, $\log(\text{likes}(u_i))$, to discretize the attribute into 8 categories. Figure 2.(a) shows the popularity distribution in our dataset. To evaluate the effect of page popularity on users' following behavior, we measure the relative popularity of each page and popularity of her followers and popularity of her followees. Results indicate that in 49.5% of cases, users like more popular users. In 12.5% of cases, users like users with the same popularity level, and in 38% of cases users like less popular users. This result matches with our expectation that users usually follow those who are more popular than themselves. Figure 2.(b) shows this behavior with respect to different popularity levels. As we can see in this figure, 24% of extremely popular users like users that are not as popular as themselves. Users with more than 2,000 and less than 10,000 likes are the most balanced group of users with respect to following and being followed by users with the same popularity level.

To evaluate the effect of users' popularity on their following (liking) behavior, we measure the homophily of each group of users with respect to their popularity level and plot the results in Figure 2.(c). As we can see in this graph, overall, followees are a better match with users than their followers, although there are some exceptions. Users with less than 100 likes highly match with those who liked them. When the popularity increases, we observe a higher homophily effect between users and those they like (follow). The maximum homophily effect belongs to users with about 100K likes. Beyond that, the trend changes and the curve touches its minimum level of similarity, which belongs to celebrities. Celebrities, usually have a non-uniform liking behavior. They follow users from different categories and different popularities, which decreases the similarity between the user and her followees. The same effect occurs with those who follow celebrities, as a celebrity has followers from a variety of categories and interests, which decreases the similarity between the celebrity user and her followers.

Neighbors Diversity

In this section, we investigate the effect of neighbor diversity on homophily. We use entropy to measure the diversity among followers and followees as follows,

$$e_i = -\sum_k P(A_k) log P(A_k) \qquad (3)$$

where A_i is the number of users that take the ith, $1 \leq i \leq k$ possible value for attribute a and e_i is the entropy of user u_i's neighbors with respect to attribute a. Higher entropy indicates the higher diversity among one's neighbors. We calculate the entropy for followers e_{i_r} and followees e_{i_e}. We summarize the results in Figure 3 considering the following possible scenario: $e_{i_r} \approx e_{i_e}, e_{i_r} > e_{i_e}$, or $e_{i_r} < e_{i_e}$.

Each bar in Figure 3 shows three values. The blue bar shows the percentage of users who have more diverse followees than followers, the red bar shows the percentage of users who have as diverse followers as followees, and the green bar the percentage of the users who have more diverse followers than followees. For both of the attributes, *political orientation* and *page category*, followees are more diverse than followers. Looking at this problem from a user popularity point of view, users with less than 1,000 likes follow the most diverse group of users. In contrast, popular users and celebrities hold the smallest percentage of diverse followees. Diversity among the follower and followees is a measure that can be used to decide which source should be used to infer users' missing information.

Neighbors' Prediction Power

In this section, we investigate the neighbors' prediction power. We use followees, followers, and the combination of followees and followers to predict users' missing information. As previously mentioned, we use weighted majority vote to infer users' missing information. Similar to the previous section, we use followees and followers to predict users's *political orientation* and *category* .

Predicting Political Orientation

In these sets of experiments, we used immediate neighbors to predict users' missing information. The results show that if we use all of the users' neighbors, including followees and followers, by using majority vote algorithm, we can achieve 75% accuracy in predicting users' political orientation. If we limit the neighbors to

Table 4: Category Consistency between Users, Their Followees, and Their Followers with respect to Different Levels of User Popularity

Neighbors	All	$\leq 1K$	$\geq 10K$	≤ 100	$\geq 1M$
Followees	39%	44%	35%	30%	30%
Followers	37%	39%	34%	33%	26%
Fe + Fr	35%	40%	33%	31%	26%

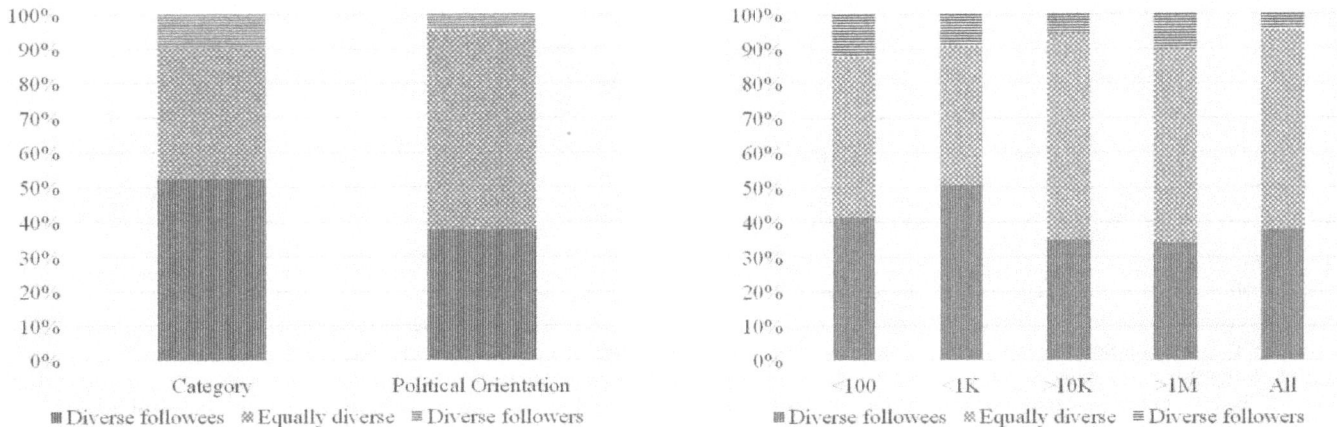

Figure 3: Neighbor diversity among followers and followees. For both attributes, page category and political orientation, followees are more diverse than followers. The figure on right shows the political orientation diversity for pages with different popularity level.

Table 5: Predicting political Orientation using Users' neighbors

Neighbors	All	$\leq 1K$	$\geq 10K$	≤ 100	$\geq 1M$
Followees	77%	78%	76%	78%	78%
Followers	73%	72%	72%	73%	72%
Fe + Fr	74%	74%	74%	74%	74%

Table 6: Page Category Prediction using Users' Neighbors

Neighbors	All	$\leq 1K$	$\geq 10K$	≤ 100	$\geq 1M$
Followees	45%	47%	40%	29%	31%
Followers	43%	36%	38%	32%	26%
Fe + Fr	43%	36%	39%	33%	28%

only the followees, the accuracy increases to 77%. By using one's followers to predict her information we are able to achieve 73% accuracy, which is less than followees and a combination of followees and followers. Table 5 shows the detailed results with respect to different levels of user popularity. The results show that in all different experiments, followees are better sources to predict users' political orientation. Though followers are not as good as followees, they can correctly predict political orientation in more than 73% of cases. Similar to the results from Section using a combination of followers and followees does not improve the accuracy compared to just using the followees.

Predicting Category

Similar to predicting political orientation, we used neighbors to predict users' category. Using all neighbors generates 43% accuracy which is less than followees with 45% accuracy and is similar to followers with 43% accuracy. Prediction results with respect to different levels of users' are reported in Table 6.

CONCLUSION

Our goal in this paper was to study homophily in directed social networks. We investigated whether one can use the neighbors in directed networks to infer users' preferences. We use a dataset of 5 million Facebook fan pages and form a directed network to conduct experiments. We divide every users' neighbors into followers and followees, and use them to infer users' personal preferences. The experiments revealed one's followees can be used to predict her preferences with 74% accuracy. With a similar setting followers

predict users' preference with 73.5% accuracy. The results show the effectiveness of both followers and followees on predicting one's preferences. Previous work on inferring missing attributes in social networks show that it is possible to predict users' personal preferences by using their own online behavior. In this study, we show that not only users' own online behavior, but also users' neighbors' behavior can be used to reveal users' attributes and preferences. Our findings raise the awareness of users over the dangers of having their privacy violated by being able to predict their preferences using individuals that follow them.

ACKNOWLEDGMENTS

We thank the anonymous reviewers for their useful comments. This research is, in part, sponsored by the Office of Naval Research grants N000141110527 and N000141410095.

REFERENCES

[1] M. A. Abbasi, S.-K. Chai, H. Liu, and K. Sagoo. Real-world behavior analysis through a social media lens. In *Social Computing, Behavioral-Cultural Modeling and Prediction*, pages 18–26. Springer, 2012.

[2] M. A. Abbasi and H. Liu. Measuring user credibility in social media. In *Social Computing, Behavioral-Cultural Modeling and Prediction*, pages 441–448. Springer, 2013.

[3] A. Chaabane, G. Acs, M. A. Kaafar, et al. You are what you like! information leakage through users' interests. In *Proceedings of the 19th Annual Network & Distributed System Security Symposium (NDSS)*, 2012.

[4] M. D. Conover, B. Gonçalves, J. Ratkiewicz, A. Flammini, and F. Menczer. Predicting the political alignment of twitter users. In *Privacy, security, risk and trust (passat), 2011 ieee third international conference on and 2011 ieee third international conference on social computing (socialcom)*, pages 192–199. IEEE, 2011.

[5] S. D. Gosling, S. J. Ko, T. Mannarelli, and M. E. Morris. A room with a cue: personality judgments based on offices and bedrooms. *Journal of personality and social psychology*, 82(3):379, 2002.

[6] J. Hu, H.-J. Zeng, H. Li, C. Niu, and Z. Chen. Demographic prediction based on user's browsing behavior. In

Proceedings of the 16th international conference on World Wide Web, pages 151–160. ACM, 2007.

[7] C. Jernigan and B. F. Mistree. Gaydar: Facebook friendships expose sexual orientation. *First Monday*, 14(10), 2009.

[8] M. Kosinski, D. Stillwell, and T. Graepel. Private traits and attributes are predictable from digital records of human behavior. *Proceedings of the National Academy of Sciences*, 110(15):5802–5805, 2013.

[9] R. Li, S. Wang, H. Deng, R. Wang, and K. C.-C. Chang. Towards social user profiling: unified and discriminative influence model for inferring home locations. In *Proceedings of the 18th ACM SIGKDD international conference on Knowledge discovery and data mining*, pages 1023–1031. ACM, 2012.

[10] B. Marcus, F. Machilek, and A. Schütz. Personality in cyberspace: personal web sites as media for personality expressions and impressions. *Journal of Personality and Social Psychology*, 90(6):1014, 2006.

[11] M. McPherson, L. Smith-Lovin, and J. M. Cook. Birds of a feather: Homophily in social networks. *Annual review of sociology*, pages 415–444, 2001.

[12] A. Mislove, B. Viswanath, K. P. Gummadi, and P. Druschel. You are who you know: inferring user profiles in online social networks. In *Proceedings of the third ACM*

[13] D. Murray and K. Durrell. Inferring demographic attributes of anonymous internet users. In *Web Usage Analysis and User Profiling*, pages 7–20. Springer, 2000.

[14] D. Quercia, M. Kosinski, D. Stillwell, and J. Crowcroft. Our twitter profiles, our selves: Predicting personality with twitter. In *Privacy, security, risk and trust (passat), 2011 ieee third international conference on and 2011 ieee third international conference on social computing (socialcom)*, pages 180–185. IEEE, 2011.

[15] D. Quercia, R. Lambiotte, D. Stillwell, M. Kosinski, and J. Crowcroft. The personality of popular facebook users. In *Proceedings of the ACM 2012 conference on Computer Supported Cooperative Work*, pages 955–964. ACM, 2012.

[16] D. Rao and D. Yarowsky. Detecting latent user properties in social media. In *Proc. of the NIPS MLSN Workshop*, 2010.

[17] C. Tan, L. Lee, J. Tang, L. Jiang, M. Zhou, and P. Li. User-level sentiment analysis incorporating social networks. In *Proceedings of the 17th ACM SIGKDD international conference on Knowledge discovery and data mining*, pages 1397–1405. ACM, 2011.

[18] R. Zafarani, M. A. Abbasi, and H. Liu. *Social Media Mining: An Introduction*. Cambridge University Press, 2014.

Understanding Mass Cooperation Through Visualization

Remy Cazabet
National Institute of Informatics
2-1-2 Hitotsubashi, Chiyoda-ku
Tokyo, japan
remy.cazabet@gmail.com

Hideaki Takeda
National Institute of Informatics
2-1-2 Hitotsubashi, Chiyoda-ku
Tokyo, japan
takeda@nii.ac.jp

ABSTRACT

We present a new type of visualization designed to help the understanding of inner mechanisms of mass cooperation. This type of cooperation is ubiquitous nowadays, not only in Online Social Networks, but also in many other situations, such as scientific research on a worldwide scale. Mass cooperation is also at the source of most complex systems. One problem to which researchers are confronted to when they study such cooperation is to build an intuitive representation of what is happening. Many tools and metrics exist to study the results of the cooperation, but sometimes, these metrics can be misleading if one doesn't really observe what the cooperation process really looks like. The main proposition of this paper is a visualization of the cooperation flow. The novelty of our approach is to represent the internal structure of the cooperation in a longitudinal perspective. Through examples, we present how one can form a rich understanding of what form the cooperation takes in a given context, and how this understanding can help to formulate hypothesis which can consequently be studied with appropriate tools such as statistical analysis.

Categories and Subject Descriptors

- [**Human-centered computing**]: Information visualization

Keywords

Mass cooperation; Complex networks; Visualization; Dynamic analysis

1. INTRODUCTION

Since the advent of the digital era, both the technical possibilities and the introduction of new behaviors have participated in the production of large databases storing tremendous amounts of varied information. Recent hot topics such as Big Data, Complex Systems and Network Analysis have been stimulated by this new access to information. One

particular topic of interest is the study of how crowds are involved in massive generation of content, whether it be on Wikipedia, Twitter, Facebook, or even through the publication of ever growing number of scientific publications. If these datasets are a stimulating opportunity, they are also a challenge. The manipulation and comprehension of such information is complex, and it is often hard for the human mind to develop a global understanding of what these data really represent. In this paper, we propose a new tool for the visualization of mass cooperation, a common object of study.

1.1 Mass cooperation definition

When several individuals are involved in a collective creation process, they can either do so in **cooperation** or in **collaboration**. In collaboration users are conscious that they want to achieve a common objective, and a typical feature is that they communicate among themselves, either in a direct or indirect manner. On the contrary, in cooperation, communication is not important and there is no centralized organization. Everyone act according to his own interest, and the result emerges at the global level. Although there is no clearly definite threshold, we consider a cooperation to be mass cooperation when it can no longer be studied exhaustively. Our visualization is already helpful with a cooperation involving a hundred elements.

The visualization we propose is suited for any kind of collective behaviors fulfilling the following properties:

- We can identify a set of successive productions concerning a same topic

- These productions make references to previous elements of the same set

- These references represent the very process of collective creation, and are not merely the result of a hidden communication.

The aim of our proposition is to provide a visualization method more efficient than the commonly used to study the internal structure of internal cooperation. We want a researcher to be able to look rapidly at several instances of mass cooperation from the same datasets, and to identify the most important productions, similarities and differences between these productions. We also want to give an idea of the depth and the width of the flow, that is, if the structure is mostly composed of chains (production a reference production b referencing production c and so on and so forth), or of stars (a 1000 productions referencing a single one).

1.2 Related Works

Several visualizations have been proposed to understand complex systems and large data in general. We introduce the most closely related to our proposition.

ThemeRiver [10] is probably the most famous of these. It allows to represents the dynamic of topics in large collections of documents.

History flows [18]also focuses on dynamic aspects. It is a tool to visualize cooperation and conflict between authors in the process of collaboration, in particular on the web.

Several works have also been done on the visualization of dynamic networks; we can cite [3] as a reference on the domain.

We can cite other related works such as [2, 14, 1, 5, 13]

2. MASS COOPERATION DATASETS

In order to illustrate the possibilities and practical applications of the tools presented in this paper, we applied them to three large datasets from different fields.

2.1 From raw data to cooperation flow

A single type of input is needed to create a cooperation flow, that is a file describing the network of the cooperation. A node in this network corresponds to a "Cooperative Production", or **CP** in the rest of this paper. A CP is any kind of production included in a cooperation flow, that is, which makes references, or is referenced, by other CPs in the same cooperation flow. Edges in the network correspond to references between these CPs. If a CP a make a reference to another b, this is reflected by the directed edge (a, b). The cooperation flow is therefore defined as a directed graph G=V,E and is composed of the following information:

- A set of vertices V, where each vertex is characterized by a quadruplet (cp, v, c, d) with:
  - cp, the cooperative production represented by this vertex
  - v, a float attribute, which can take any value
  - c, a category attribute, represented by a String
  - d, a date

- A set of edges E between these vertices. These edges cannot be reciprocal, i.e. $\nexists a, b, (a, b) \in E \wedge (b, a) \in E$.

The choice of the parameters v and c depends strongly of what we want to study.

2.2 NicoNico

NicoNico is a Japanese video-sharing platform, with functionalities similar to those of YouTube. It is especially famous for the important community of people cooperating in the creation of complex Music Videos centered on the character of Hatsune Miku. Starting from an original song, many people create videos based on it, with innovation such as dancing, singing, creating new graphics, etc. More information about this character and phenomenon can be found in [9, 11, 7]. We use the dataset described in [8] which covers all videos published on the network between January 2007 and December 2012.

Definition of a cooperation flow
In NicoNico, tags are associated with videos. We automatically detect tags corresponding to songs with more than 500 related videos. These videos compose the cooperation flow.

Nodes
Each node corresponds to a video. The date is the date of publication of the video. The v attribute is the number of views of the video. The c attribute is the main contribution of this Video, extracted from tags associated to the video. Typical possible contributions are Singing, Dancing, Original Song, 3D Videos. For more information, please refer to [8].

Edges
In NicoNico, users have the possibility to add a textual comment to the video they publish. A common practice among people involved in cooperation is to write in the comment the unique ID of all other videos they use in their own. We crawled these comments and extracted the references.

Statistics
We finally obtain 165 cooperation flows, composed by 500 to 7654 videos, with an average of 865 videos.

2.3 Twitter

We used a dataset covering the period between March 5, 2011 and March 24, and which covers most tweets published in Japan during this period. For more information, please refer to [16].

We define cooperation flow as chains of retweets, extracted as described in [6].

2.4 DBLP

Thousands of researchers around the world cooperate to improve the global scientific knowledge. We use as a dataset the DBLP database [12], and in particular the version including links between papers, as described in [15].

Our cooperation flows represent the citations of seminal papers and the citations among these papers. Our categories reflect the venues and journals in which these papers have been published.

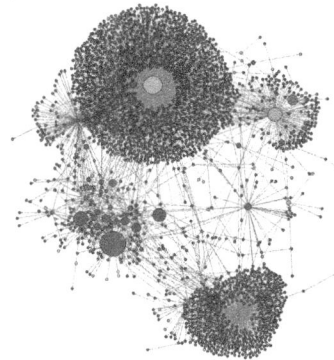

Figure 1: Network of references cleaned from transitive edges

3. PROPOSITION OF VISUALIZATIONS

Representing a cooperation involving hundreds or thousands of productions, made by heterogeneous agents, with different roles, in an extended period of time, is obviously a challenge. The most common tool used for this purpose is often the directed network. By representing cooperative productions (CP) as nodes, and their references as links, one can have a global view of the structure of the cooperation.

By using network visualizations with node-positioning algorithms, one can for instance spot visually clusters of nodes, indicators of a segmentation of the cooperation.

On the other hand, the network representation also has some drawbacks. Figure 1 depicts the network of a typical cooperation flow on NicoNico. We use Gephi, and a combination of layout algorithms to obtain the best node layout as possible. We also use and display all available information on nodes, as we will do in our own solution. The original graph being unreadable, we already improved it by removing the links forming transitive closures. We will discuss about the implications of this choice in the next section. We are now confronted to another problem, intrinsically linked to the network visualization: the node position do not encode any information, that is, we lack the longitudinal aspect.

If we take two nodes of this network, we cannot know which one is a successor of which other one. Of course, as the network is directed, this information is actually present, but is not usable by a human due to the large quantity of information. Yet, this information is important to understand the flow. The network do not represents in an intelligibly way the depth of the cooperation: we cannot differentiate a source CP, which do not user previous ones, from a leaf CP, never referenced, from a synthesizing CP referencing several different contents.

The strength of the visualization we propose is to keep the advantages of the network visualization, while addressing its identified weaknesses, by solutions designed for the specificities of cooperation flows. We keep the principles of networks: CPs are represented as nodes and references between them are represented as edges. In the following sections, we will describe the process to go from the original data, encoded as a graph, to our visualization. To give a first concrete example, the same graph as presented in Fig. 1 is represented with our method in Fig. 2.

3.1 Suppression of transitive links

As stated in the previous section, one first step to take in order to simplify the number of edges is to remove transitive ones. For each triplet of nodes a, b, c such as $(a, b), (b, c)$ and (a, c) belongs to E, we remove (a, c) from the network. We have to stress that this transformation is destructive: we will loose some information compared to the original data. However, we argue that in the specific case of cooperation flows, this information is not crucial, and might even be deceptive. First, in flows, there is a naturel order between all CPs, which is determined by their temporal location. If there is a link from b to c, and another from a to b, then we know that c is anterior to a. Furthermore, we know that a has a knowledge of c, and that a made a reference to b. Therefore, we can consider that a is using c without being aware of it, through b. This position is of course questionable, and one must check that it makes sense on the dataset he wants to use. However, in our example dataset and probably in most data coming from real cases, relying on the existence or not of these transitive links can be deceptive. Our Twitter dataset is a good example. When a user a retweets a tweet he has seen from another user b, originally published by user c, he can do it in several manners [4], but due to a restriction in the number of characters, the information about intermediaries will more likely be lost. The transitivity is already inferred in the data. More generally, when

references are chosen "manually" by the CPs authors, it is likely that all the chains of references will not be present.

3.2 Node Layout

The layout we proposed is a fix layout, which means that the same network will always be displayed in the same manner.

The idea is to emphasize the longitudinal aspect of the flow: nodes are ordered, and this order is an important information worth displaying.

x position
A x value is assigned to each node, which corresponds to the maximal number of hops between this node and a source. Sources will have a value of $x = 0$, nodes referencing them a value of $x = 1$, etc. The x value is trivially converted to match the available area for displaying.

More formally, the function can be described in a recursive manner:

$$x(n) = \begin{cases} 0 & \text{If } \nexists m, (n, m) \in E \\ max(\{x(m) : (n, m) \in E\}) & \text{Otherwise} \end{cases}$$

y position
The y position of a node n depends of 2 factors: the node ancestor of n, and the instant of n. Nodes descendant of the same node with the same x value are sorted according to their instant, the older the node, the higher the y position. For two nodes with same x value but different ancestors, they are sorted according to the y values of their ancestor. As for the x position, the y value can be trivially converted to a value in pixels accordingly to the available area for displaying. This algorithm is best translated in a recursive fashion, see Algorithm 1, with:

$succ(n)$ a function returning the successors of n ordered chronologically

$height(n)$ a function returning the height of the node n

Algorithm 1: $setY(NS)$

Data: $NS = (n_1, ..., n_x)$ nodes ordered chronologically
begin
    $CP \longleftarrow 0$
    for $n \in NS$ **do**
        if $n.y \neq null$ **then**
            $n.y \longleftarrow CP$
        $SP \longleftarrow CP$
        $setY(succ(n))$
        if $SP + heigth(n) > CP$ **then**
            $CP \longleftarrow SP + heigth(n)$

It is also necessary to add a function to ensure that all nodes with successors will be centered relatively to them, as described in Algorithm 2
Nodes with several ancestors
For synthesizing nodes, i.e. nodes with several ancestors, we consider only one of their ancestors as a reference. We choose the node with the maximal x value. In case of several ancestors with the same x value, we choose the one with the maximal y value.

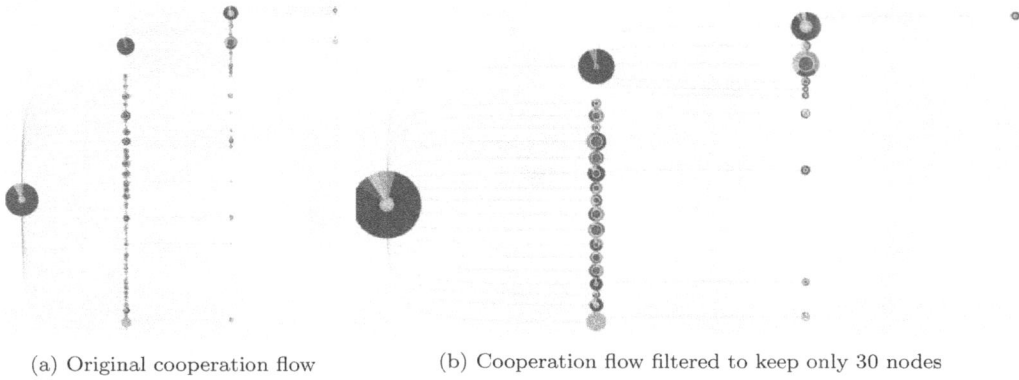

(a) Original cooperation flow   (b) Cooperation flow filtered to keep only 30 nodes

Figure 2: Effect of filtering nodes

Algorithm 2: $CenterAncestors(N)$

Data: $N = \{n_1, ..., n_x\}$ list of all displayed nodes
begin
    for $n \in N$ **do**
        if $succ(n) > 1$ **then**
            $YFirstSucc \longleftarrow min(v_x.y, \forall v_x \in succ(v))$
            $YLastSucc \longleftarrow max(v_x.y, \forall v_x \in succ(v))$
            $n.y \longleftarrow$
            $max(n.y, (YFirstSucc + YLastSucc)/2)$

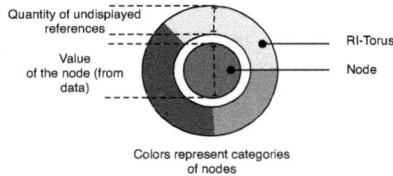

Figure 3: Schema of the representation of a node

3.3 Aspect of the nodes

Nodes are represented by two circular shapes with the same center, as illustrated in Fig. 3. The inner shape is simply a circle that represents the properties of the event, as it is common with network visualizations. The size and color of the node correspond to properties defined by the original data. The second shape is an annulus, or torus, positioned around the first circle, and which summarize the cooperation properties of the node. We will refer to it as the **RI-Torus**, for Reuse Indicator Torus.

In cooperation flows, as in most networks representing real world data, we observe a power law distribution of the degrees of nodes. The consequence is that an important proportion of CPs are leaves: they are never used by any other CP. As a consequence, instead of displaying each and every of these nodes, we summarize them in the RI-Torus. Its width for node n is proportional to the total number of nodes making a reference to n and not displayed on the graph. The tore is composed of colored sections reflecting the proportion of these nodes corresponding to each category.

For both shapes, we apply a logarithmic scale between the values and the area of the shapes, as this scale is often the most appropriate when representing data coming from complex real world data.

3.4 Filtering of nodes

If the number of nodes to display after this simple summarization is still big, the visualization can be difficult to apprehend. In this case, we propose a way to simplify the graph while keeping as much information as possible. For each node, we compute a cooperation impact value, $CO - IMP$, which represents how strong is the impact of this node in the global cooperation flow:

$$CO - IMP(n) = 1 + |\{v : path(v, n)\}|$$

where $path(v, n)$ is true if there is a path going from v to n in the network

This value corresponds to the degree that the node would have if all relations were transitive, or the number of nodes that might have reused it.

We keep for displaying only the top T nodes according to their $CO - IMP$ value, where T is a parameter. All nodes that are removed from the visualization are now summarized on the RI-Torus of their first displayed ancestor, in a way strictly equivalent as if they were a direct leaf of this node.

With this mechanism, even though we greatly simplify the complexity of the displayed network we still keep all the most influent nodes in the cooperation flow, and part of the information of other nodes is still present in the visualization, through the cooperation impact torus of their first displayed ancestor.

The effect of this simplification can be observed in the figure 2

3.5 Additional possibilities

One interesting property of this visualization is that nodes situated on overlapping y values are necessarily ordered in a chronological order from left to right. Therefore, it is possible to switch to a temporal representation without changing the y position of nodes. This possibility is present in our implementation.

4. VALIDATION OF EXPRESSIVITY

This cooperation flow visualization can be used at least for two different purposes. First, to find common proper-

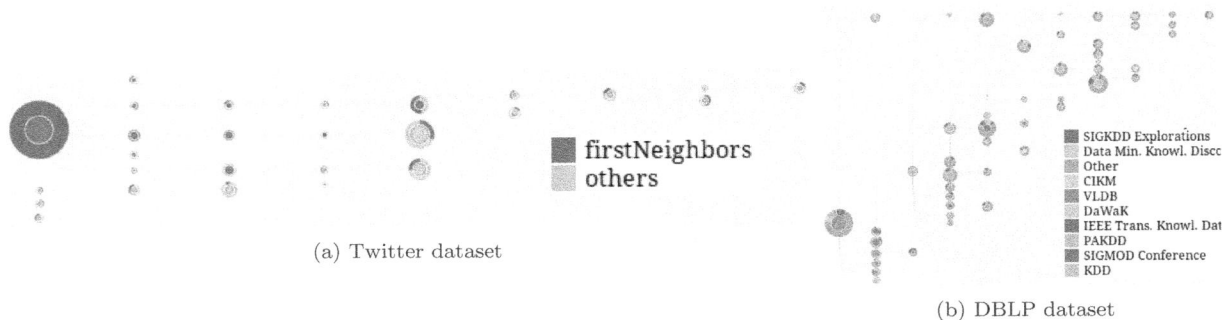

(a) Twitter dataset

firstNeighbors
others

- SIGKDD Explorations
- Data Min. Knowl. Discc
- Other
- CIKM
- VLDB
- DaWaK
- IEEE Trans. Knowl. Dat
- PAKDD
- SIGMOD Conference
- KDD

(b) DBLP dataset

Figure 4: Examples of typical cooperation flow in Twitter and DBLP

ties, common patterns, or major differences in sets of cooperation, either from the same data source or different ones. This is typical of Exploratory Data Analysis [17] needs, and we will detail this later. A second usage, intended for end-users, is to use this visualization to discover useful elements in the cooperation flow. In the research example, one can immediately spot the most cited articles on a particular topic, the anteriority between them, if reviews have been written, with the papers they cite, if the domain is split in different branches, and so on and so forth.

4.1 Exploration of example datasets

In this section, we show how the proposed visualization can be used to explore, understand, and make hypothesis on datasets. All observations made here are not scientific evidences, as they repose on manual observations of limited number of cases, but are a mean for a researcher to make hypothesis which can therefore be tested by rigorous statistical analysis, validating of refuting the initial observation. To cite Tukey [17], "[Exploratory Data Analysis] can never be the whole story, but nothing else can serve as the foundation stone - as the first step"

4.2 Deep study of one dataset: NicoNico

NicoNico is the richest and the most complex of our datasets. In fig. 2, we shown a typical flow from this network. We can make the following observations, also valid on most other flows:

1. There is only one original source, and most of the cooperation is made directly from this source, as we can judge by the large RI-Torus

2. Most important nodes for the collaboration are on the first level, they directly reference the original node only

3. The cooperation is more wide than deep, there is not much cooperation at a level greater than 3.

4. Although many categories (colors) are present, each node seems to generate a specialized cooperation: RI-Torus are mostly of a single color, not always the same.

These are only examples of observations we can make, which can later be checked easily and allow to grasp some properties of the cooperation. Most of them cannot be done directly by using a classic network visualization, because the organization is not encoded in the position of nodes. As soon as the number of nodes become important (here, the original networks contain around 2000 nodes), the information we encode in the RI-Torus is also difficult to observe.

4.3 Comparison of datasets

In fig. 4, we present two visualizations typical of the other datasets. We can immediately spot some differences. In the tweet dataset, cooperation is deeper, and we tend to see the formation of chains, long but without many bifurcations. More important nodes are not necessarily situated at the first step, but can occur deeper. There seems to be a stronger relation between the popularity of the node and its role in the cooperation. There is not a single source.

In the citation dataset, we immediately spot a large number of nodes making references to several others. These nodes with many references are important in the cooperation. Nodes at a deep level seem to generate as much cooperation as those in the first levels. There also seems to be a lesser concentration in the cooperation generation: a larger fraction of nodes are referenced by other important nodes, and the gap is less important between the top influential nodes and the ordinary ones. Exploring in further details the properties of the different datasets is beyond the scope of this paper.

5. CONCLUSION

In this paper, we have presented a graph-based visualization to explore mass cooperation. The graph based visualization we proposed is solving several problems encountered when using traditional graph visualization: we limit the number of nodes to display through a visual mean (RI-Torus) and a selection of the nodes to display, and we discussed about the balance between the loss of information and the simplification of the visualization.

In the future, we hope that other researchers will use this visualization and help to improve it, either by their remarks or extending the possibilities. In this prospect, we release its source code, altogether with an interactive online version, so as interested researchers could work with it as easily as possible. One of such amelioration could concern the visualization of cooperation flows in which most important nodes are synthesizers, that is, they make many references to previous nodes on different branches, as this makes currently the graph difficult to read.

6. ACKNOWLEDGMENTS

We thank Fujio Toriumi for collecting the Twitter dataset, and allowing us to make use of it in this work.

7. REFERENCES

[1] D. Auber. Tulip, a huge graph visualization framework. In *Graph Drawing Software*, pages 105–126. Springer, 2004.

[2] M. Bastian, S. Heymann, and M. Jacomy. Gephi: an open source software for exploring and manipulating networks. In *ICWSM*, pages 361–362, 2009.

[3] S. Bender-deMoll and D. A. McFarland. The art and science of dynamic network visualization. *Journal of Social Structure*, 7(2):1–38, 2006.

[4] D. Boyd, S. Golder, and G. Lotan. Tweet, tweet, retweet: Conversational aspects of retweeting on twitter. In *System Sciences (HICSS), 2010 43rd Hawaii International Conference on*, pages 1–10. IEEE, 2010.

[5] B.-J. Breitkreutz, C. Stark, M. Tyers, et al. Osprey: a network visualization system. *Genome Biol*, 4(3):R22, 2003.

[6] R. Cazabet, N. Pervin, F. Toriumi, and H. Takeda. Information diffusion on twitter: everyone has its chance, but all chances are not equal. In *Signal-Image Technology & Internet-Based Systems (SITIS), 2013 International Conference on*, pages 483–490. IEEE, 2013.

[7] R. Cazabet, H. Takeda, M. Hamasaki, and F. Amblard. Using dynamic community detection to identify trends in user-generated content. *Social Network Analysis and Mining*, 2(4):361–371, 2012.

[8] M. Hamasaki and M. Goto. Songrium: a music browsing assistance service based on visualization of massive open collaboration within music content creation community. In *Proceedings of the 9th International Symposium on Open Collaboration*, page 4. ACM, 2013.

[9] M. Hamasaki, H. Takeda, and T. Nishimura. Network analysis of massively collaborative creation of multimedia contents: case study of hatsune miku videos on nico nico douga. In *Proceedings of the 1st international conference on Designing interactive user experiences for TV and video*, pages 165–168. ACM, 2008.

[10] S. Havre, E. Hetzler, P. Whitney, and L. Nowell. Themeriver: Visualizing thematic changes in large document collections. *Visualization and Computer Graphics, IEEE Transactions on*, 8(1):9–20, 2002.

[11] H. Kenmochi. Vocaloid and hatsune miku phenomenon in japan. *Proc. of InterSinging 2010*, pages 1–4, 2010.

[12] M. Ley. The dblp computer science bibliography: Evolution, research issues, perspectives. In *String Processing and Information Retrieval*, pages 1–10. Springer, 2002.

[13] M. Rosvall and C. T. Bergstrom. Mapping change in large networks. *PloS one*, 5(1):e8694, 2010.

[14] P. Shannon, A. Markiel, O. Ozier, N. S. Baliga, J. T. Wang, D. Ramage, N. Amin, B. Schwikowski, and T. Ideker. Cytoscape: a software environment for integrated models of biomolecular interaction networks. *Genome research*, 13(11):2498–2504, 2003.

[15] J. Tang, J. Zhang, L. Yao, J. Li, L. Zhang, and Z. Su. Arnetminer: extraction and mining of academic social networks. In *Proceedings of the 14th ACM SIGKDD international conference on Knowledge discovery and data mining*, pages 990–998. ACM, 2008.

[16] F. Toriumi, T. Sakaki, K. Shinoda, K. Kazama, S. Kurihara, and I. Noda. Information sharing on twitter during the 2011 catastrophic earthquake. In *Proceedings of the 22nd international conference on World Wide Web companion*, pages 1025–1028. International World Wide Web Conferences Steering Committee, 2013.

[17] J. W. Tukey. Exploratory data analysis. 1977.

[18] F. B. Viégas, M. Wattenberg, and K. Dave. Studying cooperation and conflict between authors with history flow visualizations. In *Proceedings of the SIGCHI conference on Human factors in computing systems*, pages 575–582. ACM, 2004.

How You Post Is Who You Are: Characterizing Google+ Status Updates across Social Groups

Evandro Cunha[1,2], Gabriel Magno[1], Marcos André Gonçalves[1],
César Cambraia[2] and Virgilio Almeida[1]
[1]Dept. of Computer Science, [2]College of Letters - Universidade Federal de Minas Gerais, Brazil
{evandrocunha, magno, mgoncalv, virgilio}@dcc.ufmg.br, nardelli@ufmg.br

ABSTRACT

The analysis of user-generated content on the Web provides tools to better understand users' behavior and to the development of improved Web services. Here, we consider a large dataset of Google+ status updates to evaluate linguistic features among members of distinct social groups. Our study reveals that groups hold linguistic particularities – such as a tendency to use professional vocabulary, suggesting that Google+ might be employed, by certain users, for professional activities, or that members do not dissociate from their jobs when interacting in this environment. To illustrate a possible application of our outcomes, we present a classification experiment aiming to infer users' social information through the analysis of their posts, with satisfactory preliminary results. Our findings help to understand not only collective peculiarities of online social media users, but also important characteristics of the textual genre *post*, being one of the first and most comprehensive studies on this topic.

Categories and Subject Descriptors: J.5 [Computer Applications]: Arts and Humanities—*Linguistics*

Keywords: OSNs; Google+; Internet linguistics; Microtext analysis

1. INTRODUCTION

Increasingly, researchers have taken advantage of the vast amount of language data that online applications can provide, which gave rise to a new subfield of knowledge called *Internet linguistics* [5]. According to Crystal [4], the Internet plays an unprecedented role in the study of language, as it allows linguists to use rich documented datasets to investigate language use in various levels and the nature of the language employed by Web users. From this perspective, authors are concerned with understanding and describing computer-mediated communication, as well as developing tools to provide better online services. Opportunities arising in this area include the employment of collections from user-generated content websites as corpora of large-scale natural language data.

Google+ is an online social network (OSN) launched in June 2011. To better understand its typical features, the investigation of formal and functional aspects of the content shared by its members is of utmost importance. Here, we study one kind of content published in Google+: status updates, usually called *posts*. Our

focus is to characterize Google+ posts and to identify differences and similarities among linguistic aspects of texts produced by users considering their distinct social characteristics. We analyze texts from male and female members from 10 countries and 15 groups of occupations, since gender, location and job are known as factors that influence language usage in a myriad of domains [12]. Our main hypothesis is that the membership in certain social groups may influence aspects of the language employed by users when posting, reflecting patterns observed in other online and offline situations.

To our knowledge, this work is novel in that it is the first to focus on linguistic aspects of Google+ posts. Moreover, it contributes to the general literature on Internet linguistics by investigating the role of social factors in relevant aspects of language use in social media. Possible applications of this study include the development of improved Web services, as discussed in the following sections.

2. RELATED WORK

On Google+. An analysis of Google+ social graph is presented by Magno et al. [15], who studied structural properties of this network in comparison to other services and found different patterns of its usage across distinct countries. They discovered, among other findings, that Google+ is popular in countries with relatively low Internet penetration rate and that its top users are not celebrities or public figures, but mainly individuals in the IT industry.

A study on how members organize and select audiences for shared content in Google+ was conducted by Kairam et al. [11]. An interesting result is that users weigh limiting factors, like privacy, against the desire to reach a large audience. Gonzalez et al. [9] showed that, despite the recent growth of this OSN, the relative size of its largest connected component has decreased with time and that only a few users exhibit any type of activity.

On language and social factors. Literature on the relations between language and society is now really vast. Labov's [12], Trudgill's [26] and Romaine's [22] works present the main findings of decades of research, considering also the correlations between language variation and the social factors that we contemplate here.

Bell et al. [1] used computational tools to investigate differences in language styles among men and women. Their finding that women use more social words than men could be verified by our analysis. It is also worth mentioning Lakoff's [13] seminal work on language and gender, where the author indicates that a number of linguistic features can distinguish men's speech from women's.

The study of linguistic styles associated with particular professions was performed by Jones [10]. However, our approach that identified the use of professional vocabulary in posts published in an online social network seems to be an original contribution.

On language use in social media. The study of topics from Facebook posts was performed by Wang et al. [28]. They demonstrated that women are more likely to write posts about personal themes, contrasting with men, who tend to share more public subjects, like politics and sports. Even though we study another OSN, this finding relates to the prevalence of usage of words from categories like *family*, *social* and *affection* by female users in our dataset.

An investigation on how men and women differ when designating hashtags on Twitter was carried out by Cunha et al. [6], who found that, in the context of political debate, Brazilian women are more prone to use approaches based on solidarity, while men tend to employ assertive strategies. Ottoni et al. [16] examined users' descriptions on Pinterest and showed differences in the linguistic style between genders, being women more likely to use words of fondness and affection. Schwartz et al. [24] investigated the relation between language and different variables on Facebook, and found associations between personality and language use of given groups.

Studies that performed gender and location prediction of users based on the written content posted by them will be referenced ahead, where we present the results of our classification experiment.

Although we found these and other investigations on language use in OSNs, we did not find studies that considered, simultaneously, all social factors and linguistic attributes examined here.

3. METHODOLOGY

Data collection. From March 23rd to June 1st, 2012, we collected profile information and posts of Google+ users. For ethical and legal reasons, we gathered only public information revealed in users' pages and did not attempt to obtain access to information set as private. We inspected the *robots.txt* file provided by Google+, followed the corresponding sitemap to retrieve the lists of URLs of profiles to be collected and then made HTTP requests to the pages. Since we collected the complete list of profiles provided, we believe we retrieved information from all users with public pages at the time of the collection, compiling information from 160,304,954 profiles.

Posts. Among the profiles collected, only 8,564,462 set their posts as publicly available. We were able to retrieve up to the last ten status updates from each user's page, totaling 29,366,310 posts.

To select only messages generated in English, we used *langid.py* [14], a language identification tool that identified 20,928,557 posts probably written in this language. In order to increase the confidence that our posts are actually in near-standard English – thus avoiding the analysis of posts only partially produced in this language or written in dialects, mixed varieties or fused lects –, we additionally filtered texts with probability of at least .99 of being in English. After this restriction, we narrowed our dataset down to 7,414,679 posts. A manual evaluation of several filtered posts indicated that they were indeed written in near-standard English.

Since we aimed to analyze language characteristics of individuals, we alleviated the impact of copied posts, like chain letters and other highly replicated texts, by removing duplicated messages. We identified 265,100 types of texts that presented duplication, totaling 1,220,341 repeated posts, and removed them all from the dataset. Therefore, at this point we have 6,194,338 distinct Google+ posts.

Figure 1 displays a general characterization of distinct Google+ posts written in English. The first two graphics show, respectively, cumulative distribution functions of numbers of characters and words per post. On average, posts have 111.2 characters and 25.6 words. The third graphic indicates that the majority of posts have only a few sentences: 53% of them have one sentence, while 26% have two and 10% have three sentences. This shows that, even though Google+ posts are not compulsorily limited to a small number of characters like Twitter updates and Foursquare tips, they can still be considered microtexts.

Social information. Besides the posts, we collected information on users' location, gender and professional activity.

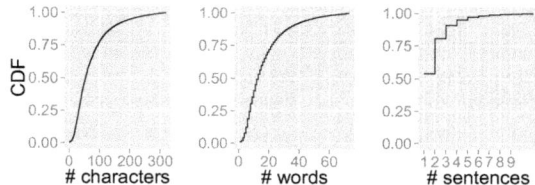

Figure 1: Cumulative distribution functions of numbers of characters, words and sentences per post

Location. We inferred users' location using information available in the field *Places lived*, in which members can create a list of places where they have lived. This is an open field, meaning that users can type any text they want to. Therefore, the same place can be written in different ways (e.g. *New York*, *NYC*, *New York City*) or using distinct geographic levels (e.g. *Los Angeles*, *California*, *USA*).

To identify an user's country, we extracted the geographic coordinates of the last location cited and translated them into a valid country identifier. In this fashion, we were able to identify the country of 22,578,898 members (14.08% of the full dataset). Remaining users set this information as private or simply did not fill this field.

Here, we consider only members located in the ten countries with most posts in English: United States (US), Great Britain (GB), India (IN), Canada (CA), Australia (AU), Indonesia (ID), Germany (DE), Philippines (PH), Malaysia (MY) and France (FR). Figure 2 summarizes the process of posts collection until this point.

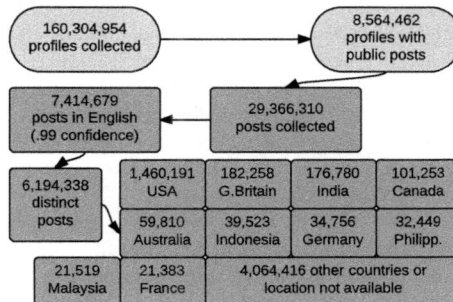

Figure 2: Description of the posts collection

Gender. Gender information is shared by 126,531,842 users (78.93% of the complete dataset) and by 770,997 users with posts collected in the ten countries studied. Considering members who set this information publicly available, 63.77% chose *male*, 34.38% chose *female* and 1.85% chose *other*. Here, we do not consider users who set their own gender as *other*.

Professional activity. The field *Occupation* is an open field, so users can type any text they want to in order to describe their activity. As a result, we gathered a very large number of different occupations and had to summarize the information introduced by users: first, we manually aggregated the most common strings present in the dataset, since the same occupation can be written in different ways (e.g. *student*, *study*, *graduate student*, *go to school*); second, we selected the top 30 occupations; third, we used the Standard Occupational Classification (SOC) by the U.S. Bureau of Labor Statistics [27] to divide these occupations into the major groups of professional activities used here. The occupations *student* and *retired*, although not shown in the SOC, are also considered in our analyses.

Table 1 shows the number of posts and users per social group in our dataset.

4. ANALYSES

In this section, we present the linguistic analyses performed on Google+ posts. They are all independent investigations, not neces-

Social group	# posts	# users	Social group	# posts	# users
Country			Occupation		
United States (US)	1,460k	494k	Student	85k	36k
Great Britain (GB)	182k	62k	Computer and math.	61k	19k
India (IN)	177k	96k	Arts and design	25k	7,9k
Canada (CA)	101k	34k	Archit. and engin.	15k	6,0k
Australia (AU)	60k	21k	Business and financ.	11k	3,9k
Indonesia (ID)	40k	24k	Media	8,3k	2,1k
Germany (DE)	35k	15k	Educ. and library	6,7k	2,2k
Philippines (PH)	32k	14k	Management	5,9k	1,9k
Malaysia (MY)	22k	10k	Sales	4,6k	1,6k
France (FR)	21k	10k	Legal	2,6k	0.8k
			Retired	2,2k	0.9k
Gender			Healthcare	1,9k	0.8k
Male	1,549k	557k	Religious	1,5k	0.4k
Female	526k	203k	Science	1,2k	0.4k
Other/NA	55k	18k	Food preparation	0.7k	0.3k
			Other/NA	1,897k	695k

Table 1: Number of posts and users per social group (round)

sarily examining the same text attributes, which makes it possible to test distinct aspects of language behavior. It is important to note that the results presented here apply only to language behavior in the specific context of Google+ and may not be valid for offline environments or even for other online social networking systems.

4.1 Misspellings

The occurrence of misspelled words in texts may signify unawareness of standard orthographic rules or carelessness during typing, due to negligence or lack of revision. Thus, calculating the extent to which misspellings emerge in our dataset might indicate how high literacy levels in English of the communities are or how concerned individuals are about the quality of their posts – since, for most users, it may not matter whether they make misspellings in OSN posts. In other cases, non-standard spellings may be on purpose, in order to create specific effects on readers.

By using a list of 4,238 common misspellings in English (available at `http://bit.ly/1ieaEOa`), that encompasses 31.3% of the whole vocabulary employed in the dataset, we investigated the occurrence of these non-standard linguistic elements in Google+ posts produced by different social groups. This list, that considers spelling differences in distinct varieties of the language, comprises misspelled items and their corresponding standard spellings, which are, therefore, the only words susceptible to misspelling in our analysis. Only cases of sequences of letters representing no standardly spelled words in English are included in the list, and homographs are not considered. We applied this approach instead of running a spelling checker on the posts in order to avoid the classification of intentional non-standard spellings (such as *gonna*, *doin'*, *ur* and many other common spellings on Web environments, which are not included in the list) as misspellings.

We calculated the fraction of misspellings per post by dividing the number of misspelled words by the number of words susceptible to misspelling. To avoid biases due to the small number of words susceptible to misspelling in some posts (e.g. if a post has only one word susceptible to misspelling, its fraction of misspellings is either 0 or 1), we did not consider posts with less than five words that appear in our list, thus evaluating 758,233 posts.

Figure 3 exhibits the average fractions of misspellings per post. It shows that, as expected, non native English speakers, with exception of French users, are more prone to make misspellings in English written posts. We also found that, in general, women's fraction of misspellings is higher than men's: we believe that the difference between topics discussed by men and women – as will be seen in Section 4.4 – does not force women to be so demanding on the formal linguistic attributes of the content published.

Figure 3 also states that workers who deal more with written texts make fewer misspellings in Google+ posts: while food and health professionals have the highest fractions of misspellings, media, legal and education professionals have the smallest ones. It is worth remembering that, by the nature of these occupations, review of written material is sometimes an activity performed daily.

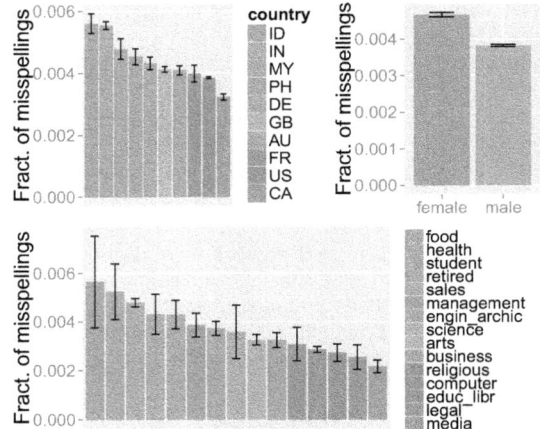

Figure 3: Average fractions of misspellings per post for different countries, genders and occupations ± standard errors

4.2 Readability and complexity

The readability of a text is the ease in which readers can properly comprehend it. A series of formulas that return numerical scores estimating the level of difficulty of texts have already been proposed [8] and should not be seen as metrics of quality of documents, since *easier* or *more difficult* texts are not necessarily *worse* or *better* texts. Here, we employ a readability index to diagnose differences in the organization of speech by distinct groups in Google+.

The Unix command *style* returns results for the Automated Readability Index (ARI), which calculates the readability of a text using the formula $ARI = 4.71 \cdot \frac{\#of\,characters}{\#of\,words} + 0.5 \cdot \frac{\#of\,words}{\#of\,sentences} - 21.43$. The ARI relies mostly on a factor of characters per word and, on a lesser extent, on a factor of words per sentence. Thus, its assumption is that the adoption of big words and the construction of large sentences are features that enhance the complexity of a text: other aspects being equal, smaller words and shorter sentences should result in increases of comprehension [25].

Figure 4 depicts average values of ARI for distinct groups. Higher scores indicate higher complexity, as they correspond to bigger words and sentences. According to our results, texts of German, French and Indian users on Google+ are the most complex ones; on the other side, posts of Malaysians, Filipinos and Indonesians are the least complex. Interestingly, native speakers of English – from Australia, Great Britain, Canada and USA – present the central values, which seems to indicate that non native English speakers must have transferred linguistic patterns of their mother tongues to the foreign language [3]. This hypothesis is strengthened when we observe that users from countries with prevalence of speakers of Indo-European languages have the highest values of ARI and those from countries with prevalence of speakers of Austronesian languages have the lowest indices. We also observed that the average number of characters per word is very similar across countries, showing that, in this case, the discriminant factor of the readability index is the number of words per sentence, which may be highly influenced by the linguistic structures of mother tongues.

ARI scores for female and male users show that posts written by men are, on average, more complex than those written by women. This fact is observed for most countries and professions. The exami-

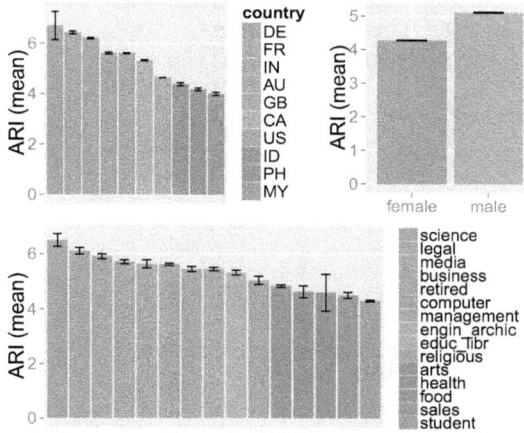

Figure 4: Average values of ARI for posts of users from different countries, genders and occupations ± standard errors

nation of the complexity of posts of users with different occupations can be related to the previous analysis on misspellings: in the same way that workers from fields more associated with written communication and traditionally elaborated texts, like legal and media professionals, publish texts with fewer misspellings, they also produce more complex posts than those from fields that do not necessarily deal with written texts, like food preparation and sales professionals. Ahead, in Section 4.4, we will advocate that: (a) men and women make distinct use of this OSN, which could explain the differences in the complexity of the posts between genders; and (b) Google+ users are often talking about their own professional activities and, therefore, about topics that ask for either more or less elaborated linguistic constructions, according to their respective occupations.

4.3 Vocabulary variability

We also considered vocabulary variability – through an entropy-based approach – across different groups, since this could add relevant insights into statistical regularities of the language employed by users. Differences of entropy values are related to the specific style of each community: lower values mean more predictable word usage, while higher ones mean more vocabulary variability.

After removing stopwords and applying stemming based on Porter's algorithm [19], we calculated Shannon's entropy of the concatenation of all posts from each group. Since the number of users in each group differs and the number of unique words is directly affected by the total number of words, we applied an under-sampling methodology across our three categories of social groups. We repeated this process 25 times and calculated the mean.

No significant differences among entropy values of different groups were found, indicating that they are not discriminant on the variability of vocabulary in the context of Google+ posts and denying our hypothesis that vocabulary variability in this OSN varies among posts written in English by users from different countries, genders and occupations.

4.4 Semantic categories of words

An interesting way of investigating language differences across groups is through the analysis of the vocabulary used by their members. Since vocabulary is a system of mapping the world, this kind of investigation reveals how groups perceive reality, indicating what the main concerns and interests of certain communities might be.

We aim to identify if some given semantic categories of words are more common in texts produced by members of particular countries, genders and occupations. To accomplish this task, we used the Language Inquiry and Word Count (LIWC) [18], a tool that

examines texts and verifies the occurrence of words previously classified as members of functional/grammatical (e.g. pronouns, articles, prepositions etc.) or semantic (e.g. social, money, religion etc.) categories. A comprehensive list of all LIWC categories, including examples of words that are part of each category, is available at `http://www.liwc.net/descriptiontable1.php`.

We calculated LIWC scores for a given category of words as the fraction of words of this category in the total amount of categorized words of a particular post. After having calculated LIWC scores for 41 categories of semantic words, we compared them across the social groups. Figure 5 shows the categories of words with most significant differences across the groups considered in this study.

We observed that users from different countries hold distinct patterns in the usage of certain semantic categories of words in their posts. For example, Indians have the highest scores in the use of words from categories such as *friend*, *humans* and *social*, while they have low scores in categories like *negative emotions*, *anger* and *time*. Also, users from most of the Western countries considered here tend to be the main users of words related to *home*, *money* and *work* and the least users of words from the categories *health*, *affection*, *positive emotions* and *family*. These categories might be revealing the topics more covered in the posts and are a sign of cultural differences among users from different countries, which is relevant for the literature on comparative cultural studies, interested in investigating cultures in global and intercultural contexts [20].

Considering gender, we found that women are more prone to use words from categories such as *family*, *home*, *friend*, *social*, *humans*, *affection* and *emotions*, while men are the main adopters of words from categories like *cause*, *motion*, *space*, *numbers*, *money* and *work*. We interpret these results suggesting that men have a tendency to use Google+ to talk about technical topics, their achievements and professional activities, while women are more likely to use this OSN to talk about their social and familial relations. These distinct approaches toward this specific online social networking service may also be the reason why men's posts are more complex and formally accurate, having fewer misspellings, as described in the Sections 4.1 and 4.2 above.

We also found a clear correlation between word usage and users' occupations. For instance, words related to religion are extremely more frequent in posts from religious professionals; the same for money vocabulary in posts from salespeople, body-related words in posts from health workers, among many others (interestingly, the category *family* is adopted mainly by retired users). This fact suggests that vocabulary employed in Google+ posts is highly related to users' working activities, indicating that this OSN may be often used for professional activities or that members do not dissociate from their jobs when interacting in Google+, maintaining their professional vocabulary even in this environment. This result has important implications for the literature on cognitive linguistics, since it reinforces the view that individuals' conceptual maps – represented by their vocabulary – is strongly related to their jobs.

As far as we are concerned, these significant differences among the vocabulary of users with different occupations have been found for the first time in online social media.

4.5 Inference of social groups

To illustrate a possible application of these results, we propose the task of inferring social characteristics of users based on linguistic analysis of their posts. This type of application is useful to assist in the development of tools aiming authorship attribution for purposes like personalization of services and identification of fake profiles.

We conducted a preliminary classification experiment using textual metrics contemplated above. For each user, we created a vector

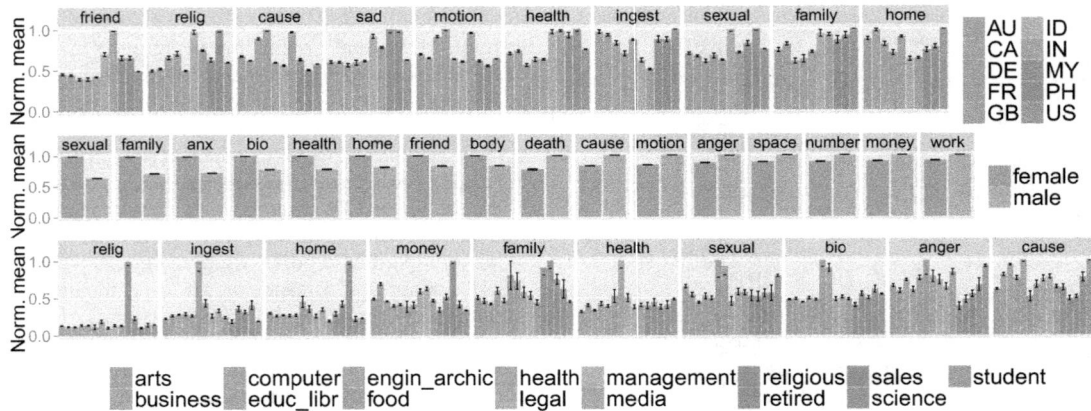

Figure 5: Semantic categories of words with most significant differences across distinct groups of users (countries, genders and occupations, respectively) ± standard errors

containing 76 features: 4 size metrics (numbers of characters, words, sentences and paragraphs per post), 7 readability indices (ARI and other indices provided by the Unix command *style*), 64 LIWC categories (including categories of semantic words and categories of grammatical and function words) and fraction of misspellings.

We sought to make inferences by using support vector machine classifier (SVM) and the *scikit-learn* library [17] to conduct the SVM classification and parametrization. For the experiments, we employed a 5-fold cross-validation technique randomly selecting a fixed number of users per class: 1,000 for countries and genders; 259 – the number of members in the smallest occupation group – for occupations. The results reported in Table 2 are the averages of the 25 runs and their respective confidence intervals at 95%.

Table 2 shows that, when using our vector of linguistic features, the SVM classifier increased in 19.7% (for genders), 83.0% (for countries) and 134.6% (for occupations) the accuracies of the inferences if compared to a random classifier. It also depicts values of F1 per class, indicating that some groups – like Indians ans religious professionals – are much more easily identified by our classifier than others – like Australians and architects/engineers.

	Accuracy random	Accuracy SVM	F1 weighted
Country	0.1000	0.1830±0.0032	0.1788±0.0027
Gender	0.5000	0.5985±0.0093	0.5768±0.0079
Occupation	0.0666	0.1563±0.0054	0.1515±0.0044

Social group	F1	Social group	F1
Country		Occupation	
India (IN)	0.2593	Religious	0.4191
Philippines (PH)	0.2365	Sales	0.2277
Indonesia (ID)	0.2030	Retired	0.1879
United States (US)	0.1910	Media	0.1761
Canada (CA)	0.1851	Business and financial	0.1465
Great Britain (GB)	0.1845	Healthcare	0.1393
France (FR)	0.1605	Legal	0.1364
Germany (DE)	0.1553	Student	0.1354
Malaysia (MY)	0.1148	Computer and mathematical	0.1227
Australia (AU)	0.0990	Arts and design	0.1177
		Education and library	0.1075
Gender		Management	0.0994
Male	0.6179	Science	0.0931
Female	0.5768	Food preparation	0.0672
		Architecture and engineering	0.0463

Table 2: Results of the inference experiments

Other studies already proposed solutions for gender classification in different online social systems. Schler et al. [23], who investigated language use in blogs, achieved up to 80.1% of accuracy in this task; Burger et al. [2], in their Twitter classifier relying only on text attributes, achieved 75.5% of accuracy; and Rao et al. [21], who also

studied Twitter, achieved up to 72.33% of accuracy. Although the accuracy of our preliminary gender classifier is not high if compared to these previous ones, we believe that they and other classifiers can benefit from the use of some of the features proposed here.

Eisenstein et al. [7] addressed the issue of inferring users' geographic location from Twitter texts. Differently from us, they only considered users from different states in the United States, which makes comparison between our and their studies quite difficult. The task of predicting the professional activity of OSN users, however, seems to be an unexplored subject, since we did not find studies regarding the inference of occupations in online systems.

We advocate, then, that our vector of linguistic features can be used in conjunction with other metrics, such as profile information, network topology and other linguistic metrics, with the goal of increasing the quality of predictors of social characteristics of members in information networks.

5. CONCLUDING REMARKS

In this study, we considered a large dataset of Google+ posts to evaluate linguistic elements among members of particular social groups. These analyses not only describe the posts, but especially identify how distinct groups differ when posting content on the Web.

To the extent of our knowledge, this work is the first to focus on language aspects of Google+ posts and one of the most extensive investigations of the role that social factors exert on language usage in an OSN. Also, we contemplated language attributes and social characteristics that have been underinvestigated in other studies on language use in social media.

Contributions of our study go beyond the mere characterization of posts – which per se is an important supplement to the literature on language use in social media –, since implications on authorship attribution may follow. For this reason, we implemented a preliminary classifier to infer social characteristics of Google+ users, which may be an useful tool to improve the task of automatically detecting fake profiles through the analysis of their linguistic behaviors and to improve language modeling focused on personalization of services.

Future work should include the analysis of other relevant linguistic and social factors, such as the topic of posts and the educational level of users. Also, it would be interesting to compare the outcomes reported here for Google+ with other popular OSNs, such as Facebook and Twitter. Another related issue to be analyzed in future studies is the question of how these different social groups express their feelings on the Web and which linguistic elements are used to indicate tones of happiness, angriness, hope and hatred, among others: are these elements also distinctive across different social groups in the context of online social networking services?

6. REFERENCES

[1] C. M. Bell, P. M. McCarthy, and D. S. McNamara. Using LIWC and Coh-Metrix to investigate gender differences in linguistic styles. In P. M. McCarthy and C. Boonthum-Denecke, editors, *Applied Natural Language Processing: Identification, Investigation, and Resolution.* Information Science Reference, Hershey, PA, 2012.

[2] J. D. Burger, J. Henderson, G. Kim, and G. Zarrella. Discriminating gender on Twitter. In *Proceedings of the Conference on Empirical Methods in Natural Language Processing*, pages 1301–1309. Association for Computational Linguistics, 2011.

[3] T. Cadierno and L. Ruiz. Motion events in Spanish L2 acquisition. *Annual Review of Cognitive Linguistics*, 4:183–216, 2006.

[4] D. Crystal. *The Language Revolution.* Polity Press, Cambridge, UK, 2004.

[5] D. Crystal. The scope of Internet Linguistics. *American Association for the Advancement of Science*, 2005.

[6] E. Cunha, G. Magno, M. A. Gonçalves, C. Cambraia, and V. Almeida. He votes or she votes? Female and male discursive strategies in Twitter political hashtags. *PLOSONE*, 9(1):e87041, January 2014.

[7] J. Eisenstein, B. O'Connor, N. A. Smith, and E. P. Xing. A latent variable model for geographic lexical variation. In *Proceedings of the 2010 Conference on Empirical Methods in Natural Language Processing*, pages 1277–1287. Association for Computational Linguistics, 2010.

[8] E. Fry. Readability. In *Reading Hall of Fame Book*. February 2006.

[9] R. Gonzales, R. Cuevas, R. Motamedi, R. Rejaie, and A. Cuevas. Google+ or Google-? Dissecting the evolution of the new OSN in its first year. In *Proceedings of the 22nd ACM International World Wide Web Conference (WWW 2013)*, 2013.

[10] N. L. Jones. Talking the talk: the confusing, conflicting and contradictory communicative role of workplace jargon in modern organizations. Master's thesis, University of Rhode Island, 2011.

[11] S. Kairam, M. J. Brzozowski, D. Huffaker, and E. H. Chi. Talking in circles: selective sharing in Google+. In *Proceedings of the ACM Conference on Human Factors in Computing Systems (CHI'12)*, 2012.

[12] W. Labov. *Principles of Linguistic Change: Social Factors.* Blackwell, Malden, MA, 2001.

[13] R. Lakoff. *Language and Woman's Place.* Harper and Row, New York, NY, 1975.

[14] M. Lui and T. Baldwin. langid.py: an off-the-shelf language identification tool. In *Proceedings of the 50th Annual Meeting of the Association for Computational Linguistics (ACL 2012)*, pages 25–30, 2012.

[15] G. Magno, G. Comarela, D. Saez-Trumper, M. Cha, and V. Almeida. New kid on the block: exploring the Google+ social graph. In *Proceedings of the ACM Internet Measurement Conference (IMC'12)*, 2012.

[16] R. Ottoni, J. P. Pesce, D. Las Casas, G. Franciscani Jr., W. Meira Jr., P. Kumaraguru, and V. Almeida. Ladies first: Analyzing gender roles and behaviors in Pinterest. In *Proceedings of the 7th International AAAI Conference on Weblogs and Social Media (ICWSM'13)*, 2013.

[17] F. Pedregosa, G. Varoquaux, A. Gramfort, V. Michel, B. Thirion, O. Grisel, M. Blondel, P. Prettenhofer, R. Weiss, V. Dubourg, J. Vanderplas, A. Passos, D. Cournapeau, M. Brucher, M. Perrot, and E. Duchesnay. Scikit-learn: Machine learning in Python. *Journal of Machine Learning Research*, 12:2825–2830, 2011.

[18] J. W. Pennebaker, C. K. Chung, M. Ireland, A. Gonzales, and R. J. Booth. *The Development and Psychometric Properties of LIWC2007.* The University of Texas at Austin and The University of Auckland, New Zealand, 2007.

[19] M. F. Porter. An algorithm for suffix stripping. *Program: electronic library and information systems*, 14:130–137, 1980.

[20] Purdue University Press. Comparative Cultural Studies. `http://bit.ly/1gDkJUL`, Retrieved in March 2014.

[21] D. Rao, D. Yarowsky, A. Shreevats, and M. Gupta. Classifying latent user attributes in Twitter. In *Proceedings of the 2nd International Workshop on Search and Mining User-Generated Contents*, pages 37–44. ACM, 2010.

[22] S. Romaine. *Language in Society: An Introduction to Sociolinguistics.* Oxford University Press, 1994.

[23] J. Schler, M. Koppel, S. Argamon, and J. W. Pennebaker. Effects of age and gender on blogging. In *AAAI Spring Symposium: Computational Approaches to Analyzing Weblogs*, volume 6, pages 199–205, 2006.

[24] H. A. Schwartz, J. C. Eichstaedt, M. L. Kern, L. Dziurzynski, S. M. Ramones, M. Agrawal, A. Shah, M. Kosinski, D. Stillwell, M. E. Seligman, et al. Personality, gender, and age in the language of social media: The open-vocabulary approach. *PLOSONE*, 8(9):e73791, 2013.

[25] C. Swanson and H. Fox. Validity of readability formulas. *The Journal of Applied Psychology*, 37(2), 1953.

[26] P. Trudgill. *Sociolinguistics: an introduction to language and society.* Penguin, London, UK, 1983.

[27] U.S. Bureau of Labor Statistics. Standard occupational classification and coding structure. `http://1.usa.gov/14INxmQ`, February 2010.

[28] Y. C. Wang, M. Burke, and R. Kraut. Gender, topic, and audience response: An analysis of user-generated content on Facebook. In *Proceedings of the ACM Conference on Human Factors in Computing Systems (CHI'13)*, 2013.

A Taxonomy of Microtasks on the Web

Ujwal Gadiraju, Ricardo Kawase, and Stefan Dietze

{gadiraju,kawase,dietze}@L3S.de

L3S Research Center, Leibniz Universität Hannover, Germany

ABSTRACT

Nowadays, a substantial number of people are turning to crowdsourcing, in order to resolve tasks that require human intervention. Despite a considerable amount of research done in the field of crowdsourcing, existing works fall short when it comes to classifying typically crowdsourced tasks. Understanding the dynamics of the tasks that are crowdsourced and the behaviour of workers, plays a vital role in efficient task-design. In this paper, we propose a two-level categorization scheme for tasks, based on an extensive study of 1000 workers on CrowdFlower. In addition, we present insights into certain aspects of crowd behaviour; the task affinity of workers, effort exerted by workers to complete tasks of various types, and their satisfaction with the monetary incentives.

Categories and Subject Descriptors

H.4 [**Information Systems Applications**]: Miscellaneous

Keywords

Crowdsourcing; Microtasks; Taxonomy; Incentive; Effort; Affinity

1. INTRODUCTION

Crowdsourcing is evolving rapidly as a means for solving problems that require human intelligence or human intervention. Over the last decade, there has been a considerable amount of work towards establishing suitable platforms and proposing frameworks for fruitful crowdsourcing. Amazon's Mechanical Turk[1] and CrowdFlower[2] are exemplary reflections of such platforms.

A large number of researchers have used these platforms in order to gather distributed and unbiased data, to validate results or to build ground truths. However, the literature

---

[1] https://www.mturk.com/mturk/
[2] http://www.crowdflower.com/

inspecting the actors involved in the crowsourcing process is rather scarce. Only a few noteworthy works have investigated best practices, the reliability of data [4], or have proposed comprehensive strategies and guidelines [7] (see Section 2).

As a consequence, without adequate knowledge of how one can effectively and efficiently exploit the wisdom of the crowd through crowdsourcing platforms, several research works are hindered by chaotic results leading to doubtful conclusions. Thus, it is essential that task administrators[3] are, to some extent, educated in crowdsource task modeling. To pave a way towards solving this problem, we present our work comprising the categorization of crowdsourced tasks, and reflect on guidelines and principles of crowsourcing tasks.

First, based on a crowdsourced survey, we present strong evidence that a large number of *workers*[4] are untrustworthy. This evidence shows that simple gold-standards (See Section 4) might not be enough to provide reliable data.

Second, after a manual exhaustive selection of reliable responses, we provide a data analysis showing that, in fact, *workers* are in a modern *gold-rush*, prioritizing monetary reward over their affinity to tasks.

Finally, we venture into determining a fine-grained goal-oriented categorization of crowdsourced tasks. This facilitates a greater understanding of the dynamics between the administrators of such tasks and the workers in the crowd, thereby increasing reliability of the results and data quality.

2. RELATED WORK

Marshall et al. profile Turkers who take surveys, and examine the characteristics of surveys that may determine the data reliability [4]. Similar to their work, we adopt the approach of collecting data through crowdsourced surveys in order to draw meaningful insights.

Kazai et al. [3], use behavioural observations to define the types of workers in the crowd. They type-cast workers as either *sloppy, spammer, incompetent, competent,* or *diligent.* By doing so, the authors expect their insights to help in designing tasks and attracting the best workers to a task. Along the same lines, Ross et al. [6] study the demographics and usage behaviors, characterizing workers on Amazon's Mechanical Turk. Complementing such existing works, as well as in contrast, our work focuses on task modeling rather

---

[3] A user responsible for deploying tasks on a crowdsourcing platform.
[4] A user that performs tasks for monetary rewards on a crowdsourcing platform.

How many men have been known to jump up from earth and touch the sun with bare hands?
- ○ Many
- ○ None
- ○ Few
- ○ Some

Figure 1: Engaging workers and checking their alertness by using questions.

than user modeling. Nevertheless, we hypothesize that the consideration of both aspects is essential for effective crowdsourcing.

In their work, Yuen et al. present a literature survey on different aspects of crowdsourcing [8]. In addition to a taxonomy of crowdsourcing research, the authors present a humble example list of application scenarios. Their short list represents the first steps towards task modeling. However, without proper organization regarding types, goals and work-flows, it is hard to reuse such information to devise strategies for task design. We solve this issue by providing an articulated categorization in terms of goals and work-flows.

In the realm of studying the reliability of crowd workers, and gauging their performance with respect to the incentives offered, Mason et al. investigate the relationship between financial incentives and the performance of the workers [5]. They find that higher monetary incentives increase the quantity but not the quality of work of the crowd workers. A large part of their results align with our findings presented in Section 4.

In their work, Geiger et al. propose a taxonomic framework for crowdsourcing processes [2]. Based on 46 crowdsourcing examples they conceive a 19-class crowdsourcing process classification. As stated by the authors, they focus exclusively on an organizational perspective, thus providing valuable insights mainly for stakeholders running crowdsourcing platforms. With a different focus, our proposed categorization intends to primarily assist microtask administrators in effectively using such platforms.

3. APPROACH

We aim to analyze tasks that are typically crowdsourced by exploiting response-based data from the workers.

We deployed a survey using the CrowdFlower platform in order to gather information about typically crowdsourced jobs. To begin with, the survey consisted of questions regarding the demographics, educational and general background of the workers. Next, questions related to previous tasks that were successfully completed by the workers, are introduced. The survey consisted of a mixture of open-ended, direct, and Likert-type questions designed to capture the interest of the workers. We restrict the participation to 1000 workers. We ask the crowd workers open-ended questions, about two of their most recent successfully completed tasks. State-of-the-art qualitative research methods [1], have indicated that relying on recent incidents is highly effective, since respondents answer such questions with more details and instinctive candor. We pay all the contributors from the crowd, irrespective of whether or not we discard their data for further analysis.

In addition, to keep the participants engaged we intersperse the regular questions with humour-evoking and amus-

ing bits as shown in Figure 1. At the same time, these questions are also used to filter out spammers or workers with malicious intentions. We do not use other sophisticated means to curtail regular crowd worker behaviour, in order to capture a realistic composition of workers (both trustworthy and otherwise), although malicious workers are discarded from our data analysis.

4. DATA ANALYSIS

In this section we present our findings from the analysis of the data, collected through the crowd sourcing process described in Section 3.

From the 1000 workers that participated in the survey, we consider the responses from 490 in our analysis. The responses from 433 workers are pruned out of consideration based on their failure to pass at least one of the so called '*gold standard*' tests. A gold standard question, is one that is designed in order to prevent malicious workers from either progressing in a task, or to identify and discard such workers during analysis. For example, consider the question in Figure 1. Malicious workers often pick and choose from the available options at random. By using two such hidden tests, we prune out workers with ulterior intentions.

We manually curated the responses from the remaining workers, and found that 77 workers tried to cheat their way through to task completion by copy-pasting the same bits in response to all open-ended questions.

Of the 490 trusted workers, 76% were found to be *Male* participants while 24% were *Female*. The average age of the male and female crowd workers was similar, at 33.7 and 33.1 years respectively. We found that 88% workers cared about their reputation as crowd workers, while 12% workers claimed that they did not care about their reputation. These workers contributed to the description of 980 tasks that they successfully completed in the past. Workers claimed that in hindsight, they could have performed better in 534 of these instances, while they responded that they could not have performed better in 282 of those tasks. Workers were unsure about a possible improvement in their performance corresponding to 164 tasks.

4.1 How do workers choose their tasks?

An interesting research question, which we set out to answer through this work, was to find out what factors influence a worker's choice in the tasks she picks to complete. Based on our survey, we gather the three most commonly stated factors that determine a worker's choice in task. An indicator could be the *monetary incentives* offered on task completion. The *interestingness* of the task itself and the *time required* to complete a task are the other factors that surfaced. However, the distribution of significance of these factors is not known. In order to determine this, we capture the responses from the workers for this question on a 5-point Likert-scale from *No Influence: 1* to *Strong Influence: 5*.

The aggregated results of the Likert-scale show that *monetary reward* (4.02) is significantly ($p < 0,01$) the most crucial factor for a worker while determining which task to complete. The factors *Time required* (3.76) for the completion of a task and *topic* (3.69) come in next with marginal difference between them.

Apart from the factors captured on the Likert-scale, we posed additional questions to the workers regarding why they chose to complete the particular tasks that they de-

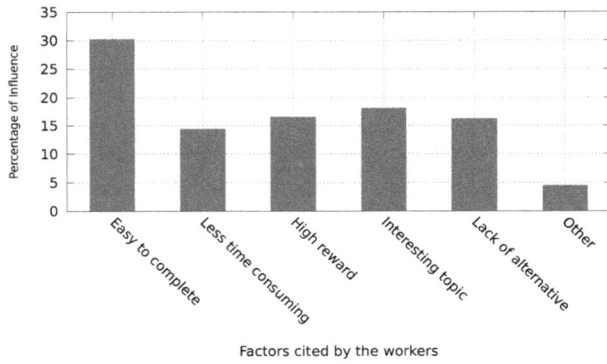

Figure 2: Factors that determine workers' choice of task based on their most recently completed tasks.

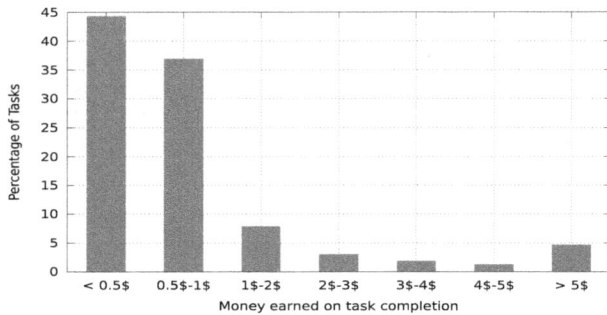

Figure 3: Money earned by workers on completing various tasks.

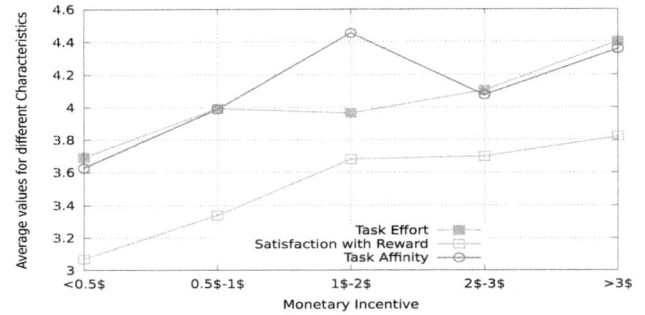

Figure 4: Distribution of effort required, task affinity, and satisfaction with reward of the workers with respect to varying task incentives.

scribed in the survey (the workers' two most recently completed tasks). Figure 2 quantifies our findings. The *ease of completion* of a task is a driving force in the task selection process of a worker. An *interesting topic*, a *high reward*, a *less time consuming* task also play a role in the choice of task of a crowd worker, albeit to a less prominent extent. It is interesting to note that a significant number of crowd workers end up completing tasks due to the *lack of other alternatives*. Additionally, we facilitated for an open-ended response when workers chose the *Other* option. Through this we found a few other minor reasons that workers cited for choosing to complete their previous tasks. For example, a few workers said they wanted to increase their overall profile accuracy, i.e. their reputation on the crowdsourcing platform.

Considering that the monetary reward is highly influential in the workers' choice of completing tasks, it is interesting to investigate the precise amount of rewards offered by the tasks. Figure 3 presents the distribution of the money earned by the workers on completion of the 980 tasks, considered in the analysis. We note that most tasks that are deployed for crowdsourcing, offer either meagre (<0.5$) or small monetary rewards (between 0.5$ and 2$). This is reasonable from the point of view of the task deployers or administrators, since most of these tasks do not require a lot of effort from the crowd workers, as confirmed from our analysis (see Figure 4).

We clearly see that the tasks that offer bigger monetary awards (>3$) are also coincidentally the tasks in which the

crowd workers are required to exert the most amount of effort. From this, we infer that the monetary rewards offered for the tasks that are typically crowdsourced, are proportional to the amount of effort that is expected for task completion by the crowd workers.

4.2 Task Affinity vs Incentive

We define *task affinity* as the tendency of a crowd worker to like the task she chooses to complete. Next, we investigate how the incentive for a given task influences the task affinity of a crowd worker. From our analysis, presented in the Figure 4 we observe that there are two subtle kinds of behaviour exhibited by the workers in the crowd. Crowd workers tend to exhibit a greater affinity to those tasks which offer higher incentives (>3$). This is understandable since the workers can earn more money by completing such tasks. On the other hand, crowd workers also depict a significant amount of affinity for tasks that offer a reasonable amount of incentive (between 1$ and 2$). This can be explained by the fact that, these tasks require significantly lesser effort from the workers.

An interesting point to note, is that although the most number of tasks deployed on crowd sourcing platforms fall under the bracket of relatively low monetary incentives, thus resulting in such tasks being completed by most workers, the workers' affinity towards these given tasks is considerably low.

We consider that a workers' approval of the monetary reward corresponding to a given task, may be subject to change on task completion. This may be attributed to the difference in the amount of effort needed for task completion when compared to the anticipated effort by a crowd worker. We capture the average satisfaction of the crowd workers with the reward they receive on task completion. Our aggregated results are presented in Figure 4. We observe that the satisfaction is proportional to the incentive of the reward that is offered.

5. CATEGORIZATION OF TASKS

From the responses collected through the crowdsourced survey, we have manually established the following classes that describe typically crowdsourced tasks. The example task descriptions presented alongside each type of task, are extracted from the responses received from workers regarding their previous micro-tasks. We categorize the tasks into

6 high-level goal-oriented classes as presented next, with each class containing sub-classes of other types of tasks. The high-level categorization is drawn based on the 'goals' of a task, while the sub-classes are based on the 'work-flow' of tasks.

5.1 Categorization Scheme

- **Information Finding**(IF)- Such tasks delegate the process of searching to satisfy one's information need, to the workers in the crowd. For example, *'Find information about a company in the UK'*, or *'Find the cheapest air fare for the selected dates and destinations'*.
- **Verification and Validation**(VV)- These are tasks that require workers in the crowd to either verify certain aspects as per the given instructions, or confirm the validity of various kinds of content. For example, *'Is this a Spam Bot? : Check whether the twitter users are either real people or organisations, or merely spam twitter user profiles'*, or *'Match the names of personal computers and verify corresponding information'*.
- **Interpretation and Analysis**(IA)- Such tasks rely on the wisdom of the crowd to use their interpretation skills during task completion. For example, *'Choose the most suitable category for each URL'*, or *'Categorize reviews as either positive or negative'*.
- **Content Creation**(CC)- Such tasks usually require the workers to generate new content for a document or website. They include authoring product descriptions or producing question-answer pairs. For example, *'Suggest names for a new product'*, or *'Translate the following content into German'*.
- **Surveys**(S)- Surveys about a multitude of aspects ranging from demographics to customer satisfaction are crowdsourced. For example, *'Mother's Day and Father's Day Survey (18-29 year olds only!)'*
- **Content Access**(CA)- These tasks require the crowd workers to simply access some content. For example, *'Click on the link and watch the video'*, or *'Read the information by following the website link'*. In these tasks the workers are merely asked to consume some content by accessing it, but do nothing further.

It is important to note that, in certain cases it may be possible for a particular job to belong to more than one of the aforementioned classes. For example, a survey about the perception of a product like the new iPhone from Apple could belong to the classes of *Surveys* as well as *Sentiment Analysis*.

Apart from these high-level categorization based on the goals of the tasks, Table 1 presents some sub-classes of the high-level classes, which are based on the work-flow of the tasks. Some sub-classes are explained below.

- Class *IF*/**Metadata Finding**- Such tasks require the users to find specific relevant information from a given data source. For example, *'Find e-mail addresses of corresponding employees from the company's websites'*.
- Class *VV*/**Content Verification**- In these tasks the crowd workers are required to verify, validate, qualify, or disqualify different aspects as dictated by the task administrators. For instance, *'Check if the following company websites describe the correct business'*.
- Class *IA*/**Categorization and Classification**- Such tasks involve the organization of entities into groups

with the same features, or assigning entities to classes according to a predetermined set of principles. For example, *'Choose the most suitable category for each URL'*.

- Class *IA* or *CC*/**Media Transcription**- These tasks require the crowd workers to transcribe (put into written form) different media like images, music, video, and so forth. For example, *'See the images and find the year on which the wine bottle was manufactured'*. The tasks also include transcribing captchas. For instance, *'Type what you see in the following Captchas'*.
- Class *IA*/**Ranking**- Here the crowd workers are required to determine the most relevant entities with respect to the search query. For example, *'Search for the given terms and click on the best three results'*.
- Class *IA*/**Content Moderation**- Here the workers are required to moderate content for guideline violations, inappropriate content, spam, or others. Independent of the kind of media (text, photos, or videos), the crowd is asked to evaluate the content against a set of rules. For example, *'Moderate images for inappropriate content (sexually explicit content)'*.
- Class *IA*/**Sentiment Analysis**- Tasks that pertain to the assessment of the sentiment towards an entity or notion, fall under this category. For example, *'What do you think of the new Samsung tablet?'*, or *'Identify if the tweets are positive, negative, or neutral'*.
- Class *CC*/**Data Collection and Enhancement**- Crowdsourcing is used to generate and enhance data. For instance, the crowd has been used in the past to create a dataset of colours by asking workers to annotate different hues and shades with labels[5].
- Class *S*/**Content Feedback**- In such tasks workers are asked to assess and provide feedback about products, entities, websites, and so forth. For example, *'Help us improve our website'*.
- Class *CA*/**Promoting**- In such tasks workers are asked to access and consume content. For example, *'Visit the webpage by clicking on the provided link'*.

5.2 Tasks as per Categorization Scheme

Based solely on the reliable data collected during the crowdsourcing process, we manually annotated each of the workers' previously completed tasks according to the categorization scheme. Figure 5 presents the distribution of these tasks, as per their categorization into the different proposed classes.

Note that certain tasks can rightly be classified into more than one class. For example, consider the task, *'Search for spam-like comments in the following content'*. This task can be classified into the classes *Verification and Validation*, as well as *Information Finding*. This is because, the goal of such a task could be either to ensure the content is spam-free, or merely find the spam comments. Consider the task, *'Identify biographies in the following'*. This task can be classified into the class *Interpretation and Analysis* since the identification of a biography relies on the workers interpretation of the classification. At the same time, the task can be classified into *Verification and Validation*, since the goal of the task could be to validate biographies.

---

[5]http://www.crowdflower.com/blog/2008/03/our-color-names-data-set-is-online

Table 1: Sub-classes of the proposed categorization for typically crowdsourced tasks.

Information Finding	Verification & Validation	Interpretation & Analysis	Content Creation	Surveys	Content Access
Metadata finding	Content Verification	Classification	Media Transcription	Feedback/Opinions	Testing
	Content Validation	Categorization	Data Enhancement	Demographics	Promoting
	Spam Detection	Media Transcription	Translation		
	Data matching	Ranking	Tagging		
		Data Selection			
		Sentiment Analysis			
		Content Moderation			
		Quality Assesment			

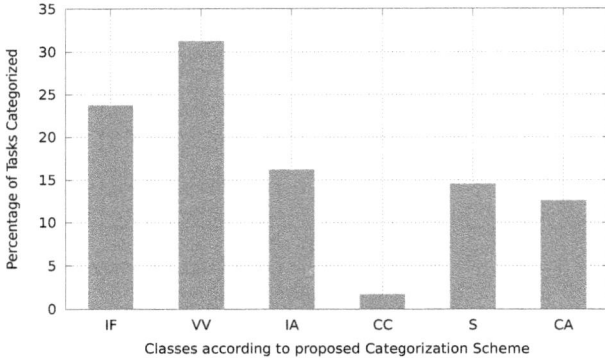

Figure 5: Distribution of tasks in the classes of the proposed Categorization Scheme.

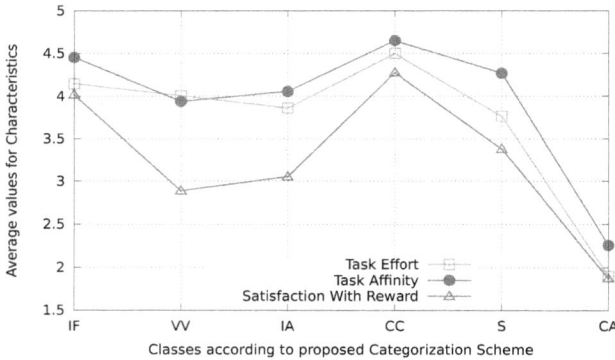

Figure 6: Distribution of task-related characteristics according to the proposed Categorization Scheme.

As a next step, we analyze the average effort that a worker needs to exert to complete a task, the task affinity, as well as the workers' satisfaction with the reward, for each of the high-level classes. The findings are presented in Figure 6. Understandably, tasks of the class *Content Creation* require the most amount of effort from the crowd workers, while those of the class *Content Access* require the least amount of effort. It is interesting to note that crowd workers like to work on tasks of the class type *Information Finding* and *Surveys* in addition to *Content Creation*. The most disparity between the effort exerted for task completion by the workers and their satisfaction with the reward, corresponds to the classes of *Verification and Validation*, and *Interpretation and Analysis*.

5.3 Tasks with Ulterior Motives

During our manual analysis of the data collected we identified several tasks with deceitful hidden motives. While such tasks may indicate legitimacy to some extent due to the work-flow they suggest to workers, there is a clear ulterior goal of deliberately manipulating third party results. For example, improving the popularity or general sentiment of particular content. In most cases, these tasks fall in the classes *Content Access* and *Content Creation*, further being masked with an additional goal such as a *Survey*. For example, '*Search for some particular terms in Google, and click on the link of our Website*', '*Watch this video on Youtube and click like*', or '*Give a five start rating to this product*'.

We also verified that in many circumstances, these tasks are followed by a survey which contains a failure guaranteed gold standard. For example, '*What's your age?*', whereas the only correct answer is an unrealistic number. At this point, the malicious task administrator has already collected his desired data and the system prevents workers from getting their reward. As a principle, crowdsourcing platforms discourage the deployment of such tasks. We hypothesize that our modeling categorization can improve the identification of deceitful tasks by the system and also by potential workers. This is a critical issue to be addressed in order to improving crowdsourcing practice.

6. CONCLUSIONS & FUTURE WORK

In this paper, we presented a meta-crowdsourcing profiling study. First, we identified high levels of malicious workers. Almost 44% of the workers did not manage to correctly answer simple attention check questions. It is important to highlight that we deliberately model our crowdsourcing task to allow such malicious behavior. These results highlight the importance of gold standards in crowdsourcing tasks and need for intelligent task modeling strategies.

At the same time, based on the manually verified reliable responses, we collected enough data to characterize workers' behaviour and preferences. Further, we thoroughly study the types of tasks that are typically crowdsourced, and as a result, we propose a goal-oriented *Categorization Scheme* for crowdsourced tasks. A fine-grained categorization of crowdsourced tasks has important implications for the user modeling of crowd workers, and recommendation of tasks. The proposed categorization of tasks, including the findings from our extensive analysis, aid in future task design and deployment. By drawing from our findings related to the task dependent characteristics, like task affinity, task effort, incentive required, and so forth, one can design tasks with higher success rates (i.e., maximizing the quality of the results with respect to the given reward).

7. REFERENCES

[1] CORBIN, J., AND STRAUSS, A. *Basics of qualitative research: Techniques and procedures for developing grounded theory.* Sage, 2008.

[2] GEIGER, D., SEEDORF, S., SCHULZE, T., NICKERSON, R. C., AND SCHADER, M. Managing the crowd: Towards a taxonomy of crowdsourcing processes. In *AMCIS* (2011).

[3] KAZAI, G., KAMPS, J., AND MILIC-FRAYLING, N. Worker types and personality traits in crowdsourcing relevance labels. In *Proceedings of the 20th ACM international conference on Information and knowledge management* (2011), ACM, pp. 1941–1944.

[4] MARSHALL, C. C., AND SHIPMAN, F. M. Experiences surveying the crowd: Reflections on methods, participation, and reliability. In *Proceedings of the 5th Annual ACM Web Science Conference* (New York, NY, USA, 2013), WebSci '13, ACM, pp. 234–243.

[5] MASON, W., AND WATTS, D. J. Financial incentives and the performance of crowds. *ACM SigKDD Explorations Newsletter 11*, 2 (2010), 100–108.

[6] ROSS, J., IRANI, L., SILBERMAN, M., ZALDIVAR, A., AND TOMLINSON, B. Who are the crowdworkers?: shifting demographics in mechanical turk. In *CHI'10 Extended Abstracts on Human Factors in Computing Systems* (2010), ACM, pp. 2863–2872.

[7] WILLETT, W., HEER, J., AND AGRAWALA, M. Strategies for crowdsourcing social data analysis. In *Proceedings of the SIGCHI Conference on Human Factors in Computing Systems* (New York, NY, USA, 2012), CHI '12, ACM, pp. 227–236.

[8] YUEN, M.-C., KING, I., AND LEUNG, K.-S. A survey of crowdsourcing systems. In *PASSAT/SocialCom 2011, Privacy, Security, Risk and Trust (PASSAT), 2011 IEEE Third International Conference on and 2011 IEEE Third International Conference on Social Computing (SocialCom), Boston, MA, USA, 9-11 Oct., 2011* (2011), pp. 766–773.

The AMAS Authoring Tool 2.0: A UX Evaluation

Conor Gaffney
School of Computer Science
and Statistics
Trinity College Dublin
Dublin, Ireland
+353(1)896 1335
cogaffne@scss.tcd.ie

Owen Conlan
School of Computer Science
and Statistics
Trinity College Dublin
Dublin, Ireland
+353(1)896 2158
Owen.Conlan@scss.tcd.ie

Vincent Wade
School of Computer Science
and Statistics
Trinity College Dublin
Dublin, Ireland
+353(1)896 2091
Vincent.Wade@scss.tcd.ie

ABSTRACT

Adaptive hypermedia has been well documented as being very beneficial in the domain of online education. Authoring adaptive educational hypermedia is however a complex and difficult task. There have been a number of tools developed to address the issue of authoring so as to ease the cognitive load involved in composition. This paper examines two key areas related authoring tool design: hypertext representation and User Experience (UX) design. Both of these are important factors that should be considered when designing hypertext authoring tools. The paper also presents the AMAS Authoring Tool. A new and unique authoring tool that allows non-technical Subject Matter Experts to compose adaptive activity based courses without the needing to write any code or technical languages.

Categories and Subject Descriptors

J.1 [**Administrative Data Processing**]: Education; H.1.2 [**Models and Principles**]: User/Machine Systems; H.5.2 [**Information Interfaces and Presentation**]: User Interfaces; H.5.4 [**Information Interfaces and Presentation**]: Hypertext/Hypermedia;

General Terms

Design; Experimentation; Measurement; Human Factors

Keywords

Adaptive hypermedia; authoring tools; AMAS

1. INTRODUCTION

Adaptive Educational Hypermedia (AEH) [15] has been well documented as being a beneficial approach to delivering online training [6]. AEH environments adapt to learners so as to increase the effectiveness and efficiency of the training provided [29]. Such courses are however difficult and time consuming to author [9, 31]. Over the past decade many different AEH authoring tools have been developed to assist teachers, pedagogical professionals and AEH experts in developing adaptive online courses. Such tools have however only had limited success and were primarily built as a proof-of-concept [14].

AEH authoring tools have suffered from a great many issues ranging from '*not being flexible enough*' to '*not being easy enough for non-experts to use*' [14]. The uptake of AEH authoring tools is hampered further by the fact that they primarily focus on content. While MOT [9], AHA! [12] and the ACCT [10] have been instrumental in improving the accessibility and design of AEH authoring, they are limited in their pedagogical scope. These tools allow authors to compose adaptive environments but the resultant courses do not include adaptive interactivity. Interactive learning environments include (but are not limited to) serious games [34], activity based learning [22] and online training simulations [15]. Such interactive solutions have been shown to increase the engagement of learners [10]. They can bridge the gap between theory and application by providing a safe and convenient environment for learners to practice their skill [1,40], complete relevant exercises [22] and learn through interaction with other learners. The learner is not a passive subject within an interactive learning experience but instead becomes an active participant in their own educational process [37].

There are in fact very few AEH authoring tools that allow users to create interactive adaptive eLearning solutions. The AEH authoring tools that accommodate interactivity focus primarily on simulation, such as the ACTSim [15], and eLearning games, StoryTec [27] for example. This paper presents the AMAS Authoring Tool 2.0. This is a new and unique authoring tool that allows non-technical Subject Matter Experts (SMEs) to compose adaptive activity based courses. The newest version of the authoring tool, 2.0, is an online prototype based on a previous non-web based version, 1.0.

The AMAS Authoring tool is designed to be accessible to teachers, lecturers and pedagogical designers. Non-technical users compose adaptive activity based course by configuring specialized authoring components in a graphical workflow to define the complex hypertext of adaptive online courses. This innovative approach to describing hypertext components and structuring does not require the author to write any code or rules, learn a new procedural language (such as LAG [14]) or have a deep understanding of Adaptive Hypermedia principles. Version 1.0 of the AMAS Authoring Tool incorporated these authoring principles. Authoring components and basic design of the non-web based tool were extensively examined with authentic real world study participants [15]. The first version of the AMAS Authoring Tool however lacked User Experience (UX) design. While being functional it employed a cluttered interface that gave little consideration to user engagement and experience. The key innovation of the web based 2.0 version of the authoring tool presented in this paper, was to carefully consider and implement user experience design. Improved UX design considerations and methodologies to evaluation UX design will benefit future AEH authoring tools.

To the authors knowledge this is the first AEH authoring tool that primarily focus on composing adaptive online courses that are activity based. The following section describes in further detail the motivation and key challenges involved in developing the AMAS Authoring Tool 2.0. The section concludes with description of the remaining contents of the paper.

1.1 AEH Authoring Tools: User Experience

Toolkits developed for authoring hypertext, particularly those that include the aspects required for describing the complexities of educational content and interactivity, are challenging to design [9]. Introducing authoring components that describe personalization, such as those related to adaptive dimensions [18] or adaptive rule definition [10], further increases the composition cognitive workload for an author [27]. As described by Foss and Cristea [14], authoring AEH courses is *"genuinely hard"*. To address this issue Foss and Cristea [14] present a set of imperatives that describe how eLearning authoring tools should support authors of adaptive educational hypertext. These include: a separation of concerns; use of frameworks; use of standards; adaptive functionality; simple access; a shallow learning curve and familiarity. While these imperatives assist in defining the design of AEH authoring tools they lack an important dimension in realizing their real world application, User Experience (UX). This paper proposes to extend the imperatives presented by Foss and Cristea to include user experience and engagement in the design of AEH authoring tools. User experience emphasizes the positive aspects of interaction, in particular the phenomena associated with being captivated by the application and wanting to use it frequently [7]. Inadequate UX design of AEH authoring tools may be a key factor impeding their widespread commercial and academic uptake.

As web technologies improve it has become more common for modern Adaptive Hypermedia authoring tools to be web based and accessible through a browser. This approach allows users to collaborate and easily share developed courses [19] as well as access the tools themselves. User engagement is a key concept in the UX design of web applications [26]. Visual appeal of a web page has been identified as an important factor for user engagement [32], generically in web application design and specifically in the domain of education [32]. In particular web page *'style'* has been related to positive engagement and to promote focused attention [32]. Both positive affect and focused attention are important characteristics of user engagement [26]. Web page style has been related to screen layout, graphics and the use of design principles [26]. Furthermore, it has been documented that saliency *("visually catchiness")* impacts metrics associated with user engagement. Research in neuroscience and cognitive psychology show that users view salient objects differently from the rest of the display [2]. Saliency can be linked to features such as color, edge orientation and size to engage users [2].

This paper proposes that AEH authoring tool should consider both style and saliency in their implemented design. The style of an AEH authoring tool should consider such factors as symmetry and balance while insuring the interface does not become cluttered or overloaded with content and workflow authoring components. Saliency should be applied to the central authoring component of the AEH authoring tool to insure they are prominent within interface. For example, if an AEH authoring tool employs 'concepts' as its most important authoring component, such as the GAT [35], the representation of those concept components should be *'visually catchy'*. Similarly, an authoring tool that focuses on

dialogue to develop adaptive soft skill simulations, the ACTSim [15] for example, the dialogue authoring components should be more salient compared to rest of the interface. In the case of the AMAS Authoring Tool 2.0, it employs nodes and links to describe the narrative of hypertext so as to allow complex structures to be designed [28]. These visual representations of hypertext are central to the tool and are the most important aspect of the design and as such should be visually salient within the interface.

The remainder of this paper is organized as follows. Section 2 presents a brief description of state of the art work that is related to this research. The following section describes the presents the design of the AMAS Authoring Tool, including version 1.0 and 2.0. The fourth section presents the evaluation of the AMAS Authoring Tool with respect to UX design. The final section outline the conclusion of this paper.

2. RELATED WORK

The first AMAS Authoring Tool, 1.0, was developed with an examination of the state of the art of a range of authoring tools. These included AuthorAR [24], ASK Learning Design Toolkit (ASK-LDT) [36], ACTSim [15], the GRAPPLE Authoring Tool (GAT) [35] and Learning Activity Management Systems (LAMS) [11]. The 1.0 version of the AMAS Authoring Tool was developed as a standalone system that was installed and run on a personal computer. The first version of the AMAS Authoring Tool was thoroughly examined with respect to course authoring approaches, authoring components and course/personalization representation. The next generation of the AMAS Authoring Tool, 2.0, was built as an online tool that could be accessed through a web browser. Employing the successful design aspects of the first version of the AMAS Authoring Tool, the most recent prototype design focused on improving the UX design of the toolkit. This section briefly outlines relevant related work with respect to hypertext authoring tools highlighted for their UX design approach.

Hypertext can be structured within authoring tools to support a many different composition objectives [20]. Various approaches have been employed to describe hypertext links and linking, for example: Presto [13], MyLifeBits [17] and Haystacks [21]. Hyper Text Editing System [41] and Hypercard [8] were early hypertext authoring tools that were somewhat limited in their UX design and representation of hypertext. For example, neither employed a workflow view that employed nodes and links. Such representative approaches of workflow have become more commonplace; for example, Storyspace [4] and Tinderbox [5]. As version 1.0 of the AMAS Authoring Tool was designed with nodes and edges employed to define the complex course workflow, examination of the state of the art in UX design was limited to tools that employed a similar approach. The two standout tools identified with respect to UX design were StoryTec [27] and HypeDyn [28].

StoryTec is an authoring tool used to develop adaptive digital educational games. It is designed to allow multiple user groups, such as game designers, artists and domain experts, to collaborate directly in a single interface. As such, the authoring tool is required to capture important information in multiple views; these include the Story Editor, Stage Editor, Property Editor and Object Browser. All the functions for editing the game are based on simple authoring concepts instead of programming languages or other more technical approaches. Although StoryTec employs multiple views and windows they are realized in a clear concise UX style design. More specifically, evaluation study participants rated the *"ergonomics of StroyTex positively"* [27]. The interface scored well with respect to suitability to task, controllability, conformity with user expectation and suitability for individualization. Participants in a comparison study with e-Adventure [38] also preferred StoryTec. The Story Editor view is particularly relevant with respect to the research described in this paper. It defines a games visual overview with nodes and edges that outlines the workflow of an entire story. These include all paths through the game as well as the adaptive controls. The interface is designed with a high level of saliency and employs clean edges and contrasting colors and color gradient to emphasize game components and links.

HypeDyn [28] is a hypertext authoring tool used to compose interactive multiple-points-of-view stories. These are complex hypertext narrative structures that allow the same story to be presented from different perspectives. Hypertext is represented with node and edge workflow visualization. HypeDyn provides additional visual representations and mechanisms to support authorial decisions in the process of composing a multiform story. For example, conditional links and conditional content nodes are employed to define different paths and narrative perspectives. There are two aspects of HypeDyn that make it a particularly relevant authoring tool with respect to the research described in this paper. The first is that the interface is simplistic and minimalist insuring a UX design that does not overwhelm a user. Secondly, it employs additional representation of hypertext to support authoring that is presented with a high level of saliency with contrasting node representation and node size. Representing such complex structures of hypertext is on of the key challenges addressed in this research. The following section presents the design of the AMAS Authoring Tool.

3. THE AMAS AUTHORING TOOL

Describing complex structures of hypertext such as those required for defining adaptive educational courses is a complex issue. Mitchell and McGee [28] summaries Bernsteins [4] observation that *"the inability of current hypertext authoring tools to represent more complex structures, such as montages, makes it difficult to perceive, manipulate and understand these patterns"*. The issue of representing hypertext within the AMAS Authoring Tool is addressed in the following section that describes the design of 1.0 version. This is followed by a section that addresses the UX design principles that were introduced into version 2.0 of the AMAS Authoring Tool.

3.1 Version 1.0

The first version of the AMAS Authoring Tool was developed with two sets of system requirements; *architectural* and *interface* requirements. Architectural requirements relate to the preexisting AMAZE architecture [22] with which the authoring tool needed integrate. The AMAZE architecture required the authoring tool provided three separate models to define the complex hypertext structures: an Activity Model, Adaptivity Model and Content Model. The interface requirements, developed with an analysis of the state of the art of authoring tools, defined several requirements related to the user interface. These included a clear separation between activities and content, accessible adaptivity controls and an easy-to-use intuitive visualization. The key challenge to be addressed by the first authoring tool was capture the hypertext complexities in a manner that satisfied both of these sets of requirements.

The visualization design of the first version of the AMAS Authoring Tool was initially based on the use of nodes and edges

as had been implemented in a number of similar authoring tools including the ASK-LDT and LAMS. This simplistic approach was extended to allow several different types of authoring components to be included and nested within one another. Authoring component types included Activities, Tasks, Topics and Tags. Activities are a high level grouping components that can be used to indicate the beginning and end of lessons or academic terms. Activity nodes include compartments where Tasks can be placed and configured in a workflow. The 'Task' authoring components are in fact a homogeneous set of pre-defined exercises or assignments that learners must complete as part of their online course. Examples of Tasks presently available in the authoring tool include WebQuest; Display Content; Group Discussion; Quiz; Revise Course; Group Presentation; Forum; and Additional Reading. Task nodes include a compartment that allows Topics and Tags to be added. The Topic authoring components are used to define content within an online activity based course. Topics can be text based, include images or link to external web content. Personalization within the AMAS Authoring Tool is controlled with Tag authoring components. Tags can be placed on Tasks to indicate that those components are relevant to particular sets of learners. Employing different types of authoring component and nesting them within one another in a single model is similar to the approaches employed by the LAMS and ACTSim authoring tools. Furthermore, the use of different node types to represent key authoring components can also be seen in HypDen. This approach to structuring, as presented in Figure 1, allows very complex hypertext formations to be represented and is the key innovation of the first version of the AMAS authoring.

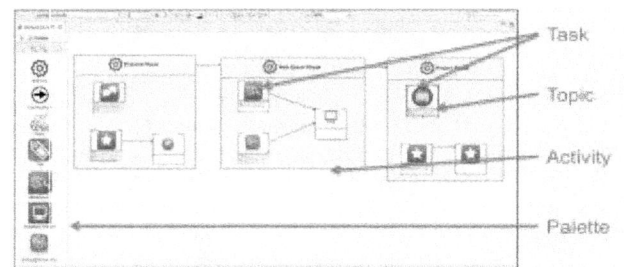

Figure 1: Screenshot of AMAS Authoring Tool 1.0

The AMAS Authoring Tool interface is composed of two primary areas, the Palette and Canvas. The Canvas is the area where a course workflow is constructed. The Palette is the area that contains the main functionality for authoring. It includes the operations for selecting and connecting appropriate authoring components to be placed in the Canvas. The approach, similar to the MOT3.0 design [14], was to employ functional authoring components that are elementary but contained within them complex functionality hidden from the SME; simple building blocks that allow complex adaptive hypertext models to be defined.

The first version of the AMAS Author Tool was successfully evaluated with authentic real world pedagogical professionals including teachers, lecturers and course design experts. The main objective of this evaluation was to examine the accessibility of the authoring component design; could non-technical Subject Matter Experts compose adaptive activity based courses with the provided composition functionality? The evaluation was very successful. All participants in the study completed a task of creating the outline of an adaptive activity based course in their domain. Both quantitative and qualitative data gathered during the evaluation indicated that participants found the authoring tool intuitive, accessible and easy to use. Further details of version 1.0 are presented in the authors' previous publications [16].

While there were some aspects of the UX design that were examined in the first study, the orientation of the Canvas and Palette and user interpretation of the icons for example, the style of the interface was not scrutinized. There was also some criticisms of the tool, for example, one participant in the study commented that they found it difficult to view the workflow and a *"different color canvas might work as better contrast"*. In the authors view, with the knowledge that that there was little time afforded to UX design, the first version of the authoring tool was rather clunky and lacked design sophistication. Furthermore, there is a lack of saliency about the interface, no one part of the tool looks more or less important than the other. The objective of the first AMAS Authoring Tool prototype was functionality. However, the basic UX design cannot be completely ignored, one user in the first evaluation did comment that the interface *"presentation is excellent in that, visually, it is attractive. One isn't bombarded with overcrowding of icons/information overload"*. The following section presents the initial prototype of the AMAS Authoring Tool 2.0.

3.2 Version 2.0

The objective of the second version of the AMAS Authoring Tool was to create an online tool that employed the same basic authoring components and principles defined in first version but delivered them in a cleaner interface that improved user experience. Both StoryTex and HypeDyn were used as design templates as they employ intuitive uncluttered interfaces. The AMAS Authoring Tool 2.0 implemented three UX design improvements.

The first UX improvement was to simplify the node design of the graph interface, a strategy employed in both the StoryTex and HypeDyn interfaces. Version 1.0 of the authoring tool implemented nodes that were very icon-centric which resulted in graph components being indistinguishable from each other in a workflow and within nested components. For example, it was difficult for users to distinguish between two Tasks in the interface if they were close together. The design was improved in version 2.0 by removing the icon and employing simple line based node. In future design implementation, to distinguish between different component types, the icon could be included again but in less visually intrusive manner; for example reduced in size and placed in a small part of the node.

The second design innovation was to simplify the Palette area so as to allow the Canvas space and course workflow to become more salient within the interface. Version 1.0 of the authoring tool employed Canvas and Palette icons that were identical and equal in dimension. This resulted in a users eye being drawn equally to both the Palette and Canvas. The Palette was simplified by removing the icons. Furthermore, a uniform style was implemented across the Palette and remainder of the interface, excluding the Canvas, so as to improve saliency.

The final design improvement of second version of the authoring tool was to upgrade the Canvas area visualization with a more contrasting background to allow authoring components to become more prominent. This concept was also carried over to the directional link connections between authoring component, which were improved by changing their color, and moving the directional indicator to a more central position. Figure 2 presents a screenshot of the initial prototype of the second version of the AMAS Authoring Tool.

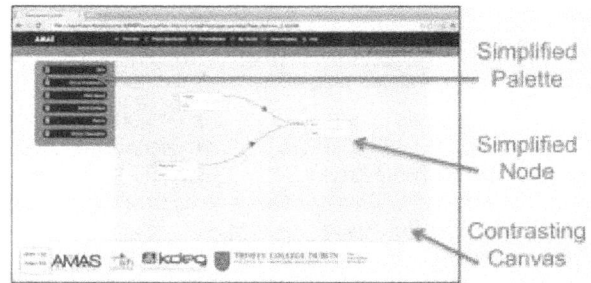

Figure 2: Screenshot of AMAS Authoring Tool 2.0 Prototype

The initial prototype does not yet include all of the authoring components implemented in version 1.0. Presently, the prototype allows six different Task types to be added to the Canvas. These Tasks can be edited and connected but there are no Activities, Topics or Tags. The authoring tool was however suitably mature to evaluate the UX design as related to interface style. As the missing components and their nesting structure was successfully evaluated in the previous study their exclusion could be tolerated from a user experience style point of view. It was however important that users could interact with the tool in some manner and could construct a simple activity based course with the tool. The details of the UX evaluation are presented in the following section.

4. EVALUATION

The evaluation of the AMAS Authoring Tool prototype 2.0 focused on the UX design style of the interface. This evaluation objective was decomposed into four relevant UX areas that could be examined: *'style'*, color, look & feel and familiarity.

Tullis and Albert define three main characteristics of user experience [39] when evaluating design 1) a user is involved, 2) that user is interacting with a product or system and 3) the users' experience is of interest, and observable and measurable

To accommodate these principles, a user-based trial was employed to evaluate the authoring tool prototype. Participants in the study were required to complete a short assignment using the prototype and report on their experience via a questionnaire. The questionnaire was employed to gather both quantitative and qualitative data. Quantitative data was gathered with a five point Likert scale (Strongly Agree to Strongly Disagree). Qualitative data was gathered with questions that allowed participants to enter text-based answers.

A total of eight authentic non-technical real world users participated in the study. Participants ranged form a diverse set of teaching backgrounds with over 80 years combined teaching experience. They included three K12 teachers, three pedagogical design experts and two university lecturers. While eight users may not be statistically significant numerous studies have shown that little more is learnt from user based applications when evaluation participant numbers exceeds five [30]. The results of the experiment, while not completely accurate and dependable, are indicative of the potential strengths and weaknesses of the authoring tool.

The evaluation assignment required participants to add and, if appropriate, connect three Tasks in the Canvas area to create the outline of a simple course in their preferred domain. The participants were then asked to complete a questionnaire that consisted of six questions relating to UX design style.

4.1 Results

The results of the usability evaluation are described below with respect to each of the evaluation goals previously outlined.

'Style': There were two questions assigned to evaluating the *'style'* of user interface. The first was a Likert scale which asked participants if the liked the 'style' of the interface. The second question asked if the participant had any comments relating to the 'style'. Addressing the first question, seven participants agreed or strongly agreed with liking the 'style' of the interface, while one neither agreed nor disagreed. Qualitative data also reflected positively on the 'style'. Two participants both commented that the authoring tool was *"easy to use"*, one of those participants also commented that it was a *"good design"*. Another participant commented that it was a *"simple design"* that had *"a nice clean interface"*.

Color: Lindgaard [23] defines color as being related to a very strong visual appeal within the area of UX design. All eight participants either agreed or strongly agreed with the statement *"I liked the color scheme of the authoring tools interface"*. One participant commented that the interface incorporated a *"good color"* scheme while another commented that it *"holds [your] attention"*. One participant however commented that the color scheme should *"maybe not use such a harsh black"*.

Look & Feel: To evaluate the look and feel of the UX interface design, participants were provided with a list of words and asked to select those words that they felt accurately described the authoring tool. The participants were provided with a list of thirteen words [25]. The results of the evaluation are presented in Figure 3. The word selected by most participants, seven in total, was 'orderly', 'calm' and 'functional' were selected by six participants, while 'focused' and 'minimalists' were selected by five participants in the study. None of the participants selected words with negative connotations, such as 'cluttered' or 'chaotic'.

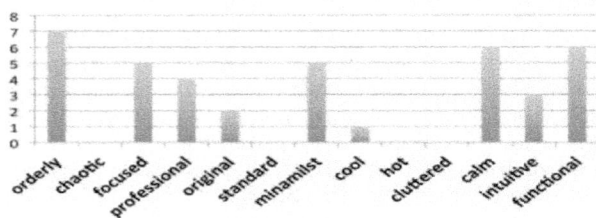

Figure 3: Interface Look & Feel Evaluation Results

Familiarity: To evaluate the familiarity of AMAS Authoring Tool 2.0 prototype participants were asked if it reminded them of any digital based systems such as other authoring tools, web applications or mobile apps. Five of the eight participants were not reminded of any other systems. One participant commented that the authoring tool reminded them of *"mindmap tools"* and was also similar to Prezzi. Another participant commented that the interface reminded them of Microsoft Access due to the approach of *"linking and normalizing tables of data"*. Finally, one participant commented that the interface reminded them of *"a flight map"*.

Discussion: Generally the evaluation of the 2.0 authoring tool UX design was very positive. Quantitative and qualitative results related to the *'style'*, color and look & feel were all favorable. As only three of the five participants were reminded of other digital systems it cannot be said that the authoring tool incorporates a sense of familiarity. However, some participants could be

described as less non-technical than others. As such, they may simply not interact with a great deal of technology and so are less likely to be reminded of similar systems.

The final question in the questionnaire allowed participants to add any additional comments that they might have relating to the 2.0 authoring tool. One consistent issue was associated with the font size within the Task nodes. Three participants in the study commented that the text was too small: *"script in graph component very small"*; *"size of print in 'nodes' is very small"*; and the *"text [could] be bigger"*. There were also a number of comments relating to the prototypes early stages of development. For example, one participant commented that they were not *"able to undo"* operations, a feature that has not yet been added. Another participant commented that they would like to employ *"swim lanes"* to assist in defining their course. Activity authoring components, which were not included in the prototype, would adequately suffice as swim lanes. One participant in the study was concerned that the *"canvas could become very crowded depending on course"* – such concerns have been noted in the authors previous publications where the introduction of navigational aids addressed the issue of large complex models [15].

Finally, the authors are also aware that only eight user participated in the study. Although eight participants may not be statistically significant [43] they are representative of the relatively small number of users at which the AMAS Authoring Tool is targeted. The results from the evaluation are indicative of the potential UX design strengths and weaknesses of the authoring tool.

5. CONCLUSION

This paper has presented the AMAS Authoring Tool 2.0. This is a new and unique Adaptive Educational Hypermedia authoring tool that allows non-technical Subject Matter Experts to compose adaptive online activity based courses. SMEs can compose activity based courses that include sophisticated personalization without the need to define complex rules or employ technical languages such as LAG [14].

The paper began with an introduction describing the motivation behind the research. It included a description of related work and presented the design of the first and second version of the AMAS Authoring Tool. The final section of the paper described the findings a preliminary evaluation. The paper has presented two key innovations related to hypertext authoring tools and AEH authoring tools. The first key innovation relates to the importance of UX style within online hypertext authoring tools, an approach to implementing UX style in interfaces and a methodology for its evaluation. The second key innovation relates to the representation of complex hypertext with the use of different node types and structured nesting. In particular, how complex hypertext structures in the domain of adaptive educational hypermedia can be realized in an accessible and user-friendly manner. It is no longer sufficient for hypertext authoring tools to simply be functional; they must also engage non-technical users.

Future work will primarily comprise of the completion of the 2.0 version of the AMAS Authoring Tool to include all authoring components that were implemented version 1.0. This will be completed in a manner that is suited to the UX design that has already been implemented.

6. ACKNOWLEDGMENTS

This work was funded by Science Foundation Ireland via grant 08/IN.1/I2103.

7. REFERENCES

[1] Alessi, S. M., S. R. Trollip 2001 Multimedia for learning : methods and development. *Chapter 7: Simulations*, 213-268 . Allyn and Bacon.

[2] Arapakis, J.M. Jose & P.D. Gray. 2008 Affective feedback: An investigation into the role of emotions in the information seeking process. *In Proc. SIGIR2008*, ACM press 395-402.

[3] Ardissono, L., Gena, C., Torasso, P., Bellifemmine, D., Difino, A., Negro, B. 2004. Personalized Digital Television – Targeting Programs to Individual Viewers, *Journal of Human-Computer Interaction*, volume 6, pp.3-26.

[4] Bernstein. M. 2002. Storyspace 1. In HYPERTEXT '02:*Proceedings of the thirteenth ACM conference on Hypertext and hypermedia*, pages 172,181, New York,NY, USA, 2002. ACM.

[5] Bernstein. M. 2003 Collage, composites, construction. In HYPERTEXT '03: Proceedings of the fourteenth ACM conference on Hypertext and hypermedia.

[6] Brusilovsky, P. 2012. Adaptive Technologies for Training and Education: Chapter 3 Aaptive Hypermedia for Education and Training. *Edited by Paula J. Durlach, Alan M. Lesgold.* Cambridge University Press.

[7] Carmagnola, F., Cena, F., Console, L., Grillo, P., Vernero, F., Simeoni, R., & Perrero, M. 2009 iDYNamicTV: a social adaptive television experience. *In Proceedings of the 20th ACM conference on Hypertext and hypermedia* (pp. 375-376). ACM

[8] Conklin. J., 1987 Hypertext: An introduction and survey. *Computer*, 20(9):17{41}

[9] Cristea, A., C. Stewart 2004. Authoring of Adaptive Hypermedia. *Advances in Web-Based Education: Personalized Learning Environments*. Information Science Publishing.

[10] Dagger, D., V. Wade 2005. Evaluation of adaptive course construction toolkit (ACCT). 3rd International Workshop on Authoring of Adaptive and Adaptable Educational Hypermedia, 12th International Conference on Artificial Intelligence in Education, 18-22 July 2005, Amsterdam, Netherlands.

[11] Dalziel, J. R. 2006. Lessons from LAMS for IMS Learning Design. *In ICALT* (Vol. 6, pp. 1101-1102)

[12] De Bra, P., N. Stash, D. Smits, C. Romero, S. Ventura 2007. Authoring and management tools for adaptive educational hypermedia systems: The AHA! case study. *Studies in Computational Intelligence*, Vol. 62, 285-308. Springer..

[13] Dourish, P., Edwards, W., LaMarca, A. and Salisbury, M. 1999. Presto: an experimental architecture for fluid interactive document spaces. *ACM Transactions on Computer-Human Interaction*. 6, 2 (1999), 133-161

[14] Foss, Jonathan GK, Alexandra I. Cristea, and Maurice Hendrix. 2010 Continuous use of authoring for adaptive educational hypermedia: a long-term case study. *In Advanced Learning Technologies (ICALT)*, IEEE 10th International Conference on, pp. 194-196. IEEE, 2010

[15] Gaffney, C. 2013 Authoring Adaptive Soft Skill Simulations. *PhD. Computer Science. Dublin, Trinity College Dublin.*

[16] Gaffney, C., I. O'Keeffe, A. Staikopoulos O. Conlan, V. Wade "A Training Framework for Authoring Adaptive Educational Hypermedia Authoring Tools" Paper Accepted at the Ninth European Conference on Technology Enhanced Learning, (EC-TEL) Graz Austria, 2014.

[17] Gemmell, J., Bell, G. and Lueder, R. 2006. MyLifeBits: a personal database for everything. *Commun. ACM.* 49, 1 (2006), 88-95.

[18] Harrigan, M., M. Kravčík, C. Steiner, V. Wade. 2009. What Do Academic Users Really Want from an Adaptive Learning System? *User Modeling, Adaptation, and Personalization Lecture Notes in Computer Science,* Vol. 5535, 454-460. Springer.

[19] Huang. M.H. 2003. Designing website attributes to induce experiential encounters. *Computers in Human Behavior*, 19, 4

[20] Jones, W., & Anderson, K. M. 2011. Many views, many modes, many tools... one structure: Towards a Non-disruptive Integration of Personal Information. *In Proceedings of the 22nd ACM conference on Hypertext and hypermedia (pp. 113-122). ACM*

[21] Karger, D.R. 2007. Unify Everything: It's All the Same to Me. In Personal Information Management (William Jones and Jaime Teevan, Eds). University of Washington Press

[22] Keeffe, I.O. et. al: 2012 Personalized Activity Based eLearning, In 12th International Conference on Knowledge Management and Knowledge Technologies

[23] Lindgaard, G. 2007 Aesthetics, visual appeal, usability, and user satisfaction: What do the user's eyes tell the user's.

[24] Lucrecia, M., Cecilia, S., Patricia, P., & Sandra, B. 2013. AuthorAR: Authoring tool for building educational activities based on Augmented Reality. *In Collaboration Technologies and Systems (CTS), 2013 International Conference on* (pp. 503-507). IEEE

[25] McAlpine,R. 2000. How to evaluate a web site. *Webpagecontent*: http://www.webpagecontent.com/arc_archive/62/5/

[26] McCay-Peet, L., Lalmas, M., & Navalpakkam, V. 2012. On saliency, affect and focused attention. *In Proceedings of the SIGCHI Conference on Human Factors in Computing Systems* (pp. 541-550). ACM

[27] Mehm , F., Konert, J., Göbel, S., & Steinmetz, R. 2012. An authoring tool for adaptive digital educational games. *In 21st Century Learning for 21st Century Skills* (pp. 236-249). Springer Berlin Heidelberg

[28] Mitchell, A., & McGee, K. 2009. Designing hypertext tools to facilitate authoring multiple points-of-view stories. *In Proceedings of the 20th ACM conference on Hypertext and hypermedia* (pp. 309-316). ACM

[29] Mustafa, Y., M. Sharif. 2010. An Approach to Adaptive E-Learning Hypermedia System based on Learning Styles (AEHS-LS): Implementation and Evaluation. *International Journal of Library and Information Science*, Vol. 3, Issue 1, 15-28. Academic Journals.

[30] Nielsen, J., R. Molich (1990) *"Heuristic Evaluation of User Interfaces."* Conference on Human Factors in Computing Systems, Amsterdam, Netherlands. ACM.

[31] Nurjanah, D., H. Davis 2012. Improving the Workspace Awareness of Authors in Asynchronous Collaborative Authoring of Learning Designs. *EdMedia - World*

Conference on Educational Media and Technology, Denver, USA, 26-29 June. AACE.

[32] O'Brien H., E. Toms. 2010. The development and evaluation of a survey to measure user engagement. *JASIST* 61, 1

[33] OReilly, T. 2005. What Is Web 2.0. Design Patterns and Business Models for the Next Generation of Software.

[34] Peirce, N., O. Conlan, V. Wade 2008. Adaptive Educational Games: Providing Non-invasive Personalised Learning Experiences. *2nd IEEE International Conference on Digital Games and Intelligent Toys Based Education*, 17-19 Nov, Banff, Canada. IEEE.

[35] Ploum, E.L.M., 2009. Authoring of Adaptation in the GRAPPLE Project. *Technische Universiteit Eindhoven*

[36] Sampson, D., Karampiperis, P., & Zervas, P. 2005 ASK-LDT: a web-based learning scenarios authoring environment based on IMS learning design.International *Journal on Advanced Technology for Learning* (ATL), 2(4), 207-215

[37] Tanner, J., G. Stewart, M. Totaro, M. Hargrave 2012. Business Simulation Games: Effective Teaching Tools Or Window Dressing? *American Journal Of Business Education*, Vol. 5, Issue 2. The Clute Institute.

[38] Torrente, J., Del Blanco, Á., Marchiori, E. J., Moreno-Ger, P., & Fernández-Manjón, B. 2010. *< e-Adventure>:* *Introducing educational games in the learning process.* In Education Engineering (EDUCON), 2010 IEEE (pp. 1121-1126). IEEE

[39] Tullis and Albert 2010. Measuring the User Experience: Collecting, Analyzing and Presenting Usability Metrics.

[40] Uibu, K., E. Kikas 2012. Authoritative and authoritian-inconsistent teachers' preferences for teaching methods and instructional goals. *International Journal of Primary, Elementary and Early Years Education.* Taylor and Finch.

[41] van Dam, S. Carmody, T. Gross, T. Nelson, and D. Rice.1969 A hypertext editing system for the /360. *In Proceedings of the Conference in Computer Graphics.*

[42] Vogl,S., Halbmayer,P., Lichtenberger, C., Rauscha, H., Rodler, D., Mullner, W. 2008. Media space navigator: navigating videocontent on IPTV portals, *Proc. EuroITV 2008, Changing television environments,* Salzburg, Austria.

[43] Woolrych, A., G. Cockton. 2001. Why and When Five Test Users aren't Enough. *1st International Conference IHM-HCI, Lille, France,* Vol. 2, 105-108. September 2001. Cépaduès éd.

Balancing Diversity to Counter-measure Geographical Centralization in Microblogging Platforms

Eduardo Graells-Garrido
Universitat Pompeu Fabra
Barcelona, Spain
eduard.graells@upf.edu

Mounia Lalmas
Yahoo Labs
London, UK
mounia@acm.org

ABSTRACT

We study whether geographical centralization is reflected in the virtual population of microblogging platforms. A consequence of centralization is the decreased visibility and findability of content from less central locations. We propose to counteract geographical centralization in microblogging timelines by promoting geographical diversity through: *1)* a characterization of imbalance in location interaction centralization over a graph of geographical interactions from user generated content; *2)* geolocation of microposts using imbalance-aware content features in text classifiers, and evaluation of those classifiers according to their diversity and accuracy; *3)* definition of a two-step information filtering algorithm to ensure diversity in summary timelines of events. We study our proposal through an analysis of a dataset of Twitter in Chile, in the context of the 2012 municipal political elections.

Categories and Subject Descriptors

H.3.3 [**Information Storage and Retrieval**]: Information Search and Retrieval—*Information Filtering*

Keywords

Information Filtering; Information Diversity; Geolocation.

1. INTRODUCTION

Microblogging sites are social platforms where, worldwide, users are able to participate; there are no physical barriers. However, geography still plays an important role in the way user content is generated [1, 8, 18, 19, 25], not always in a fair manner. When population distribution is imbalanced, it is expected that content shared on social platforms is also imbalanced, but in centralized populations, content from non-central locations may itself be driven by the central locations, further increasing the imbalance. This causes two problems: on one hand, the voice of less populated and non-central locations is lost in a timeline flooded with content

from few locations. On the other hand, algorithms to classify content become biased because of the over-representation of content generated from centralized places, particularly when algorithms rely on representative documents for modeling. For instance, predicting that all content is about the centralized and most populated location will lead to high accuracy, in spite of the absence of geographical diversity.

In Chile, around 40% of its population live in its capital, Santiago, and public policy and media are biased towards the needs of the capital [23]. A common saying is *"Santiago is not Chile"*, referring to the fact that the capital is not representative of the country, yet media outlets concentrate in Santiago and government policies are tailored towards its needs. Given the climatic, geographical and cultural diversity of Chile, centralization is a serious problem.

Motivated by the above situation, we address two research questions: **Q1)** *When centralization is present in the physical world, is it reflected in the virtual population of microblogging platforms?* **Q2)** *How to generate geographically diverse event-specific timelines?* We study both questions through a case study using a dataset from Chile focusing on the microblogging platform Twitter. On October 28, 2012, we crawled microposts, or *tweets*, published in the context of municipal elections held in Chile that day [24]. This event was locally relevant throughout the country, making it a good dataset for our research questions as local events have denser discussion networks than global events [25].

Many tweets are not associated with a geographical location, so we need to geolocate their content to provide geographical meta-data. To this end, we geolocate users by querying a high precision gazetteer [10, 15, 22]. Then, to geolocate tweets we extend previous work [9] by considering content features aware of user locations. These features are based on TF-IDF (which has superior performance than topic modeling for recommendation tasks [20]) and allow us to train classifiers with a number of features that are several orders of magnitude smaller than typical bag of words approaches. To overcome the false sense of accuracy introduced by imbalance, we consider both accuracy *and* diversity when evaluating, because *accuracy is not enough* [13]. Then, building on prior work [7, 16] we define an information filtering algorithm to generate a diverse timeline with a focus on geographical diversity that summarizes an event.

Our work makes the following contributions: *1)* we show that centralization from the physical world is reflected in a spatially representative sample of the Chilean virtual population in Twitter; *2)* we address population imbalance from a content perspective, while previous work has focused on a network perspective [22]; *3)* to evaluate classifiers considering accuracy and diversity, we define a *D-measure* based on the F-measure used in Information Retrieval [2]; and *4)* we evaluate our information filtering algorithm, and find that timelines generated with our approach ensure geographical diversity, and are more diverse than plain timelines based on popularity.

2. METHODOLOGY

We focus on timelines from microblogging platforms. Even though our definitions are general, we restrict ourselves to Twitter. Twitter is a microblogging platform where users publish status updates called *tweets* with a maximum length of 140 characters. Users can *follow* other users, establishing directed connections between pairs of users. When user A *follows* user B, tweets and *re-tweets* made by B will show up in A's timeline. A timeline is a list of tweets in reverse chronological order. Users can annotate tweets using *hashtags*, i.e. keywords that start with the hash character **#**.

Problem Definition. We define our problem as follows: *1)* given an event E (defined as a set of hashtags and special keywords) relevant to a country C, with a set of locations L, collect all tweets related to E generated in C in a tweet set T_E; *2)* given all users U who published tweets in T_E, predict (if possible) a location from L for all users $u \in U$; *3)* considering the users U_L who were geolocated, aggregate their interactions to find if geographical centralization is present; *4)* aggregate the content from U_L into location documents, and use these to build a location classifier P such that given an arbitrary tweet, predicts its location; *5)* using the output from P applied to all tweets in T_E, filter T_E to produce a summary tweet set T_θ, with $|T_\theta| \leq |T_E|$, which is more geographically diverse, i.e. $geodiversity(T_\theta) \geq geodiversity(T_E)$.

Geolocating Users. To geolocate users we rely on the self-reported location in user profiles. Instead of querying external services using profile locations as input [15], we build an ad-hoc gazetteer from official location names, from lists of known toponyms extracted from Wikipedia [10, 22] and from labeled user profiles. Then, to geolocate a user u, we query the gazetteer with u's self-reported location.

Location Interactions. In previous work, two locations become connected if someone from location A follows someone from location B [12]. In our context this is not meaningful, because such connectivity may not convey an interaction between two users that is relevant to the event E. Hence, we consider *1-way interactions* between locations through mentions and retweets [19] by building an adjacency matrix: $M_{i,j} = mentions(L_i, L_j) + retweets(L_i, L_j)$, where $mentions(L_i, L_j)$ is the number of tweets from location L_i (those tweets whose author has been geolocated to that location) that mention one or more accounts from location L_j, and $retweets(L_i, L_j)$ is the number of times that tweets from L_j have been retweeted by users from L_i.

Measuring Centralization. From the adjacency matrix we build an undirected graph with self-connecting edges removed, and estimate the edge weights with a normalized *geometric mean* of information flow:

$$weight(i,j) = \frac{\sqrt{M_{i,j} \times M_{j,i}}}{\max\{\sqrt{M_{i,j} \times M_{j,i}} | \forall l_i, l_j \in L : i \neq j\}}$$

It is likely that this matrix represents a fully connected graph. Because information does not always follow geodesic

paths, and because we want to weight information paths, over this graph we estimate *random-walk weighted betweenness centrality* [17]. To confirm the presence of centralization, we consider the estimated centrality as the *observed centrality in location interactions*, which is compared to the *expected centrality in location interactions*. The expected centrality is the random walk betweenness centrality estimated in the interaction graph, considering edge weights as the normalized geometric mean of location populations. A considerable deviation from the expectations is a strong signal of centralization.

Document Location Representation. Our initial assumption is that each location will have several local words and hashtags that characterize it. These hashtags, among other words like place names, people names and vernacular words, will have more weight in their corresponding documents than global, non local words. Hence, we consider that a tweet talks about a particular location if its content resembles or is similar enough to the aggregated content of that location. To build a *location corpus* of $|L|$ *location documents*, we consider the set of geolocated users U_L. Each document is the aggregation of tweets originating from those locations, leaving out *replies*, *mentions* and *retweets* to avoid repeated content between different documents. We represent each location document d as a vector $\vec{d} = [w_0, w_1, \ldots, w_n]$, where w_i represents the vocabulary word i weighted according to its locality by using TF-IDF [2]:

$$w_i = freq(w_i, d) \times log \frac{|L|}{|l \in L : w_i \in l|}$$

Classifying Tweets using Location Similarity. To predict a location for a given document $\vec{d}$, we build a feature vector $\vec{f_d}$ containing the similarity of $\vec{d}$ with each location document from the location corpus. In this way, we consolidate all similarities in a single vector: $\vec{f_d} = [f_0, f_1, \ldots, f_{|L|}]$, where f_i is the cosine similarity between the document $\vec{d}$ and the location document $\vec{l_i}$:

$$cosine\_similarity(\vec{d}, \vec{l_i}) = \frac{\vec{d} \cdot \vec{l_i}}{\| \vec{d} \| \| \vec{l_i} \|}$$

We use the feature vectors and their corresponding author geolocations to train classifiers based on *Support Vector Machines* (SVM) [6] and *Naive Bayes*. We define that a prediction is correct if the location predicted for a tweet matches the author location. Although this approach may give *false positives* (a user tweets about other locations) or *false negatives* (a user tweets about the event from a generic point of view), this assumption is also made in previous work [5, 10] because the usage of the self-reported location in geolocation allows to assign only one location to every user, which we find acceptable when considering events where users are expected to have a single location.

Evaluating Geographical Diversity. To find how different classifiers behave when considering geographical diversity, we define *geographical diversity* as the normalized *Shannon entropy* [11] with respect to locations:

$$geodiversity = \frac{-\sum_{i=1}^{|L|} p_i \log p_i}{log|L|}$$

where p_i is the fraction of predictions for location i, and L is the set of locations ($|L| > 1$). To balance classifier accuracy and geographical diversity, based on the *F-measure* [2], we define a *D-measure* as the harmonic mean between accuracy and *geographical diversity*:

$$D_\beta = (1 + \beta^2) \cdot \frac{geodiversity \cdot accuracy}{(\beta^2 * geodiversity) + accuracy}$$

where β establishes the weight given to diversity: D_1 gives equal weight to accuracy and diversity, $D_{0.5}$ gives more weight to accuracy, and D_2 gives more weight to diversity.

Filtering Information Streams. Given an event of interest E and a set of related tweets T_E, we generate a summary tweet set or timeline T_θ, where T_θ contains s tweets. To maximize geographical diversity of T_θ, we consider a greedy algorithm from prior work [7]. This algorithm generates T_θ from an *information entropy* perspective, where entropy is estimated in terms of several features extracted from tweets. Since the complexity of those dimensions can be greater than those of geography (for instance, consider the number of hashtags in an event and the number of locations), the entropy contribution of these dimensions is higher than the entropy contribution of geography. Thus, diversity can still be optimal even in the absence geographical diversity.

To inject geographical diversity, we extend [7] by adding a sidelining step [16] when considering tweets for inclusion in T_θ, that is, tweets from a location previously selected in the previous iterations of the algorithms will not be considered for a given number of turns. Additionally, for user interests to be represented, we introduce popularity into the input features, which has been established as a valuable feature for tweet recommendation [3, 4].

For each tweet t, we consider a vector representation $\vec{v_t}$ with the following features:

1. *Presence of links*: whether the tweet contains an URL.
2. *Time bucket*: n^{th} time-window of 5 minutes since the start of E.
3. *Annotated hashtags*: topical information for each tweet.
4. *Geography*: defined as the location the tweet content is most likely to be about using our text classifiers.
5. Author's number of *followers*.
6. Author's *hub dimension* ($\frac{followers}{friends}$).
7. Author's *global tweet count*.
8. *Popularity*: number of times the tweet has been retweeted.

For a given tweet set T', with k different vector representations of its elements ($k \leq |T'|$), we estimate its *Shannon entropy* [11]: $H_{T'} = -\sum_{i=1}^{k} p(\vec{v_{t_i}}) \log p(\vec{v_{t_i}})$. Then, to create a summary tweet set T_θ of size s, where *turns* is the number of times a location is not considered for addition ("*it is sidelined*") and t_l is the predicted location for tweet t, we define the following information filtering algorithm:

1. Define a dictionary mapping *sidelined* where $sidelined[l] = 0, \forall l : l \in L$.
2. Start by selecting a tweet t from the most popular ones from T_E as initial seed in T_θ. Set $sidelined[t_l] = turns$.
3. For all tweets in T_E which are not in T_θ, build a tweet set T_c, where every tweet t in T_c satisfies the following: its addition to T_θ maximizes H_{T_θ}.
4. For all tweets in T_c, leave out those where $sidelined[t_l] > 0$, and select randomly a tweet t' from the remaining most popular tweets.
5. Set $sidelined[l] = sidelined[l] - 1, \forall l : l \in L, l \neq t'_l$
6. Set $sidelined[t'_l] = turns$
7. Repeat step 3 unless $|T_\theta| = s$.

Data	#	Fraction
User Accounts	199951	–
w/ Location Text	131625	65.83%
All Tweets	886813	–
RTs	306377	34.55%
w/Mentions or Replies	252525	28.48%
w/Hashtags	274592	30.96%
w/Geo. Coordinates	66196	7.46%
Vocabulary Size	65516	–

Table 1: Our information space: main types of data crawled during the #municipales2012 event. *w/* means *with*.

Level	# Users	# Tweets
Country	18902 (9.45%)	112321 (12.67%)
Region	420 (0.21%)	3385 (0.38%)
Province	2048 (1.02%)	15186 (1.71%)
Municipality	53436 (26.72%)	355224 (40.06%)
Geolocated	74806 (37.41%)	486116 (54.82%)

Table 2: Number and geographical level of geolocated accounts using the self-reported location.

3. CASE STUDY: CHILE

The administrative locations of Chile are defined according to the following hierarchy: *municipality* → *province* → *region* → *country*. In our work, we consider the 15 Chilean regions, as is the level at which Chilean centralization is characterized [23]. The most populated and centralized region is *Región Metropolitana (RM)*.

Dataset. Our dataset is composed of tweets crawled on October 28, 2012, related to the municipal elections held in Chile. The event had a distinctive hashtag, #municipales2012, which among other related hashtags (e.g. #túdecides), keywords (e.g. vote), location and candidate names were used as queries to the *Twitter Streaming API*.[1] Table 1 gives an overview of the dataset after removing unrelated tweets and tweets not in Spanish. The fraction of tweets with geographical coordinates is very low (7.46%) and the fraction of tweets with hashtags is less than a third (30.96%).

Virtual Population. To initialize the gazetteer, we loaded a list of 1978 toponyms from previous work [9]. Table 2 contains the number of users and tweets per location level. Only 37.41% of the participating accounts could be geolocated, although those accounts produce 54.82% of the event content, a reasonable amount to build the corpus of location documents. Figure 1 (left top) shows the number of accounts per region, showcasing the imbalance in population distribution. The mean rate of regional twitter accounts per 1000 inhabitants is 2.65, indicating that the proportion of accounts in each region is similar (see Figure 1, top right). To explore the representativity of the sample, we estimate the *Pearson product-moment correlation coefficient* between virtual and physical population, and between account rate and household Internet Access Rate in Chile [14]. Because of population imbalance, we estimate the correlation of the logarithms of population, obtaining 0.95 ($p < 0.01$, Figure 1 bottom left). The user and household Internet access rates correlate at 0.68 ($p < 0.01$, Figure 1 bottom right).

[1] https://dev.twitter.com/docs/streaming-apis, accessed 2-July-2014.

Region	Tweet Share	Incoming Share	Import %	RM Import %	Export %	RM Export %	Exp./Imp.	Expected Centrality	Observed Centrality
I	2.52	1.90	16.01	9.14	36.81	29.64	3.06	0.04	0.01
II	2.71	1.60	26.66	13.43	56.72	46.66	3.60	0.05	0.02
III	0.72	0.44	45.11	24.58	66.47	54.66	2.41	0.04	0.01
IV	2.34	2.13	54.04	35.90	58.04	48.36	1.18	0.06	0.02
V	10.06	5.77	46.02	30.29	69.07	60.64	2.62	0.10	0.09
VI	1.43	0.67	64.51	38.96	83.44	71.52	2.77	0.07	0.01
VII	2.78	1.39	38.62	24.04	69.25	57.97	3.58	0.07	0.02
VIII	8.23	5.25	37.63	23.80	60.22	51.51	2.51	0.10	0.07
IX	3.19	1.89	33.83	18.92	60.75	49.36	3.03	0.07	0.03
X	2.39	1.28	35.95	20.31	65.60	53.37	3.40	0.07	0.02
XI	0.33	0.14	61.76	30.15	83.33	68.59	3.10	0.02	0.00
XII	1.13	1.03	56.81	36.48	60.28	50.65	1.15	0.03	0.01
XIV	2.46	1.95	32.54	20.11	46.71	37.92	1.82	0.04	0.03
XV	0.85	0.59	50.80	27.45	65.67	53.48	1.85	0.03	0.01
RM	**58.87**	**73.97**	**29.12**	**70.88**	**10.95**	**89.05**	**0.30**	**0.19**	**0.76**

Table 3: Information trade in terms of proportion of outgoing and incoming tweets for the Chilean regions. Centrality is estimated from the adjacency matrix of interactions.

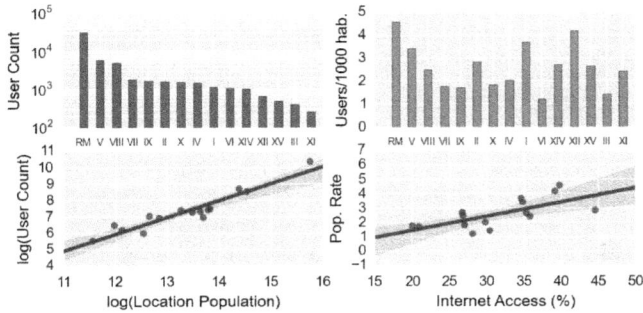

Figure 1: Top: Distributions of population according to Chilean regions (left) and user rates per 1000 inhabitants (right). Bottom: linear regressions of: logarithms of physical population with Twitter accounts (left), Internet access rate with Twitter account rate (right).

Therefore, we consider our sample spatially representative of the physical population at the regional level.

Location Interactions. As defined in Section 2, we build the adjacency matrix of 1-way interactions and its corresponding graph. We observe in Table 3 that *RM* produces the majority of tweets (58.87%) and receives most of the incoming interactions (73.97%). The ratio of exported/imported tweets shows an interesting pattern: the only region with a ratio below 1 is *RM*, suggesting the presence of centralization. Then, we estimate *random walk betweenness centrality* [17] considering the edge weights defined in Section 2. Table 3 shows both expected and observed centralities for all locations: *RM* is, indeed, the most central location (0.76 expected, 0.19 observed), having the only increased and highest difference between observed and expected centralities. Therefore, in the context of our dataset, there is centralization in location interactions.

Content Location Classifiers. After building the location corpus, we apply TF-IDF to find the most discriminating hashtags and keywords for each location. To remove noise, when building location documents we discarded hashtags and keyword appearing in less than 5 different tweets. Most of the found discriminative keywords can be categorized in: *a)* toponyms, like #laserena (IV) and coyhaique (XI); *b)*

names of candidates from the corresponding region: #soria (I) and arellano (VI); and *c)* local adaptations of event hashtags: #municipalesmag (XII) and #municipalesfm (V). This result validates our assumptions about local vocabulary.

Using the location documents and the set of tweets from the geolocated users, we build the feature vectors corresponding to each tweet. We evaluated the following classifiers using a 10-fold stratified cross-validation: SVM Linear Kernel (*one versus one* multiclass strategy), SVM Linear Kernel (*one versus all* multiclass strategy) [21], SVM RBF Kernel and Naive Bayes. We divided the set of tweets from geolocated users in 10 groups, maintaining the proportions of users' tweets in each group, and then ran 10 iterations to evaluate the classifiers. In each iteration we trained each classifier using 9 tweet groups and tested predictions with the remaining group. In this way, each tweet was used nine times for training and one time for evaluation. We did not consider retweets and replies to avoid duplicate tweets in training and evaluation sets. Then, we estimated the geographical diversity of the set of predictions of each classifier, and calculated the *D-measure* at $\beta = \{0.5, 1, 2\}$. To evaluate results of our approach, we considered the following baselines: *a) Trivial Classifier*, which predicts the most common location in the dataset (*RM*); *b) Best Cosine Similarity*, which predicts the location with the highest cosine similarity between the tweet content and the location documents, as in [9]; and *c) SVM* and *Naive Bayes* classifiers trained with *bag of words*, with vocabulary size 65516. Results are reported in Table 4.

In terms of accuracy, SVM has the best performance in both scenarios (using similarity features and bag of words), which aligns with previous work on imbalanced populations [22]. However, not all classifiers show diversity: some of them have entropy 0, which means that they are behaving in the same way as the trivial classifier. Although geographical diversity is important in our context, accuracy is needed to avoid inconsistent results. Thus, we consider $D_{0.5}$, in which the best scores are for *Cosine Similarity* (0.60) and *SVM Linear1vsA* (0.58). We believe *SVM Linear1vsA* is a better solution, as *Cosine Similarity* has worse performance when considering finer location granularity [9] and SVM has proven to be robust at different levels [22]. Note that even without our features *SVM Linear1vsA* had a considerable amount of diversity (but still lesser than with our approach).

Approach	Acc.	Geo. Div.	D_1	$D_{0.5}$	D_2
SVM Linear1vs1	0.68	0.34	0.45	0.56	0.38
SVM RBF	0.68	0.34	0.45	0.56	0.38
SVM Linear1vsA	0.68	0.38	0.49	0.58	0.41
Naive Bayes	0.58	0.00	–	–	–
Cosine Similarity	0.62	0.54	0.58	0.60	0.56
W-SVM Linear1vs1	0.58	0.00	–	–	–
W-SVM RBF	0.58	0.00	–	–	–
W-SVM Linear1vsA	0.68	0.27	0.39	0.52	0.31
W-Naive Bayes	0.58	0.00	–	–	–
Trivial	0.58	0.00	–	–	–

Table 4: Evaluation results at regional level of our classifiers using a 10-fold stratified cross validation. Classifiers prefixed with *W-* use normalized word counts, while other classifiers use TF-IDF weighting according to locations.

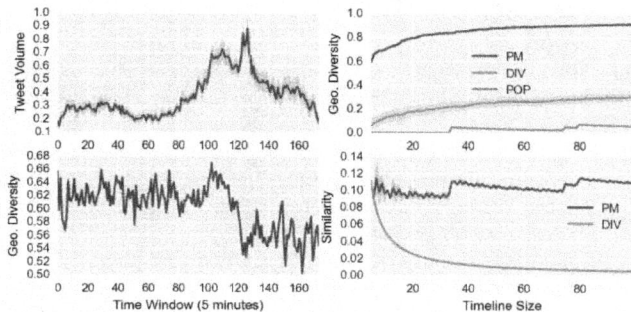

Figure 2: Tweet volume during the event (top left) and corresponding geographical diversity (bottom left). Normalized geographical diversity for timeline sizes between 5 and 100 (top right). Jaccard similarity between generated timelines using filtering and the popularity sampling for timeline sizes between 5 and 100 (bottom right).

Temporal Geographical Diversity. Figure 2 shows tweet volume (top left) and geographical diversity (bottom left) of the dataset: from morning to afternoon, activity increased steadily as the elections were being held. At night, specific events regarding unexpected results raised the level of activity above expectation. Before this peak, geographical diversity had a mean value of 0.62; after, the mean geographical diversity was 0.55, a decay explained by the unexpected defeat of several candidates in some locations, shifting the discussion in a natural way towards fewer locations.

Filtering Algorithm. Because geographically diverse content exists, we evaluate if our information filtering algorithm produces geographically diverse summary timelines. We consider the following baselines against our *Proposed Method* (PM): *B1) Popularity Sampling* (POP): we select the s most popular tweets in terms of retweets; *B2) Diversity Filtering* (DIV): an implementation of [7] considering the tweet predicted location as a geographical feature. We estimate the $s = 100$ most popular tweets for POP, and run DIV and PM a hundred times (POP runs only once because the outcome is always the same for the same input). At every timeline size $i \in [5, 100]$ we estimate: *1)* the geographical diversity of POP, DIV and PM; *2)* the Jaccard similarity between DIV and POP, and between PM and POP (defined as $J(A, B) = \frac{|A \cup B|}{|A \cap B|}$). Our algorithm consistently shows greater geographical diversity than POP and DIV (Figure 2 top right),

indicating that our sidelining step produces the needed effect of *geodiversification*. The lack of geographical diversity in POP could be a consequence of centralization, as even on the imbalanced population distribution at least 41.13% of the tweet share is generated outside of RM (see Table 3). In terms of the similarity with POP, our method is much more similar than DIV (Figure 2 bottom right). Because we modified the baseline algorithm from [7] to start with one the most popular tweets instead of a random selection, the initial similarity is the same as in our method. However, as the timeline size increases, the similarity to POP tends to become 0, whereas our method maintains a similarity between 0.09 and 0.12 (Figure 2 bottom right). Hence, our method has a stronger representation of user interests than DIV.

4. DISCUSSION

System biases affecting how people behave should be considered in system design. In this line, we explored how *systematic biases from the physical world are reflected on microblogging platforms*. In the case of Chile, we confirmed that centralization happens in Twitter when the population from the physical world is centralized (Table 3).

Then, we proposed text features for geolocation and found that *similarity features help classification in biased scenarios* (see Table 4). In this aspect, when using SVM the *one vs all* approach [21] is better than *one vs one*, as it has greater diversity with our features and it does not become over-fitted when using the *bag of words* approach. In terms of scalability, similarity features are orders of magnitude smaller than the vocabulary size in the *bag of words* approaches. Moreover, a classifier trained over similarities should tolerate new vocabulary without needing re-training, as it is built over how similar a given text is to the location documents instead of word distributions.

Finally, to balance event-summary timelines from a geographical perspective we defined an information filtering algorithm based on previous work. In an off-line evaluation, our algorithm outperformed the baselines in terms of geographical diversity while still maintaining desirable properties such as information diversity and representation of user interests.

Limitations. Critics might rightly say that other approaches could have led to better precision and higher recall than our ad-hoc gazetteer. We analyzed the representativity of the sample of geolocated users and found that it was spatially representative of the population. The focus of our work is not o identify the exact user geolocation, but to use the latter to promote diverse timelines. Our approach is thus sufficient for this work.

Future Work. It remains to be seen if centralization is stronger at other geographical levels, as well as the behavior of the similarity features when classifying tweets. Because our results need to be explained from user perspectives in qualitative terms, a long-term longitudinal study is needed to evaluate the real effect of incorporating these results (e.g. promoting geographical diversity) into microblogging platforms and their user interfaces.

Acknowledgments. We thank Bárbara Poblete for many fruitful discussions about this work. This work was partially funded by Grant TIN2012-38741 (Understanding Social Media: An Integrated Data Mining Approach) of the Ministry of Economy and Competitiveness of Spain.

5. REFERENCES

[1] Ricardo Baeza-Yates, Christian Middleton, and Carlos Castillo. The Geographical Life of Search. In *Web Intelligence and Intelligent Agent Technologies, 2009. WI-IAT'09. IEEE/WIC/ACM International Joint Conferences on*, volume 1, pages 252–259. IET, 2009.

[2] Ricardo Baeza-Yates and Berthier Ribeiro-Neto. *Modern information retrieval: the concepts and technology behind search, 2nd. Edition*. Addison-Wesley, Pearson, 2011.

[3] Jilin Chen, Rowan Nairn, Les Nelson, Michael Bernstein, and Ed Chi. Short and tweet: experiments on recommending content from information streams. In *Proceedings of the SIGCHI Conference on Human Factors in Computing Systems*, pages 1185–1194. ACM, 2010.

[4] Kailong Chen, Tianqi Chen, Guoqing Zheng, Ou Jin, Enpeng Yao, and Yong Yu. Collaborative personalized tweet recommendation. In *Proceedings of the 35th international ACM SIGIR conference on Research and development in information retrieval*, pages 661–670. ACM, 2012.

[5] Zhiyuan Cheng, James Caverlee, and Kyumin Lee. You are where you tweet: a content-based approach to geo-locating twitter users. In *Proceedings of the 19th ACM international conference on Information and knowledge management*, pages 759–768. ACM, 2010.

[6] Corinna Cortes and Vladimir Vapnik. Support-vector networks. *Machine learning*, 20(3):273–297, 1995.

[7] Munmun De Choudhury, Scott Counts, and Mary Czerwinski. Identifying relevant social media content: leveraging information diversity and user cognition. In *Proceedings of the 22nd ACM conference on Hypertext and hypermedia*, pages 161–170. ACM, 2011.

[8] Ruth Garcia-Gavilanes, Daniele Quercia, and Alejandro Jaimes. Cultural Dimensions in Twitter: Time, Individualism and Power. In *International AAAI Conference on Weblogs and Social Media*, 2013.

[9] Eduardo Graells-Garrido and Bárbara Poblete. #Santiago is not #Chile, or is it?: a model to normalize social media impact. In *Proceedings of the 2013 Chilean Conference on Human-Computer Interaction*, pages 110–115. ACM, 2013.

[10] Brent Hecht, Lichan Hong, Bongwon Suh, and Ed H Chi. Tweets from Justin Bieber's heart: the dynamics of the location field in user profiles. In *Proceedings of the 2011 annual conference on Human factors in computing systems*, pages 237–246. ACM, 2011.

[11] Lou Jost. Entropy and diversity. *Oikos*, 113(2):363–375, 2006.

[12] Juhi Kulshrestha, Farshad Kooti, Ashkan Nikravesh, and Krishna P Gummadi. Geographic dissection of the Twitter network. In *Proceedings of the 6th International AAAI Conference on Weblogs and Social Media (ICWSM)*, 2012.

[13] Sean M McNee, John Riedl, and Joseph A Konstan. Being accurate is not enough: how accuracy metrics have hurt recommender systems. In *CHI'06 extended abstracts on Human factors in computing systems*, pages 1097–1101. ACM, 2006.

[14] Gobierno de Chile Ministerio de Desarrollo Social. CASEN Survey. `http://observatorio.ministeriodesarrollosocial.gob.cl/casen_obj.php`, 2011. [In spanish; Online; accessed 2-July-2014].

[15] Alan Mislove, Sune Lehmann, Yong-Yeol Ahn, Jukka-Pekka Onnela, and J Niels Rosenquist. Understanding the demographics of Twitter users. In *Proceedings of the Fifth International AAAI Conference on Weblogs and Social Media (ICWSM'11), Barcelona, Spain*, 2011.

[16] Sean A Munson, Daniel Xiaodan Zhou, and Paul Resnick. Sidelines: An Algorithm for Increasing Diversity in News and Opinion Aggregators. In *Third International AAAI Conference on Weblogs and Social Media*, 2009.

[17] Mark EJ Newman. A measure of betweenness centrality based on random walks. *Social networks*, 27(1):39–54, 2005.

[18] Bárbara Poblete, Ruth García, Marcelo Mendoza, and Alejandro Jaimes. Do all birds tweet the same?: characterizing Twitter around the world. In *Proceedings of the 20th ACM international conference on Information and knowledge management*, pages 1025–1030. ACM, 2011.

[19] Daniele Quercia, Licia Capra, and Jon Crowcroft. The social world of Twitter: Topics, geography, and emotions. In *The 6th international AAAI Conference on weblogs and social media*, 2012.

[20] Daniel Ramage, Susan T Dumais, and Daniel J Liebling. Characterizing Microblogs with Topic Models. In *ICWSM*, 2010.

[21] Ryan Rifkin and Aldebaro Klautau. In defense of one-vs-all classification. *The Journal of Machine Learning Research*, 5:101–141, 2004.

[22] Dominic Rout, Kalina Bontcheva, Daniel Preoţiuc-Pietro, and Trevor Cohn. Where's@ wally?: a classification approach to geolocating users based on their social ties. In *Proceedings of the 24th ACM Conference on Hypertext and Social Media*, pages 11–20. ACM, 2013.

[23] Wikipedia. Centralismo en Chile — Wikipedia, The Free Encyclopedia. `http://es.wikipedia.org/wiki/Centralismo_en_Chile`, 2013. [In spanish; Online; accessed 2-July-2014. Title translation: "Centralization in Chile"].

[24] Wikipedia. Elecciones municipales de Chile de 2012 — Wikipedia, The Free Encyclopedia. `https://en.wikipedia.org/wiki/Chilean_municipal_election,_2012`, 2013. [Online; accessed 2-July-2014].

[25] Sarita Yardi and Danah Boyd. Tweeting from the Town Square: Measuring Geographic Local Networks. In *Proceedings of the Fourth International AAAI Conference on Weblogs and Social Media*, 2010.

Inferring Nationalities of Twitter Users and Studying Inter-National Linking

Wenyi Huang*
Information Sciences and
Technology
Pennsylvania State University
University Park, PA 16802
harrywy@gmail.com

Ingmar Weber
Qatar Computing Research
Institute
Doha, Qatar
iweber@qf.org.qa

Sarah Vieweg
Qatar Computing Research
Institute
Doha, Qatar
svieweg@qf.org.qa

ABSTRACT

Twitter user profiles contain rich information that allows researchers to infer particular attributes of users' identities. Knowing identity attributes such as gender, age, and/or nationality are a first step in many studies which seek to describe various phenomena related to computational social science. Often, it is through such attributes that studies of social media that focus on, for example, the isolation of foreigners, become possible. However, such characteristics are not often clearly stated by Twitter users, so researchers must turn to other means to ascertain various categories of identity. In this paper, we discuss the challenge of detecting the nationality of Twitter users using rich features from their profiles. In addition, we look at the effectiveness of different features as we go about this task. For the case of a highly diverse country—Qatar—we provide a detailed network analysis with insights into user behaviors and linking preference (or the lack thereof) to other nationalities.

Categories and Subject Descriptors

Applied Computing [**Law, social and behavioral sciences**]: Sociology; Computing methodologies [**Machine Learning**]: Supervised learning by classification

Keywords

Twitter; Qatar; nationality inference; user classification

1. INTRODUCTION

The availability of large amounts of social media data has created new possibilities to study social phenomena at large scale through the lens of online behavior. To obtain insightful results and to "link" these online data to offline, "real-world" variables, it is often useful to have detailed social media user attributes such as gender, age or nationality. Though inferring gender and age from a user's social media presence has been studied before, the latter has, to the best of our knowledge, not been explored. A likely reason for this gap is that in most countries the population is dominated by the "native" nationality. Even in the US, which is often perceived as a country of immigrants, only about 13% of the population are foreign-born[1] and of those, about 45% are American citizens,[2] leaving just over 7% of "foreigners." Due to this nationality skew, even a trivial American-or-Not classifier would have an accuracy of 93% by always reporting "American." However, in Qatar, the *majority* of the population is foreigners, exceeding 85%. This creates a range of challenges related to the identification of national identity. We are interested in potential correlations between national identity and social capital [2], and are curious to know if asking questions about nationality as it manifests on Twitter can lead to different or better understandings of how the two are linked (or not).

To explore this question, we created a classifier that detects the likely nationality of Twitter users based on a range of features, including language, the hashtags they use, and the geographical location of their social ties. We then perform a feature analysis, which leads to an interesting discovery regarding patterns related to the use of particular hashtags, such as #disappointed or #takemeback. These hashtags have a negative connotation, and are linked to people of particular nationalities.

Regarding a definition of a "nationality," we take a simplified approach given our goal: you (a Twitter user) have the nationality that others (CrowdFlower workers) believe you have. We argue that this approach is acceptable for several reasons. First, challenges regarding perception of national origin and impartial treatment are known [22]. Regardless of how individuals self-identify as one nationality or another, the *impression* others have of them factors into conduct and actions (ibid.) Second, we also evaluated the quality of crowdsourced data on a subset of users who explicitly state their nationality in their Twitter profile as in "An American living in Doha" (details in Section 4.3). The agreement between self-stated nationality and crowdsourced labels was 91.86%, which validates the reliability of our crowdsourced data.

2. RELATED WORK

Related work involves user classification on Twitter for attributes ranging from political orientation to gender. In addition, researchers have explored the use of Twitter messages (and similar data) to study a wide range of cultural phenomena.

2.1 Twitter User Classification

Rao et al. [16] introduced the work of classifying latent user attributes including gender, age, regional origin, and political orientation using simple features such as n-gram models, presence of emoticons, number of followers/following and retweet frequency.

---

*The work was done while the author was an intern at QCRI.

---

[1] http://www.census.gov/how/infographics/foreign_born.html
[2] http://www.migrationinformation.org/datahub/state.cfm?ID=US\#3

In [9], the authors extended this work by introducing a two phase architecture for classifying Twitter users. The first part is using basic features for classification, and the second part is to use social graph-information to update classification result. The interesting result is that the first phase alone achieves good performance which is hard to improve by the social graph information. The idea of using information from neighborhood context for classification was first introduced by Pennacchiotti and Popescu [12]. Zamal, Liu, and Ruths extended the previous work by augmenting the user features and neighboring features and boosted the performance of gender, age, political orientation classifications [23]. Burger, Henderson, and Zarrella [3] conducted a study that used only text content for determining the gender of Twitter users. They also included a human performance study using Amazon Mechanical Turk and claimed that the trained model performed better than human assessment. In addition, Cheng et al. [4], Hecht et al. [7] and Mahmud et al. [8] have looked at inferring Twitter user location based on tweet text. Unlike previous research, our study begins to explore the question of nationality detection—a new classification task.

2.2 Social Media and Social Studies

Poblete et al. [13] analyzed and compared Twitter user language, sentiment, content, and network properties in the ten most active countries. In [6], the authors study behavioral patterns on Twitter and associated them with three different cultural dimensions: pace of life, individualism, and power distance. They found that country-level behavior derived from Twitter strongly correlates with said dimensions. Santani and Gatica-Perez [17] presented an analysis of languages used in Switzerland to examine multiculturalism. They used Foursqaure data, and presented a descriptive analysis of linguistic differences and similarities in multiple cities. In our analysis we also came across negative sentiments and worries. This is related to work that looks at the geographical differences in well-being and happiness [14, 15, 18, 10].

3. DEMOGRAPHICS OF QATAR

Geographically, Qatar is located in the center of the Middle Eastern Countries. Although it is a small country, Qatar is one of the wealthiest countries in terms of per-capita income in the world due to oil and gas exploitation. Qatar is currently in a job and construction boom, partly related to the 2022 FIFA World Cup, which is attracting a lot foreign workers. As a result, the country has experienced a significant shift in its population composition, doubling in size to about 2 million in 7 years. Figure 1 shows the population as of 2012, according to the Qatar Statistics Authority and Qatar's Permanent Population Committee [11]. We can see that the demographic composition is very diverse with only 15% of the total population being Qataris, while the rest is mixed, and includes large fractions of Indians, Nepalese, and Filipinos. These statistics show the "offline" demographics of Qatar. Conversely, in our study, we analyze "online" nationalities as found on Twitter.

4. DATASET CONSTRUCTION

To study the online nationality distribution of Qatar, we chose Twitter as a platform due to its wide popularity and relative ease of data access through public APIs. To find a significant number of Twitter users based in Qatar, we made two constraints when querying the APIs: Users should either (i) explicitly state in their profile that they are located in Qatar (in the free text "location" field) or (ii) have at least one geo-tagged tweet originating from Qatar.

A total number of 51,449 candidate Twitter user profiles were collected between April 2013 and June 2013. For these users, we

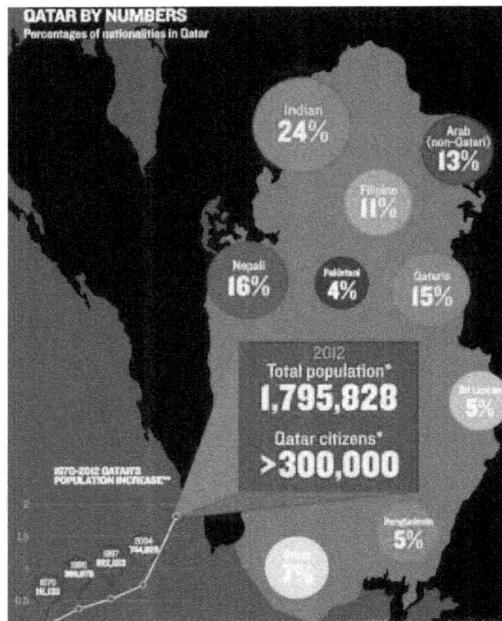

Figure 1: A Glimpse into Qatar's "offline" Demographic.

queried the API to collect all their publicly available tweets (up to 3,200). In total, 54,075,860 tweets were collected. In addition to the tweets' content, we obtained additional meta information such as the (latitude, longitude) for geo-tagged tweets, and information about the device used to post the tweets. To filter out inactive profiles, we restricted our study to 35,780 users who had at least 10 tweets and at least 5 followers and 5 friends.[3] Furthermore, we collect follower and friend user profiles of these 35,780 users, yielding a total of 5,572,765 profiles including their self-declared location. We also obtained profile pictures of the 35,780 Twitter users.

4.1 Preprocessing

A user's nationality is rarely explicitly stated in the profile (e.g. "I am American"), making simple rule-based approaches inappropriate to build a training set. So, to obtain ground truth, and a reasonably sized training set, we turned to crowdsourcing to tag the data. To make the job easy for people to tag, we first preprocessed our data as follows:

- We use language detection tools by Shuyo, Nakatani [19] and run the code on all collected tweets. We calculated tweet language distributions for each Twitter user. In the crowdsourcing jobs, we show the top 3 languages used in tweets for every user.

- We use an R library to convert latitude/longitude pairs from geo-tagged tweets to countries. In the crowdsourcing jobs, we show the top 3 locations along with a small sample of geo-tagged tweets from each location for every user.

- Since most people state their location in natural language, e.g. "NYC," "New York City," and so on, we employed a state-of-the-art geo-coder to map these free texts to explicit countries. We used the Yahoo! Placemaker API[4] for this extraction. We show the top 3 self-stated countries of a user's followers and friends in the crowdsourcing jobs.

---

[3]We are using Twitter's terminology where a "friend" denotes a "followee," the compliment of a follower.
[4]http://developer.yahoo.com/yql/console/\#

238

- We also show other information about the Twitter users available from the Twitter API, such as their name, screen name, profile picture, biography, a link to a homepage, location, time zone, and interface language.

4.2 Data Labeling

We use the Crowdflower platform[5] for crowdsourcing. To create as-easy-as-possible micro-tasks for the contributors, we recreate Twitter profile pages and provide the preprocessed information about each user in the labeling interface. Figure 2 shows an example of our crowdsourcing job.

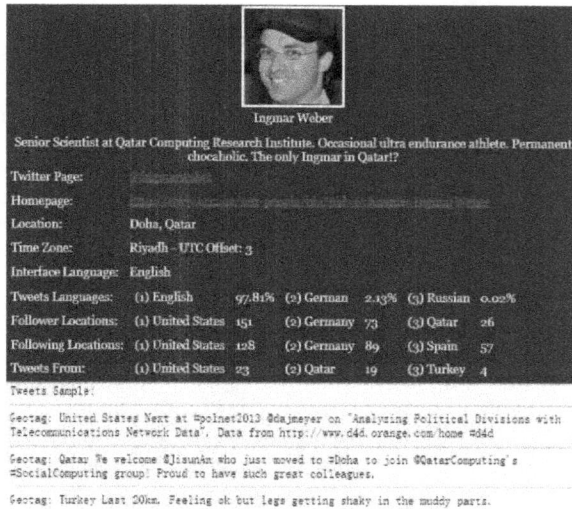

Figure 2: An example of a crowdsourcing task.

To ensure that the contributors correctly understood instructions, and to remove bots and spammers, we created 100 "gold" samples for the so-called "quiz mode." Potential contributors will first only see "gold" samples and must correctly tag at least 8 out of 10 gold samples before they can access non-gold units. For each contributor, we also require at least 3 trustful labels with higher than 66.6% agreement, which means at least two people agreed with each other. If such an agreement is not attained on the first 3 tags, we will require more people to tag the data until the agreement reaches 66.6%.

With respect to nationality group, we divided the Twitter users into 6 groups: Qatari (QA), non-Qatari Arab (ARA), Westerner (WES), Indian Subcontinent (IN), Southeast Asia (SA) and others (OTH). These simplified groups are based on the Social and Economic Survey Research Institute (SESRI) of Qatar University and in other statistics concerning the country's population. We assigned a group Unclear (UN) for Twitter profiles where Crowdflower contributors think there is not enough information to classify them into any of the 6 defined groups.

The tagging process lasted about a week. Figure 3 provides the results of the crowdsource tagging: The online demographics of Twitter users in Qatar is very different from the statistics in Figure 1. We attribute this difference to the fact that many expatriates from the Indian Subcontinent or from Southeast Asia come to Qatar to perform manual labor. Their salaries are often insufficient to permit purchases like smartphones or computers, and access to such devices is difficult. In addition, there is a possibility that unawareness and/or disinterest in Twitter leads to lack of tweet activity, and ability to post and/or read in native languages may not be available.

5 http://crowdflower.com/

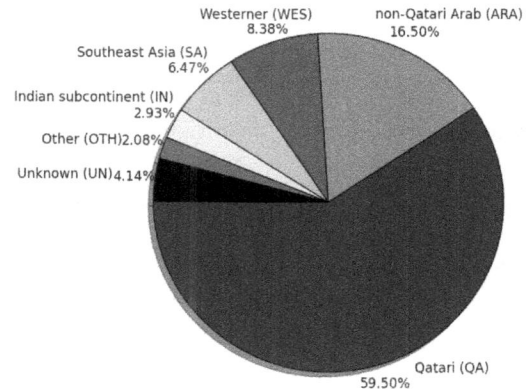

Figure 3: "Online" demographics of Twitter users in Qatar.

4.3 Data Validation

To validate the correctness of the crowdsourced data, we introduced "hidden gold" data to our crowdsource job. Among 35,780 users, 1,210 stated their own nationalities in the profiles. We randomly selected and hand-checked a subset of these users and got 467 profiles which we were 100% sure about their nationalities. For these users, we replaced the nationality words that appeared in their profiles with "XXX" and shuffled them into our crowdsource job. Contributors on Crowdflower.com will be assigned to tag these "hidden gold" data randomly.

After the tagging process was complete, we evaluated the correctness of these "hidden gold" data, which shows that 91.86% of the validation set were correctly tagged.

5. CLASSIFICATION MODEL

In this section, we describe how to build classifiers using the ground truth labels from the crowdsourced data. First, we introduce the features we use for training the classifiers.

5.1 Features

Twitter offers a range of user information with different characteristics, so we chose to first include as much information as possible when generating the features.

Location-related features. There are 4 types of location-related features: 1) Followers' Locations, 2) Friends' Locations, 3) Self-stated Location and 4) geo-tagged tweets' locations. Each feature vector is a 196 dimensional vector with each dimension representing a country;

Time zone. A vector of 24 dimensions with each dimension representing a possible time zone;

Language related features. Due to the limitation of language detection tools, there are 20 possible dimensions for the language-related vector covering the most prominently spoken languages, but it is missing many less-common languages;

HashTags. We collected 7,057 different HashTages which appear more than 5 times in our dataset;

Profile picture features. We use Faceplusplus,[6] a facial recognition API, to estimate basic information from profile pictures. The feature is a three dimensional vector with one dimension representing gender, one representing race, and one for age;

Name ethnicity. We use a name ethnicity detection toolkit by [20] and get a 10 dimensional vector with each dimension representing an ethnicity;

6 http://www.faceplusplus.com/

UTF-8 charset type We check the charset used by each user in their profile, and their tweets. A vector with 209 dimension was formed, with each dimension representing the percentage of a type of charset (in UTF-8).

Tweet source. We collected 571 different utilities that Twitterers used to post tweets.

Mentioned users. Twitter users mentioned in Tweets (people you actually interact with)-this feature includes 3 sub features: 1) self-stated location of mentioned user, 2) interface language of mentioned user, 3) time zone of mentioned user.

Table 1 shows a complete list of features.

Feature	Description & Example
follower loc	[QA: 20, US: 1 , ...]
following loc	similar to follower loc
self loc	[UAE, UK, ...]
geo tag loc	similar to follower loc
time zone	[Abu Dhabi]
tweets lang	[EN: 70.7%, ES: 20.5%, UN: 8.8%]
interface lang	[EN: 1]
hashtag	[#love: 1 , : 1, #Mubarak: 1, ...]
race	[White: 91%, Yellow: 7%, Black: 2%]
age	[Age: 31, age_confidence: 83%]
gender	[Male: 1, gender_confidence : 98%]
name eth	[English: 89%, German: 9%, French: 2%]
charset	[Arabic: 25.1%, Basic Latin: 45.8% , ...]
source	[Twitter for iPhone: 312, Mobile Web: 3 ...]
mention loc	similar to follower loc
mention time zone	similar to time zone
mention lang	similar to interface lang

Table 1: Feature descriptions and examples.

5.2 Gradient Boosted Tree

Gradient Boosted Tree [5] is an effective off-the-shelf procedure for classification. The main advantages of Gradient Boosted Tree are that 1) it can handle data of mixed-type features, and 2) it is very robust regarding outliers in input space. In our case, we may have a lot of noisy data in our constructed feature space, and Gradient Boosted Tree can perform robustly in both training and predicting. Because the dataset is highly unbalanced, we performed our experiments and evaluations using stratified 5-fold cross-validation.

6. RESULT

The best performance of Gradient Boosted Tree was achieved with a number of trees= 300 and the best overall accuracy is 83.8%. In Table 2, we show the overall classification performance (Precision, Recall, F_1 score) for each nationality group. Due to the unbalanced data distribution, we can see that the performance for less populated groups is not very high.

	Pre.	Rec.	F_1
QA	86.67%	95.37%	90.81%
ARA	82.96%	71.16%	76.56%
WES	70.86%	70.62%	70.64%
SA	93.35%	90.48%	91.89%
IN	82.19%	71.13%	76.00%
OTH	78.67%	40.72%	53.54%
UN	30.78%	15.13%	20.16%

Table 2: The average Precision, Recall and F_1 scores for each nationality group.

For a detailed analysis of the trained model, we show the confusion matrix of the classification results in Table 3. Combining the results from Table 2 we can see that the low performance of classifying non-Qatari Arabs is due to the confusion with the group of Qatari citizens. In the following section, we explain why such classification is so challenging.

				Predicted Label			
	QA	ARA	WES	SA	IN	OTH	UN
QA	5439	143	63	10	9	2	37
ARA	404	1125	25	1	5	4	17
WES	125	28	567	12	12	14	45
SA	24	5	16	561	2	0	12
IN	41	2	16	2	200	1	19
OTH	27	10	66	4	0	81	11
UN	216	45	48	11	16	1	60

Table 3: The confusion matrix of the trained classifier.

Table 4 shows the normalized confusion matrix of the human-tagged tweets. As described in section 4.2, the ground truth labels are based on majority votes from the crowdsource workers. This normalized confusion matrix describes the judging agreement among different people. This is trivially "biased" towards a low confusion and low error rate, as when two out of three judges agree on anything, correct or not, it is considered the gold standard. With this caveat in mind, the confusion matrix shows that the performance of human labeling is better than our classification model. However, we can also see from the matrix that it is difficult for humans to distinguish between the Qatari group (QA) and non-Qatari Arabs (ARA). In addition, compared to classification model, unclear labels (UN) appear more frequently when people are confused about the users' nationality (such as "Qatar born, Egyptian blood"). Overall, the human labeling confusion matrix also indicates that our data collection process is satisfactory for further studies.

				Labeling Label			
	QA	ARA	WES	SA	IN	OTH	UN
QA	5158	259	92	8	7	7	169
ARA	86	1418	16	1	1	2	53
WES	27	8	721	3	1	7	32
SA	13	1	10	578	0	2	12
IN	8	2	11	2	239	2	12
OTH	5	3	8	0	0	172	8
UN	76	30	40	11	7	5	224

Table 4: The normalized confusion matrix of the human labelling.

6.1 Feature Analysis

All features do not contribute equally to the classification model. In many cases, the majority of the features contribute little to the classifier and only a small set of discriminative features end up being used. Here, we discuss the importance of different features.

The relative depth of a feature used as a decision node in a tree can be used to assess the importance of the feature. Here, we use the expected fraction of samples each feature contributes to as an estimate of the importance of the feature. By averaging all expected fraction rates over all trees in our trained model, we could estimate the importance for each feature. It is important to note that feature spaces among our selected features are very diverse. The impact of the individual features from a small feature space might not beat the impact of all the aggregate features from a large feature space. So apart from simply summing up all feature spaces within a feature (i.e. sum of all 7, 057 importance scores in hashtag feature), which is referred to as un-normalized in Figure 4, we also plot the normalized relative importance of each features, where each feature's importance score is normalized by the size of the feature space.

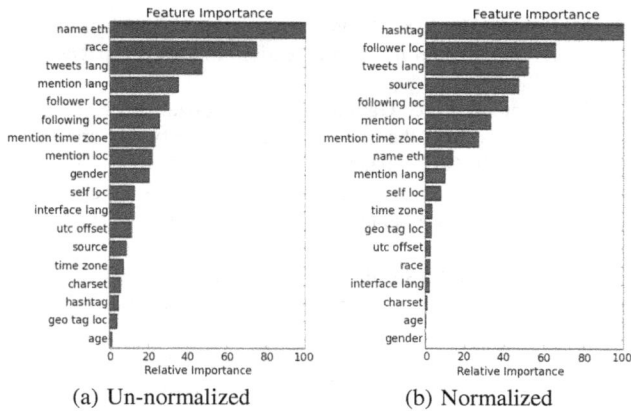

Figure 4: Relative Feature Importance when training the models.

It is not surprising that the hashtag feature—with the largest ranked feature space—ranked first in the un-normalized plot. However, in the normalized plot, this feature ranked very low. One explanation is that *some* hashtags will be quite useful in classification, but the majority of hashtags are often not useful. To justify the explanation, we study the most popular hashtags when training the classifiers in Section 6.1.1. Location-related features like followers/following location and mentioned users' locations are often dominant features. These features, however, are only ranked second (for follower locations) and fifth (for following locations) in un-normalized ranking, being ranked fifth/sixth in normalized ranking. The relative ranking of these can potentially be explained by the fact that many people follow pop stars or international news agencies, but non-famous users are unlikely to be followed by many international users. Tweet language is the third most important feature in both evaluation metrics. We presume that most expatriates from non-Arab countries are unlikely to understand or tweet in Arabic. In the following sections, we take a look at the details of some of the most influential features.

By comparing these two figures, we provide a guideline of feature selection; if you want one feature (or small feature group) to work (to some degree) all the time, then name ethnicity and race are the best choice. But if you want more accurate result, features with a large feature space size (i.e. hashtags) will help improve classification models.

6.1.1 Hashtags

In Figure 5, we plot the most influential hashtags for training the classifier using the Gephi [7] toolkit. Red dots represent Twitter users labeled as Qatari, green dots represent non-Qatari Arabs, blue dots represent Westerners, cyan dots represent Southeast Asians, and yellow dots represent people from the Indian subcontinent. The large gray nodes (mostly overlapped by the textual hashtags) represent each hashtag. This color scheme will be used throughout the remainder of the paper.

From this figure, we observe that certain hashtags are only used by certain groups. For example #IPL (Indian Premier League) only appears among people from the Indian subcontinent, #ihatequotes is used among people from Southeast Asia, and #No_thirsty_in_Qatar are most used among Qataris. Such hashtags serve as "sufficient" features, which means that if such hashtags appear in one's tweets, the classifier will has sufficient information to infer your nationality group. However such "sufficient" features

[7] https://gephi.org/

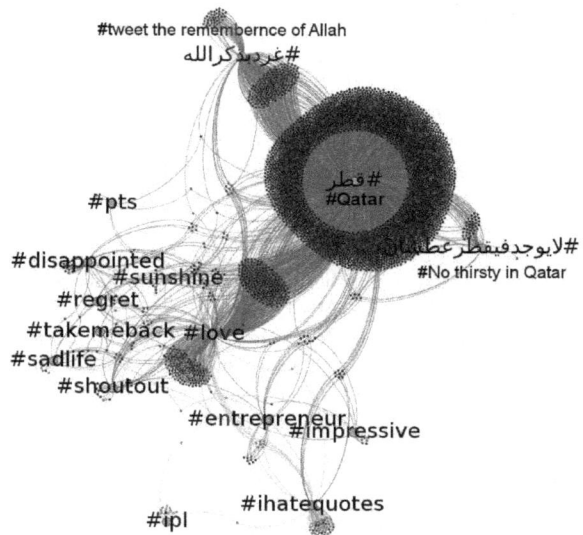

Figure 5: Top 15 important hashtags when training the classifers.

(hashtags) appear comparatively rare as we could see from the figure. Most hashtags provide little information about your nationality (for example #Qatar (in English) #Doha (in English)). This supports our findings in Section 6.1—that the hashtag feature plays an important role in training the classifier. However, if averaged by the size of the feature set, it is not that important because most hashtags contribute very little to the classifier.

Also, this figure shows that the language used in hashtags also provides important information about nationality groups as non-Arab people rarely use Arabic hashtags, and they rarely retweet Arabic hashtags. This is likely due to the language barrier. Also we see that if an Arabic hashtag is related to Qatar, it is most likely tweeted by Qataris.

Compared to Arabs, others are more willing to express personal feelings - at least in English. For example, the hashtag #love has a low percentage of Arab users attached to it when compared to the overall fraction of such users. In addition, foreign expatriates have a much higher probability of expressing negative emotions in tweets. Hashtags like #sadlife, #disappointed, #takemeback are mostly tweeted by this population.

7. CONCLUSIONS

We built a classification model to address the question of how to identify nationalities of Twitter users. We collected the Twitter user profiles from Qatar, and used crowdsourcing to label the dataset. We used Gradient Boosted Tree to model the data and trained a classifier to detect the nationality of Twitter users based on a number of features. A feature analysis study was performed, and we discovered some interesting patterns of user features. The distribution of the inferred online Twitter nationalities does not match the offline reality, mostly due to a selection bias of who is online and on Twitter. However, our methodology is useful for detecting general trends, and—importantly—will serve as a foundation for future work. Exploring the link between social capital, cultural capital [2], and Twitter use and relationships in Qatar are all rich areas of study. Going forward, we plan to combine traditional offline surveys with online data mining approaches. This combination may help unbias online results, e.g. through the use of appropriate re-weighting factors, and it could enrich more limited and structured surveys with rich and multi-faceted analyses.

8. REFERENCES

[1] E. Badger. Map the iphone users in any city, and you know where the rich live, 2013.

[2] P. Bourdieu. *Distinction: A social critique of the judgement of taste*. Harvard University Press, 1984.

[3] J. D. Burger, J. Henderson, G. Kim, and G. Zarrella. Discriminating gender on twitter. In *EMNLP*, pages 1301–1309, 2011.

[4] Z. Cheng, J. Caverlee, and K. Lee. You are where you tweet: a content-based approach to geo-locating twitter users. In *CIKM*, pages 759–768. ACM, 2010.

[5] J. H. Friedman. Stochastic gradient boosting. *Computational Statistics & Data Analysis*, 38(4):367–378, 2002.

[6] R. O. G. Gavilanes, D. Quercia, and A. Jaimes. Cultural dimensions in twitter: Time, individualism and power. In *ICWSM*, 2013.

[7] B. Hecht, L. Hong, B. Suh, and E. H. Chi. Tweets from justin bieber's heart: the dynamics of the location field in user profiles. In *Proceedings of the SIGCHI Conference on Human Factors in Computing Systems*, pages 237–246. ACM, 2011.

[8] J. Mahmud, J. Nichols, and C. Drews. Where is this tweet from? inferring home locations of twitter users. In *ICWSM*, 2012.

[9] A. Mislove, S. Lehmann, Y.-Y. Ahn, J.-P. Onnela, and J. N. Rosenquist. Understanding the demographics of twitter users. In *ICWSM*, pages 554–557, 2011.

[10] L. Mitchell, M. R. Frank, K. D. Harris, P. S. Dodds, and C. M. Danforth. The geography of happiness: Connecting twitter sentiment and expression, demographics, and objective characteristics of place. *PLOS One*, 8, 2013.

[11] C. M. Paschyn. Anatomy of a globalized state. *Think. Issue 2*, 2012.

[12] M. Pennacchiotti and A.-M. Popescu. A machine learning approach to twitter user classification. In *ICWSM*, pages 281–288, 2011.

[13] B. Poblete, R. O. G. Gavilanes, M. Mendoza, and A. Jaimes. Do all birds tweet the same?: characterizing twitter around the world. In *CIKM*, pages 1025–1030, 2011.

[14] D. Quercia, J. Ellis, L. Capra, and J. Crowcroft. Tracking "gross community happiness" from tweets. In *CSCW*, pages 965–968, 2012.

[15] D. Quercia, D. Ó. Séaghdha, and J. Crowcroft. Talk of the city: Our tweets, our community happiness. In *ICWSM*, 2012.

[16] D. Rao, D. Yarowsky, A. Shreevats, and M. Gupta. Classifying latent user attributes in twitter. In *SMUC*, pages 37–44, 2010.

[17] D. Santani and D. Gatica-Perez. Speaking swiss: languages and venues in foursquare. In *ACM Multimedia*, pages 501–504, 2013.

[18] H. A. Schwartz, J. C. Eichstaedt, M. L. Kern, L. Dziurzynski, R. E. Lucas, M. Agrawal, G. J. Park, S. K. Lakshmikanth, S. Jha, M. E. P. Seligman, and L. H. Ungar. Characterizing geographic variation in well-being using tweets. In *ICWSM*, 2013.

[19] N. Shuyo. Language detection library for java, 2010.

[20] P. Treeratpituk and C. L. Giles. Name-ethnicity classification and ethnicity-sensitive name matching. In *AAAI*, 2012.

[21] W. Xie, C. Li, F. Zhu, E.-P. Lim, and X. Gong. When a friend in twitter is a friend in life. In *WebSci*, pages 344–347, 2012.

[22] I. P. Young and J. A. Fox. Asian, hispanic, and native american job candidates: Prescreened or screened within the selection process. *Educational Administration Quarterly*, 38(4):530–554, 2002.

[23] F. A. Zamal, W. Liu, and D. Ruths. Homophily and latent attribute inference: Inferring latent attributes of twitter users from neighbors. In *ICWSM*, pages 387–390, 2012.

Sociolinguistic Analysis of Twitter in Multilingual Societies*

Suin Kim
KAIST
Republic of Korea
suin.kim@kaist.ac.kr

Ingmar Weber
Qatar Computing
Research Institute
iweber@qf.org.qa

Li Wei
Birkbeck,
University of London
li.wei@bbk.ac.uk

Alice Oh
KAIST
Republic of Korea
alice.oh@kaist.edu

ABSTRACT

In a multilingual society, language not only reflects culture and heritage, but also has implications for social status and the degree of integration in society. Different languages can be a barrier between monolingual communities, and the dynamics of language choice could explain the prosperity or demise of local languages in an international setting. We study this interplay of language and network structure in diverse, multi-lingual societies, using Twitter. In our analysis, we are particularly interested in the role of bilinguals. Concretely, we attempt to quantify the degree to which users are the "bridge-builders" between monolingual language groups, while monolingual users cluster together. Also, with the revalidation of English as a *lingua franca* on Twitter, we reveal users of the native non-English language have higher influence than English users, and the language convergence pattern is consistent across the regions. Furthermore, we explore for which topics these users prefer their native language rather than English. To the best of our knowledge, this is the largest sociolinguistic study in a network setting.

Categories and Subject Descriptors

J.4 [**Social and Behavioral Sciences**]: Sociology

Keywords

Multilingualism; Sociolinguistics; Topic Modeling; Social Media

1. INTRODUCTION

The language we speak is an integral part of our culture. We use it to communicate, to transmit facts and emotions, and to navigate the social environment surrounding us. In multilingual societies such as Canada or Switzerland, the spoken language can even

---

*This work was done while the first author was at Qatar Computing Research Institute.

be a political statement with wide-ranging implications. In some cases, governments subsidize programs to save a language from disappearing. At the individual level, people who are fortunate to be bilingual constantly make a choice in favor of or against one or the other language. Anecdotally, even after mastering a second language many people continue to count (and swear [14]) in their mother tongue. At the societal level, the question arises to which degree bilinguals are the "glue" that keeps multilingual societies together.

We study the phenomena of multilingual societies and the role that bilinguals play in them by using large amounts of Twitter data. Social media data has the fascinating component of also containing a *network*. These social links allow us to investigate the interaction between a user's language and their social surroundings. Understanding this interaction has a number of potential implications:

- *Preservation of a language.* Assuming that you are bilingual and that all of your friends understand English reasonably well, but not all understand your native language. Should you switch your language to maximize your audience size?

- *Social capital*[8] *and potential issues of segregation.* Is it possible to build social ties across language barriers? Which role do bilinguals play in this "bridge-building"?

- *Social status and language assimilation.* Eliza Doolittle in George Bernard Shaw's "Pygmalion"/"My Fair Lady" underwent a huge change in social status by learning a new language, though just a "high class dialect" in this case. Generally, are there elite languages in multi-lingual societies?

- *Language selection.* How do bilinguals choose one language over the other for a given topic? Do they prefer their mother tongue for issues "close to the heart"? Correspondingly, is the same topic discussed differently in different languages?

We explore these questions with large-scale Twitter data from several multilingual societies. We analyze the Twitter following behavior to uncover whether monolingual users form tightly connected clusters, what bridging roles multilingual users play, and which language groups show higher social status. We apply language processing to analyze the amount of language usage depending on the surrounding network, and probabilistic topic modeling to discover the differences in topics in different languages by multilingual users. Methodologically, we propose metrics for quantifying language use and network diversity in multilingual Twitter network, and we illustrate techniques from machine learning applied to multilingual tweets.

2. RELATED WORK

There is now widespread recognition among linguists that social media such as Twitter are highly multilingual and provide an immense volume of real-world language data. Several studies in sociolinguistics have explored Twitter and other online language [6, 9, 3, 22, 12, 34, 17, 2, 4], and in particular, social scientists have examined the strategic use of multilingualism on Twitter in recent political movements [30]. However, these studies are limited in scope, which require computational tools for a systematic analysis of multilingualism that involves both network analysis and language processing at a large scale.

More recently, sociolinguists, together with computer scientists, have tried to map out linguistic diversity through spatial and temporal analyses of multilingual Twitter. Studies by [5] and [24] have revealed the extensive use of a large number of different languages in Manchester, discovering Twitter users in Manchester are connected globally and use languages other than those recorded in the local census. Similarly, [25] used Twitter to detect the extent of multilingualism in London, which revealed that there are specific geographical concentrations of monolingual users of different languages. The processes of language shift, language attrition, language loss, language endangerment and language death were also investigated [19, 15, 18, 23, 31]. The related but different process is competition between different groups of language users [33, 29]. While groups with more socio-economic power often have a crucial impact on the spread of particular language, the size of the speaker group also plays a significant role. It has been shown that a single monolingual speaker of a particular language may hold the key to the survival of the language in the bilingual community, as the bilingual speakers try to accommodate the monolingual speaker [16, 20]. It then follows that relatively low number of language users could have a snowballing effect and prompt the majority to use a specific language in Twitter. A number of mathematical models for language competition have been proposed [1, 10, 28].

Social scientists, especially sociolinguists, have long been interested in the role language plays in the formation of social networks and in how structures of social networks impact on language practices [26, 13]. Relatively little is known about the role multilingualism plays in forming these networks and how the virtual networks impact on multilingual practices. While it is expected that speakers would identify themselves more easily with others who share the same languages, therefore forming language-specific clusters, it is not clear how monolinguals and bilinguals would pattern in relation to each other. Understanding the pattern of connections between monolingual and bilingual speakers would not only offer a new perspective on multilingualism on the social media, but also provide new insights into the societal structures and human relations in multilingual societies.

3. DATA COLLECTION AND LANGUAGE DETECTION

We collected Twitter data (recent tweets and friend/follower lists) from two countries (Qatar, Switzerland) and Quebec province in Canada. We identified Twitter accounts from two sources. First, we used Twitter streams provided by GNIP as part of a trial period. These streams comprise (i) about 28 hours of Firehose stream (ii) two weeks of decahose stream, both around June to August 2013. Users with at least one geo-tagged tweet from Qatar and Switzerland are considered as candidates. Another source of Twitter accounts is the location information from the public user profile

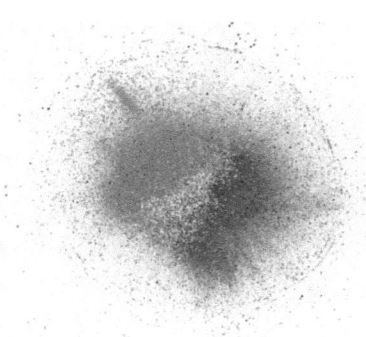

Figure 1: Visualization of Qatar Twitter network. Each node and edge represents user and followings in the Twitter networks. Each node is colored by the language usage from corresponding user's tweets. AR-EN Bilingual users are located between monolingual clusters.

Figure 2: Language distribution of the Twitter users for each region. The upper bar illustrates the distribution of language usage, and the lower bar shows the distribution of mono-, bi-, and trilingual users. For all regions there are < 1% of trilingual users.

using Followerwonk[1]. To capture users with only the city names, for each of the three countries we compiled lists of cities with more than 10^6 inhabitants, along with the names translated into multiple languages using Wikipedia entries. After identifying users from the regions of interest, we used the Twitter API to crawl all their *friends* (= *followings*) and *followers*, and up to 3,200 recent tweets for each user. Table 1 shows the statistics of the Twitter data. We ignored inactive users with fewer than 5 tweets. Then, we classified the language used in each tweet, which is not a trivial task because a large number of tweets contain very little information for language classification [24] and a single tweet can mix multiple languages. To optimize language classification accuracy against these challenges, we aggregated all tweets for each user into a document of tweets. After removing mentions, hashtags, and URLs, we used Compact Language Detector 2 [2] and detected the top three languages with their approximate percentages of the text bytes in the document. We define users as speaking a language if they have $\geq$ 15% of text bytes written in the respective language. Figure 2 shows the distribution of language usage.

---

[1]https://followerwonk.com/bio
[2]https://code.google.com/p/cld2/

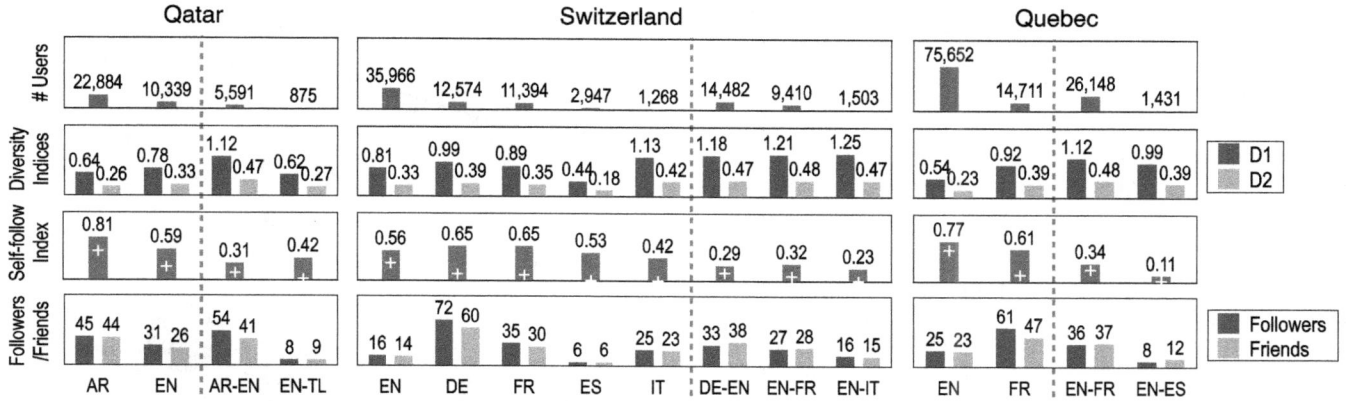

Figure 3: Network measurements for lingua groups in each multilingual region. Diversity indices D_1 (Eq. 2) and D_2 (Eq. 3) are calculated based on the distribution of the edges toward the lingua groups. *Self-follow Index* (Eq. 4) measures the probability that a new edge from a user would be directed to another user in the same lingua group. $+$ marks the baseline for *Self-follow Index*, based on purely random edges.

4. QUANTIFYING LANGUAGE USE AND NETWORK CHARACTERISTICS

In this section, we present a quantitative analysis for discovering social structure in the multilingual societies. After labeling each user by the language they tweet, we created a network for each region with nodes representing users and directed edges representing Twitter following relationships. Table 1 shows the statistics and network measurements for the five networks.

We first define a *lingua* as a mono- or multi-lingual combination of languages. We also define S is the set of all possible linguae, for instance, {EN, AR, AR-EN, DE-EN-FR, ...}. The "lingua group", U_i^r, is the set of users speaking lingua i in region r. We quantify the distribution of linguae for each region r using Shannon entropy:

$$H(r) = -\sum_{i \in S} p_i^r \log_2 p_i^r, \qquad (1)$$

where p_i^r indicating the fraction of users speaking lingua i over the Twitter population of our data in region r. Higher $H(r)$ indicates that there is an even distribution of linguae over the population, and the entropy value for each region is shown in Table 1. As Figure 2 shows, Switzerland has the most diverse distribution of linguae, followed by Qatar and Quebec.

DATA STATISTICS			
Region	#Users	#Edges	#Tweets
Qatar	41,782	1,496,491	43,305,962
Switzerland	83,777	2,187,340	51,725,870
Quebec	110,434	3,074,463	73,676,397

NETWORK MEASUREMENTS			
Region	$H(r)^*$	Avg. degree	GCC** (%)
Qatar	1.403	71.63	99.50
Switzerland	2.195	52.22	98.77
Quebec	1.097	55.68	99.57

Table 1: Data Statistics and network measurements. Edges (directed) represent followings. See Eq. 1 for *$H(r)$, for which higher value indicates that the distribution of languages in the region is less skewed. **GCC, node coverage of the greatest connected component over the network, is calculated with undirected edges.

Figure 1 shows the visualization of the networks. We used Gephi[3] software for plotting with the Yifan Hu graph layout algorithm. For the purpose of illustration, we highlighted the bilingual users. This visualization shows that monolingual users cluster together, while bilinguals are located between the two monolingual groups. To quantify this observation, we measured the diversity of outlinks for each lingua group. We first labeled and grouped users by the lingua. Then, we counted the edges between the groups. To calculate this, we define e_{ij}^r as the edge from user i to j in region r, pointing from Twitter follower i to the friend j. E_{ij}^r is the set of respective edges. Then we define P_{ij}^r as the proportion of the number of edges from i to j over the all outgoing edges from i. Formally,

$$|E_{ij}^r| = \sum_{a \in U_i^r, b \in U_j^r} e_{a,b}^r = \sum_{e \in E_{ij}^r} e \quad \text{and}$$

$$P_{ij}^r = |E_{ij}^r| / \sum_{k \in S} |E_{ik}^r|.$$

Diversity Measures. We first define D_1, based on Shannon Entropy of outgoing links for language subgroup i in region r, so that a lower D_1 indicates that outgoing edges will be more concentrated to a single lingua group. And we define D_2 using Simpson Index, the special version of inverse True diversity:

$$D_1(r, i) = -\sum_{j \in S} P_{ij}^r \log_2 P_{ij}^r \qquad (2)$$

$$D_2(r, i) = 1 - \sum_{j \in S} (P_{ij}^r)^2 \qquad (3)$$

D_2 is used in [21] as *Participation coefficient*, to measure how a node's connections are 'well-distributed', and from definitions, a lingua group with lower D_1 or D_2 has more concentrated outlinks into the small set of lingua groups. Since these metrics can only quantify the general shape of distribution, whether it is diverse or concentrated, we define *Self-follow index*, the probability of making a homogeneous connection when creating new edge from each user in a group. Higher intra-edges with lower inter-edges indicate the average user tends to follows another from the same language group. We call self-follow index of a lingua group as the average of self-follow index of all users in the group. The self-follow index

---

[3] http://gephi.org

of user a, region r and lingua group i is defined as

$$P(a) = (\sum_{b \in U_i^r} e_{a,b}^r)/(\sum_{j \in S} \sum_{b \in U_j^r} e_{a,b}^r). \qquad (4)$$

Monolinguals Cluster Together. For all three regions, we found that monolingual groups consistently show lower D_1 scores than multilingual groups. As in D_1, monolingual groups have higher D_2 when compared to the multilingual groups in the same region except for the English monolinguals. Figure 3 shows both D_1 and D_2 for each group. We also found that monolingual lingua groups have higher self-follow index than any bilingual groups in all regions. The results from three diversity metrics and Intra-Inter edge ratio suggests that users in monolingual subgroups have a strong tendency to follow users inside of the same subgroup, while bilinguals do not.

Users of Local Language have Higher Influence. We explore the question of language use and social status, which we estimate simply with the number of followers, as studies have shown that tweets from a user with a high in-degree are more likely to be retweeted [11, 32]. We first look at the mean and median of the number of followers and friends of users in each lingua group within the network. This is to approximate the user's intra-region social status by excluding the effect toward the outside of the network in our data. To minimize the effects of outliers we removed the top and bottom 10% of users for the number of followers and friends. Figure 3 shows the average number of followers and friends for each lingua group in three regions, and median strictly followed the mean numbers. In all three regions and all lingua groups, we found that the number of friends is always larger than the number of followers. Also, for all three regions, users tweeting in the local language have more followers and friends, even when there are more English monolinguals in the dataset, such as in Switzerland and Quebec. This phenomenon shows that users tweeting in the local language exert higher influence within the regional network.

5. ANALYSIS OF BILINGUAL GROUPS

In this section, we analyze questions such as: Do bilinguals act as bridges between monolingual groups? Is there a pattern of language convergence where, say, when your audience contains a certain fraction of English-only speakers you switch to English?

Bilinguals and English Act as Bridges. The previous section showed that monolinguals form clusters. Now we analyze the mono- and bilingual bridges that glue multilingual societies together, as well as help to avoid language-ghettoization. We first visualize how monolingual and multilingual users follow each other. Figure 4 shows the ratio of follows among lingua groups in the three regions. A node represents a lingua group, and the size of a node corresponds to the relative number of users in that group. We only show nodes for the lingual groups that are represented in Figure 3. Only edges with weight higher 10% are shown to avoid visual clutter. To calculate the numbers underlying the figure, we first get the follow distribution toward lingua groups for each user, then averaged the distributions for all users in the same lingua group. We found that bilingual groups bridge monolingual groups. The key findings are (i) English acts as a hub language, meaning monolingual groups are connected through a X-EN bilingual group, or through the EN group, (ii) Bilingual group X-Y bridges two monolingual groups X and Y, (iii) In-group following takes the largest proportion for monolingual groups, and (iv) Monolingual users do not follow monolingual users of another language.

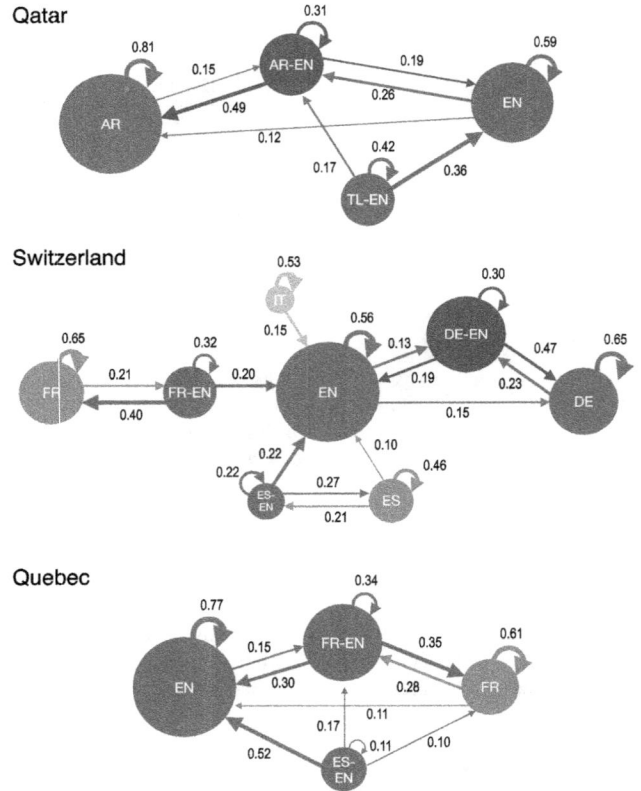

Figure 4: Following patterns among lingua groups. The color of an edge corresponds to the source color of the edge. Following distribution normalized for each user and averaged over group. The number for each edge corresponds to the ratio of the followings over all from source group. Edges having weight > 0.10 are shown.

For all three regions, we found that English users communicate with bilingual groups. Specifically, monolingual groups are strongly connected with respective bilingual groups, which in turn are connected to the EN group. Such connection property forms a star-shaped network with EN group as a hub. Our observation that English acts as a hub language revalidates the prior finding that English is used as a lingua franca in Twitter.

Language Convergence Consistent Across Regions. Given that the tweets are broadcast to every follower, how should multilinguals choose their language? A game-theoretic approach with an objective of "maximizing the audience" might predict that it requires the users to switch to the language of largest fraction. This could then quickly lead to a global convergence to a single lingua franca and pose a threat to the preservation of language. We investigate this issue by looking at the language distribution of bilingual users on Twitter. A user who at least occasionally tweets in different language has a choice and could use either language. How does their tweet mixing ratio, i.e., the fraction of tweets in English, depend on the mixing ratio of their followers, i.e., the average tweet mixing ratio of their followers, bilingual or not? If we were to observe a steep, threshold-like shape of the curve for English, where bilinguals predominantly use English as soon as a small fraction of their followers use only English, then this would spell trouble for the "native" languages.

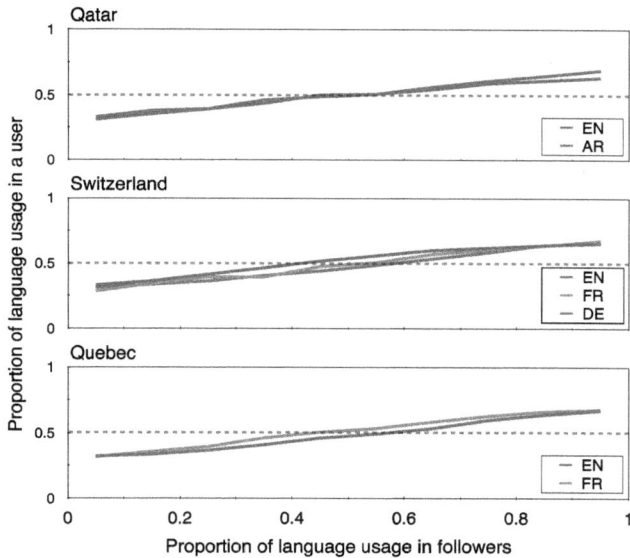

Figure 5: Trendline for the relation between language usage of a bilingual user and their monolingual friends. The X-axis indicates the average percentage of monolingual followers for a user and the language of interest. The Y-axis indicates the average percentage of a bilingual user's tweets in that language.

Figure 5 plots the language distribution of a bilingual user's monolingual friends on the x-axis and the language distribution of bilingual users with the corresponding language distribution among followers on the y-axis. To draw a trend line, we divide the x axis into ten bins, and average users' proportion of language usage for each bin. Users having < 5 followers in the induced network are filtered out. The observed pattern is very consistent among languages and geographical regions. Simply put, bilingual users "mimic" the language mix observed among their followers.[4] Though the equality does not hold for users at either end of the spectrum, say, with 90% English among their followers, this is likely an artifact as we only consider bilinguals. While it is still possible that a large number of users have already been converted to monolingual users, The very smooth and consistent pattern suggests that the language conversion process is more gradual than one might have expected.

Bilinguals Post Different Stories in Different Language. To gain a deeper understanding of the role of bilingual users in a multilingual society, we analyze the contents of the tweets from bilingual users. To observe any systematic differences in language use, we use a parallel set of tweets containing the same hashtags in two languages, train a topic model on those tweets to reveal the differences in the topics of the same hashtags. For this analysis, we train latent Dirichlet allocation model [7] to discover the topics and analyze any differences in information depending on the language. We did not use the Polylingual topic model[27], as it requires a corpus of documents in different languages with similar topics. After running LDA for each language and we translated the top words into English. We avoid the topic alignment problem by using the set of translated hashtag pairs. For instance, we use (#suisse - #switzerland) for EN-FR in Switzerland, and respective country hashtag pairs for other regions. We set the number of topics for each set,

---

[4]We observed nearly identical plots when we also included bilingual followers for the x-axis and "bucketed" them according to their tweet mixing ratio.

QATAR, AR-EN BILINGUAL		
#	Label	Top words
قطر#	development	national doha development vision
	government	government national qa foundation
	emir/god	hamad bin god sheikh tamim emir
	gcc countries	doha egypt kuwait bahrain uae
#qatar	national day	day national doha gcc about today
	sports event	doha volleyball football uae photo
	photography	instagram katara instagood love
	recruitment	job please send cv recruitment org
SWITZERLAND, EN-FR BILINGUAL		
#suisse	politics	more country politics no federal
	news/radio	ch news tar info thank you radio
	recruitment	job manager head senior engineer
	ski	ski weather romandie snow rentals
#switzerland	scenery	lake sun sky sunset beautiful night
	greeting	love like time good show morning
	party/club	club dj party enjoy welcome house
	wine/fashion	fashion valais basel wine beautiful

Table 2: Part of the topics discovered from tweets containing country hashtags and are posted by bilinguals. Topics are manually labeled from the top words. We translated the most frequent words into English. We do not display stopwords and region names. For all three regions, tweets containing local language hashtag are mainly of informative/political/debatable topics, while tweets containing English hashtag are event/tour/enjoyment topics.

$k = 10$, and after fitting the model we use Google translate service to translate words into English. We set $\alpha = 50/k$ and $\beta = 0.01$ for LDA. Table 2 shows the part of topics from two regions. We found that from all bilingual groups in three regions, bilingual users post *informational and political* tweets for the local audience in local language. They, on the other hand, post *events, tourism, photography*, and other *leisure-related* tweets in English for the non-local audience. These results show that our methodology of identifying bilingual Twitter users and analyzing the topics of their tweets can reveal the semantics of communications among multiple language speakers in a multilingual society.

6. CONCLUSION

We presented a large-scale computational analysis of language use and network characteristics of the language-based groups in multilingual societies using Twitter data. Using the extensive set of tweets from monolingual and bilingual users from Qatar, Switzerland, and Quebec, we first discovered that monolingual users cluster together, while bilinguals do not. Then, we revealed that users speaking local language have more influence than others. Additionally, we have shown that, surprisingly, the language-mixing ratio of bilingual users closely mirrors the mix of their followership. Then we showed that bilinguals bridge between monolinguals with English as a hub, while monolinguals tend not to directly follow each other. Finally, with the statistical topic model, we discovered that bilinguals express informative/political/debatable topics in a local language, while posting event/tour/enjoyment topics on the English.

Acknowledgements

This research was funded by the MSIP (Ministry of Science, ICT & Future Planning), Korea in the ICT R&D Program 2014.

7. REFERENCES

[1] D. M. Abrams and S. H. Strogatz. Linguistics: Modelling the dynamics of language death. *Nature*, 2003.

[2] J. Androutsopoulos. Language choice and code-switching in german-based diasporic web forums. *The multilingual Internet*, 2007.

[3] J. Anis. Neography: Unconventional spelling in french sms text messages. *The multilingual Internet*, 2007.

[4] A.-S. Axelsson, Å. Abelin, and R. Schroeder. Anyone speak swedish? tolerance for language shifting in graphical multi-user virtual environmnets. *The multilingual Internet*, 2007.

[5] G. Bailey, J. Goggins, and T. Ingham. http://mlm.humanities.manchester.ac.uk/reports/Twitter%20and%20Language%20Diversity.pdf.

[6] S. Bergsma, P. McNamee, M. Bagdouri, C. Fink, and T. Wilson. Language identification for creating language-specific twitter collections. In *LASM*. ACL, 2012.

[7] D. M. Blei, A. Y. Ng, and M. I. Jordan. Latent dirichlet allocation. *JMLR*, 2003.

[8] P. Bourdieu. *Distinction: A social critique of the judgement of taste*. Harvard University Press, 1984.

[9] S. Carter, W. Weerkamp, and M. Tsagkias. Microblog language identification: Overcoming the limitations of short, unedited and idiomatic text. *Language Resources and Evaluation*, 2013.

[10] X. Castelló, V. M. Eguíluz, and M. San Miguel. Ordering dynamics with two non-excluding options: bilingualism in language competition. *New Journal of Physics*, 2006.

[11] M. Cha, H. Haddadi, F. Benevenuto, and P. K. Gummadi. Measuring user influence in twitter: The million follower fallacy. *ICWSM*, 2010.

[12] S. Climent, J. Moré, A. Oliver, M. Salvatierra, I. Sànchez, and M. Taulé. Can machine translation enhance the status of catalan versus spanish in online academic forums? *B. Danet & S. Herring (Eds.), The multilingual Internet*, 2007.

[13] X. Daming, W. Xiaomei, and L. Wei. 15 social network analysis. *The Blackwell guide to research methods in bilingualism and multilingualism*, 2008.

[14] J.-M. Dewaele. Blistering barnacles! what language do multilinguals swear in? *Estudios de Sociolinguistica*, 2004.

[15] N. C. Dorian. *Language death: The life cycle of a Scottish Gaelic dialect*. University of Pennsylvania Press Philadelphia, 1981.

[16] N. C. Dorian. *Investigating obsolescence: Studies in language contraction and death*. Cambridge University Press, 1992.

[17] M. Durham. Language choice on a swiss mailing list. *JCMC*, 2003.

[18] J. A. Fishman. *Reversing language shift: Theoretical and empirical foundations of assistance to threatened languages*. Multilingual matters, 1991.

[19] S. Gal. *Language shift: Social determinants of linguistic change in bilingual Austria*. Academic Press New York, 1979.

[20] L. A. Grenoble and L. J. Whaley. *Endangered languages: Language loss and community response*. Cambridge University Press, 1998.

[21] R. Guimera and L. A. N. Amaral. Functional cartography of complex metabolic networks. *Nature*, 2005.

[22] C. K.-M. Lee. Linguistic features of email and icq instant messaging in hong kong. *The multilingual Internet*, 2007.

[23] W. Li. *Three generations, two languages, one family: Language choice and language shift in a Chinese community in Britain*. Multilingual Matters, 1994.

[24] M. Mainguy, Y. Nakai, and M. Takayama. http://mlm.humanities.manchester.ac.uk/reports/Mapping%20Mancunian%20Multilingualism%20on%20Twitter.pdf.

[25] E. Manley. http://urbanmovements.co.uk/2012/10/23/detecting-languages-in-londonstwittersphere/.

[26] L. Milroy. *Language and social networks*. B. Blackwell, 1987.

[27] D. Mimno, H. M. Wallach, J. Naradowsky, D. A. Smith, and A. McCallum. Polylingual topic models. In *EMNLP*, pages 880–889, 2009.

[28] J. W. Minett and W. S. Wang. Modelling endangered languages: The effects of bilingualism and social structure. *Lingua*, 2008.

[29] S. S. Mufwene. *Language evolution: Contact, competition and change*. Continuum International Publishing Group, 2008.

[30] T. Poell and K. Darmoni. Twitter as a multilingual space: The articulation of the tunisian revolution through #sidibouzid. *NECSUS*, 2012.

[31] M. S. Schmid. *Language attrition*. Cambridge University Press Cambridge,, UK, 2011.

[32] B. Suh, L. Hong, P. Pirolli, and E. H. Chi. Want to be retweeted? large scale analytics on factors impacting retweet in twitter network. In *SocialCom*. IEEE, 2010.

[33] R. Wardhaugh. *Languages in competition: Dominance, diversity, and decline*. B. Blackwell, 1987.

[34] M. Warschauer, G. R. E. Said, and A. G. Zohry. Language choice online: Globalization and identity in egypt. *JCMC*, 2002.

Co-Following on Twitter

Venkata Rama Kiran Garimella[*]
Aalto University
Espoo, Finland
kiran.garimella@aalto.fi

Ingmar Weber
Qatar Computing Research Institute
Doha, Qatar
iweber@qf.org.qa

ABSTRACT

We present an in-depth study of co-following on Twitter based on the observation that two Twitter users whose followers have similar friends are also similar, even though they might not share any direct links or a single mutual follower. We show how this observation contributes to (i) a better understanding of language-agnostic user classification on Twitter, (ii) eliciting opportunities for Computational Social Science, and (iii) improving online marketing by identifying cross-selling opportunities.

We start with a machine learning problem of predicting a user's preference among two alternative choices of Twitter friends. We show that co-following information provides strong signals for diverse classification tasks and that these signals persist even when the most discriminative features are removed.

Going beyond mere classification performance optimization, we present applications of our methodology to Computational Social Science. Here we confirm stereotypes such as that the country singer Kenny Chesney (@kennychesney) is more popular among @GOP followers, whereas Lady Gaga (@ladygaga) enjoys more support from @TheDemocrats followers.

In the domain of marketing we give evidence that celebrity endorsement is reflected in co-following and we demonstrate how our methodology can be used to reveal the audience similarities between not so obvious entites such as Apple and Puma.

1. INTRODUCTION

How much does following a particular set of people reveal about your interests? Does the fact that you follow @Starbucks make it more likely that you follow @TheDemocrats as well? And can Twitter users be grouped in a meaningful way by looking at whether their followers have similar friends[1]?

Such questions are relevant to at least three lines of research. First, there is lots of work on user classification on Twitter, e.g., [7, 8, 3]. Such classifiers often rely on language-specific tools such as stemming or dictionaries with special terms. Our work shows that

---

[*]Most of this work was done while the author was at QCRI.

[1]We use the term "friend" as Twitter terminology referring to another Twitter user that a user follows.

such information might not be required and a language-agnostic method using a user's friends as features achieves ROC-AUC of .80-.85 for a wide range of binary classification tasks. Second, online social networks are becoming a more and more important data source for Computational Social Science [16, 6]. We contribute to this area by showing how things such as "lifestyle politics" can be studied by using co-following information. Lastly, Twitter with its user base of several hundreds of millions is an important advertising and marketing platform. We show how followership-based similarity methods can be used to identify accounts with a similar audience in terms of interests which could create cross-selling opportunities.

Most of our analysis is centered around 18 rivalries such as @GOP vs. @TheDemocrats or @McDonalds vs. @BurgerKing. In many cases the two alternatives are arguably interchangeable and one might not expect a big difference between the interests of the followers of, say, @Hertz and @Avis. For each of these seed pairs we obtained up to 2,000 random followers. Their friends are used to construct feature vectors and we perform an in-depth analysis of the co-following behavior. We also construct the same kind of vectors for a set of popular musicians, and in all cases the basic hypothesis is that users following similar users are similar and that this propagates to their friends. Our findings include the following.

1. Using *solely* language-agnostic co-following information provides strong signals concerning a user's preference even among arguably interchangeable choices such as @Hertz or @Avis.

2. Such classification is robust with respect to the removal of the most strongly and often obviously related co-following features.

3. Aggregated signals from the general crowd work better for distinguishing binary preferences than relying on the most similar users in a k-NN fashion.

4. A feature analysis confirms stereotypes such that @ladygaga is more popular among @TheDemocrats followers, but also reveals less expected patterns such as that @SnoopDogg followers tend to prefer @Pepsi over @CocaCola.

5. There is evidence that celebrity endorsement works as following a celebrity increases the probability of following the related product.

6. Groups of related Twitter accounts, such as musicians, can be mapped in a simple manner by looking at their followers' friends.

7. Such a mapping reveals Republicans' preference for Miller's beers, Democrats' preference for Budweiser, and the fact that Apple and Puma target a similar, metropolitan audience.

To the best of our knowledge, this is the first such study of co-following on Twitter. We hope that both our analysis and our tools will be of interest to researchers working on user classification, Computational Social Science, or on social media marketing.

2. RELATED WORK

A key assumption to group users based on the similarity of their followers' friends is that following is an expression of topical interests or demographic similarity, rather than personal contacts. Kwak et al. [15] observe that Twitter is more of a news source than a social network, which is *good* for our applications as this indicates that follower/friend links are more related to user interests than social connections.

Related to our approach of using co-following to measure user similarity is the work in [2] where An et al. use the common audience of two Twitter accounts as a measure of closeness. This differs fundamentally from our methodology as we use *second order* co-following. Concretely, two accounts that do not share a single follower are considered similar by us if their followers share many friends. We believe that such an approach is preferable to break out of the "homophily ghetto" where users follow what their friends follow. It also allows for a more far-reaching notion of similarity that could be used to, say, align political parties in different countries on a common spectrum, even if no user follows parties in two distinct countries [24].

Several papers have looked at various Twitter user classification tasks, typically for (i) political orientation in the US, (ii) gender, and (iii) age [19, 21, 26, 7, 8, 3]. This line of work usually involves a broad set of features, including textual content, network and activity based features, as well as a variety of classification approaches that make use of label-propagation across social links. Our approach differs from these in a number of ways. First, the binary classification task of "does the user follow A or B" is different. Second, we do not use any content-based features. Third, we do not use any retweet signals as we are not interested in the sparse network of interests that users strongly engage with, but rather the larger network of "weak interests". Fourth, we do not make use of label-propagation across social links as we are not interested in methods that work for (and re-inforce) "information bubbles" but we are looking for approaches that can be transferred to completely new domains where users do not yet have any direct social ties. Finally, the actual classification performance is of less interest to us than an understanding of how much information is contained in co-following and how this could be used for different applications.

Our mapping and visualization of similar accounts is conceptually similar to community detection/clustering which also identifies groups of related accounts [17, 18, 11]. Our approach, presented in Section 5 is different from these, as we do not require a global view of the entire network as we are only interested in understing the relative positions of the main users. Also, we do not want to find communities induced by friends-of-friends type links. Rather we strive for a similarity-only based approach that can easily be transferred to domains without any friends-of-friend links.

Determining which of two alternatives a Twitter user is more likely to follow is related to friend recommendation or link prediction as, in a sense, we are suggesting which of the two links should be formed. Intuitively, transitivity and mutuality of links are important signals for link prediction [12] but, as discussed previously, we do not want to use such "three people you follow also follow X" information as it leads to a different type of application, closer to community detection. User similarity based on user attributes has also been used as a feature for link prediction [25, 13]. But this work still partly relies on mutuality and transitivity, which is equivalent to re-enforcing partisan camps without noting any existing similarities in terms of shared interests. For example, such approaches would most likely fail to pick up the similarity between @Puma and @TheAppleInc that we observe. Weber et al. [24] present applications of the idea of second order co-following for making out-of-context recommendations of musicians and politicians.

3. DATA

Our data set is constructed around a set of *Twitter seed accounts*. These accounts correspond to "rivalries" between two entities such as @CocaCola vs. @Pepsi or @Samsung vs. @TheAppleInc. The full list of 18 account pairs can be found in Table 1. The list of these rivalries was obtained from Fortune.com.[2] Later, we also look at *groups* of seed accounts, namely, Twitter accounts for (i) popular musicians, and (ii) all the 18 rivalries combined. In all cases, we first obtained a list of all the accounts' followers. From this list we then sampled uniformly at random a set of 2,000 followers. For each of the sampled followers we obtained the full list of their Twitter friends, i.e., users that they follow. The sampling of 2,000 followers was done in order to make this step of acquiring the friends feasible (due to the strict rate limits of the Twitter API). The seed accounts pertaining to the corresponding rivalry/group were removed from these friends lists and the remaining ones were treated as a feature vector with each dimension corresponding to a Twitter account being followed. Users who followed *only* seed accounts were dropped. For the cases of rivalries, we also imposed the constraints that the followers were located in the United States. This was done to avoid picking up differences in international market penetrations, rather than within-US cultural differences.

We used this data to construct a binary classifier for which we created train and test splits, each consisting of ~1,000 users. Note that even though 2,000 users were sampled, due to limitations in the Twitter API, the actual number of users for which we could get the friends varies between 1,800-2,000. This could be due to changes in users' privacy settings, accounts getting blocked and so on. For constructing the training vectors, we only considered users who were followed by at least two users in our training set. That is, if only one of the thousands of users in the training set followed @phdcomics, then following @phdcomics would not be used as a feature. This serves as a simple method for reducing the dimensionality as well as removing unimportant dimensions. This is analogous to the text mining scenario of removing rare tokens with a frequency 1.

4. CO-FOLLOWING AND BINARY PREFERENCES

In this section we look at how much a user's choice of Twitter friends reveals about their preference among two alternatives such as @CocaCola vs. @Pepsi. We do this with different research questions in mind. First, we approach things from a machine learning perspective with an evaluation of the corresponding binary classification task. Next, we do a feature analysis to see which arguably irrelevant features, such as musicians followed, provide information about a user's soft drink or political preferences.

Feature Vectors Using IDF. As a preprocessing step, we transformed our binary X-follows-Y vectors to an IDF-weighted alternative. To illustrate why, imagine that almost everybody follows @SuperCelebrity. Then following @SuperCelebrity is not very informative or discriminative and is given a very low IDF weight. For each of the 18 rivalries, we compute the IDF scores of the friends of the followers of the seed 36 seed rivals. In total, 63,853 (N) followers of the seed accounts were used (= 36 x 2,000, minus cases with fewer than 2,000 followers and blocked/deleted/private accounts). We computed the IDF of each of their friends, obtaining one IDF-weighted vector for each of the 63,853 followers.

---

[2] http://bit.ly/1o6WMqf

$$IDF(user_i) = log\left(\frac{N}{|followers(user_i)|}\right), \qquad (1)$$

where $followers(user_i)$ indicates the followers of a particular user, from the set of followers sampled for the seed rival accounts. Each of these IDF-weighted vectors was then normalized in 2-norm and, for a given seed account, all of its followers normalized vectors are summed up. This summed vector is then re-normalized in 2-norm to give the final "global" summary vector for the seed account.

4.1 Machine Learning Performance

In this section we evaluate how much information co-following provides for the task of classifying users according to their binary preference. The ground truth is the single account that the test user actually followed. The feature dimensions corresponding to the following of the seed accounts are always removed and, later, we also remove strongly correlated features such as following @BarackObama for the @GOP vs. @TheDemocrats task. Empty vectors, after removing the seed accounts (for users following only the seed accounts) are ignored. Our main performance measure is the area-under-curve (AUC) for the Response Operating Characteristic Curve (ROC) as computed by using a toolkit provided by Goadrich, et al. [9]. We also report AUC for the Precision-Recall Curve (PR) though AUC-ROC will be the default. A value of 0.5 indicates a random, unskilled prediction model.

Note that we are more interested in understanding the relative performance when, say, the most discriminative features are removed than we are in achieving the highest possible classification accuracy. The accuracy could always be improved further by using other algorithms (SVM, Maximum Entropy, etc.), other feature sets (textual data, interaction features, network features, etc.), or incorporating other techniques (label propagation, community detection, etc.). Our focus is more on understanding issues such as robustness under feature removal, relative performance on sparse test vectors or opportunities for Computational Social Science arising from feature analysis.

Global vs. Local Approach. To determine whether you fall into group A or B, is it more useful to know (i) what the general, average members of A and B are like, or (ii) which if any of the two contains a small number of members just like you? The answer to this question has applications both for the design of classification algorithms and for understanding the structure of groups of followers. We try to answer this question by comparing two different classification strategies. First, a "global" method using the single IDF-weighted summary vector described above. This method also includes information about fairly rare friends as it aggregates information from about 2,000 followers. Second, a "local" approach, that uses a k-nearest neighbor classifier. It then assigns each test vector to the class with the largest number of close neighbors among the top k. For k-NN we experimented with a range of values for k from 1 to 9 in increments of 2. There was a clear tendency for higher values of k to perform better and so we stuck to a choice of k=9. We did not experiment with larger values as the general trend of a more and more global approach performing better was our main objective, rather than identifying an optimal value of, say, k=135.

The performance of the binary classification is shown in Table 1. The global approach always performs better than the local approach, showing that the it is worth aggregating the long tail of rare co-follower relations. The AUC-ROC averaged across the 18 tasks is 0.81.

Removing Obvious Co-following Signals. Discovering that following @BarackObama on Twitter is an indication for following

Rivalry	Global	Local
@Budweiser vs. @MillerCoors	0.86 (0.91)	0.80 (0.85)
@FedEx vs. @UPS	0.73 (0.73)	0.69 (0.72)
@GM vs. @Ford	0.75 (0.86)	0.69 (0.76)
@GOP vs. @TheDemocrats	0.91 (0.95)	0.86 (0.93)
@Hertz vs. @Avis	0.92 (0.93)	0.91 (0.92)
@InsideFerrari vs. @lamborghini	0.92 (0.95)	0.87 (0.93)
@jcpenney vs. @Sears	0.75 (0.82)	0.67 (0.72)
@McDonalds vs. @BurgerKing	0.78 (0.79)	0.68 (0.70)
@MercedesBenz vs. @bmw	0.89 (0.93)	0.86 (0.91)
@Nike vs. @Reebok	0.78 (0.74)	0.73 (0.68)
@NikonUSA vs. @CanonUSAimaging	0.83 (0.85)	0.78 (0.83)
@pepsi vs. @CocaCola	0.69 (0.76)	0.65 (0.73)
@PUMA vs. @adidas	0.77 (0.84)	0.69 (0.73)
@SamsungMobile vs. @TheAppleInc	0.95 (0.96)	0.92 (0.94)
@Starbucks vs. @DunkinDonuts	0.80 (0.87)	0.72 (0.82)
@Target vs. @Walmart	0.78 (0.86)	0.69 (0.79)
@thewanted vs. @onedirection	0.79 (0.88)	0.76 (0.84)
@Visa vs. @MasterCard	0.71 (0.72)	0.62 (0.59)

Table 1: Performance comparison for the 18 binary classification tasks (detecting preference among rivaling alternatives) in terms of AUC-ROC (AUC-PR) for both the global and local similarity-based approaches.

@TheDemocrats rather than @GOP is obvious. Similarly, following @CokeZero correlates positively with following @CocaCola. As we were more interested in studying the *non-obvious* dependencies we investigated the classification performance when the most predictive features are removed. Note that this is the *opposite* of what normal feature selection does.

Concretely, for each binary setting we rank features as follows. For each rivalry pair A, B, we look at the absolute differences in the feature values listed in A's and B's summary vectors. These absolute differences are then sorted in descending order. Features with a large difference correspond to accounts that are typically more followed by the followers of one seed account, but not the other one.

In order to check the influence of the top features, we removed the top 10, 20, 50, 100 and 200 most obvious features and compared the AUC in each case. Note that in this setting, since we remove the most influential features, the size of the test set might change (because some users might only follow these influential users). In order to compensate for this, we tried two variants, one considering only users who have more than 201 followers, so that the size of the test set is fixed and the other with a varying test set size. The results of the former case are presented in Figure 1, though results in both cases are comparable. The y-axis indicates AUC averaged across all the rival groups. We note a gradual decrease in the mean AUC as we remove more features, which is in line with what is expected.

For our later "mapping" analysis (Section 5), we take a similar approach to remove the top 20 features for each of the A vs. non-A classification problems, where A iterates over all the seed accounts and the non-A group pools all non-A seeds.

4.2 Feature Analysis

Correlation with Lifestyle. Apart from using it for user classification and targeted advertising, co-following patterns are also of interest in their own right and can serve to answer questions in Computational Social Science. For instance, there is academic work that looks at "lifestyle politics" such as the correlation between political leaning and television preferences or the stereotype

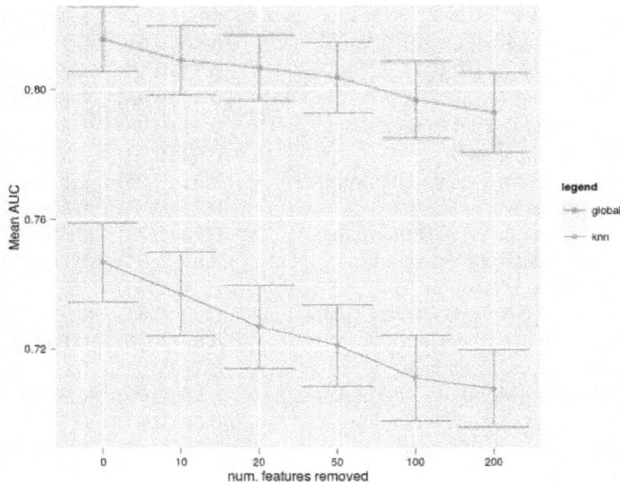

Figure 1: Average AUC across the 18 binary classification tasks (detecting preference among rivaling alternatives) as more and more features are removed, but the test set size is fixed. Only users with more than 201 followers are considered. Error bars indicate the standard error across the tasks.

	@GOP	@TheDemocrats
Music 1	@kennychesney (64)	@ladygaga (24)
Music 2	@jakeowen (122)	@aliciakeys (57)
Music 3	@taylorswift13 (139)	@SnoopDogg (62)
Sports 1	@espn (125)	@rolandsmartin (66)
Sports 2	@runnersworld (143)	@bubbawatson (79)
Sports 3	@AdamSchefter (178)	@NBA (188)
News 1	@WSJ (12)	@nytimes (11)
News 2	@HumanEvents (77)	@cnnbrk (21)
News 3	@toddstarnes (107)	@NYTimeskrugman (23)
	@Pepsi	@Cocacola
Music 1	@SnoopDogg (1)	@maroon5 (8)
Music 2	@Nickiminaj (2)	@davidguetta (19)
Music 3	@Drake (5)	@Pitbull (28)
Sports 1	@shaq (3)	@SInow (99)
Sports 2	@ochocinco (20)	@kaka (103)
Sports 3	@DwightHoward (42)	@chicagobulls (206)
News 1	@Rapup (120)	@cnnbrk (55)
News 2	@Life (133)	@WSJ (81)
News 3	@MTVnews (339)	@TheOnion (183)

Table 2: List of differentiating co-following features from different WeFollow classes, for @GOP vs. @TheDemocrats, and @Pepsi vs. @Cocacola. The numbers in parentheses indicate the absolute position of this feature in our ranking irrespective of the topic (Music, Sports or News).

that liberals like lattes [5, 4, 20]. Our approach contributes to this by offering a language-agnostic tool to use online data to quantify such effects at scale. In this section, we use the feature ranking described previously to generate the top, discriminative features (such as following @BarackObama to predict a @GOP or @TheDemocrats preference). As an example, we look at the rivalries between @TheDemocrats vs. @GOP, and @Pepsi vs. @Cocacola. For both cases we look at the top discriminative co-following features from the http://WeFollow.com categories Music, Sports and News.[3] Table 2 shows some examples of the insights we can get from co-following patterns. The lifestyle correlations for the political rivalry @GOP vs. @TheDemocrats can be inspected to make intuitive sense with, e.g., @nytimes being more popular among @TheDemocrats followers.[4] For @Pepsi vs. @CocaCola many observations can be explained by the fact that @Pepsi targets the younger "New Generation".

Celebrity Endorsements. An interesting side note of examining the top features is the detection of celebrity endorsements. By observing these features, we found out that celebrity endorsements go hand in hand with who people follow. Some examples include Derrick Rose (@drose) for Adidas; Kevin Durant (@KDTrey5) for Nike; SnoopDogg (@SnoopDogg), Nicki Minaj (@NickiMinaj) and Drake (@drake) for Pepsi, and Maroon 5 (@maroon5) and David Guetta (@davidguetta) for Cocacola, etc. This observation has interesting applications in marketing campaigns and recommendation systems and deserves more analysis in the future.

5. MAPPING THE TWITTERSPHERE VIA CO-FOLLOWING

In this section we look at whether a co-following based similarity can be used to map the relative positions of players from domains such as music. Though our maps can be seen as "community de-

tection", the approach and interpretation is very different. Whereas traditional community detection algorithms use direct social links and, e.g., would try to find clusters with unusually high triadic closure [17], our approach relies on more indirect and high-order links. As an example, imagine two football clubs that are fierce rivals and who would definitely not follow each other. Fans and Twitter followers of either club might also not follow the other one. However, their fans might jointly follow many other accounts related to sports news. Due to this co-following of the clubs' followers we would consider the clubs as similar in terms of their audiences' interests. This approach also opens up opportunities for cross-marketing and cross-selling: if two Twitter accounts from different domains share a similar followership then they might consider cross-posting or otherwise combining their forces. Note again that they do not have to share even a single follower to be considered similar as we look at second-order following relations, namely, the friends of their followers.

Technically, we did the following: For each of the ~2,000 followers of an account, we constructed the IDF vector for the users they follow.[5] We then computed the pair-wise cosine similarity between these feature vectors. Since we need distances, we used (1 - cosine similarity) as the measure of distance. We then used the classical, Metric Multi-Dimensional Scaling [23] (MDS) on this data with the $cmdscale()$ function in $Matlab$. Note that MDS is a *lossy* embedding and that even though two points appear close in the 2-dimensional plane, they might be far apart in the original high dimensional space. Therefore, all conclusions and observations we derived from such mappings in the following have also been validated using the high dimensional similarity information.

5.1 Popular Musicians

To see if our approach generalizes to diverse domains such as music, we decided to map popular musicians on Twitter. To this

---

[3] A small number of mislabeled entries were removed. For example, @AgainAmerica was incorrectly listed in the Music category.

[4] The New York Times is generally perceived to have a liberal bias, see http://en.wikipedia.org/wiki/The_New_York_Times#Political_persuasion_overall.

---

[5] The total number of followers (N) for Musicians was 38,358.

end we obtained a list of the top 22 musicians from `http://wefollow.com/interest/music`.[6]

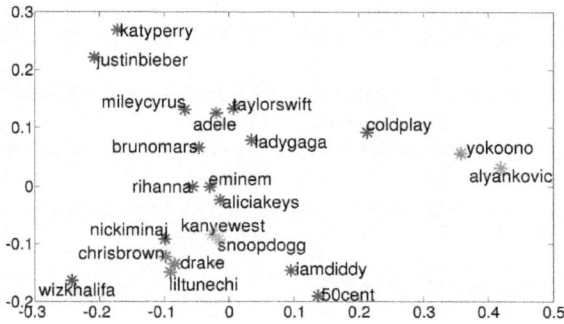

Figure 2: A 2D MDS similarity map of popular musicians. Similarity measures are derived from their followers' aggregated friends.

Figure 2 shows the map that was obtained using MDS on the musicians data. Most of the observed structure corresponds to musical genres. For example, Lil Wayne (@liltunechi), Chris Brown (@chrisbrown) and Drake (@drake) are rappers and are co-mapped together in the map, marked in red. Similar is the case of Snoop Dogg (@snoopdogg) and Kanye West (@kanyewest), marked in green, both of which are hip hop artists. However, there are also surprising things that emerge such as the relative closeness of "Weird Al" Yankovic (@alyankovic), famous for musical parody, and Yoko Ono (@yokoono), both marked in orange. Though very different musical genres, both arguably appeal to an older, more educated audience. This already hints at applications of such analysis for the identification of cross-selling opportunities.

5.2 Combination of All Rivals

To show the full generalizability of this mapping approach also *across* domains we combined all the 36 Twitter accounts from the 18 rivalries and mapped them in a common space in Figure 3. As one would expect, many rivals such as @Target vs. @jcpenney and @thewanted vs. @onedirection are comparatively close as their followers share similar interests. However, the relative distances across rivalries also makes sense. For example, the beer brand @MillerCoors is closer to @GOP than to @TheDemocrats and the opposite holds for @Budweiser. This makes sense as it has been observed before that "Republicans are also big fans of Miller Lite and Coors Light, but Democrats drink more Budweiser" [10, 22], though, some studies show that the opposite is true [1]. Sometimes, studies such as this one are inconclusive and show conflicting results based on the demographics studied (such as voters vs. just politically leaning but not necessarily voting), sampling methods used, etc. Similarly, @GM and @Avis are very close in the low-dimensional embedding. Again, this makes sense as "[s]ince the late 1970s, Avis has featured mainly General Motors (GM) vehicles"[7]. Also noteworthy is the closeness between @PUMA and @TheAppleInc. Though there does not appear to be any formal alliance, both brands try to create a similar image of themselves. Puma targets the "sports lifestyle" trend with persona attributes such as metropolitan and international [14] which, arguably also applies to Apple. We believe that such a mapping is useful to

quickly generate hypotheses for lifestyle politics and similar research areas that can then be investigated in depth. It is important to note that even if some of these findings were not to hold "offline" in all cases, these Twitter-only findings are still useful for online advertising as they definitely provide a signal.

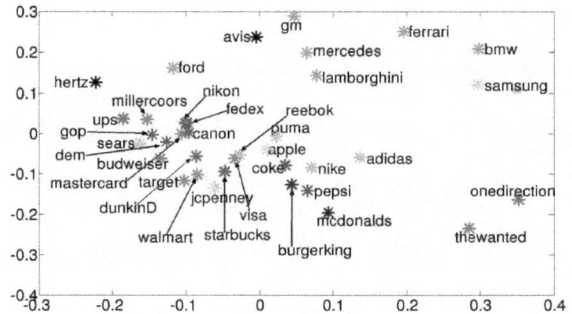

Figure 3: A 2D MDS similarity map of all the 18x2 rivals. Similarity measures are derived from their followers' aggregated friends. Rival pairs are represented by stars of the same color. Some labels have been shortened due to space constraints. dunkinD represents DunkinDonuts and dem., Democrats.

6. CONCLUSIONS

We presented an in-depth study of co-following behavior on Twitter which contributes to (i) a better understanding of language-agnostic user classification on Twitter, (ii) eliciting opportunities for Computational Social Science, and (iii) improving online marketing by identifying cross-selling opportunities. Concretely, we used the similarity of followers' friends to predict a users' preferences and to group main Twitter users according to their audiences' similarities. We showed that such language-agnostic co-following information provides strong signals for diverse classification tasks and that these signals persist even when the most discriminative features are removed. Rather than solely focusing on the classification task, we presented applications of our methodology to the area of Computational Social Science and confirmed stereotypes such as that @ladygaga (also an LGBT activist) is more popular among @TheDemocrats followers than among @GOP followers. In the domain of marketing we gave evidence that celebrity endorsement is reflected in co-following and we demonstrated how our methodology can be used to reveal the audience similarities between Apple and Puma and, less obviously, between Nike and Coca-Cola. To the best of our knowledge, this is the first systematic study that shows how co-following on Twitter can be used for a variety of applications. Our main focus in this paper was to introduce the concept of (second order) co-following and examine how it works for a wide range of settings, rather than the algorithm itself. In future, we would like to focus more on the algorithmic perspective and extend our work by looking deeper into aspects such as comparing co-following to, e.g., methods which use the tweet content and user profile or compare the plots generated by MDS with other community detection algorithms.

---

[6]We removed 4 accounts from the initial list that corresponded to media/producers rather than musicians or bands.
[7]`http://en.wikipedia.org/wiki/Avis_Rent_a_Car_System`, accessed on Jan 20, 2014.

7. REFERENCES

[1] Republicans, democrats split on olive garden, other food issues, February 2013. http://newsfeed.time.com/2013/02/27/republicans-democrats-split-on-olive-garden-other-food-issues/.

[2] J. An, M. Cha, P. K. Gummadi, and J. Crowcroft. Media landscape in twitter: A world of new conventions and political diversity. In *ICWSM*, 2011.

[3] P. Barbera. Birds of the same feather tweet together: Bayesian ideal point estimation using twitter data. In *PolNet*, 2013. https://files.nyu.edu/pba220/public/barbera_birds_july2013.pdf.

[4] J. Bernstein, R. E. Bromley, and K. T. Meyer. Republicans and golf, democrats and outkast: Or, party political culture from the top down. *The Forum*, 4(3), 2006.

[5] J. Blakley. The zogby/lear center survey on politics and entertainment, 2008. http://www.learcenter.org/html/projects/?cm=zogby/08.

[6] C. Cioffi-Revilla. Computational social science. *Wiley Interdisciplinary Reviews: Computational Statistics*, 2(3):259–271, 2010.

[7] R. Cohen and D. Ruths. Classifying political orientation on twitter: It's not easy! In *ICWSM*, 2013.

[8] M. Conover, B. Gonçalves, J. Ratkiewicz, A. Flammini, and F. Menczer. Predicting the political alignment of twitter users. In *SocialCom/PASSAT*, pages 192–199, 2011.

[9] J. Davis and M. Goadrich. The relationship between precision-recall and roc curves. In *ICML*, pages 233–240, 2006.

[10] P. Doyle. Favorite beers of republicans and democrats, October 2012. http://www.bostonmagazine.com/news/blog/2012/10/01/favorite-beers-republicans-democrats/.

[11] S. Fortunato. Community detection in graphs. *Physics Reports*, 486(3-5):75–174, 2010.

[12] S. A. Golder and S. Yardi. Structural predictors of tie formation in twitter: Transitivity and mutuality. In *SocialCom/PASSAT*, pages 88–95, 2010.

[13] C. Hutto, S. Yardi, and E. Gilbert. A longitudinal study of follow predictors on twitter. In *CHI*, pages 821–830, 2013.

[14] T. Kahute. Puma brand communication analysis, 2006. http://www.scribd.com/doc/35130565/Puma-Brand-Analysis.

[15] H. Kwak, C. Lee, H. Park, and S. Moon. What is twitter, a social network or a news media? In *WWW*, pages 591–600, 2010.

[16] D. Lazer, A. S. Pentland, L. Adamic, S. Aral, A. L. Barabasi, D. Brewer, N. Christakis, N. Contractor, J. Fowler, M. Gutmann, et al. Life in the network: the coming age of computational social science. *Science*, 323(5915):721, 2009.

[17] M. E. J. Newman. Modularity and community structure in networks. *PNAS*, 103(23):8577–8582, 2006.

[18] Y. Pan, D.-H. Li, J.-G. Liu, and J.-Z. Liang. Detecting community structure in complex networks via node similarity. *Physica A: Statistical Mechanics and its Applications*, 389(14):2849–2857, 2010.

[19] M. Pennacchiotti and A.-M. Popescu. Democrats, republicans and starbucks afficionados: user classification in twitter. In *KDD*, pages 430–438, 2011.

[20] D. D. Posta, Y. Shi, and M. Macy. Why do liberals drink latte?, 2013. under review.

[21] D. Rao, D. Yarowsky, A. Shreevats, and M. Gupta. Classifying latent user attributes in twitter. In *SMUC*, pages 37–44, 2010.

[22] M. Shannon and W. Feltus. What your beer says about your politics, September 2012. http://www.nationaljournal.com/blogs/hotlineoncall/2012/09/what-your-beer-says-about-your-politics-27.

[23] L. Vaughan. Visualizing linguistic and cultural differences using web co-link data. *Journal of the American Society for Information Science and Technology*, 57(9):1178–1193, 2006.

[24] I. Weber and V. R. K. Garimella. Using co-following for personalized out-of-context twitter friend recommendation. 2014.

[25] D. Yin, L. Hong, and B. D. Davison. Structural link analysis and prediction in microblogs. In *CIKM*, pages 1163–1168, 2011.

[26] F. A. Zamal, W. Liu, and D. Ruths. Homophily and latent attribute inference: Inferring latent attributes of twitter users from neighbors. In *ICWSM*, 2012.

A Behavior Analytics Approach to Identifying Tweets from Crisis Regions

Shamanth Kumar, Xia Hu, Huan Liu
Computer Science & Engineering, School of CIDSE, Arizona State University
{shamanth.kumar, xia.hu, huan.liu}@asu.edu

ABSTRACT

The growing popularity of Twitter as an information medium has allowed unprecedented access to first-hand information during crises and mass emergency situations. Due to the sheer volume of information generated during a disaster, a key challenge is to filter tweets from the crisis region so their analysis can be prioritized. In this paper, we introduce the task of identifying whether a tweet is generated from crisis regions and formulate it as a decision problem. This problem is challenging due to the fact that only ~1% of all tweets have location information. Existing approaches tackle this problem by predicting the location of the user using historical tweets from users or their social network. As collecting historical information is not practical during emergency situations, we investigate whether it is possible to determine that a tweet originates from the crisis region through the information in the tweet and the publishing user's profile.

Categories and Subject Descriptors

H.2.8 [**Database Management**]: Database Applications—*Data mining*

Keywords

crisis tweets; user behavior in tweets; situational awareness

1. INTRODUCTION

Social media, particularly Twitter, has been a popular medium to discuss and report disaster related information. As an information dissemination platform Twitter has been used with varying success in several recent crises and mass emergency situations. For example, during Hurricane Sandy in 2012, people published videos and images of the damage caused by the storm. The continued usage of Twitter as a platform to submit crisis related information motivates us to identify relevant information during a crisis. As Twitter is a globally visible information medium the high volume of tweets generated during a crisis makes this a challenging

task. It is reasonable to assume that first-hand reports on a crisis such as reports of damage, originate in the crisis region. Therefore, we propose to study the problem of identifying information generated from crisis regions.

Twitter facilitates the geotagging of tweets, which is a process by which precise location information can be appended to a tweet. However, a recent investigation [14] has shown that only a small fraction (~1%) of all tweets contain location information. Thus, it is necessary for us to find alternate methods to identify a tweet's location. Recent approaches to tweet location identification leverage the geographic bias in the language of the tweet [2]. However, these techniques do not consider the topic bias in the information stream during a crisis. Thus, it is much harder under these circumstances to determine whether a tweet is generated inside the crisis region. These challenges motivate us to to identify tweets from crisis region.

Identifying the user's location is another alternative, which can be accomplished using the social network information [19] and the user's historical tweets [3, 11]. Typically, identifying and extracting additional information such as a user's network, or his tweet history during a crisis is not practical due to the API constraints imposed by Twitter. These approaches also fail when there is insufficient network, or content history. Hence, we cannot apply these techniques to identify tweets from crisis region. Recent studies have also shown that a user's location may not necessarily correspond to the location of the tweet [4], due to user mobility. Thus, it is more reasonable to identify the location of a tweet.

In this paper, we conduct a study of crisis tweets to gain deeper insight into their characteristics and to specifically answer the following questions: 1) Do tweets inside crisis region express different behavioral patterns and can these patterns be used to identify tweets from crisis region when explicit location information is unavailable. Our contributions are the following:

- We formally define the novel problem of identifying tweets from a crisis region and highlight the challenges;
- We conduct a study of tweets from major crises to discover behavioral patterns in Section 2; and
- We propose an approach to identify tweets from crisis region in Section 3.

Problem statement: Given a crisis C associated with a crisis region R, and a collection of tweets relevant to the crisis T, where each tweet $t \in T$ contains tweet data t_d, including the tweet text and the user's profile information t_u, but does not include the location information. For each such tweet $t \in T$, we need to decide whether the tweet is

Table 1: Dataset Characteristics

Dataset	# Tweets	# Retweets	# Geotagged Tweets	# Inside Tweets	# Outside Tweets
EQ Japan	2,734,431	1,223,609	105,669	44,119	28,953
FL Mississippi River	157,435	72,377	3,042	944	1,355
HUR Sandy	4,344,308	2,203,262	58,092	36,324	15,455
SP OWS	10,722,020	5,039,152	95,313	43,489	38,557
WF AZ	8,679	2,865	213	85	35

generated from inside the crisis region, i.e., $t \in R$ or the tweet is generated from outside the crisis region, i.e., $t \notin R$.

2. BEHAVIORAL PATTERNS IN TWEETS

We begin with a study of the characteristics of crisis tweets to identify distinct behavioral patterns.

2.1 Datasets

To conduct this study, we collected tweets pertaining to major crises in 2011 and 2012. All the data was collected using our tweet monitoring platform TweetTracker [10] through parameters specified by virtual volunteers from the NGO Humanity Road[1] and analysts from various governmental agencies monitoring the crises. Specifically, three types of parameters were used to collect the tweets: keywords/hashtags, geographic regions, and userIDs.

Preparing the dataset: To study the characteristics of the tweets, we must first identify tweets originating in the crisis region. The affected region for each crisis was decided based on the nature and scale of the crisis. For example, as Hurricane Sandy affected the entire East coast of the United States, we consider the region extending from Florida to New York as the crisis region R. Once a crisis region was determined, tweets from crisis region were identified through the geotagging information explicitly provided by the users. As the location information is voluntarily provided, we assume that it is accurate. Geotagged tweets which contained only a link or no content at all were removed. From Table 1, it can be observed that geotagged tweets typically comprised a small fraction of the data. The distribution of the tweets is presented in Columns 5 and 6 in Table 1.

2.2 Tweets From Crisis Regions

Previous studies have shown that the primary application of Twitter during a crisis involves information dissemination [9, 8]. In [18], the authors investigated the characteristics of tweets generated using mobile devices. In [22], the authors investigated the utility of linguistic features to detect tweets with situational awareness. Motivated by these studies, we propose to conduct a study of the characteristics of crisis tweets along the following dimensions: device usage behavior, attention seeking behavio, resource sharing behavior, and the originality of information.

Below we investigate the differences in these behaviors in crisis tweets. For each identified behavior, we will follow the following procedure to compare the behavior in the tweets. Comparison of the likelihood of a behavior is performed by computing the *Likelihood Ratio*. The *Likelihood Ratio* is indicative of how likely is the behavior to be exhibited by tweets inside crisis region when compared to tweets from outside the crisis region. Given a behavior b, its *Likelihood Ratio* can be computed as:

$$LR_b = \frac{P(b|inside)}{P(b|outside)}, \qquad (1)$$

where P(b|inside) is the likelihood of the behavior to be exhibited in tweets from inside crisis region and P(b|outside) is the likelihood of the behavior to be exhibited in tweets from outside crisis region. If $LR_b > 1$, then the tweets inside the crisis region are more likely to express the behavior and the magnitude of the ratio indicates how likely this is. Further, to establish the significance of the differences in the observed behavior, we employ statistical tests.

Testing statistical significance: To establish that the difference in the behavioral patterns is statistically significant, we will employ the two tailed t-test. For all the comparisons, we set the significance level $\alpha = 0.05$. Let μ be the mean of the number of tweets exhibiting the behavior inside crisis region and μ_0 be the mean of the number of tweets exhibiting the behavior outside crisis region. The null hypothesis H_0 for the test can be defined as:

H_0 : the tweets inside the crisis region and tweets outside the crisis region demonstrate similar behavior, i.e., $\mu = \mu_0$.

If the p-value of the test is below the chosen significance level, then we can accept the alternate hypothesis i.e., $\mu \neq \mu_0$ and conclude that the difference in the behavior observed in the two types pf tweets is statistically significant. Otherwise, we accept the *null hypothesis* and conclude that the behavior in the two types of tweets is similar.

2.2.1 Is the usage of mobile devices more prevalent inside crisis region?

Mobile devices are ubiquitous. The usage of capable mobile devices such as smartphones is increasing rapidly. In the United States alone, the usage of smartphones has exceeded 60% of all mobile subscribers[2]. Therefore, we begin with an investigation of the usage of mobile device during a crisis.

Each tweet is associated with a client or an application which was used to publish it. From the client, it is possible to determine whether the tweet was published using a mobile device. As there are no explicit resources to distinguish between mobile and non-mobile clients, below we present a strategy to perform this task.

Procedure to identify mobile clients: In our datasets, we observed that the popularity of clients followed the power law distribution, where only a few clients were used to publish most tweets. As mobile clients need to be identified manually, we focus our effort on the most popular 100 clients from each dataset. Our investigations show that the top 100 clients account for more than 94% of the tweets in all the datasets. Among these clients, some clearly indicate their mobile nature. For example *Ubertwitter for Android*. For others, we visited the associated homepage where additional information was available. If a client indicated that it was an API, provided a desktop tool, or it was a bot, then it was

---

[1] http://www.humanityroad.org

[2] http://bit.ly/1bgXMlX

Table 2: Behavioral characteristics in tweets: I

Dataset	LR_{mobile} (p-value)	$LR_{hashtag}$ (p-value)	$LR_{resource}$ (p-value)	$LR_{retweet}$ (p-value)
EQ Japan	2.35 (0.0)	0.06 (0.0)	2.37 (0.0)	0.11 (3.14E-85)
FL Mississippi River	0.86 (6.046E-4)	0.72 (4.53E-8)	0.79 (1.44E-4)	0.89 (0.55)
HUR Sandy	1.07 (5.25E-56)	1.34 (6.37E-102)	1.50 (3.26E-222)	0.40 (7.51E-23)
SP OWS	0.96 (3.99E-6)	0.86 (9.27E-131)	1.03 (0.0)	0.81 (3.856E-10)
WF AZ	0.46 (0.01)	2.59 (5.04E-6)	1.51 (0.04)	2.47 (0.30)

classified as a non-mobile source, otherwise it was considered to be a mobile client.

Using the annotated clients, we investigated the tweets published using mobile clients. We set the behavior b in Equation 1 to *mobile* and compute LR_{mobile}. We found that the tweets from crisis region were more likely to be generated using mobile devices in two datasets. In the case of *EQ Japan*, tweets from crisis region were more than twice as likely to be published using a mobile device. Natural disasters are typically associated with the failure of utilities and increased mobility of users, such as during Hurricane Sandy[3] and we observed this behavior in the two biggest events in our data: EQ Japan and HUR Sandy. A summary of LR_{mobile} is presented in column 2 in Table 2. The results were found to be statistically significant (p-values from the test are presented next to the ratio).

2.2.2 Are tweets from crisis region more likely to seek visibility?

Hashtags are typically used to indicate the topic of a tweet and for organizational purposes. However, studies have shown that the use of multiple hashtags indicates an effort to seek visibility [16]. The usage of multiple hashtags allows a tweet to be indexed under these hashtags and increases the chances of a tweet to be seen by a wider audience. To investigate this behavior in crisis tweets by setting the behavior b in Equation 1 to *hashtag*. The results show that tweets inside crisis region are less likely to include multiple hashtags in the tweet. We observed that this pattern was consistent across most datasets. Crises typically have specific popular hashtags associated with them. In addition, the usage of multiple hashtags reduces the amount of information that can be included in the tweet, which might explain this behavior. The $LR_{hashtag}$ for the datasets are presented in Column 3 of Table 2.

2.2.3 Are tweets from crisis region more likely to share an external resource?

Twitter messages are restricted to 140 characters. Thus, longer content and media such as images and videos can only be shared through external references. Therefore, we investigate whether tweets inside crisis region are more likely to share external resources. We measure $LR_{resource}$ by setting the behavior b in Equation 1 to *resource*. The $LR_{resource}$ for the datasets is summarized in Column 4 of Table 2. In this study, we only consider original tweets. Our study shows that the tweets from crisis region were more likely to contain URLs in most of the datasets. During a crisis, we expect the tweets from crisis region to contain links to resources such as videos and images describing the impact. For example, during Hurricane Sandy images of the flooding in the streets and the subway were widely shared by the local residents[4].

---

[3]http://ti.me/1neNTZB
[4]http://bit.ly/1sgSj9h

Table 3: Behavioral characteristics in tweets: II

Dataset	LR_{action} (p-value)	$LR_{entities}$ (p-value)
EQ Japan	0.34 (0.0)	0.43 (0.0)
FL Mississippi River	1.10 (3.08E-10)	0.86 (9.63E-13)
HUR Sandy	0.93 (1.28E-55)	0.93 (9.38E-76)
SP OWS	1.08 (4.50E-112)	0.98 (7.07E-5)
WF AZ	0.97 (0.83)	1.06 (0.55)

2.2.4 Are tweets from crisis region more likely to be a retweet?

There are several ways to publish tweets. When tweets posted by another user are forwarded by a user, the tweet is called a retweet. Retweets are characterized by the inclusion of the symbol "RT" at the beginning of the tweet. Typically retweets constitute a large part of crisis related tweets. Therefore, we study the originality of tweets from crisis region. We measure $LR_{retweet}$ by setting the behavior b in Equation 1 to *retweet*. The results in Column 5 of Table 2 show that the tweets from crisis region are more original and less likely to be a retweet. As first hand information is more readily available inside crisis region, it is reasonable to expect tweets from crisis region to contain original information and this is confirmed by the results.

2.2.5 Are tweets from the crisis region more likely to indicate an action?

Action words imply that the user publishing the tweet is performing an action. Verbs are typically used to indicate an action, such as leaving, moving etc. in the context of a crisis. To detect verbs in a tweet, we use the Ark NLP Part-Of-Speech (POS) tagger [15]. To study this behavior, we measure LR_{action}. The results are presented in Column 2 of Table 3. Our study shows that the tweets from crisis region are less likely to contain action words in a majority of the datasets. The results were also found to be statistically significant in most of the datasets studied.

2.2.6 Are tweets from crisis regions more likely to reference entities?

Entities typically refer to the names of people, buildings, or specific locations. During a crisis, such entities may refer to people and landmarks in the crisis region etc. Proper nouns are typically associated with names of people and places. Therefore, we employ the Ark POS tagger to identify the proper nouns in tweets. By analyzing proper nouns contained in the tweets we can determine whether the tweets reference entities. We set the behavior b in Equation 1 to *entity* and describe the results in Column 3 of Table 3. We expect that the first hand reports from crisis regions would be more likely to reference local entities who may be affected/involved in the crisis, thus providing situational awareness to first responders and other responding agencies. However, LR_{entity} for the datasets shows that tweets from crisis regions are less likely to reference entities. This might be due to the quick propagation of the information regard-

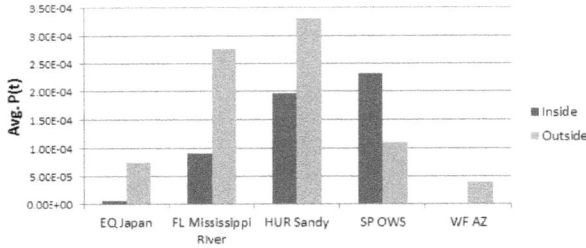

Figure 1: Avg. probability of tweets in various crises data ing local entities outside the region after a crisis leading to frequent references in tweets from outside the region.

2.2.7 Are tweets from the crisis region novel?

Novel content indicates original information and not merely a tendency to publish popular content. To answer this question, we construct a unigram language model assuming the tweets are constructed using the bag-of-words strategy. The likelihood of each word $P(w)$ is estimated using the Maximum-Likelihood approach as

$$P(w) = \frac{c(w \in W)}{\sum_w c(w)}, \quad (2)$$

where $c(w)$ is the count of the word in the corpus. The probability of a tweet ($P(t)$) is computed as

$$P(t) = \Pi_{w \in W} P(w). \quad (3)$$

In Figure 1, we present a comparison of the average probability of a tweet in each dataset. The experiment shows that tweets inside crisis region are generally more novel.

From the above study we have three key insights on tweets from crisis regions: 1) they are associated with original content and are more likely to discuss novel topics, which reaffirms previous findings on the information dissemination behavior of tweets during crisis, 2) they are less likely to seek attention, and 3) they are more likely to use external resources to convey their message.

3. USING BEHAVIORAL PATTERNS

Using the insights from the above study, we extract the following different types of features to model a tweet:

Mobile Features: Using the annotated list from Section 2.2.1 we identify if a tweet is published using a mobile client.

Resource Features: We constructed features indicating the presence of a URL and the number of URLs. In addition, we consider if the URLs point to an image or a video. References to Foursquare location are considered separately as an indication of location information.

Textual Features: Patterns in tweets, such as whether a tweet is a retweet, a directed message, or contains a user mention as well as the usage of hashtags. Positive and negative emoticons are distinguished using a list of popular happy and sad emoticons[5]. The quality of tweets is measured through punctuations, character, and word length.

Linguistic Features: References to actions and entities in tweets is measured using both the presence and the frequency of part-of-speech tags including proper nouns, verbs, and pronouns. Additionally, given a tweet t with vocabulary w, we compute and use the probability of the most probable word ($max_w P(w)$), the least probable word ($min_w P(w)$),

[5] http://en.wikipedia.org/wiki/List_of_emoticons

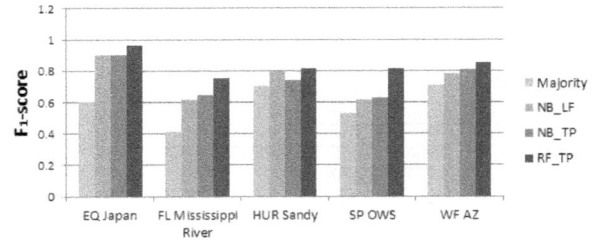

Figure 2: A comparison of the F_1 score

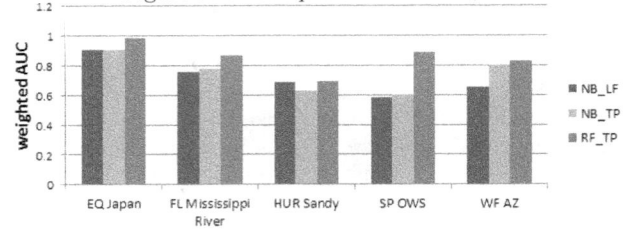

Figure 3: A comparison of the weighted AUC score

and the probability of the tweet ($P(t)$) computed using the language model previously discussed.

User Features: From the user's profile, the user's familiarity with the medium is extracted through the number of status messages and the user's network activity.

Baseline Approaches: As the we only consider the tweets collected during crises and the profile of the publishing user as the available information, we cannot directly compare with other location prediction approaches, such as [11] and [2] as they require historical data. Therefore, we propose to use the following baselines:

- **Majority** - Since there is class imbalance, we consider predicting the majority class as a baseline.
- **Verma et al. (LF)** identified various linguistic features such as the unigrams and their raw frequency and the POS tags and demonstrated their effectiveness in identifying tweets containing situational awareness. Thus, we apply this model to our problem as a baseline. It should be noted that this strategy leads to a very large number of features which was generally proportional to the number of instances.

All experiments were performed using implementations in Weka [6] and the results were generated using 5-fold cross validation with 80% training data and 20% test data.

3.1 Evaluating the Performance

We evaluated our approach using the naive Bayes and *random forest* classifier. Comparisons with the baseline approaches are made using the F_1 score computed as

$$F_1 = \frac{2 * (precision * recall)}{precision + recall}. \quad (4)$$

Figure 2 summarizes the performance of the naive Bayes classifier applied to the baseline (NB_LF) and the proposed model (NB_TP). We find that our approach performs better than the baseline with significantly greater efficiency due to the compact representation. In addition, the random forest classifier (RF_TP) using the proposed features performed considerably better than the naive Bayes classifier.

To account for class imbalance, we also present the weighted AUC score in Figure 3. We omit the "majority" baseline

Table 4: Arizona wildfires summary created using Z_i

Summary Tweets
it's really smokey and hazy today. #wallowfire
smoke near eagar #wallowfire http://twitpic.com/5ci9i7
wildfire info: wallow fire pm update 6/19/11 (wallow wildfire) http://bit.ly/mdoigp #azfire #wallowfire
#wallow fire swept thru greer.
glenwood gazette - breaking news: #wallowfire 06/10/11 map http://t.co/xr8e23b

Table 5: Arizona wildfires summary created using Z_o

Summary Tweets
wildfires wreaking havoc in arizona. http://bit.ly/jsgwpv
#arizona - y su bonito glowing bird suena en radio paranoia :)
rt @radionoisefm cel mai devastator incendiu din a.. http://bit.ly/jtshyl #12 #ore #arizona #devastator #dublat #incendiu
hello #arizona, #bringit http://instagr.am/p/f4ife/
1600 quadratkilometer wald durch brand vernichtet #arizona

here as it was significantly worse than the other approaches. The proposed approach outperformed the baseline in almost all datasets. We verified the statistical significance of the results using the Wilcoxon-Signed Rank test. We compare the baseline (NB_LF) and our approach (NB_TF), treating them as a paired sample. The observed p-value was 0.0019 and the improvement was statistically significant at $\alpha = 0.05$.

3.2 Importance of Features

To evaluate the importance of different feature classes we constructed a *logistic regression* classifier. This classifier learns a weight for each feature, which can be interpreted as a measure of the feature's importance for the prediction task. The overall rank of a feature across different datasets was determined by the sum of its rank on each dataset. Lower rank values indicate that a feature is important across the datasets. Our investigation revealed that linguistic features were the most important class of features. This can be attributed to the novelty of tweets from crisis region. Textual features such as the use of punctuations were found to be more useful than reference to entities and action words. User related features were the least important class of features for the task, thus suggesting that prediction can be reasonably performed with just the information contained in tweets.

4. CASE STUDY: ARIZONA WILDFIRES

Tweets from crisis region can be used to obtain situational awareness and can be used to generate post-crisis summarization of the event from the perspective of tweets. In the task of event summarization, the goal is to identify a small number of representative tweets from the entire corpus, which can describe the event or a crisis. In this case study, we will use the task of event summarization to demonstrate that the application of our approach enables the generation of a more meaningful summary of the crisis.

Extracting representative tweets from topics derived from the tweets is a commonly used approach to event summarization [5]. To illustrate the differences between the two sets of tweets, we will summarize the Arizona Wildfires (WF AZ). First, the proposed model is used to classify all tweets whose location information is unknown. Then, the following procedure is applied:

- Extract 10 topics Z_i from tweets inside and Z_o from tweets outside crisis region.
- For each detected topic, rank tweets t with vocabulary w by its perplexity score defined as $perplexity(t) = exp\left(\frac{-log P(t|z)}{|w|}\right)$.
- Create a summary of the crisis by picking the 5 most relevant tweets from the top 10 tweets in the topic.

The extracted summaries in Tables 4 and 5 show that the summary created using Z_i has more relevant information and it highlights the relevance of our approach.

5. RELATED WORK

Social media services have been extensively studied as social sensors to monitor important events occurring in the real world. In particular, recent research has focused on the analysis of the use of social media during emergencies [20], including earthquakes [12], riots [17], wildfires [21], etc. Seeking high-quality social media data pertaining to crisis serves as the basis of these studies and motivates this study to identify tweets from crisis regions.

Identifying a user's home location using social media data[7] is an interesting and important problem. The existing research on this topic can be divided into two groups. The first set of research methods assume that a user's tweets might contain distinct features due to their proximity to the region. Cheng et al. [2] estimated a Twitter user's home city based on the content of their tweets. Mahmud et al. [11] used an ensemble of statistical and heuristic classifiers to infer the home location of Twitter users at different granularities by using the content information and their tweeting behavior. However, topic specific variation of content has not been investigated. These approaches also rely on the availability of a user's tweet history, which is not readily available during a crisis. The second set of research methods assume that a user's home location is strongly correlated with his friends' home location. Backstrom et al. [1] estimated the home location of Facebook users using user-supplied address data and the network of associations between members. But, due to the API limitations it is not practical to extract network information during a crisis under time constraint. Therefore, these approaches cannot be directly applied to our data.

The problem of recognizing eyewitness tweets was independently investigated in [13]. While the authors evaluated whether linguistic features could be used to identify such tweets, here we analyzed several kinds of behavioral patterns in tweets from crisis regions.

6. CONCLUSIONS AND FUTURE WORK

Identifying tweets from crisis regions is becoming increasingly important due to information overload on Twitter. In this paper, we used tweets from several crises to conduct a study of the tweet characteristics and behavior and used the observations to build a novel method to detect tweets from crisis regions. Through experiments, we demonstrated that our approach is successful in identifying such tweets. As part of our future work, we will investigate the impact of the size of training data on the performance of the model as the process of filtering tweets from crisis regions should be initiated as soon as possible. We also plan to study the temporal effects on patterns in crisis tweets.

Acknowledgments

This work was supported in part by the Office of Naval Research grants N000141110527 and N000141410095.

7. REFERENCES

[1] L. Backstrom, E. Sun, and C. Marlow. Find Me If You Can: Improving Geographical Prediction with Social and Spatial Proximity. In *Proceedings of the 19th international conference on World wide web*, pages 61–70, 2010.

[2] Z. Cheng, J. Caverlee, and K. Lee. You Are Where You Tweet: A Content-Based Approach to Geo-Locating Twitter Users. In *CIKM*, pages 759–768, 2010.

[3] Z. Cheng, J. Caverlee, and K. Lee. A Content-driven Framework for Geolocating Microblog Users. *ACM Trans. Intell. Syst. Technol.*, 4(1):2:1–2:27, 2013.

[4] E. Cho, S. A. Myers, and J. Leskovec. Friendship and mobility: User Movement in Location-Based Social Networks. In *Proceedings of the 17th ACM SIGKDD international conference on Knowledge discovery and data mining*, pages 1082–1090, 2011.

[5] F. C. T. Chua and S. Asur. Automatic Summarization of Events From Social Media. *Technical Report*, 2013.

[6] M. Hall, E. Frank, G. Holmes, B. Pfahringer, P. Reutemann, and I. H. Witten. The WEKA Data Mining Software: An Update. *ACM SIGKDD Explorations Newsletter*, 11(1):10–18, 2009.

[7] B. Hecht, L. Hong, B. Suh, and E. H. Chi. Tweets From Justin Bieber's Heart: The Dynamics of the Location Field in User Profiles. In *Proceedings of the SIGCHI Conference on Human Factors in Computing Systems*, pages 237–246, 2011.

[8] T. Heverin and L. Zach. *Microblogging for Crisis Communication: Examination of Twitter Use in Response to a 2009 Violent Crisis in the Seattle-Tacoma, Washington, Area.* ISCRAM, 2010.

[9] A. L. Hughes and L. Palen. Twitter Adoption and Use in Mass Convergence and Emergency Events. *International Journal of Emergency Management*, 6(3):248–260, 2009.

[10] S. Kumar, G. Barbier, M. A. Abbasi, and H. Liu. TweetTracker: An Analysis Tool for Humanitarian and Disaster Relief. In *ICWSM*, 2011.

[11] J. Mahmud, J. Nichols, and C. Drews. Where Is This Tweet From? Inferring Home Locations of Twitter Users. In *ICWSM*, 2012.

[12] M. Mendoza, B. Poblete, and C. Castillo. Twitter Under Crisis: Can We Trust What We RT? In *Proceedings of the first workshop on social media analytics*, pages 71–79, 2010.

[13] F. Morstatter, N. Lubold, H. Pon-Barry, J. Pfeffer, and H. Liu. Finding Eyewitness Tweets During Crises. In *Workshop on Language Technology and Computational Social Science*, 2014.

[14] F. Morstatter, J. Pfeffer, H. Liu, and K. M. Carley. Is the Sample Good Enough? Comparing Data from Twitter's Streaming API with Twitter's Firehose. *ICWSM*, 2013.

[15] O. Owoputi, B. OŠConnor, C. Dyer, K. Gimpel, N. Schneider, and N. A. Smith. Improved Part-Of-Speech Tagging for Online Conversational Text with Word Clusters. In *Proceedings of NAACL-HLT*, pages 380–390, 2013.

[16] R. Page. The Linguistics of Self-Branding and Micro-Celebrity in Twitter: The Role of Hashtags. *Discourse & Communication*, 6(2):181–201, 2012.

[17] P. Panagiotopoulos, A. Z. Bigdeli, and S. Sams. "5 Days in August"–How London Local Authorities Used Twitter during the 2011 Riots. In *Electronic Government*, pages 102–113. 2012.

[18] M. Perreault and D. Ruths. The Effect of Mobile Platforms on Twitter Content Generation. In *ICWSM*, 2011.

[19] D. Rout, K. Bontcheva, D. Preotiuc-Pietro, and T. Cohn. Where's @Wally?: a Classification Approach to Geolocating Users Based on their Social Ties. In *HT*, pages 11–20, 2013.

[20] T. Sakaki, M. Okazaki, and Y. Matsuo. Earthquake Shakes Twitter Users: Real-Time Event Detection by Social Sensors. In *Proceedings of the 19th international conference on World wide web*, pages 851–860, 2010.

[21] S. Sinnappan, C. Farrell, and E. Stewart. Priceless Tweets! A Study on Twitter Messages Posted During Crisis: Black Saturday. 2010.

[22] S. Verma, S. Vieweg, W. J. Corvey, L. Palen, J. H. Martin, M. Palmer, A. Schram, and K. M. Anderson. Natural Language Processing to the Rescue? Extracting "Situational Awareness" Tweets During Mass Emergency. In *ICWSM*, 2011.

Finding Mr and Mrs Entity in the City of Knowledge

Vanessa Lopez, Martin Stephenson, Spyros Kotoulas, Pierpaolo Tommasi
Smarter Cities Technology Centre, IBM Research, Ireland
{vanlopez, martin_stephenson, Spyros.Kotoulas, ptommasi}@ie.ibm.com

ABSTRACT

More and more urban data is published every day, and consequently, consumers want to take advantage of this body of knowledge. Unfortunately, metadata and schema information around this content is sparse. To effectively fulfill user information needs, systems must be able to capture user intent and context in order to evolve beyond current search and exploration techniques. A Linked Data approach is uniquely positioned to surface information and provide interoperability across a diversity of information sources, from consumer data residing in the original enterprise systems, to relevant open city data in tabular form. We present a prototype for contextual knowledge mining that enables federated access and querying of entities across hundreds of enterprise and open datasets pertaining to cities. The proposed system is able to (1) lift raw tabular data into a connected and meaningful structure, contextualized within the Web of Data, and (2) support novel search and exploration tasks, by identifying closely related entities across datasets and models. Our user experiments and prototype show how semantics, used to consolidate city information and reuse assets from the Web of Data, improve dataset search and provide users effective means to explore related entities and content to fit their information needs.

1. MOTIVATION

Smart City applications rely on large amounts of data retrieved from sensors, devices, social networks, open data portals or government authorities, often in the form of tabular data, but with little and incomplete schema information. The need to make city-specific information easy to consume and combine is rapidly increasing day-by-day, but given the complexity of the domain, extreme heterogeneity, diversity of the data, and lack of a priori defined schemas and semantics, this proves a difficult task. It is exactly this lack of semantics that make text-based approaches ill-suited for this environment. On the other hand, the cost of classical data integration approaches is prohibitive since it would require a common model built ahead of time, covering very broad domains and/or an N-to-N integration, which scales badly.

In this information jungle, semantic technologies have been proposed for making both city data and open data easier to consume, and, as such, improving interoperability and discoverability of datasets by reusing standard vocabularies, linking to external sources, as well as enabling richer querying [1][2][3]. The advantages of such systems lies in their ability to integrate data in an incremental manner: they lower the entry cost by importing datasets as they are, and mapping them to other sources incrementally, without the need for global integration, pre-defined schemas, or even linking the entire input. At the same time they fully exploit the Web-wide wealth of resources rich in meaning and structure published as Linked Open Data (LOD) [4].

In this paper, we propose a system to make a diverse set of heterogeneous enterprise city data searchable and interoperable with any well-formed open data in tabular form. Raw data is ingested, annotated, and transformed into a meaningful and connected structure, in order to be accessed and queried on demand and in context based on space, time and semantic relations to other relevant open data. This goes beyond classical document search or entity search, since it largely relies on externally available models to disambiguate, organize and query non-semantic data. To achieve this, data is semantically uplifted, entities and relations between them are extracted and aligned to well-known vocabularies and widely used LOD resources. Different views and explorations paths are exposed according to dynamically chosen models, allowing users to profit from the expressive power of semantic standards while hiding the complexity behind services exposed in an intuitive and easy-to-use interface. We propose a data-centric approach that extends the state-of-the-art in three dimensions:

- Information needs: requires understanding complex user information needs and context across different sources, without requiring significant expertise from data publishers or consumers (fit for use).
- Relevance model: uses an open set of dimensions for relevance, not only based on web popularity, document term-frequency or spatio-temporal relevance, but also based on other types of semantic and contextual relations across entities and models.
- Search Scope: ingestion, integration and search of different types of information sources - structured and semi-structured, customer data (e.g., city databases) and open data (LOD, spreadsheets).

This paper is structured as follows. A motivating scenario and key challenges are presented in Section 2. We position against related work in Section 3. The approach and realization of the components for uplifting; mining semantic annotations from distributed sources and contextual retrieval based on semantic relatedness are presented in Sections 4 and 5. Experiments and conclusions are presented in Sections 6.

2. SCENARIO AND CHALLENGES

We use publicly available and widely-used vocabularies and ontologies to annotate, transform and combine both raw customer data, stored in relational tables, and relevant open city data, which often comes in the form of spreadsheets made for consumption by humans, into meaningful linked data[1].

---

[1] Due to confidentiality we can't describe the customer data in greater detail. Data often refers to, but not limited to, city operations, such as business, event management, incidents, etc., as described in http://www.ibm.com/developerworks/industry/library/ind-intelligent-operations-center/

The resulting consolidated multi-faceted information, including linked and urban data, is used to bootstrap search and exploration and expose it to users, moving from catalogue-based content management to searching and querying for entities and their relations across sources, aggregating information into meaningful views. For example, consider a field worker that would like to explore all known factors affecting safety and contributing to insecurity in impoverished urban areas, in order to prioritize onsite inspection: poor housing, crime rates in the area, access to food, transport or services (e.g., location of markets, hospitals) and other barriers related to the population, such as rates of single parent households, low income population, lower levels of education, or behavioral health problems – such as ambulance calls out due to substance abuse, etc. The required information is coming from different domains and sources of unknown structure. The relevant correlations depend on the user task.

In this paper, we propose an approach to extract entities and uncover relevant links and content to support the users perform more intelligent tasks for searching and exploring city data, for which the following *research challenges* are identified:

1. Semantic Uplift: creating good quality Linked Data from enterprise data silos and raw open city data with minimal cost.
2. Contextual Retrieval: determining whether a particular source, a subset of it, or a set of them, is relevant for a user given task. In particular: (1) allow for more complex queries, understand user intent and the meaning of the content; and (2) allow users to explore combine relevant information into views.
3. Entity Linking: discovering relevant connections across data both a priori and on-demand.
4. Distributed Access: integrating and query data residing in different source systems.

3. STATE OF THE ART

Data is published by cities in various portals, e.g. in London[5] and Chicago[6], allowing users to explore the relevant datasets through keyword search or by navigating through their catalogues. However, there is limited semantic meaning or descriptions associated to the datasets (column names and values), and no mechanism to refine explorations and queries across sources, or to help users discover related datasets.

QuerioCity[3] was our first approach to provide semantic context for the data and metadata published in *DubLinked.ie* without the need to ETL data. It follows a centralised graph-based approach with a focus on data-view manipulation and tracking provenance. For every step on the publishing process (capture metadata, convert content into a tabular RDF representation, entity extraction, linking, user validations, and data-view merging) a new data-view that merges all previous graphs is generated, and querying implies querying the union of these graphs. This allows having multiple modifications and interpretations of the same data by different publishers. The drawback is the significant added cost on indexing this data. Other publishing platforms exist for automating the lifting of tabular data into semantic data, and interlinking datasets with existent LOD datasets [7][8]. Differently from previous approaches, here we propose a light-weight approach, where we consider the distributed nature of RDF and that is able to ingest any customer data and relevant open data available, as long as it follows a tabular representation (e.g., relational tables, CSV files). The data is virtualized into RDF, exposed and contextualized with any reference ontologies and models of choice in the Web of data.

A number of tools and recommendations by the W3C are used for automatically converting tabular data (mostly CSV) and relational tables into RDF[9][10]. There are two main approaches. The

Direct Mapping approach automatically generates RDF using the tables names for classes and column names for properties. Each row/line becomes a resource, with one of the columns uniquely identifying the entity. This approach allows to quickly obtain RDF from a relational database or tabular file but without using any vocabulary. The other approach provides a standardized mapping language, R2RML[14], allowing to assign vocabulary terms to the database schema, mapping column names to RDF properties.

Following this paradigm, in [2], a set of tabular data from the Norwegian directorates *FactPages* is transformed into a relational database, a Linked open dataset, and an ontology, adding more semantics in each step. As stated in [2] there is added value in having a semantic representation on top of a relational one, in terms of improving data quality, without adding too much overhead on the step of converting CSV to relational tables and relational tables to RDF. A semantically enriched dataset can be queried using SPARQL and used for automated reasoning, facilitating the combination of information in arbitrary ways and the integration with other datasets or vocabularies.

These recommendations and approaches however do not solve the issues of (1) automatically reusing well-known vocabularies and schemas; (2) extracting spatial / temporal entities, datatypes and object properties when often entities are not linked (no foreign keys). Furthermore, it is based on the assumption that each row is an entity; (3) allowing users to explore and aggregate relevant data across sources.

Extracting structured data from Web tables for search is attracting interesting from search engines [15][16]. In [16] columns in web tables are associated with labels (types), if the values in that column can be matched as values of the type. In [17] tables are associated to concepts in a knowledge taxonomy. In [18] an approach is proposed for finding related tables on the Web to facilitate the reuse of existing datasets and improve table search. It is based on Entity Complement (union of tables with similar schemas and complementary entities), and Schema Complement (table join - adding more columns about the same set of entities).

4. APPROACH

In what follows, we describe our approach and implementation. To allow incremental integration and uplift (research challenge 1) we use a set of reference ontologies to annotate and act as common anchors, and therefore integrate through common topics and entities (no silos) our data against. Information can then be retrieved by following the relevant relationships across entities in different sources in a given context (research challenge 2). The set of reference ontologies is open, and new reference ontologies can be added at any time, incrementally adding new annotations in the *context store* and therefore automatically aligning each data source with the new model (research challenge 3).

To abstract from the infrastructure of each source, information is accessed from distributed sources as RDF (research challenge 4). Extracted semantic annotations (using the reference ontologies), links and schema information resides in a centralized context store based on Jena TDB, where different graphs are created and associated for each source to keep provenance.

In here we present a flexible architecture (Figure 1) for which the following functionality and main contributions are exposed: (1) The Data Server for automatic data ingestion and virtualization (Section 4.1); and (2) The Application Server to semantically uplift entities from open and enterprise data to specified ontologies in order to provide services for contextual information retrieval (Section 4.2). The demo UI accesses the system via RESTful APIs to hide the complexity of the back end (Section 5).

New datasets, reference ontologies or annotation sources can be configured and added at any time and, any number of SPARQL end points can be configured, in order to meet potential scalability requirements. Their location, access details (SPARQL end point, RDF file or Jena repository), and associated graph name are given in a configuration file. There are two configuration files, one to specify the LOD sources use as annotators and the other one for the virtualized RDF repositories containing the data. A singleton class is implemented to read the configuration files and store the associations between a graph and their connection details. A factory class is implemented to access and query the different sources accordingly. Currently, various APIs are implemented to access sources in different SPARQL end points: a local copy of DBpedia in Virtuoso[11], the virtualized RDF through both OpenRDF Sesame[12] and SNORQL stores[13], RDF files (e.g., schema.org) or a Jena TDB repository (for the context store). A federated query mechanism is implemented to query the corresponding graph / repository given an entity or annotation.

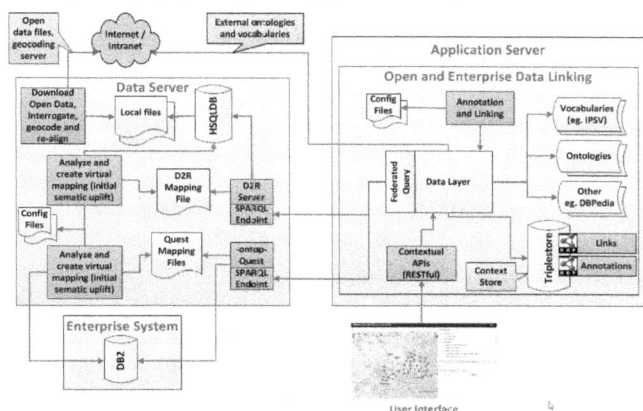

Figure 1. Architecture and components diagram

4.1 Distributed Virtual RDF

The semantic layer enables de-coupling from the infrastructure of each source, in addition to allowing each data source owner to implement her own data access control policies; this provides the ability to expose only a selected subset of information if required. The original enterprise data resides in the original relational systems and is accessed though virtual RDF.

Tabular files need to be first downloaded and linked to a relational database. We are using HSQLDB (Version 2.2.5), as it has the capability to allow the data to reside in the tabular file (as opposed to directly importing the data into the database). Building a simple database schema from a CSV is similar to the process of extracting a semantic representation from the relational table. As table names and column names we use the CSV file and the columns in the first line of the file. The datatypes are determined by examining the data: numbers, *booleans*, date values are converted into the correct format. Primary keys are created, if an identifier column cannot be identified, using auto-increment numeric values.

When the user requests to integrate an open data file, they have the option to geocode the file also. If the user selects this option the header line of the file is downloaded and presented to the user, who can then select the relevant header columns that represent the address to be geocoded. The address information (extracted for each row as it is processed) is passed to a Singleton geocoder class that uses a factory pattern to determine what geocoder to use to geocode the address (the geocoder to use, currently the Google Geocoding API, is specified in a configuration file). In this way new implementations of the geocoder can be dropped in by writing a

new class that adheres to the interface defined in the factory pattern. The geocoder factory passes back the latitude and longitude of the requested address, which are added as new data to the end of the current row of data.

Two different RDF virtualization technologies are used: D2R Server (d2rq.org) for the open data tabular files (as it supports SPARQL 1.1) and onto Quest [30] for the DB2 Enterprise data (as it supports the IBM DB2 database, whereas D2R does not).

A set of vocabularies and ontologies are used for defining the virtual RDF mappings, which specify a translation from the database sources to the virtual RDF graphs. These mappings determine how SPARQL queries are rewritten into SQL queries. The virtual RDF is exposed using multiple SPARQL end points, based on both SNORQL and OpenRDF Sesame (Version 2.7.6).

There are methods for direct mapping of a relational database to a mapping file (e.g., the D2R server can automatically generate such a map); they produce a basic mapping file that maps each table to a new RDFS class that is based on the table's name, and maps each line on the table to an instance and each column to a property based on the column's name. As we require more powerful set of initial mappings, our system directly writes the mapping files, implementing a rule-based entity extraction mechanism (specified in a configuration file) to specify commonly used one to one mappings between database property values and known RDF properties. In particular, to detect geographical entities (using the WGS84[19] vocabulary to create properties for certain header labels with cell values corresponding to decimals number between -90 and 90), recognizing the column with names for instance labels (*rdfs:label*), contact information (using VCARD[20]), and temporal properties (using OWLTime[21]). Note that temporal properties (dates, month, year) are not always part of the table itself but they need to be inferred from the table titles (e.g., *Crime Stats May 2013*).

In addition, values are mapped to literals for datatype properties. *XSD datatypes* are given according to *SQL datatypes* or extracted from the values (string, integer, boolean, date). Or if object properties are detected - if the column is a foreign key - or for string (non-numeric) repeating values (below a threshold variance percentage) - values are mapped to URIs, e.g., city names.

4.2 Semantic uplift and linking to the web of data

Significant added value (in terms of interoperability, discoverability and sanitizing data) can be obtained by reusing popular vocabularies and ontologies, such as the Integrated Public Service Vocabulary (IPSV)[22] used by UK public sector organisations, W3C Dublin core[23], schema.org, and other LOD sources that cover a wider domain and geographical information, notably DBpedia, considered the hub for the web of data[24]. External sources are used to annotate and catalogue the data, therefore give meaning and context, and providing common anchors across otherwise isolated data sources, without requiring the creation of a common model.

For each dataset in the virtualized RDF repository, we extract the schema information and store it in the centralized context store: class types, datatypes and object properties, class objects and their set of possible instances, domains and ranges. We also include the instances' labels, if known, for indexing purposes. Then, for each dataset class in the context store, we use index searches and string similarity metrics (e.g., Jaccard, Jaro, Levenshtein [25]) on the localname or label to annotate classes and properties with URIs found in the external sources used as annotators, as well as to find *owl:sameAs* links for instances. The annotations are stored in an annotation graph, linking the source URI and the annotation URI with a confidence score.

The annotations for the dataset class label, often partially matching the short table titles, are used to populate the property *dcterms:subject* [23] for all entities extracted from the dataset, as they often indicate the topic of the dataset. Besides syntactic mappings (string similarity), the structure of the ontologies used to annotate the data can also be used to disambiguate and assign the confidence score to the candidate annotations. For example, if the dataset class is labeled *Street furniture licenses* the properties *dcterms:subject* are added to link this term to the DBpedia terms *Street_furniture* and *License* (as well as similar terms in IPSV). The annotations for a property labeled *Pole light num* within the domain of this dataset would be annotated with the DBpedia term *Street_light* rather than *Lightning* (as a storm), capturing how close the URIs are in the graph (*Street_light* is connected to *Street_furniture* through the property *dcterms:subject* in DBpedia). However, in many cases correct annotations are not related to others in the same dataset (e.g., a property named *Outside_house_num*), thus the confidence store will be lower.

These annotations and scores are used, as shown in Section 5, to capture the meaning of content and context in our shared RDF stores – i.e., to find and rank related entities or datasets by analyzing the ontological taxonomy and relationships between the annotations in background knowledge sources (namely, alternative names, redirects, common *dcterms:subject*, *skos:broader/narrower*, or any other semantic relationship).

However capturing user intent requires providing proactivity and guidance to ease the burden for users on discovering and interacting with data to solve complex exploratory tasks beyond full text index searches. The main challenge for contextual exploration and search is to be able to determine whether a particular source or a subset of it is relevant for a given user task, as well as considering its connections to other relevant related sources. In this sense, two disparate datasets about diverse topics and intent, such as *Ambulance Call Outs* and the *Register of Fats and Oils Licenses* may both be relevant in the context of a user searching for hospitals, because the latter contains the locations of services establishment for which a license has been granted, where establishments can be filter by type (hospital, restaurants, supermarkets). To capture user intent search and exploration services (contextual APIs) are provided, as described next.

5. REALIZATION

The previous components are integrated into an interface[2], giving users the possibility to publish new datasets and providing contextual access in response to user needs. The following backend API and REST services are provided to expose the functionality of the system, so UI developers and users do not require having any knowledge of Linked Data or SPARQL.

Catalogue-based dataset and entity explorations

Datasets can be explored according to the virtualized repositories where they belong (as said before, in our prototype, we currently have one repository for customer data and another one for open data), or by following any given reference taxonomical model. In our scenario, the IPSV hierarchy is selected as the reference model for catalogue exploration because of its wide coverage of city related topics. Datasets are organized into a hierarchical view of subcategories in the reference model, allowing an easy and thematic browsing of the data. The alignment is done automatically when the entity representing the dataset type is annotated with this model (*dcterms:subject*). Thus a dataset may

sit in more than one subcategory, as we do not attempt to decide what is the best category but rather what categories may be appropriate. To avoid users having to navigate through empty categories, only the part of the tree for which there are datasets is shown. For example the *Sidewalk Café Permits* dataset sits under the IPSV categories (from the deepest subcategory to the root): *Food related licenses* (the subject annotation), *Business licenses*, *Business practice and regulations* and *Business and industry*.

The user can click on a dataset to display the tabular data (generated from their representation in RDF), the annotations of a dataset, or select one or many datasets to plot the spatial (mappable) entities in a map. By clicking on any of these entities the user can explore its properties and attributes.

Spatial entity search and faceted filtering

Users can ask for all data (entities) within a geographic region by drawing a bounding box (e.g., everything known about an address). Behind the scenes, a SPARQL query is used to extract all entities URIs and labels with *Wgs84:lat* and *Wgs84:lon* values inside the bounding box. Entities from different datasets can be overlaid on the map, and datasets can be spatially related by drawing a bounding box, e.g., to discover *crime* hot spots near establishments with *sidewalk cafe permits*. The user can further refine the query by applying faceted filtering, filtering entities by suggesting restrictions while preventing dead-ends, e.g., to plot only crime spots related to robberies (where *robbery* is either a property or a property value for the *Minneapolis Crime* dataset).

Semantic keyword-based search

Besides performing full-text ranked searches based on Lucene[27] to discover entities matching the keyword search, the query is semantically expanded with lexically related words as given by the annotation sources. For example, the *Crime Data* dataset is returned as a result for the keyword search *Fire*. This is because *Fire* is semantically related to *Arson*, a datatype property in the *Minneapolis Crime* dataset. *Fire* is lexically annotated with a set of LOD URIs, among others *IPSV:613*, which preferable label is *Fire* and is related to the concept *IPSV:612*, also known as *Arson*, through the property *skos:related*. As such, query expansion is performed with all semantically related words (smoke, fire brigade, arson, etc.). Duplicated matches are removed and grouped by the datasets they belong to. Entity level matches (classes, properties, ranges, and instances) and their provenance can be displayed per user request, and optionally these entities can be plot in the map. Datasets are ranked by the number of matches, weighted by the average of their score (a number between 0-1).

If no matches are found for compound terms, they are recursively split into their constituents, e.g., *public health Minneapolis* would get datasets with results for both *public health* and *Minneapolis*.

Related dataset and entity search

As datasets are aligned with ontologies, the ontological annotations can be used to identify heterogeneous datasets or entities that are closely related or relevant to a given one. Three criteria are combined to find related datasets for a given one.

Topic based: the subject of the entities from different datasets is the same or related (linked), indicating correspondence between topics. An example is shown in Fig. 2.A where the *Police Cad* dataset is related to *Crime Data* dataset by the graph path connecting the subjects for both datasets. The *Police* and *Crime* subjects are linked through the broader IPSV concept *Crime and law enforcement*.

Content based: datasets with related content even if the purpose (topic) is different, i.e., they have properties sharing the same

---

[2] The website is not publicly available because of customer data confidentiality but videos showcasing the interface are available at http://dublinked.ie/sandbox/queriolift/

annotations. Also, if the values of an object property are connected to annotation entities in other datasets, in the example in Fig. 2.B, the instance value *Theft* for the property *Problem* in *Police Cad* has a *owl:sameAs* link to the DBpedia term *Category:Theft*, which is the broader term of *Category:Robbery*, an annotation property in *Crime Data*.

Entity co-reference: different datasets describing similar entities. Datasets, such as *Sidewalk Café Permits* and *Liquor Permits* are related because they share a few instance entities with the same label, e.g., establishments with both sidewalk café permits and liquor permits (same name across both datasets).

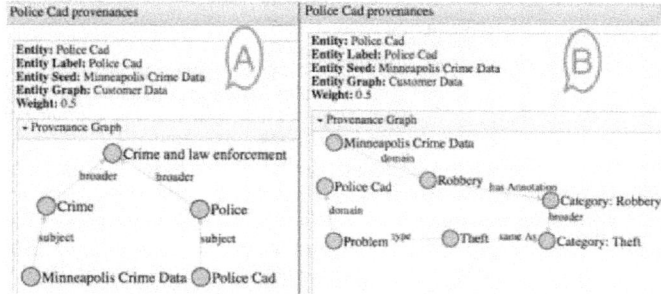

Figure 2. Provenance graphs for related datasets

As for all services, the search for related datasets is performed on demand through efficient SPARQL queries or SPARQL federation across distributed sources. Related datasets are ranked by summing the relevance weights for the *provenance graphs* (*pv*) obtained for each criterion. The weight is calculated according to how significant the entity-level matches are – i.e., for the content-based provenance graph: how many annotations are matched (*num_anns_common*) out of the total for the input dataset (*total_anns_input*), as well as, considering the average confidence score (*WSc*) of each matched annotations to assign weighs to the different criteria when combined. The following formula, used to calculate the score (*Sc*) of a related dataset with respect to an input, responds to the intuition that datasets are more similar if the share more labels/annotations and share labels/annotations with large weights.

$$Sc\_dataset = \sum_{pvi} Avg(W_{Sc\_anns\_common}) * \frac{num\_anns\_common}{total\_anns\_input}$$

6. EXPERIMENT AND CONCLUSIONS

We also tested the usability of the system to support users to perform more complex information retrieval tasks beyond keyword search. We use customer data and relevant open datasets extracted from various portals including geocommons.com and dublinked.ie, for Dublin (Ireland), Minneapolis (Minnesota, USA), as well as some national-level datasets for the USA. In total over a hundred datasets, which were automatically integrated, semantically annotated and linked in less than one hour, producing approximately 1 million virtualized data triples in two SPARQL end points (one for open data and one for customer data,) and almost 190.000 schema triples and annotations stored in the centralized and indexed context store.

We simulated a scenario, where 5 evaluators (all IT experts but not necessarily knowledgeable about semantic standards) are asked to use the system in order to answer the given complex tasks in Table 1. The order of the queries presented to each user was randomized. In Table 1, on the right of the question, we show the minimum number of steps as determined by the authors (min. navigation links /features needed) to get an answer. The features counted are: semantic search, catalogue exploration, displaying tabular data or entity information, plotting entities in a map,

faceted filtering – including the use of negations/exclusion, drawing a bounding box to visualize all entities within, and looking for related datasets and provenance graphs.

The results are shown in Table 1. We evaluate on the number of users which succeeded to find satisfactory answers for the task (*S*), the average number of steps (links / features, including failed attempts) needed by the user to get an answer (*Avg. link*) and the average time to get the answer (essentially measuring the time the user needs to get some business insight)

Domain (datasets)	Question (min. navigation links)	Avg link	S	Avg time
Health (2)	Q1: Find the addresses of all health centers and hospitals in Dublin (4)	5.6	5	2m41s
Environment transport (2)	Q2: Train stations near beaches in Malahide (3)	4.4	5	4m6s
Transport (2)	Q3: Find the number of total spaces for parking areas near Howth station (4)	6.25	5	2m17s
Environment (1)	Q4: Number of readings in Dublin 15 of pollutants over 40 (PM10) in 2012 (4)	5.4	5	1m53s
Environment ,buildings (2)	Q5: The name of the garda station near air pollution sensors in Dublin 15 (4)	5.4	5	2m41s
Public safety Business (2)	Q6: Which cafes are near robbery crimes areas in Minneapolis (5)	7.6	4	3m52s
Public safety (1)	Q7: Spots in Minneapolis with more than 10 car thefts and 10 arson crimes (3)	5.6	4	2m04s
Business (2)	Q8: All places holding both a liquor license and sidewalk permits in Minneapolis (2)	7.2	5	3m40s
Public safety recreation(2)	Q9: All police disturbances near the Creekview center (5)	9.2	5	3m46s

Table 1. Questions of the test, by categories, and results

All users were successful in all tasks, except for **Q6** and **Q7** for which two different users (one for each query) gave up. For **Q6** users would often attempt to find the answers in the *Police Cad* dataset (one of them gave up when she could not find it there), while the answer is found by applying faceted filtering on the property *robberies* in the *Crime* dataset (or as a result from the keyword search *robbery*) and overlaying the results with entities from the *Sidewalk Café Permits* dataset on the map. In **Q7**, one user gave up before realizing he could apply more than one facet filter in the same dataset. All users live in Dublin, therefore they completed the tasks from **Q1** to **Q5** using less navigation links on average, as they knew where to look on the map. For most tasks, users started by using keyword search or catalogue exploration. When catalogue exploration fails, such as when looking for *hospitals* in **Q1**, users will use keyword search to find information hidden in the datasets. The geocoded *Fats and Oils Licenses* dataset is returned as result of this search, where *hospital* is a boolean datatype property. The user can plot in the map the entities for which *hospital* is true in this dataset (faceted filtering), together with all entities from the *Health Centers* dataset. Besides searching and catalogue exploration, plotting a dataset (or matched entities) on the map and displaying entity and tabular data were features used in all queries. Facets were used in more than half of the queries. The bounding box feature was not use often, although it is the faster way to answer **Q3** and **Q5** (e.g., by drawing a bounding box near *Howth station* for **Q3** and near the pollution sensors in **Q5**). Finally, all queries were answered in less than 6 minutes, and in average in less than 4 minutes.

In sum, a semantic approach, able to exploit in an integrated way the combination of information spaces defined by the LOD datasets and the city data is well suited to address the timely issue of data consumption in the context of cities. Here, we presented a lightweight and incremental information sharing approach, as well as an end-user application, to consume city data online. Our main contributions are twofold: (1) Open modeling, where organizations can expose new distributed information based on their models (ontologies/schemata) of choice at any time and without the need to ETL data; (2) Web integration by uplifting data to existing models and exploit overlap across ontologies and data to infer hidden links across entities on demand, in response to user searches or contextual explorations.

REFERENCES

[1] Ding, L., Lebo, T., Erickson, J.S., DiFranzo, D., et al.: A portal for linked open government data ecosystems. Web Semantics 9(3), 2011

[2] Skjaeveland, M., Lian, E., Horrocks, I. Publishing the Norwegian Petroleum Directorate's FactPages as Semantic Web Data. Proc. of the International Semantic Web Conference, ISWC 2013

[3] Lopez, V., Kotoulas, S., Sbodio, M.L., Lloyd, R. Guided Exploration and Integration of Urban Data. Proc. of Hypertext 2013

[4] Kotoulas, S., Lopez, V., Lloyd R., Sbodio, M.L., Lecue, F., et al. SPUD- Semantic Processing of Urban Data. Web Semantics, 2014

[5] London: data.london.gov.uk/

[6] Chicago: data.cityofchicago.org/

[7] Scharffe, F., Atemezing, G., R., T., Gandon, F., et al. Enabling linked-data publication with the datalift platform. In (AAAI'12) Workshop on Semantic Cities, 2012

[8] Maali, F., Cyganiak, R., Peristeras, V.: A publishing pipeline for linked government data. In: Extended Semantic Web Conference. (2012) 778{792

[9] http://www.w3.org/2001/sw/rdb2rdf/p

[10] Han, L., Finin, T., Parr, C., Sachs, J., Joshi, A.: Rdf123: From spreadsheets to rdf. In: 7th International Conference on The Semantic Web. (2008) 451-466

[11] http://virtuoso.openlinksw.com

[12] www.openrdf.org

[13] https://github.com/kurtjx/SNORQL

[14] http://www.w3.org/TR/r2rml/

[15] Cafarella, M.J., Halevy, A., Madhavan, J. Structured data on the Web. Communications of the ACM., 54(2), 2011

[16] Venetis, P., Halevy, A.Y, Madhavan, J., Pasca, M., et al. Recovering semantics of tables on the web. PVLDB, 4(9): 528-538, 2011

[17] Wang, J., Wang H., Wang Z, and Kenny Q. Zhu: Understanding tables on the web. Proc. of the international conference on Conceptual Modeling (ER'12), 2012.

[18] Das Sarma, A., Fang, L., Gupta, N., Halevy, A., Lee. H., et al. Finding Related Tables. Proc. of SIGMOD 2012

[19] WGS84 geo-coordinates: http://www.w3.org/2003/01/geo/

[20] www.w3.org/TR/vcard-rdf

[21] OWL Time ontology: *www.w3.org/TR/owl-time/*

[22] http://doc.esd.org.uk/IPSV/2.00.html

[23] http://dublincore.org/specifications

[24] Bizer, C., Lehmann, J., Kobilarov, G., Auer, S., Becker, C., Cyganiak, R., Hellmann, S. DBpedia - A crystallization point for the Web of Data. Web Semantics, 7(3), 154–165, 2009

[25] Cohen, W, Ravikumar, P., Fienberg, S., E.: A Comparison of String Distance Metrics for Name-Matching Tasks. In IJCAI Workshop on Information Integration, 2003, http://secondstring.sourceforge.net

[26] Mendes, P, Jakob, M., Garcia-Silva, A., Bizer, C. DBpedia spotlight: shedding light on the web of documents. Proc of I-Semantics, 2011

[27] http://lucene.apache.org/core/

[28] Lopez. V., Unger, C., Cimiano, P., Motta, E. Evaluating Question Answering over Linked Data. Web Semantics, 21(0), 2013

[29] http://webdatacommons.org/webtables/

[30] OntoQuest: http://ontop.inf.unibz.it/?page_id=7

Self-Adaptive Filtering Using PID Feedback Controller in Electronic Commerce

Zeinab Noorian [*]
Department of Computer
Science
University of Saskatchewan
Saskatoon,Canada
zen951@mail.usask.ca

Mohsen Mohkami [*]
Department of Computer
Science
University of Saskatchewan
Saskatoon,Canada
m.mohkami@cs.usask.ca

Julita Vassileva
Department of Computer
Science
University of Saskatchewan
Saskatoon,Canada
jiv@cs.usask.ca

ABSTRACT

The performance of e-marketplaces plays a crucial role in attracting and retaining buyers. For example, a variation in the delivered Quality of Services (QoS) can frustrate buyers and they leave the e-marketplace, causing revenue loss. The inherent uncertainties of open marketplaces motivate the design of reputation systems to facilitate buyers in finding honest feedback from other buyers (advisers). Defining the threshold for acceptable level of honesty of advisers is very important, since inappropriately set thresholds would filter away possibly good advice, or the opposite - allow malicious buyers to badmouth good services. However, currently, there is no systematic approach for setting the honesty threshold. We propose a self-adaptive honesty threshold management mechanism based on PID feedback controller. Experimental results show that adaptively tuning the honesty threshold to the market performance enables honest buyers to obtain higher quality of services in comparison with static threshold values defined by intuition and used in previous work.

Keywords

Trust modeling, Reputation systems, Credibility mechanism, Honesty Threshold, e-commerce

1. INTRODUCTION

Open electronic marketplaces are uncertain places. They consist autonomous self-interested participants that act and interact flexibly and intelligently [14]. Validating testimonies and reviews of different products provided by buyers is challenging, since participants neither feel obliged to provide truthful reputation information nor even to share their experiences with their peers.

The performance of an e-commerce systems is a function of a large number of parameters, such as information quality with respect to the accuracy of provided feedback [2], buyers satisfaction and their net benefits [3], service quality of providers, and assurance including the adopted credibility and security measures [20].

[*] Authors equally contributed on the paper.

Designing reputation systems for open marketplaces seems to be an effective approach to ensure that only participants with satisfactory qualities can prosper [8, 22]. Reputation systems assist buyers in their decision making process by providing them with trustworthiness assessment techniques to thoroughly evaluate the credibility of other buyers (advisers), considering various parameters and environmental circumstances.

Although different trust and reputation systems [6, 17, 21] have shown very promising results in accurately modeling the trust of participants, there are certainly opportunities for further optimization with respect to the accuracy of the model. More specifically, existing reputation systems perform under the assumption of the existence of a honesty (credibility) threshold to retain only trustworthy advisers. The credibility threshold sets a decision boundary on the behavioral model of advisers and characterized them as honest and malicious. These systems suffer from a lack of a systematic approach for adjusting the credibility threshold to the dynamic environmental conditions.

Defining the threshold for acceptable level of honesty of advisers is very important. A low threshold will result in a plenty of possible advisers, but the quality of advice may be low. On the other hand, a higher credibility threshold leads to the contribution of a smaller number of advisers and can make it impossible to find advisers. Clearly, adjusting a threshold value is a trade-off between the number of credible advisers and the risk of being misled by deceptive peers.

This paper proposes a method by feedback on the performance of the marketplace in terms of QoS metrics to dynamically determine appropriate value for honesty threshold to optimize the market performance. We built a controller that monitors the quality of e-marketplace and uses a PID feedback controller technique [19] to determine new values for the honesty threshold. Buyers then dynamically re-evaluate their network of trustworthy advisers according to the new recommended value.

Our approach was validated experimentally by integrating our PID-based honesty threshold controller into a simulated e-marketplace with different population tendency. Experimental results show that adaptively tuning the honesty threshold to the market performance enables honest buyers to obtain higher quality of services and more accurately detect malicious advisers in comparison with the static threshold values defined based on designer intuition that are used in previous work.

This research situates well within the context that Jøsang and Golbeck outline as the central concern for future research in multi-agent trust modeling. According to [9], artificially adjusting the credibility threshold value might be inappropriate since one of the ways in which trust models can fail to be robust is in relying on a set of untrustworthy advisers. The methods we outline in this paper seek to address this concern.

2. RELATED WORK

Abdul-Rahmanand and Hailes [1] proposed a model for supporting trust in virtual communities, based on direct experiences and reputation. This trust model uses four degrees of belief to typify agent trustworthiness. However, there are certain aspects of their model that are ad-hoc and limited such as the four trust degrees and fixed weightings assigned to the feedback- which are simply added up without any mathematical justification. Zhang [30] proposed a personalized approach for handling unfair ratings in centralized e-marketplaces. In this model, advisers share their ratings about some sellers. To estimate the credibility of advisers, buyers exploit a probabilistic approach and model advisers' trustworthiness by integrating the public and private reputation components about advisers. Noorian [15, 16] proposed a two-layered cognitive filtering approach to detect and disqualify unfair advisers. The credibility of advisers is evaluated according to the similarity degree of advisers' opinions with those of buyers, as well as their behavioral dispositions in feedback provision. Beta Filtering Feedback [27] and RATEWeb [13] evaluate the ratings based on their deviations from the majority opinion. The basic idea of the proposed method is that if the reported rating agrees with the majority opinion, the raters credibility is increased, and otherwise - decreased. However, unlike other models, RATEweb does not simply discard the rating, if it disagrees with the majority opinion; instead, RATEWeb decreases the credibility of the rater by a certain degree. Wang [26] proposed super-agent framework for reputation management for service selection environment where agents with more capabilities act as super-agents and become responsible for collecting, managing and providing reputation information. Buyers adopt reinforcement learning approach to model the trustworthiness of super-agents. BLADE [21] provides a model for buyers to interpret evaluations of advisers using a Bayesian learning approach. This model does not discard all unreliable ratings; rather, it learns an evaluation function for advisers who provide ratings similar to their direct experience. BLADE applies a strict judgment on the credibility of feedback providers. For example, BLADE discounts the ratings of advisers with an honesty degree of 0.7.

These existing trust models, however, do not address how they distinguish trustworthy advisers from untrustworthy ones. That is, these models can not answer the following questions: 1) How to define the acceptable level of honesty, trustworthiness and/or similarity of an adviser?, 2) How to define the credibility adjustment threshold? To the best of our knowledge, in the existing literature, the honesty threshold has been either explicitly initialized by a central server, as in [23, 26, 28, 30] or has been subjectively determined by buyers according to their behavioral characteristics as presented in [13, 15]. Gorner [5] proposes an empirical methodology to limit the number of advisers that should be maintained in the social network of buyers. However, in their proposed approach system designer should empirically experiments different values for thresholds in the simulated marketplace- performing under presumption settings- to determine the optimal value, which makes it difficult to be adopted to the real-world marketplaces. Another approach that addresses the aforementioned questions is FIRE [7], which defines an adaptive inaccuracy tolerance threshold based on the sellers' performance variation to specify the maximal permitted differences between the actual performance and the provided ratings. This work is different from our approach, however, since in FIRE each buyer filters away advisers based on their local obser-

vation on a quality of the sellers, and thus this model suffers from the risk of unfair judgment of advisers.

3. CREDIBILITY EVALUATION MECHANISM

Suppose that a buyer c sends a query to advisers requesting information about sellers $P = \{p_1, p_2, .., p_j, .., p_m\}$ on the outcomes of the interactions between the advisers and sellers occurring within a time threshold t (which diminishes the risk of changeability in sellers' behaviour). Adviser a_i responds by providing a rating vector R_{ij} for each seller, for example p_j. It contains a tuple $\langle r, s \rangle$, which indicates the number of successful (r) and unsuccessful (s) interaction outcomes with seller p_j respectively. Once the evidence is received, for each R_{ij}, buyer c calculates the expected value of the probability of a positive outcome ($P_r(R_{ij})$) for seller p_j based on a beta distribution [10] as follows:

$$P_r(R_{ij}) = \frac{r+1}{r+s+2} \qquad (1)$$

Clearly, $0 < P_r(R_{ij}) < 1$ and as it approaches 0 or 1, it indicates *unanimity* in the body of evidence [25]. That is, particularly large values of s or r provide better intuition about an overall tendency and quality of sellers. In contrast, $P_r(R_{ij}) \approx 0.5$ (i.e. $r \approx s$) signifies the maximal conflict in gathered evidence, resulting in increasing the uncertainty in determining the quality of sellers. Based on these intuitions, we are able to calculate the degree of reliability and certainty of ratings provided by advisers. More formally, let x represent the probability of a successful outcome for a certain seller. Based on the Definitions (1) and (3) in [25], the *reliability degree* of each R_{ij} can be defined as follows:

$$Conf(R_{ij}) = \frac{1}{2} \int_0^1 \left| \frac{x^r(1-x)^s}{\int_0^1 x^r(1-x)^s \, dx} - 1 \right| \, dx \qquad (2)$$

Theoretical analysis [25] demonstrates that, for a fixed ratio of positive and negative observations, the reliability increases as the number of observations increases. On the contrary, given a fixed number of observations, as the extent of conflict increases, the reliability of the provided observations decreases accordingly. That is, reliability is at a minimum when $P_r(R_{ij}) = 0.5$. As such, the less conflict in their ratings, the more reliable the advisers would be.

However, buyer c should not strictly judge the advisers with rather low reliability in their R_{ij} as deceptive advisers since this reliability factor could signify both the dishonesty of advisers and the dynamic and fraudulent behaviour of sellers reported by the advisers. For example, some malicious sellers may supply satisfactory quality of products in some situations when there is not much at stake and act conversely in other occasions associated with a large gain.

To address this ambiguity, buyer c computes $P_r(R_{cj})$ and $Conf(R_{cj})$ based on her personal experience, R_{cj}, with a set of sellers P with whom the advisers also have experience.[1] Through the comparison of advisers' metrics with the buyer's experience, the buyer would have more trust in those advisers with a similar rating pattern and satisfactory level of honesty. More formally, buyer c measures an average level of dishonesty of a_i by:

$$D_h(a_i) = \frac{\sum_{j=1}^{|P|} | P_r(R_{cj}) - P_r(R_{ij}) |}{|P|} \qquad (3)$$

---

[1] Here, we choose a set of sellers $P \subset \{p_1, ..., p_m\}$ with whom buyer c has sufficient experience, to make sure that the buyer has sufficient knowledge to judge the advisers.

It may also happen that an honest adviser lacks experience with sellers. Thus, despite her inherent honesty, its reliability degree is low and it should not be highly trusted. To address this, we introduce an uncertainty function $U_n(a_i)$ to capture the intuition of information imbalance between c and a_i as follows:

$$U_n(a_i) = \frac{\sum_{j=1}^{|P|} | Conf(R_{cj}) - Conf(R_{ij}) |}{|P|} \quad (4)$$

Given the level of dishonesty of adviser a_i, the honesty of the adviser could be calculated as $1 - D_h(a_i)$. Similarly, given the uncertainty of adviser a_i, the certainty of the adviser would be $1 - U_n(a_i)$. Thus, a credible adviser should achieve higher honesty and certainty simultaneously. The *credibility degree* of adviser a_i is then calculated by reducing her honesty based on her certainty degree as follows:

$$CR(a_i) = (1 - D_h(a_i)) \times (1 - U_n(a_i)) \quad (5)$$

To retain only the most trustworthy advisers, an *honesty threshold*, β where $0 \leqslant \beta \leqslant 1$, is used to determine behavioral patterns of advisers. That is, if $CR(a_i) \geq \beta$, a_i will be counted as a *credible* adviser. In contrast, if $CR(a_i) < \beta$, a_i will be detected as *malicious* adviser and would be filtered out from the buyer c's advisers network.

4. PID-BASED CREDIBILITY THRESHOLD MANAGEMENT

Inspired by the existing electronic commerce quality models[2] [2, 3, 20], we consider two factors that contribute to performance of e-marketplaces, including, 1) market liquidity (denoted by $Mliq$) and 2) buyers satisfaction.

Market liquidity describes a marketplace's ability to facilitate trading of the products promptly without transaction cost (i.e., having to considerably reduce their price) [4]. It also denotes the ability of buyers to find products with desirable features, when needed. However, the open nature of e-commerce, the existence of variety of products with competing features, and the lack of honesty enforcement mechanism make buyers uncertain in discovering the best-suited transaction partners (i.e., trust-wise and profit-wise),thus affecting the liquidity of the market.

Buyer satisfaction can be measured using the ratio of transactions with successful outcome to all the transactions conducted by buyers.

Through the proposed credibility threshold management, each buyer can further adjust her social network of credible advisers by considering the overall performance of the e-marketplace. For example, a marketplace with poor performance might imply that a considerate amount of advisers and sellers might be malicious. In this case, each buyer might want to carefully check other buyers' qualification as her advisers by increasing the credibility threshold β. In other words, when the community is populated with deceitful advisers, buyers would find it difficult to access honest feedback about sellers. Hence, the buyers should require more credible advisers by increasing β. This can help them to detect and exclude more dishonest advisers from their network, and thus obtain opinions of higher quality advisers.

If $\text{SuccessNum}_{(c)}$ denotes the number of successful outcomes achieved by c in a time stamp t, $\text{transactionNum}_{(c)}$ indicates the number of transactions conducted within t, $\text{purchaseNum}_{(c)}$ denotes the number of transactions that c initially *intended* to perform

within t as indicated in its purchase mission [3], we can formulate the *transaction success rate* and the *transaction rate* of the buyer c denoted by $tp(c)$ and $tr(c)$ for the time stamp t as follows:

$$tp(c) = \frac{\text{SuccessNum}_{(c)}}{\text{transactionNum}_{(c)}} \quad (6)$$

$$tr(c) = \frac{\text{transactionNum}_{(c)}}{\text{purchaseNum}_{(c)}} \quad (7)$$

To accurately adjust β, the central server should have a global observation of the system performance. Therefore, buyers are asked to periodically share their $tr(c)$ and $tp(c)$ with the *e-marketplace central server* (ECS). The values of $tr(c)$ and $tp(c)$ reflect the behavior of participants in the e-marketplace. For example, having a high transaction rate $tr(c)$ but a low transaction success rate $tp(c)$ signifies the situation in which a buyer c is misled by dishonest advisers in her network; therefore, could not find high quality sellers. Given these quality metrics, we propose the performance measures for e-commerce systems as follows:

$$Q(t) = \frac{2 * tp(t) * Mliq(t)}{tp(t) + Mliq(t)} \quad (8)$$

Where $Mliq(t) = \frac{\sum_{i=1}^{n} tr(c_i)}{n}$ and $tp(t) = \frac{\sum_{i=1}^{n} tp(c_i)}{n}$ are the average of all $tr(c)$ and $tp(c)$ shared by buyers at time stamp t, and $Q(t)$ is the *harmonic mean* of the e-commerce quality metrics described above. Since the performance of the marketplace is a function of these quality metrics, we use a harmonic mean to balance them by mitigating the impact of the one with a larger value and aggravating the impact of the other with a lower value.

To adjust β accordingly, ECS adopts the idea of feedback controller, specifically, ***Proportional-Integral-Derivative*** (**PID**) controller [24]. Given a designated goal in a system, called the reference r, the feedback control system calculates the error by differentiating the actual outcome, called y, and the reference r. PID controllers provide a means to minimize the error in a system based on the received feedback [19].

In e-commerce systems, the ultimate goal is to maximize the performance of marketplaces in terms of buyers' satisfaction degree and market liquidity, achieving $Q(t) = 1$, so we initialize the goal r to $r = 1$. We designate error, $e(t)$, in the e-commerce system as the difference between the actual performance of the system $Q(t)$ and the goal r which is $e(t) = r - Q(t)$.

In the ideal e-commerce systems in which no malicious buyers exist $Q(t)$ could converge to one. However, in a realistic situation where the marketplace is populated with different participants with various behavioral dispositions, it is not reasonable to expect the perfect performance of the system; therefore, the system will have $Q(t) < 1$.

Given these values, ECS calculates a new value for β that improves $Q(t)$ to reach the idealistic goal $r = 1$. To this end, ECS incorporates PID controller to determine the extent that it has to change the value of β.

The new recommended value of β for the next time stamp $t + 1$ is formulated as follows:

$$\beta(t + 1) = \beta(t) + \beta_0(t + 1) \quad (9)$$

in which $\beta_0(t+1)$ is formalized using the PID controller presented as,

---

[2] We ascribe the performance of the e-commerce system only to the quality of its participants (buyers and sellers) in conducting transaction.

[3] We assume that buyers have a pre-determined purchase missions such that they enter the market to buy certain products.

$$\beta_0(t+1) = k_p e(t) + k_i \int_0^t e(\tau)d\tau + k_d \frac{de(t)}{dt} \qquad (10)$$

Where k_p, k_i, and k_d are the coefficients that leverage the contribution of *Proportional* **P**, which captures the error $e(t)$ calculated in the time stamp t, *Integral* **I**, which accumulates all errors from the start of the e-marketplace, and *Derivative* **D**, which calculates the deviation of current error $e(t)$ from its previous value $e(t-1)$, respectively.

Since in the e-marketplace it is unrealistic to expect $Q(t)$ reaches the value of r (due to the activity of malicious participants), ECS would stop adjusting β if $Q(t)$ reaches a stable point.

More formally, ECS updates the value of β for the next time stamp $t+1$, given the following conditions:

$$\beta(t+1) = \begin{cases} \beta(t) + \beta_0(t+1) & |Q(t) - Q(t-1)| > \sigma \\ \beta(t) & \text{otherwise} \end{cases} \qquad (11)$$

Where σ is a trigger threshold.

5. EXPERIMENTS

In our experiments below, we explore that how systematically determining the value of threshold can yield important gains in trust modelling accuracy of different buyers and improve the quality of the electronic marketplace.

5.1 Experimental Settings

The e-marketplace environment used for experiments is populated with self-interested buyers and sellers, and is operated for 20 days. We initialize the e-marketplace with 100 buyers in total, each of which has a maximum of 5 requests everyday.

Buyers (advisers) are divided into two groups: honest buyers (ones with high credibility), and dishonest buyers (ones with low credibility). Honest advisers generate ratings that differs *at most* by 0.2 points from their actual ratings. In contrast, dishonest advisers generate ratings that differs *at least* by 0.2 points from the actual experience. For example, if the seller's QoS value was 0.9, then the honest adviser would generate a value between (0.7 and 0.9), and dishonest adviser would generate a value between (0.1 and 0.69).

We assume there exist 80 sellers and 20 product types and every 4 of the sellers supply products with the same features. Sellers offer same price for products. We further assume the utility of each product is a value randomly distributed within [50,70] for all sellers[4]. Half of sellers, who supply the same kind of product, are high-performance with QoS values in the range (0.8-1.0). On the contrary, low-performance sellers generate QoS value in a range of (0-0.2). For example, if the seller's QoS is 0.3, the utility of its product is 60 and the price is 5, a buyer's *actual profit* of carrying out a transaction with that seller would be $0.3 * 60 - 5 = 12$.

Buyers calculate the credibility degree of advisers through the presented *Credibility Evaluation Mechanism*. A buyer, e.g. c, calculates the trustworthiness of sellers e.g. p_j through weighted aggregation of advisers ratings, $r_{(a_i)}$, with its own recent experiences $r_{(c)}$, presented as follows:

$$\tau_{(p_j)} = \omega . r_{(c)} + (1-\omega) \frac{\sum_{i=1}^n CR_{(a_i)} * r_{(a_i)}}{\sum_{k=i}^n CR_{(a_i)}} \qquad (12)$$

Buyers subjectively decide to conduct a transaction if $\tau_{(p_j)} > T$ where T indicates the transaction threshold. We further set the

---

[4]In this e-marketplace, we consider products as equally important and offer rather similar utility. Dealing with products with different range of utility is remained for future work.

threshold T to be 0.6. Also, ω is determined based on Equation 18 presented in [18].

The buyer c's expected utility of carrying out a transaction with a seller p_j can be formalized as follows:

$$Exp_c^{p_j} = \tau_{(p_j)} * V_{p_j} - p_s \qquad (13)$$

where V_{p_j} and p_s indicate the utility of the product promised by p_j and the price of the product, respectively. Also, a loss of a buyer c in conducting transaction with p_j can be captured as the difference of its actual profit $Act_c^{p_j}$, and its expected utility presented as,

$$Loss_c^{p_j} = Exp_c^{p_j} - Act_c^{p_j}. \qquad (14)$$

We conduct comparative experiments in e-marketplace where 50% of buyers are honest and 50% of them are malicious. We evaluate the performance of the e-marketplace in different environmental settings, adopting the fixed $\beta = 0.5$ versus the PID-based β approach.

The e-marketplace operates for a period of 20 days and the reported results for each day are the average of 10 runs.

5.1.1 Evaluating the Market Liquidity of the Simulated e-marketplace

We first measure the *market liquidity* by examining the transaction rate of different groups of buyers. Upon arrival, buyers randomly select sellers based on their promised utility (up to round 2). After acquiring sufficient experiences they establish their social network of trustworthy advisers, adopting different honesty threshold approaches: 1) the fixed β and 2) the PID-based β, which is initialized to 0.5. Given the initial setting of β, buyers have a similar transaction rate in initial days. However we observe that as β increases, the transaction rate of the honest buyers increases while the transaction rate of dishonest advisers decreases (Figure 2).

From Figures 1 and 2 , we notice that in both honesty threshold management approaches, honest buyers have higher transaction rates compared to the dishonest ones. However, comparative results indicate that in a PID-based β honest buyers have higher transaction rate than their counterparts in the fixed β approach. The adaptive approach of ECS in adjusting β, based on the quality of marketplaces, results in 1) increase of honest buyers' transaction rate, and 2) detection and isolation of more dishonest advisers. Note that, even though the value of β gradually increases and the dishonest advisers are mostly filtered away, the honest buyers cannot conduct all the transactions they initially intended (i.e., $tr(c) < 1$). This is due to a lack of experience of buyers and advisers with the sellers that they intend to make transactions with.

5.1.2 Evaluating Buyers' Satisfaction in the Simulated e-marketplace

In order to measure *buyers satisfaction* rate we compare the transaction success rate, total profit and loss gained by different buyers. We observe that, honest buyers provided with the PID-based β conduct more successful transactions (Figures 4), and are more satisfied with their transaction outcomes (Figure 5) than other honest buyers in the fixed β approach (Figure 3). Results suggest that in both honesty threshold management approaches, honest buyers have higher transaction success rates and gain larger profit compared to the dishonest ones. However, comparative results indicate that in a PID-based β honest buyers conduct more satisfactory transaction; and dishonest buyers conduct less satisfactory transaction than their counterparts in the fixed β approach.

The profit difference between honest buyers and dishonest buyers with a PID-based β is much larger than that of fixed β (Figure 5). The results suggest that in the e-marketplaces in which buyers

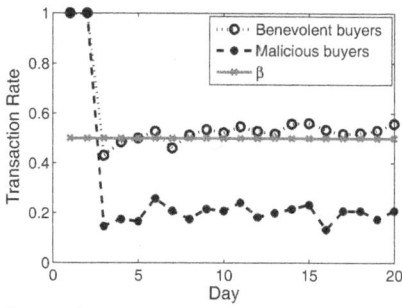

Figure 1: The market liquidity of e-commerce system when buyers adopt fixed β

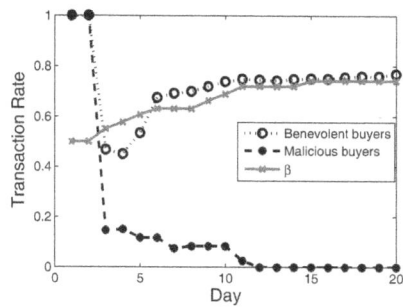

Figure 2: The market liquidity of e-commerce system when buyers adopt PID-based β

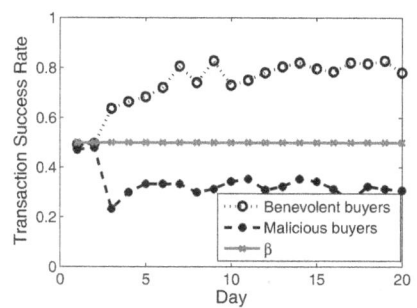

Figure 3: The transaction success rate of buyers adopt fixed β

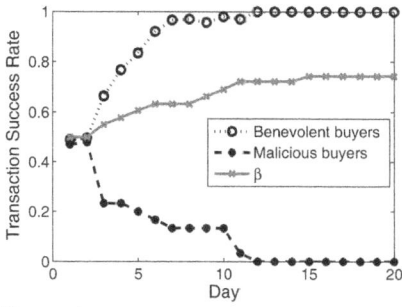

Figure 4: The transaction success rate of buyers adopt PID-based β

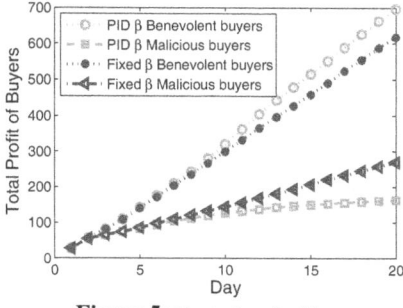

Figure 5: The total profit of buyers

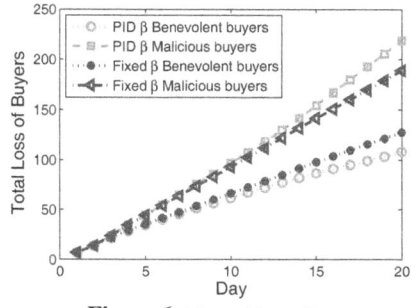

Figure 6: The total loss of buyers

are equipped with a credibility evaluation mechanism with fixed β dishonest buyers have a good chance of making profit by behaving deceitfully in the environment. This problem is especially important in competitive e-marketplaces where sellers have limited inventories and good sellers are scarce. On the contrary, as many of the dishonest buyers are detected in a PID-based β mechanism, they have a small chance to access genuine feedback and to mislead other buyers with their corrupted information.

Finally, as depicted in Figure 6, honest buyers in a PID-based β approach are able to predict the expected utility of sellers more accurately and gain lower level of loss compared with their counterparts in the fixed β approach. Experimental results further show that the loss difference between honest buyers and dishonest buyers with a PID based β is much larger than that of fixed β in a balance e-marketplace.

6. SUMMARY AND FUTURE WORKS

In this paper, we design a controller to evaluate the honesty threshold, which serves as decision boundary to separate participants based on their behavioral characteristics.

The proposed controller monitors the quality of e-marketplace and uses a PID feedback controller technique to determine new values for the honesty threshold to adapt to the changing marketplace. In the existing literature, the choice of values for this "magic" threshold is usually left to the designers implementing a particular system.

Experimental results show that using a principled method to evaluate the value of honesty threshold will provide an improvement to the accuracy of credibility mechanisms in classifying different group of participants. We have also seen that the threshold parameter should be modestly sized depending on the quality of marketplaces in terms of market liquidity and buyers satisfactions- allowing dishonest advisers to be filtering away. With the presenta-

tion of the array of comparative results, the value of employing our PID-based credibility threshold management for setting threshold becomes apparent. Our methods are in fact demonstrating that employing a principled approach results promote the honest buyers and demote the dishonest ones more effectively than the static approach in which the threshold value is selected arbitrarily by system designers.

An interesting direction for future work would be to improve the feedback controller method by adopting different dynamic performance metrics supported in the market microstructure literature [12], in addition to those considered here. Furthermore, since the buyers' contribution in providing feedback is an essential elements in the performance monitoring of the marketplace, a useful direction for future work would be the incorporation of an incentive mechanism to promote more participation (in terms of providing honest feedback) from the buyers.

It also would be useful to explore some extensions to our proposed mechanism. For example, we could propose a more comprehensive approach for credibility mechanism which considers the buyers subjectivity in assessing trustworthiness and the performance of the entire e-marketplace. We then conduct experiments to evaluate the effectiveness of PID-based threshold adjustment in improving the quality of e-marketplace where buyers with different behavioral characteristics exist.

We will also develop more extensive experimentation to continue to validate our model. We are particularly interested in empirically demonstrating how different credibility mechanisms [16, 29] guided by our PID-based threshold adjustment are able to handle marketplaces where strategic buyers collude with each other. This problem has been acknowledged as an important consideration by several researchers in the field [11, 30] and if addressed in a convincing manner would continue to provide valuable encouragement for the use of web-based agents for electronic marketplace.

7. REFERENCES

[1] A. Abdul-Rahman and S. Hailes. Supporting trust in virtual communities. In *System Sciences, 2000. Proceedings of the 33rd Annual Hawaii International Conference on*, pages 9–pp. IEEE, 2000.

[2] S. J. Barnes and R. Vidgen. Measuring web site quality improvements: a case study of the forum on strategic management knowledge exchange. *Industrial Management & Data Systems*, 103(5):297–309, 2003.

[3] W. H. Delone. The delone and mclean model of information systems success: a ten-year update. *Journal of management information systems*, 19(4):9–30, 2003.

[4] M. Fleming. Measuring treasury market liquidity. *FRB of New York Staff Report*, (133), 2001.

[5] J. Gorner, J. Zhang, and R. Cohen. Improving trust modeling through the limit of advisor network size and use of referrals. *Electronic Commerce Research and Applications*, 12(2):112–123, 2013.

[6] Y. Haghpanah and M. desJardins. Prep: a probabilistic reputation model for biased societies. In *Proceedings of the 11th International Conference on Autonomous Agents and Multiagent Systems-Volume 1*, AAMAS '12, pages 315–322, 2012.

[7] T. D. Huynh, N. R. Jennings, and N. R. Shadbolt. Fire: An integrated trust and reputation model for open multi-agent systems. In *In Proceedings of the 16th European Conference on Artificial Intelligence (ECAI*, pages 18–22, 2004.

[8] A. A. Irissappane, S. Jiang, and J. Zhang. A framework to choose trust models for different e-marketplace environments. In *IJCAI*, 2013.

[9] A. Jøsang and J. Golbeck. Challenges for robust trust and reputation systems. In *Proceedings of the 5th International Workshop on Security and Trust Management (SMT 2009), Saint Malo, France*, 2009.

[10] A. Josang and R. Ismail. The Beta reputation system. In *Proceedings of the 15th Bled Electronic Commerce Conference*, 2002.

[11] R. Jurca and B. Faltings. An incentive compatible reputation mechanism. In *Proceedings of the second international joint conference on Autonomous agents and multiagent systems*, AAMAS '03, pages 1026–1027, New York, NY, USA, 2003. ACM.

[12] A. Madhavan. Market microstructure: A survey. *Journal of Financial Markets*, 3(3):205–258, 2000.

[13] Z. Malik and A. Bouguettaya. Rateweb: Reputation assessment for trust establishment among web services. *The VLDB Journalâ€"The International Journal on Very Large Data Bases*, 18(4):885–911, 2009.

[14] L. Mui, M. Mohtashemi, and A. Halberstadt. Notions of reputation in multi-agents systems: a review. In *Proceedings of the first international joint conference on Autonomous agents and multiagent systems: part 1*, AAMAS '02, pages 280–287, New York, NY, USA, 2002. ACM.

[15] Z. Noorian, S. Marsh, and M. Fleming. Multi-layer cognitive filtering by behavioral modeling. In *The 10th International Conference on Autonomous Agents and Multiagent Systems - Volume 2*, AAMAS '11, pages 871–878, 2011.

[16] Z. Noorian, S. Marsh, and M. Fleming. Prob-cog: An adaptive filtering model for trust evaluation. In *IFIPTM*, pages 206–222, 2011.

[17] Z. Noorian and M. Ulieru. The state of the art in trust and reputation systems: a framework for comparison. *J. Theor. Appl. Electron. Commer. Res.*, 5:97–117, August 2010.

[18] Z. Noorian, J. Zhang, Y. Liu, S. Marsh, and M. Fleming. Trust-oriented buyer strategies for seller reporting and selection in competitive electronic marketplaces. *Autonomous Agents and Multi-Agent Systems*, pages 1–38, 2013.

[19] H. Ozbay. *Introduction to feedback control theory*. CRC Press, 2000.

[20] A. Parasuraman, V. A. Zeithaml, and A. Malhotra. Es-qual a multiple-item scale for assessing electronic service quality. *Journal of service research*, 7(3):213–233, 2005.

[21] K. Regan, P. Poupart, and R. Cohen. Bayesian reputation modeling in e-marketplaces sensitive to subjectivity, deception and change. In *Proceedings of the National Conference on Artificial Intelligence*, volume 21, page 1206. AAAI Press, 2006.

[22] J. Sabater and C. Sierra. Review on computational trust and reputation models. *Artificial Intelligence Review*, 24(1):33–60, 2005.

[23] W. L. Teacy, J. Patel, N. R. Jennings, and M. Luck. Travos: Trust and reputation in the context of inaccurate information sources. *Autonomous Agents and Multi-Agent Systems*, 12(2):183–198, 2006.

[24] A. Visioli. *Practical PID control*. Springer, 2006.

[25] Y. Wang and M. P. Singh. Formal trust model for multiagent systems. In *IJCAI*, pages 1551–1556, 2007.

[26] Y. Wang, J. Zhang, and J. Vassileva. A super-agent framework for reputation management and cimmunity formation in decentralized systems. *Computational Intelligence*, 2014.

[27] A. Whitby, A. Jøsang, and J. Indulska. Filtering out unfair ratings in bayesian reputation systems. In *Proc. 7th Int. Workshop on Trust in Agent Societies*, 2004.

[28] L. Xiong and L. Liu. Peertrust: Supporting reputation-based trust for peer-to-peer electronic communities. *IEEE Transactions on Knowledge and Data Engineering*, 16:843–857, 2004.

[29] J. Zhang. *Promoting Honesty in Electronic Marketplaces: Combining Trust Modeling and Incentive Mechanism Design*. PhD thesis, School of Computer Science, University of Waterloo, 2009.

[30] J. Zhang and R. Cohen. Evaluating the trustworthiness of advice about seller agents in e-marketplaces: A personalized approach. *Electronic Commerce Research and Applications*, 2008.

On the Choice of Data Sources to Improve Content Discoverability via Textual Feature Optimization

Elizeu Santos-Neto[1]   Tatiana Pontes[2]   Jussara M. Almeida[2]   Matei Ripeanu[1]

[1]University of British Columbia
Vancouver, BC, Canada
{elizeus, matei}@ece.ubc.ca

[2]Universidade Federal de Minas Gerais
Belo Horizonte, MG, Brazil
{tpontes, jussara}@dcc.ufmg.br

ABSTRACT

A large portion of the audience of video content items on the web currently comes from keyword-based search and/or tag-based navigation. Thus, the textual features of this content (e.g., the title, description, and tags) can directly impact the view count of a particular content item, and ultimately the advertisement generated revenue. More importantly, the textual features can generally be optimized to attract more search traffic.

This study makes progress on the problem of automating tag selection for online video content with the goal of increasing viewership. It brings two key insights: first, based on evidence that existing tags for YouTube videos can be improved by an automated tag recommender, even for a sample of well curated movies, it explores the impact of using information mined from repositories created by different production modes (e.g., peer- and expert-produced); second, this study performs a preliminary characterization of the factors that impact the quality of the tag recommendation pipeline for different input data sources.

Categories and Subject Descriptors

H.4 [**Information Systems Applications**]: Miscellaneous

General Terms

Measurement

Keywords

peer-production; social tagging; video popularity

1. INTRODUCTION

Given the sheer volume content owners currently generate (e.g., YouTube receives 100 hours of video per minute [23]), they often offload online publication and monetization tasks to specialized content management companies. Content managers publish, monitor, and promote the owner's content, and usually there is a revenue sharing agreement between the content manager and the content owner (e.g., the ad revenue associated with the content).

Although viewers may reach a content item starting from many 'leads' (e.g., an e-mail from a friend or a promotion campaign in an online social network), a large portion of viewers relies on keyword-based search and/or tag-based navigation to find videos. An argument supporting this assertion is the fact that 10.5% of the unique YouTube visitors come from Google.com searches [24].

HT'14, September 1–4, 2014, Santiago, Chile.
Copyright © 2014 ACM 978-1-4503-2954-5/14/09 $15.00.
http://dx.doi.org/10.1145/2631775.2631815

With the integration of Google and YouTube search, one might expect that the volume of search traffic that leads to views on YouTube will only increase. Moreover, YouTube is the third most popular site on the web; behind Facebook and Google [25].

Consequently, the textual features of video content (e.g., the title, description, comments, and tags, in the case of YouTube) have a major impact on the view count of each item and ultimately on the revenues of the content manager and owner [9,22].

Experts can produce these textual features via manual inspection of a content object, a practice still used today. This solution, however, is manpower intensive and limits the scale at which content managers can operate. More importantly, even for well curated online videos, there is evidence that their textual features can be further improved to attract more search traffic [18].

Therefore, mechanisms to support this process (e.g., automating textual feature suggestion) are desirable. It has been shown that simple suggestions have positive results: for example, title suggestions on eBay have benefitted both sellers, who increased revenue, and buyers, who found relevant products faster [9].

With the ever-increasing volume of user-generated content available on the Web, there is a plethora of sources from which an automated mechanism that suggests textual features (tags, in particular) could extract candidate terms. For example, *Wikipedia* (a peer-produced encyclopedia), *MovieLens* and *Rotten Tomatoes* (social networks where movie enthusiasts collaboratively catalog, rate, and annotate movies), *New York Times movie review* section, or even *YouTube* comments are potential sources of candidate keywords to annotate user-generated videos.

This study starts from the observation that textual features, such as tags currently available for YouTube videos, can generally be further optimized to attract more search traffic, and hence, increase content viewership [18]. With this in mind, we investigate the value of various information repositories such as the aforementioned ones, when used as input for tag recommendation algorithms that aim to boost video-content popularity. In particular, we categorize the data sources as peer- or expert-produced according to their production mode. The following research questions drive our investigation:

Q1. *How do peer- and expert-produced input data sources compare with regards to their impact on the performance of tag recommenders for boosting content popularity?*

Q2. *Do peer-production aspects, such as the number of contributors to a data source, influence the effectiveness of tag recommenders that aim to increase content popularity?*

It is worth highlighting that this work uses recommender algorithms in a different context than many previous studies: our goal is *not* to design novel and more efficient tag recommendation algorithms, but rather explore the impact of the choice of the input data source. While previous work proposes tag recommenders that aim to maximize relevance or diversity [1,6,12,15,17], this study focuses on comparing the outcomes of using different sources of information when recommending tags to boost video popularity.

To this end, *we adopt the following methodology*:

(i) We construct a ground truth by recruiting '*turkers*' from Amazon Mechanical Turk (AMT), asking them to watch a set of YouTube videos and provide the keywords they would use to search for these videos (§3);

(ii) We implement an experimental tag recommendation pipeline and couple it with different input data sources (§2, §4),

(iii) We evaluate the impact of data source choice on the quality of the tag recommendations provided (§5.1, 5.3).

In summary, *the contributions of this work are*:

- A comparison of the relative value of using different information sources as inputs for tag recommenders that aim to boost content popularity. The relative value of an information source is evaluated by accuracy and rank distance metrics (described in §4.4), which compare the tags suggested by the recommenders to the ground truth. This comparison reveals that: *(i)* repositories with structured information about the contents of the videos (e.g., actor names, genre classification) provide better tags than unstructured ones; *(ii)* combining sources with different characteristics regarding the production mode (i.e., experts and peers) and the structure of data (e.g., presence or absence of an schema) leads to better results; and, *(iii)* some peer-produced sources (e.g., *MovieLens*) lead to surprisingly good performance despite their lack of structure and central coordination.

- An analysis of the characteristics of data sources shows that the number of peers who produced data to an item correlates with the recommendation quality extracted from this data source.

This paper builds on our own previous effort [18], where we show that textual features of YouTube videos can be optimized to attract more traffic. The quest to improve content visibility is not new - the Search Engine Optimization field has seen uninterrupted attention. Multiple avenues are available ranging from some that are viewed as abusive (e.g., link-farms) to perfectly legitimate ones (e.g., better content organization, good summaries in the title-bar of webpages). Our exploration falls in this latter category.

2. CONTEXT FOR OUR ASSESSMENT

This section describes the context in which we investigate the effectiveness of different information sources as inputs for tag recommendation algorithms, and presents the formal statement of the recommendation problem used as a backdrop in our work.

Annotating a video with tags that match the terms users would use to search for it increases the chance that users view the video. This is because most information services, and search in particular, rely on tags as main source of description of the rich media content (e.g., videos). Various textual sources related to the video and whose content can be automatically retrieved (e.g., movie reviews, comments) can be used as input sources for recommenders to suggest tags for items. Our study focuses on movies but it can easily be extended to other types of content.

A recommendation pipeline that implements this idea is schematically presented in Figure 1: data sources feed the pipeline with textual input data. Next, the textual data is pre-processed by filters to both clean and augment it (e.g., remove stopwords,

detect named entities). This processing step provides candidate keywords for the recommenders. The recommendation step uses the candidate keywords (and their related statistics, e.g., frequency and co-occurrence) to produce a ranked list according to a scoring function implemented by a given tag recommender. As the space available for tags provided by video sharing websites (e.g., *YouTube* or *Vimeo*) is limited, the selection of the most valuable candidate keywords is constrained by a budget, often defined by the number of words or characters. Thus, the final step consists of solving an instance of the 0-1-knapsack problem that selects a set of tags from the list produced by the recommender.

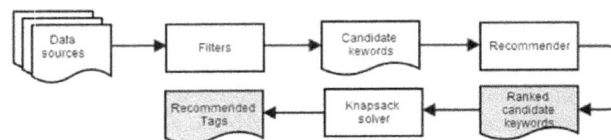

Figure 1. The recommendation pipeline.

The recommendation pipeline is composed of four main elements:

- *Data Sources*. Provides the input textual data used by the recommenders. In particular, we are interested in peer-produced data sources, as well as expert-produced. Discussion in §4.1.

- *Filters*. The raw textual data extracted from a data source is filtered to minimize noise. We consider simple filters such as stopwords and punctuation removal, lowercasing, and named entity detection (we leverage *OpenCalais.com*). The goal is to both clean and augment the input data.

- *Tag Recommender*. Starting from a set of candidate keywords together with relevant statistics (e.g., frequency, co-occurrence), a recommender scores the candidate keywords. There are many ways of defining scoring functions; and, it is *not* our goal to advocate a specific scoring function or recommender. Instead, our intention is to investigate the influence of the choice of data source on overall performance. Discussion in §4.2.

- *Knapsack Solver*. After ranking candidate keywords, those that best fit the budget are selected. Here the budget is expressed in terms of the number of characters, as done in *YouTube*, where the one can use up to 500 characters for tags. This step is formulated as 0-1-knapsack problem, whose objective is to select a set of tags that maximizes the recommender score function while respecting the total constraint.

Our goal is to evaluate how the choice of the data source used as input for this recommendation pipeline impacts the quality of the recommended tag-set. Specifically, we aim to compare peer- and expert-produced information sources in the context of tag recommendation tasks that attempt to improve video popularity. Intuitively, a high quality solution for the tag recommendation problem is a good approximation of the query terms users would use to search for a video. Next, we discuss how to build a ground truth that enables comparing data sources.

3. THE GROUND TRUTH

The ideal ground truth to understand the impact of tags on content popularity in YouTube would consist of experiments that vary the set of tags associated to videos and capture their impact on the number of views attracted. However, collecting this ground truth requires having the publishing rights for the videos, and implies executing experiments over a considerable duration.

We built a ground truth by setting up a survey using the Amazon Mechanical Turk (AMT). The survey asks participants to watch a video and answer the question: '*What query terms you would use* to search for this video?'. The rationale is that these terms would, if used as tags to annotate the video, maximize its retrieval by the *YouTube* search engine (and indirectly maximize viewership) while still being relevant to the video. Next, we briefly summarize our methodology to build the ground truth. More details in [18].

Content Selection. We asked *turkers* (i.e., AMT workers) to watch movie trailers, not the actual movies. The reason is that the trailers are generally shorter (about five minutes or less), which encourage them to watch more trailers and add more keywords.

Our dataset has 382 movies selected to meet two constraints: first, their trailers must be available on *YouTube*; second, to enable comparisons, they had to have reviews available via the *NY Times* movie reviews API, and records in the *MovieLens* catalog.

Survey. For each video, we collected answers from three turkers who were asked to associate 3 to 10 keywords to each video (as search queries are typically of this length [7]). Each participant was paid $0.30 per task (leading to a total cost of $345 for the survey). We followed AMT pay guidelines: our pay rate amounts to an hourly rate of $3/hour, which is way cheaper than the wage of a dedicated 'channel managers'. We performed simple quality control by inspecting each answer to avoid accepting spam.[1]

4. EXPERIMENTAL SETUP
We present the data sources, recommenders, and metrics used.

4.1 Data Sources
We focus on comparing the effectiveness of *peer-* and *expert-produced* sources as input to tag recommenders in the context of content promotion. The position of a data source in this spectrum (Figure 2) depends on whether data is produced collaboratively or by a single expert. *IMDb* was not considered, as it did not have an API by the time we did this study. Next, we describe data sources:

MovieLens is a web system where users collaboratively build a catalog of movies. Users can create and update movie entries; annotate movies with tags; review and rate movies. Based on previous users' activities and ratings, *MovieLens* suggests movies that a user may like to watch. For our evaluation, we use only the tags users produce while collaboratively annotating the movies. This data is a trace of tag assignments available on the Web [26].

Wikipedia is an encyclopedia where users collaboratively write articles [27]. These pages are the sources of candidate keywords for recommending tags for their respective movies.

NY Times reviews are written by critics who can be considered experts on movies. We leverage the review page of a movie as the source of candidate keywords for the tag recommender. Reviews are collected via the New York Times API [28].

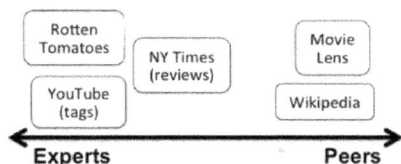

Figure 2. Illustration of the space of data sources we explore.

Rotten Tomatoes is a portal where users can rate and review movies. They also have access to all credits information: actors, directors, producers, synopsis, etc. The portal links to critics' reviews as well. This information can be considered as produced

by experts (likely the film credits are obtained directly from the producers, while the critics' reviews are similar to those from *NY Times*). This is available via the Rotten Tomatoes API [29]. In the experiments, we divide Rotten Tomatoes into two data sources: *Rotten Tomatoes* (with the credit information); and, *RT Reviews* (with the critics' reviews). While users can review the movies as well (qualified as peer-produced information), these were *not* accessible via the API at the time of our investigation.

YouTube. We collect the tags already assigned to the *YouTube* videos in our sample from the HTML source of each video's page to test if they can be further optimized. *YouTube* figures in the expert-produced end of the spectrum, as only the publisher can assign tags to the video. It is reasonable to assume that publishers aim to optimize videos' textual features to attract more views.

4.2 Recommenders
The experiments use two tag recommendation algorithms that process the input provided by the data sources. In particular, we use FREQUENCY and RANDOMWALK primarily because they harness some fundamental aspects of the tag recommendation problem that state-of-the-art methods [1,2,11,19] also use (i.e., tag frequency, and tag co-occurrence patterns). We note that the methodology we describe and the ground truth can be used to evaluate other, more sophisticated, recommender algorithms.

The *FREQUENCY* recommender scores the candidate keywords based on how often each keyword appears in the data provided by a data source. Given a movie title, our pipeline finds the documents in the data source that match the title and extracts a list of candidate keywords. For example, in *Wikipedia*, the candidate keywords to a given movie are extracted from the *Wikipedia* page about the movie. Hence, the frequency of a keyword is the number of times it appears in that page. Similarly, in *MovieLens*, the frequency is the number of times a tag is assigned to a movie.

The RANDOMWALK recommender harnesses both the frequency and the co-occurrence between keywords. The co-occurrence is detected differently depending on the data source. In *MovieLens*, two keywords co-occur if they are assigned to the movie by the same user, while in *NY Times*, *Rotten Tomatoes*, and *Wikipedia* two keywords co-occur if they appear in the same page related to the movie (i.e., review, movie record, and movie page, respectively). RANDOMWALK builds a graph where each keyword is a node and an edge connects two keywords if they co-occur. The initial node score is proportional to the individual frequency of each keyword obtained from the data source. This recommender is executed until convergence and the final node scores are used to rank the candidate keywords [4,11,20].

4.3 Budget Adjustment
To make the comparison fairer, we adjust the budget used by the knapsack solver to the size of the tag set of each movie in the ground truth. The reason for using a budget per video is that otherwise, a uniform larger budget, would bias the F3-measure we use (see definition below), as the number of recommended tags would be always larger than the ground truth size.

4.4 Success Metrics
The final step is to estimate, for each combination of videos, input data sources, and tag recommender, the quality of the recommended tag-set compared with the ground truth. To this end, we use three metrics: F3-measure, generalized τ distance [5], and the Normalized Discounted Cumulative Gain (NDCG).

Let T_v and S_v be the set of distinct words in the ground truth and the recommended tag-set, respectively, for video v.

F3-measure for video v is defined as:

$$F_3(v) = \frac{10 \cdot P(v) \cdot R(v)}{9 \cdot P(v) + R(v)}$$

$P(v) = \frac{|T_v \cap S_v|}{|S_v|}$ is the precision, and $R(v) = \frac{|T_v \cap S_v|}{|T_v|}$ is the recall. This measure weighs equally all tags in the ground truth, and thus ignores that multiple 'turkers' may suggest the same tag, a strong indication that the tag has higher value to help discover the video.

Generalized τ Distance [5] is used to address this issue, allowing the comparison between two ranked lists. Given a video, we compare its ground truth (sorted by the number of turkers who assigned the tag to the video) and its recommended tag-set (sorted by the recommender score function). It is similar to the traditional Kendall τ distance, but it relaxes the constraint that the two lists have the same elements by introducing a penalty parameter to account for elements that are in only one list. This metric however weighs equally all order inversions.

NDCG is introduced to compensate for this, penalizing order changes at the top of the list. It is computed as follows:

$$NDCG(T_v, S_v) = \frac{\sum_{j=1}^{|S_v|} \frac{2^{f(w_j,v)}-1}{\log(j+1)}}{\sum_{i=1}^{|T_v|} \frac{2^{f(k_i,v)}-1}{\log(i+1)}}$$

$f(\cdot, v)$ is the frequency of a tag in the ground truth (i.e., number of turkers who assigned the tag to v); i and j are the positions of a tag in the ground truth and in the recommended tag set, respectively. If a tag $w \in S_v$ and $w \notin T_v$, $f(w, v) = 0$.

5. EXPERIMENTAL RESULTS

This section presents our experimental results. First, we analyze the influence of individual data sources on the recommendation performance (§5.1). We then compare two sets of combined data sources (grouped into expert and peer-produced) (§5.2). Finally, we explore factors that may explain the observed performance of some peer-produced data sources (§5.3).

5.1 Individual data sources' performance

We aim to assess the value of peer- versus expert-produced information, in the context of tag recommendation to improve content popularity. To this end, we compare the performance of different data sources of candidate tags for each recommender.

Figure 3 shows the complementary cumulative distribution functions (CCDFs) of the F3-measure for each individual data source as the input for the two recommenders. We note that *RottenTomatoes* provides significant improvements over the existing tags on *YouTube*. Also, *MovieLens* is significantly better than the other three data sources (*NYTimes*, *RT Reviews*, and *Wikipedia*), though *it* provides minor improvements compared to *YouTube*. Using a Kolmogorov-Smirnov Test, we confirm that the difference in recommender's performance for each pair of data sources is statistically significant and varies from 0.18 to 0.74 (depending on the data source, recommender, and metric).

To put these results in perspective, we note that *Rotten Tomatoes*, besides providing expert-produced information, incorporates a schema for the information provided (i.e., actors, and directors names). Thus, an explanation for its good performance is that searchers tend to use names of entities related to the movie being searched. Therefore, by using an input rich of highly accurate named entities, it is more likely that a recommender is successful.

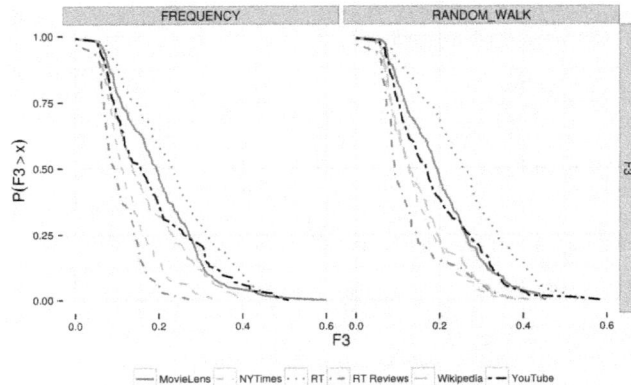

Figure 3. CCDF of F3-measure for each data source used as input for FREQUENCY (left) and RANDOMWALK (right).

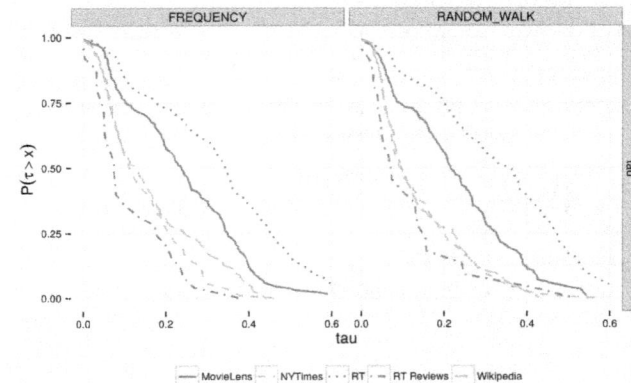

Figure 4. CCDF of τ for each data source used as input for FREQUENCY (left) and RANDOMWALK (right).

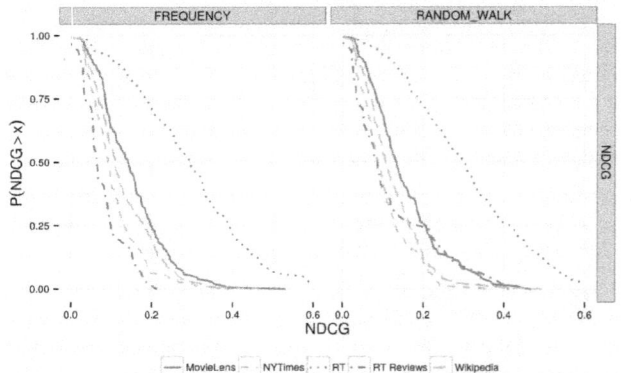

Figure 5. CCDF of NDCG for each data source used as input for FREQUENCY (left) and RANDOMWALK (right).

In fact, we inspected the ground truth and after aggregating the top-5 most frequent keywords for each movie, around 50% of the top-10% most frequent keywords are named entities.

Although it might be intuitive that accurate named entities improve recommendation, the good performance of *MovieLens* compared to the others is important. In particular, one would expect that the candidate keywords extracted from expert-produced reviews (*NYTimes* and *RT Reviews*) or peer-produced fact pages (*Wikipedia*) match what users use to search. However, the relative superiority of *MovieLens* suggests that keywords produced via collaborative annotation may be more effective than those produced by either collaborative text editing or by experts.

Figure 4 and Figure 5 show the performance of all data sources except *YouTube* in terms of τ and NDCG. These metrics consider the tags ranked according to their scores; *YouTube* was removed since it lacks ordering based on the tags relative importance. The results for τ and NDCG are qualitatively similar to those observed for F3-measure: the relative order among data sources is unchanged – *Rotten Tomatoes*, *MovieLens*, *Wikipedia*, *NYTimes*, and *RT Reviews*, from best to worst performance. These metrics highlight that biasing by tag popularity in the ground truth widens the distance between *Rotten Tomatoes* and the other sources.

5.2 Combining the data sources

This section investigates the relative performance of combinations of data sources. In particular, the experiment considers two groups – peer-produced (*MovieLens* + *Wikipedia*) and expert-produced (*NYTimesReviews* + *RTReviews*). Additionally, we compare to *Rotten Tomatoes* (which provides the best individual result) and *YouTube* as baselines for comparison.

The CCDF of the F3-measure for each group of data sources (Figure 6) leads to three observations: *(i)* the performance of both recommenders using the *peer-produced* data source is significantly better than using the *expert-produced data*; *(ii)* for the FREQUENCY recommender, the performance of the *peer-produced* data source is comparable to that of *Rotten Tomatoes* (which has the advantage of having highly accurate named entity information as discussed); *(iii)* the *peer-produced* data source provides improvement relative to the tags currently assigned to the *YouTube* videos (statistically significant for FREQUENCY).

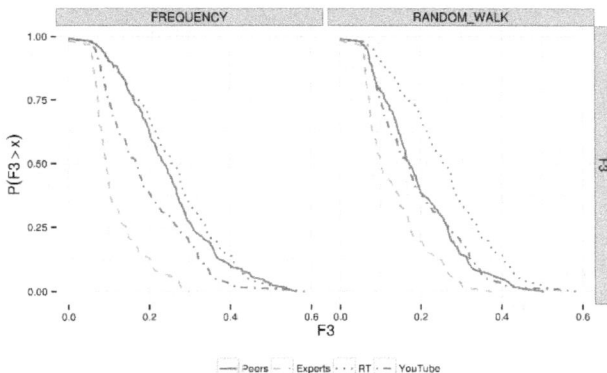

Figure 6. CCDF of F3-measure (similar for τ and NDCG).

Although *Wikipedia* alone leads the recommenders to poor performance, combining it with *MovieLens* leads to better quality tags, as the results for the FREQUENCY recommender using the *Peers* data source shows (Figure 3 vs. Figure 6). On the other hand, this combination seems to dilute important co-occurrence information that can be harnessed by the RANDOMWALK recommender when using only *MovieLens*, as the relative performance between RANDOMWALK with *Peers* compared to *YouTube* suggests (Figure 3 vs. Figure 6).

5.3 Is the number of contributors a factor?

This section investigates whether the number of peers that produce tags for a movie in the *MovieLens* has predictive power in terms of the quality of the recommendation produced (One can rephrase this as "How many peers is an expert worth?"). To this end, we compute the correlation between the number of users who annotated a movie and the recommendation performance.

A Spearman's rank correlation between the number of users and F3-measure of 0.31 indicates a mild positive correlation between

these aspects. Thus, the number of contributors partially explains the value added by the *MovieLens* to the recommenders' performance. One potential reason for such mild correlation is that the choices of keywords to tag a movie or search for it may be driven by different purposes: although 'boring' might be used as a tag to annotate a movie (to express an opinion about it), it is unlikely that users search for the same movie using that term.

6. RELATED WORK

The related literature falls into two broad categories: automated content annotation and tag value assessment. Most related efforts on automated content annotation focus on suggesting tags to annotate items such that they maximize the relevance of the tags given the content [1,3,9,13,20], while a few authors propose to leverage other aspects such as diversity [1]. However, previous studies fail to account for the potential improvement on popularity of the annotated content – a valuable aspect to content managers and publishers, as they monetize based on their audience.

To the best of our knowledge, Zhou et al. [21] study is the closest to ours. We consider the search portion of traffic that reach videos, while they approach the problem of boosting content popularity by proposing ways to leverage the related video recommendations by connecting a video to already popular ones.

This work differs from previous studies as it concentrates on evaluating the impact of data source choice instead of aiming to design a new recommendation algorithm, as other studies that propose new tag recommenders [6,10,15,17,19].

Along the lines of comparing peer- and expert-produced tags, Lu et al. [14] study the value of collaboratively produced tags to create content indices. The authors compare tags to the Library of Congress Subject Headings regarding their ability to index and classify content efficiently. They show that tag can help extending expert-assigned subject terms by improving the accessibility of content in library catalogs. Similarly, Heymann et al. [8] study the quality of tags for classification of content; and Santos-Neto et al. [16] investigate the value of tags for exploratory search from the perspective of information seekers. Our work differs from these efforts, as we focus on the aggregate value of sources of tags in a different context (i.e., for improving content popularity).

7. SUMMARY

A large portion of user traffic received by a video on the web originates from keyword-based search. Consequently, the textual features of online content may directly impact the popularity of a particular item, and ultimately the ad-generated revenue.

Based on the evidence that tags assigned to a sample of YouTube videos can be optimized to attract more traffic [18], this study compares different types of data sources (peer- and expert-produced) with the goal of understanding their relative value individually or combined to recommend tags. We find that, in the context of popularity boosting, peer-produced sources can add value compared to the best expert-based baseline. Finally, our experiments show the number of contributors in a peer-produced source partially explains its positive influence on the performance of tag recommendation for boosting content popularity.

8. ACKNOWLEDGMENTS

This research is partially funded by the InWeb (MCT/CNPq/INCTWeb 573871/2008-6), University of British Columbia, NSERC (Natural Sciences and Engineering Research Council of Canada), and by the authors' individual grants from CNPq, CAPES and FAPEMIG.

9. REFERENCES

1. Belém, F., Martins, E., Almeida, J., and Gonçalves, M. Exploiting Novelty and Diversity in Tag Recommendation. In P. Serdyukov, P. Braslavski, S. Kuznetsov, et al., eds., *Advances in Information Retrieval SE - 32*. Springer Berlin Heidelberg, 2013, 380–391.

2. Belém, F., Martins, E.F., Pontes, T., Almeida, J., and Gonçalves, M. Associative tag recommendation exploiting multiple textual features. *SIGIR*, (2011).

3. Chirita, P.-A., Costache, S., Nejdl, W., and Handschuh, S. P-TAG. *Proceedings of the 16th international conference on World Wide Web - WWW '07*, ACM Press (2007), 845.

4. Clements, M., de Vries, A.P., and Reinders, M.J.T. Optimizing single term queries using a personalized markov random walk over the social graph. (2008).

5. Fagin, R., Kumar, R., and Sivakumar, D. Comparing top k lists. *SODA '03*, Society for Industrial and Applied Mathematics (2003), 28–36.

6. Guan, Z., Bu, J., Mei, Q., Chen, C., and Wang, C. Personalized tag recommendation using graph-based ranking on multi-type interrelated objects. ACM (2009), 540–547.

7. He, B. and Ounis, I. Query performance prediction. *Information Systems 31*, 7 (2006), 585–594.

8. Heymann, P., Paepcke, A., and Molina, H.G. Tagging human knowledge. *WSDM*, ACM (2010), 51–60.

9. Huang, S., Wu, X., and Bolivar, A. The effect of title term suggestion on e-commerce sites. ACM (2008), 31–38.

10. Jäschke, R., Marinho, L., Hotho, A., Schmidt-Thieme, L., and Stumme, G. Tag Recommendations in Folksonomies. In J. Kok, J. Koronacki, R. Lopez de Mantaras, S. Matwin, D. Mladenic and A. Skowron, eds., *Knowledge Discovery in Databases: PKDD 2007*. Springer Berlin / Heidelberg, Warsaw, Poland, 2007, 506–514.

11. Konstas, I., Stathopoulos, V., and Jose, J.M. On social networks and collaborative recommendation. *SIGIR*, ACM (2009), 195–202.

12. Krestel, R. and Fankhauser, P. Language Models and Topic Models for Personalizing Tag Recommendation. *2010 IEEE/WIC/ACM International Conference on Web Intelligence and Intelligent Agent Technology*, IEEE (2010), 82–89.

13. Liu, D., Hua, X.S., Yang, L., Wang, M., and Zhang, H.J. Tag ranking. ACM (2009), 351–360.

14. Lu, C., Park, J.-R., and Hu, X. User tags versus expert-assigned subject terms: A comparison of LibraryThing tags and Library of Congress Subject Headings. *Journal of Information Science 6*, 6 (2010), 763–779.

15. Marinho, L.B. and Schmidt-Thieme, L. Collaborative Tag Recommendations. In C. Preisach, H. Burkhardt, L. Schmidt-Thieme and R. Decker, eds., *Data Analysis, Machine Learning and Applications*. Springer Berlin Heidelberg, 2008, 533–540.

16. Neto, E.S., Figueiredo, F., Almeida, J., Mowbray, M., Gonçalves, M., and Ripeanu, M. Assessing the Value of Contributions in Tagging Systems. *Social Computing / IEEE International Conference on Privacy, Security, Risk and Trust, 2010 IEEE International Conference on 0*, (2010), 431–438.

17. Rendle, S. and Schmidt-Thieme, L. Pairwise interaction tensor factorization for personalized tag recommendation. *Proceedings of the third ACM international conference on Web search and data mining - WSDM '10*, ACM Press (2010), 81.

18. Santos-Neto, E., Pontes, T., Almeida, J., and Ripeanu, M. Towards Boosting Video Popularity via Tag Selection. *Workshop on Social Multimedia and Storytelling*, (2014).

19. Sigurbjörnsson, B. and Zwol, R. van. Flickr tag recommendation based on collective knowledge. *17th International World Wide Web Conference*, ACM (2008), 327–336.

20. Wang, C., Jing, F., Zhang, L., and Zhang, H.J. Image annotation refinement using random walk with restarts. ACM (2006), 647–650.

21. Zhou, D., Bian, J., Zheng, S., Zha, H., and Giles, C.L. Exploring social annotations for information retrieval. *17th International World Wide Web Conference*, ACM (2008), 715–724.

22. Zhou, R., Khemmarat, S., Gao, L., and Wang, H. Boosting video popularity through recommendation systems. *Databases and Social Networks on - DBSocial '11*, ACM Press (2011), 13–18.

23. YouTube Statistics. http://www.youtube.com/yt/press/statistics.html.

24. Search terms to reach YouTube. http://www.alexa.com/siteinfo/youtube.com#keywords.

25. Site ranking. http://www.alexa.com/topsites/global.

26. GroupLens Dataset. http://www.grouplens.org/taxonomy/term/14.

27. Pulp Fiction's Wikipedia Page. http://en.wikipedia.org/wiki/Pulp_Fiction_(Film).

28. NYT Developer API. http://developers.nytimes.com/.

29. Rotten Tomatoes Developer's API. http://developer.rottentomatoes.com/.

On the Predictability of Talk Attendance at Academic Conferences

Christoph Scholz   Jens Illig   Martin Atzmueller   Gerd Stumme

Knowledge and Data Engineering Group, University of Kassel
Wilhelmshöher Allee 73, D-34121 Kassel, Germany
{scholz, illig, atzmueller, stumme}@cs.uni-kassel.de

ABSTRACT

This paper focuses on the prediction of real-world talk attendances at academic conferences with respect to different influence factors. We study and discuss the predictability of talk attendances using real-world face-to-face contact data and user interests extracted from the users' previous publications. For our experiments, we apply RFID-tracked talk attendance information captured at the ACM Conference on Hypertext and Hypermedia 2011. We find that contact and similarity networks achieve comparable results, and that combining these networks helps to a limited extent to improve the prediction quality.

1. INTRODUCTION

Academic conferences facilitate scientific exchange, collaboration and innovation, e. g., fostered by social contacts and interesting talks. A major task for conference attendees is the selection of talks relevant to their research. Conference guidance systems such as *Conference Navigator* [27] and CONFERATOR [4, 5], support this with the possibility of creating a personalized schedule. Picking talks manually, however, may become complex due to the large amount of available talks at a conference. Furthermore, conversations with other attendees and changes in the conference schedule can influence the talk selection.

Recommendation components of conference guidance systems can support their users by presenting suggestions of talks which the system determined as most interesting for the respective user. Such recommendations influence the user's decision e. g., due to recommended talks which were otherwise not considered. Therefore, recommender systems should ideally always be evaluated in an online scenario, where influence is part of the evaluation.

In this paper, we focus on the predictability of real talk attendances, i. e., we try to find models imitating the actual decision process without recommendation influence. However, online recommender evaluation options are often not available. In such contexts, it is reasonable to evaluate recommender systems on a prediction setting. This is partially valid since good predictions are also good recommendations to the extent that the user does not repent the predicted decisions.

For our evaluation, we use real-world talk attendance data which was collected using the CONFERATOR system. The CONFERATOR applies active RFID technology developed by the SocioPatterns consortium (http://www.sociopatterns.org) for the localization as well as for the measurement of face-to-face contacts between researchers during the conference, e. g., during the coffee breaks. Given such RFID data and collected content information of scientific papers, we derive a set of social interaction networks [3]. Based on these, we investigate the potential of social contact information and content-similarity for predicting real-world talk attendance decisions. In particular, we analyze the potential of combining different information sources for improving the overall prediction quality. Our contribution can be summarized as follows:

1. We present the first study about the predictability of visited talks at academic conferences on real world data.
2. We analyze different influence factors concerning the predictability of talks at academic conferences. In particular, we study the influence of face-to-face contacts and user interest on the talk attendance decision.
3. We consider and adapt state-of-the-art unsupervised link prediction methods for the talk prediction problem
4. We present an in-depth analysis of talk attendance predictability using different performance metrics and investigate the influence of different interaction networks, e. g., derived from social contact and content information, for this task.

The rest of this paper is structured as follows: Section 2 discusses related work. Section 3 gives a detailed overview of the RFID setup and the collected dataset. In Section 4, we discuss the algorithms used for the prediction task. After that, Section 5 presents a detailed evaluation using the dataset collected at ACM Hypertext 2011. Finally, Section 6 summarizes our results.

2. RELATED WORK

In this section, we discuss related work concerning the talk prediction problem at academic conferences.

2.1 Analysis of Human Contact Patterns

The analysis of offline social networks, focusing on human contacts, has been largely neglected. [12, 14] presented an analysis of proximity information collected by devices based on Bluetooth communication. However, in all these experiments it was not possible to detect reliable face-to-face contacts. The SocioPatterns collaboration developed an infrastructure that detects face-to-face proximity (1-1.5 meters) of individuals [9]. One of the first experiments using this kind of proximity tags was done by by Cattuto et al. in [2]. In [19] the authors analyzed the connection between research interests, roles and academic jobs of conference attendees.

An extended version of this article can be found in [24]

2.2 Talk Recommendation and Prediction

Content-based and collaborative-filtering approaches [1] are common for general recommendation tasks. Collaborative filtering methods utilize common item ratings of users, while content-based recommenders make use of properties of the recommended items. For the specific case of talk recommendation, items are talks, while author, title, and abstract are content-properties.

Minkov et al. [21] as well as Pham et al. [22] simulated talk attendances and collected explicit user feedback in form of questionnaires about the generated recommendations. Minkov et al. [21] trained a RankSVM [16] classifier by supervision from a training part of their user feedback and evaluated on a test set. They combine a content-based approach with a collaborative dimensionality reduction that is optimized across users. [22] apply content-boosted collaborative filtering. They calculate similar users according to common co-authors and commonly bookmarked talks in the conference management system *Conference Navigator* [27]. Lee and Brusilovsky [17] apply boosted collaborative filtering to *Conference Navigator* bookmarks. They calculate most similar users based on a weighted average of Jaccard coefficients on common co-authors and commonly referenced publications. They provide two textual example statements from evaluation forms but no quantitative evaluation. In contrast, we quantitatively test the predictability of real talk attendances in an RFID-based dataset.

3. DATASETS

In the following section, we first outline the active RFID technology that we used to collect the RFID datasets. Next, we describe the collected data in more detail.

RFID-Setup.

At the Hypertext 2011 conference we asked each participant to wear an active RFID tag. One decisive factor of these active RFID tags is the possibility to detect other active RFID tags within a range of up to 1.5 meters, which allows us to create human face to face contact networks. We call these active RFID tags *proximity tags* in the following. Each proximity tag sends out tracking signals to RFID readers placed at fixed positions in the conference area. These tracking signals are used to transmit proximity information to a central server and for determining the position of each conference participant [23] [20]. For more information about the proximity tags we refer to Barrat et al [7].

Face-to-Face Contact Data.

We collected the face-to-face contact data at the 22nd ACM Conference on Hypertext and Hypermedia 2011 (HT 2011) in Eindhoven. Table 1 provides a summary on the characteristics of the collected face-to-face proximity dataset. The contact length distribution, diameter, average degree, and average path length of G are similar to the results presented in [6, 15]. For more details on the applied dataset, we refer to, e.g., [10] and [19] .

	HT 2011
$|V|$	68
$|E|$	698
$Avg.Deg.(G)$	20.53
$APL(G)$	1.76
$d(G)$	4
$AACD$	529

Table 1: Collected dataset at HT 2011. Here d is the diameter, AACD the average aggregated contact-duration (in seconds) and APL the average path length.

Talk Attendance Data.

For our analysis, we focus on the parallel talks at HT 2011. Overall, 14 parallel talks took place in two rooms. For our prediction analysis it is essential to determine whether or not a participant attended a talk. Therefore, we installed one RFID reader in each conference room. Whenever we detected a signal of a participant in a conference room we know that this participant must have been in this room and determine the attendance information accordingly. Overall, we observed 359 visited talks from 53 conference participants.

Full-Text Data.

For our prediction task, we also consider the content of all papers. For each conference participant, we crawled all papers that are listed in DBLP since 2006. In total, we crawled 707 papers. With the full-text data we created bag-of-words models representing the paper profiles of each participant. For the participants' bag-of-words-model construction, we used the Porter Stemmer algorithm [26] and removed all stop words.

4. ALGORITHMS

In this section, we describe the algorithms used for the prediction of talks at academic conferences. Focusing on unsupervised methods, we use the *Hybrid Rooted PageRank* algorithm, an extension of the *rooted PageRank* algorithm, for prediction.

4.1 Rooted PageRank

The *rooted PageRank* predictor (RPR) [18] is an adaptation of the *PageRank* algorithm [8] for the link prediction task. The *rooted PageRank* predictor score between participants r and y is defined by the stationary probability distribution of participant y under the following random walk [18]:

- With probability α, jump to r.
- With probability $1 - \alpha$, jump to a random neighbor of the current node.

For the *weighted rooted PageRank (WRPR)* predictor, the random walk selects a random neighbor n of the current node c with probability $\frac{w(c,n)}{\sum\limits_{c \to d} w(c,d)}$, where $w(c,d)$ is the weight of the edge (c, d).

4.2 The Hybrid Rooted PageRank Method

In this section, we describe the *Hybrid Rooted PageRank* algorithm, first presented in [10]. This algorithm is an unsupervised machine learning method and extends the *rooted PageRank* algorithm. *Hybrid Rooted PageRank* combines the information of different networks. To do so, it computes the stationary distribution of nodes under the following random walk: In each step, the walk jumps to root node r with probability α; with probability $1 - \alpha$ the walk selects a given network with respect to a given probability distribution. From the current node c, a link in this network is then selected to a random neighbor n of node c with probability $\frac{w(c,n)}{\sum\limits_{c \to d} w(c,d)}$, where $w(c,d)$ is the weight of the edge (c,d). If no link exists in the chosen network (i.e., if the node is isolated), then the algorithm jumps back to the root node. In this way, one can integrate different networks for the prediction of links.

5. EVALUATION

In this section, we analyze the predictability of talk attendance at academic conferences. Specifically we study the influence of face-to-face contacts and user interests on this prediction problem. Furthermore, we consider combinations of different knowledge sources given as social interaction networks.

5.1 Evaluation Method

For our talk prediction task, we use AUC [13] to evaluate a global ranking. For each triple of two parallel talks t_1 and t_2 and a talk attendee, we calculate two predictor scores, one for t_1 and one for t_2. This generates a ranking of all positive and negative decisions for predicting a talk. AUC evaluation rewards a predictor's ability to rank correct decisions before wrong decisions according to the ground truth. An ideal predictor ranks all correct decisions above all wrong predictions and achieves thus an AUC score of 1.0, while a purely random predictor achieves a score of 0.5.

5.2 Predictability of Talk Attendance

In this subsection we study and discuss the predictability of talk attendance at academic conferences.

5.2.1 Talk and Session Attendance Statistics

We first present statistics about the talk and session attendance behavior at HT 2011 for the parallel talks. Overall, the 53 conference participants attended 194 sessions. Most of the participants did not change a session during HT 2011. At this conference, only in $7\%(\frac{14}{194})$ of all cases, the corresponding participant changed the session. In $69\%(\frac{134}{194})$ of all cases the participants visited all talks of the session.

5.2.2 Influence Factors of Talk Attendance Using Face-To-Face Contact Networks

In this section, we study the influence of conference face-to-face contacts on the attendance of talks. In particular, we analyze the probability that two participants attended the same talk, based on the current face-to-face contact behavior between these two participants. In the following, we apply a t-test for determining the significance of our observations and plot the 95% confidence intervals of the results. First, we assume that there exists no face-to-face contact between two conference participants until the start of talk t. In Figure 1(a), we observe that the probability is nearly random (i. e., probability is 50.8%) that these two participants visit the same talk t, if there exists no prior face-to-face contact. In addition, we analyze the probability that two participants visit the same talk, when there exists a face-to-face contact till the end of the conference. We observe that the probability here is slightly increased (probability is 55.5%) to attend the same talk, if there will exist a face-to-face contact till the end of the conference. It is interesting to see that the probability is 58.74%, if already a prior face-to-face contact exists, before the talk starts. This result highlights the influence of face-to-face contacts on the talk attendance. Furthermore, we analyzed whether a face-to-face contact during the coffee break will influence the probability to attend the same talk of the next session. In Figure 1(a), we see that that the probability is 65.5% to attend the same talk of the next session, if there exists a face-to-face contact in the coffee-break before the session.

In addition, we consider the connection between a participant and the presenter of a talk. We study here, whether a participant p will attend the talk of this presenter q, when there exists a face-to-face contact between participants p and q. In Figure 1(b), we plot the probability to join the talk of presenter q, given that there exists a face-to-face contact with presenter q with a minimum contact duration of $t \geq 20$ seconds. We observe that the probability is 61% that participant p attends the talk of presenter q, when there exists a face-to-face contact between participants p and q. Note that the probability is 50.8% if there exists no face-to-face contact. Focusing more and more on stronger ties (contacts greater than a given threshold) between these two participants we see that the probability increases almost linearly to attend the talk of presenter q. The

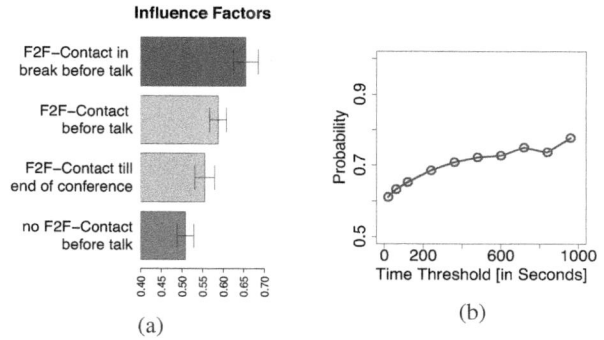

Influence Factors

(a) (b)

Figure 1: (a) Analysis of factors concerning the prediction of talks. Here we plot the probability that two participants visit the same talk, given that 1. there is a face-to-face contact in the coffee break before the next talk is going to start, 2. there exists a face-to-face contact before the next talk is going to start 3. there exists a face-to-face contact till the end of the conference, 4. there exists no face-to-face contact.
(b) Given a face-to-face contact between participant p and a presenter q. The y-axis shows the probability that participant p visits the talk of presenter q. The x-axis defines here the minimum contact duration between participants p and q.

probability to attend the talk reaches 77.78%, if there exists a face-to-face contact with duration greater than 960 seconds.

5.2.3 Predictability of Talk Attendance based on User Interests

We also investigated to what extent conference participants at HT 2011 decided for their attended talks based on the topics of the talks. This is motivated by the general conception that, next to social interactions, personal interest in the presented topics is another major influence factor for talk attendance decisions. We simply assume that personal interest is reflected by previous publications. Although this introduces limitations with respect to novel upcoming topics, it is based on observable facts. We downloaded all accessible publications of a user with a publication date before the beginning of the conference. From these, we counted word occurrences into bag-of-word models. All bag-of-word models were generated after removing stopwords, stemming word tokens using the porter stemmer, and tf-idf weighting. In the most simple setup, we estimate similarities between a visitor's interest and the topic of a talk by calculating the cosine similarity between the respective bag-of-word vectors. For each user and time slot, we predict the talk with the higher cosine similarity to the participants' interest model. In order to avoid further influence factors in our experiments, we evaluate content-based influence on a core of our dataset. In this core, only those 51 out of the original 53 users are retained, for which we were able to download at least one prior publication. To model topics of talks, we build bag-of-word vectors directly from the presented papers in the proceedings. For additional experiments, we also limit to bag-of-word models derived only from abstracts or paper titles.

Motivated by the intuition that people might make their talk attendance decisions based on one or two talks rather than on all talks of the session, and that participants do not change sessions, we also predict talk attendance session-wise. We tried two session-wise options for prediction. For the first option, we predict the session with the higher maximum similarity of all talks in the respective session.

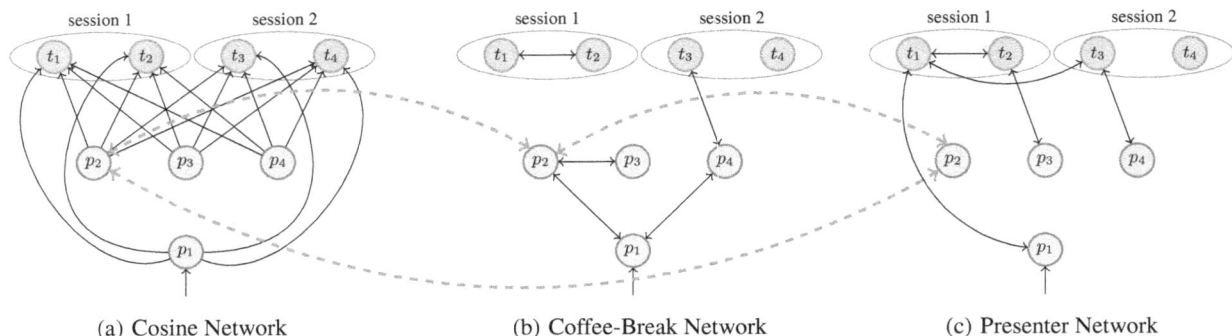

(a) Cosine Network   (b) Coffee-Break Network   (c) Presenter Network

Figure 2: Example illustrations of the *Hybrid Rooted PageRank* networks for talk prediction. Graph (a) shows the structure of a cosine (user interests) network connecting persons $p_1, ..., p_4$ with the presenters of the talks $t_1, ..., t_4$ for which attendance is to be predicted. Graph (b) shows the coffee-break network linking persons for whom face-to-face contact have been measured in the coffee-break before the talk. Graph (c) is the presenter network, containing face-to-face contacts at any time before the talks to be predicted. Dashed links show an example part of identity relations holding between all nodes with equal labels.

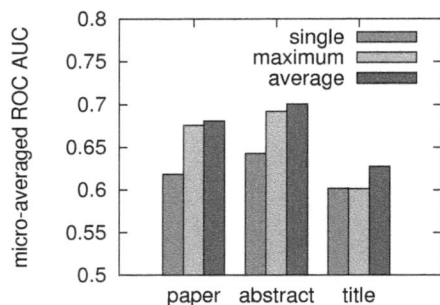

Figure 3: AUC values for content-based talk prediction based on cosine similarity depending on the talk representation and whether the decision is predicted for each talk separately or once for all talks of a session by either maximum or average talk similarity

For the second option, we choose the session with the higher average talk similarity. Figure 3 depicts the area under the ROC curve results for the ranked list of all 337 individual decisions of each certain participant for a certain talk. For building up this global ranking, we first normalized all cosine scores of each particular person and time-slot by dividing by their sum.

As can be seen from Figure 3, session-wise prediction constantly achieves superior AUC scores. This is in accordance to our finding that only few people change between parallel sessions. This can be interpreted as an indication that the decision of a participant for one of the session is usually a consideration of one or more of the most interesting talks. For the global prediction ranking measured by the AUC, the average attendee-talk similarity constantly results in the best results.

It can also be seen that, with title-based models, the maximum predictor scores much lower than with paper or abstract based models. This may be due to sparsity leading to to wrong decisions based on few overly weighted word matches in one of the talks' titles.

Interestingly, the results with abstract-based talk models constantly compare favorably to full-paper models in all settings. Potential explanations are the summarizing character of abstracts and

the fact that people often do not have the opportunity to read the full paper before choosing the talk to attend. In order to decrease sparsity problems, we also experimented using dimensionality reduction like for example used by [25] which is similar to *Latent Semantic Indexing* [11]. However, the results did not lead to a clear improvement.

5.2.4 Predictability of Talk Attendance Using the Hybrid Rooted PageRank Predictor

In this section, we analyze the predictability of talk attendance using a combination of different networks. For this analysis, we use the *Hybrid Rooted PageRank* (HRPR) algorithm (see section 4.2) as predictor. The advantage of this algorithm is that we can analyze and compare the predictive power of different networks and combinations of these networks. Using the HRPR-algorithm, we combine the information of the paper-similarity network, the aggregated face-to-face contact network (of the coffee break before the next talk is going to start), and the presenters face-to-face contact network. The structure of these graphs is illustrated in Figure 2. Note that the hybrid rooted random walk selects a network with respect to a given probability distribution $P = (p_1, p_2, p_3)$. In our experiments, we studied all parameter combinations with $p_1 + p_2 + p_3 = 1$ and $p_1, p_2, p_3 \in \{0.0, 0.1, 0.2, ..., 1.0\}$. Assume we want to predict, whether participant p attends talk t_1 or talk t_2. The predicted talk is then given by the talk t_i, where p_i is the presenter of talk t_i, p_j the presenter of talk t_j and $HRPR(p, p_i) > HRPR(p, p_j)$.

We start by analyzing the predictive power for each network separately. In Figure 4(a), we observe that the paper-similarity network performs best with an AUC-value of 0.630. Using just the face-to-face contact network of the coffee-break does not work as well as using the paper-similarity network. Here the AUC-value is 0.596. In contrast to the coffee break's face-to-face contact network, the presenter network contains just the links from the presenter of the next talk that is going to start. We observe that using just the presenters face-to-face contact network does not perform very well and works worse than using just the face-to-face contact network. This is because most participants do not have a face-to-face contact to a presenter before the presenter's talk starts. Hence, the presenter network is rather sparse and does not provide major predictive power on its own. The AUC-value for the presenter network is

0.474. In this context, the observation that the face-to-face contact network works better than the presenter networks suggests that links between participants help to improve the predictive power.

Furthermore, we analyze, whether the combination of different networks increases the predictability of talk attendance at academic conferences. In Figure 4(a), we observe that the best result can be obtained by combining the information of all networks. However, the increase of predictability by combining the information of different networks is rather small, and we do not know the parameter combinations leading to the best results. The result just gives an indication that a combination can help to increase prediction quality. In our analysis, we handle the presenter network as an additional network. This gives us the possibility to weight a link between a participant and presenter separately. We observe here that the predictability could not be increased when we combine the presenter network and the face-to-face contact network.

In Section 5.2.1, we observed that most participants visited all talks in one session. It was also unlikely that a participant changed a session. Despite this observation, it is natural to assume that a participant is not interested in each talk of one session. We argue here that, in most cases, at most one or two talks of a session are the cause for attending the session. Therefore, for each network, we merge the nodes of all presenters in one session. The merged nodes thus represent the whole session. The weight vectors for in- and out-going edges are calculated as the re-normalized sum of the respective individual nodes' weight vectors. Results of the experiments with the merged network are depicted in Figure 4(b). Compared to Figure 4(a), we observe a clear increase in talk prediction quality. Considering the best tested parameter combinations, the AUC score increases from 0.638 to 0.703.

We also observe that, for each parameter combination, combining all networks performs better, when we merge the presenter nodes. Unlike the model where we do not merge the presenter nodes of one session, we observe that the combination of the presenter network and the face-to-face contact network increases the prediction quality significantly, when we merge the presenter nodes. Considering the best parameter combinations for the presenter and face-to-face contact network, the prediction quality increases from 0.61 to 0.685 AUC.

A further interesting point is that a minimal fraction of the face-to-face contact network or paper-similarity network increases the predictive power of the presenters face-to-face contact network from 0.61 to 0.661 and 0.655. To our surprise, this trend can not be observed for the face-to-face contact network results.

6. CONCLUSIONS

In this paper, we analyzed the predictability of talk attendance at academic conferences. Specifically, we studied the influence of face-to-face contacts and user interests on the talk attendance. We showed that the probability of two participants attending the same talk is nearly random, if there exists no contact before the talk is going to start. In this context, the probability (that two participants attend the same talk) is significantly increased if there exists a contact in the break before the talk. Next, we analyzed the influence of user interests on talk attendance. We observed, that prediction based on user-interest alone achieves better results than prediction based solely on face-to-face contact data. We showed that a combination of different networks helps to further improve the prediction accuracy. However, the increase of predictability was rather small. Another important observation is that the combination of all information belonging to one session, i. e., merging the presenter nodes, significantly improves prediction accuracy.

AUC values, HRPR

PaperSim / Presenter	0	0.1	0.2	0.3	0.4	0.5	0.6	0.7	0.8	0.9	1
0	59.6	58.2	60.4	61.1	62.8	62.8	63.0	62.6	63.1	63.3	63.0
0.1	57.3	61.9	62.4	62.7	63.5	63.6	63.1	63.6	63.1	63.6	
0.2	57.3	63.1	62.7	63.1	63.2	63.0	63.5	63.8	63.6		
0.3	56.6	63.8	63.4	63.7	62.5	63.0	62.9	63.7			
0.4	56.7	63.3	63.1	63.0	62.4	62.9	63.1				
0.5	56.1	63.4	62.5	61.9	61.9	61.2					
0.6	55.5	63.1	62.0	60.8	61.5						
0.7	56.1	61.4	60.7	60.5							
0.8	54.6	59.8	58.8								
0.9	52.7	56.0									
1	47.4										

(a) Single Variant

AUC values, HRPR

PaperSim / Presenter	0	0.1	0.2	0.3	0.4	0.5	0.6	0.7	0.8	0.9	1
0	61.1	56.6	57.4	60.2	62.4	64.7	66.2	68.0	68.5	68.1	67.0
0.1	68.5	62.5	63.4	65.3	67.4	68.9	69.3	68.8	68.8	70.3	
0.2	67.1	66.5	66.5	68.1	68.5	68.9	69.5	69.3	69.2		
0.3	65.5	67.9	68.2	68.7	68.7	68.2	68.0	69.2			
0.4	67.8	69.0	69.4	68.8	68.5	67.9	67.5				
0.5	67.0	69.5	69.0	68.4	67.2	67.4					
0.6	68.2	69.8	68.9	67.8	66.4						
0.7	67.5	69.3	68.4	65.7							
0.8	66.8	68.9	66.2								
0.9	66.1	65.5									
1	61.0										

(b) Merged Variant

Figure 4: AUC values for the talk prediction task using the *Hybrid Rooted PageRank* as predictor. The x-axis represents the probability to choose the paper-similarity network in the random walk of $HRPR$, the y-axis the probability to choose the presenter network. The probability to choose the coffee-break network is then defined as 1-x-y. The z-axis displays the AUC-value for the defined (by the x and y axes) parameter combinations. In (a) we present the predictability-results, without merging the presenter nodes, in (b) we merge the presenter notes.

7. REFERENCES

[1] G. Adomavicius and A. Tuzhilin. Toward the Next Generation of Recommender Systems: A Survey of the State-of-the-Art and Possible Extensions. *Knowledge and Data Engineering*, 17(6), 2005.

[2] H. Alani, M. Szomszor, C. Cattuto, W. V. den Broeck, G. Correndo, and A. Barrat. Live Social Semantics. In *Intl. Semantic Web Conference*, pages 698–714, 2009.

[3] M. Atzmueller. Data Mining on Social Interaction Networks. *Journal of Data Mining and Digital Humanities*, 1, 2014.

[4] M. Atzmueller, M. Becker, M. Kibanov, C. Scholz, S. Doerfel, A. Hotho, B.-E. Macek, F. Mitzlaff, J. Mueller, and G. Stumme. Ubicon and its Applications for Ubiquitous Social Computing. *New Review of Hypermedia and Multimedia*, 20(1):53–77, 2014.

[5] M. Atzmueller, D. Benz, S. Doerfel, A. Hotho, R. Jäschke, B. E. Macek, F. Mitzlaff, C. Scholz, and G. Stumme. Enhancing Social Interactions at Conferences. *it+ti*, 3:1–6, 2011.

[6] M. Atzmueller, S. Doerfel, A. Hotho, F. Mitzlaff, and G. Stumme. Face-to-Face Contacts at a Conference: Dynamics of Communities and Roles. In *Modeling and Mining Ubiquitous Social Media*, volume 7472 of *LNAI*. Springer Verlag, Heidelberg, Germany, 2012.

[7] A. Barrat, C. Cattuto, V. Colizza, J.-F. Pinton, W. V. den Broeck, and A. Vespignani. High Resolution Dynamical Mapping of Social Interactions with Active RFID. *CoRR*, abs/0811.4170, 2008.

[8] S. Brin and L. Page. The Anatomy of a Large-Scale Hypertextual Web Search Engine. *Computer Networks*, 30(1-7):107–117, 1998.

[9] C. Cattuto, W. Van den Broeck, A. Barrat, V. Colizza, J.-F. Pinton, and A. Vespignani. Dynamics of Person-to-Person Interactions from Distributed RFID Sensor Networks. *PLoS ONE*, 5(7):e11596, 07 2010.

[10] Christoph Scholz and Martin Atzmueller and Alain Barrat and Ciro Cattuto and Gerd Stumme. New Insights and Methods For Predicting Face-To-Face Contacts. In *Proc. 7th Intl. AAAI Conference on Weblogs and Social Media*, 2013.

[11] S. Deerwester, S. Dumais, G. Furnas, T. Landauer, and R. Harshman. Indexing by Latent Semantic Analysis. *Journal of the American Society for Information Science 41*, pages 391–407, 1990.

[12] N. Eagle, A. Pentland, and D. Lazer. From the Cover: Inferring Friendship Network Structure by using Mobile Phone Data. *Proceedings of The National Academy of Sciences*, 106:15274–15278, 2009.

[13] J. A. Hanley and B. J. McNeil. The Meaning and Use of the Area under a Receiver Operating Characteristic (ROC) Curve. *Radiology*, 143(1):29–36, Apr. 1982.

[14] P. Hui, A. Chaintreau, J. Scott, R. Gass, J. Crowcroft, and C. Diot. Pocket Switched Networks and Human Mobility in Conference Environments. In *Proceedings of the 2005 ACM SIGCOMM workshop on Delay-tolerant networking*, WDTN '05, pages 244–251, New York, NY, USA, 2005. ACM.

[15] L. Isella, J. Stehlé, A. Barrat, C. Cattuto, J.-F. Pinton, and W. V. D. Broeck. What's in a Crowd? Analysis of Face-to-Face Behavioral Networks. *Journal of Theoretical Biology*, 271:166–180, 2011.

[16] T. Joachims. Optimizing search engines using clickthrough data. In *Proceedings of the Eighth ACM SIGKDD International Conference on Knowledge Discovery and Data Mining*, KDD '02, pages 133–142, New York, NY, USA, 2002. ACM.

[17] D. Lee and P. Brusilovsky. Exploring Social Approach to Recommend Talks at Research Conferences. In *COLLABORATECOM 2012 - 8th IEEE International Conference on Collaborative Computing: Networking, Applications and Worksharing*, Oct. 2012.

[18] D. Liben-Nowell and J. M. Kleinberg. The Link Prediction Problem for Social Networks. In *Proc. 12th Intl. Conference on Information and Knowledge Management (CIKM)*, pages 556–559, New York, NY, USA, 2003. ACM.

[19] B.-E. Macek, C. Scholz, M. Atzmueller, and G. Stumme. Anatomy of a Conference. In *Proc. 23rd ACM Conference on Hypertext and Social Media*, pages 245–254, New York, NY, USA, 2012. ACM Press.

[20] M. Meriac, A. Fiedler, A. Hohendorf, J. Reinhardt, M. Starostik, and J. Mohnke. Localization Techniques for a Mobile Museum Information System. In *Proceedings of WCI*, 2007.

[21] E. Minkov, B. Charrow, J. Ledlie, S. Teller, and T. Jaakkola. Collaborative Future Event Recommendation. In *Proceedings of the 19th ACM International Conference on Information and Knowledge Management*, CIKM '10, pages 819–828, New York, NY, USA, 2010. ACM.

[22] M. C. Pham, D. Kovachev, Y. Cao, G. M. Mbogos, and R. Klamma. Enhancing Academic Event Participation with Context-aware and Social Recommendations. In *Proceedings of the 2012 International Conference on Advances in Social Networks Analysis and Mining (ASONAM 2012)*, ASONAM '12, pages 464–471, Washington, DC, USA, 2012. IEEE Computer Society.

[23] C. Scholz, S. Doerfel, M. Atzmueller, A. Hotho, and G. Stumme. Resource-Aware On-Line RFID Localization Using Proximity Data. In *Proc. ECML/PKDD 2011: European Conference on Machine Learning and Principles and Practice of Knowledge Discovery in Databases*, pages 129–144, Heidelberg, Germany, 2011. Springer.

[24] C. Scholz, J. Illig, M. Atzmueller, and G. Stumme. On the predictability of talk attendance at academic conferences. *CoRR*, abs/1407.0613, 2014.

[25] H. Schütze. Automatic Word Sense Discrimination. *Computational Linguistics*, 24(1):97–123, 1998.

[26] C. van Rijsbergen, S. Robertson, and M. Porter. New Models in Probabilistic Information Retrieval. 1980.

[27] C. Wongchokprasitti, P. Brusilovsky, and D. Para. Conference Navigator 2.0: Community-Based Recommendation for Academic Conferences. In *Proc. Workshop Social Recommender Systems, IUI'10*, 2010.

Twitter in Academic Conferences:
Usage, Networking and Participation over Time

Xidao Wen
University of Pittsburgh
Pittsburgh, USA
xiw55@pitt.edu

Yu-Ru Lin
University of Pittsburgh
Pittsburgh, USA
yurulin@pitt.edu

Christoph Trattner
Know-Center
Graz, Austria
ctrattner@know-center.at

Denis Parra
PUC Chile
Santiago, Chile
dparra@ing.puc.cl

ABSTRACT

Twitter is often referred to as a backchannel for conferences. While the main conference takes place in a physical setting, attendees and virtual attendees socialize, introduce new ideas or broadcast information by microblogging on Twitter. In this paper we analyze the scholars' Twitter use in 16 Computer Science conferences over a timespan of five years. Our primary finding is that over the years there are increasing differences with respect to conversation use and information use in Twitter. We studied the interaction network between users to understand whether assumptions about the structure of the conversations hold over time and between different types of interactions, such as retweets, replies, and mentions. While 'people come and people go,' we want to understand what keeps people staying engaged with the conference on Twitter. By casting the problem as a classification task, we find different factors that contribute to the continuing participation of users to the online Twitter conference activity. These results have implications for research communities to implement strategies for continuous and active participation among members.

Categories and Subject Descriptors: H.2.8 [**Database Management**]:Database Applications—*Data mining*

Keywords: Twitter; academic conferences; usage; interactions; retention

1. INTRODUCTION

Twitter, as one of the most popular microblogging services, has been raised as the backchannel of academic conferences [19]. There is a considerable amount of research into understanding the users' behavior on Twitter during academic events. Researchers look into why people tweet [17, 19], and what people tweet from a small number of conferences [5, 12, 23].

In this work, we collect data about a larger set of academic conferences over five consecutive years, and provide in-depth analysis on this temporal dataset. We are particularly interested in the following research questions:

RQ1: Do users use Twitter more for socializing with peers or for information sharing during conferences? How has such use of Twitter during conferences changed over the years?

RQ2: What are the structures of conversation and information sharing networks in individual conferences? Have these network structures changed over time?

RQ3: Do users participate on Twitter for the same conference over consecutive years? To what extent can we predict users' future conference participation?

To answer these questions, we crawled a dataset that consists of the tweets from 16 Computer Science conferences from 2009 to 2013. We examined Twitter in conferences by characterizing its use through retweets, replies, etc. We studied the structure of conversation and information-sharing by deriving two networks from the dataset, conversation and retweet network. Furthermore, to understand the factors that drive users' continuous participation, we propose a prediction framework with usage and network metrics.

As a result of our analyses, we found: (i) an increasing trend of informational usage (URLs and retweets) compared to the stable pattern of conversational usage (replies and mentions) of conferences on Twitter over time; (ii) the conversation network is more fragmented than the information network, and the former becomes more fragmented over the time; and (iii) that the number of timeline tweets, users' centrality in information networks, and number of contacts in conversation networks are the most relevant features to predict users' continuous participation. These results summarize the online user participation of a real research community, which in turn helps to understand how it is perceived in online social networks and whether it is able to attract recurring attention over time.

The rest of the paper is structured as follows: The next section surveys Twitter used as a backchannel in conferences. Then, Section 3 describes the dataset in this study and how we obtained it. Section 4 presents the experiment setup, followed by section 5 which provides the results. Section 6 summarizes our findings and concludes our paper with discussion of the future work.

2. RELATED WORK

Twitter usage has been studied in events as diverse as politics [10, 21], sports [9, 25], and natural disasters [1, 15]. However, research that studies Twitter as a backchannel in academic conferences is closer to our work. Ebner et al. [5] studied tweets posted during the ED-MEDIA 2008 conference, and they argued that micro-blogging can enhance participation in the usual conference setting. They conducted a survey over 41 people who used Twitter during conferences, finding that people who actively participate via Twitter are not only physical conference attendants, and that the reasons people participate are sharing resources, communicating with peers, and establishing an online presence [17].

Considering another area, Letierce et al. [12] studied Twitter usage by the semantic web community during the conference ISWC 2009. They further analyzed three conferences [11] and they found that analyzing Twitter activity during the conference helps to summarize the event (by categorizing hashtags and URLs shared), and that the way people share information online is affected by the use of Twitter. In another study, Ross et al. [19] investigated the use of Twitter as a backchannel within the community of digital humanists. By studying three conferences in 2009 they found that the micro-blogging activity during the conference is not a single conversation but rather multiple monologues with few dialogues between users and that the use of Twitter expands the participation of members of the research community. With respect to applications, Sopan et al. [20] created a tool that provides real-time visualization and analysis for backchannel conversations in online conferences.

In [24], we investigated the use of Twitter in three conferences in 2012 related to user modeling research communities. We classified Twitter users into groups and we found that the most senior members of the research community tend to communicate with other senior members, and newcomers (usually masters or first year PhD students) receive little attention from other groups, challenging Reinhardt's assumption [17] about Twitter being an ideal tool to include newcomers in an established learning community.

Compared to previous research and to the best of our knowledge, this article is the first one studying a larger sample of conferences (16 in total) over a period of five years (2009-2013). This dataset allows us to generalize our results to Information and Computer Science and also to analyze trends of Twitter usage over time.

3. DATASET

Previous studies on analyzing the tweets during conferences examined a small number of conferences [4, 12]. For each conference, they collected the tweets that contain the conference official hashtag in its text, for example, #kidneywk11, #iswc2009. They produced insights of how users employ Twitter during the conference, but their results are limited considering that they analyzed at most three conferences. On the other hand, we are interested in studying trends of the usage and the structure over time, where we aimed to collect a dataset of tweets from a larger set of conferences over several years. Following the list of conferences in Computer Science listed in *csconf.net*, we used the Topsy API[1] to crawl tweets by searching for the conference hashtag. With regard to the time period of the conference, as summarized by [17], Twitter activities can happen at different stages of a conference: before a conference, during a conference, and after a conference. For this purpose we set the search time window to be seven days before the conference until seven days after the conference, in order to capture most of the Twitter activities about the conference.

Conference dataset. For this study, we focused on the conferences that had Twitter activity from 2009 to 2013. The crawling process took two weeks in December 2013. We aggregated 109,076 tweets from 16 conferences over the last five years.

User-Timeline dataset. We acknowledge that users would also interact with other users without the conference hashtag, and therefore we additionally constructed the timeline dataset by crawling the timeline tweets of those users who participated in the conference during the same period (users from the conference dataset). Table 1 shows the statistics of our dataset. In addition, we publish the detailed information about each conference[2].

---

[1]http://topsy.com

[2]https://github.com/xidaow/twitter-academic

	2009	2010	2011	2012	2013
#Unique Users	1,114	2,970	3,022	**5,590**	5,085
#Conference Tweets	8,125	18,107	19,308	**34,424**	27,549
#Timeline Tweets	228,923	608,308	589,084	**1,025,259**	939,760

Table 1: Properties of the dataset collected in each year.

Random dataset. Any pattern observed would be barely relevant unless we compare with a baseline, because the change might be a byproduct of Twitter usage trends overall. Hence, we show the conference tweets trend in comparison with a random sampled dataset. Several sampling methods about data collection from Twitter have been discussed in [18]. Unfortunately, none of those approaches are applicable to this study, as most of them drawed the sample from the tweets posted during limited time period through Twitter APIs. Sampling from the historical tweets (especially for the tweets in the five year period) via Twitter APIs seems to be a dead end. To overcome this issue, we again used Topsy API, for which it claims to have full access to all historical tweets. As Topsy does not provide direct sampling APIs, we then wrote a script to construct a sample from all the tweets in the Topsy archive and to ensure the sampling process is random and the sample acquired is representative of the tweets. To eliminate the diurnal effect on Twitter, we randomly picked two-thirds of all the hours in each year, randomly picked two minutes from the each hour as our search time interval, and randomly picked the page number in the returned search result. The query aims to search for the tweets that contain any one of the alphabetical characters (from a to z). The crawling process took two days in December, 2013. As each query returned us 100 tweets, we were able to collect 5,784,649 tweets from 2009 to 2013. Our strategy was designed to create a quasi-random sample using the Topsy search APIs. To examine the quality of our sample, we compared our dataset with the statistics of Boyd et al. [3]. In 2009, 21.8% of the tweets in our random dataset contain at least one URL, close to 22% as reported in their paper. The proportion of tweets with at least one '@user' in its text is 37%, close to 36% in Boyd's data. Moreover, 88% of the tweets with '@user' begin with '@user' in our sampled data, comparable to 86% of Boyd's. These close distributions support the representativeness of our dataset during 2009, then we extended the sampling method for the ongoing years.

4. METHODOLOGY

In this section we describe our experimental methodology, i.e., the metrics used, analyses and experiments conducted to answer the research questions.

4.1 Analyzing the Usage

We examined the use of Twitter during conferences by defining the measurements from two aspects: information usage and conversation usage. We want to use these measures to understand different usage dimensions and whether they have changed over time.

Conversation usage. With respect to using Twitter as a medium for conversations, we defined features based on two types of interactions between users: Reply and Mention ratios. For instance, @Alice can reply to @Bob, by typing '@Bob' at the beginning of a tweet, and this is recognized as a reply from @Alice. @Alice can also type @Bob in any part of her tweet except at the beginning, and this is regarded as a mention tweet. We computed the Reply Ratio to measure the proportion of tweets categorized as replies and the Mention Ratio respectively, but considering mentions.

Information usage. For the informational aspect of Twitter use during conferences, we computed two features to measure how it changed over the years: URL Ratio and Retweet Ratio. Intuitively, most of the URLs shared on Twitter during conference time are linked to additional materials such as presentation slides, publication links, etc. We calculated the URL Ratio of the conference to measure which proportion of tweets are aimed at introducing information to Twitter. The URL Ratio is simply the number of the tweets with 'http:' over the total number of the tweets in the conference. The second ratio we used to measure informational aspects is Retweet Ratio, as the retweet plays an important role in disseminating the information within and outside the conference. We then calculated the Retweet Ratio to measure the proportion of tweets being shared in the conference. To identify the retweets, we followed a fairly common practice [3], and used the following keywords in the queries: 'RT @', 'retweet @', 'retweeting @', 'MT @', 'rt @', 'thx @'.

We computed the aforementioned measures from the tweets in the conference dataset (tweets that have the conference hashtag in the text, as explained in Section 3). Following the same approach, we computed the same measures from the tweets in the random dataset, as we wanted to understand if the observations in conferences differ from general usage on Twitter.

4.2 Analyzing the Networks

To answer the research question *RQ2*, we conducted a network analysis following Lin et al. [13], who constructed networks from different types of communications: hashtags, mentions, replies, and retweets; and used their network properties to model communication patterns on Twitter. We followed their approach and focused on two networks derived from our dataset: conversation network, and retweet network. We defined them as follows:

- Conversation network: We built the user-user network of conversations for *every conference each year*. This network models the conversational interactions (replies and mentions) between pairs of users. Nodes are the users in one conference and one edge between two users indicates they have at least one conversational interaction during the conference.
- Retweet network: We derived the user-user network of retweets for *each conference each year*, in which a node represents one user and a directed link from one node to another means the source node has retweeted the targeted one.

The motivation for investigating the first two networks comes from the study of Ross et al. [19], who stated that: a) the conference activity on Twitter is constituted by multiple scattered dialogues rather than a single distributed conversation, and b) many users' intention is to jot down notes and establish an online presence, which might not be regarded as an online *conversation*. This assumption is also held by Ebner et al. [17]. To assess if the validity of these assumptions holds over time, we conducted statistical tests over network features, including the number of nodes, the number of edges, density, diameter, the number of weakly connected components, and clustering coefficient of the network [22].

We constructed both conversation and retweet networks from the users' timeline tweets in addition to the conference tweets, as we suspect that many interactions might happen between the users without using the conference hashtag. Therefore, these two datasets combined would give us a complete and more comprehensive dataset. Furthermore, we filtered out the users targeted by messages in both networks who are not in the corresponding conference dataset to assure these two networks only capture the interaction activities between conference Twitter users.

4.3 Analyzing Continuous Participation

To understand which users' factors drive their continuing participation in the conference on Twitter, we trained a binary classifier with some features induced from users' Twitter usage and their network metrics. From our own experience of attending the same conference repeatedly, we know that one reason is that we had valuable experience in the past –quality research and social connections, to

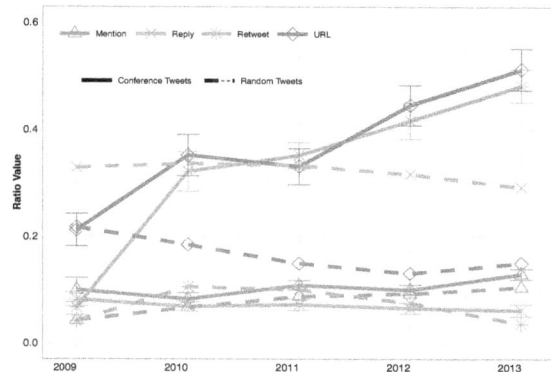

Figure 1: Usage pattern over the years in terms of proportion of each category of tweets. Continuous lines represent conference tweets, dashed lines a random dataset from Twitter.

be more specific. We expect that a similar effect exists with respect to the continuous participation on Twitter. Users' decision of whether or not to return to the conference possibly depends on their experience with the conference via Twitter in the past – valuable information and meaningful conversations. To capture both ends of a user's Twitter experience, we computed the usage measures, as described in Section 4.1, and user's network position [13] in each of the networks: conversation network and retweet network, as discussed in Section 4.2. Measures for user's network position are calculated to represent the user's relative importance within the network, including degree, in-degree, out-degree, HIT hub score [8], HIT authority score [8], PageRank score [16], eigenvector centrality score [2], closeness centrality [22], betweenness centrality [22], and clustering coefficient [22].

Dataset. We identified 14,456 unique user-conference participations from 2009 to 2012 in our dataset. We then defined a positive continuing participation if one user showed up again in the same conference he or she participated in via Twitter last year, while a negative positive continuing participation if the user failed to. For example, @Alice posted a tweet with '#cscw2010' during the CSCW conference in 2010, we counted it as one positive continuing participation if @Alice posted a tweet with '#cscw2011' during the CSCW conference in 2011. By checking these users conference participation records via Twitter in the following year (2010-2013), we identified 2,749 positive continuing participations. We then constructed a dataset with 2,749 positive continuing participations and 2,749 negative continuing participations (random sampling [7]). **Features**. In the prediction dataset, each instance consisted of a set of features that describe the user's information *in one conference in one year* from different aspects, and the responsive variable was a binary indicator of whether the user came back in the following year. We formally defined the key aspects of one user's features discussed above, in the following:

- Baseline: This set only includes the number of timeline tweets and the number of tweets with the conference hashtag, as the users' continuous participation might be correlated with their frequencies of writing tweets. We consider this as the primary information about a user and this information will be included in the rest of the feature sets.
- Conversation: We built this set by including the conversation usage measures (Mention Ratio and Reply Ratio) and network position of the user in the conversation network.
- Information: Different from the previous one, this set captures the information oriented features, including the information usages (Retweet Ratio, URL Ratio) and user's position in the retweet network.

Feature		2009	2010	2011	2012	2013
Conversation	#Nodes	165.313 ± 50.358	323.688 ± 100.481	385.625 ± 100.294	649.313 ± 202.518	622.188 ± 142.485
	#Edges	342.188 ± 126.758	660.625 ± 240.704	688.500 ± 227.768	1469.000 ± 643.431	1157.813 ± 344.484
	In/Out degree	1.446 ± 0.153	1.567 ± 0.161	1.502 ± 0.086	1.646 ± 0.144	1.618 ± 0.088
	Density	0.044 ± 0.020	0.010 ± 0.002	0.007 ± 0.001	0.005 ± 0.001	0.004 ± 0.000
	Clustering Coefficient	0.066 ± 0.015	0.086 ± 0.014	0.074 ± 0.008	0.070 ± 0.009	0.078 ± 0.006
	Reciprocity	0.172 ± 0.034	0.210 ± 0.029	0.237 ± 0.023	0.195 ± 0.022	0.203 ± 0.017
	#WCCs	4.750 ± 0.911	13.438 ± 3.243	16.625 ± 4.118	26.750 ± 6.956	29.188 ± 5.930
Retweet	#Nodes	87.063 ± 30.005	355.500 ± 107.412	476.813 ± 117.641	720.875 ± 210.047	734.375 ± 153.998
	#Edges	116.375 ± 46.124	722.125 ± 258.400	940.938 ± 277.384	1676.250 ± 693.462	1431.625 ± 351.722
	In/Out degree	0.981 ± 0.102	1.607 ± 0.129	1.653 ± 0.114	1.760 ± 0.143	1.728 ± 0.094
	Density	0.121 ± 0.048	0.009 ± 0.001	0.006 ± 0.001	0.004 ± 0.000	0.003 ± 0.000
	Clustering Coefficient	0.051 ± 0.016	0.078 ± 0.010	0.063 ± 0.008	0.048 ± 0.008	0.060 ± 0.006
	Reciprocity	0.053 ± 0.018	0.066 ± 0.010	0.054 ± 0.005	0.058 ± 0.008	0.070 ± 0.006
	#WCCs	6.250 ± 1.627	6.500 ± 1.780	5.375 ± 1.341	6.625 ± 1.326	6.625 ± 1.998

Table 2: Descriptive statistics (mean± SE) of network metrics for the retweet and conversation networks over time. Each metric is an average over the individual conferences.

- Combined features: A set of features that utilizes all the features above to test the combination of them.

Evaluation. We used Information Gain to determine the importance of individual features in WEKA [6]. Then we computed the normalized score of each variable's InfoGain value as its relative importance. To evaluate the binary classifier, we deployed different supervised learning algorithms and used the area under ROC curve (AUC) to determine the performance of our feature sets. The evaluation was performed using 10-fold cross validation in the WEKA machine learning suite.

5. RESULTS

In the following sections we report on the results obtained for each of our analyses.

5.1 Has usage changed?

We answer this question by the results presented in Figure 1, which shows the overtime ratio values of different Twitter usage in the conferences accompanied by their corresponding values from the random dataset.

We can highlight two distinct patterns first. The trends we observed for the information usage ratios are similar. The Retweet Ratio increases (6.7% in 2009, 48.2% in 2013) over the years (one-way ANOVA, $p < .001$) along with URL Ratio (21.2% in 2009, 51.3% in 2013; one-way ANOVA, $p < .001$). Noticeably, Retweet Ratio rapidly increased from 2009 to 2010 but rather steadily gained afterward. We believe this could be explained by the Twitter interface being changed in 2009, when they officially moved 'Retweet' button above the Twitter stream [3]. On the other hand, rather stable patterns can be observed in both conversational measures: Reply Ratio (8.2% in 2009, 6.1% in 2013) and Mention Ratio (10.0% in 2009, 12.9% in 2013). Therefore, as we expected, *Twitter behaved more as an information sharing platform during the conference, while the conversational usage did not seem to change over the years.*

Figure 1 also presents the differences between the ratio values in the conference dataset and the baseline dataset, as we want to understand if the trend observed above is the reflection of Twitter usage in general. During the conferences, we observed a higher Retweet Ratio and URL Ratio. We argue that it is rather expected because of the nature of academic conferences: sharing knowledge and their valuable recent work. The Mention Ratio in the conference is slightly higher than it is in the random dataset, because the conference is rather an event of people interacting with each other in a short time period. However, we observe a significant difference in Reply Ratio. Users start the conversation on Twitter using the conference hashtag to some extent like all users, but most users

who reply (more than 90%) usually drop the hashtag. Although it is still a public discussion on Twitter, we guess that users tend to keep it semi-public to their listeners. However, a deeper analysis which is outside the context of this research should be conducted to assess this assumption, since in some cases users would drop the hashtag simply to have more characters available in the message.

5.2 Has interaction changed?

Table 2 shows the evolution of the network measures. Each metric is an average over all the individual conferences in each year from 2009 to 2013. We first highlight the similar patterns over years observed from both networks: conversation network and retweet network. During the evolution, several types of network measures increase in both networks: (i) the average number of nodes; (ii) the average number of edges; and (iii) the average in/out degree. This suggests that more people are participating in the communication network.

Then, we compare these two networks in terms of the differences observed. Table 2 shows that the average number of weakly connected components in conversation network (#WCC) grows steadily over time from 4.750 components on average in 2009 to a significantly larger 29.188 components in 2013, with the CHI conference being the most fragmented (#WCC=87, #Nodes=2117). However, the counterpart value in retweet network is almost invariable, staying between 5.375 and 6.625 on average. The former metric supports the assumption of Ross et al. [19] in terms of the scattered characteristic of the activity network (i.e. multiple non-connected conversations). The #WCC suggests that the retweet network is more connected than the conversation network.

Not surprisingly, the reciprocity in the conversation network is significantly higher than the one in the retweet network ($p < .001$ in all years; pair-wise t-test). This shows that the conversations are more two-way rounded interactions between pairs of users while people who get retweeted do not necessarily retweet back. Both results are rather expected. The mentions and replies are tweets sent to particular users, and therefore the addressed users are more likely to reply back due to social norms. Yet, the retweet network is more like a star network, and users in the center do not necessarily retweet back.

Moreover, we observe that the average clustering coefficient in conversation network is higher than the one in retweet network, in general. We think that two users who talked to the same people on Twitter during conferences are more likely to be talking to each other, while users who retweeted the same person do not necessarily retweet each other. However, the significant difference is only found in 2012 ($p < .05$; t-test) and 2013 ($p < .001$; t-test). We tend to believe that it is the nature of the communication on Twitter,

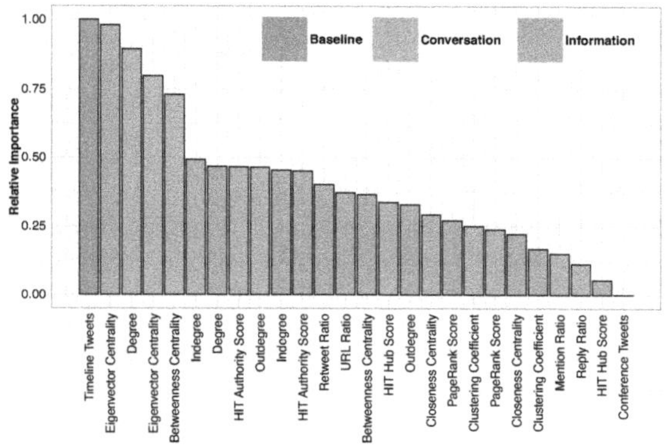

Figure 2: Relative Importance of the features.

Feature Sets	RF	ADA	Bagging	LR	SVM
Baseline	0.654	0.713	**0.716**	0.714	0.63
Baseline+Conversation	0.728	0.754	**0.774**	0.742	0.659
Baseline+Information	0.74	0.761	**0.771**	0.74	0.655
Combined	0.753	0.775	**0.787**	0.754	0.662

Table 3: Area under the ROC curve (AUC) for predicting continuing participation in the coming year with different feature sets and learning algorithms. The best algorithm for each feature set is highlighted. Methods used are Random forest (RF), Adaptive Boosting (ADA), Bagging, logistic regression (LR), and support vector machines (SVM).

but we need more observations and further analysis to support this guess.

5.3 What keeps the users returning?

The results of the prediction model are shown in Table 3, the Bagging approach achieved the highest performance across all the feature sets. Furthermore, baseline features achieved better performance when they are accompanied with conversation features than with the information features. This suggests that the conversation features have more predictive powers in inferring the users' continuous participation. Finally, the combination of all the features reached the best performance.

We further examine the importance of features in the combined set based on their information gain measures. Figure 2 shows the relative importance of different features. First, it is interesting that two features in the baseline have distinct importance: the number of one user's conference tweets produced the least information gain, while the number of timeline tweets has the least information gain. This suggests that the user is more likely to return because she has been highly active on Twitter in general; the number of conference tweets tends to be an incident of many factors, for instance, users could have fewer conference tweets because she does not have time to tweet during the conference or the Internet connection is not available.

We observe that the user's eigenvector centrality score from the information network has a higher importance (second lead in all the features). As the user with a higher eigenvector centrality score means that they and their neighbors have higher values in this measure, we interpret this as these users play important roles in information spreading during conferences. We conjecture these users are influential members in the conference so they are more likely to participate in the future.

Furthermore, we observe that three measures of the conversation network are also prominent: degree centrality, eigenvector centrality, and betweenness centrality. We know from the definitions of these measures that: higher value in the degree centrality of the user means more people this user has talked to in the conference on Twitter; higher eigenvector centrality value suggests the user has conversed with users that are also active in this network; and higher betweenness centrality indicates the user has served as the bridge of different groups of people. We suspect users' conversational experience and their roles are linked to their decisions of the return in the next year.

6. DISCUSSION AND CONCLUSIONS

In this paper, we investigated how Twitter has been used in academic conferences and how this has changed over the years. We attempted to study the usage, the network structures, and participation of the users during conferences on Twitter. We addressed our research with three questions.

To answer the first research question *RQ1*, we computed four features to quantitatively measure two aspects of Twitter use at conferences: information usage and conversation usage. Our results show that researchers are using Twitter in 2013 in a different way than they did in 2009 with respect to favoring more the information sharing value of Twitter, however their Twitter conversation interactions in 2013 do not differ much from five years ago.

Then, to answer the second research question *RQ2*, we constructed the conversation network and the retweet network for each conference and use network properties to measure how people interacted over the years. Our results show that with more people participating over time, the conversations turn scattered into small groups, while the information flow (retweets) stays mainly within a giant component.

Finally, to answer the third research question *RQ3*, we trained a binary classifier with features extracted from the Twitter usage, network positions of the user and achieve the best prediction performance using the combination of conversation features, information features, and baseline features. We also found that the most influential factors that drive users' continuous participation are being active on Twitter, being central in the information network and talking with more people.

We acknowledge the limitations of this work. First of all, we claimed to obtain the quasi-random tweets from the historical tweets, however this approach still needs refinement on the choices of several parameters, although we achieved reasonable results compared to other studies[3]. Second, we assumed conference hashtags as the medium with which users shared information and interacted with others during and about the conference. Although this is adopted by related studies, we may have collected incomplete data because some tweets that do not contain the conference hashtag however still are about the conference. Last but not least, we conducted our analysis on 16 Computer Science conferences, but the findings might not be generalized to all the computer science conferences since users in different sub-domains may show different Twitter usage. In future work, we plan to extend our study to a larger set of conferences across different domains in the field such as Information Systems and Data Mining, in order to see whether users in these conferences behave differently in Twitter.

Acknowledgments: This work is supported by the Know-Center and the EU funded project Learning Layers (7th Framework Program, Grant Agreement 318209). The Know-Center is funded within the Austrian COMET Program - Competence Centers for Excellent Technologies - under the auspices of the Austrian Ministry of Transport, Innovation and Technology, the Austrian Ministry of Economics and Labor and by the State of Styria. COMET is managed by the Austrian Research Promotion Agency (FFG).

---

[3]As of the time we wrote this paper, we did not find other statistics for random sample that can serve as a comparison with our study. However, later, Liu et al. [14] provided statistics in their study and their results similar to ours.

7. REFERENCES

[1] F. Abel, C. Hauff, G.-J. Houben, R. Stronkman, and K. Tao. Twitcident: fighting fire with information from social web streams. In *Proceedings of the 21st international conference companion on World Wide Web*, pages 305–308. ACM, 2012.

[2] P. Bonacich. Factoring and weighting approaches to status scores and clique identification. *Journal of Mathematical Sociology*, 2(1):113–120, 1972.

[3] D. Boyd, S. Golder, and G. Lotan. Tweet, tweet, retweet: Conversational aspects of retweeting on twitter. In *System Sciences (HICSS), 2010 43rd Hawaii International Conference on*, pages 1–10. IEEE, 2010.

[4] T. Desai, A. Shariff, A. Shariff, M. Kats, X. Fang, C. Christiano, and M. Ferris. Tweeting the meeting: an in-depth analysis of twitter activity at kidney week 2011. *PloS one*, 7(7):e40253, 2012.

[5] M. Ebner. Introducing live microblogging: How single presentations can be enhanced by the mass. *Journal of research in innovative teaching*, 2(1), 2009.

[6] M. Hall, E. Frank, G. Holmes, B. Pfahringer, P. Reutemann, and I. H. Witten. The weka data mining software: An update. *SIGKDD Explor. Newsl.*, 11(1):10–18, Nov. 2009.

[7] H. He and E. A. Garcia. Learning from imbalanced data. *IEEE Trans. on Knowl. and Data Eng.*, 21(9):1263–1284, Sept. 2009.

[8] J. M. Kleinberg. Authoritative sources in a hyperlinked environment. *JOURNAL OF THE ACM*, 46(5):604–632, 1999.

[9] J. Lanagan and A. F. Smeaton. Using twitter to detect and tag important events in live sports. *Artificial Intelligence*, pages 542–545, 2011.

[10] A. O. Larsson and H. Moe. Studying political microblogging: Twitter users in the 2010 swedish election campaign. *New Media & Society*, 14(5):729–747, 2012.

[11] J. Letierce, A. Passant, J. Breslin, and S. Decker. Understanding how twitter is used to spread scientific messages. 2010.

[12] J. Letierce, A. Passant, J. G. Breslin, and S. Decker. Using twitter during an academic conference: The# iswc2009 use-case. In *ICWSM*, 2010.

[13] Y.-R. Lin, B. Keegan, D. Margolin, and D. Lazer. Rising tides or rising stars?: Dynamics of shared attention on twitter during media events. *CoRR*, abs/1307.2785, 2013.

[14] Y. Liu, C. Kliman-Silver, and A. Mislove. The tweets they are a-changin': Evolution of twitter users and behavior. 2014.

[15] M. Mendoza, B. Poblete, and C. Castillo. Twitter under crisis: can we trust what we rt? In *Proceedings of the first workshop on social media analytics*, pages 71–79. ACM, 2010.

[16] L. Page, S. Brin, R. Motwani, and T. Winograd. The pagerank citation ranking: Bringing order to the web, 1999.

[17] W. Reinhardt, M. Ebner, G. Beham, and C. Costa. How people are using twitter during conferences. *Creativity and innovation Competencies on the Web*, page 145, 2009.

[18] B. Rieder. The refraction chamber: Twitter as sphere and network. *First Monday*, 17(11), 2012.

[19] C. Ross, M. Terras, C. Warwick, and A. Welsh. Enabled backchannel: conference twitter use by digital humanists. *Journal of Documentation*, 67(2):214–237, 2011.

[20] A. Sopan, P. Rey, B. Butler, and B. Shneiderman. Monitoring academic conferences: Real-time visualization and retrospective analysis of backchannel conversations. In *Social Informatics (SocialInformatics), 2012 International Conference on*, pages 62–69. IEEE, 2012.

[21] A. Tumasjan, T. O. Sprenger, P. G. Sandner, and I. M. Welpe. Predicting elections with twitter: What 140 characters reveal about political sentiment. *ICWSM*, 10:178–185, 2010.

[22] S. Wasserman and K. Faust. *Social network analysis: methods and applications*. Cambridge University Press, Cambridge; New York, 1994.

[23] K. Weller, E. Dröge, and C. Puschmann. Citation analysis in twitter: Approaches for defining and measuring information flows within tweets during scientific conferences. In *Proceedings of Making Sense of Microposts Workshop (# MSM2011). Co-located with Extended Semantic Web Conference, Crete, Greece*, 2011.

[24] X. Wen, D. Parra, and C. Trattner. How groups of people interact with each other on twitter during academic conferences. In *Proceedings of the Companion Publication of the 17th ACM Conference on Computer Supported Cooperative Work & Social Computing*, CSCW Companion '14, pages 253–256, New York, NY, USA, 2014. ACM.

[25] A. Zubiaga, D. Spina, V. Fresno, and R. Martínez. Classifying trending topics: a typology of conversation triggers on twitter. In *Proceedings of the 20th ACM international conference on Information and knowledge management*, pages 2461–2464. ACM, 2011.

A Rating Aggregation Method for Generating Product Reputations

Ahmad Abdel-Hafez
Queensland University of
Technology
Brisbane, Australia
a.abdelhafez@qut.edu.au

Yue Xu
Queensland University of
Technology
Brisbane, Australia
yue.xu@qut.edu.au

Audun Jøsang
University of Oslo
Oslo, Norway
josang@mn.uio.no

ABSTRACT

Many websites offer the opportunity for customers to rate items and then use customers' ratings to generate items reputation, which can be used later by other users for decision making purposes. The aggregated value of the ratings per item represents the reputation of this item. The accuracy of the reputation scores is important as it is used to rank items. Most of the aggregation methods didn't consider the frequency of distinct ratings and they didn't test how accurate their reputation scores over different datasets with different sparsity. In this work we propose a new aggregation method which can be described as a weighted average, where weights are generated using the normal distribution. The evaluation result shows that the proposed method outperforms state-of-the-art methods over different sparsity datasets.

Keywords

Reputation Model; Ratings Aggregation; Uncertainty

1. INTRODUCTION AND BACKGROUND

People are increasingly dependent on information online in order to decide whether to trust a specific object or not. Therefore, reputation systems are an essential part of any e-commerce or product reviews websites, where they provide methods for collecting and aggregating users' ratings in order to calculate the overall reputation scores for products, users, or services [1].

One of the challenges that face any reputation model is its ability to work with different datasets, sparse or dense ones. Within any dataset some items may have rich rating data, while others, especially new ones, have low number of ratings. Sparse datasets are the ones that contain higher percentage of items which do not have many ratings or users who didn't rate many items. However, with the increased popularity of rating systems on the web particularly, sparse datasets become denser by time as ratings build up on the dataset. On the other hand, most of the existing reputation models don't consider the distribution of ratings for an item, which should influence its reputation. In this paper, we propose to consider the frequency of ratings in the rating aggregation process in order to generate reputation scores. The purpose is to enhance accuracy of reputation scores using any dataset no matter whether it is dense or sparse. The proposed methods are weighted average methods, where the weights are assumed to reflect the distribution of ratings in the overall score. An important contribution of this paper is a method to generate the weights based on the normal distribution of the ratings, other weighting factors can be easily combined into our proposed methods.

Many methods used weighted average as an aggregator for the ratings, where the weight can represent user's reputation, time when the rating was given, or the distance between the current reputation score and the received rating. Shapiro [2] proved that time is important in calculating reputation scores; hence, the time decay factor has been widely used in reputation systems [2, 3, 4, 5]. On the other hand, Riggs and Wilensky [6] performed collaborative quality filtering, based on the principle of finding the most reliable users. Lauw et al. introduced the Leniency-Aware Quality (LQ) Model [7] which is a weighted average model that uses users' ratings tendency as weights. Using fuzzy models are also popular in calculating reputation scores because fuzzy logic provides rules for reasoning with fuzzy measures [8, 9]. Jøsang and Haller introduced a multinomial Bayesian probability distribution reputation system based on Dirichlet probability distribution [4]. This model is probably the most relevant method to our proposed method because this method also takes into consideration the count of ratings.

2. NORMAL DISTRIBUTION BASED REPUTATION MODEL (NDR)

In this section we will introduce a new aggregation method to generate product reputation scores. In this paper we use arithmetic mean method as the Naïve method. Our initial intuition is that rating weights is the frequency of rating levels, because the frequency represents the popularity of users' opinions towards an item. Another fact we consider in deriving the rating weights is the distribution of ratings. Like many "natural" phenomena, we can assume that the ratings fall in normal distribution. In our case, it will provide different weights for ratings, where the more frequent the rating level is, the higher the weight the level will get.

Suppose that we have n ratings for a specific product P, represented as $R_P = \{r_0, r_1, r_2, \ldots, r_{n-1}\}$ where r_0 is the smallest rating and r_{n-1} is the largest rating, i.e., $r_0 \leq r_1 \leq r_2 \leq \cdots \leq r_{n-1}$. In order to aggregate the ratings, we

HT'14, September 1–4, 2014, Santiago, Chile.
ACM 978-1-4503-2954-5/14/09.
http://dx.doi.org/10.1145/2631775.2631779.

need to compute the associated weights with each rating, which is represented as $W_P = \{w_0, w_1, w_2, \ldots, w_{n-1}\}$. The weights to the ratings will be calculated using the normal distribution density function given in Equation (1), where a_i is the weight for the rating at index $i, i = 0, \ldots, n-1$, μ is the mean, σ is the standard deviation, and x_i is supposed to be the value at index i; the basic idea is to evenly deploy the values between 1 and k for the rating scale $[1, k]$ over the indexes from 0 to $n-1$. k is the number of levels in the rating system.

$$a_i = \frac{1}{\sigma\sqrt{2\pi}} e^{-\frac{(x_i - \mu)^2}{2\sigma^2}}, \text{ where } x_i = \frac{(k-1) \times i}{n-1} + 1 \quad (1)$$

We deploy the values of x_i between 1 and k, where $x_0 = 1$ and $x_{n-1} = k$. In Equation (1), the value of the mean is fixed, i.e., $\mu = \frac{(k+1)}{2}$. However, the value of σ is the actual standard deviation value extracted from the ratings to this item; hence, each item in the dataset will have different flatness for its normal distribution curve. The generated weights in Equation (1) is then normalized so the summation of all weights is equal to 1, hence, we create the normalized weights vector $W_P = \{w_0, w_1, w_2, \ldots, w_{n-1}\}$ using Equation (2).

$$w_i = \frac{a_i}{\sum_{j=0}^{n-1} a_j}, \text{ where } \sum_{i=0}^{n-1} w_i = 1 \quad (2)$$

In order to calculate the final reputation score, which is affected by the ratings and the weights, we need to sum the weights of each level separately. We partition all ratings into groups based on levels, $R^l = \{r_0^l, r_1^l, r_2^l, \ldots, r_{|R^l|-1}^l\}$, $l = 1, 2, \ldots, k$, for each rating $r \in R^l$, $r = l$. The set of all ratings to item p is $R_P = \bigcup_{l=1}^{k} R^l$. The corresponding weights for the ratings in R^l are represented as $W^l = \{w_0^l, w_1^l, w_2^l, \ldots, w_{|R^l|-1}^l\}$. The final reputation score is calculated as weighted average for each rating level using Equation (3), where LW^l stands for level weight.

$$NDR_p = \sum_{l=1}^{k} \left(l \times LW^l \right), \text{ where } LW^l = \sum_{j=0}^{|R^l|-1} w_j^l \quad (3)$$

We will do a slight modification to our proposed NDR method by combining uncertainty principle, introduced by Jøsang and Haller Dirichlet method [4]. This enhancement is important to deal with sparse dataset, because when the number of ratings is small, the uncertainty is high. Inspired by the Dirichlet method in [4], the NDRU reputation score is calculated using Equation (4) which takes uncertainty into consideration. C is a priori constant which is set to 2 in our experiments, and $b = \frac{1}{k}$ is a base rate for any of the k rating values.

$$NDRU_{p1} = \sum_{l=1}^{k} \left(l \times \left(\frac{n \times LW^l + C \times b}{C + n} \right) \right) \quad (4)$$

3. EXPERIMENT AND DISCUSSION

The dataset used in this experiment is the MovieLens dataset which is publicly available and widely used in the area of rec-ommender systems. The dataset contains about 1 million anonymous ratings of approximately 3,706 movies. In this dataset each user has evaluated at least 20 movies, and each movie is evaluated by at least 1 user. Three new

Table 1: MAE results for the 5 fold rating prediction experiment

Dataset	Naïve	LQ	Dirichlet	NDR	NDRU
4RPM	0.556	0.5576	**0.5286**	0.5614	0.5326
6RPM	0.561	0.5628	0.5514	0.5608	**0.5498**
8RPM	0.5726	0.5736	0.5705	0.5693	**0.5676**
ARPM	0.7924	0.7928	0.7928	**0.7851**	0.7853

datasets were extracted from the original dataset (ARPM) in order to test the different reputation models for different levels of sparsity. The sparsest dataset created has only 4 ratings per movie randomly selected from users' ratings to this movie(4RPM). For the second and the third datasets, each movie has 6 (6RPM) and 8 (8RPM) randomly selected ratings, respectively.

The experiment is to predict an item rating using the item reputation score generated by reputation models. The hypothesis is that the more accurate the reputation model the closer the scores it generates to actual users' ratings. For one item, we will use the same reputation score to predict the item's rating for different users. In this experiment we use the training dataset to calculate a reputation score for every movie. Secondly we will use these reputation scores as rating prediction values for all the movies in the testing dataset and will compare these reputation values with users' actual ratings in the testing dataset. The Baseline methods we will compare with include the Naïve method, Dirichlet reputation system proposed by Jøsang and Haller [4], and the Leniency-aware Quality (LQ) model proposed by Lauw et al. [7]. The mean absolute error (MAE) is used to measure the accuracy of rating prediction. Equation (5) shows how to calculate the MAE.

$$MAE = \frac{\sum_{i=1}^{n} |p_i - r_i|}{n} \quad (5)$$

The experiment is done as a five-fold cross validation, where every time a different 20% of the dataset is used for testing. This method ensures that each user's data has been used five times; four times in training and one time in testing. We record the MAE in each round for all the implemented methods, and at the end we calculate the average of the five MAE values recorded for each reputation model. We have tested the ratings prediction accuracy using the four previously described datasets. From the results in Table 1, we can see that the NDR method produces the best results when we use it with dense datasets, and that the Dirichlet method is the best with sparse datasets. Most importantly, the NDRU method, provides good results in any case, and can be used as a general reputation model regardless of the sparsity in datasets.

4. CONCLUSIONS

In this work we have proposed a new aggregation method for generating reputation scores for items or products based on customers' ratings, where the weights are generated using a normal distribution. The method is also enhanced with adding uncertainty part by adopting the idea of the work proposed by Jøsang and Haller [4]. The results of our experiments show that our proposed method outperforms the state-of-the-art methods in ratings prediction over a well-known dataset.

5. REFERENCES

[1] Resnick, P., Kuwabara, K., Zeckhauser, R. Friedman, E.: Reputation Systems. Communi-cations of the ACM, 43(12), pp. 45-48. (2000).

[2] Shapiro, C.: Consumer Information, Product Quality, And Seller Reputation. The Bell Journal of Economics,13(1), pp. 20-35. RAND. (1982).

[3] Ayday, E., Lee, H., Fekri, F.: An Iterative Algorithm For Trust And Reputation Management. Proceedings of the International Symposium on Information Theory, pp. 2051-2055. IEEE. (2009)

[4] Jøsang, A. and Haller, J.: Dirichlet Reputation Systems. Proceedings of the Second International Conference on Availability, Reliability and Security, pp. 112-119. IEEE. (2007).

[5] Leberknight, C. S., Sen, S., Chiang, M.: On The Volatility Of Online Ratings: An Empirical Study. E-Life: Web-Enabled Convergence of Commerce, Work, and Social Life, pp. 77-86. Springer Berlin Heidelberg. (2012).

[6] Riggs, T., Wilensky, R.: An Algorithm For Automated Rating Of Reviewers. Proceedings of the First ACM/IEEE-CS joint conference on Digital libraries, pp. 381-387. ACM.. (2001).

[7] Lauw, H. W., Lim, E. P., Wang, K.: Quality and Leniency in Online Collaborative Rating Systems. ACM Transactions on the Web (TWEB), 6(1), 4. (2012).

[8] Sabater, J., Sierra, C.: Reputation And Social Network Analysis In Multi-Agent Systems. in Proceedings of the first international joint conference on Autonomous agents and multiagent systems. pp. 475-482. (2002).

[9] Bharadwaj, K. K., Al-Shamri, M. Y. H.: Fuzzy Computational Models For Trust And Reputation Systems. Electronic Commerce Research and Applications, 8(1), pp. 37-47, (2009).

A Focused Crawler for Mining Hate and Extremism Promoting Videos on YouTube

Swati Agarwal, Ashish Sureka
Indraprastha Institute of Information Technology, Delhi (IIIT-D)
New Delhi, India
swatia@iiitd.ac.in, ashish@iiitd.ac.in

ABSTRACT

Online video sharing platforms such as YouTube contains several videos and users promoting hate and extremism. Due to low barrier to publication and anonymity, YouTube is misused as a platform by some users and communities to post negative videos disseminating hatred against a particular religion, country or person. We formulate the problem of identification of such malicious videos as a search problem and present a focused-crawler based approach consisting of various components performing several tasks: search strategy or algorithm, node similarity computation metric, learning from exemplary profiles serving as training data, stopping criterion, node classifier and queue manager. We implement a best-first search algorithm and conduct experiments to measure the accuracy of the proposed approach. Experimental results demonstrate that the proposed approach is effective.

Categories and Subject Descriptors

H.5.4 [**Hypertext/Hypermedia**]: Navigation; K.4.2 [**Social Issues**]: Abuse and crime involving computers; D.2.8 [**Metrics**]: Performance measures; H.3.1 [**Content Analysis and Indexing**]: Linguistic processing

Keywords

Social Media Analytics; Focused Crawler; Hate and Extremism Detection; Video Sharing Website; Online Radicalization.

1. RESEARCH MOTIVATION AND AIM

Research shows that YouTube has become a convenient platform for many hate and extremist groups to share information and promote their ideologies. The reason is because video is the most usable medium to share views with others [1]. Previous studies show that extremist groups put forth hateful speech, offensive comments and messages focusing their mission [3]. Social networking allows these users

HT'14, September 1–4, 2014, Santiago, Chile.
ACM 978-1-4503-2954-5/14/09.
http://dx.doi.org/10.1145/2631775.2631776 .

(uploading extremist videos, posting violent comments, subscribers of these channels) to facilitate recruitment, gradually reaching world wide viewers, connecting to other hate promoting groups, spreading extremist content and forming their communities sharing a common agenda [2] [6]. The presence of such extremist content in large amount is a major concern for YouTube moderators (to uphold the reputation of the website), government and law enforcement agencies (identifying extremist content and user communities to stop such promotion in country). However, despite several community guidelines and administrative efforts made by YouTube, it has become a repository of large amounts of malicious and offensive videos [5]. Detecting such hate promoting videos and users is a significant and technically challenging problem. 100 hours of videos are uploaded every minute, that makes YouTube a very dynamic website. Hence, locating such users by keyword based search is overwhelmingly impractical. The work presented in this paper is motivated by the need of a solution to combat and counter online radicalization. We frame our problem as: identifying such videos promoting hate and extremism on YouTube. The research aim of the work presented in this paper is to investigate the application of a focused crawler (best-first search) based approach for retrieving YouTube user-profiles promoting hate and extremism. To investigate the effectiveness of contextual features such as the title of the videos uploaded, commented, shared, and favourited for computing the similarity between nodes in the focused crawler traversal and to examine the effectiveness of subscribers, featured channels and public contacts as links between nodes.

2. BEST-FIRST SEARCH CRAWLER

The proposed method is a multi-step process primarily consists of three phases, Training Profile Collection, Statistical Model Building and Focused Crawler. We perform a manual analysis and a visual inspection of activity feeds and contextual metadata of various YouTube channels. We collect 35 positive class channels (promoting hate and extremism) used as training profiles. We build our training dataset by extracting the discriminatory features (user activity feeds such as titles of videos uploaded, shared, favourited & commented by the user and profile information) of these 35 channels using YouTube API[1]. We build a statistical model from these training profiles by applying character n-gram based language modeling approach. We build a focused crawler (best-first search) which is a recursive process.

---

[1]https://developers.google.com/youtube/getting_started

Algorithm 1: Focused Crawler- Best First Search

Data: Seed User U, Width of Graph w, Size of Graph s, Threshold th, N-gram Ng, Positive Class Channels U_p
Result: A connected directed cyclic graph, Nodes=User u

```
1   for all u ∈ Up do
2   |   D.add(ExtractFeatures(u))
    end
    Algorithm BFS(U)
3   |   while graphsize < s do
4   |   |   userfeeds Uf ←ExtractFeatures(U)
5   |   |   score score ←LanguageModeling(D, Uf, Ng)
6   |   |   if (score <th) then
7   |   |   |   U.class ←Irrelevant
    |   |   else
8   |   |   |   U.class ←Relevant
9   |   |   |   Hashmap Usorted·InsertionSort(U, score)
    |   |   end
    |   |   for i ← 1 to w do
10  |   |   |   Hashmap Ugraph.add(Usorted(i))
    |   |   end
    |   |   for all Ug ∈ Ugraph do
11  |   |   |   fr = Extract_Frontiers(Ug)
12  |   |   |
13  |   |   |   Hashmap Ucrawler.add(fr)
    |   |   end
    |   |   for all Ufr ∈ Ucrawler do
14  |   |   |   BFS(Ufr)
15  |   |   |
    |   |   end
    |   end
    end
```

Algorithm 2: Frontier Extraction for a YouTube User

Data: User u
Result: Frontiers of a channel
Algorithm $Extract\_Frontiers(U)$

```
1   |   usubs ←u.getSubscribers()
2   |   ufc ←u.getFeaturedChannels()
3   |   ucon ←u.getFriends()
```

It takes one YouTube channel as a seed (a positive class channel) and extract it's contextual metadata (user activity feeds and profile information) using YouTube API. We find the extent of textual similarity between these metadata and training data by using statistical model (build in phase 2) and LingPipe API [2]. We implement a binary classifier to classify a user channel as relevant or irrelevant. A user channel is said to be relevant (hate and extremism promoting channel) if the computation score is above a predefined threshold. If a channel is relevant, then we further extend it's frontiers (links to other YouTube channels) i.e. the subscribers of the channel, featured channels suggested by the user and it's contacts available publicly. We extract these frontiers by parsing users' YouTube homepage using jsoup HTML parser library [3]. We execute focused crawler phase for each frontier recursively which results a connected graph, where nodes represent the user channels and edges represent the links between two users.

Inputs to the algorithm is a seed (a positive class user) U, width of graph w i.e. maximum number of children of a node, size of graph s i.e. maximum number of nodes in graph, threshold th for classification, n-gram value Ng for similarity computation (language modeling), and a lexicon of 35 positive class channels U_p. We compare each training profile with all profiles and compute their similarity score for each mode. We take an average of these 35 scores and compute the threshold values. The proposed method (Algorithm 1) follows the standard best-first traversing to explore relevant user to seed input. Best-First Search examines a node in the graph and finds the most promising node among it's children to be traversed next [4]. This priority of nodes (users) is decided based upon the extent of similarity with the training profiles. A user with the similarity score above

[2] http://alias-i.com/lingpipe/index.html
[3] http://jsoup.org/apidocs/

a specified threshold is said to be relevant and allowed to be extended further. If a node is relevant and has the highest priority (similarity score) among all relevant nodes then we extend it first and explore it's links and discard irrelevant nodes. We process each node only once and if a node appears again then we only include the connecting edge in the graph. Steps 1 and 2 extract all contextual features for 35 training profiles using a feature extraction algorithm and build a training data set. Steps 4 and 5 extract all features for seed user U and compute it's similarity score with training profiles using character n-gram and language modeling. Steps 6 to 8 represent the classification procedure and labeling of users as relevant or irrelevant depending upon the threshold measures.

BFS method has non-binary priority values assigned to each node. The priority values are the similarity score, which is computed by comparing the users' contextual metadata (user activity feeds and profile information) with training profiles. Steps 9 and 10 make a list of top w (maximum number of children, a node can have) users among relevant users based upon their similarity score, sorted in a decreasing order. Steps $11 - 13$ extracts frontiers of a user channel using Algorithm 2. Steps 14 and 15 repeat Steps $3 - 13$ for each frontier extracted. We execute this function till we get a graph with desired number of nodes or there is no more node is left to extend.

Table 1: Best-First Search Confusion Matrix

		Predicted	
		Relevant	**Irrelevant**
Actual	**Relevant**	921	314
	Irrelevant	125	67

3. PERFORMANCE EVALUATION

The crawler requires exemplary documents or training examples to learn the specific characteristics and properties of documents in the training dataset. A statistical model (text classifier) needs to be built from a collection of documents pertaining to a predefined topic. We create a list of 35 user-ids used as training profiles. The 35 user ids consists of 612 videos and hence the training is performed on 612 videos. We obtain the training dataset by manually searching (keyword based) for anti-India hate and extremism promoting channels using YouTube search and traversing related video links (using the heuristic that videos on similar topic will be connected as relevant on YouTube). We select 10 random positive class (hate and extremist) channels for creating test dataset. Each user works as a seed input to the focused crawler. To evaluate the effectiveness of our solution approach we execute our focused crawler several times for various configurations and seed. Table 1 shows the confusion matrix for binary classification performed during Best-First Search approach. Given the input of 10 seed users and 6 modes (pair of threshold and n-gram values) we get different number of connected users in each iteration. To measure the accuracy of our proposed approach we collect results of all 60 iterations and classify 1046 (921 + 125) users as relevant and 381 (314 + 67) as irrelevant users. There is a misclassification of 25.42% and 65.10% in predicting the relevant and irrelevant users respectively.

4. REFERENCES

[1] Hsinchun Chen, Dorothy Denning, Nancy Roberts, Catherine A. Larson, Ximing Yu, and Chunneng Huang. The dark web forum portal: From multi-lingual to video. In *ISI*, pages 7–14. IEEE, 2011.

[2] Maura Conway and Lisa McInerney. Jihadi video and auto-radicalisation: Evidence from an exploratory youtube study. In Daniel Ortiz-Arroyo, HenrikLegind Larsen, DanielDajun Zeng, David Hicks, and Gerhard Wagner, editors, *Intelligence and Security Informatics*, volume 5376 of *Lecture Notes in Computer Science*, pages 108–118. Springer Berlin Heidelberg, 2008.

[3] Lacy G McNamee, Brittany L Peterson, and Jorge Peña. A call to educate, participate, invoke and indict: Understanding the communication of online hate groups. *Communication Monographs*, 77(2):257–280, 2010.

[4] S. Rawat and D.R. Patil. Efficient focused crawling based on best first search. In *Advance Computing Conference (IACC), 2013 IEEE 3rd International*, pages 908–911, Feb 2013.

[5] Ashish Sureka, Ponnurangam Kumaraguru, Atul Goyal, and Sidharth Chhabra. Mining youtube to discover extremist videos, users and hidden communities. In Pu-Jen Cheng, Min-Yen Kan, Wai Lam, and Preslav Nakov, editors, *Information Retrieval Technology*, volume 6458 of *Lecture Notes in Computer Science*, pages 13–24. Springer Berlin Heidelberg, 2010.

[6] Yilu Zhou, Edna Reid, Jialun Qin, Hsinchun Chen, and Guanpi Lai. Us domestic extremist groups on the web: link and content analysis. *Intelligent Systems, IEEE*, 20(5):44–51, 2005.

Spatio-Temporal Quality Issues for Local Search

Dirk Ahlers

NTNU – Norwegian University of Science and Technology
Trondheim, Norway
dirk.ahlers@idi.ntnu.no

ABSTRACT

Geographic search is routinely used in many services and applications that exploit the availability of Web content which is related to a real world place, region or object. However, do you trust the location information? Who has not made the experience that the restaurant you went to has just moved to another part of the city or shut down? Local search returns located results, e.g., extracted entities located in a certain spot or area, but their quality can be difficult to judge. Compared to normal Web search, local Web search has additional inherent issues due to factors such as insufficient semantics, ambiguity of references, imprecise mapping, or unknown status of the real-world entities described in documents. We present selected issues and features of geospatial quality and credibility based on spatial, temporal, and topical indicators as an additional measurement of spatial relevance.

Categories and Subject Descriptors

H.3.3 [**Information Storage and Retrieval**]: Information Search and Retrieval

Keywords

Search quality; credibility; location-aware search; geospatial Web retrieval; entity extraction; temporal retrieval

1. INTRODUCTION

Location is an important and successful feature in Web information retrieval. Scenarios include the planning of a business trip or a vacation, the search for a new house, the decision for a school or university or something as simple as where to buy groceries [1, 5]. The reliability of search results becomes even more crucial in a location-based or mobile scenario where it can be much more difficult to judge the reliability of information short of actually visiting a place. Consider a user's dissatisfaction who drove all the way to an out-of-business restaurant that was, however, shown in

HT'14, September 1–4, 2014, Santiago, Chile.
ACM 978-1-4503-2954-5/14/09.
http://dx.doi.org/10.1145/2631775.2631792 .

a list of results of recommended restaurants. The difference in perception to Web search can be explained by the fact that a result document matches the query in some way, but a result entity carries the implied assumption that it is actually represented in the real world – and it is much easier to check a document than it is to check an actual place. In short, the existence of information about a place is expected to be a proxy for the existence of the place itself.

As an example, consider a query about the "Museum of Modern Art" (MoMA). The usual result would be the information about its exhibitions, its homepage (www.moma.org) and of course its location. Normally this would be given as 11 West 53rd Street, Manhattan, New York, NY, USA, or, with less granularity, as New York, USA. However, the query is broader than the example suggests. There is also the San Francisco Museum of Modern Art (SFMOMA) and of course many more museums with this exact name around the world. Optimally, these multiple occurrences are identified, disambiguated, and treated separately.

The issue becomes more interesting when taking more complex situations into account. For example, changes in the real world can leave marks in the Web that can be challenging to interpret. A special event took place between 2002 and 2004. The MoMA underwent renovations and was closed during that time. The museum itself was unavailable to visitors, but parts of the collection were exhibited elsewhere, some in the MoMA QNS which was located at 33rd Street and Queens Boulevard. When further searching for MOMA in Queens, the P.S.1 Contemporary Art Center comes up at 22-25 Jackson Ave, Long Island City, NY, USA. Yet this is is a separate entity only affiliated on some exhibitions with the MOMA. A major part of the collection was further shown in Berlin during 2004 under the name "Das MoMA in Berlin" at the museum Neue Nationalgalerie at Potsdamer Straße 50, 10785 Berlin, Germany, which received a large media response. Nowadays, the exhibition is gone, but many Web pages still mention it and it turns up in local search engines. So in their own right, all of these results would be valid for a certain period of time only.

Figure 1 shows a result set for "museum of modern art" on a global scale, highlighting New York and Berlin; the cutout shows Manhattan and Queens. For these three results, their lifespan is plotted in the graph; the shaded shapes give an estimate on expected pages mentioning the place. Web resources may not always match very well to the entity lifespan and the evidence for a new entity is usually much better than that for its disappearance. While a global search could very well judge the MoMA in New York to be the most important

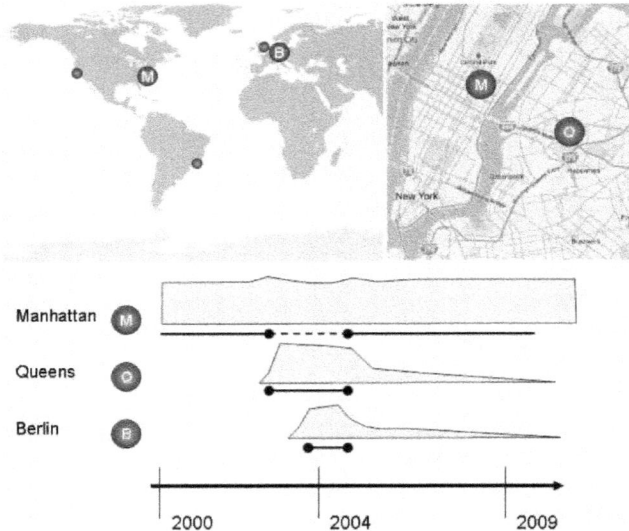

Figure 1: Example of temporal changes for entities

one, there usually would be results all over the map. A local search within Berlin would still find strong evidence for its presence.

This article presents an initial discussion of credibility issues influencing geospatial search quality and relevance.

2. QUALITY AND RELEVANCE

The Web is a major information source, but also contains inaccuracies, omissions, outdated pages, or even adversaries. Thus, retrieval techniques have to address the information credibility issue to deliver high-quality results. Geospatial Web search engines [4] face similar issues, but often on different levels or, due to the spatial processing, from entirely new angles. User requirements include not only relevance, but also features such as freshness and diversity [18] or reliability. In Geographic Web information retrieval [13], results are ranked based on the relevance of the documents to a query on content and spatial features [9, 10, 16]. Our aim is to address location data quality to lay the ground for higher-level quality models. Then, quality and credibility is added as another dimension of relevance:

$$
\begin{aligned}
Relevance(q, doc) \;=\; & Rel_{Content}(q_{content}, doc_{content}) \otimes \\
& Rel_{Spatial}(q_{spatial}, doc_{spatial}) \otimes \\
& Credibility_{Spatiotemporal}(q, doc)
\end{aligned}
$$

Going into more detail, we understand geospatial credibility not only as individual data quality, but as a new compound measure across a variety of features and sources such as reliability, authority, trustworthiness, quality, correctness, up-to-dateness, completeness, availability, and finally, physical existence in the real world. Note that credibility not only depends on the documents in the index, but also on the query, as different queries can have different expectations or requirements.

2.1 Selected Factors

Credibility indicators can be derived from features such as presence of keywords, references, named entities, detectable

patterns, times and dates, linkage patterns, or external sources, to name just a few. However, in many cases even these features are not completely accurate or carry a certain uncertainty [6, 11], as well as their extraction process, either implicit or explicitly annotated. Therefore, the following factors indicate uncertain data on multiple levels.

Temporal features are strongly connected to geospatial information [7]. A question for museums in the vicinity implicitly has a temporal aspect in that the museums should be there at the time of the question. Web pages frequently appear, disappear, move, or change. Similarly, the location references on them and those in the real world do the same when businesses are created, move, change name or owner, or are closed. For the example of the MoMA Berlin, it would usually take some time to show up in search results. More importantly, it is more difficult to detect its closing. An opening of a new place thus is harder to detect than a closing or a move of a business. This also applies to compound or aggregate measures.

Geoparsing and Geocoding issues to consider include extraction errors, wrong matches, and granularity, [12, 17]. In the example, using only broad granularity would identify both the Manhattan and Queens buildings as New York.

Entity and Relation Extraction plays a major role in location credibility within entity-oriented search such as company or people search [8, 17, 3]. Issues arise with incomplete entities due to varying levels of detail or spellings of names, imprecision in extraction etc.

External Data Integration of spatial domain knowledge is necessary for, e.g., validation, but it may also already carry inaccuracies [2] and might change over time.

Aggregation can increase the reliability of results that are based on multiple sources [15, 3, 14]. For example, some pages may show outdated information or report different names for a museum. We would have to identify MoMA with Museum of Modern Art and similar names, yet distinguish them from the MoMA QNS and maybe even from the museum store within the same building, while considering the temporal changes.

Visualization and interaction can draw user's attention to the reliability of information or may compute aggregate mappings to achieve its goals [14]. This is especially important as items on a map tend to be trusted more by users since mapped data "feels" more accurate.

3. CONCLUSION

We have discussed quality and credibility issues in geospatial Web information retrieval on an initial selection of spatiotemporal features. Ultimately, they should be incorporated into an improved model for relevance ranking. Temporal issues are only one aspect of a more complete model of credibility, but they show up in many features and are underlying non-considered causes for certain cases of lowered result quality. Future work will investigate cross-relations and propose solutions or mitigations for certain issues as well as connect these issues with requirements and implications for different application scenarios. We believe that these issues will have to play a bigger role in future geospatial retrieval systems and open up interesting research questions towards improved trust and quality.

4. REFERENCES

[1] D. Ahlers. *Geographically Focused Web Information Retrieval*. OlWIR, Oldenburg, Germany, 2011. PhD Thesis.

[2] D. Ahlers. Assessment of the Accuracy of GeoNames Gazetteer Data. In *GIR '13*, 2013.

[3] D. Ahlers. Business Entity Retrieval and Data Provision for Yellow Pages by Local Search. In *Integrating IR technologies for Professional Search Workshop @ ECIR2013*, 2013.

[4] D. Ahlers. Towards a development process for geospatial information retrieval and search. In *WWW '13*. 2013.

[5] D. Ahlers and S. Boll. Location-based Web search. In A. Scharl and K. Tochterman, editors, *The Geospatial Web*. Springer, 2007.

[6] I. Askira Gelman and A. L. Barletta. A "quick and dirty" website data quality indicator. In *WICOW '08: Proceeding of the 2nd ACM Workshop on Information Credibility on the Web*, 2008.

[7] K. Balog and K. Nørvåg. On the use of semantic knowledge bases for temporally-aware entity retrieval. In *ESAIR '12*, 2012.

[8] M. J. Cafarella, J. Madhavan, and A. Halevy. Web-Scale Extraction of Structured Data. *SIGMOD Rec.*, 37(4):55–61, 2008.

[9] P. D. Clough, H. Joho, and R. Purves. Judging the Spatial Relevance of Documents for GIR. In *ECIR'06*, 2006.

[10] P. Ehlen, R. Zajac, and K. B. Rao. Location and Relevance. In *LocWeb '09*, 2009.

[11] B. J. Fogg, J. Marshall, O. Laraki, A. Osipovich, C. Varma, N. Fang, J. Paul, A. Rangnekar, J. Shon, P. Swani, and M. Treinen. What Makes Web Sites Credible?: A Report on a Large Quantitative Study. In *CHI '01*, 2001.

[12] D. W. Goldberg, J. P. Wilson, and C. A. Knoblock. From Text to Geographic Coordinates: The Current State of Geocoding. *URISA Journal*, 19(1):33–46, 2007.

[13] C. B. Jones and R. S. Purves. Geographical Information Retrieval. *International Journal of Geographical Information Science*, 22(3):219 – 228, 2008.

[14] C. Kumar, W. Heuten, and S. Boll. A Visual Interactive System for Spatial Querying and Ranking of Geographic Regions. i-KNOW '13, 2013.

[15] R. Lee, D. Kitayama, and K. Sumiya. Web-based Evidence Excavation to Explore the Authenticity of Local Events. In *WICOW '08*, 2008.

[16] B. Martins, M. J. Silva, and L. Andrade. Indexing and Ranking in Geo-IR Systems. In *GIR '05*, 2005.

[17] Y. Morimoto, M. Aono, M. E. Houle, and K. S. McCurley. Extracting Spatial Knowledge from the Web. In *SAINT '03*. 2003.

[18] I. Szpektor, Y. Maarek, and D. Pelleg. When relevance is not enough: Promoting diversity and freshness in personalized question recommendation. WWW '13, 2013.

A Two-tier Index Architecture for Fast Processing Large RDF Data over Distributed Memory

Long Cheng[1,2,3], Spyros Kotoulas[2], Tomas E Ward[1], Georgios Theodoropoulos[4]

[1] National University of Ireland Maynooth, Ireland   [2] IBM Research, Ireland
[3] Technische Universität Dresden, Germany   [4] Durham University, UK

long.cheng@tu-dresden.de,   spyros.kotoulas@ie.ibm.com,   tomas.ward@nuim.ie,   theogeorgios@gmail.com

ABSTRACT

We propose an efficient method for fast processing large RDF data over distributed memory. Our approach adopts a two-tier index architecture on each computation node: (1) a light-weight primary index, to keep loading times low, and (2) a dynamic, multi-level secondary index, calculated as a by-product of query execution, to decrease or remove inter-machine data movement for subsequent queries that contain the same graph patterns. Experimental results on a commodity cluster show that we can load large RDF data very quickly in memory while remaining within an interactive range for query processing with the secondary index.

Categories and Subject Descriptors

H.2.4 [**Systems**]: Distributed Databases, Query Processing

Keywords

Distributed RDF Processing; Dynamic Indexing

1. INTRODUCTION

Responding to the rapid growth of Linked Data, several approaches for distributed RDF data processing have been proposed [18, 16, 10, 15], along with clustered versions of more traditional approaches [9, 2, 17]. Depending on the data partitioning and placement patterns, these solutions can be divided into four categories: (1) *Similar-size partitioning*: Partitions containing similar volumes of raw triples are placed on each computation node without a global index. During query processing, nodes provide bindings for each triple pattern and formulate the intermediate (or final) results using *parallel joins* [18, 15]. (2) *Hash-based partitioning*: Exploiting the fact that SPARQL queries often contain "star" graph patterns, triples under this scheme are commonly hash partitioned (by subject) across multiple machines and accessed in parallel at query time [16, 11]. (3) *Sharded/Partitioned indexes*: Perhaps the approach closest to centralized stores, triple indexes in the form of SPO, OPS etc are distributed across the nodes in a cluster and stored as a B-Tree [9, 17]. (4) *Graph-based partitioning*: Graph partitioning algorithms

are used to partition RDF data in a manner that triples close to each other can be assigned to the same computation node. SPARQL queries generally take the form of graph pattern matching so that sub-graphs on each computation node can be matched independently and in parallel, as much as possible [10].

In general, the techniques outlined above operate on a trade-off between loading complexity and query efficiency, with the earlier ones in the list offering superior loading performance at the cost of more complex/slower querying and the latter ones requiring significant computational effort for loading and/or partitioning. In this paper, we are proposing an efficient parallel way that *combine the loading speed of similar-size partitioning with the execution speed of graph-based partitioning.*

2. OUR APPROACH

The main elements of our approach are: (1) We maintain a local light-weight primary index supporting very fast data loading and retrieval. (2) Secondary indexes supporting non-trivial access patterns are built dynamically, as a byproduct of query execution. In the following, we refer to the primary index as (l_1) and secondary indexes as 2nd-level (l_2), 3rd-level (l_3), etc.

Triple Encoding. We first transform RDF terms into 64-bit integers and represent statements using this encoding. We utilise a distributed dictionary encoding method as described in our previous work [8]. The overall implementation strategy for each node and the corresponding data flow are shown in Figure 1.

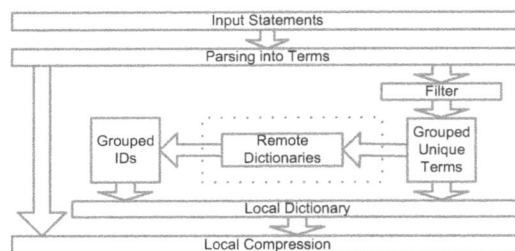

Figure 1: Workflow of triple encoding at each node.

Every statement in the input set is parsed and split into individual *terms*, namely, *subject*, *predicate*, and *object*. Duplicates are locally eliminated, and the extracted set of *unique* terms is then divided into individual groups according to their hash values. The groups of unique terms are then pushed to the responsible remote dictionaries for encoding. After that, every node builds a local dictionary, for encoding the parsed statements, based on the grouped

HT'14, September 1–4, 2014, Santiago, Chile.
ACM 978-1-4503-2954-5/14/09.
http://dx.doi.org/10.1145/2631775.2631789.

unique terms and the corresponding group of ids received from remote nodes.

Primary Index. After encoding, we build the primary index l_1 for the encoded triples at each node. We use a modified *vertical partitioning* approach [1] to decompose the local data into multiple parts. Triples in [1] are placed into n two-column *vertical tables* (n is number of unique properties), and all the *subjects* in each table are sorted. In comparison, we only insert each tuple in an **unordered** list in a corresponding *vertical table*. To support multiple access patterns, we build additional tables. By default, we build $P \rightarrow SO$, $PS \rightarrow O$ and $PO \rightarrow S$, corresponding to the most common access patterns. Note that there is no communication over the network for this step.

Parallel Hash Joins. Once we have built the primary index, we can compute SPARQL queries through a sequence of lookups and joins. For a basic graph pattern (BGP), looking up the results can be implemented in parallel and independently for each node. Regardless, a *join* between any two sub-queries can not be executed independently since we have no guarantee that join keys will be located on the same node. We adopt the parallel hash-join implementation here, namely, results of each subquery are redistributed among computation nodes by hashing the values of their join keys, so as to ensure that the appropriate results for the join are co-located [18].

Secondary Indexes. For join operations, as we have to redistribute all results for each triple pattern as well as the intermediate results, data transfers between each node become costly. To remedy this shortcoming, we employ a bottom-up dynamical programming parallel algorithm to build secondary indexes ($l_2 ... l_n$), based on each query execution plan.

For simplification, here, we just give a simple example to show the process of building the 2nd-level index l_2 based on a join between two basic graph patterns. As shown in Algorithm 1, the first three steps (lines 1-3) is actually a *parallel hash joins* processing. Regardless, after that, the redistributed results will be kept locally in l_2, according to the non-variables appearing in the responsible BGP. For instance, the redistributed results of the BGP <?s p1 ?o> will be added into the vertical table $p1 \rightarrow SO$ of l_2.

Algorithm 1 Implementation of building l_2 at each node

Phase 1: Tuple redistribution
1: retrieve result r_i ($i = 1, 2$) of each BGP from the index l_1
2: redistribute r_i to all nodes according to hash values of join keys
Phase 2: l_2 index building
3: implement local joins and formulate outputs
4: insert received tuples r'_i into local l_2

Since the index is constructed by a simple *copy* of the redistributed data, which is introduced by a *join* of a query, the secondary indexes can be re-used by other queries that contain patterns in common. In fact, according to the terminology regarding *graph partitioning* used in [10], the 2nd-level index on each node will construct a 2-hop subgraph, the 3rd-level one will be a 3-hop subgraph, and l_k will become to k-hop subgraph. This means that our method essentially does dynamic graph-based partitioning starting from an initial equal-size partitioning, based on the query load. Therefore, our approach can combine their advantages on fast data loading and efficient querying.

3. EVALUATION

Platform. We use 16 IBM iDataPlex® nodes with two 6-core Intel Xeon® X5679 processors, 128GB of RAM and a single 1TB SATA hard-drive, connected using Gigabit Ethernet. We use Linux kernel version 2.6.32-220 and implement our method using X10 [3] version 2.3, compiled to C++ with gcc version 4.4.6.

Setup. We load LUBM(8000), containing about 1.1 billion triples, and run the two most complex queries Q2 and Q9. As we do not support RDF inference, we use a modified version shown in the Appendix. To focus on analyzing the core performance only, we do not count the time spent on *parsing*, *planning*, *dictionary lookup* or *result output* as described in [4].

Data Loading. We load 1.1 billion triples and build three primary indexes (on P, PO and PS) in memory. As shown in Table 1, it takes 254 seconds to encode triples and 86 seconds to build the primary index l_1, for an average throughput of 540MB or 3.24M triples per second. This is faster than any other implementation in the literature.

Table 1: Time to load 1.1 billion triples using 192 cores

Triple encoding:	254 seconds
Building l_1 (P, PO, PS):	86 seconds
Total:	**340 seconds**

Data Querying. We examine the runtime of Q2 and Q9 using l_1, l_2 and l_3. Meanwhile, we also record the time cost to build indexes. Figure 2 shows that the secondary index can obviously improve the query performance. Moreover, the higher the level of index is, the lower the execution time. At the same time, we can also see that the operation of building a high-level index is very fast, taking only hundreds of *ms*, which is extremely small compared to the query execution time.

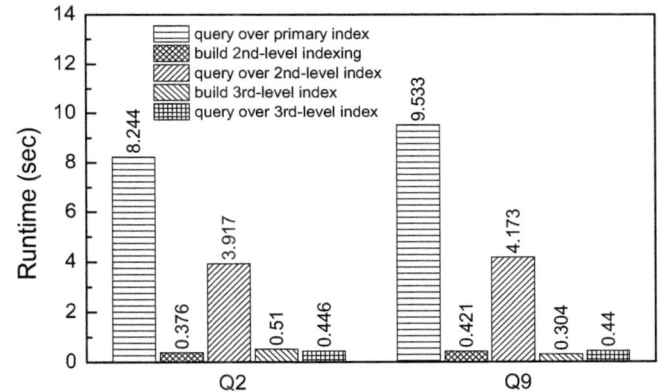

Figure 2: Runtime over different indexes using 192 cores.

4. CONCLUSION

In this work, we propose a dynamic two-tier index architecture designed for fast processing large RDF data over distributed memory. Our experimental results demonstrate that the approach can both load and query large RDF datasets quickly.

We will investigate extensions to our design through the application of methods for *skew handling* [15, 5, 6, 7], *index size reduction* [14] and *incremental sorting* [12, 13] which should further improve performance. Our long term goal is to develop a highly scalable distributed analysis framework for extreme-scale RDF data.

Acknowledgments. This work is supported by the Irish Research Council and IBM Research Ireland.

5. REFERENCES

[1] D. J. Abadi, A. Marcus, S. R. Madden, and K. Hollenbach. Scalable semantic web data management using vertical partitioning. In *Proceedings of the 33rd International Conference on Very large Data Bases*, VLDB' 07, pages 411–422, 2007.

[2] B. Bishop, A. Kiryakov, D. Ognyanoff, I. Peikov, Z. Tashev, and R. Velkov. OWLIM: A family of scalable semantic repositories. *Semantic Web*, 2(1):33–42, 2011.

[3] P. Charles, C. Grothoff, V. Saraswat, C. Donawa, A. Kielstra, K. Ebcioglu, C. Von Praun, and V. Sarkar. X10: An object-oriented approach to non-uniform cluster computing. *ACM SIGPLAN Notices*, 40(10):519–538, 2005.

[4] L. Cheng, S. Kotoulas, T. Ward, and G. Theodoropoulos. Runtime characterization of triple stores. In *Proceedings of the 15th IEEE International Conference on Computational Science and Engineering*, CSE' 12, pages 66–73, 2012.

[5] L. Cheng, S. Kotoulas, T. E. Ward, and G. Theodoropoulos. QbDJ: A novel framework for handling skew in parallel join processing on distributed memory. In *Proceedings of the 15th IEEE International Conference on High Performance Computing and Communications*, HPCC' 13, pages 1519–1527, 2013.

[6] L. Cheng, S. Kotoulas, T. E. Ward, and G. Theodoropoulos. Efficient handling skew in outer joins on distributed systems. In *Proceedings of the 14th IEEE/ACM International Symposium on Cluster, Cloud and Grid Computing*, CCGrid' 14, pages 295–304, 2014.

[7] L. Cheng, S. Kotoulas, T. E. Ward, and G. Theodoropoulos. Robust and efficient large-large table outer joins on distributed infrastructures. In *Proceedings of the 20th European Conference on Parallel Processing*, Euro-Par' 14, pages 258–269, 2014.

[8] L. Cheng, A. Malik, S. Kotoulas, T. E. Ward, and G. Theodoropoulos. Efficient parallel dictionary encoding for RDF data. In *Proceedings of the 17th International Workshop on the Web and Databases*, WebDB' 14, 2014.

[9] O. Erling and I. Mikhailov. Virtuoso: RDF support in a native RDBMS. In *Semantic Web Information Management*, pages 501–519. Springer, 2010.

[10] J. Huang, D. J. Abadi, and K. Ren. Scalable SPARQL querying of large RDF graphs. *Proceedings of the VLDB Endowment*, 4(11):1123–1134, 2011.

[11] M. Husain, J. McGlothlin, M. M. Masud, L. Khan, and B. M. Thuraisingham. Heuristics-based query processing for large RDF graphs using cloud computing. *IEEE Transactions on Knowledge and Data Engineering*, 23(9):1312–1327, 2011.

[12] S. Idreos, M. L. Kersten, and S. Manegold. Database cracking. In *CIDR*, pages 68–78, 2007.

[13] S. Idreos, M. L. Kersten, and S. Manegold. Self-organizing tuple reconstruction in column-stores. In *Proceedings of the 2009 ACM SIGMOD International Conference on Management of Data*, SIGMOD '09, pages 297–308, 2009.

[14] K. Kim, B. Moon, and H.-J. Kim. R3F: RDF triple filtering method for efficient SPARQL query processing. *World Wide Web*, pages 1–41, 2013.

[15] S. Kotoulas, J. Urbani, P. Boncz, and P. Mika. Robust runtime optimization and skew-resistant execution of analytical SPARQL queries on PIG. In *Proceedings of the 11th International Semantic Web Conference*, ISWC' 12, pages 247–262. 2012.

[16] K. Rohloff and R. E. Schantz. High-performance, massively scalable distributed systems using the MapReduce software framework: The SHARD triple-store. In *Programming Support Innovations for Emerging Distributed Applications*, 2010.

[17] B. Thompson and M. Personick. Bigdata: The semantic web on an open source cloud. In *International Semantic Web Conference*, 2009.

[18] J. Weaver and G. T. Williams. Scalable RDF query processing on clusters and supercomputers. In *The 5th International Workshop on Scalable Semantic Web Knowledge Base Systems*, SSWS' 09, 2009.

APPENDIX

The rewritten LUBM SPARQL queries Q2 and Q9 used in our evaluation are as follows.

Q2: select ?x ?y ?z where { ?x rdf:type lubm:GraduateStudent. ?y rdf:type lubm:Department. ?z rdf:type lubm:University. ?y lubm:sub OrganizationOf ?z. ?x lubm:memberOf ?y. ?x lubm:undergraduate DegreeFrom ?z.}

Q9: select ?x ?y ?z where { ?x rdf:type ub:GraduateStudent. ?y rdf:type ub:FullProfessor. ?z rdf:type ub:Course. ?x ub:advisor ?y. ?y ub:teacherOf ?z. ?x ub:takesCourse ?z.}

Spatial Hypertext Modeling for Dynamic Contents Authoring System based on Transclusion

Ja-Ryoung Choi
Dept. of Multimedia Science
Sookmyung Women's University
Seoul, Korea
j2arlove@gmail.com

Sungeun An
Dept. of Multimedia Science
Sookmyung Women's University
Seoul, Korea
imsung110@gmail.com

Soon-Bum Lim
Dept. of Multimedia Science
Sookmyung Women's University
Seoul, Korea
sblim@sookmyung.ac.kr

ABSTRACT

This paper proposed a web content collecting model to reuse a variety of web contents based on Transclusion. Transclusion is a model for collecting existing web contents and including them into a new document. However, Transclusion lacks consideration of copyright issues and dynamic changes. Therefore, we classified Transclusions into three different types based on copyright restrictions: Trans-quotation, Trans-reference and Trans-annotation. Then we represented Transclusions in each different type of spatial hypertext model. Also, we designed RVS(ReVerse Syndication) model in order to trace the dynamic changes.

Categories and Subject Descriptors

H.5.4 **[Information Interfaces and Presentation]**: Hypertext/Hypermedia – *Navigation, User issues*

General Terms

Design; Human Factors; Theory.

Keywords

Transclusion; Spatial hypertext; Dynamic contents.

1. INTRODUCTION

Web technologies have evolved to give users the ability to produce and consume web content. For example, when making textbook or lecture notes, authors access to various web contents and collect the pieces they want to reuse and paste it in their documents. But as web is open to everyone, illegal content reproduction issues arise. Moreover, web contents are subject to change, and they cause dynamic changes such as content loss, update and modification made by various authors. In order to solve such issues, we proposed a web content collecting model. In this paper, to reuse various web contents, we classified Transclusions into three different types based on copyright restrictions. All of these are effectively managed by strong connection with the original source, so as to adapt to dynamic changes of web contents.

2. RELATED WORK

Project Xanadu is an existing technique for collecting and connecting documents and files on web[1]. Based on unbreakable links for connecting to original sources, Project Xanadu is designed to provide a view of two documents on one screen, with full support on versioning. Transclusion proposed by Project Xanadu is a technique for the inclusion of existing content into a new document. Contents authors actually do not make a copy of an existing document, but make a reference to the virtually stored original content.

TED(Transclusions in Enterprice Documents) system is one of such examples. This system proposed multiple classes of XML-based transclusions[2,3]. As the original content changes, the referenced content on target document is revised accordingly.

WARP system is another study of Transclusions. WARP is a web-based dynamic spatial hypertext that runs in a web browser. WARP has the ability to transclude other spatial hypertexts as collections[4]. Project Breadcrumbs is another study similar to WARP[5].

3. SPATIAL HYPERTEXT MODEL FOR TRANSCLUSION

In this system, we classified Transclusions into three different types based on copyright restrictions: Trans-quotation, Trans-reference and Trans-annotation. These restrictions are concerned about the rights on source reproduction and distribution (see Figure 1).

- **Trans-quotation**

  In cases where both source reproduction and distribution are allowed, Trans-quotation includes a direct quote from its original source.

- **Trans-reference**

  In cases where source distribution is allowed but not source reproduction, Trans-reference includes a quote paraphrased by user from its original source.

- **Trans-annotation**

  In cases where neither source reproduction nor distribution is allowed, Trans-annotation separates content from the original source. Since direct quotation is not allowed for this type, users can access the original contents through the link address instead.

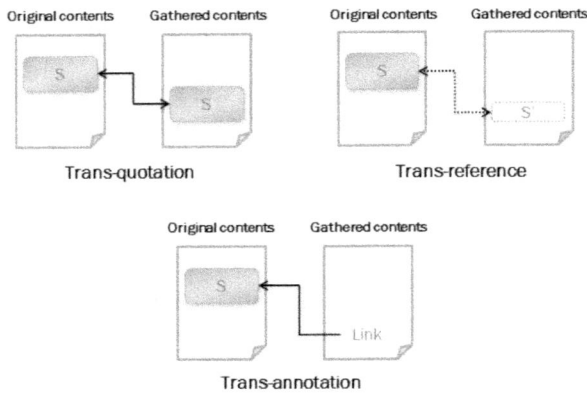

Figure 1. Classification of Transclusions

Each Transclusion is expressed in a different form of spatial hypertext model. Trans-quotation is displayed as it is because directly quoted. If users want to see the original content web page, they can click on the transcluded region. For Trans-reference, when users place the cursor over the transcluded region, the original web document pops up; so as to see where the quote came from and what it originally states. Since copyright restrictions are quite strict for Trans-annotation, its transcluded region contains only URL address that takes users to the original source web page.

4. DYNAMIC CONTENTS SYNDICATION MODEL

The web content collecting model is based on Transclusion to reuse web contents. Metadata for tracking information is designed to manage this system. Tracking information contains necessary information to maintain connection to its original content, and the concept of this metadata is opposite concept of RSS.

As Figure 2 shows, existing RSS is created by the content provider, whereas RVS(Reverse Syndication) is created by the content collector. Using this RVS model, the content collector is able to trace dynamic changes such as content loss or update.

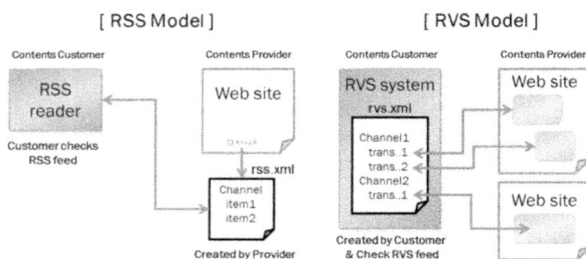

Figure 2. RSS Model vs. RVS Model

Figure 3 describes the RVS metadata structure in RELAX NG format. Since RVS is an XML document, we described the structure of RVS document using RELAX NG; which is a schema language for XML. It has <rvs> as a root node, <document> and <channel> as child nodes. <channel> node records information of web contents collected by users, and has child nodes as follows: <title>, <link>, <description>, <copyright>, <pubDate>, <category>, <managingEditor>, <language>, <ttl>, <skipDays> and <transclusion>. In order to trace the original source,

<transclusion> node records portions of the content that have been referenced by users. Such RVS file enables continuous connection with the original source, enabling us to check for updates.

Figure 3. Metadata structure for Dynamic Contents Syndication

5. CONCLUSION

In this paper, we designed a system that collects various web contents and displays them as spatial hypertext. We analyzed patterns of web content, and classified Transclusions into Trans-quotation, Trans-reference and Trans-annotation. These Transclusions are displayed as transcluded regions. Also, we defined RVS model for metadata to adapt to dynamic changes. This model can show whether there is any change in the original document.

The system will be evaluated in terms of the feasibility of e-Book. Concluding from this evaluation, the paper will explore the future work necessary to enhance the model that automatically handles problem with dynamic changes.

6. ACKNOWLEDGMENTS

This research is supported by Ministry of Culture, Sports and Tourism(MCST) and Korea Creative Content Agency(KOCCA) in the Culture Technology(CT) Research & Development Program 2014.

7. REFERENCES

[1] T.H. Nelson. The new XANADU structure for the web[Online], http://xanadu.com/nxu, 2001.

[2] A.D. Iorio, J. Lumley. From XML inclusions to XML transclusions. In Proceedings of the 20th ACM conference on Hypertext and hypermedia (pp. 147-156), 2009.

[3] A.D. Iorio, et al. Towards XML Transclusions. In Proceedings of the First Workshop on New Forms of Xanalogical Storage and Functions, ACM Hypertext Conference (pp. 23-28), 2009.

[4] L.Francisco-Revilla, F. M.Shipman, WARP: a web-based dynamic spatial hypertext. In Proceedings of the 15th ACM conference on Hypertext and hypermedia (pp. 235-236), 2004.

[5] L.Francisco-Revilla, A.Figueira, Adaptive spatial hypermedia in computational journalism. In Proceedings of the 23rd ACM conference on Hypertext and social media (pp. 313-314), 2012.

TagRec: Towards A Standardized Tag Recommender Benchmarking Framework

Dominik Kowald
Know-Center
Graz University of Technology
Graz, Austria
dkowald@know-center.at

Emanuel Lacic
KTI
Graz University of Technology
Graz, Austria
elacic@know-center.at

Christoph Trattner
Know-Center
Graz University of Technology
Graz, Austria
ctrattner@know-center.at

ABSTRACT

In this paper, we introduce *TagRec*, a standardized tag recommender benchmarking framework implemented in Java. The purpose of *TagRec* is to provide researchers with a framework that supports all steps of the development process of a new tag recommendation algorithm in a reproducible way, including methods for data pre-processing, data modeling, data analysis and recommender evaluation against state-of-the-art baseline approaches. We show the performance of the algorithms implemented in *TagRec* in terms of prediction quality and runtime using an evaluation of a real-world folksonomy dataset. Furthermore, *TagRec* contains two novel tag recommendation approaches based on models derived from human cognition and human memory theories.

Categories and Subject Descriptors

H.2.8 [**Database Management**]: Database Applications—*Data mining*; H.3.3 [**Information Storage and Retrieval**]: Information Search and Retrieval—*Information filtering*

Keywords

personalized tag recommendations; recommender framework; recommender evaluation; Java

1. INTRODUCTION

In recent years social tagging has become an important instrument of Web 2.0, which allows users to collaboratively annotate and search content. In order to support this process, current research has attempted to improve the performance and quality of tag recommendations. However, although various tag recommender approaches and experiments exist, most of them use different data pre-processing methods and evaluation protocols, making it difficult for researchers to reproduce these experiments and to compare these approaches with other algorithms.

To tackle this issue, we developed *TagRec*, a standardized tag recommender benchmarking framework that provides researchers with methods for data pre-processing, data modeling, data analysis and recommender evaluation against state-of-the-art baseline

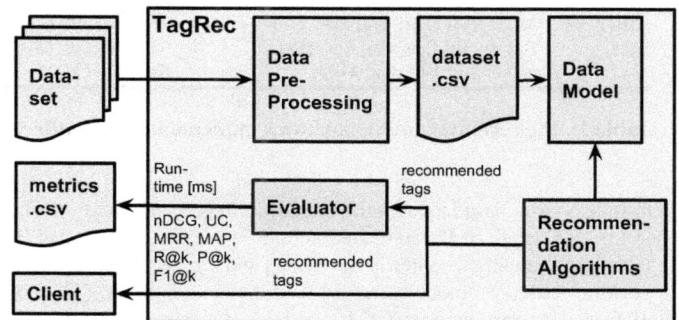

Figure 1: *TagRec* system architecture.

approaches. The purpose of *TagRec* is not only to increase the reproducibility in the tag recommender research but also to decrease the workload of developers who implement or test a new algorithm for tag recommendations.

2. SYSTEM OVERVIEW

TagRec was fully implemented in Java apart from the FM and PITF algorithms that were provided as a C++ framework by the University of Konstanz. TagRec is open-source and can be downloaded via Github[1].

Figure 1 shows the system architecture of *TagRec*, which consists of four main components:

Data pre-processing. *TagRec* offers various methods for data pre-processing: (1) parsing and processing of social tagging datasets, such as CiteULike, BibSonomy, Delicious, LastFm, MovieLens and Flickr, into the system's data format; (2) *p*-core pruning; (3) training/test set splitting (e.g., leave-one-out, time-based or 80/20 splits) [3] and (4) creating Latent Dirichlet Allocation [6] topics for category-based algorithms, such as 3Layers [4, 10].

Data model. The data model of *TagRec* is generated from simple .csv files that contain the bookmarks (i.e., the combination of user-id, resource-id, timestamp and assigned tags) in a folksonomy. Furthermore, the data model is fully object-oriented and provides distinct classes and powerful methods for modeling and analyzing the relationship and interactions between users, resources and tags (e.g., the number of times a specific tag has been assigned to a target resource or the time since the last usage of a specific tag in the tag assignments of a target user).

Recommendation algorithms. This component is the main part of *TagRec* and contains the implementations of the various algorithms shown in Table 1. Along with the state-of-the-art approaches

---

[1]https://github.com/learning-layers/TagRec/

Algorithm	Name	Authors
MP	Most popular tags	Jäschke et al. [3]
MP_u	Most popular tags by user	Jäschke et al. [3]
MP_r	Most popular tags by resource	Jäschke et al. [3]
$MP_{u,r}$	Mixture of MP_u and MP_r	Jäschke et al. [3]
CF_u	User-based Collaborative Filtering	Marinho et al. [8]
CF_r	Resource-based Collaborative Filtering	Marinho et al. [8]
$CF_{u,r}$	Mixture of CF_u and CF_r	Marinho et al. [8]
APR	Adapted PageRank	Jäschke et al. [3]
FR	FolkRank	Jäschke et al. [3]
FM	Factorization Machines	Rendle et al. [9]
PITF	Pairwise Interaction Tensor Factorization	Rendle et al. [9]
LDA	Latent Dirichlet Allocation	Krestel et al. [6]
LDA&LM	Mixture of LDA and $MP_{u,r}$	Krestel et al. [6]
3L	3Layers	Seitlinger et al. [10]
3LT	Time-dependent 3L	Kowald et al. [4]
GIRP	Temporal Tag Usage Patterns	Zhang et al. [11]
GIRPTM	Mixture of GIRP and MP_r	Zhang et al. [11]
BLL	Base Level Learning Equation	Kowald et al. [5]
BLL+C	Mixture of BLL and MP_r	Kowald et al. [5]

Table 1: Tag recommender algorithms implemented in *TagRec*.

to folksonomy-based tag recommendations (e.g., Collaborative Filtering, FolkRank or Pairwise Interaction Tensor Factorization) [7] the engine contains two newly developed and recently published algorithms based on models derived from human cognition (3L and 3LT) and human memory (BLL and BLL+C) theories. All algorithms implement a common interface which, making it easy to develop and integrate new approaches. The predicted tags generated by the different algorithms can be forwarded either to the evaluation engine or directly to a client application.

Evaluator. This component evaluates the algorithms based on a training/test set split of a dataset with respect to standard Information Retrieval (IR) metrics, such as Recall ($R@k$), Precision ($P@$), F1-score ($F1@k$), Mean Reciprocal Rank (MRR), Mean Average Precision (MAP), Normalized Discounted Cumulative Gain (nDCG) and User Coverage (UC) [2]. Moreover, the evaluation engine offers data post-processing to limit the evaluation to users with the minimum or maximum number of bookmarks.

3. RESULTS

To show the functionalities of *TagRec*, we evaluated and compared a selection of the implemented algorithms in terms of recommender quality and runtime using a real-world folksonomy dataset gathered from the image sharing portal Flickr. The dataset contained 9,590 users, 864,679 resources, 127,599 tags and 3,552,540 tag assignments and was split into a training and test set using the leave-one-out pre-processing method of *TagRec* (i.e., the latest bookmark for each user was used for testing and the rest for training). To quantify the prediction quality of the approaches, the set of well-known Information Retrieval metrics available in *TagRec* ($R@k$, $P@k$, $F1@k$, MRR, MAP, nDCG and UC) was used (see also [5]).

The first plot in Figure 2 shows the recommender quality of the various approaches in the form of recall/precision plots for $k = 1$ - 10 recommended tags. The results show that all algorithms, except for the simple MP approach, perform reasonably well on the dataset and that the two newly developed approaches based on human cognition (3LT) and human memory (BLL+C) theories perform best.

The runtime comparison is shown in the second plot in Figure 2, which indicates the full time required for providing tag recommendations for all user-resource pairs in the Flickr test set. Clearly, the BLL+C and 3LT approaches, which performed best in the recom-

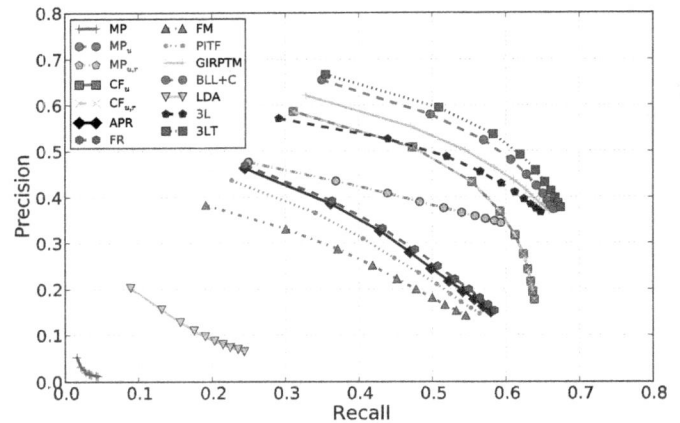

(a) Recommender quality

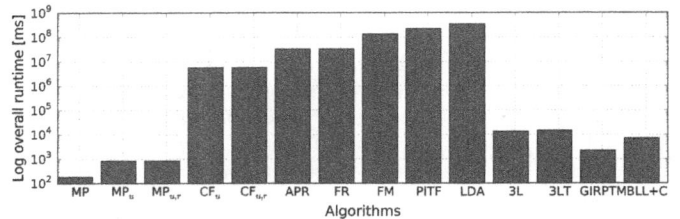

(b) Recommender runtime

Figure 2: Evaluation results for the Flickr dataset showing the quality and overall runtime of the recommender algorithms.

mendation quality experiment, also provided a reasonable runtime in contrast to the more complex algorithms, such as LDA, APR, FR, FM and PITF.

4. CONCLUSIONS & FUTURE WORK

In this work we presented *TagRec*, a standardized tag recommender benchmarking framework that provides researchers with methods for data pre-processing, data modeling, data analysis and recommender evaluation in a reproducible way. *TagRec* was fully implemented in Java and contained a rich set of state-of-the-art tag recommender algorithms along with two newly developed and published tag recommendation mechanisms based on models derived from human cognition (3L and 3LT) and human memory (BLL and BLL+C) theories.

In the future we plan to expand the framework by using more algorithms for tag recommendations and, especially, by content-based methods [1] since at the moment *TagRec* focuses on folksonomy-based approaches. Furthermore, we would like to adapt the implemented algorithms and evaluation procedures in order to also provide resource and user recommendations.

Acknowledgments: This work is supported by the Know-Center and the EU funded project Learning Layers (7th Framework Program, Grant Agreement 318209). The Know-Center is funded within the Austrian COMET Program - Competence Centers for Excellent Technologies - under the auspices of the Austrian Ministry of Transport, Innovation and Technology, the Austrian Ministry of Economics and Labor and by the State of Styria. COMET is managed by the Austrian Research Promotion Agency (FFG).

5. REFERENCES

[1] I. Cantador, A. Bellogín, and D. Vallet. Content-based recommendation in social tagging systems. In *Proceedings of the fourth ACM conference on Recommender systems*, pages 237–240. ACM, 2010.

[2] R. Jäschke, F. Eisterlehner, A. Hotho, and G. Stumme. Testing and evaluating tag recommenders in a live system. In *Proceedings of the third ACM conference on Recommender systems*, pages 369–372. ACM, 2009.

[3] R. Jäschke, L. Marinho, A. Hotho, L. Schmidt-Thieme, and G. Stumme. Tag recommendations in social bookmarking systems. *Ai Communications*, 21(4):231–247, 2008.

[4] D. Kowald, P. Seitlinger, C. Trattner, and T. Ley. Forgetting the words but remembering the meaning: Modeling forgetting in a verbal and semantic tag recommender. *arXiv preprint arXiv:1402.0728*, 2014.

[5] D. Kowald, P. Seitlinger, C. Trattner, and T. Ley. Long time no see: The probability of reusing tags as a function of frequency and recency. In *Proc.*, WWW '14. ACM, 2014.

[6] R. Krestel and P. Fankhauser. Language models and topic models for personalizing tag recommendation. In *Proc.*, pages 82–89. IEEE, 2010.

[7] L. Marinho, A. Nanopoulos, L. Schmidt-Thieme, R. Jäschke, A. Hotho, G. Stumme, and P. Symeonidis. Social tagging recommender systems. In F. Ricci, L. Rokach, B. Shapira, and P. B. Kantor, editors, *Recommender Systems Handbook*, pages 615–644. Springer US, 2011.

[8] L. B. Marinho and L. Schmidt-Thieme. Collaborative tag recommendations. In *Data Analysis, Machine Learning and Applications*, pages 533–540. Springer, 2008.

[9] S. Rendle and L. Schmidt-Thieme. Pairwise interaction tensor factorization for personalized tag recommendation. In *Proc.*, WSDM '10. ACM, 2010.

[10] P. Seitlinger, D. Kowald, C. Trattner, and T. Ley. Recommending tags with a model of human categorization. In *Proc.*, CIKM '13, pages 2381–2386. ACM, 2013.

[11] L. Zhang, J. Tang, and M. Zhang. Integrating temporal usage pattern into personalized tag prediction. In *Web Technologies and Applications*, pages 354–365. Springer, 2012.

SocRecM: A Scalable Social Recommender Engine for Online Marketplaces

Emanuel Lacic
Graz University of Technology
Graz, Austria
elacic@know-center.at

Dominik Kowald
Know-Center
Graz, Austria
dkowald@know-center.at

Christoph Trattner
Know-Center
Graz, Austria
ctrattner@know-center.at

ABSTRACT

This paper presents work-in-progress on *SocRecM*, a novel social recommendation framework for online marketplaces. We demonstrate that *SocRecM* is easy to integrate with existing Web technologies through a RESTful, scalable and easy-to-extend service-based architecture. Moreover, we reveal the extent to which various social features and recommendation approaches are useful in an online social marketplace environment.

Categories and Subject Descriptors

H.2.8 [**Database Management**]: Database Applications—*Data mining*; H.3.3 [**Information Storage and Retrieval**]: Information Search and Retrieval—*Information filtering*

Keywords

social recommender engine; online marketplaces; recommender framework; recommender evaluation; Apache Solr

1. INTRODUCTION

Recommender systems aim at helping users find relevant information in an overloaded information space. Although various recommender frameworks are available nowadays, there is still a lack of frameworks that address such important aspects in recommender systems research as: easy integration into an existing infrastructure, scalability, hybridization and social data integration. To tackle these issues, we implemented *SocRecM*, a scalable and easy-to-integrate online social recommender framework whose purpose is not only to decrease the workload of developers via an easy-to-use framework but also to provide recommendation algorithms that utilize social data obtained from various data sources (e.g., Facebook, Twitter, etc.).

2. SYSTEM OVERVIEW

The first prototype of *SocRecM* was implemented in Java and can be found online as open-source software [1]. Figure 1 shows the

[1] https://github.com/learning-layers/SocRec

HT'14, September 1–4, 2014, Santiago, Chile.
ACM 978-1-4503-2954-5/14/09.
http://dx.doi.org/10.1145/2631775.2631783.

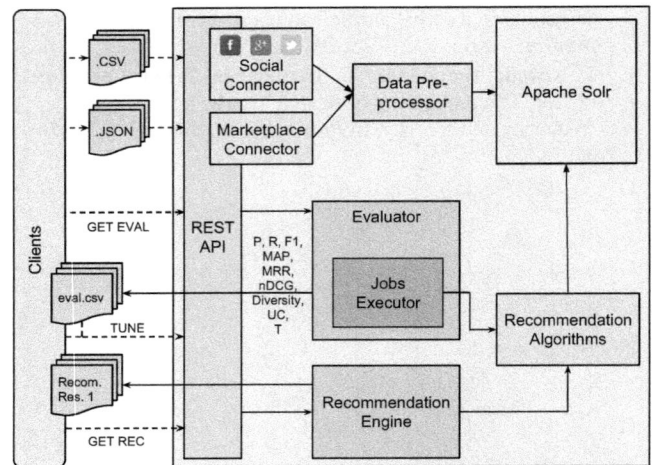

Figure 1: *SocRecM* system architecture.

system architecture of *SocRecM*. As featured, the engine can easily be integrated into a RESTful API for communicating with client applications. The *SocRecM* API provides methods for uploading marketplace and social data into the engine and for querying resource recommendations and benchmarking results. The marketplace and social data are gathered via respective connectors and pre-processed to be indexed by Apache Solr, which in turn offers powerful search and content analyzing functionalities (e.g., facets or MoreLikeThis queries) that are used by the recommendation algorithm implementations. Currently, *SocRecM* contains four types of algorithms to recommend resources (in our case products) to users: MostPopular (MP), Collaborative Filtering (CF) [6], Content-based (C) [5] and Hybrid Recommendations (CCF) [1] (see also [4]). These algorithms are calculated based on either marketplace features, such as purchases (CF_p), title (C_t) and description (C_d) or social features, such as likes (CF_l), comments (CF_c), interactions(CF_{in}), social stream content data (C_{st}), groups (CF_g) and interests (CF_i). Additionally, the algorithms and data features are incorporated into hybrid algorithms (CCF_m for marketplace and CCF_s for social features).

The recommendation algorithms are invoked by the evaluator component and its jobs executor in order to evaluate them with respect to various IR metrics (e.g., Recall (R), Precision (P), nDCG, User Coverage (UC), etc.) [2, 7]. The evaluation results are further used in *SocRecM* to tune the parameters of the algorithms, especially in the case of the hybrid approaches. Furthermore, the algo-

(a) Rec. quality (experiment 1) (b) UC (experiment 1)

(c) Rec. quality (experiment 2) (d) UC (experiment 2)

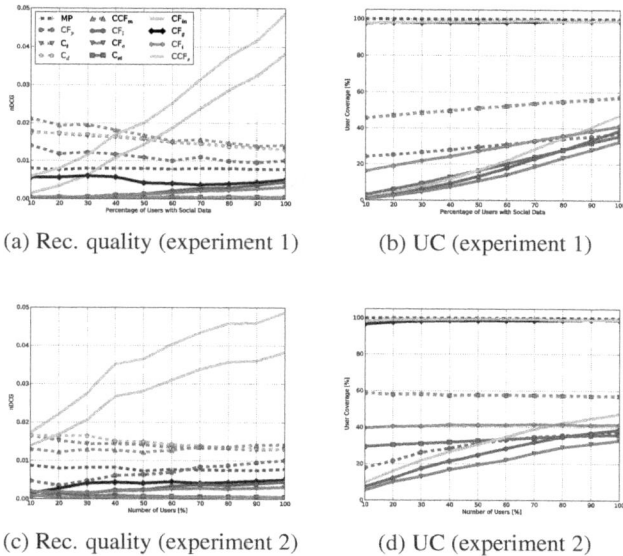

Figure 2: Results of the two experiments in terms of recommendation accuracy (nDCG) and User Coverage (UC).

rithms are called by the recommendation engine in order to forward the recommended resources back to the client.

3. RESULTS

To demonstrate the effectiveness of our approach under different scenarios we conducted two "virtual" experiments with a social dataset gathered from the virtual world of SecondLife, which provides both: detailed marketplace purchase data and social data collected from users in the virtual world (similar as in [9]). The dataset contains 126,356 users, 122,360 products, 265,274 purchases, 1,839,783 social interactions, 510,145 social stream contents, 260,137 groups and 88,371 interests and was split into a training and test set using the method proposed in [4]. The experiments described bellow were conducted using an IBM System x3550 server with two 2.0 GHz six-core Intel Xeon E5-2620 processors, a 1TB ServeRAID M1115 SCSI Disk and 128 GB of RAM using one Apache Solr 4.3.1 instance in the back-end.

The first experiment demonstrated how the recommendation quality in terms of the nDCG and User Coverage (UC) metrics [3] could be improved if the users' social data were provided in addition to the marketplace data. To simulate this, we extracted all users from our dataset that have both the marketplace and social data (10,996 users). Out of this subset, we randomly selected 10% of users and replaced them with users that only provided marketplace data. We continued until 100% of the data consisted of users with only marketplace data in their profiles. As demonstrated in plots (a) and (b) of Figure 2, the recommendation approaches based on marketplace data alone are fairly constant regardless of how many users have social data in their profiles. This was expected since the number of users neither increased nor decreased throughout the experiment. However, it is apparent that although the recommenders based on the users' interactions perform best (CCF_s and CF_{in}), they depend greatly on the number of social profiles in the dataset. An interesting finding in this context was that the content-based approach based on the users' social stream contents (CF_{st}) performed as poorly as the recommender based on the users' interests (CF_i).

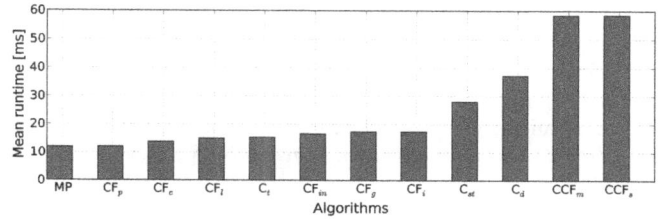

Figure 3: Mean runtime of the algorithms in *SocRecM*.

In the second experiment we simulated a cold-start scenario for a new social marketplace system, under which we assumed that all new users provided social data as it was the case with the start of Spotify, to determine if and how the recommendation quality would be affected by an increasing number of social users. In order to conduct this experiment, we once again extracted all users from the dataset with both marketplace and social data (10,996) and eliminated the rest. Using these data, we created 10 different sets with an increasing number of users and evaluated the recommendation approaches on them, as shown in plots (c) and (d) in Figure 2. As the number of users with marketplace and social data increased, the approaches based on the social data (CCF_s and CF_{in}) delivered a much higher prediction quality than those that used only the marketplace data (e.g., CF_p). Moreover, the user coverage of the hybrid approaches based on the social data (CCF_s) was much higher than the one based on the marketplace data (CCF_m). Comparing CF_p with CF_{in}, shows that although both algorithms have a higher user coverage with more users, the social features ultimately provide better results.

In addition to the recommendation quality, we compared the mean runtime (i.e., the time needed to calculate recommendations for a user) of the recommendation approaches shown in Figure 3. In general these results demonstrate that *SocRecM* is capable of providing near real-time recommendations for users since the maximum mean test time was only 58 milliseconds for the hybrid approaches CCF_m and CCF_s.

4. FUTURE WORK

In the future, we plan to further extend our framework using different approaches to make sense of social data provided by users in a social marketplace environment. For example, we would like to implement a topic modeling approach based on LDA to combine comments with purchase data or to derive topics from the user's social stream to calculate similarities between users. Furthermore, we are interested in extending our framework to generate recommendations based on the user's geo-location data (e.g., [8]). Last but not least, we are interested in developing novel hybridization approaches for diverse social data sources to further increase the predictive power of our recommender framework.

Acknowledgments: This work is supported by the Know-Center and the EU funded project Learning Layers (Grant Nr. 318209). The Know-Center is funded within the Austrian COMET Program - Competence Centers for Excellent Technologies - under the auspices of the Austrian Ministry of Transport, Innovation and Technology, the Austrian Ministry of Economics and Labor and by the State of Styria. COMET is managed by the Austrian Research Promotion Agency (FFG).

5. REFERENCES

[1] R. Burke. Hybrid recommender systems: Survey and experiments. *User modeling and user-adapted interaction*, 12(4):331–370, 2002.

[2] J. L. Herlocker, J. A. Konstan, L. G. Terveen, and J. T. Riedl. Evaluating collaborative filtering recommender systems. *ACM Transactions on Information Systems (TOIS)*, 22(1):5–53, 2004.

[3] K. Järvelin and J. Kekäläinen. Cumulated gain-based evaluation of ir techniques. *ACM Trans. Inf. Syst.*, 20(4):422–446, Oct. 2002.

[4] E. Lacic, D. Kowald, D. Parra, M. Kahr, and C. Trattner. Towards a scalable social recommender engine for online marketplaces: The case of apache solr. In *Proc.*, WWW '14. ACM, 2014.

[5] M. J. Pazzani and D. Billsus. Content-based recommendation systems. In *The adaptive web*, pages 325–341. Springer, 2007.

[6] J. B. Schafer, D. Frankowski, J. Herlocker, and S. Sen. Collaborative filtering recommender systems. In *The adaptive web*, pages 291–324. Springer, 2007.

[7] B. Smyth and P. McClave. Similarity vs. diversity. In D. Aha and I. Watson, editors, *Case-Based Reasoning Research and Development*, volume 2080 of *LNCS*, pages 347–361. Springer, 2001.

[8] M. Steurer and C. Trattner. Acquaintance or Partner? Predicting Partnership in Online and Location-Based Social Networks. In *Proc. ASONAM'13*. IEEE/ACM, 2013.

[9] Y. Zhang and M. Pennacchiotti. Predicting purchase behaviors from social media. In *Proceedings of the 22Nd International Conference on World Wide Web*, WWW '13, pages 1521–1532, 2013.

Cross-Hierarchical Communication in Twitter Conflicts

Zhe Liu*
College of Information Sciences and Technology
The Pennsylvania State University
University Park, Pennsylvania 16802
zul112@ist.psu.edu

Ingmar Weber
Qatar Computing Research Institute
PO Box 5825, Doha, Qatar
iweber@qf.org.qa

ABSTRACT

Social hierarchy plays an important role in shaping the way individuals interact with each other. In this study, we propose three metrics: equality, diversity, and reciprocity to evaluate the social hierarchical differences in cross-ideological communication on Twitter. We do this within the context of three diverse conflicts: Israel-Palestine, US Democrats-Republicans, and FC Barcelona-Real Madrid. In all cases, we collect data around a central pair of Twitter accounts representing the two main parties. Our results show in a quantitative manner that social hierarchy can be considered a factor that impacts individual's communication in Twitter conflicts. As one of the first literatures in this area, we demonstrate social hierarchy's effect in online environments.

Categories and Subject Descriptors

J.4 [**Social and Behavioral Sciences**]: Sociology

Keywords

Conflict, social hierarchy, Twitter, social network

1. INTRODUCTION

Social stratification has been proved to play a substantial role in shaping the way people interact and perceive others, and has been investigated in sociological studies. The recent advent of social networking sites has provided great data sources for researches on social stratification. Besides the advantages of large data size, social networking sites also contain rich interactions between cross-ideological individuals [1]. Studying such kind of cross-hierarchical communication, especially in conflicts, can be very important, as lately "digital hate" on Twitter grows at an alarming speed [2]. In order to empirically understand how cross-hierarchical communication happens in Twitter conflicts, in this study we asked questions like: How much does the social hierarchy matter in cross-ideological communication? And how universal are such patterns across different types of polarized conflicts?

For our study, we choose three conflicts of very different natures, and identify likely supporters of either camp by using retweet signals of certain seed node in combination with additional rules. We validate our ideological labels, as well as all other labels used for this project, through extensive crowd-sourced evaluation. We evaluated the cross-hierarchical communication in all conflicts via three assessment metrics namely, (i) equality, (ii) diversity, and

---

* The work was done while the author was an intern at QCRI.

HT'14, September 1–4, 2014, Santiago, Chile.
ACM 978-1-4503-2954-5/14/09.
http://dx.doi.org/10.1145/2631775.2631788

(iii) reciprocity. We find that individuals from the bottom class initiate the most communication toward their foes in the topmost social hierarchical level. Although those bottom people tend to mention a diverse audience inter-ideologically, under most cases they get ignored and receive no response back. We believe our results advances people's understanding of the opportunities and limitations provided by Twitter for facilitating cross-hierarchical interactions.

2. DATA COLLECTION AND LABELING

To automatically detect users with similar or different ideologies, we started with three pairs of opposing seed users: @AlqassamBrigade and @IDFSpokesperson, @TheDemocrats and @GOP, and @FCBarcelona_es and @realmadrid. We intentionally chose these Twitter accounts as seed nodes considering their key roles in well-known Twitter conflicts. For each of the seed nodes, we obtained up to 3,200 of its latest tweets using the Twitter API. As retweet often indicates endorsement and preference of a message, then for each tweet we identified up to 100 retweeters and labeled them as the supporters of the corresponding seed node. To remove mediators and neutral intervenors, such as peace movement organizations and journalists, we first identified the top retweeted accounts from each side. After manually removing those with neutral leanings (e.g. @BBCBreaking, @Reuters, etc.), we kept only the top 10 influential ones from each camp. We next labeled users who retweeted the top 10 influential accounts from one side 4 times less than from the other side as with neutral or unclear leanings in the conflict, and eliminated them from our datasets. Here we chose 4 as the threshold because it provided the most reasonable balance between the classification accuracy and the size of data for later analysis, compared to other values ranging from 2 to 5. We validated our classification results via CrowdFlower (crowdflower.com) by assigning 100 random users in each ideology to the HIT workers. By comparing user's pre-assigned ideology to the majority-voted label obtained from CrowdFlower, we found that our classification method worked well over all three datasets, yielding an average accuracy of 96.2%. With the classified users, we extracted all mentions between them as interactions between ideological-friends and foes. The descriptions of our collected data sets were shown in Table 1.

Table 1. Properties of the three collected datasets

Conflict	#Users	#Inter-Interaction	#Intra-Interaction
PA-IL	9,937	4,829	178,255
DEM-REP	17,869	20,257	576,848
FCB-RMFC	28,218	21,089	152,799

Next, we split the classified users into four social hierarchical groups according to their number of followers, including: the top 1%, top 1%-10%, 10%-70%, and 70%-100% users. The division is arbitrary, but we think that given the specialty of the top and bottom users in Twitter, our grouping scheme can be most useful in comparing the communication patterns across social hierarchies. Also, we believe, that the number of followers at least partly indicates a person's degree of influence on the social network [3], even though it may not fully represent the social "status" of an individual in real world.

3. ANALYSIS OF CROSS-HIERARCHICAL COMMUNICATION

We adopted three assessment metrics, namely equality, diversity, and reciprocity, to explore the cross-hierarchical communication flows. One-way ANOVA tests with post-hoc Tamhane's T2 analyses were utilized to determine statistical significance at a p value of 0.05 or less.

Equality requires all individuals to engage and contribute equally in communication. People in lower hierarchies are supposed to participate less, as they are expected to have little power or control over outcomes. We quantify a user's engagement by the total number of mentions each individual makes to their ideological-foes.

Diversity measures the degree of variation in an individual's conversational network. We adopt a metrics called E-I ratio to measure the diversity of one's communication. The E-I ratio captures the extent to which one's communication network is composed of individuals that are across ideologies as compared to within ideologies. The E-I ratio is calculated as:

$$EI_i = \frac{E_i - I_i}{E_i + I_i}$$

where E_i = number of ideological-foes user i has mentioned, I_i = number of ideological-friends user i has mentioned. The E-I ratio ranges from -1 to 1. The closer the E-I index is to -1, the more likely an individual only talks to ideological-friends.

Reciprocity refers to dyadic information exchanges between individuals. It is assumed that individuals in lower social hierarchies engage in more dyadic interactions than individuals in higher hierarchical levels since communication constructed from the higher-ranked individuals are more often one-to-many interactions. To evaluate the reciprocity levels across ideologies and hierarchies, we adopted the maximum length of inter-ideological conversations as the measurement.

4. RESULTS

Figure 1 showed the conditional probability of a communicator interacting with another, given their social hierarchies. Here we used the PA - IL conflict for illustration purpose and only reported findings that can be generalized to all three datasets. The results were visualized using parallel sets, with the width of the bar denoted the number of interactions existed cross-hierarchical levels. We saw that except the bottom-most level, users from the other three hierarchies have about the same probabilities of being mentioned by their friends. However, under an inter-ideological context, we noticed that users in the top-most hierarchical level have the highest chance of receiving a mention initiated by their foes, which is even higher than the sum of the probabilities derived from the remaining three levels. This indicated that people are more willing to attack or challenge "authorities". Besides, under both conditions, there is very little chance that the bottom 30% of users will be mentioned by either their friends or foes. In addition, from viewing the width of all "ribbons", we found that users from the bottom-most hierarchical level maintain the highest probability of initiating a mention of the top 1% of users.

The ANOVA results on equality demonstrated no significant social hierarchical difference, except on the DEM-REP dataset (F $_{(3, 6977)}$ = 27.45, p = 0.00). Tamhane's T2 tests further revealed that only users in the bottom group are involved in significantly less

interactions with their ideological-foes, whereas, the other three social hierarchical groups did not differ on the total number of interactions that they initiated. In that sense, we claim that in general, social hierarchy has little or no effect on user's participation in cross-ideological communication.

The one way ANOVA tests on E-I ratio also showed significant differences for all three datasets (PA-IL: F $_{(3, 7374)}$ = 25.29, p =0.00; DEM-REP: F $_{(3, 15963)}$ = 24.06, p = 0.00; and FCB-RMCF: F $_{(3, 22004)}$ = 62.34, p = 0.00). Tamhane's T2 further revealed that the second hierarchical group of both political datasets had the significantly lowest E-I ratio, indicating that people in that social hierarchy are more insular toward their ideological-foes. In contrast, the bottom hierarchy exhibited the highest tendency towards inter-ideological communications.

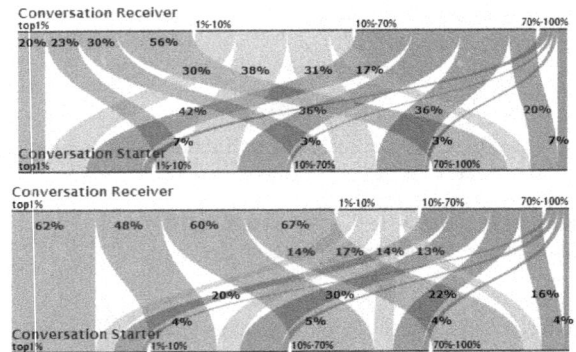

Figure 1: Intra (above) and inter-ideological (below) communication across hierarchies.

Social hierarchy also demonstrated significant impact on the continuity of inter-party discussions on PA-IL (F $_{(3, 3768)}$ = 4.60, p = 0.00) and FCB-RMCF (F $_{(3, 7593)}$ = 10.24, p = 0.00) datasets, whereas the DEM-REP data failed to demonstrate such difference on inter-ideological conversation length (F $_{(3, 104774)}$ = 27.56, p = 0.06). Post hoc analyses further revealed that in general conversation starters from the bottom hierarchy had significantly less back and forth exchanges in cross-ideological conversations.

5. CONCLUSION

We present an initial analysis on the effect of social hierarchy on cross-ideological communication in Twitter conflicts. Our results provided evidence that people in the bottom social hierarchy tend to be aggressive toward their ideological-foes in the upper classes, however, more than often they tend to be ignored by their adversaries. In addition, our results showed that the two political conflicts revealed approximately the same cross-hierarchical communication characteristics, whereas the sports-related contradiction exhibited quite different patterns. Future work will involve the investigation of other aspects of inter-ideological communications, such as tweet politeness or informativeness.

6. REFERENCES

[1] Liu, Z., and Weber, I. Predicting ideological friends and foes in Twitter conflicts. *WWW companion 2014*

[2] D. MacMillan. Twitter aids rise of web-based hate forums. http://www.bloomberg.com/news/2013-05-07/twitter-aids-rise-of-web-based-hate-forums-report-finds.html. May 2013.

[3] Kwak, C. Lee, H. Park, and S. Moon. What is twitter, a social network or a news media? *WWW2010*

A DSL Based on CSS for Hypertext Adaptation

Alejandro Montes García, Paul De Bra, George H. L. Fletcher, Mykola Pechenizkiy
Department of Mathematics and Computer Science
Eindhoven University of Technology
Eindhoven, the Netherlands
{a.montes.garcia, p.m.e.d.bra, g.h.l.fletcher, m.pechenizkiy}@tue.nl

ABSTRACT

Personalization offered by Adaptive Hypermedia and Recommender Systems is effective for tackling the information overload problem. However, the development of Adaptive Web-Based Systems is cumbersome. In order to ease the development of such systems, we propose a language based on CSS to express personalization in web systems that captures current adaptation techniques.

Categories and Subject Descriptors

H.5.4 [**Information Interfaces and Presentation**]: Hypertext/Hypermedia

General Terms

Languages, Theory

Keywords

Adaptation Language; Adaptive Systems; Personalization

1. INTRODUCTION

The web is an enormous hyperspace where users face the problem of information overload. Adaptive web-based systems (AWBS) tackle this problem by displaying only the information that is meaningful for the user. The development of AWBS can be cumbersome and time consuming [4]. Moreover, two kinds of adaptation coexist and are not unified namely, pre-authored (e. g. AHA [10]), and data-driven adaptation (e. g. collaborative recommender systems [2]).

To ease the development of AWBS, we propose a Domain Specific Language [11] (DSL) to express adaptation and only adaptation. This way adaptation is decoupled from the business logic and by doing so, easier integration with existing applications is enabled. The syntax of this DSL must capture the state-of-the art techniques [14] without distinguishing between data-driven and pre-authored adaptation.

We took CSS as a starting point of our DSL because of its usage is widespread in web-based systems and it already

HT'14, September 1–4, 2014, Santiago, Chile.
ACM 978-1-4503-2954-5/14/09.
http://dx.doi.org/10.1145/2631775.2631782.

defines some rules that can be used for adaptation purposes (e. g. hiding fragments). For this reason it will be easy for CSS developers to develop a fully adaptive system, but also, it will be easy to integrate our language in CSS authoring tools for non proficient CSS developers. This approach also roots our work in the Dexter-based [13] AHAM model [9], that contemplates a layer for presentation specifications.

Adaptation languages for AWBSs already exist [5, 16, 18, 10, 19, 8, 3, 12] but they either do not capture all the adaptation techniques or do not do it in a way that is decoupled from the web system and easy to learn by developers.

2. ELEMENTS OF THE LANGUAGE

2.1 Selectors

Selectors are the elements of our language that allow the developer to express which DOM nodes will be modified and under which conditions. If we map the DOM nodes to the atomic fragments in AHAM [9] it becomes clear that the adaptation modifies entire DOM nodes.

We distinguish three types of selectors that are useful in a language to express adaptation in AWBS namely, item selectors, user selectors and context selectors. The first ones select nodes from the DOM tree to be modified by the adaptation rules, while the latter ones select to what type of user or in which context the rules will be applied.

An **item selector** is used to select nodes from the DOM tree to be modified by the adaptation rules. CSS defines a set of selectors [6], and their usage is widespread in web systems development, therefore we will use them.

To ease the development as much as we can and develop an approach as close to the standards as possible, we propose **user selectors** (or queries) based on media queries [17]. Media queries are part of the W3C recommendation and their usage is widespread in web development. While those aim to select to which type of device the rules contained inside should be applied, user queries follow the same approach but selecting users instead of devices.

We allow arbitrary features in user queries. The interpreter will search them in the User Model, if those are not found, the query will be evaluated to false and the rules will not be applied. If a feature starts with `min-` or `max-`, its first characters will be deleted and the interpreter will look for the rest and evaluate to true if the value in the UM is higher or lower than the expected. We use `min` and `max` instead of $\leq$ or $\geq$ to stay within the CSS syntax.

It is desirable also to adapt content according to context features. We define **context selectors** the same way as user selectors. Media queries already do some context adaptation related to device properties. We add the time and location features shown below to provide a wider adaptation effect.

- `min-hour`/`max-hour`: Hour in which the adaptation will start/stop to be executed.
- `date`: Date in which the adaptation will be executed.
- `min-date`/`max-date`: Date in which the adaptation will start/stop to be executed.
- `weekday`: Days of the week in which the adaptation will be executed.
- `centre`: A point on the Earth in which the adaptation effect will be provided.
- `radius`: How far a user can be from the previous point.

To connect queries with a logical OR, the user/context queries have to be separated by commas. A logical AND is achieved by nesting them. Different features of one query can also be separated by the keyword **and** to require that every feature is true.

2.2 Adaptation Rules

Adaptation rules are used to select the adaptation effects to be provided. For some techniques, standard CSS rules can be used, e.g. hiding fragments. However, for other techniques we have to extend the CSS rules keeping the CSS syntax. Our new rules will be transformed to calls to javascript functions. The following rules have been defined:

- `append(url|HTML)`: Gets the content from `url` or takes it from `HTML` and appends it to the selected node.
- `insert(url|HTML)`: Similar to append, but deleting the previous content.
- `reorder-nodes`/`reorder-links(strategy)`: Reorders the subnodes (or links contained in an unordered list) according to a strategy (data-driven or expert-based).
- `trim-at(int)`: Trims the text contained in the node at a specified position.
- `fisheye-doi([0.0-1.0])`: Sets the selected value as the value the DOI function has to take in that node.
- `update-attribute(attr,val)`: Sets the attribute named `attr` to be equal to `val` in the selected node.
- `delete-node(bool)`: Deletes the selected node, the boolean indicate whether the content inside the node should be deleted (true) or kept (false).

3. USE CASE SCENARIO

To better illustrate our language, let's consider a use case motivated by the CHIP project [1]. CHIP aims to create personalized tours in the Rijksmuseum by using a server-side adaptation engine. Listings 1 and 2 show a possible implementation of some parts of CHIP using our approach.

Listing 1: adapt.amf

```
#artworks {
  reorder-nodes: CB-recommender;
}
@user(max-art-knowledge: 30) {
  .description {
    trim-at: 200;
    append: <a>Open description</a>;
  }
  a.advanced {
    delete-tag: false;
}}
@context(centre:52.36,4.88 and radius:5m){
```

```
  a.next {
    update-attribute: href, ./room2.html;
}}
@context(min-date: 17/03/2014 and max-date
    : 21/03/2014) {
  @context(centre:52.4,4.88 and radius:5m){
    #special {
      display: block;
      append: <p>Picasso exhibition only
          this week</p>;
}}
  @user(min-surrealism-interest: 50) {
    #upcoming {
      append: <li>Dalí exhibition</li>
}}}
```

Listing 2: HTML file from Rijksmuseum

```
<head>
  <link href="adapt.amf" title="wibaf"/>
  <script src="wibaf.js"/>
</head><body>
  <div style="display:none" id="special"/>
  <div id="artworks">
    <div id="art-cachopo">
      <h2>Cachopo</h2><p class="description">
      This <a href="impress.html" class=
      "advanced">impressionist</a>...</p>
    </div>...</div>
    <ul id="upcoming"><li>Room 3 will be
      renovated soon</li></ul>
    <a class="next" href="./r1.html">Next</a>
</body>
```

Analyzing Listing 1, we see that in the first three lines, the artworks are reordered with the data-driven rule **reorder-nodes**, which is an example of **sorting fragments**.

After that, users with a knowledge in art lower than 30 are targeted. Two adaptation techniques are applied to them. First **stretchtext** is applied to the description of the artworks. After that, links to concepts with the class **advanced** are deleted but the anchor is preserved, i.e. **link hiding**.

Then a case of **guidance** is shown. The current room is detected in and the links to the next room are updated.

The last block is used to display a message if the user is in the right room, saying that there is an special exhibition this week. Then, if the user is interested in surrealism, a list element is appended to the list of upcoming events. Both are examples of the **inserting fragments** technique.

4. CONCLUSIONS AND FUTURE WORK

We have demonstrated a CSS-based DSL for adaptation. Our proposed language supports the expression of common data-driven and expert-driven adaptation techniques.

In order to use our language, a Javascript interpreter is being developed at the same time as an adaptive application that uses it. Our interpreter is in an early stage of development but already shows some interesting functionality such as selecting rules according to context and user features.

Future work in this line consists of providing a implementations of methods that perform adaptive operations. Moreover, this language has to be complemented with another one to support the expression of user modeling. In addition, the UM elements should be mapped to ontologies [7] to achieve cross-site integration and enhance personalization [15].

5. ACKNOWLEDGEMENTS

The preparation of this article has been supported by the TUE and Adversitement B.V. under the project WiBAF.

6. REFERENCES

[1] L. Aroyo, R. Brussee, L. Rutledge, P. Gorgels, N. Stash, and Y. Wang. Personalized museum experience: The Rijksmuseum use case. In J. Trant and D. Bearman, editors, *Museums and the Web 2007*, volume 4511 LNCS, pages 385–389, Toronto, Canada, Apr 2007.

[2] M. Balabanović and Y. Shoham. Content-based, collaborative recommendation. *Communications of the ACM*, 40(3):66–72, Mar 1997.

[3] A. Berlanga and F. J. García Peñalvo. Towards reusable adaptive rules. In *Proceedings of the 4th International Workshop on Adaptive Hypermedia and Collaborative Web based Systems*, ICWE 2004, Berlin, Germany, Jul 2004.

[4] P. Brusilovsky, J. Eklund, and E. Schwarz. Web-based education for all: A tool for development adaptive courseware. *Comput. Netw. ISDN Syst.*, 30(1-7):291–300, Apr. 1998.

[5] F. Bry and M. Kraus. Adaptive hypermedia made simple with HTML/XML style sheet selectors. In P. Bra, P. Brusilovsky, and R. Conejo, editors, *Adaptive Hypermedia and Adaptive Web-Based Systems*, volume 2347 of *Lecture Notes in Computer Science*, pages 472–475. Springer Berlin Heidelberg, 2002.

[6] T. Çelik, E. J. Etemad, D. Glazman, and I. Hickson. Selectors Level 3. W3C Recommendation 29 September 2011. http://www.w3.org/TR/2011/REC-css3-selectors-20110929/. Accessed: December 12th, 2013.

[7] F. Cena, A. Dattolo, P. Lops, and J. Vassileva. Perspectives in semantic adaptive social web. *ACM Trans. Intell. Syst. Technol.*, 4(4):59:1–59:8, Oct. 2013.

[8] A. Cristea and L. Calvi. The three layers of adaptation granularity. In P. Brusilovsky, A. Corbett, and F. Rosis, editors, *User Modeling 2003*, volume 2702 of *Lecture Notes in Computer Science*, pages 4–14. Springer Berlin Heidelberg, 2003.

[9] P. De Bra, G.-J. Houben, and H. Wu. AHAM: A dexter-based reference model for adaptive hypermedia. In *Proceedings of the 10th ACM Conference on Hypertext and Hypermedia : Returning to Our Diverse Roots: Returning to Our Diverse Roots*, HT' 99, pages 147–156, Darmstadt, Germany, 1999. ACM.

[10] P. De Bra, D. Smits, and N. Stash. The design of AHA! In *Proceedings of the 17th Conference on Hypertext and Hypermedia*, HT '06, pages 171–195, New York, NY, USA, 2006. ACM.

[11] A. V. Deursen, P. Klint, and J. Visser. Domain-specific languages: An annotated bibliography. *ACM SIGPLAN Notices*, 35(6):26–36, Jun 2000.

[12] S. Hagemann and G. Vossen. Web page augmentation with client-side mashups as meta-querying. In N. Nguyen, M. Le, and J. Świątek, editors, *Intelligent Information and Database Systems*, volume 5990 of *Lecture Notes in Computer Science*, pages 23–32. Springer Berlin Heidelberg, 2010.

[13] F. Halasz and M. Schwartz. The dexter hypertext reference model. *Commun. ACM*, 37(2):30–39, Feb. 1994.

[14] E. Knutov, P. De Bra, and M. Pechenizkiy. AH 12 years later: a comprehensive survey of adaptive hypermedia methods and techniques. *New Review of Hypermedia and Multimedia*, 15(1):5–38, 2009.

[15] K. Koidl, O. Conlan, and V. Wade. Towards cross site personalisation. In *Web Intelligence International Conferences*, volume 1 of *WI '13*, pages 542–548, Atlanta, USA, Nov 2013.

[16] M. Kraus, F. Bry, and K. Kitagawa. XML document adaptation queries (XDAQ): An approach to adaptation reasoning using web query languages. In F. Bry, N. Henze, and J. Małuszyński, editors, *Principles and Practice of Semantic Web Reasoning*, volume 2901 of *Lecture Notes in Computer Science*, pages 113–127. Springer Berlin Heidelberg, 2003.

[17] F. Rivoal. Media Queries. W3C Recommendation 19 June 2012. http://www.w3.org/TR/2012/REC-css3-mediaqueries-20120619/. Accessed: December 12th, 2013.

[18] D. Smits and P. De Bra. GALE: A highly extensible adaptive hypermedia engine. In *Proceedings of the 22nd ACM Conference on Hypertext and Hypermedia*, HT '11, pages 63–72, New York, NY, USA, 2011. ACM.

[19] N. Stash, A. I. Cristea, and P. De Bra. Adaptation languages as vehicles of explicit intelligence in adaptive hypermedia. *International Journal of Continuing Engineering Education and Life Long Learning*, 17(4):319–336, 2007.

Fake Tweet Buster:
A Webtool to Identify Users Promoting Fake News on Twitter

Diego Saez-Trumper
Universitat Pompeu Fabra
Barcelona, Spain
dsaez-trumper@acm.org

ABSTRACT

We present the "Fake Tweet Buster"[1] (FTB), a web application that identifies tweets with fake images and users that are consistently uploading and/or promoting fake information on Twitter. To do that we mix three techniques: (i) reverse image searching, (ii) user analysis and (iii) a crowd sourcing approach to detected that kind of malicious users on Twitter. Using that information we provide a credibility classification for the tweet and the user.

Categories and Subject Descriptors

H.4.2 [**Types of Systems**]: Decision support; H.3.3 [**Information Storage and Retrieval**]: Information Filtering

General Terms

Experimentation, Human factors

Keywords

Social networks; Fake tweets; Fake Photos; News; Credibility; Webtool; Tools

1. INTRODUCTION

Nowadays social media, and more specifically Twitter, is one of the Battlefields for political confrontations. Although that the majority of the people involved in these discussions are using this tool to express their opinions and support their positions in a good manner, there are also people using dirty tricks to win this battle. Specifically, we focus on users that deliberately post fake photos of news. This phenomeno is increasing in the last years, and the goal of those "fakers" is to delegitimize their opponents or to show that their positions have more support that it really has[2]. The usual way to do this, is to take an old photo (e.g. a photo of a demonstration in country X from two years ago), and

---

[1]http://grupoweb.upf.edu/fake-buster

present it as new (e.g. say that is a demonstration in country Y, right now). The sophistication of these fake photos can include some retouch or cropping, but often is just the same photo with a new "title". However, without knowing the context (sometimes people in other countries are following conflicts through Twitter) could be difficult to know if those photos are fake or not. Futhermore, sometimes these photos become viral, and even some newspapers can publish them [1]. Therefore, there are two types of people publishing this kind of images: malicious users that intentionally post fake information, and naive users that believes on that information. The goal of the "Fake Tweet Buster" (FTB) application is to help normal users to check the credibility of a Tweet and also to detected malicious users that are consistently uploading and/or promoting fake information on Twitter. To that, we propose a online application, very easy to use (just copy/paste the tweet url), that returns a credibility score for a given tweet.

2. RELATED WORK

In 2010 Mendoza *et al.*[8] study the tweets during the earthquake in Chile, finding that rumors propagates in a different way than the actual news. In 2011 Castillo *et al.* [5] studied tweets' credibility using posting behavior, text characteristics, and the citation of external sources, to classify tweets as credible or not credible.

Some user's characteristics such as are account's age, number of tweets and followers has been also found to be correlated with tweets credibility[6, 7]. Although that the FTB application focus in tweets with photos, exploding information's, we also take in account the users characteristics.

To the best of our knowledge, beyond the research done in this area, there are no online services available to detect users that are intentionally posting fake photos on twitter.

3. HOW IT WORKS?

"Fake Tweet Buster" works as follows:

- **Step 1:** The user copy/paste a Tweet url or and Tweet account URL.

- **Step 2:** FTB returns a panel showing similar images, a small text description of the image (See the "Best guess for this image" description in Reverse image search description), the original twitter account that posted that image, the account history (what

Original Tweet

Tweet: Oppression in Venezuela #SOSVenezuela
Date: 3-3-2014

Account Information:
Source Account: @SOSVenezuela___
Created at: 3-1-2014
Followers: 45
Tweets: 20

Similar Images

Date: 8-9-2011

Google's *best guess* for this image:
student protest in chile

Our Guess: Fake
Your guess: ◯ Fake   ◯ Legitimate   ◯ Not Sure

Figure 1: A photo from the student protest in Chile in 2011 that was *tweeted* as a Venezuelan demonstration in 2014.

other FBT users opined about that account) and a credibility score based on those informations.

- **Step 3:** FTB user is asked to tag that tweet as Fake or Legitimate.

We use three approaches to identify whether a tweet is legitimate or fake:

- **Reverse image search:** It is a technique that uses a image as query, and the search engine returns similar images. Reverse image search can be used to find out where a photo comes from. For FTB we use two popular reverse image search services: Google Images [3] and TinEye [4]. Google Images has a feature called "Best guess for this image" that returns the textual query that matches better with the image. TinEye, that has a smaller database than Google (i.e. less images to compare with), allows to sort the results by date, allowing to discover the image's "age". Using the two results (text related and image's age), we can know if the photo is new or old, and in which context it appears. Therefore, we can estimate if the photo seems to be related with the tweet or not. For example, imagine a Tweet with a photo claiming that this image is a demonstration in Country X, in 2014. Now, applying reverse image search, we found that the "Best guess for this image" does not refer to Country X, but to Country Y, and that the photo is from 2012. Hence, that photo seems to be fake.

- **User analysis:** Using the Twitter API we obtain the number of tweets, number followers, and the age of an account to determinate if this is suspicious or not. New accounts with an small amount of tweets and followers tends to be more suspicious that an old account with a lot of tweets and followers.

- **Crowd sourcing:** We include a panel with all the information about the photo and the twitter account that posted it and then ask FTB's users to tag that account as fake or legitimate.

4. FUTURE WORK

We will improve our model using the crowd sourced information, that will be a dataset of manually tagged (as fakers or legitimate) accounts. We also want to implement the methodology described in [5] to use the tweet text and posting behavior to classify tweets as credible or not.

4.1 Acknowledgements

This work has been partially funded by the "Understanding Social Media: An Integrated Data Mining Approach" (TIN2012-38741) project from the Spanish Economy and Competitiveness Ministry.

5. REFERENCES

[1] Austrian Newspaper Apologizes for Fake Syria Photo. http://www.imediaethics.org/News/3284/Austrian_newspaper_apologizes_for_fake_syria_photo.ph.

[2] 'Fake' Images Shared on Venezuela Protests. http://www.bbc.com/news/magazine-26258335.

[3] Google images. http://images.google.com.

[4] Tineye. http://www.tineye.com.

[5] C. Castillo, M. Mendoza, and B. Poblete. Information Credibility on Twitter. In *Proceedings of World Wide Web Conference (WWW)*, pages 675–684. ACM Press, Feb. 2011.

[6] A. Gupta and P. Kumaraguru. Credibility ranking of tweets during high impact events. In *Proceedings of the 1st Workshop on Privacy and Security in Online Social Media*, PSOSM '12, pages 2:2–2:8, New York, NY, USA, 2012. ACM.

[7] A. Gupta, H. Lamba, and P. Kumaraguru. $1.00 per RT #BostonMarathon #PrayForBoston: Analyzing Fake Content on Twitter. In *Eigth IEEE APWG eCrime Research Summit (eCRS)*, page 12. IEEE, 2013.

[8] M. Mendoza, B. Poblete, and C. Castillo. Twitter under crisis: can we trust what we rt? In *Proceedings of the first workshop on social media analytics*, pages 71–79. ACM, 2010.

Inferring Social Ties from Common Activities in Twitter

Umang Sharma
Indian Institute of Technology
Guwahati
s.umang@iitg.ernet.in

Abhishek Suman
Indian Institute of Technology
Guwahati
abhishek.suman@iitg.ernet.in

Saswata Shannigrahi
Indian Institute of Technology
Guwahati
saswata.sh@iitg.ernet.in

ABSTRACT

We investigate the extent to which we can infer social ties between a pair of users in an online social network Twitter, based on their common activities defined by the number of common celebrity profiles they are following. In this work, we analyze the list of celebrities that a set of Twitter users are following in December 2013 to infer the social ties that existed between these users till July 2009. We use two probabilistic models given by Kossinets et al. [Science, 2006] and Crandall et al. [PNAS, 2010] for this purpose. The model of Kossinets et al. is meant to give an upper bound for the probability of friendship between a pair of users, whereas the model by Crandall et al. is supposed to give an almost accurate estimate of the same. We observe that the model of Kossinets et al. is able to give an upper bound whereas the model given by Crandall et al. is unable to give an almost accurate estimate for our dataset. However, the model by Crandall et al. is observed to provide a correct estimate of the probability of friendship between the users when we consider following a particular type of celebrity profile, e.g. CEO, Author etc., as the activity of a user.

ACM Classification Keywords: H.1.0: Information Systems - MODELS AND PRINCIPLES - General

Keywords: Social Networks; Inferring Social Ties

1. INTRODUCTION

Online social networks like Twitter, Facebook etc. have become increasingly widespread over the last decade. Users of these social networking sites either create friendships or follow other users. They are also involved in a wide variety of online activities like commenting on other user's posts, liking other profiles, playing online games, rating movies etc. The motivation behind this work is to understand how much private information such as friendship can be inferred from the online activities of the users in Twitter. Earlier works have shown how social ties between individuals in a network can be inferred by analyzing its anonymized versions [2, 7] or the common online behaviour such as visiting similar web sites [8] and tagging or commenting on similar content with

similar keywords [9]. In this work, we investigate the extent to which online social ties between individuals can be inferred based on the common celebrity profiles they follow on Twitter. We analyze two models given by Kossinets et al. [5] and Crandall et al. [3] to see how accurately they fit in our setting.

2. EXPERIMENTAL SETUP AND DATA SET

We use the data from a social networking website Twitter (www.twitter.com). Using the data from the website [6], we obtain a list of *celebrity profiles* on Twitter in July 2009, where a celebrity profile is defined to be a user profile which had at least 10,000 followers at that time. From the website http://an.kaist.ac.kr/traces/WWW2010.html [6], we also get the list of all Twitter users along with their followees till July 2009. We define *active users* to be those non-celebrity users who had been following at least 1000 other users on Twitter in July 2009. We identify a total of 21,626 active users. The public API of Twitter is used to collect the data of the celebrity profiles that these *active users* are following in December 2013. We are interested to infer the friendship between these active users, that existed till July 2009, based only on the celebrity profiles they have started following between August 2009 and December 2013. This is done to avoid the cases where the users explicitly make friendship with other users on Twitter who are following the same celebrity profiles. We define following a celebrity profile to be an *activity* by a user. Also, two users are assumed to be *friends* if they follow each other on Twitter.

To begin with, we take the entire set of 6,499 celebrity profiles and consider following these celebrity profiles by the users, as their activities. Based on these activities, we infer the probability of friendship between the users. Thereafter, we identify particular type of celebrities such as Authors, Entrepreneurs, Organization CEOs, Musicians/Music company and News Sources. There are a total of 115 CEOs, 147 Authors, 213 Entrepreneurs, 64 Music related and 158 News Source related celebrity profiles in our dataset. Based on each of these types of celebrities, we infer the probabilities of friendship between the users.

3. PROBABILISTIC MODELS STUDIED
3.1 Model of Kossinets and Watts

Kossinets and Watts [4, 5] used a data set encoding the full history of email communication among roughly 22,000 students over one year period at a large U.S. University. From the communication traces, they constructed a network, joining two people by a link at a given instant if they had ex-

HT'14, September 1-4, 2014, Santiago, Chile.
ACM 978-1-4503-2954-5/14/09.
http://dx.doi.org/10.1145/2631775.2631785

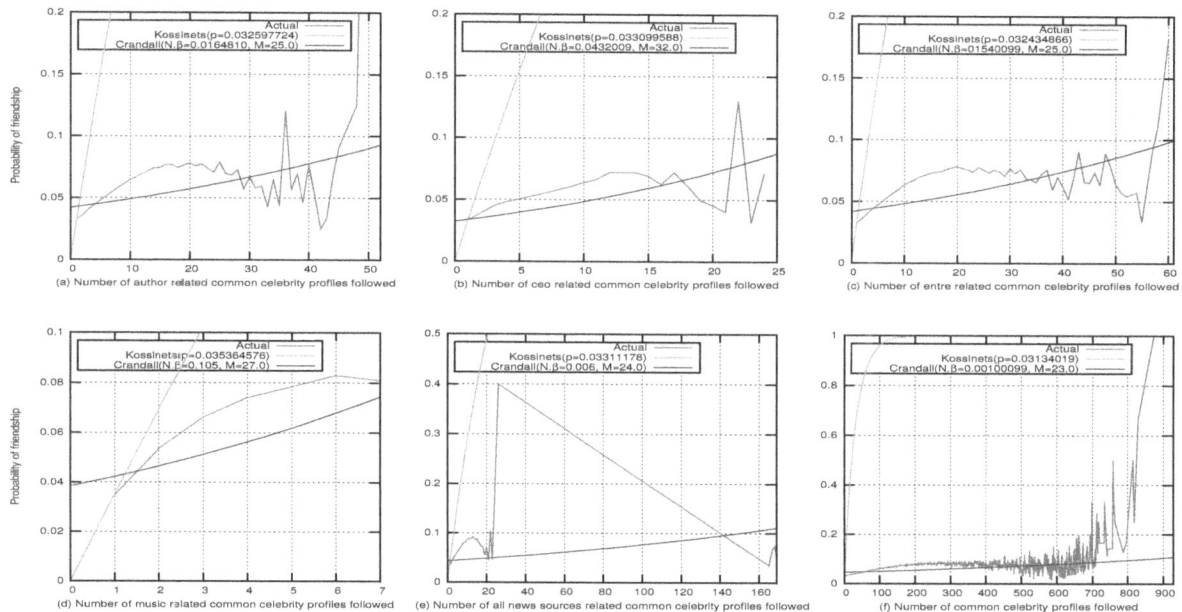

Figure 1: Plots (a)-(e) show the probability of friendship vs the number of common celebrity profiles being followed by a pair of users for a particular type of celebrity profile. The celebrity types considered are (a) authors, (b) CEOs, (c) entrepreneurs, (d) music related and (e) news sources. The plot (f) shows the probabilities of friendship when following any of the celebrity profiles is considered as an activity.

changed emails in each direction at some point in the past 60 days. They also had the information about the class schedule of each student. In this way, each class became a *common activity* and two students shared an activity if they had taken a class together. The authors computed the probability of friendship as a function of the number of shared activities, and came up with a simplified baseline model describing what one might have expected the probabilities to be with all the activities being independent of each other. Their claim was that the baseline plot always lies above the actual data plot. So, if F is the event of two students being friends, C_k is the event of two students attending k common classes and p is the probability that the two students with a single common class are friends, then $P(F|C_k) \leq 1-(1-p)^k$.

3.2 Model of Crandall et al.

Crandall et al. [3] investigated the problem of inferring social ties based on co-occurrences in space and time. They used a large scale dataset from a popular photo sharing site Flickr. The photos in Flickr have time stamp and geo-tags associated with them, which indicates when and where they were taken. Apart from this, Flickr also allows users to befriend each other. The authors define a spacio-temporal co-occurrence between two Flickr users as an instance in which they both took photos at approximately the same place and at approximately the same time. Specifically, their model divides the surface of the earth into grid-like cells. They say that two people A and B co-occurred in a given $s \times s$ cell C, at temporal range t, if both A and B took photos geo-tagged at a location inside the cell C within t days of each other. The formulation of the simple model provided by Crandall et al. is as follows. Let N be the number of cells and M be the number of people in the network. The network has

$\frac{M}{2}$ disjoint edges with each person being friend with only another person. Also, let β be the probability with which each such pair decides everyday to visit a place together. The choice of the location is made uniformly at random. Let F be the event of two individuals being friends, C_k be the event that two individuals visit the same location on k consecutive days and p_1 be the probability that two friends visit the same location on a particular day. Then,

$$P(F|C_k) = \frac{p_1^k}{p_1^k + (\frac{1}{N})^k \cdot (M-2)}.$$

4. EXPERIMENTAL RESULTS AND OBSERVATIONS

It can be observed from Figure 1 that the probability distribution obtained from the model given by Kossinets et al. lies above the one obtained from the actual data in all the plots from (a) through (f), as claimed by the authors. In order to apply the model by Crandall et al., we minimize the Kolmogorov-Smirnov statistics between the distribution inferred by their model and the one from the actual data, using the Java API [1]. We see that the K-S test accepts the hypothesis that the distribution obtained from the actual data and the one from the model by Crandall et al. are similar for all the plots from (a) through (e). In plot (f) where the entire set of celebrity profiles are considered irrespective of their types, the K-S test rejects the hypothesis that the distribution obtained from the model by Crandall et al. matches the one from the actual data. We conclude that the model by Crandall et al., having a very simple underlying network structure, is not sufficient to infer the friendship probabilities for the Twitter users that we consider. It's an interesting open problem to give a new model to estimate the friendship probabilities in this kind of setting.

5. REFERENCES

[1] JMSL numerical library 6.1-class KolmogorovTwoSample.

[2] L. Backstrom, C. Dwork, and J. Kleinberg. Wherefore art thou r3579x? anonymized social networks, hidden patterns, and structural steganography. *Proceedings of the 16th International World Wide Web Conference.*, pages 111–125, 2007.

[3] D. J. Crandall, L. Backstromb, D. Cosleyc, S. Surib, D. Huttenlocherb, and J. Kleinberg. Inferring social ties from geographic coincidences. *Proceedings of the National Academy of Sciences*, 99(12):1–6, 2010.

[4] D. Easley and J. Klienberg. *Networks, Crowds and Markets: Reasoning about a highly connected world.* Cambridge University Press, 2010.

[5] G. Kossinets and D. J. Watts. Empirical analysis of an evolving social network. *Science*, 311(12):88–90, 2006.

[6] H. Kwak, C. Lee, H. Park, and S. Moon. What is twitter, a social network or a news media? *Proceedings of the International conference on World wide web*, pages 591–600, 2010.

[7] A. Narayanan and V. Shmatikov. De-anonymizing social networks. *Proceedings of the 30th IEEE Symposium on Security and Privacy.*, pages 173–187, 2009.

[8] F. Provost, B. Dalessandro, R. Hook, X. Zhang, and A. Murray. Audience selection for online brand advertising: Privacy-friendly social network targeting. *Proceedings of the International Conference on Knowledge Discovery and Data Mining.*, pages 707–716, 2009.

[9] R. Schifanella, A. Barrat, C. Cattuto, B. Markines, and F. Menczer. Folks in folksonomies: Social link prediction from shared metadata. *Proceedings of the Third ACM International Conference on Web Search and Data Mining*, pages 271–280, 2010.

FoP: Never-ending Face Recognition and Data Lifting.

Julien Subercaze
Université de Saint-Etienne,
10, rue Tréfilerie
Saint-Étienne, F-42000, France
julien.subercaze@univ-st-etienne.fr

Christophe Gravier
Université de Saint-Etienne
10, rue Tréfilerie
Saint-Étienne, F-42000, France
christophe.gravier@univ-st-etienne.fr

ABSTRACT

In this demonstration, we present `Faces of Politics (FoP)`, a face detection system from pictures illustrating news articles. The first iteration of the face recognition model propelling `FoP` was trained using Freebase data about politicians and their pictures. `FoP` is a never-ending system: when a new face is recognized, the learned model is updated accordingly. At this step, `FoP` is also giving data in return to the LoD cloud that fed him in the first place: it leverages visual knowledge as Linked Data.

Categories and Subject Descriptors

H.3.5 [**Information Systems**]: Information storage and retrieval—*Online Information Services*; I.2.6 [**Artificial intelligence**]: Learning—*Learning*

Keywords

face recognition; data lifting; never-ending learner

1. INTRODUCTION

The size of the Web makes it difficult to leverage knowledge from all this corpus in a single shot. Learning structured knowledge from the Web is therefore an incremental process. This process never ends, even if it is only because new data is generated daily. This principle was popularized by NELL, the never-ending learner [3], that has been running continuously, and has learnt more than 50 millions of facts by itself. This principle was recently applied at a Web scale for multimedia data by the same group of researchers[4]. In `FoP`, we are interested in a particular sort of multimedia data: the presence of people in the image. In this demonstration we are focusing on images of politicians. Ultimately, `FoP` will be able to continuously learn new representation of people in a picture from people already known in its database.

2. RELATED WORK

With the assumption that video objects are an opaque information nutshell for crawlers, [6] presents a generic crowdsourcing framework for automatic and scalable semantic annotations of HTML5 videos. This framework is easing the leveraging of Linked Data based on the Event Ontology[1], which includes the `Agent` class whose instances can be persons. Another related work is the Flickr wrapper [2]. This latter intends to extend Wikipedia with user-generated semantic annotations on Flickr pictures. However, the linkage possibility are limited to declare that a picture is "related" to a Wikipedia page (related can be pretty vague), and it is not possible to link only a sub-part of the picture (e.g. faces). [5] presented FANS, a face annotation framework. The FANS inner model is first trained using a manually constructed dataset resulting from google queries on 6,025 persons. By applying a Locality-Sensitive Hash function to the natural feature points of detected faces, the authors demonstrated a scalable Web image retrieval engine. However, FANS do not interact with the Web of Data, and the model is not evolving with time.

3. FOP ARCHITECTURE

The `FoP` system data leveraging flow is illustrated in Figure 1. The exchange of data between `FoP` and the LoD-cloud is giving rise to raising edges of data called "`ticks`", while the falling edges (from the LoD-cloud to `FoP`) are respectively called "`tocks`".

3.1 Tocks

`Tocks` are data queried from the LoD-cloud that enrich the `FoP` learner. The first `tock` drived the training of a first face recognition model. For this, the Local Binary Patterns algorithm [1] is a very robust face recognition algorithm that is less sensitive to lighting conditions than other standard algorithms. Moreover it is not computationally expensive to perform an update of the model, which is a unique feature among holistic methods [7]. Face recognition algorithms are however very sensitive to parameters settings. We conducted several tests to determine the best parameter set to use at `tock` phase. The task of face recognition is still a hard research issue : it is not possible to maintain high values for both precision and recall. As our system will handle a large volume of pictures, and that our goal is to provide data with the highest level of correctness, we trade recall for precision. In order to determine the best parameter that

---

[1]http://motools.sourceforge.net/event/event.html

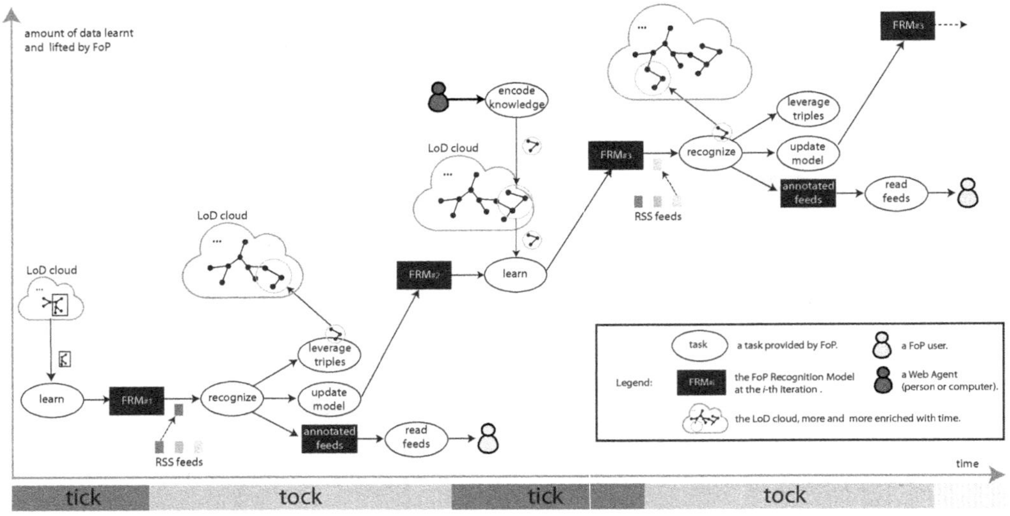

Figure 1: Never-ending face recognizing and semantizing tick/tock model.

maximize precision while preserving recall, we learnt a first model with French politicians in national news. We extract the list of living politicians having government positions in France along to their pictures in Freebase. We then use these pictures and their associated resource to train a first version of the face recognition model. For this first model, we experimentally set the single parameter (which is the maximum authorized distance between two pictures to be considered neighbors) of the Binary Local Pattern algorithm to 57. This value maximizes the recall for a near-perfect precision (0.97). However, the recall still remains low (0.15) and very few pictures would be handled. That is the reason why other **tocks** occur at regular interval of time. At further **tocks**, FoP queries again the Freebase database for new Picture–Person links. At each **tock**, the FoP face recognition model is therefore enhanced using LoD-based data. FoPgives knowledge back to the LoD based data at **tick**.

3.2 Ticks

A **tick** is initiated by receiving an update of one of the RSS feeds to which FoP has subscribed. For each article FoP extracts pictures, detects faces, and matches them against the previously trained model. If a person is recognized using the face recognition model, we validate its presence by searching the article text for his/her name. If validated, annotated feeds articles are added to the internal database, and the model is updated using the newly detected face. A **tick** can therefore also generate model updates of the FoP recognition model. Updating the model allows us to overcome the initial low recall issue. For a threshold of 57, we maintain a very high precision (above .93). In the mean time, recall greatly improved from .15 to .35. For greater values of the threshold the recall improvement is far greater but it implies serious degradation of the precision to unacceptable values, that would result in falsely labeled pictures. Aside from updating the model and storing annotated feeds articles for later consultation by FoP users, FoP leverages Linked Data at **ticks**. The ontology for me-

dia resources (`ma-ont`[2]) defines media fragment as sub-parts of a media. Mediafragments[3] makes it possible to specify rectangular clipping of images by appending its coordinates to the original URI. This is particularly useful for identifying several persons in a picture, since one can specify the region where the face of a person is located. Due to domain coverage shortcomings of `ma-ont`, we defined an object property `IsInPicture` whose domain is a `foaf:Person` and whose range is the intersection of `ma-ont#Image` and `ma-ont#MediaFragment`. This enables to search for pictures containing multiple people. For example one is able to retrieve in one query pictures containing both France's president and prime minister.

4. DEMONSTRATION OVERVIEW

Our FoP never ending learner is available online at `http://demo-satin.telecom-st-etienne.fr/facesofpolitics`.

In this demonstration, FoP is subscribing to the major French politicians news feeds. We will showcase the following to the conference attendees. First, through the FoP user interface we shall demonstrate FoP in action by accessing latest feeds with recognized person(s). We will present discovered persons along the part of the multimedia in which they were found, along the context of the original feed article. Second, by switching to another GUI area, we will query FoP data using SPARQL. The demonstration will encompass article retrieval based on the presence of one known person in the FoP triplestore. Then, we will also demonstrate how it is possible to create a curation of articles from different RSS feeds by specifying several persons that must be present in the article illustration.

Moreover, we also provide a public SPARQL endpoint and a Web interface in order to query the Linked Data leveraged by FoP to LOD-cloud resources. Full RDF Dumps and a public SPARQL endpoint are also available at the FoPwebsite.

---

[2]`http://www.w3.org/TR/mediaont-10/`
[3]`http://www.w3.org/TR/media-frags/`

5. REFERENCES

[1] T. Ahonen, A. Hadid, and M. Pietikainen. Face description with local binary patterns: Application to face recognition. *Pattern Analysis and Machine Intelligence, IEEE Transactions on*, 28(12):2037–2041, 2006.

[2] C. Becker and C. Bizer. flickr wrappr–precise photo association, 2011.

[3] A. Carlson, J. Betteridge, B. Kisiel, B. Settles, E. R. Hruschka Jr, and T. M. Mitchell. Toward an architecture for never-ending language learning. In *AAAI*, 2010.

[4] X. Chen, A. Shrivastava, and A. Gupta. Neil: Extracting visual knowledge from web data. December 2013.

[5] S. C. H. Hoi, D. Wang, I. Y. Cheng, E. W. Lin, J. Zhu, Y. He, and C. Miao. Fans: face annotation by searching large-scale web facial images. In *WWW (Companion Volume)*, pages 317–320, 2013.

[6] T. Steiner, R. Verborgh, R. Van de Walle, M. Hausenblas, and J. G. Vallé s. Crowdsourcing event detection in youtube video. In M. Van Erp, W. R. Van Hage, L. Hollink, A. Jameson, and R. l. Troncy, editors, *Proceedings of the 1st workshop on detection, representation, and exploitation of events in the semantic web*, pages 58–67, 2011.

[7] W. Zhao, R. Chellappa, P. J. Phillips, and A. Rosenfeld. Face recognition: A literature survey. *ACM Computing Surveys (CSUR)*, 35(4):399–458, 2003.

Why You Follow: A Classification Scheme for Twitter Follow Links[*]

Atsushi Tanaka[†]
a.tanaka@mbs.co.jp

Hikaru Takemura[‡]
takemura@dl.kuis.kyoto-u.ac.jp

Keishi Tajima
tajima@i.kyoto-u.ac.jp

Graduate School of Informatics, Kyoto University, Sakyo, Kyoto 606-8501 Japan

ABSTRACT

Twitter is used for various purposes, such as, information publishing/gathering, open discussions, and personal communications. As a result, there are various types of follow links. In this paper, we propose a scheme for classifying follow links according to the followers' intention. The scheme consists of three axes: user-orientation, content-orientation, and mutuality. The combination of these three axes can classify most major types of follow links. Our experimental results suggest that the type of a follow link does not solely depend on the type of the followee nor solely on the type of the follower. The results also suggest that the proposed three axes are highly independent of one another.

Categories and Subject Descriptors

H.3 [**Information Storage and Retrieval**]: Information Search and Retrieval

Keywords

Micro-blogging; social network; link classification

1. INTRODUCTION

The most distinctive feature of Twitter is its mechanism of *follow*. By the mechanism of follow, one can use Twitter to gather information as with RSS readers, to share discussions as in discussion forums, and to have communication with friends as in SNSs (Social Network Services). Because Twitter is used for these various purposes, the reason behind each follow link differs from case to case. A user may follow a famous singer because the user is a fan, may follow a news media for gathering information, may follow a technical expert for participating in a discussion led by the expert, and may also follow a friend for daily conversations.

[*]This work was supported by JSPS Kakenhi 26540163.

[†]Currently at Mainichi Broadcasting System, Inc.

[‡]Currently at Yahoo Japan Corporation

HT'14, September 1–4, 2014, Santiago, Chile.
ACM 978-1-4503-2954-5/14/09.
http://dx.doi.org/10.1145/2631775.2631790.

Information on the intentions behind links is useful in various applications, e.g., user recommendation [4, 20], link prediction [18, 5, 1], or information diffusion analysis [15, 8]. For example, some studies proposed Twitter user recommendation method based on the topic similarity between users [4]. If the target user follows some user because he is interested in the information in the tweets by the followee, we should recommend other users with similar tweets. However, if the target user follows the user because he is a fan of the followee, or if it is because they are friends, it does not make sense to recommend other users with similar tweets.

In order to classify follow links in Twitter, we first need to design a classification scheme. The selection of classification categories or axes can, however, be subjective. The goal of this research is to find a set of very primitive and independent classification axes in order to avoid such subjectivity.

2. THREE AXES FOR CLASSIFICATION

Based on our survey of the real Twitter data and the classification schemes in the existing studies [9, 7, 11, 19, 17], we propose the following three axes: (1) *user-orientation*, (2) *content-orientation*, and (3) *mutuality*.

User-orientation is an axis representing whether the follower is interested in the followee user itself. *If a user follows some user and it cannot be replaced with another user with very similar tweets, that follow link is user-oriented.* For example, a follow link to some pop idol by a fan of the idol, or a follow link to a friend, is usually very user-oriented.

On the other hand, content-orientation means whether the follower is interested in specific information in the tweets. *If the original reason of a follow link would be lost once the followee user stopped tweeting about a specific topic, that follow link is content-oriented.* For example, follow links to news media are usually content-oriented.

Notice that user-orientation and content-orientation are not exclusive. For example, suppose a user follows `bbcbusiness` because he thinks it is the most reliable. He does not want to switch to other similar news media, and will not follow `bbcbusiness` if it stops tweeting about business news. That link is both user-oriented and content-oriented.

Mutuality means *whether a follower expects to have mutual communication*. Notice that reciprocal follow links do not necessarily mean mutuality if they do not intend to have mutual communication. In fact, there are many Twitter accounts that automatically follow back to all the followers.

Figure 1 shows how some popular link types are plotted in the classification space generated by these three axes. (Note that it does not mean that all follow links are classified into

Table 1: Classification Precision with Various Feature Sets and the Baseline (Majority Class Method)

features used	A	B	C	A+B	A+C	B+C	A+B+C	majority
3 binary SVMs combined	30.97	36.95	33.52	36.95	34.08	**50.20**	42.70	30.63
3 binary decision trees combined	25.30	48.36	33.52	43.58	27.29	**54.91**	43.26	30.63
8-class SVM	38.07	43.81	32.72	46.93	37.51	43.26	**50.28**	32.72
8-class decision tree	28.01	51.32	35.67	49.16	29.93	**55.87**	50.12	32.72

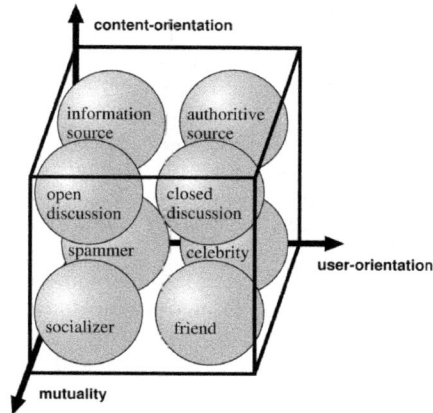

Figure 1: Some link types in our classification space.

Table 2: Breakdown of the Data Set

$m=1$	$u=1$	$u=0$	$m=0$	$u=1$	$u=0$
$c=1$	126	23	$c=1$	410	244
$c=0$	40	29	$c=0$	149	232

Table 3: Features Used for Link Classification

category	features
(A) followee	ratio of information lists/community lists including the followee, those listed in (B)
(B) follower	# of followees, followers, reciprocal follows, lists, reciprocal follower ratio, reciprocal followee ratio
(C) relation	number of lists including both followee and follower, reciprocity, frequency of replies, frequency of RT

these eight types.) Links to friends are user-oriented and have mutuality, but usually not content-oriented. Links to celebrities from the fans are user-oriented, but not content-oriented nor have mutuality. Links to authoritative information sources are both content-oriented and user-oriented, but do not have mutuality. Links to non-authoritative information sources, e.g., a bot tweeting weather reports, are content-oriented but not user-oriented, and do not have mutuality. If a user follows some users for joining a discussion on some topic, these links are content-oriented and have mutuality. If the discussion is closed to specific users, or led by authoritative people, the links are also user-oriented.

Spammers randomly follow many users just for getting "follow-backs" and distributing advertisement [12, 16]. *Socializers* also try to increase followees and followers, no matter who they are. Follow links by them are neither user-oriented nor content-oriented. The purpose of spammers is to send advertisements, so links by them do not have mutuality, while socializers expect to have mutual communication, so links by them have mutuality. In this way, the three axes can classify the most typical types of follow links.

3. PROPERTIES OF THE AXES

An important question is whether our three classification axes are really classifying follow links, or they are simply classifying the followee or the follower. For example, follows to celebrities are usually user-oriented and not content-oriented. Another question is whether the three axes are independent of one another. In order to answer to these questions, we conducted some experiments.

First, we create a data set consisting of 1,253 links by using a questionnaire to 44 Twitter users on a crowdsourcing service. Table 2 shows the breakdown of the data set, where u, c, m denotes the three axes, and 1/0 means yes/no.

Next, we constructed SVMs and decision trees that classify follow links along the three axes by using three types of features: (A) properties of the followee, (B) properties of the follower, and (C) properties of the relation between

them. Table 3 shows the concrete list. (We omit the details.) We ran the classifiers with various combinations of feature sets (A), (B), and (C). We also compared two approaches: classification by three binary classifiers corresponding to the three axes, and classification by a single 8-class classifier corresponding to the combination of the three axes.

The result was evaluated with 10-fold cross validation. Table 1 shows the precision of classification into eight classes. It also includes the precision by the majority class method for comparison. For three out of four methods, B+C achieves the highest precision, and for one method, A+B+C achieves the highest precision. These results suggest that the type of a link does not solely depend on the followee nor solely on the follower. We can also see that the difference between the precision by three binary classifiers and that by one 8-class classifier are not significant, which suggests that the three axes are highly independent.

4. RELATED WORK

There have been research on Twitter user classification based on their purposes [7], on spam user detection [12, 16], and on classifying users into human users, bots, and cyborgs [3]. These studies classify users, while we classify each follow link. The type of a follow link does not solely depend on the followee nor solely on the follower, as explained above.

There have been also research on the classification of links in SNS into positive links and negative links [13, 14, 10]. Their target is, however, Wikipedia and message boards like Slashdot, where negative links are frequently found. In our limited survey, we found no negative links in Twitter.

There have been research on predicting the reciprocity between two Twitter users [2, 6]. Reciprocity, however, does not necessarily imply mutuality as explained before.

5. CONCLUSION

We proposed three primitive axes that can classify most popular types of Twitter follow links. Our experimental results suggest that the type of a link does not depend solely on the followee nor the follower, and also suggest that the three proposed axes are highly independent of one another.

6. REFERENCES

[1] L. Backstrom and J. Leskovec. Supervised random walks: predicting and recommending links in social networks. In *Proc. of WSDM*, pages 635–644, 2011.

[2] J. Cheng, D. M. Romero, B. Meeder, and J. M. Kleinberg. Predicting reciprocity in social networks. In *Proc. of IEEE Third International Conference on Social Computing (SocialCom)*, pages 49–56, Oct. 2011.

[3] Z. Chu, S. Gianvecchio, H. Wang, and S. Jajodia. Who is tweeting on twitter: human, bot, or cyborg? In *Proc. of ACSAC*, pages 21–30, 2010.

[4] J. Hannon, M. Bennett, and B. Smyth. Recommending twitter users to follow using content and collaborative filtering approaches. In *Proc. of RecSys*, pages 199–206, 2010.

[5] M. Hasan and M. Zaki. A survey of link prediction in social networks. In *Social Network Data Analytics*, pages 243–275. Springer, 2011.

[6] J. E. Hopcroft, T. Lou, and J. Tang. Who will follow you back?: Reciprocal relationship prediction. In *Proc. of CIKM*, pages 1137–1146, Oct. 2011.

[7] A. Java, X. Song, T. Finin, and B. Tseng. Why we Twitter: Understanding microblogging usage and communities. *Proc. of KDD*, pages 56–65, 2007.

[8] M. Kim, D. Newth, and P. Christen. Modeling dynamics of meta-populations with a probabilistic approach: Global diffusion in social media. In *Proc. of CIKM*, pages 489–498, 2013.

[9] B. Krishnamurthy, P. Gill, and M. Arlitt. A few chirps about twitter. In *Proc. of WOSP*, pages 19–24, 2008.

[10] J. Kunegis, A. Lommatzsch, and C. Bauckhage. The slashdot zoo: mining a social network with negative edges. In *Proc. of WWW*, pages 741–750, 2009.

[11] H. Kwak, C. Lee, H. Park, and S. Moon. What is twitter, a social network or a news media? In *Proc. of WWW*, pages 591–600, 2010.

[12] K. Lee, J. Caverlee, and S. Webb. The social honeypot project: protecting online communities from spammers. In *Proc. of WWW*, pages 1139–1140, 2010.

[13] J. Leskovec, D. Huttenlocher, and J. Kleinberg. Predicting positive and negative links in online social networks. In *Proc. of WWW*, pages 641–650, 2010.

[14] J. Leskovec, D. Huttenlocher, and J. Kleinberg. Signed networks in social media. In *Proc. of CHI*, pages 1361–1370, 2010.

[15] D. M. Romero, B. Meeder, and J. M. Kleinberg. Differences in the mechanics of information diffusion across topics: idioms, political hashtags, and complex contagion on twitter. In *Proc. of WWW*, pages 695–704, 2011.

[16] E. Tan, L. Guo, S. Chen, X. Zhang, and Y. Zhao. Unik: Unsupervised social network spam detection. In *Proc. of CIKM*, pages 479–488, 2013.

[17] S. Wu, J. M. Hofman, W. A. Mason, and D. J. Watts. Who says what to whom on twitter. In *Proc. of WWW*, pages 705–714, 2011.

[18] D. Yin, L. Hong, X. Xiong, and B. D. Davison. Link formation analysis in microblogs. In *SIGIR*, pages 1235–1236, 2011.

[19] D. Zhao and M. B. Rosson. How and why people twitter: the role that micro-blogging plays in informal communication at work. In *Proc. of GROUP*, pages 243–252, 2009.

[20] G. Zhao, M. L. Lee, W. Hsu, W. Chen, and H. Hu. Community-based user recommendation in uni-directional social networks. In *Proc. of CIKM*, pages 189–198, 2013.

Buon Appetito - Recommending Personalized Menus*

Michele Trevisiol
trevisiol@acm.org

Luca Chiarandini
luca.chiarandini@upf.edu

Ricardo Baeza-Yates
rbaeza@acm.org

Web Research Group
Dept. of Information and Communication Technologies
Universitat Pompeu Fabra, Barcelona, Spain

Yahoo Labs
Barcelona, Spain

ABSTRACT

This paper deals with the problem of *menu recommendation*, namely recommending menus that a person is likely to consume at a particular restaurant. We mine restaurant reviews to extract food words, we use sentiment analysis applied to each sentence in order to compute the individual food preferences. Then we extract frequent combination of dishes using a variation of the Apriori algorithm. Finally, we propose several recommender systems to provide suggestions of food items or entire menus, *i.e.* sets of dishes.

Categories and Subject Descriptors

H.4 [**Information Systems Applications**]: Miscellaneous

Keywords

Recommender Systems, Food-word Recognition, Sentiment Analysis, Menu Recommendation.

1. INTRODUCTION

The quality of a restaurant is strongly related to the quality of the served food and drinks. In this work, we tackle the problem of *menu recommendation, i.e.*, the task of recommending good menus to people looking for a restaurant. In the following we will refer to "dishes" or "food items" for food and drinks indistinguishably and to "menu" as the set of food items a person is going to consume. Recommending menus to people may be useful in a number of ways. For example, it allows customers to pick the restaurants that offer dishes which are more in line with their tastes, or it may make them try new dishes which they have never tried before but are among the top-rated choices offered by the restaurant. In this work we use User Generated Content (UGC) to recommend menus and dishes to people. Analyzing and extracting the meaningful information from the user reviews of

---

*This work was done while the first two authors were PhD interns at Yahoo Labs Barcelona.

HT'14, September 1–4, 2014, Santiago, Chile.
ACM 978-1-4503-2954-5/14/09.
ACM http://dx.doi.org/10.1145/2631775.2631784 .

the places. We use Natural Language Processing (NLP) to extract information from public reviews of restaurants, performing Sentiment Analysis to estimate the user preference associated to each dish. We then build menus by finding sets of dishes that appear often together weighting them with the *positive* and *negative sentiments* previously extracted. Finally, we propose several recommender systems able to recommend dishes and menus and evaluate them quantitatively. Our results indicate that sentiment analysis at the sentence level helps to improve the quality of the recommendations. We are not aware of other research that exploit user reviews, extracting sentiments of each food item, in order to build profiles for people and restaurants to design a menu recommender system. Our approach is versatile as can be easily extended to recommend products or services of businesses based on the reviews of users, as is not strictly related to food items and restaurants.

Related Work Previous work about place recommendation within Yelp, are based on hidden factors [6], extraction of subtopics [4], or optimization for mobile devices [1]. A different problem related to reviews is extracting keywords in order to improve readability [10]. The majority of related work is about recipe recommendation (*e.g.*, [3, 9, 8, 5]) where the ingredients or the recipes are usually explicitly rated by users. However they deal with explicit user ratings and require a dataset of recipes' feedback. The studies done on recipes are very different from our, and they cannot be applied on a general textual review service. Our work differs from previous on basic aspects, first we use User Generated Content, which includes a degree of complexity due to noise and language use. We do not rely on structured databases of recipes, in which a complete knowledge is available, but deal with fragmented information extracted solely from the user reviews of restaurants. Moreover, we are dealing with the problem of menu recommendation not in an abstract way, as a standalone problem, but contextualized to the user environment. This means that we are not just recommending food to people but rather recommending dishes *at a particular restaurant*. The recommendation task is constrained by these factors but the result is more related to everyday life applications.

2. ANALYSIS

In this paper, we use a collection of user's reviews of places on Yelp, a popular online urban guide that contains a list of business (*e.g.*, restaurants, coffee shops) and allows people to write reviews about their experiences at each place. Reviews also contain a rating, expressed as number of "stars" (from 1 to 5, 1 being the worst and 5 being the best rating). In total, the dataset contains 11,537 businesses, 43,873 users, and 229,907 reviews. In order to reduce noise and sparsity, we split a review in sentences, we remove stopwords in each sentence, and we lemmatize all the words. In order to capture the most popular food in reviews, we use three publicly available sources[1] building a dictionary of around 9,000 food items. We then extract the food words from each review (at the sentence-level) obtaining an average of 4.7 food words per review, meaning that users tend to comment more than one dish. Sentiment analysis is the use of NLP techniques to identify subjective information from text. We are interested in understanding the *polarity* of a text, *i.e.*, the amount in which it is positive or negative, and to do that we use the LIWC 2007 [7] dictionary of sentimentally-annotated words. Given a text, we define the sentiment score with $S = \frac{p-n}{p+n}$, where p is the number of positive words, and n is the number of negative words. Moreover, we compare the sentiments extracted by the entire review with the sentiments extracted on each sentence of the same review. We observe that in the case of sentiment of sentences, there is a majority of positive and negative, while review sentiments are more mixed (*i.e.*, $-1 < S < +1$). Indeed, mixed sentiments occur only in 12% of the sentences, against 57% in the case of review-level sentiment analysis. Our experiments shown that splitting by sentence allows us to get a more precise, clean, and localized characterization of the text.

From Dishes to Menus. A menu is a set of dishes which are served during the same meal, and we are interested in detecting menus that people often like. We apply an extension of the Apriori algorithm [2] that deals with *fuzzy* sets, sets whose elements have degrees of membership that in our case are represented by the sentiments extracted from the sentences. Note that for each review, the membership of each food word is the averaged sentiment that it receives in each sentence, normalized to fall into the interval $[0, 1]$.

3. RECOMMENDATION EXPERIMENT

We implement 3 recommender systems and a simple baseline which predict which food items will be present in each given new review. In order to have a meaningful dataset, we consider only users with an average number of food items per review greater or equal to the global average (4.7). We pick 80% of the data as train set (from which we build the user and place profile to train the recommenders), and the remaining as test set. Our evaluation is done on the top K food items (@K) where K represents the number of food items for each test review. All the approaches are based on user and restaurant profiles built on the training data, the first one on the dishes frequently consumed by the user, whereas the latter one on the dishes frequently ordered in the restaurant. Based on the findings showed in Section 2, we propose the following algorithms: (a) `avg-sent`, return the most frequent positive food items that belong to both the user and restaurant profiles, but discarding food items that have a sentiment smaller than the average sentiment in either the user or the restaurant profile; (b) `user-words`, a standard collaborative-filtering recommender that estimates

[1] *WordNet*: (wordnet.princeton.edu), *Oregon State University Food Glossary* (food.oregonstate.edu), and *BBC Food*: (www.bbc.co.uk/food).

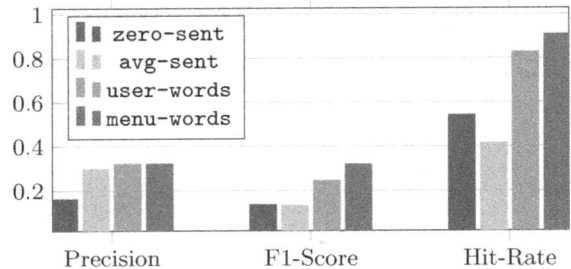

Figure 1: Performance of the sentiment-based recommender systems among different evaluation metrics.

the similarity of the users' tastes in order to rate any food item that belong to the restaurant (the items are weighted with the positive sentiments); (c) `menu-words`, uses the frequent and good menus extracted with the Fuzzy Apriori algorithm, in this case the profiles are built by sets of food words (item sets), the menus. Finally we implement also a baseline, `zero-sent`, that does not consider the sentiments and simply recommend the most frequent items that belong to both the user and the restaurant profiles.

Results Discussion. The results of the recommender systems (Figure 1) are evaluated with Hit-Rate in addition of Precision and F1-Score, in order to highlight the coverage of the algorithms. At a first glance the sentiment-based approaches outperform the baseline showing that sentiment analysis boosts the precision of the recommended food items, thus increasing the probability of recommending dishes that the user will actually order at the restaurant. However, the `full-sent` has significantly worse performance in term of F1-Score and Hit-Rate compared to the `*-words` algorithms, this is due because its strong filtering that might reduces at zero the items to recommend. Among the last two algorithms, the results show interesting insights. Even if `user-words` is slightly better in term of Precision, it decreases in term of Recall and F1-Score. Whereas the recall and precision of `menu-words` are very close to each other meaning that including the most frequent and good good menus considerably boosts the overall accuracy. Moreover in terms of Hit-Rate, `menu-words` is showing the biggest coverage, with around 90% of the users receiving at least one relevant recommendation, whereas `user-words` is slightly smaller.

4. CONCLUSIONS

We introduced the novel problem of menu recommendation for restaurants, describing for the first time how to build a sentiment-based menu recommender system. We use the Fuzzy Apriori algorithm to extract frequent and good food items. We compared different algorithms showing how the sentiment analysis and the menu lead to increase the performance in term of Precision, F1-Score and Hit-Rate. Further work includes inverting the recommendation task such as to recommend restaurants given the dishes a person may want to eat, or even, to recommend the most appealing menus to the restaurants based on the reviews.

Acknowledgments

This work was partially funded by Grant TIN2012-38741 (Understanding Social Media: An Integrated Data Mining Approach) of the Ministry of Economy and Competitiveness of Spain.

5. REFERENCES

[1] C. Biancalana, A. Flamini, F. Gasparetti, A. Micarelli, S. Millevolte, and G. Sansonetti. Enhancing traditional local search recommendations with context-awareness. In *User Modeling, Adaption and Personalization*, pages 335–340. Springer, 2011.

[2] M. Delgado, N. Marín, D. Sánchez, and M.-A. Vila. Fuzzy association rules: general model and applications. *Fuzzy Systems, IEEE Transactions on*, 11(2):214–225, 2003.

[3] J. Freyne and S. Berkovsky. Recommending Food : Reasoning on Recipes and Ingredients. *User Modeling, Adaptation, and Personalization*, 6075:381–386, 2010.

[4] J. Huang, S. Rogers, and E. Joo. Improving restaurants by extracting subtopics from yelp reviews. In *iConference*, pages 1–5, Germany, 2014. Round One Yelp Data Challenge Winners, 2013.

[5] F.-f. Kuo, C.-T. Li, M.-K. Shan, and S.-y. Lee. Intelligent menu planning: Recommending Set of Recipes by Ingredients. In *Proceedings of the ACM multimedia 2012 workshop on Multimedia for cooking and eating activities - CEA '12*, page 1, New York, New York, USA, 2012. ACM Press.

[6] J. McAuley and J. Leskovec. Hidden factors and hidden topics. In *Proceedings of the 7th ACM conference on Recommender systems - RecSys '13*, pages 165–172, New York, New York, USA, 2013. ACM Press.

[7] J. W. Pennebaker, M. E. Francis, and R. J. Booth. Linguistic inquiry and word count: Liwc 2001. *Mahway: Lawrence Erlbaum Associates*, page 71, 2001.

[8] C.-y. Teng, Y.-r. Lin, and L. A. Adamic. Recipe recommendation using ingredient networks. In *Proceedings of the 3rd Annual ACM Web Science Conference on - WebSci '12*, pages 298–307, New York, New York, USA, 2012. ACM Press.

[9] M. Ueda, M. Takahata, and S. Nakajima. User âĂŹ s Food Preference Extraction for Personalized Cooking Recipe Recommendation. In *Proc. of the Second Workshop on Semantic Personalized Information Management: Retrieval and Recommendation*, 2011.

[10] J. Wang. *Clustered Layout Word Cloud for User Generated Online Reviews*. PhD thesis, Virginia Polytechnic Institute and State University, 2012.

AiRCacher: Virtual Geocaching Powered with Augmented Reality

Gianluca Tursi
NetAtlas s.r.l.
Turin, Italy
gianluca.tursi@netatlas.it

Martina Deplano
Computer Science department
University of Turin, Italy
deplano@di.unito.it

Giancarlo Ruffo
Computer Science department
University of Turin, Italy
ruffo@di.unito.it

ABSTRACT

Nowadays, smartphones and digital networks are being heavily used as data sources for research on social networks. Our daily experiences, interactions and transactions are recorded thanks to the digital traces that users leave behind their activities, both individual and social. In this work, we describe AiRCacher, a mobile app for virtual geocaching enhanced with Augmented Reality. By following gamification and Game With A Purpose design approaches, the aim is to bring people outside and make them move, by hiding and seeking virtual caches. As a side effect of their gaming activity, they became like social sensors able to provide geo-located social data. Therefore, the aim of our work is to carry out data analyses about users' outdoor behaviors, by looking for several findings such as trending places for different cache's typologies, and the detection of interesting events emerging from the concentration of caches in specific places.

Categories and Subject Descriptors

H.5.m [**INFORMATION INTERFACES AND PRESENTATION**]: Miscellaneous; J.4 [**SOCIAL AND BEHAVIORAL SCIENCES**]: Sociology

General Terms

Design

Keywords

Augmented Reality; Social sensor; Geolocation; Geocaching; Gamification

1. INTRODUCTION

Starting from the concept of users as social sensors [4, 3, 6, 5] and the worldwide success of Geocaching[1], our idea

---

[1] http://www.geocaching.com

HT'14, September 1–4, 2014, Santiago, Chile.
ACM 978-1-4503-2954-5/14/09.
http://dx.doi.org/10.1145/2631775.2631778.

is to transform the concept of *cache* in a virtual one, by improving the user experience with the Augmented Reality. While performing their activities, users can became data sources, thanks to the technologies of their mobile devices, such as GPS. Several analyses can be carried out following this concept, from the detection of an earthquake through Twitter [6], to the description of human habits through their GPS mobile devices [4, 3].

In the AiRCacher system, a cache is a virtual container where the user can add messages, photos and videos. They can share these content with everyone, or decide to dedicate them to a single friend or a selected group of friends. Thanks to the addition of gamified solutions [2] to these virtual activities, our aim is to collect information about the users' behavior and patterns related to geocaching activities.

This work follows the concept explored in [1]: using game elements to encourage users to use geo-social systems, and providing important data about the performed actions as a side effect of the game [7]. A lot of information could be collected from the users game activity, such as favorite places where caches being hidden, trend places in specific moments, preferences on caches typology, and common paths between two caches.[2]

2. AIRCACHER OVERVIEW

2.1 Purpose

The scientific aim of AiRCacher project is to collect data about users behaviors, habits and movements. By providing the users with a gamified geocaching app powered with augmented reality, we try to stimulate them to spend time outdoor hiding and seeking their caches. Gamification aspects are used to engage the users, bring them outside and motivate them to be more active.

2.2 Architecture

AiRCacher has been developed with a client-server architecture. From the client-side point of view, the innovation is the addition of the Augmented Reality to the geocaching experience. Several features are provided to the users, as described in Section 2.3.
On the server-side, a SQL database has been developed, and the communication part is provided by JSON.

---

[2] Disclaimer: the iOS version of the app has been fully developed by NetAtlas company (http://www.aircacher.com) and it is downloadable for free from the App Store.

2.3 Functionalities

The main menu is divided into six sections: Seek, Hide, Profile, Leaderboards, Logs, and Tour. The three main functionalities are described below.

Hide: The hiding activity starts from the visualization of the geolocalized map. The user can choose the position of the cache by using his own location or by positioning the pin in another place of the map. After that, some information can be added to the cache: name of the cache, description, object to add inside it, and specific addressees. Different points are collected by the user, depending on the characteristics of these details. After hiding the cache, the user can share the news by posting it on Facebook.

Seek: The user can seek close caches. In the map view (See Fig.1(a)), all the caches are shown and identified with different pins depending on their status (close/far, found/to be found, restricted/public). When the user is close enough to a cache, its pin becomes activated (by changing its icon from the binoculars to the magnifying glass) and the user can start using the Augmented Reality to look for the cache. In the Augmented Reality view (See Fig.1(b)), the radar shows the location of the cache and an hot-air balloon appears when the user focus on the correct position. By touching the hot-air balloon, the player can collect the cache, see its content, add something new inside it and share the new finding with friends, by posting it on Facebook.

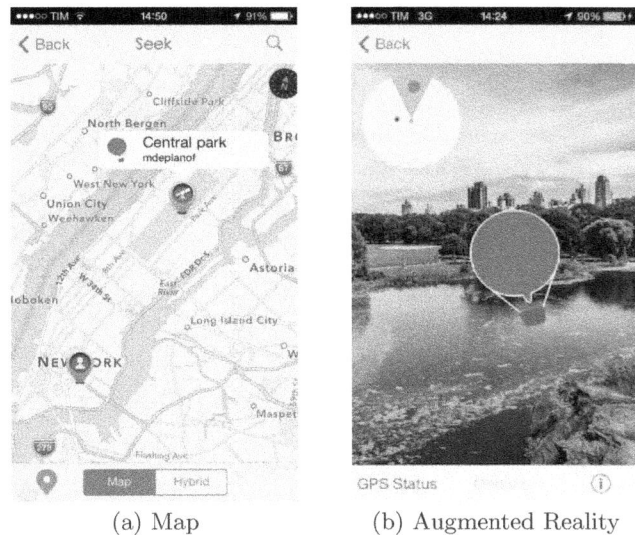

Figure 1: Seek modality: map with a far cache with the binoculars icon (a); Augmented Reality view for a close cache, identified by the hot-air balloon (b)

Profile: All the personal information about the user can be shown. In particular, in Fig.2(a) we can see the user's name, nickname, points, actual level, progression bar to the nest level, and the number of hidden and found caches. On the other hand, in Fig.2(b) the statistics of the user's activity are shown, divided in "seeker" and "hider" statistics.

3. USE CASE SCENARIO

Bob wants to dedicate a virtual cache to Alice, his girlfriend. He decides to hide the cache on the top of the Times Square's staircase, the place where he first met Alice. He

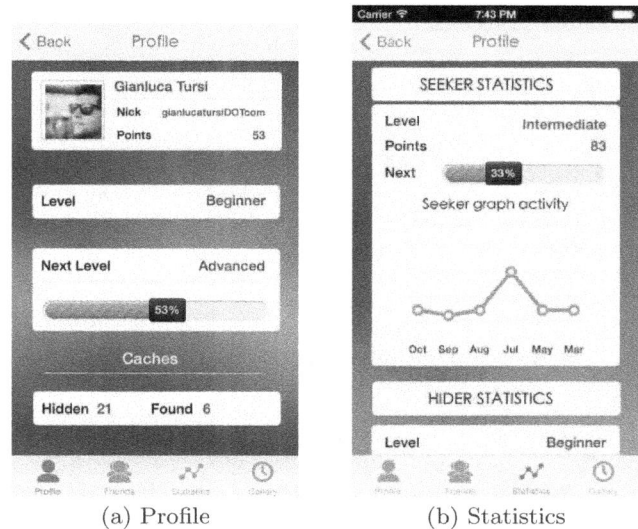

Figure 2: Profile section: personal information (a), and statistics divided into "Seeker" and "Hider" (b)

adds the YouTube url of their favorite song. He also collects some points, rising the ranking of the AiRCacher community. Alice receives a push notification of the dedicated cache and she is the only user allowed toseek and find it, because Bob set the restricted modality during hiding. Alice goes to Time Squares and, when she is near the cache, she enters the Augmented Reality mode to seek her hot-air baloon through the radar visualization. Once she taps on the hot-air balloon on the screen, she collects some points and she can watch the video linked to the cache.

4. CONCLUSIONS AND FUTURE WORK

The main goal of the AiRCacher app is to collect data about geolocated users' activities, by taking advantage of their social sensing feature. While performing their activities, indeed, users can became important and accurate data sources, thanks to their mobile devices' technology. On the other hand, starting from the actual relevance of gamification elements, we think that these incentives can be able to drive people to spend more time outdoor, to move around and to socialize in order to hide and seek virtual caches. New gamified solutions are under development with the aim to enhance the user experience by providing more engaging and social activities.

Future work will be focus on analyzing users' behaviors and looking for interesting findings, such as trend places where users hide their caches, or common paths and patterns among them. Event detection analysis will be carried out when the system will be populated by a big number of users. In particular, by following the creation of a big amount of caches in a specific place, some inference could be done about the cause of this concentration.

Moreover, the Android version is now under development and it will be available soon.

5. REFERENCES

[1] M. Deplano and G. Ruffo. Gwap as a tool to analyze, design, and test geo-social systems. In D. Kanellopoulos, editor, *Intelligent Multimedia Technologies for Networking Applications: Techniques and Tools*, chapter 16, pages 380–407. IGI Global, 2013.

[2] S. Deterding, D. Dixon, R. Khaled, and L. Nacke. From game design elements to gamefulness: defining "gamification". In *Proceedings of the 15th International Academic MindTrek Conference: Envisioning Future Media Environments*, MindTrek '11, pages 9–15, New York, NY, USA, 2011. ACM.

[3] N. Eagle. Mobile phones as sensors for social research. *Emergent technologies in social research. Oxford University Press, New York*, pages 492–521, 2011.

[4] A. Pentland. Reality mining of mobile communications: Toward a new deal on data. *The Global Information Technology Report 2008–2009*, page 1981, 2009.

[5] G. Sagl, B. Resch, B. Hawelka, and E. Beinat. From social sensor data to collective human behaviour patterns: Analysing and visualising spatio-temporal dynamics in urban environments. In *Proceedings of the GI-Forum 2012: Geovisualization, Society and Learning*, pages 54–63, 2012.

[6] T. Sakaki, M. Okazaki, and Y. Matsuo. Earthquake shakes twitter users: real-time event detection by social sensors. In *Proceedings of the 19th international conference on World wide web*, pages 851–860. ACM, 2010.

[7] L. Von Ahn. Games with a purpose. *Computer*, 39(6):92–94, 2006.

Author Index

www.ingramcontent.com/pod-product-compliance
Lightning Source LLC
Chambersburg PA
CBHW080915220326
41598CB00034B/5577